WAYS OF THINKING OF EASTERN PEOPLES

India, China, Tibet, Japan

WAYS OF THINKING OF EASTERN PEOPLES: INDIA-CHINA-TIBET-JAPAN

Hajime NAKAMURA

REVISED ENGLISH TRANSLATION
EDITED BY PHILIP P. WIENER

University of Hawaii Press
Honolulu

First edition 1964, 1966, 1968, 1971

Paperback edition

93 92 91 90 89 88 12 11 10 9 8

Library of Congress Card Number 64-63438
ISBN 0-8248-0078-8
Manufactured in the United States of America

FOREWORD

The appearance of a revised English edition of Professor Nakamura's work will be warmly welcomed by scholars and by laymen who seek to understand the complex societies of Asia with whose destinies the West is ever more intimately involved. It is surely appropriate that this should be the first major publication of the East-West Center at the University of Hawaii, for Mr. Nakamura is concerned with two problems that are crucial for the development of better mutual understanding between East and West.

The first of these problems is the identification in some meaningful way of the "East" and the "West." How may one define such entities, and how may systematic comparisons be made that will bring into bold relief basic differences and similarities? In the four and a half centuries from the European "discovery" of Asia to the present period of intensified culture contact, Europeans and Asians alike have learned all too little about each other. False antitheses and monolithic comparisons have persisted from one generation to the next; knowledge is difficult to attain, understanding is more so, and resort to cliché generalization proves irresistible. In recent times some of these clichés have been dressed up in new jargons so that thousands of unwary readers have been led to believe that they were being given new magic keys that would open the door to the "Oriental mind," "Oriental logic" or what-not. But the keys opened doors into dream worlds inhabited only by clichés and phantasies.

Professor Nakamura sweeps aside this flotsam and sets out to analyze, with rigor and objectivity, the characteristic thought-patterns of four Asian peoples as these are revealed in their languages, their logic, and their cultural products. In this analysis he speaks neither of an "Oriental mind" nor of an undifferentiated "West." Rather he speaks of the Indians, the Chinese, the Tibetans, and the Japanese out of solid understanding of their distinctive cultures and histories. And when he speaks of the West, it is with full awareness of the mutiplicity of traditions that have contributed to Western civilization. He seems to me to demonstrate the level of understanding that can be reached once we transcend the ancient myth of the "East" and the "West" as monoliths.

The second major problem dealt with in this study is equally relevant to the need for mutual understanding between the peoples of Asia and the West. Mr. Nakamura poses it this way: It is clear that no people in the world today is isolated from those world-wide movements of thought and belief that everywhere tend to transform men's lives and the values they live by. Yet each people is engaged, consciously and unconsciously, in selecting among the manifold influences which reach them and then of adapting and modifying those elements which they select. What governs this process and how does it come about that out of it cultures emerge which are amalgams—certain elements of them being native and distinctive, others clearly derived from one or another world-wide movement? Mr. Nakamura believes that there are clues to this process in the long history of Buddhism which began and evolved in India and then invaded, one by one, all the historic societies of Central, East, and Southeast Asia. Indians, Chinese, Tibetans, and Japanese were continuously engaged in selecting and adapting elements from the evolving tradition of Buddhism. The ways in which they did this reveal certain long-continuing and distinctive modes of thought, certain key values and attitudes which governed the scope of the borrowing and the process of adapting Buddhist ideas. These peoples' experience with Buddhism, when properly understood, in turn helps to explain their differences one from another and their widely variant responses to Western culture in our time. This is the great theme to which Mr. Nakamura addresses himself in this volume.

The magnitude of this study, involving as it does four civilizations, four literary traditions, two and a half millenia of history, and a host of analytical problems, inevitably directs attention to its author. What sort of man is he and under what circumstances did he conceive and carry through this impressive work? Mr. Nakamura completed the original Japanese version of his study in 1947 when he was in his middle thirties. Portions of the work in its early stages were developed as part of a broader project on language and culture headed by Professor Kichinosuke Ito, but the scope and method of the book are distinctively Mr. Nakamura's own. He graduated from Tokyo Imperial University in 1936 and received the degree of Doctor of Letters (*Bungaku Hakase*) in 1943. In 1957 he was awarded the Imperial Prize of the Academy of Japan for his four-volume history of early Vedānta philosophy. Since 1954 he has been Professor of Indian and Buddhist Philosophy at the University of Tokyo.

Professor Nakamura was trained at Tokyo University in Indian and Buddhist studies—fields which necessarily involved him in the study of the cultures and the Buddhist traditions of China, Tibet, and Japan. In the course of this training he acquired the broad knowledge of languages and cultures requisite for such a study as this. From the beginning of his career, however, his intellectual interests carried him beyond the traditional confines of Indology and Buddhology. He emerged as a major force in the modernization of Indian studies in Japan, and his publications have ranged over a wide field: studies of ancient Indian history, studies on the character of primitive Buddhism, studies of Indian philosophic traditions, notably Vedānta, articles on the living traditions of modern India, a book on the nature of religion in modern Japan, and numerous publications on problems of language and culture and on East-West cultural relations.

The catastrophe which befell Japan in 1945 ushered in a period of great intellectual and spiritual ferment. Japanese intellectuals asked themselves fundamental questions about their nation and their culture, about the potential of a new Japan in a new world order. One facet of this great effort of reappraisal and projection was comparative study which, it was hoped, would give the Japanese a fresh view of their culture and society, their myths and their values. Mr. Nakamura, as the preface to the Japanese edition indicates, was drawn to this new effort at national self-knowledge through intercultural comparisons. His training in Indian and Buddhist studies led him to examine four societies (including his own) which had been affected in different ways by their experience with Buddhism. Other intellectual influences dictated the methods he was to use.

Western philosophy has long been one of Mr. Nakamura's major interests, and the approaches used in this volume were shaped by these interests. Mr. Nakamura was first introduced to the thought of such British and American philosophers as Russell and Dewey. At this stage he also read widely in the writings of Deussen, Keyserling, and Schopenhauer. After reading Professor Shinkichi Sudo's *Logic,* he went on to study the German logicians. He has long been deeply interested in Windelband's "problem approach" to the history of philosophy.

Like many scholars throughout the world, Mr. Nakamura has been greatly influenced by the general breakdown of absolutist philosophies. He was impelled to ask the question, not, are these views in accord with some absolute system, but rather how it is that some men in some societies come to hold such views? How will men's behavior be affected by those views, and under what altered conditions will they change them? In formulating questions of this kind, Mr. Nakamura was influenced by Marx, Max Weber, and by Professor Watsuji, whose book, *Climate,* explored the problem of the relation between environment and thought. Thus in the present book Mr. Nakamura uses the study of philosophic ideas to carry through an inquiry that lies largely beyond the traditional scope of philosophy. This inquiry seeks to analyze the modes of thought or "ways of thinking" of the four Asian peoples—those distinctive and slowly evolving ways in which people sort and classify experience, argue with one another, and make value judgments or practical decisions. For such an analysis, he has been concerned with a whole range of phenomena which might be classified as social-historical, psychological, and linguistic.

The design of this comparative study of modes of thought was developed out of the intellectual interests we have noted. Each of the four sections of the study is developed on a common plan. First there is some discussion of language and logic, of the characteristic ways in which each of these Asian peoples habitually made certain types of judgment and inferences. In each section the author then proceeds to the manifestations of these patterns in formal philosophical writing, in literature, and in individual and group behavior. In each section Buddhism is used, in the manner described earlier, as a kind of chemical precipitant to isolate those indigenous habits of thinking that are most enduring and resistant to change.

Mr. Nakamura is aware that explicit logic and philosophical formulations of all kinds are the particular property of the small educated elites in the societies he is considering. But, if I interpret him correctly, he regards the philosophizing of the elite as a kind of translation into more general and abstract terms of the problems encountered in the common life of the society. And, in turn, folk sayings, proverbs, everyday thought reflect a translation downward or a seeping downward of what the philosophers have voiced. To find evidence of how this occurred and of how Buddhist ideas and values entered into this process in the four societies, Mr. Nakamura has cast a wide net. He has combed folk literature, prayers and the scriptures of popular cults, collections of proverbs, descriptions of everyday life and, wherever possible, he has used the accounts of foreign observers whose fresh eyes often register characteristics that escape the native critic of his own society. Thus, in the end we are shown not only how each elite grappled with the problems of Buddhist thought and belief but also how this process affected habits of thought and modes of behavior in the society as a whole.

The present revised English edition reflects at many points the development of Mr. Nakamura's thought in the period since 1947. When the first Japanese version was written, Japan was only beginning to emerge from the isolation of years of war and military rule. Since that time Mr. Nakamura has read widely in newer writings in the fields of philosophy, anthropology, and linguistics. During 1951–1952, he visited Stanford University where his work was the focus of a year-long faculty seminar. Again in 1962–1963 he discussed his findings with a seminar of scholars at the East-West Center. Portions of his book, certain lines of argument, and much of the documentation have been revised in the light of the author's experiences over the last fifteen years.

It is a pleasure to present this revised English edition to the Western reader. In its pages scholar and layman alike will find a wealth of insight into the range of great problems with which Mr. Nakamura is concerned. He will also, I think, come to admire its author as a tireless explorer on the frontiers of knowledge, a scholar whose virtuousity in research is matched by his relentless drive towards new understandings.

ARTHUR FREDERICK WRIGHT

Yale University

EDITOR'S PREFACE

Professor Nakamura's book was the basis of conferences held at the East-West Center, in 1962–1963, where everyone agreed that the existing English version, now out of print, deserved highly to be replaced by a more readable, updated, and revised edition. With the help of the Senior Scholars and the department of Research Translations of the Institute of Advanced Projects at the East-West Center, and through close collaboration with the author and with our colleagues at the University of Hawaii, especially with Professor Kenneth K. Inada, my editorial task has been directed at providing a more correctly printed and revised text incorporating many new features. Among these are a new Foreword by the distinguished Far Eastern scholar, Professor Arthur F. Wright, who has been intimately acquainted with the evolution of Mr. Nakamura's studies; he and Professor Charles A. Moore have encouraged us to produce this new edition.

The renouned sinologue Professor P. Demiéville has recently said of Dr. Nakamura's work: "No statement or hypothesis is enunciated in this book without resting on some document duly indicated in the footnotes. . . . It is a comparative study of 'the ways of thinking' characteristic of the peoples of India, China, Tibet, and Japan, with an Introduction and Conclusion on East Asia in general. . . . They are treated in a broad manner, as "cultural phenomena" (*bunka genzō* in Japanese), through language chiefly but also bringing in psychology, sociology, esthetics, and logic . . . all without pedantry, in a lively and at times humorous tone which holds your interest. . . . I was particularly struck by the part on Japan which occupies nearly half the work, for it constitutes a national self-criticism, wholesome and sharp, such as you would not have thought written by a Japanese. . . . The myth of an "Oriental mind" common to the whole of East Asia is denounced without beating around the bush. . . . The claim of Western thought to universality does not escape any better off." (*T'oung Pao*, vol. L, 1–3 [1963], pp. 287ff.)

Professor Nakamura's numerous emendations and additions of new material to the text of both the original Japanese edition and first English version have resulted in the following changes. The Introduction has been enlarged, recent studies on Indian, Chinese, Tibetan, and Japanese thought and culture have been utilized, entirely new chapters on Tibet have been added, the chapters on Japan have been re-organized, and an Index has been compiled (since none existed in the first English version). Bibliographical notes have been revised to include more recent references, and more titles have been translated; more dates of authors and leaders of thought have also been discussed.

The breadth and plasticity of Professor Nakamura's thinking are evidenced by his willingness to revise even his basic ideas and interpretations, such as the greater emphasis in this edition on socio-cultural traditions and environmental influences than on innate, national, or racial traits.

I am greatly indebted to the author for broadening the scope of my own interests in the history of ideas, since I have learned so much from his work about the myriad aspects of the profound thought and culture of Eastern peoples. It has been an honor as well as an edifying experience to collaborate with so eminent a Japanese scholar as Professor Hajime Nakamura.

PHILIP P. WIENER

East-West Center, University of Hawaii
City University, New York

ACKNOWLEDGMENTS

On the occasion of publishing a new English edition of this work, the author would like to offer a few words of thanks to those who worked to bring it to completion.

This work has had a long history. The late Professor Kichinosuke Ito of the University of Tokyo, who was commissioned by the Ministry of Education Committee of Japan to promote the comparative study of the ways of thinking of different peoples, asked me to collaborate in this study during the year 1945–1946. I accepted his proposal, proceeded with the necessary research, and submitted reports to the committee.

Since then, I have continued to develop my studies further. I first wished to determine the procedure I should adopt and the form in which I should embody the results. I realized that if I was not clear on methodology, I would not achieve the scientific accuracy desired. Hence, in order to pursue the study systematically, I adopted the following methods: When possible, I aimed to isolate the characteristic features of the ways of thinking of each people by analyzing their typical forms of judgment and inference; such features are, I believe, most clearly revealed in these forms of expression. I have refrained from discussing them *in toto;* but occasionally using the characteristic features thus isolated, I intended to proceed with investigations of concrete cultural phenomena which also reflect the ways of thinking and the thought-processes of each people. To clarify the particular ways in which Buddhism and Indian logic were introduced from India into China, Tibet, and Japan—that is, how a universal religion and logic came to be adapted to the native characteristics of each people—constituted the special focus of my research. I therefore applied *the same methods* in investigating the ways of thinking of each people. (Concerning the Japanese ways of thinking, I realized I had to deal also with the problem of the introduction and modification of Confucianism. However, as this problem lies beyond my ability, I touched upon it only occasionally.) The contrasts and comparisons with Occidental ways of thinking were not a separate topic but were made an integral part of the study. As a result, I took special care to indicate the contrasts presented by the ways of thinking of ancient Occidental peoples in that part of my study in which Indian ways of thinking are explained. Although the ancient Indians and the ancient Occidentals were ethnographically and linguistically related, there are many differences in their individual ways of thinking. I feel that a clarification of these differences is a scientific problem of great importance. I do not refer to a study of differences in their philosophical theories of culture, but to a specific and positive study of the characteristic features of their ways of thinking exhibited in linguistic and cultural phenomena.

When Dr. Charles B. Fahs, Director of the Rockefeller Foundation came to Tokyo in 1950, he urged a tentative translation of some chapters of this work (published in Japanese in 1948–1949) into English, on the advice of Professor Shunsuke Tsurumi. A grant was conferred by the Rockefeller Foundation on the Institute for the Science of Thought, Tokyo. A board for the translation was established; the chapters "Introduction" and "Japanese Ways of Thinking" were translated by its members.

When the author went to Stanford University as visiting professor of philosophy in September 1951, a seminar was established by the faculty for discussing the contents of the translated portions, the members being Professors John David Goheen (Philosophy), Arthur F. Wright (History), Nobutaka Ike (Political Science), Bernard Joseph Siegel (Anthropology), Bert Alfred Gerow (Anthropology), David Shepherd Nivison (Chinese Philosophy), Donald Herbert Davidson (Philosophy), Thomas Carlyle Smith (History), and Raymond K. Waters (Japanese). The session was held every other week, and reports were distributed each time. Some parts of the translation were criticized and revised.

After the author left America in July 1952, Professors Nivison and Waters continued the work of editing the English manuscript, which was thus brought to partial completion. Some portions of the chapter on "Chinese Ways of Thinking" were translated by the author during his stay in London in 1952, and were later edited by Professor Wright and distributed by the Committee for Chinese Thought at Aspen, Colorado.

This work was taken up by the Japanese National Commission for UNESCO, Government of Japan, as the first attempt to translate philosophical works by Japanese scholars. The Editorial Board, set up by the Commission for this task, helped the Secretariat in the arrangements for translation. The author was requested to collaborate in the project on August 21, 1958. The translation of the whole work was finished in June 1959. Finally it was published in 1960 by the Japanese National Commission for UNESCO under the title: THE WAYS OF THINKING OF EASTERN PEOPLES.

Now we are going to present a new different English translation, chiefly based upon the revised Japanese text, published in 1961–1962 by the Shunjusha Company, Tokyo.

When I stayed at the East-West Center, University of Hawaii, from August 1962 to January 1963, Senior Scholars there—Homer H. Dubs, Professor Emeritus of Oxford, Professor Philip P. Wiener, Chairman of the Department of Philosophy, City University of New York, and Daya Krishna, Assistant Professor of Saugar University, India—came to take interest in this work, and formed a group to hold sessions regularly at the suggestion of Professor Charles A. Moore. Their remarks and criticisms were very helpful in rewriting the work.

The help of Professor Wiener, who has long experience in scholarly editing as the executive editor of the JOURNAL OF THE HISTORY OF IDEAS, was most valuable; he devoted a great deal of his time to editing this work, rewriting most of it, suggesting references to Western thought, and eliminating errors of printing and inconsecutive passages. Anne Magura was good enough to type the whole manuscript rewritten by him.

In April 1963, Professor Wiener came to Japan, and during his two-month stay, he continued to collaborate with me on the revisions and rewriting of my work. Professor Kenneth Inada kindly checked the manuscripts after receiving the revisions from Professor Wiener. Professor Ryusaku Tsunoda of Columbia University, a master of Japanese studies in America, then staying at the Center as Senior Scholar, did not spare his time in giving valuable assistance. Professor Walter Maurer, also at the East-West Center, helped in the part on India.

I greatly appreciate the thoughtful arrangements made possible by Alexander Spoehr, Chancellor of the East-West Center, Edward W. Weidner, Vice-Chancellor of the Center, Minoru Shinoda, Director of the Translation Bureau, and Professor Winfield E. Nagley, Chairman of the Department of Philosophy, all of whom enabled us to fulfil the task. Last, but not least, I am heartily thankful to Professor Arthur F. Wright of Yale University who kindly honored me by contributing a new Foreword to this edition.

Herewith I express my sincere gratitude to these scholars, without whose assistance this work could not be brought to the public.

Hajime Nakamura

June 1963

CONTENTS

WAYS OF THINKING OF EASTERN PEOPLES

India, China, Tibet, Japan

INTRODUCTION

Ways of Thinking of East Asian Peoples

Our sense of belonging to one world has never been keener than at present. Yet the emphasis today on this evident fact itself implies that while every individual is affected by the quickening flow of world events, he is still strongly influenced by the ways of living and thinking in his own nation and culture.

It is commonly said that following the Meiji Restoration in 1868, Japan in less than a century rapidly and skillfully adopted and assimilated Western civilization; this acceptance was selective and beneficial in several respects. But may we say that it is actually being accepted in its entirety? And how much the less may this be said of those great peoples of Asia, the Indians and the Chinese? For despite their close relations with Westerners for several hundred years, industrialism and capitalism have failed in many respects to replace their traditional ways; it is not surprising therefore that verbal expressions, beliefs, ritual practices, etc. show few signs of being easily transformed. Western thought, from its first arrival in these lands, was theoretically rather well understood among the educated classes as a part of their general cultivation. And yet it certainly did not govern completely the practical and concrete behavior of many of these peoples. How are we to explain this? We cannot dismiss these phenomena simply by labels like "cultural lag," "backward peoples," or "Asiatic underdevelopment," but must rather seek the answer in the cultural characteristics and traditional ways of thinking of each group of people.

There has long been a tendency to think in terms of a dichotomy between East and West, presupposing two mutually opposed cultural sets of values labeled "Occidental" and "Oriental." Thus the Oriental way of thinking is represented as "spiritual," "introverted," "synthetic" and "subjective," while the Occidental is represented as "materialistic," "extroverted," "analytic," and "objective." This sort of explanation by paired opposites is now rejected as too simple; the cultures of the "Orient" and "Occident" are too diversified and each one is extremely complex. If we inquire into what these words refer to, we are struck by the fact that the sense of each is composite, embracing a range of various narrower concepts. For example, the Greek and Hebrew civilizations, among the historical components of Western civilization, differ markedly from each other. Moreover, the civilization formed by the fusion of these strains is divisible into the ancient, medieval, and modern periods, each of which has its peculiar characteristics; and further, modern Western civilization takes on different characteristics from nation to nation. Consequently, without a thorough grasp of these differences it is impossible to generalize accurately about the ways of thinking of Westerners.

So likewise in the case of Eastern peoples,[1] we must first explain the characteristic ways of thinking in each of their diverse cultures. If we are to hazard any conclusions about Eastern peoples as a whole, it must be as a tentative hypothesis in a comparative study of the data. Generalized conclusions drawn before such individual preparatory studies have been made will perforce be hasty and dogmatic. Thus, in order to deal with the ways of thinking of Eastern peoples, it is first necessary to examine the ways of thinking of each of the peoples individually. However, such a study of all the peoples of the East is, from a practical point of view, impossible at this time. I intend to concentrate on India, China, Tibet, and Japan. My reason is that among these four peoples alone did there exist—however imperfectly—a study of traditional Buddhist logic, which came first from India to the other three areas, and then developed independently in each. I believe that the various other peoples of the East have nearly the same ways of thinking as one or another of these four. Specifically, one may say that Ceylon, Burma, Thailand, and western Indo-China (Cambodia and Laos) are akin to India. Central Asia and Mongolia are akin to pre-Communist Tibet. Manchuria, Korea, and eastern Indo-China (Vietnam) are akin to China. Thus, an examination of the ways of thinking of these four is, in effect, a study of the most influential peoples of the East. It is only after such a study, if at all, that a generalized view of the ways of thinking of Eastern peoples can emerge.

"Ways of Thinking" and Other Terms

In order to prepare an explanation for the problems raised above, I shall first define several related concepts as they appear in this work.

(1) "Rules of logic" (formerly called "Laws of Thought") are those explicitly expressed formal rules put forward by logicians. When interpreted, such rules usually claim to give universally valid results, that is, to lead from true assumptions to only true conclusions. Traditional logic claimed special priority for the "laws" of identity, contradiction, and the

excluded middle; alternative systems suggest other rules. The rules of logic do not purport to describe how people think. Hence the present work, not being a work in logic, does not deal with thinking from a logical and formal point of view. But, of course, it is a historical fact that certain people have at certain times accepted, organized, and promulgated logical systems and rules, and from this fact, among others, conclusions can be drawn about how people think. In this sense alone, the present book is concerned with viewing rules of logic and logical systems as cultural products of reflective thinking.

(2) The phrase "ways of thinking" refers to any individual's thinking in which the characteristic features of the thinking habits of the culture to which he belongs are revealed. "Ways of thinking" as here used will designate especially ways of thinking about concrete, empirical questions, which may, on many occasions, involve also value-judgments and questions of values in ethics, religion, aesthetics, and other such human concerns. The thinker need not himself be aware of any way of thinking when he is engaged in operations of thinking. However, his ways of thinking are, in fact, conditioned by his culture's habits and attitudes when he communicates his thoughts. I have adopted the phrase "ways of thinking" in the title of this work as the main subject of our study.

On some logical or other specialized problems all members of a society or a group may think in the same way. But concerning informal or non-technical problems of daily experience, the individuals constituting one and the same people do not necessarily think in the same way, and so we can only point out a general tendency of the thinking of the people concerned. Thus, as each individual may think in a slightly different way, our work can only mention the predominant tendencies of each people.

(3) Following one or more of several "ways of thinking"—as defined above—any thinker might develop a coherent, self-conscious system of thought. We call this system and its tradition a "system of thought." For example, any well-organized, coherent system of theology or philosophy is a "system of thought." We refer to such systems only when they have affected or reflected ways of thinking of most people in Far-Eastern countries.

Ways of Thinking and Language

In studying the ways of thinking of a people, we find one of the first clues in their language. Language is basic to the cultural life of a people; so basic that when a special language system comes into being, we may say that a people has come into being. The existence of a common language and culture serves as a criterion for the identification of a people.

Even though linguistic activity is common to all mankind, a universal language has never been adopted by all people, and consequently there has never been a worldwide speech community. Several international languages have been devised, and some have, moreover, actually begun to be used for international communication. These, however, are languages used only by people who, faced with the actual situation of many different languages existing in conflict, wish to overcome this confusion. Practically speaking, these languages are also in a sense only *special* artifacts.

Forms of linguistic expression become, in the inner consciousness of people, norms for psychologically ordering in a fixed pattern and carrying to conclusion the operations of thought. Therefore the special forms for developing the effectiveness of a given language, especially the grammar of that language and more especially its syntax, express the more conscious ways of thinking of the people using the language, and what is more, may be said to explicate such ways of thinking.

Are philosophical ideas or traditional thought relative to language? For some time a good deal of discussion has taken place in Western scholarly circles concerning the relation between linguistic forms and ways of thinking. Many scholars[2] believe that between the two there exists some sort of parallel development and mutual correspondence. However, there are other scholars[3] who either deny such parallel development and mutual correspondence entirely or assert that the relationship is not a significant one. Recently, especially in America, the relation between language and action based upon communication has been discussed as one of the most important philosophical problems.

Recognizing that many theories exist as to the relationship between linguistic forms and ways of thinking, in this work I have nevertheless followed what seems to be the general assumption that between the two there is a close relationship of correspondence or parallel development—that language is a representation in sound, writing, or gesture of the concept produced in the operation of thinking.

If there is such an intimate relationship between the operations of language and thinking, it is worthwhile and indeed necessary to inquire into forms of linguistic expression as a key to the study of forms and ways of thinking.

Studies have already been partially undertaken which attempt to clarify the differences between the ways of thinking of various peoples, using as a key the differences in the forms of grammatical construction in the languages used by these peoples. For example, Wilhelm von Humboldt thought it possible to study the differences between the structural aspects of different languages by making a study of such questions as how a given form of grammatical structure is handled in each language, what sort of grammatical position it has, and what sort of relationship it has to other grammatical forms. As one instance of this, he made an investigation of duals.[4] Thus, with this method as a key, he proposed to attack the problem of the forms of thinking of a people. Again, the sinologist Granet said, "Just as linguistic research permits the analysis of the *mechanism* of thoughts transmitted in language, in the same way the analysis of the guiding principles of thought can verify the analysis of its means of expression."[5] Taking this position he endeavored to explain the ways of thinking of the Chinese people as a whole, by using the analytical study of the Chinese language as a key.

In this work it is my aim to carry out an investigation of a broad scope with regard to the most important peoples of the East, following a similar scheme of analysis for each people.[6] The procedure I have followed with each people is to study their forms of expressing judgments and inferences as initial clues to their ways of thinking, and then to attempt to elucidate these ways of thinking by analyzing the various cultural phenomena correlated with them. But for comparative purposes I have placed particular emphasis upon Buddhism—a cultural phenomenon common to all.

Ways of Thinking and Logic

Although the forms of linguistic expression raise many different problems, since we are concerned with ways of thinking it will be proper for us to give primary emphasis to the forms of judgment and inference. These are the basic forms for expressing the operations of thinking. I shall postpone for the present such questions as what varieties of forms of judgment and inference there are, and how these varieties ought to be classified, for these are, properly speaking, problems of logic.[7] Accordingly, although it would be desirable to examine the special characteristics of the ways of thinking of each people, taking up all the forms of expression of judgment and inference one by one, yet insofar as the problem of their classification is concerned, the actual fact is that the content of logic in this respect is not yet definitely fixed. I would like to select for consideration merely those judgments and inferences which are fundamental or especially characteristic.

First, as to judgments, I shall consider the most fundamental and simple forms, namely judgments of identity, judgments of classification, judgments of inference, and judgments of existence.[8] In Western logic the problem of *impersonal judgments* has been widely discussed but propositions (such as "it is raining," for example), which in the West are considered impersonal judgments, cannot be so considered in Japanese and

Chinese, differing as they do from Western languages in their linguistic forms. Furthermore, in the ancient Indian language, which is on a par with Western languages in its linguistic forms, very often the same idea is not an impersonal judgment but is expressed as a judgment with a subject ("it is raining" equals *"devo varṣati"* i.e. "the god of rain causes rain"). Consequently, since the question how to classify the "impersonal judgment" must first be argued out logically, in this work comparisons of the linguistic forms of various languages in the matter of the impersonal judgment will not be carried out as an independent topic, but will merely be discussed as an illustration of the relation of language to logic. Moreover, in recent years there have been many logicians who have emphasized the "judgment of relation" (*relational statements*).[9] However, inasmuch as the views of scholars vary as to the meaning of the concepts of "relational judgments," in the present work it will suffice to discuss such judgments only when necessary, without bringing them together and examining them under an independent heading.

Moreover, among the various forms of inference, I should like to call attention especially to the forms of expression of simple types of inference. In Western formal logic this problem used to be examined under the "syllogism"; but in everyday life we very often demonstrate a conclusion by advancing only one premise in the manner "x, therefore y." We must in addition consider the joining together of several inferences. However, the compound syllogism—i.e. a form which joins together complete syllogisms—is in actual fact seldom used; in almost all situations a form is used which links together abbreviated syllogisms. This is called in formal logic the *sorites* or chain argument. We must, of course, also be concerned with the question of how these chains of inference are differently applied by various peoples.[10] We shall seek these forms of expression which exhibit especially clearly the typical features of the ways of thinking of a given people; but even better material is sometimes offered by logic, whether developed or adopted by the people. Since the original name for logic, ἡ λογικὴ τεχνή, means skill in regard to *logos* (word), the features of the ways of thinking which are unconsciously embodied in language may possibly become explicit in logic and may moreover be displayed in a systematized, organized state. In this sense, logic is one of the most important keys for the study of the features of the ways of thinking of a people. Accordingly, by studying Eastern logical works and at the same time comparing them with those of the West, we should be able to comprehend some features of the conscious ways of thinking of the various Eastern peoples. Logic in the East originally appeared in India, but when it was introduced into Tibet, China, and Japan, it was studied in different ways in each place, and in each country it was considerably modified. Although logic should be the most universal form of learning, as a matter of historical fact it has by no means been formulated or transmitted to these other peoples in a universal language. Naturally, the characteristic features of ways of thinking, differing with each people, are reflected in the mutual differences of native or imported patterns of logic when the latter are tied to the structure of a given language.

But it ought to be noted here that those who have mastered logic and actually apply it are the *intellectual class* of any people. Some of the intellectual class within a given society think in conformity with logic, and logic becomes a standard for them in the orderly statement of the content of their thoughts.[11] In spite of the fact that the masses use language constantly every day, their use of logical forms of expression is almost non-existent. Consequently, it is incorrect to say that logic regulates the ways of thinking of a given people to the same extent as do linguistic forms. It is impossible to hold that conclusions obtained from the examination of the systems of logic of the past are directly applicable to the entire people who study this logic. In order to take logic as a key for the examination of the ways of thinking of a given people, it is necessary to take into consideration just such facts as these.

The comparison of the systems of logic of East and West is in itself a large problem and an independent topic of study. Since it is impossible to discuss this problem fully in this work, I shall discuss it *only insofar as it is related to the ways of thinking of peoples in general.*

Ways of Thinking and Cultural Phenomena

Here, as above, we shall not concern ourselves with logical systems as such, nor shall we deal mainly with questions of *comparative philosophy.*[12] The reason is that, in studying the ways of thinking of a given people, one should consider the ways of thinking adopted by most of the members of that group. In doing so, it is preferable not to consider exclusively the characteristic ways of thinking of individual philosophers. Of course, every philosopher, however great, is conditioned by events in a certain region of space and time. His thinking cannot, moreover, avoid a certain continuity with that of his associates, as a member of a particular society. Thus, the ways of thinking of philosophers cannot be freed completely from national or historical traditions. On the other hand, however, a great philosopher not infrequently follows a way of thinking which differs from that of the nation which gave him birth. Indeed, a philosopher is often considered great for this very reason. Therefore, the ways or patterns of thinking of individual philosophers will generally be referred to only when necessary. However, it will be pertinent to inquire whether the ways or patterns of thinking of the majority of the philosophers of a given people exhibit certain common tendencies.

On the other hand, I shall take up, in my study of the ways of thinking of a people, the characteristic popular sayings, proverbs, songs, mythology, and folklore of that people. Nor will it be out of place to include within the limits of this study generally current expressions even when found in the writings of formal philosophers. One must, however, exercise considerable caution in determining which of the numerous expressions found among the people are universal and truly characteristic of the people. In addition, such things as myths, religious scriptures, the arts (music, painting, architecture, etc.), and works of literature in general must, of course, be considered as important sources for our study. Since such documents abound among all peoples, one must choose as source material those which are *particularly cherished by the people in question.* Those works which are not esteemed by the people, even though they may be interesting from the point of view of the modern reader, will be of little significance as sources for determining the ways of thinking common to the entire people. But, on the other hand, works which furnish a critique of the ways of thinking of a given people written by *foreigners,* in spite of the fact that the people in question may know nothing of such works, are very important sources in that they clarify the differences between the ways of thinking of the two nations involved.

Ways of Thinking as Revealed in the Pattern of Adoption of a Foreign Culture

The *modern* investigator draws his conclusions about the ways of thinking of peoples by the method of comparative study, with linguistic forms, logic, and general cultural phenomena furnishing the bases for such study. There are, however, instances of a given people, in the course of its history, elucidating concretely its own ways of thinking which differ from those of another people. This insight is furnished by the way in which one people adopts the ways or patterns of thinking of another. One people does not generally adopt the ways or patterns of thinking of another culture straightaway, but rather criticizes the "alien" ways, selects from them, and modifies them in the very course of adoption. In this process the characteristics of the ways of thinking of both peoples are clearly indicated. The problem of the interplay of cultures has been investigated a great deal, but such studies have been made mainly from the historical and philological point of view. The subject has not been sufficiently explored from the standpoint of ways of thinking. It is this problem to which I address myself in this book.

Regarded from the standpoint of ways of thinking, the reception of a universal religion, among the various phenomena of cultural diffusion, would seem to furnish a most valuable clue to the understanding of the characteristic ways of thinking of a people. In what form does this people adopt the universal religion, and in what way is the religion modified? Now the most widespread religion in the East is, of course, Buddhism. (In the case of Japan, Confucianism should also be considered.) As a clue to the characteristic ways of thinking of the Eastern peoples it will be important to study how they modified Buddhism. There have been many studies of the spread (adoption, from the point of view of the people) of Buddhism. These too have been principally historical and philological, and it appears that there has been no consideration of the problem from the standpoint of ways of thinking. This is the problem I should like especially to consider.

The Order in Which the Ways of Thinking of Various Eastern Peoples will be Considered

In accordance with the methodology outlined above, I intend to proceed with this study in the following way. First, in my study of each of the Eastern peoples, I shall bring out the characteristics of their ways of thinking as discernible in the forms of expression of the simplest judgments and inferences. These characteristics are among the most fundamental to the ways of thinking of a people. Next I shall examine the ways in which such characteristic ways of thinking operate in connection with actual cultural phenomena (especially the mode of acceptance of Buddhism). These phenomena most certainly have a socio-psychological relationship with the characteristics discernible in the mode of expression of simple judgments and inferences. My study will concern itself with this relationship.

In studying the characteristics of the ways of thinking of Eastern peoples, the question arises as to the proper order in which to deal with the several peoples. In my opinion, studying India, China, and Japan in that order follows best the actual historical order. Since the Indians are, as Aryans, said to be of the same ethnic, linguistic, and cultural (Indo-European) family as Occidentals, I shall first contrast these two groups and point out their differences from the standpoint of their ways of thinking. Then I shall discuss the Chinese, who are a completely different people in origin. Lastly I shall come to Japan, which was influenced culturally by India and China (note that in contrast to this, pre-modern India had no cultural influence from Japan and only some from China). One would have to discuss India and China even if one began with

Japan. Therefore, out of practical considerations I have decided upon the first-named order. Further, Tibet, although not an important region from the political or economic point of view, cannot be overlooked in *a consideration of ways of thinking,* in that it was there that Indian logic found widest acceptance. Consequently we shall give collateral consideration to the ways of thinking of the Tibetans.

I should further like to point out here that "the Chinese" as used in this book refers to the Han people. "Chinese national" is a *political* concept, whereas "the Chinese," "the Tibetans," are cultural concepts. In a consideration of the ways of thinking, the Chinese and the Tibetans must, of course, be distinguished.

Various Cultural Phenomena and the Ways of Thinking of East Asian Peoples.

Are there any common features in the ways of thinking of Eastern peoples despite the variety of their cultures? In Japan as well as in the West we often hear people maintain that a certain trait is "Oriental" or "Eastern."[13] However, the East-West dichotomy has been challenged and strongly denied.[14]

Bertrand Russell points out that man is perennially engaged in three basic conflicts: (1) against Nature, (2) against other men, and (3) against himself.[15] Inheriting this classification, Huston Smith says: "Roughly these may be identified as man's natural, social, and psychological problems. The great surviving cultural traditions are also three—the Chinese, the Indian, and the Western. It helps us to understand and relate the unique perspectives of these three traditions if we think of each as accenting one of man's basic problems. Generally speaking, the West has accented the natural problem, China the social, and India the psychological."[16] Now it is well known that Asia includes several cultural areas. But the term "Orient" or "the East" is still used unfortunately as if it referred to one culture common to all Eastern countries.

Let us inquire further into the meaning implied by this term, Eastern or Oriental. First of all, it is generally said that in the East man's individual existence is not fully realized, but that the individual is subordinated to the universal. Hegel, for instance, asserted that God or the Absolute in the East has the feature of *"das Allgemeine"* (the Universal).

"The fundamental principles of the various religions of the East are that the single Substance alone is the True, and an individual has no value in itself, nor is capable of attaining any value so long as it is by itself, apart from that which exists in and for itself (*das Anundfürsichseyende*), the Absolute; that an individual is only capable of assuming true value by uniting itself with Substance, when this individual, however, is no longer a 'Subject' but is dissolved into the unconscious."[17]

And regarding the difference between Eastern and Western thoughts, he says: "On the contrary, with the Greek religion or Christianity the 'Subject' is aware of its freedom; and we ought to think in this manner." In the philosophy of the East, however, "The negation of the finite is real. But that negation is one in the sense that an individual only attains its freedom in unity with what is substantial."

Hegel had only a limited knowledge of the classics of the East, acquired through his reading of translations; his views, however, are shared by many Western people even nowadays. To what extent then are Hegel's statements true? Indeed, a blind subordination to authority in some form or other has prevailed in some countries of the East. Is it possible for us to assert that in the West "the self was free" and devoid of such subordination? The complete, unquestioning faith in authority during the Middle Ages in the West and the subsequent destruction or regimentation of alien cultures did not occur in the East. Was this phenomenon of "being united with Substance" as Hegel called it, not illustrated, in some cases, in the West as well as in the East?

It is often said that the peoples of the East are *intuitive* and accordingly not systematic or orderly in grasping things; by contrast the Westerners are said to be "postulational" or *logical,* and that they try to grasp things systematically and by orderly planning. Indeed, the ways of thinking of the Chinese or the Japanese may be characterized as "intuitive." But in the case of the Indians this label is hard to apply. For example, the intricate arguments of the Abhidharma literature are logical and can never be called intuitive. There is no need to refer to the difficult literature of theology in order to point out how far removed from any intuitive grasp is that complicated, fantastic, and strange set of sentiments symbolized in Indian paintings and sculptures. Indian art urges us to form a complicated association of ideas, and leads the spectator into a strange, fantastic atmosphere.

Secondly, it is often asserted that the ways of thinking of the Eastern peoples are *synthetic,* and that of the Westerners *analytic.* The Chinese word, for instance, gives us the impression that it is synthetic, but it is more properly set in a stage prior to analysis. So long as it has yet to pass through the process of analysis, it would hardly be called synthetic. On the other hand, it is generally recognized by scholars that the Indians showed a great skill in the analysis of linguistic or psychological phenomena. We cannot say that only Westerners have a tendency to be analytical. For example, Indian grammar was most advanced in the analysis of words and phrases, but very weak in its consideration of the synthetic construction of sentences, while, on the other hand, Greek grammar has left an excellent achievement concerning syntax which deals with the synthetic field of words and phrases. Therefore, it is unjustifiable to characterize the ways of thinking of the Eastern peoples simply as "synthetic."

Let us next consider the problem of *knowledge*. Max Weber says, "The premise which is common in the last analysis to all philosophies and soteriologies in Asia is that knowledge—whether it be that of books or mystical *gnosis*—is the only absolute way leading to supreme bliss in this world as well as in the next world. A careful examination would reveal the fact that 'knowledge' does not mean knowing the things of this world, nature, social life, or laws regulating both nature and man. Rather, it is the philosophical knowledge of the 'meaning' of life and the world. It is naturally understood that such a knowledge cannot be replaced by Western empirical learning, and that it should never be sought by empirical means, if we are to do justice to the purpose proper to that learning."[18]

Indeed, it is true that knowledge as conceived by the East Asian people has connotations which for the most part bear out the definition given above. But in the history of Western thought, we are able to note the existence of a similar religio-philosophical connotation. The word *gnosis* itself here is Greek, but a gnostic inclination is also seen in various religions in the western part of Asia, and is not peculiar to India and China alone. In the West, too, it explicitly appeared in Neo-Platonists like Plotinus, and may be traced back to Plato. It is generally presumed that such philosophical schools might have been influenced by Indian or Persian philosophy or thought, but this relationship is yet to be clarified. Under the influence of Greek philosophy the Gnostics arose in a movement to elevate the Christian faith to the level of knowledge. Likewise in the Middle Ages, such an inclination is said to be noticeable in some of the Christian mystics who were regarded as heretics, such as Tauler or Eckhart.

Let us consider the next problem. There are some people who maintain that all the principal religions of the world originated in Asia; therefore, if we label the whole area including the western part of Asia "East," the East might be said to be *religious,* whereas Europe (and America) or the West non-religious. Such a view was fairly dominant in Japan prior to the Pacific War, and it has never completely disappeared. However, as pointed out above, among the East Asian peoples, the Indians in particular are extremely religious, but the spiritual disposition of the Japanese or the Chinese could never be termed religious. On the contrary, there is some evidence that Western people are far more religious than the Japanese or the Chinese.

In the same way, the contention that has repeatedly been made that the Western civilization is *"materialistic,"* while the East Asian civilization is *"spiritual,"* is erroneous. A non-religious race can never be "spiritual." Of course, it all depends on what one means by "religious" and "spiritual."

Ancient civilization and its continuation in modern Western culture, which restored the ancient culture, were superior in scientific research and application of material science (technology), and consequently, the West with all its power was able to make advances on the East. The East Asian peoples, menaced by this invader, labeled the West "materialistic"; on the other hand, the West characterized the less advanced East itself as "soulful" or "spiritual." As far as the inability to control material nature is concerned, a similar feature can be seen in the aborigines of Africa as well as of America, and so is in no way peculiar to East Asia alone. For equally good reasons, the justification for defining the East as "internal" or "subjective," and the West as "external" or "objective" is also highly questionable.

Furthermore, it would be a very superficial observation to single out the East as "being ethical," for ethics is a part of every and any society. Observing that some of the traditional ethics of the Japanese and Chinese are not practiced in the modern West, some conservative Japanese, trying to preserve the ethics of old, have made this dubious claim. In connection with the above observation, Eastern thought is often regarded as metaphysical, and it is said that the basis of the Eastern metaphysical thought is "nothingness peculiar to the East."[19] It is well-known that "nothingness" was propounded in the philosophies of Lao-tzŭ and Chuang-tzŭ. On the contrary, Indian philosophy generally inquires into the "existent." The meaning of "existent," however, is different from that of Greek philosophy. In Indian philosophy in general, there is a mental tendency to seek a transcendent substantial basis for "what is real." In the case of Śaṁkara, the ultimate being of the world is the "real," and it is rather the phenomenal world which is void, so that his thought is diametrically opposed to the thoughts of Lao-tzŭ and Chuang-tzŭ, so far as literal understanding goes. In Buddhism, especially in Mahāyāna Buddhism, "voidness" is expounded but it is different from "nothingness"; this fact is often emphasized by the Indian Buddhists.[20] These two ideas were either identified or confused when the method known as *Ko-yi* (the evaluation and interpretation of Buddhism through the doctrines of Chinese thoughts, such as Confucianism, Tao-ism, etc.) was practiced after the introduction of Buddhism into China. Master Chia-hsiang,[21] however, repeatedly affirmed that Buddhist "voidness" and the "nothingness" of Lao-tzŭ's or Chuang-tzŭ's were not to be equated. Therefore, it is very dangerous for us to qualify the whole of Eastern thought with the term "nothingness peculiar to the East." (However, if the term is used to refer just to one aspect of the thought, there would be no objection. Or if a modern philosopher sets up such an idea as a result of his own contemplation, then he is free to do so, but this has nothing to do with the historically verified thought of the East.) Moreover, it could not possibly be averred that the East is metaphysical and the West is not so. Among the East Asian peoples, most of the Chinese, and the Japanese in particular, have been much more non-metaphysical than the Westerners.

Returning to the fundamental problem of the ways of thinking, it is often said that Westerners are *rationalistic,* but that East Asians are *irrationalistic*. Such characterizations seem to have acquired general acceptance and usage especially after World War II. It is particularly emphasized that the Japanese are anti-rationalistic. Indeed, the Japanese have shown in the past a distaste for systematical and logical ways of thinking. But when we consider the question more deeply, in practice the Japanese generally tend to follow certain customs and a code of conduct. Their devotion to a limited social code is a general tendency, upon which they base their criterion for moral evaluation. Accordingly, in this sense we can claim rationality for them—if "rational" is the correct term for behavior in accordance with rules.

At first sight the Chinese give us the impression of being indifferent to logical exactitude. The ways of expression in the Chinese language are extremely ambiguous, and the historical fact that there has never been a development of formal logic (apart from the short lived Mohist school) among the Chinese seems to support this view. To be indifferent to rules of formal logic, however, is not necessarily to be irrational. It is widely known that Chinese thought, due to its rationalistic character, exerted a great influence upon the philosophy of enlightenment of the modern West. Max Weber says: "Confucianism is extremely rationalistic since it is bereft of any form of metaphysics and in the sense that it lacks traces of nearly any religious basis—to such a degree that it is questionable whether it is proper to use the term 'religious ethics.' At the same time, it is more realistic than any other system, outside of Bentham's ethical system, in the sense that it lacks and excludes all measures which are not utilitarian."[22] If "rational" means thinking in a practical utilitarian way then it is the Chinese rather than the Westerners who are far more rationalistic. And it is due to this rationalistic character that Chinese thought inspired the thinkers of the period of the Enlightenment, such as Voltaire and Wolff, and came to serve as their weapons against the shackles of medieval Scholastic traditions.

Although the Indians did not achieve as remarkable a development in the field of natural science as the West, they conducted far more elaborate speculations than the Westerners of antiquity and the Middle Ages with respect to the theory of numbers, the analysis of psychological phenomena, and the study of linguistic structures. The Indians are highly rationalistic insofar as their ideal is to recognize eternal laws concerning past, present, and future. The thought represented by Tertullian's aphorism, *"credo quia absurdum,"* or "I believe because it is absurd," had no receptivity in India. The Indians are, at the same time, logical since they generally have a tendency to sublimate their thinking to the universal; they are at once logical and rationalistic. On the contrary, many religions of the West are irrational and illogical, and this is acknowledged by the Westerners themselves. For example, Schweitzer, a pious and most devoted Christian, says, "Compared to the logical religions of East Asia, the gospel of Jesus is illogical."[23] In this sense, the East is more rational, and conversely, the West is more illogical. A rationalistic attitude is seen consistently in Dharmakīrti's Buddhist logic or in the natural philosophy of the Vaiśeṣika school of India. Consequently, we cannot prudently adopt the classification that the East is irrationalistic and the West rationalistic.

Some writers make a distinction between the rationalism of the East and that of the West. For example, Max Weber says, "The practical rationalism of the West is extremely different in nature from that of the East, notwithstanding the outward or actual similarity of the two. The post-renaissance rationalism was especially rationalistic in the sense that it abandoned the restrictions of tradition and believed in the power of reason in nature."

This statement appears to be well grounded. The thought-tendency, however, which was bent on disregarding traditional authority or restriction appeared as early as the turbulent days of the so-called *"Ch'un-ch'iu,"* Spring and Autumn Annals (722–481 B.C.), to the beginning of the Ch'in dynasty (221–206 B.C.) in China; and in India it was prominent in urban society during the period of the advent of the Buddha in the 6th century B.C., and even afterwards it was propagated by naturalistic philosophers and logicians. In modern Japan as well, the germination of free thought is faintly perceived. Accordingly, it is indeed beyond doubt that disregard for conventional authority and restriction was dominant in the modern West, and was weak in East Asia, but this is merely a difference of degree or extent; it is not a difference in essence. And even if that thought-tendency were influential in the modern West, it was not so in the Middle Ages; therefore, it would be improper to distinguish the East and West on this point.

In connection with this, a *nostalgic conservatism* is very conspicuous among the Chinese, and it can also be seen to a considerable degree among the Japanese, while in India it was once partly forsaken. The Moslems, who make up a fairly large part of the Indian sub-continent, have disengaged themselves from the religions of the Indian people; therefore, nostalgic conservatism cannot be called a general feature of East Asia.

Although this nostalgic conservative character is partly common to both the Indians and the Chinese, the former are more prone to exalt the universal law underlying the past, present, and future. Thus, the basis of these two similar nostalgic characters harbors a difference in outlook or thought.

Again, we find that many people think that the character of the East Asians is their *passivity*. There is evidence that this has been a conspicuous feature of the way of thinking of the Chinese and the Indians. Among the same East Asians, however, the Japanese in particular are highly sensitive to the transition of things. Buddhist teachings and Confucian learning alike have been transformed into something dynamic in character since their introduction to Japan. Therefore, it is impossible to sum up the ways of thinking of the East Asians in general as merely being "passive." And although the thinking of the Westerners might indeed be called "dynamic," the idea of evolution or development in phenomenal existence or in history has manifested itself clearly only in modern times and could not possibly have been clear to ancient thinkers.

It is often pointed out that India, China, and Japan are situated in the monsoon zone, so that the three countries have a climatic trait in common. People living in the zone are said to be generally passive and submissive to objective nature and lacking in the will to conquer it by means of rational and measured thinking, and as they move en masse, they are easily subordinated by a specific authority, so that they dislike to assert themselves positively. Accordingly, when various thoughts are found opposed to one another, they are likely to recognize their rational force, and to compromise and synthesize, rather than to adopt one of them alternatively to the exclusion of others.

Therefore, it is often contended that in contrast to Western thought the spirit of tolerance and mutual concession is a salient feature of Eastern thought. The religion of the West at times is harsh and even emphasizes struggle for the sake of keeping the faith and condemning unbelievers:

"If any man come to me, and hate not his father, and mother, and wife, and children, and brethren, and sisters, yea, and his own life also, he cannot be my disciple." (Luke, 14.26.)

"I am come to send fire on the earth; and what will I, if it be already kindled?—Suppose ye that I am come to give peace on earth? I tell you, Nay; but rather division: For from henceforth there shall be five in one house divided, three against two, and two against three. The father shall be divided against the son, and the son against the father; the mother against the daughter, and the daughter against the mother; the mother-in-law against her daughter-in-law, and the daughter-in-law against her mother-in-law." (Luke, 12.49–53.)

Such aggressive thoughts as expressed here did not appear at all in the religions of East Asia. Throughout the religious world of India a more tranquil and peaceful atmosphere has prevailed from time immemorial. Gotama and Mahāvira ended their lives in peace. Perceiving the fact that in China a perfect freedom of faith had been preserved since ancient times, Voltaire, who has been called the "Apostle of the freedom of faith," was utterly fascinated by Chinese law.[24] Although in Japan, the principle of the freedom of faith has not fully been realized where political influence was exerted, due to the interference of the state, hatred against the heretic has been mild among the people in general. Even the Jōdo Shin sect, the most clear cut sect in its uncompromising attitude toward the other faiths, advises that in order to spread the faith it is wiser to wait calmly for a suitable opportunity rather than to force the situation.[25]

With the Indian people, self-conscious reflection on the impact of oneself against other selves is not clearly evidenced. Underneath this fact lies the view that all men are one in essence. And such a view as this seems to be shared by the other peoples of East Asia, though in different degrees.

The idea of tolerance and mutual concession is based on admitting the compatibility of many different philosophical views of the world. The Indians are prone to tolerate the co-existence of philosophical thoughts of various types from the metaphysical viewpoint; the Chinese are inclined to try to reconcile and harmonize them from a political and practical viewpoint; and the Japanese tend to emphasize the historical and physiographical features of such diverse thoughts. Interference with religions on the part of the state was not found in Hindu India, but in China it occurred to a considerable degree, and in Japan it was occasionally extreme. Consequently, we hesitate to sum up these standpoints with one adjective "Asiatic." While in the West, in modern times, the spirit of tolerance and mutual concession was preached especially by the thinkers of the Enlightenment and by the Pietists, in Asia, especially Iran, heretical views on religion were relentlessly persecuted.

It is often pointed out, particularly by Westerners, that Eastern thought has a tendency toward *escapism,* and that it is rather indifferent toward social and political action. They say that Christianity preaches the importance of practice within this world but religions of East Asia teach man to shun this world.[26] Such criticism seems to have become common in the West. In relation to this, especially concerning the traits of the religions of Asia, Max Weber says, "Indifference to the world was the attitude taught them,—whether in the form of external escapism, or in actions indifferent to this world, although taking place in this world. Accordingly, it is resistance to the world and to our participation in it."[27] Weber goes on to say: "The fundamental creed of Protestant ethics in the modern West is 'inner-worldly' asceticism. It attempted to rationalize this world ethically by accepting the will of God positively, rather than to tend toward escapism as in the case of meditation.[28] Daily conduct is elevated, through rationalization, to the level of god-sent vocation, and this is also man's assurance of happiness. In contrast with this, religions of the East hold nothing but a herd of meditative, fanatic, or insensitive devotees and they regard any inner-worldly practice as nonsense and are anxious to leave this world. Not that Buddhist monks have no practice at all, but, since their ultimate objective was to escape the 'cycle' of transmigration (*saṁsāra*), their conduct could never have undergone any thorough, inner-worldly rationalization."[29]

Indeed, the ethics of Protestantism may have been as Max Weber described it. But Western thought in and prior to the Middle Ages has not always been characterized by an attitude of inner-worldly rationalization. "A herd of meditative, fanatic, or insensitive devotees" did exist in the West in the past as well as in the East. That the religious men of the East were engaged in *inner-worldly activity* is a fact beyond doubt. The religion that pervaded the various countries of East Asia was Mahāyāna Buddhism which stresses such *inner-worldly activity*. Yet we can see in the religion of Iran a tendency also toward the worldly.

In relation to this, it is often asserted that the East Asian people contemplate nature and attempt the identification of man and nature by meditation, whereas the Westerners attempt to conquer nature. The attempt on the part of man, however, to assert himself and to conquer nature was not uncommon in East Asia. In China and India as well, the construction of canals, banks, water tanks, and ramparts was undertaken. On the other hand, the yearning for nature appeared also in the West, in which people sought to return to nature. Accordingly, on this point also, it is very difficult for us to make a clear distinction between the two spheres. Concerning problems of philosophy, the opposition of subject and object, for instance, was already taken up in ancient Indian philosophy. The reason why natural science has made remarkable progress in the West, especially in modern times, will be considered on another occasion. In any case, the attitudes toward nature as found in the West and the East are difficult to define or distinguish.

Max Weber states that during or prior to the Middle Ages, the ascetic life in the Christianity in the West had been tinged with a *rational* character: "Its object was to overcome the state of nature (*status naturae*), to rid man of his dependence upon the power of irrational impulse and upon nature and the world, to subordinate man to the rule of a deliberate scheme, and to place man's conduct under the incessant self-examination and the *evaluation* of ethical significance. Herein lies the world-historical significance of the monk's life of the West in contrast to that of East Asia—viewed not from the whole of it, but from the general type. . . ."[30] From the viewpoint of the rationalization of life, however, the workaday practices at Zen monasteries in Japan are extremely rationalistic, and, as was pointed out before, the social work of Japanese priests prior to the Middle Ages was very extensive. We agree with Weber's opinion that it is difficult to make a clear distinction between the East and the West on this particular point.

After having examined what has heretofore been designated as features peculiar to Eastern thought, we find ourselves in reality incapable of isolating a definite trait which can be singled out for contrast with the West. It appears possible for us to recognize a few similarities common to the nations in East Asia; however, it is impossible to regard them as common Eastern features and to compare them with those of Western thought as if they were non-existent in the West. These features were regarded as "Eastern" because they were conspicuous in certain countries in a certain period or among certain peoples. Accordingly, it is also certain that those common features are not without some basis in human nature.

Thus, we must acknowledge the fact that there exists no single "Eastern" feature but rather that there exist diverse ways of thinking in East Asia, characteristic of certain peoples but not of the whole of East Asia. This can be affirmed by way of comparison among the cultures of the East Asian nations, and by noting the fact that Buddhism was received by various nations of East Asia according to the character of the recipients; this clearly testifies to the cogency of our viewpoint. In other words, Buddhism, whose basic principles are universal and transcend the distinction of social classes and nations, has been adopted with certain modifications, modifications which were made according to the features peculiar to the ways of thinking of each recipient nation.

Of course, there can be similarities in ways of thinking among the Buddhists of various nations, even if they may differ in nationality, since Buddhism is a world religion and it has especially exercised a profound influence over the spiritual and social life of the East Asian peoples. Buddhism, insofar as it is a single religion, should be basically consistent wherever it may be found. (The problem of the general or common features of Buddhist sects is not treated within this book, for the problem belongs to the philosophy of religion.) It is only natural that some common traits should be perceived so long as an overwhelming number of East Asians are Buddhists. However, we cannot generalize from the facts of

Buddhism to the East Asian nations as a whole,[31] because the East Asian nations are not all necessarily Buddhist. To say that there are similarities and parallelisms among Buddhists of the East Asian nations is not tantamount to showing the parallelisms and similarities of the East Asian nations as a whole. Whether the conclusions regarding the Buddhists as a whole are applicable to, for instance, the Indians—in general they are non-Buddhists—must be considered separately.

According to the above considerations, the inevitable conclusion is that *there are no features of the ways of thinking exclusively shared by the East Asians as a whole,* unless they are universal traits of human nature in the East and West. Furthermore, if the ways of thinking differ according to the cultural history of each people, then we should expect the cultures formed by these nations to be heterogeneous. Sokichi Tsuda recently remarked that the three nations, India, China, and Japan, have established respectively their own distinct cultures.[32] As far as the ways of thinking or folk-traits of each nation are concerned, it seems proper for us to admit this cultural pluralism in order to begin our study of the fascinating diversity of human nature which led Pope to his famous saying: "The proper study of mankind is man."

Universal and Particular Aspects of East Asian Thought and Culture

THE CONCEPT OF THE "EAST" AND PREVIOUS COMMENTS ON IT

We have clarified in the previous chapter that there is no way of thinking generally applicable to the East Asians. Why then are such phrases as "East Asian thought" or "East Asian culture" used as if they were axiomatic concepts? I believe the answer is an historical one. The Japanese people were thrown into spiritual confusion due to their abrupt acceptance of Western culture after the Meiji Restoration in 1868. In Japan, prior to this period, Chinese and Indian thought intermingled with traditional Japanese thought, and they existed in harmony, oblivious of any peculiar differences. As a result, Japanese thought was regarded as being at one with Chinese and Indian thought, and thus the phrase "East Asian thought" came to be applied to all three countries, as identical. The people advocating the necessity of preserving the old Japanese cultural tradition especially emphasized the importance of East Asian thought; at the same time, almost invariably, such people have been "Orientalists." Admittedly, an exclusive minority with nationalistic tendencies did their utmost to rid Japanese culture of the remains of the influence coming from the Indian and the Chinese cultures. This faction maintained that they would pay their respect only to things proper to

Japan, but as the predominant part of old Japanese culture owed much of its substance to India and China, such a narrow-minded attitude was not shared by liberal intellectuals in general. They paid, instead, attention to the similarity and affinity between the old Japanese culture and the cultures of East Asia in general. Accordingly, despite the difference of geographical location between "Japan" and "East Asia," the conflict between the two has been scarcely felt. Along with the attitude which maintained the superiority of Japanese culture, the following view was generally held: "The Japanese are the most ingenious people in regard to accepting foreign culture. They assimilated the essential elements of the culture of East Asia. Buddhism and Confucianism are examples. Hereafter Japan might well avail itself of progressive traits of Western civilization and thereby build a new culture."

However, as we point out in this book, the way in which the Japanese received the cultures of India and China led to serious modifications and even distortion; they did not accept and assimilate these cultures in their entirety. There is a fundamental discrepancy between the old Japanese culture and the cultures of other countries in East Asia. We must not overlook this fact.

Taking notice of this situation, it has already been observed even by the Japanese scholars on East Asia that the culture of East Asia is far from being a unified entity. "Whatever amount of space may be allotted to the area which should be called 'East Asia,' as far as cultural significance is concerned, it never existed from ancient times as a unified world; there has existed no single history called the cultural history of East Asia, and accordingly, it is fundamentally impossible for us to assume that there is a single culture to be called the culture of East Asia."[33] The scholars who advocate this view deny the cultural unity of East Asia but some go so far as to impute a unity to the culture of the West: "On the whole, the West has evolved, moved by a single world history, though the nations existing therein had their own singular cultural traits and were not without their own national histories."[34] At the same time it is emphasized that the Western culture is the same as world culture. "At present, modern culture, world culture, that is to say, Western culture is not opposed to Japan's culture, but is rather reflected in and constitutes a development of Japanese culture itself."[35] This view expressed by a respected scholar on East Asia is shared and supported by a good number of intellectuals at present. However, when such an observation is analyzed, it is found that there are two premises presupposed: (1) the unity of Western culture, (2) the identity of Western culture with world culture. These two premises are formulated in opposition to the idea of the unity of the culture of East Asia. We must, however, examine and criticize these two premises.

First, concerning the unity of Western culture, there is no doubt that European countries throughout past ages developed a culture by keeping in close communication with one another spiritually and materially. However, can we rightfully claim that Western culture is a single, unified entity? Western culture may be traced back to two cultural currents, Greek and Judeo-Christian, but it is historical fact that they conflicted with each other. These two currents were compromised and blended with each other in the Middle Ages somehow or other, but in modern times a certain number of Westerners, certain materialists and positivistic scientists, do not subscribe to the Western religious tradition. Furthermore, in Western culture, there are many conflicting trends of thought, and we have already pointed out that the features of the ways of thinking which are generally called "Oriental" are also found among the ways of thinking of the Westerners.[36] It is one thing to admit that there was a close relationship among the Western nations and it is another to acknowledge *the unified character of the ways of thinking* of these nations. Therefore, as far as the ways of thinking are concerned, we must disavow the *cultural unity* of the West as we did in the case of the East. The cultural character of the West is in the final analysis nothing but that of a variegated type or an approximation to it. In any case it cannot be established as unique at all.

Next, let us deal with the contention that Western culture can be equated with world culture. It is generally acknowledged that the unification of the world was accomplished by Western nations with their dominance of power in the world in recent times. It goes without saying that no people or nation can exist isolated from the West politically or economically. In other fields as well, such as mathematical and natural sciences, learning, art, etc., the influence of Western culture is decisive. This is the reason it is generally thought that the world was unified and at the same time westernized. The unification of the world, however, is only outstanding in regard to man's efforts to control, and utilize material nature; while on the side of language, ethics, religion, art, customs, etc., the spiritual traditions of each nation can be altered only with much difficulty. For instance, the Westerners arrived in India for the first time towards the end of the fifteenth century and, at last, she came to be ruled by them. In spite of their skillful ruling policy, the Christian population in India is only a little over two per cent of the whole population; the majority of Indians professing Christianity consists of either the outcast from the Hindu society or the lowly, while the majority of the whole populace embraces the popular faiths, derived from ancient times. In China the situation is somewhat similar. The fact that the nations of the East refuse to be altered easily in their ways of thinking or their social customs, even in the face of the thought or cultural influence of the West, should not be characterized merely as due to the backwardness or retardation of the East Asian people. Some scholars report that the characters of the ways of thinking which we have delineated mainly in terms of how Buddhism was received, presented themselves in the case of Christianity as well. If it were true, then it follows that the ways of thinking of various nations have been unexpectedly firm enough to retain their cultural peculiarities to this day.

The East Asian people and their cultures will not be regarded as inferior or backward. In some cases it is as advanced as the West. For example, it is common to the West, India, China, or Tibet that culture has developed from the integral language form to the analytical one. We shall refer to this fact later. In some phases, the principal nations of the world have gone through a common process of progress. Such a common process of progress is also seen in the field of religion, ethics, social institutions, political organizations, etc. Research into the cultural contributions of various nations as seen from the viewpoint of their interrelationship is necessary. In different times, there are different social structures, and different forms in the contrast of social classes. In spite of that, there is something unchangeable that has survived to this day, and here, I have attempted to define this. I do not mean to say that something traditional or constant is always superior to the ever-changing products of dynamic historical and social processes, but it is well to realize that while the world is making progress in new directions, many traditional cultural traits of its varied peoples are still able to enrich the world with their distinctive contributions.

EAST ASIAN THOUGHT AND ITS UNIVERSALITY

It may be noted that those who contend that westernization is the same as universalization have the following view in mind: "Cultures of East Asia are subordinate after all to Western culture. The characteristics of various ways of thinking of the East Asian people are to be overcome some day by those of the Westerners. Western culture is in possession of universality, while Eastern culture is not." For example, Max Weber says, "The cultural phenomena which promoted the development of universal meaning and applied science happened to appear in the West, and in the West alone." And he has conducted sociological research into almost all the religious systems the world over in the light of the question, "Upon what kind of chain of conditions was the above fact dependent?"[37] In Japan on the other hand, Dr. Tsuda observed likewise that Chinese thought, for example, is incapable of assuming universality.[38] However, what is meant after all by "being incapable of assuming universality"? Eastern thinkers find the scientific knowledge or techniques which arose in the modern West can be understood or assimilated with ease and without change. But with respect to other cultural fields, is it possible for us to say that anything born of the culture of the West is capable of assuming universality, whereas all the cultural products of other nations are not? When we look back over the history of mankind, we can see the traces of Eastern influence upon the West. It is often observed that in the Bible there are traces from the stories of the Buddhist scriptures or that a part of Greek philosophy was influenced by Indian philosophy; these assertions may be vague and have not been fully worked out. However, the fact that in the parables or stories current in the Middle Ages of the West the influence of the Indian civilization appears acknowledged by scholars.[39] Among others, the fact that the concept of the Buddhist "Bodhisattva" was transferred to the West and made into a canonized Catholic saint should not be overlooked in spite of its triviality.[40] There is also the fact that the life story of the Indian Śākyamuni was brought over to the West, where it was transformed into the life of one of the Catholic saints; subsequently, it was carried to Japan by Christian (*Kirishitan*) missionaries, but neither Buddhists nor Christians were aware of its background.[41] In modern times, however, by means of translations Eastern thought has become increasingly familiar to the West. As a result, the influence of Eastern thought on the intellectual history of France[42] and Germany has been indeed remarkable. Chinese thought especially served as an impetus to the Enlightenment in Europe and inspired such people as Voltaire and Wolff. Likewise, Indian thought contributed to the formation of Romanticism in Germany. The movement by the brothers Schlegel, the philosophy of Schopenhauer, the thought of Keyserling in modern times, etc. could not be imagined without the influence of Indian thought. W. von Humboldt spoke highly of the Indian *Bhagavadgītā* as the most beautiful and most profound philosophical work in the world; Schopenhauer called the *Upaniṣads* "The consolation of my life and death" and found in that philosophical epic the fountainhead of his thought. Count Keyserling concluded his book *Travel Diary of a Philosopher* with the following lines: "The turmoil of the world after the great war can be saved only by the Bodhisattva Ideal." Professor Charles Morris, a philosopher in contemporary America, has given the name "Maitreyan Way" to the path upon which the world should tread in the future. In America also, pragmatists like John Dewey have shown a keen interest in the practical social aspects of Eastern thought. Northrop's comparative studies of East and West have been done from a methodological viewpoint. In England, Germany, or America, groups of people who call themselves "Buddhists," though very few in number, have formed small organizations.[43] Thus, if Eastern thought should come to be understood more deeply, the possibility of its influence looms larger.

Even within the confines of East Asia, a great cultural interchange was accomplished in the past. Buddhism spread over almost the whole of Asia. To what extent Confucianism regulated the actual life of Japan is yet to be studied; however, there is no doubt that it held a kind of regulating power in the actual, social life of Japan. According to one scholarly Confucian, it was not until the beginning of the introduction of Confucianism that a moral code prevailed in Japan.[44] Confucian scholars such as Ogiu Sorai, Dazai Shuntai, Yamagata Shūnan, and others, thought also that in ancient Japan there was no philosophy which could be regarded as ethics, and it was not until the advent of Chinese Confucianism that morality came into being. Particularly, Dazai Shuntai believed that in ancient Japan from the beginning there was lacking any sign of ethical awareness, and that it was not until the introduction from China of the "Way of the Sage" or "The Teaching of the Sage" that the Japanese became interested in ethics. "In Japan from the beginning there has never been such a conception as 'the Way.' In recent years, however, Shintoists are said to be solemnly teaching the 'way of our country' as if it were profound, yet whatever they are teaching is nearly all fabrication and interpolation of later times. The fact that there were originally no Japanese equivalents to the Confucian list of the greatest virtues, benevolence (*jen*), righteousness (*yi*), propriety (*li*), harmony or music of the soul (*yüeh*), filial piety (*hsiao*), and brotherly respect (*t'i*); the absence of these words is proof that there was no such concept as 'the Way' (*Tao*) in Japan, and so the lack of Japanese equivalents reveals that their origin is not to be placed in Japan. From the time of the mythical gods to somewhere around the fortieth Emperor (ca. 645 A.D.), for want of decorum, marriages were held among parents, children, brothers, uncles, and nieces. In the meantime communication was established with foreign countries so that *the way of the Sage of China* came to be diffused in Japan. The result was that the Japanese people became acquainted with decorum and more acutely conscious of the ways of civilized society. The most lowly of society at present regard people who have behaved against decorum as no better than beasts; this is all due to the influence of the teaching of the Sage."[45] While from the viewpoint of the Buddhists, prior to the introduction of Buddhism, Japan was utterly in the dark, it was not until that time that people were saved, and Buddhism and its enlightening virtues were received with rejoicing. For instance, Rennyo (1415–1499) expressed his feeling of joy in the following manner:

"The spread of Buddhist teachings in this country (Japan) can be traced back to the time of the Emperor Kimmei (in the sixth century), when Buddhist teachings first arrived in Japan. The Tathāgata's teaching was not widespread prior to that time; people did not at all hear the way to Enlightenment. Having been born in an age when the Buddhist teaching is widespread, we are now fortunate enough to have heard the way of deliverance from the world of birth and death, though we do not know what good causes brought this happiness about. Indeed we are now able to meet whatever is difficult to meet."[46]

Nichiren also says: "In ancient days prior to the advent of Buddha-Dharma, people knew neither the Buddha nor the Dharma. Yet after the struggle between Moriya and Jōgū Taishi (Prince Shōtoku), some people came to believe in the Buddha and others did not."[47]

How can we contend that there was no universality in the teaching which impressed so many people as being the universal teaching? Those who deny the cultural singleness of the East are prone to disavow the universality of Eastern thought. But logically speaking, it is inconsistent to deny the universality of Eastern thought as a consequence of disavowing the singleness of the East, dividing it into a number of wholes, and at the same time recognizing a mutual (or unilateral) influence among these cultural wholes. We must avoid this inconsistency. We deny the singleness of the East but affirm the establishment of a number of cultural wholes. And it is because of this that we should like to acknowledge a *universal significance* in certain aspects of various thought-systems established in East Asia. It is by no means true that all these systems have universality, but we should recognize it in some aspects of them. What we can state the universal aspects are would depend on the analysis of the cultural conditions.

If we take the standpoint of those who favor an impartial objective examination of the thoughts which mankind has produced, it follows that we could not possibly say that Western thought alone is universal and that the thoughts of other nations have no universal significance. The ancient Greeks, or at least some of them,[48] had acknowledged that the philosophical thoughts of other nations had their individual significance. Also among the modern philosophers of the West there are a good many who hold such a view.[49] Nevertheless, there are some who would attribute universal superiority especially to Western thought alone, perhaps because they wish to display the power of the modern West to control nature or are fascinated by it alone.

Indeed it is a fact that the modern world is being unified by dint of the political and military pressure of the West, but this does not affirm the insignificance of the cultures of the non-Western nations. In the ancient West, for instance, Greek culture still held its position of leadership even under the political and military rule of Rome, while India was gorgeously adorned by the flowers of culture, in spite of the oft-repeated dominance by foreign peoples during her long history. We ought not to disregard the cold fact that culture is subject to political, military pressure, but at the same time we must not forget the dignity of man which no power can subdue.

Customary and conventional as the phrase may be, if we remember this fact, it would not be meaningless for us to emphasize the significance of "East Asia" at present. There is a great significance in knowing East Asia and developing its diverse cultures. Originally such concepts as East Asia, the East, or the Orient were set in opposition to the Occident. In spite of their obscure connotation, these words came to be used by peoples, long subjected to oppression by the military and political superiority of the Westerners, as an attempt to preserve their respective cultural traditions. Indeed the famous slogan "Asia is one" uttered by Okakura Tenshin is not free from inaccuracy and is not in accordance with the facts of the history of thought. But the nations of East Asia, which have long cherished the desire to preserve and develop the respective cultures of their own, have inadvertently associated themselves with this slogan, because of the common feeling that *they shared the same objective.* It was a sort of common impulse aiming at defending their respective cultures against the rule of the West.

The desire on the part of various nations to preserve and develop their respective cultural traditions is justifiable. We ought to respect this desire. In that case, however, it behooves each nation to see to it that while being critical of foreign cultures they remain critical also of their own indigenous culture. That is, with modesty and self-awareness a new culture may be formed through enlightened self-criticism.

The neglect of criticism and the mere affirmation and preservation of the past would be tantamount to annihilating one's own culture. However, if it accepts foreign cultures uncritically, it would be merely blind acceptance, and consequently, no positive contribution toward forming a new culture for mankind will have been made.

From this standpoint, studies in East Asia should reflect something more than the mere tastes of dilettanti, and should be ready to contribute more positively to forming a fresh culture. There have been people who regard the learning and the scientific methods established in the modern West as the only absolute ones, and such a thought-tendency seems to remain fairly influential at present. This may be only natural but we ought to be critical as well as appreciative of the learning and sciences of the modern West. Learning in the future may be reformed and developed by Western advances reinforced by the results of studies in Eastern cultures.

COMPARATIVE STUDY OF WAYS OF THINKING AND PHILOSOPHY

A study of ways of thinking of the East Asians, at the same time, should be compared critically with the studies of Western philosophy. It goes without saying that we must compare above all the philosophical systems of East Asia with those of the West. Deussen once speculated as follows: "Suppose that there exists a certain planet in the solar system, say, Mars or Venus, inhabited by human beings or other beings with their culture flourishing and with an established philosophy. Suppose we come to know their philosophy through one of the beings living there, who had entered into the sphere of our terrestrial gravitation after being shot out in a missile. In that case we might undoubtedly take an enormous interest in the results of their philosophy, and we might carefully compare and examine their philosophy and ours. If there should be some difference, we would determine which side is true, and if it should be found that there is no difference between the two, then this would imply that the truth of the outcome of the philosophical contemplation of both sides had been substantiated. Although in this case we would have to take into account the natural and inevitable sophistication of pure reason, as Kant put it. This may be wishful thinking, but we have a similar situation in Indian philosophy, for Indian philosophy has taken a course of development independent of Western philosophy."[50]

He then proceeds to say, "Here, people may raise the following question: We are living in an age which has attained such a remarkable stage of development, that would it not be a childish and inappropriate attempt for us to learn something from the ancient Indians? To know the view of the world of the Indians, however, is profitable. We are enabled thereby to realize that we have fallen into a great prejudice in favor of the whole system we have established about religion and philosophy, and that besides the way of understanding things established by Hegel as the only possible and reasonable one, there exists as yet another one totally different from Hegel's."[51]

Deussen's allegation offers a number of problems over which we must ponder. As we are concerned in this book with *the ways of thinking of various nations,* we shall not treat here the significance of comparative philosophy.[52] Instead, we would here especially lay stress on the following point:

As is seen in modern Western philosophy, the concept of philosophy, which is required for instance by Kant, is not the "technical concept" (*Schulbegriff*) but the "general human concept" (*Weltbegriff, conceptus cosmicus*). He was not merely looking for the "epistemological system which was to be sought for only as a branch of learning, and which regards as its object nothing more than the unity of knowledge, that is, the logical perfection of cognition." With him, the ideal of philosophy was to be the "learning of the relationship between all cognitions and the essence of human reason." A philosopher was not the technician of reason but the legislator of human reason (*Gesetzgeber der menschlichen Vernunft*).[53] Therefore, for him the truth to be given by the supreme philosophy is *nothing but what is already latent in the minds of all people.* It may perhaps be due to such a standpoint that in his metaphysics the commonsensical view about religio-ethics held generally by Westerners seems to be lurking.

In the "a priori dialectic," in his work *Kritik der reinen Vernunft,* Kant made an inquiry into the nature of such ideas as the soul, freedom, God, etc. and contended that they are concepts not of the Understanding but of Reason; therefore, in regard to natural cognition they are not structural as in the case of a category, but regulative, and that there is a danger of substituting an image for the Idea or guiding concept and thus misunderstanding its meaning. According to his philosophy, however, an Idea is in no way an image. He therefore rejected the phenomenal status of these Ideas but recognized their metaphysical function. And it is well-known that Kant grounded his practical philosophy (ethics) on these regulative Ideas.

It is this regulative function that constitutes the "general human concept" lying behind the metaphysical reality of such Ideas. It is not certain whether he himself was aware of it, but in any case there was a traditional religio-ethical concept among Westerners which made him set up these Ideas, for his Ideas are not necessarily taken for granted among East Asians in general. For example, the thought which recognizes the metaphysical reality of soul as a permanent substance was rejected by Buddhism. Buddhists try to ground the establishment of ethics without setting up the idea of the immortality of soul as a condition. As for the idea of God, neither Buddhists nor Jains accept God as the creator of the universe. In Eastern thought in general, especially in Indian thought, gods are possessed of no meaning or any importance. Indian people generally are inclined to base their ethics on a *domain free from God's authority.* This view did not enter into Kant's philosophical vision. Despite commentaries written from various viewpoints, the attempt to understand Kant's thought mainly as initiating an epoch and a stage of development to be made by mankind's society and thought, is one-sided. As far as this point is concerned, Kant's philosophy is after all nothing but a philosophical and theoretical expression of the Protestant pietism in modern Western culture.

What we have said in the above is only an example, but in any case if we introduce various ways of thinking of East Asians into philosophical speculation, then we should have a wider and more fruitful basis for the critical consideration of the philosophical thoughts of the West.

If, however, we should admit any of the philosophical thoughts of the West indiscriminately, then we would be committed to nothing but *a blind adherence to authority,* already conspicuous among Japanese intellectuals. What the German philosophers have taken as the "universal human concept" (*Weltbegriff*) was after all restricted by the historical tradition of the German people's cultural and social life, so that the attempt by the West to foist the concept on Eastern society, admitting a universal significance only for it and neglecting their circumstances, is a kind of non-critical attitude in the formation of culture. Among ideas that Western philosophers have taken up as "universal human concepts," there are not a few that seem to a majority of Japanese to have been transformed into "technical concepts."

By reflecting upon the seemingly irrelevant ways of thinking of the East Asians, we can be *critical* of the philosophical thoughts of the West.[54] And as a result of the criticism, we should be able to acquire an efficient basis for going forward towards the establishment of a new and truly universal philosophy.

The Cognitive and the Existential Basis for the Differences in Ways of Thinking

In the following pages, we shall occasionally disclose the traits of ways of thinking of various nations in respect to their forms of expression of judgment and deduction among the peoples of East Asia, and then consider how these traits are expressed in various cultural phenomena, particularly how they have influenced Buddhism, as a universal religion, to assume different phases. In that case, we have adopted the method of inferring other traits when possible, from among some typical expression-forms of judgment and deduction. The former method proves to be the means to know the latter. Therefore, the traits seen in expression-forms of judgment and deduction are the cognitive basis (*ratio cognoscendi, jñāpaka hetu*).

Here several questions arise: What is the existential basis (*ratio existendi, kāraka hetu*) which brings about the differences in ways of thinking among nations? By what causes were such differences of expression-forms or ways of thinking brought about?

These questions cannot easily be solved here, because they are difficult questions which concern the foundations not only of philosophy but of all the sciences and humanities. The general glimpse which we shall have from a limited range of observation might help us in solving these questions.

Unverified theories have been proposed to explain why various nations show differences in ways of thinking. First of all, the features of ways of thinking seem to have nothing to do with the blood or lineage of nations. That is to say, the features of ways of thinking are not explicable by alleged racial propensities. Being left to live among a numerically greater and stronger people, a minority group naturally becomes accustomed to the new social and cultural environment and finally takes on the same traits and ways of thinking as the dominant majority. A good example of this process of acculturation, is seen, for instance, in the familiar case of Japanese emigrants who have settled down abroad. The fact is that even the so-called "Aryan race" which was divided into East and West, that is to say, the Europeans and the Indians, came to show different features of ways of thinking. It seems that the Indians are not pure Aryans, after all, but a hybrid of Aryans and aborigines, hence such differences appear; however, there is also evidence to the contrary. Although the inhabitants of Pakistan are trying even at present to keep their "pure Aryan blood," they have already discarded the religion of their ancestors and embraced Mohammedanism. Accordingly, there is no intrinsic relationship between physiological or racial lineage and peoples' ways of thinking.

Another fairly common theory for our consideration refers us to differences of climatic environment.[55] It is believed that such physical causes as climate, weather, geology, the nature of the soil, and topography of a certain locale, account for the differences in the ways of thinking among peoples; for instance, the differences of the ways of thinking between the Europeans and the Indians in the Aryan lineage might have been derived from or dependent upon such differences of climatic environment. Even the climatic or topographic environment, however, does not possess a singular or decisive influence over the differences of man's ways of thinking. If it were so, then the theory of climatic determinism would be established. But the real facts testify to the opposite. It very often happens that the selfsame people living in one and the same climatic environment changes its ways of thinking under the influence of the thought of other nations. Although the ways of thinking of an isolated people become set and hardly changeable, they can yet be changed to a considerable degree under the influence of other nations. This fact can easily be understood if we go through the history of each nation. If we stick to the climatic environment alone as its decisive cause, then we can never explain the changes of ways of thinking or thought-patterns of a nation—that is, its intellectual history.

Also in this connection, no geographical environment or topography constitutes a decisive factor, either. As is often said, India and China belong to the Continent, so that the nature of the cultures born there is *continental,* while that of the Japanese culture is *insular,* and indeed, they do create a contrasting impression. Among other things, Japan is an island nation, out of the reach of any great foreign invasion, so that she has preserved the ancient culture and even keeps such cultural products intact as have already been lost in the mainland of Asia. In the island of Ceylon, to cite another instance, the most primitive of all forms of Buddhist orders in other countries have been preserved. Therefore, it is true that an island nation is characterized by the tendency to conservatism which preserves the traditional ancient culture intact, but a nation on the continent is not without such a conservative character. The anti-progressive or static character of traditional Chinese culture has often been pointed out. And it is astonishing that a part of the Indian population still preserves the Vedic culture as it was established three thousand years ago. Anti-progressivism or conservatism is seen in many of the countries mentioned above. Accordingly it is impossible to draw the conclusion that the geographical environment or topography, continental or insular, is the only factor which determines the differences in the ways of thinking of peoples.

Ought we not to recognize the existential basis of the difference of ways of thinking, not in the natural scientific conditions of heredity and physical environment, but in the material conditions which have to do with man's social behavior? What emerges here is a theory which attaches great importance to economic conditions in the social life of humanity. Historical materialism may be an example of such a theory. Since the criticism of materialism would constitute an independent theme of study, it is impossible for us to refer to it here. As a result of our inquiry into the ways of thinking of the East Asian peoples, we shall not hesitate to conclude as follows: *The theory of the materialistic view of history or economic view of history is incapable of explaining in its entirety the fact of the different ways of thinking which vary according to the thought and culture of people.* Needless to say, the materialistic view of history emphasizes that the sum total of the productive relations in a certain period, or the economic structure of society can alone provide the material base upon which the juridical and political superstructure is established, and in accordance with which a certain social or class consciousness is also formed. Despite the fact that it affords a number of solutions to problems of social organization or social thought, it does not adequately explain other cultural problems. As a matter of fact, to what extent will the standpoint of the materialistic or economic view of history suffice to explain the differences of ways of thinking among peoples which are disclosed in our studies?

Differences of productive types cannot explain many totally opposed variants of ways of thinking; for example, the fact that the Chinese people attach so much importance to concrete individuality; while the Indians seek abstract universality, and in contrast to the Chinese people who are empirical, sensuous, and realistic, the Indian people are imaginative, otherworldly, and metaphysical. It is said that in the East Asian society people generally inherited the same type of agricultural production from ancient times and that there should be little divergence of type among agricultural nations. This is the very reason why the phrase "Asiatic productive type" is used as if the uniformity of type is taken for granted by economists and sociologists, though, of course, whether it is true that there is such uniformity is a serious question. In economics the "Asiatic productive type" might well be admitted, but so far as ways of thinking is concerned, we shall reject the use of the word "Asiatic" as an unclear and highly questionable concept. According to my opinion, ways of thinking vary according to the cultural traditions of the peoples respectively concerned. The concept of the "Asiatic productive type" does not explain the historical and cultural grounds upon which the differences of ways of thinking existing among Asian nations have arisen. Consequently, as far as this point is concerned, the materialistic view of history or the general economic view of history has in its dogmatic monolithic approach exposed its fatal weak point.

In this connection, it is often maintained by scholars that the absence of the city-state in East Asian society has produced the characteristics common to East Asian thought. It is true that the *"polis"* or *"civitas"* was never established in East Asia, and the "bourgeois" in the Western sense of the word has never existed in East Asia. *"Shimin"* (Japanese for citizen) is merely a coined word; *"Chōnin"* (inhabitant of a town) is not identical with citizen.[56] The absence of a city-state might have been the actual basis for the appearance of thought-characteristics *common to all the East Asian nations,* but it is impossible for us to explain thereby the *differences* in their ways of thinking.

After such considerations, the following hypothesis emerges; namely, a unique religious ideology is the determining factor of the distinctiveness of the social and economic life of each nation. Apparently this hypothesis was intended to correct other thoughts such as the materialistic view of history. Max Weber, a representative of such an idealistic view, says:

"An idea shapes the world's course just as a switchman directs man's motivated interests on to a track."[57] Attaching great importance[58] to the influence of religious ideas on social life, economics, and ethics, he examined the relationship between religion and social life in almost all the important nations of the world. The result of his study must be highly valued, but the study of cultural factors, in addition to religion, cannot neglect the characteristics of ways of thinking in every people. Most Indians have certain general characteristics common to Hindus, Jains, and Moslems, and most Chinese have characteristic ways of thinking shared by the devotees of Confucianism, Taoism, and Buddhism. Now it is not unusual to find the same person regarding himself a follower of many religions. The fact that this eclecticism occurs among the Japanese with Shintoism, Confucianism, Buddhism, and Christianity shows that in Japan there is a tendency, characteristic of Japan's culture, to transcend all sectarian distinctions of religions. A foreign religion has often wholly transformed the ways of thinking of a nation, and at the same time the ways of thinking peculiar to a nation have reciprocally changed the foreign religion itself.

Therefore, we have to pay attention to the fact that historical circumstances of a nation count to a great extent in bringing about a difference of thought types. We shall point out the fact that the view of most Indians about human relations favors the identity or fusion of the self with others, in contrast to the primitivistic Westerners' view which insists on the hostile and antagonistic relations of individuals in the "state of nature." The development of such a difference of thought-forms is considered to be due to the historical evolution of the society which different conquerors and ruling people formed in India and in the West. In the case of the West, the Greeks, for instance, formed their city-state (*polis*) after conquering the older inhabitants. They had come as adventurers and invaders amidst a foreign people, and first of all built a safety-zone encircled by stone walls so as to keep the common enemy out of their own world. They thought that they would thereby succeed in protecting themselves against the power of the dead souls of the enemy, and would at the same time be protected against assault from the living enemy around them, so long as the city provided them a refuge.[59] Against their expectations, however, the Aryans who invaded India did not face any such violent resistance on the part of the aborigines, so that their society was less menaced by the aborigines. They constructed *puras* (fortresses) on hills, wherein they confined themselves only in such emergencies, as an enemy invasion or flood, while in ordinary times living outside the *puras*. The differences of historical background in regard to social evolution, as illustrated above, continue to shape the ways of thinking of every nation for a long enough time to come. The differences of historical background, however, can be affected and seriously modified by future historical changes. Consequently, past evolution is not possessed of any absolute significance as a cultural determinant.

The question:—What is the existential basis or empirical factors which determine or explain the characteristics of a people's way of thinking?—yet remains unsolved. The question then is: Are not the expression-forms of judgment and deduction which we adopt as the cognitive means for studying the characteristic ways of thinking, working at the same time as an *existential basis?* Generally speaking, since the grammar and its syntax, which regulate the expression-form of judgment and deduction, do not easily change,[60] they are not only expressive of the characteristic ways of thinking of a nation but in return they also regulate them for some time. In other words, it is probable that the ways of working of a thought-form might in turn be qualified by its language-form. Therefore, as far as this point goes, the expression-forms of thought employed in language are the existential basis for the characteristics of ways of thinking of a people. But this relationship of language to thought is by no means absolute in nature. A grammar or a syntax might change on account of social unrest or as a result of a contact with foreign languages. In such cases, the ways of thinking would have undergone a change. The change of ways of thinking of a nation depends upon the many historical changes that affect the cultural customs and habits of its people.

According to the above considerations, we may offer, in the last analysis, the following hypothesis: There is no such thing as a single fundamental principle which determines the characteristic ways of thinking of a people. Various factors, as mentioned above, related *in manifold* ways, each exerting its influence, enter into the ways of thinking of a people. If we deal with the question of the existential basis which brings about differences of ways of thinking, we see no way left for us but to take the standpoint of pluralism. The attempt to seek out an isolated single cause looks alluring but it is destined to fail to grasp the complexities of social change. We are obliged to recognize in this case also the principle of "Things are born of various conditions" which Buddhism put forth against the monistic metaphysical theory. In what order, then, do these elements make themselves felt? This is a question to be contemplated upon and investigated again in the future. Here we cannot dwell upon this question in detail, and even if we try to get a general perspective, it would be difficult for us to offer a single order in response. Since the thinking function is one which in the long run affects man's conduct and practice, it might have to be said that it is conditioned by how man stands at a certain point of time. Man is a historical being and is all the time subject to the currents of history, so that he should heed both the predictable aspects of history, and at the same time, the unpredictable factor of chance. For instance, such an accidental event in which a nation comes into contact with another culture can bring about an unexpected change of affairs of a more serious nature than the nation in question had ever expected.

The ways of thinking of a people have the double relation of being conditioned by the products of man's own creation, and, at the same time, of qualifying them in return. In some cases we can also see the phase on which each one of the above mentioned sundry cultural factors is in turn characterized and formed by the ways of thinking of a people. It is an independent subject of study to clarify the operation of the mutual factors in both relations. In this book, however, we shall have practically attained the objective of our study, if we succeed in clarifying the following two points: In the first place, *there are some characteristic differences* in the ways of thinking of East Asian nations. In the second place, with regard to all people, there is a *certain logical and human connection* among these characteristics.

Attention should also be paid in this connection to the fact that in the history of every people there is a distinction of periods, such as the ancient, the middle, and the contemporary, according to which the ways of thinking of peoples naturally differ. This fact we do not mean to deny. But at the same time we also ought to recognize the fact that in every nation there are special thought-tendencies which have persisted throughout these historical stages. The more communication progresses, the closer the intercourse between nations becomes, and the more the world becomes unified, the less will be the disparity of ways of thinking among nations. Notwithstanding this fact, however, it will never be easy for any people totally to sever itself from the traditional habits and customs of the past. In order to balance variations in the ways of thinking of nations and to create a new-world culture, we need first of all to reflect upon and ascertain the characteristic ways of thinking of diverse peoples. Of course, it goes without saying that we should equally consider how they underwent changes in the course of history. The overall renovation of ways of thinking of nations will not be easily accomplished by taking only external or institutional measures such as reforms of land-ownership, economic, and political systems. For the purpose of building a new culture aspiring to truth, a rigorous criticism of the ways of thinking of nations ought continually to be made.

PART I INDIA

CHAPTER 1 INTRODUCTION

By what method can we grasp the special features of the traditional ways of thinking of the Indians? Going back to the various cultural phenomena of Indian history in order to examine them thoroughly and impartially for characteristic traits will not be an easy task. If a student, neglecting methodology, judged on the basis of his selected and partial data that Indian cultural characteristics were of a peculiar sort, he might perhaps reach the right conclusion but he would more probably draw wrong conclusions. For instance, studies of ancient Indian society have often resulted in completely opposite conclusions; those based on Brahmanic literature clash with those derived from Buddhist sources. In our present study of the ways of thinking we face a similar danger, because it is impossible to exhaust all extant sources and data.

In order to formulate *objective* conclusions, we must consider the methodology to be employed. First, we shall lay stress on the expression of culture in language; in this chapter we shall examine some of the major problems related to linguistic expression. It is important, as a first step, to compare the Indian language with the Greek and Latin languages with respect to their grammars and syntaxes. If we had some concrete examples of Greek or Latin translation of the Indian languages or vice versa, they would be very convenient for our study, but unfortunately we have nothing like them. Although the *Bhagavadgītā,* a famous religious book of India, and the *Dhammapada,* sacred verses of Buddhists, have been translated into modern languages by European scholars, the Greek and Latin translation of the former book and the Latin translation of the latter offer us important data for reference.[1] The archeological relics and epigraphs, in which Indian languages are written together with European classical languages, are limited only to certain coins so they are of little use in our present study.

Secondly, as a source of data we must lay stress on the way the Indians have taken to foreign cultures; but we regret that the evidence here has not been too clear. This is due to the fact that they did not accept Chinese culture (although Dr. S. K. Chatterjee has recently indicated some Chinese influence on Indian culture); the degree to which they accepted Greek culture has yet to be clarified sufficiently. But it is a fact that to a certain degree they accepted Greek and Latin cultures, a fact which must be considered as a part of our investigation.

Thirdly, we must lay stress on the criticisms of Indian thought by foreigners as important data for our study. In ancient times some Greeks, Romans, and Chinese criticized Indian thought from their respective standpoints. And there were some Japanese who criticized Indian thought, basing their criticism on the Chinese translation of sacred Buddhist books. Again, it is a well known fact that in modern times many European scholars have examined and criticized Indian thought.

Lastly, we must select data from the works written by the Indians themselves. This appears simple, but in reality the problem of selection is very difficult. What should we choose from so many available sources? From what sources can we learn the characteristics of peoples' ways of thinking? First of all, we consider those literatures which have been considered autochthonous by the majority of people. For example about "*the Praśnottararatnamālikā*" (Treasure garland of question and answer),[2] Brahmanic tradition says it was written by the Vedāntist Śaṁkara, Jain tradition says it was written by the Jain King Amoghavarṣa or the Jain Vimala, and Buddhist tradition says it was written by a Buddhist; we can really find its Tibetan translation in the Tibetan Tripiṭaka. From all of this we can say that this book is an important datum, though it is relatively unknown, in our examination of the general ways of thinking or cultural tendencies of Indian traditions. Again the *Kural*, which has been called the Veda in the Tamil language, has been admitted as the sacred book by each of the Jain, Buddhist, Vaiṣṇava, and Śaiva religions. Thus, it falls into the same category as that of the *Praśnottararatnamālikā*.

On the other hand, even though a book is well known to foreigners, if its thought content had not been known widely to the Indians, we should be very careful when we use it as a datum for our investigation. As only a limited number of books will be admitted by the followers of any religion as their authority, we must carefully compare all sources with one another on each point. Especially, when the same sentence is found in various books belonging to different religions of India,[3] this general acceptance may be referred to in judging the characteristics of the ways of thinking of a people.

We shall be able to reach the right conclusion by which the characteristics of the ways of thinking of a people will be shown, when we shall have compared various sources with each other and examined all the relevant data. In the following, we shall combine the conclusion gained through examining occasionally these data with the conclusion gained through examining the forms of judgment and inference; and then around these results, we shall consider synthetically the dominant characteristics of the ways of thinking of the Indians.

CHAPTER 2 STRESS ON THE UNIVERSAL

Preponderance of Abstract Notions

Indian people are inclined to consider the universal seriously in expressing their ideas of things. This can be easily seen in the fact of their verbal usage in which they have so great an inclination to use abstract nouns. In Sanskrit, an abstract noun is formed by adding -tā (f.) or -tva (n.) suffix to the root. These suffixes correspond to $\tau\eta$ (Greek), -tas (Latin), -tät (German), -té (French), -ty (English), and etymologically they have a close connection. In these European languages, however, abstract nouns are not often used except in scientific essays or formal sentences, while in Sanskrit they are often used even in everyday speeches. For example, "He becomes old,"[1] "Er wird alt," is expressed in Sanskrit "He goes to oldness": *vṛddhatāṁ* (-tvaṁ, -bhāvaṁ) *gacchati* (*āgacchati, upaiti,* etc.); "The fruit becomes soft," "Die Frucht wird weich" is expressed in Sanskrit "The fruit goes to softness": *phalaṁ mrdutāṁ* (-tvaṁ, -bhāvaṁ, mārdavaṁ) yāti; "He goes as a messenger," "Er geht als Bote" is expressed "He goes with the quality of messenger": *gacchati dautyena;* "A man was seen to be a tree" is expressed "A man was represented by the quality of tree" (*pumān kaścid vṛkṣatvenopavarṇitaḥ*).[2] The European languages express the individual by its attribute or quality realized concretely by the individual itself, while the Sanskrit expresses the individual only as one of the instances belonging to the abstract universal.

In Sanskrit, furthermore, any noun or adjective can become an abstract noun by addition of -tā or -tva suffix, i.e., the abstract noun can be made without limit in Sanskrit. On the contrary, in the Greek or Latin language the abstract noun is made by addition of -$\tau\eta$ or -tas, and does not allow such freedom. Here we can also find one of the Indian tendencies to think anything abstractly and universally.

Expressions with cognate objects appear more often in early Indian languages than in European languages. In English there are some expressions with cognate objects as "to fight a battle," "to die a hard death," "to live a good life," etc., but such usage is limited. On the contrary, in classical Indian languages such expressions have been widely and freely allowed through all the ages.[3] Therefore it is often impossible to translate from Sanskrit directly into the European languages; e.g., *kāmakāmaḥ* = *amori dediti* (desiring desire or given to love) in A. W. Schlegel's Latin translation of Dhp., 83 (those in pursuit of their desire), *abhijñānābhijñātiḥ* (possessed of occult power), *varṣaṁ varṣate, tapas tapate,* etc.

That Indians were at home in abstract speculation can be seen in their skillful expression of the ideas of numbers. A large number or an infinitesimal number often appears in religious books and literary works. This reveals their rich imagination and analysis. The decimal system of Arabic numerals based on the place notation, had been invented by the Chinese and Indians, and the Arabians only transmitted it to European countries. The manner of writing numbers in a linear horizontal order appears in ancient Chinese, but our circular sign for zero was invented by the Indians. In Sanskrit zero is called "*śūnya*" which is translated as "*kung*" by the Chinese word for "empty" in the Chinese Buddhist canons. A dot was used for zero in the ancient Chinese place system.

We are impressed by one of the main features of most philosophical thinking in India, namely a predominant way of minimizing the particular in the logical sense. This does not mean that the Indians did not develop the concept of the individual.[4] They did. The Sanskrit equivalent of individual is *vyakti*. But *vyakti* did not play much of a role in the history of Indian logic.

Most Indian thinkers are apt to emphasize universal concepts and to subordinate the concrete individual and the particular perception to the universal. Even in the Vaiśeṣika philosophy of atomic naturalism, which organized objectively the most advanced, logically coherent system of natural philosophy in India, there is no direct awareness of the concretely perceived individual. Instead, the Vaiśeṣika philosophers used the technical term *antya viśeṣa*[5] to represent the principle of particularity or what the Western scholastic metaphysicians called the principle of individuation.

Of course, in other pluralistic philosophical systems in India there was more attention to the concept of the individual, and its unique meaning was investigated. In ancient India there were frequent debates between the Individualist and the Universalist concerning the meaning of a word. The Individualist (*Vyaktivādin*) held that the individual (*vyakti*) is the denoted sense of a word, whereas the Universalist (*Jātivādin*) held that the universal (*jāti*) is the denoted sense of a word. For example, when we are asked to bring a cow, it is only obvious that what is requested is an individual cow and not a universal existing in the entire class of cows, said the Individualist, whereas the Universalist said that the universal form of the cow is implied in this case.[6]

But in Indian philosophy for the most part, the position of the perceived individual was minimized in favor of the *inferred* particular and the *conceived* universal, differing from the schools of European philosophy in which the individual, the particular, and the universal were all given equal consideration with respect to their meanings and logical status.

Even Indian realists and pluralists esteemed universals. In giving the definition of "substance" some of them said, "A substance is that which is endowed with the genus of substance."[7] This is a purely verbal definition, or a truism which teaches us nothing new about the thing to be defined, but they were satisfied, perhaps because of their very tendency to reify concepts.

We are aware of the opinion that there is a strain in Indian philosophy which also stressed individualism. But the individual soul is given the metaphysical status of a permanent substance "co-eternal with God"; as Dr. D. M. Datta says: "Emphasis on the importance of the individual is common to all the Indian systems of philosophy. It is worthy of special note that even those who believe in God as the creator do not hold that the individual soul is created by God. God creates only the material objects, including the human body. But the soul is co-eternal with God."[8]

Even the Buddhists who did not believe in a soul as a permanent substance believed in the potential Buddhahood of every individual. However, Indian esteem for the individual raised problems concerning its metaphysical sense of "the essence of living things," but it was only in the logical sense of the word that Buddhist thinkers admitted the significance of the individual (*vyakti*). With them the individual meant "the thing in itself" (*svalakṣaṇa*), which is just an instant or moment in any given situation in the transient course of time; it is the extreme concrete and particular (*kiñcid idam*—the *hoc aliquid*).[9] Mental construction or judgment (*kalpanā, adhyavasāya*) comes later.[10]

This way of thinking appears not only in their philosophy but also in their daily speech; e.g., in Sanskrit *the plural form* of the abstract noun often appears, i.e., *lakṣmyaḥ* means "happiness of a person," *kīrtayaḥ* means "honor of a person" and *bhayeṣu* (lit. in horrors) means "when he was filled with horror" (*bhayakāleṣu*). There are a few expressions like this in European languages, but they are generally used with special meaning, while in Sanskrit many plural forms of abstract nouns are used in a meaning not dissimilar to its singular form. Moreover, in modern European languages, like German and French, the exactly opposite phenomenon can be seen, i.e., the plural form of a proper noun designates those who bear the name, families including all servants and maids, or those who can be ascribed to that person's type; e.g., "*die Goethe*" means "the family of Goethe," "men who are self-centered like Goethe" or "people who have a brilliant talent"; "*les Périclès*" means "people who are conceited about their talent like *Périclès*."[11] In short, Europeans generally think of the abstract notion of an abstract noun as constructed solely by means of the universal meaning which is extracted from daily experience, so that they represent it in the singular form; on the contrary, the Indians think of the abstract notion as what is included within experienced facts and so fused with them that the essential principle is often represented in the plural form. And again, modern European people lay stress on the significance of the individual, so that they can easily classify a man by a type consisting of those who are similar to a special person, and thus change a proper noun into a common noun; on the contrary, the Indians tend to neglect the significance of the individual, so that such expressions as "die Goethe" or "les Périclès" do not appear at all.

According to the way of thinking of most Indians, therefore, the essence of the individual or the particular is no more than the universal by virtue of which the individual or the particular is grounded and realized. The tendency of most Indians is to lay stress on the significance of the universal only, and they almost neglect the significance of the individual or the particular. From this a characteristic way of thinking is introduced; i.e., the difference between that which possesses an attribute and the attribute itself is not clarified adequately by the Indians, and the difference between that which supports a substance and the substance itself is not clarified. In Indian languages there are many examples of "κατ' ἐξοχήν"; i.e., a common noun was extended to a proper noun; e.g., *buddha* (literally, he who has won enlightenment) became a proper noun for Śākyamuni, The Buddha, and *jina* (literally, one who has won) became the proper name of Jina (Vardhamāna). As a result of the same thinking process, the neuter singular form of an adjective sometimes fulfills the function of an abstract noun, e.g., *śuci* (pure, pureness), *sthira* (= solid, solidity = *sthairya*), *ślāghya* (excellent, excellence); or again the neuter singular form of an adjective sometimes fulfills the function of a collective noun, e.g., *palita* (gray, gray hair).[12] So in Sanskrit there are similar cases where the distinction between abstract "solidity" and a concrete "solid" thing is not clarified in the actual language, even though it may be clarified by using an abstract noun.

In short, these linguistic phenomena in Indian languages may have resulted from the fact that the earlier Indians were unaware of the significance of the inherent or attributive judgment.[13] Now the characteristic way of thinking mentioned above is seen in the structure of the Indian languages and reveals some important differences when compared with other peoples' forms of thought and expression. In this way of thinking, the distinction between an attribute and a ground of that attribute is almost always neglected, so that the Indians can hardly distinguish between substantive and adjective as two parts of speech. In Sanskrit grammar, these two show little difference in regard to declension, composition, and derivation. Especially in the Vedic literature, it is very difficult for us to find out which is substantive and which is adjective among many terms that indicate the same object. Even in classical Sanskrit, an adjective is used as a substantive, e.g., *suhṛd* (goodhearted, a friend), *tapana* (burning, the sun). On the contrary, in classical European languages, regarding the inherent judgment, the distinction between substantive and adjective is fairly fixed and occurs with little variation except in special instances.

The inclination to lay stress on the universal appears to some degree among the ancient Europeans in their languages. An adjective takes a form corresponding to the gender and number of the noun which it modifies, both in classical European and Indian languages, and it does not appear in its original form; e.g., ἀνὴρ ἀγαθός, *vir bonus* (good man), γυνὴ ἀγαθή, *mulier bona* (good woman). Such a grammatical rule of declension makes a speaker understand clearly that the essence of a conception expressed by an adjective is different from the specific attribute indicated by the adjective which modifies some concrete thing. Plato touched the problem of "Virtue itself as to its universality" after he had examined human virtue (ἀρετή), by analyzing the general idea into the virtue of man, of woman, of child, of slave, and so on. Plato's intellectual procedure would have been very natural and rational for the Greek people at that time; the problem, however, of whether it is possible to pursue abstract "virtue in general" apart from concrete deeds becomes a difficult question in modern ethics. But in India the conception, which was represented by an adjective, had more importance than the individual that was modified by the adjective; and the significance of individual things, which embodied the conception represented by the adjective, was reduced to almost nothing for the Indians.

Abstract Conceptions Treated as Concrete Realities

As a result of the Indian propensity for the abstract notion, in their way of thinking an abstract idea is expressed as if it were a concrete object, i.e., in their thinking process the universal is easily endowed with substantiality. Already in the Brāhmaṇas, which offer explanations of the Vedic sacrifices, abstract ideas are treated as if they were on the same plane as concrete things. This has been stated as follows: "The most remarkable characteristic of this age was that they gave spiritual powers, mysterious powers, and the role of deities without personification to the concrete elements of which the universe was constructed (heaven, sky, earth, sun and moon, stars and compass-directions, soil, water, fire, wind, and ether; years and months; seasons; animals, plants, and minerals, and so on), to the elements which were necessary for their rituals (the apparatus, rhythm, curse, and name, and so on), to the physical and mental organs, functions, qualities, abstract conceptions, numerals, and so on; in other words, to all sorts of phenomena in the natural world and human life, especially in a religious ceremony."[14] It seems that Brahmin priests of ancient India were certainly engaged in such speculations in accordance with this way of thinking. The word "*brahman,*" the original meaning of which was the magical power of spells used freely by Brahmins, became at the same time the name of the Brahmins themselves merely by changing the position of its accent; by the same thinking process "*kṣatriya,*" the name of the royal family, came from the word "*kṣatra,*" the original meaning of which was the reigning power. Here the essential nature of a thing is identified with the realizer of its power, and an abstract noun is used as a common noun; i.e. the Indians expose their thinking to the so-called charge of "reification" by fictitiously endowing every notion with substance.

According to the description in some *Upaniṣads,* the Indians assumed two routes (i.e. the *devayāna* and the *pitṛyāna*) which a man follows after he is dead.[15] One who goes the way of *devayāna* (the way of the gods) enters successively into the flame of his cremation, from the flame into the day; from the day into the half-month while the moon waxes; from the half-month of the waxing moon into the six months while the sun goes north; from these months into the world of the gods—the sun, the moon, the lightning-fire; and then he enters, guided by a person of mind (*mānasa*), into Brahman or the world of Brahmā; thus he never returns to this world. On the other hand, one who by sacrifices and austerity goes the way of *pitṛyāna* (the way of the fathers) enters successively into the smoke of his cremation and into the night; from the night into the half-month while the moon decreases, into six months while the sun goes south; from these months into the world of the ancestors' spirits; from this ancestral world into the moon where he stays to become food for the gods; then he begins to descend into space; he enters successively into the sky, air, rain, the earth; and then he enters into food (like rice and barley); he becomes a spermatozoon if he enters into the fire of a man; and then he enters into a womb of a woman to be reborn. In these steps after death, the smoke of cremation, the world of ancestors' spirits, the sun, the moon, and the lightning have some extent in space, so that it is no wonder that a dead man passes through these steps; but the night, the half-month while the moon waxes or wanes, and six months while the sun goes north or south are not anything in space but something in time, so that these descriptions in the *Upaniṣads* seem very strange, as it tells us a dead man passes through the *devayāna* or *pitṛyāna* both in space and in time. This, however, caused little wonder to the Indians at that time, who had inherited the way of thinking in the Brāhmaṇa literature as it had been. Those scholars, who wrote the Brāhmaṇa literature, thought that all abstract conceptions or ideas in space also had substantiality, and discussed them as if they were on the same level as material things in space. In this way of thinking, the day, the night, a half-month, and six months, etc. *can be expressed as if they were concrete things*. Some philosophers in the *Upaniṣads* seemed to be incapable of getting rid of such a way of thinking, and the theory of the two ways after death in the *Upaniṣads* has been adopted without change by the later Vedāntic philosophers.[16]

Thereafter, this way of thinking became popular among the common people in India. In many popular books, e.g., in the *Upamitibhavaprapañcakathā*, an educational story of the Jains, the *Prabodhacandrodaya*, a drama based on the Vedāntic philosophy, many abstract nouns are used as the main characters in them. These stories and dramas would not be read enthusiastically by Europeans but they can excite much interest among Indians.

There are many cases showing that this way of thinking has been adopted by Indian philosophers. In the Buddhist period, Pakudha Kaccāyana (c. 500 B.C.) posited pain and pleasure in addition to the earth, water, fire, wind, souls, and sky as the eternal, unchangeable, independent elements, of which all things in the universe are composed. Makkhali Gosāla of the Ājīvikas supposed good and bad fortune as well as life and death as substantial principles. With the Jains the condition or law of movement (*dharma*) and the condition or principle of non-movement (*adharma*) were also independent substances. The Sarvāstivādins, who became the most prosperous Buddhist school, maintained that all the elements admitted in Buddhism exist really in events occurring through all time, i.e. the past, the present, and the future. The principles (*dharma*) mentioned by them rather belong to psychological functions or to abstract ideas. The Vaiśeṣikas supposed the six *padārthas* (categories) as fundamental principles; they are abstract ideas that are classified into six groups and admitted as substantial elements. The philosophy of the Sarvāstivādins and the Vaiśeṣikas is called "Conceptual Realism" (*Begriffsrealismus*) by European scholars because these Indian systems are similar to the moderate Realism of European philosophy in the medieval period.

Hegel confirms our description of Indian philosophy in characterizing it as the "growing of the mind inwardly in the most abstract way" (*Fürsichwerden der Seele auf die abstrakteste Weise*), and he called it "intellectual substantiality" (*intellektuelle Substantialität*).[17] This characterization by Hegel is not correct in the case of the Vedānta Philosophy, which has been the main flow of Indian philosophy; however the endowment of concepts with substantiality can be regarded as a prominent characteristic of most schools of Indian philosophy.

CHAPTER 3 PREFERENCE FOR THE NEGATIVE

Fondness for the Negative Expression.

The Indians were led to an ultimately unlimited or indeterminate goal as the result of their leading school's way of thinking and seeking the universal. Generally, the philosophers of this school say that the universal is less limited than the individual, so that at the end of their quest for the universal they posit the undetermined.

Thus the negative character of Indian thought comes into prominence. When we take up their language as our first problem, we cannot help wondering why the Indians are so fond of the noun with the negative. For instance, the Indians say "victory or non-victory" (*jayājayau*) instead of distinguishing "Victory or defeat" and "victory or draw" as in other languages, and they say "non-one" (*aneka*) instead of "many or none." The word composed with the negative serves to express not only negative but also positive meaning. In the Indian mind "non-idleness" (*apramāda*), "non-grudge" (*avera*),[1] "non-violence" (*ahiṃsā*), etc. appeal as more positive moral virtues than "exertion," "tolerance," "peace," etc. To Europeans such a negative expression of these virtues appeals less than a positive expression for practical conduct but to most Indians these negatively expressed virtues have more power.

A yoga-disciple of the Brahmanic schools must always keep five moral precepts, i.e., non-violence (*ahiṃsā*), sincerity (*satya*), non-theft (*asteya*), chastity (*brahmacarya*) and non-acquisition (*aparigraha*).[2] Thus three of them (the words beginning with *a*—) are expressed in the negative form. The precepts which must be kept by the layman in Buddhism and Jainism are all shown in the negative form, the original meanings of which are "to rest apart from violence," "to rest apart from theft" and so on.[3] The Sarvāstivādins also enumerate negatively "non-idleness" (*apramāda*), "non-covetousness" (*anabhidhyā*), "non-wrath" (*avyāpāda*) and "non-violence" (*ahiṃsā*) among the ten great attainments of the mind. In the Brahmanic canons the various precepts are sometimes given positive expression; but in the *Vinaya-piṭaka,* in which the precepts for Buddhist monks are set forth, they are almost written in the negative form. Thus the Indians are apt to see morality in the negation of ordinary men's actions, so that they lay stress on the negative phase. Apart from the Ten Commandments of the Old Testament, showing moral precepts in a negative form seems somewhat powerless and unsatisfactory to most other people, but to the Indians, who lay stress on the negative phase and pursue the undetermined, the negative form of expression has more positive and powerful meaning.

We find it not surprising, therefore, that the Indians like to use negative conceptions even in ordinary sentences. In the classical and modern European languages the negative judgment is usually expressed by adding the negative to the finite verb in the predicate, e.g., "Er wird nicht gehen." On the other hand, in the ancient Indian languages the central conception of a sentence is expressed in negative form, e.g., "One (who attains to Enlightenment) goes to a non-meeting with the king of Death" (*adassanaṁ maccurājassa gacche* (*Dhp.*, 46) = *mortis regem non videbit.* = he will not meet with the King of Death.) Thus the Europeans and the Japanese express the negative sentence by using the positive and affirmative conception as its subject, while the Indians express it by using the negative conception as the main subject.

Again in the classical European languages, the negative of the participle of a verb is formed in the same way as the negative of the verb; on the other hand in the ancient Indian languages it is formed in the same way as the negative of a *noun* is made; e.g., *appasaṁ udayavyayaṁ* (*Dhp.*, 113) = *ortum* (*rerum*) *et interitum non animadvertens.* This linguistic phenomenon again illustrates their fondness for the negative conception.

The Indians think a negative form of judgment is not only negative but also positive and affirmative. So in Indian logic the universal negative judgment (E) is not used, and is discussed only by being changed into the universal positive obverse judgment (A); e.g., "All speeches are non-eternal." (*anityaḥ śabhaḥ*).

Grasping the Absolute Negatively

Due to their way of thinking or expressing everything negatively, the Indians pursue the Infinite or the Negative and focus on the idea of infinity in their philosophical approaches. The Absolute is expressed as the Infinite or the Negative by the Indians.

In remote times, philosophical thought about the world's creation, expressed by the poets of the *Ṛg-Veda,* reached its peak when they sang of the universal principle in the hymn called *"Nāsadāsīya"* (Then there was neither non-existence nor existence).[4] According to this hymn, in primordial antiquity there was neither non-existence nor existence, neither heaven nor space, neither death nor non-death, and there was no distinction between day and night. The whole universe was covered with darkness and was filled with rippling water devoid of light. "That One" (*tad ekam*) appeared there, by its own heat, and gave existence to desire (*kāma*). Then it realized all things in the universe using desire as the motivating power. After the creation of the universe many gods appeared too.

According to Yājñavalkya, the greatest philosopher among the wise men in the *Upaniṣads*, the highest principle in the universe is that which is free from all differential qualification. He says, "This essential being (*ātman*) is no other than pure wisdom without internality and externality. . . . It has an indestructible and imperishable quality. . . . This Ātman can be expressed only through the negative as 'not so, not so' (*neti neti*). It is incomprehensible for it cannot be perceived. It is indestructible for it cannot be destroyed. It is non-attachable for it attaches itself to nothing. It has never been restrained, disturbed, or injured."[5] In another passage he calls this highest principle the "Non-perishable" (*akṣara*), and says, "It is neither large and rough (*sthūla*) nor infinitesimal (*sūkṣma*), neither short nor long, neither burning nor moist. It has no shade, darkness, wind, space, attachment, taste, smell, eyes, ears, speeches, mind, light, vitality, mouth, quantity, internality and externality. It eats nothing and nothing eats it."[6]

We can see similar expressions in the later *Upaniṣads*: "There shines neither the sun nor the moon nor the stars. That lightning bolt also never shines. To say nothing of fire on earth!"[7] Light in the phenomenal world is almost nothing when it is compared with the Brahman, the light of the Absolute.

In early Buddhism the state of enlightenment is explained by a similar expression. "Where there exists no earth, water, fire, and wind there shines neither the sun, nor the moon, nor the stars, and there exists no darkness. When a Brahmin becomes able to perceive this by himself and becomes a saint (*muni*) by silent meditation, he shall be able to be free from materiality and non-materiality (*rūpārūpa*); pain and pleasure."[8]

Negative expressions are used very abundantly in the scriptures of Mahāyāna Buddhism. As one of the instances I would like to introduce some passages from the *Prajñāpāramitāhṛdaya-sūtra*. "Thus, these elemental things (*dharma*) all have the characteristic of voidness (*śūnyatā*); therefore they are neither created nor perished, they have neither impurity nor purity, they can neither increase nor decrease. Therefore, in the void there is neither materiality (*rūpa*) nor sensation (*vedanā*) nor imagination (*saṁjñā*) nor volition (*saṁskāra*) nor consciousness (*vijñāna*); there exist neither eyes nor ears in it nor nose nor tongue nor tactile organs nor intellect, there is neither color and shape nor sound nor odor nor taste nor tangibles nor non-sensuous objects; there exists neither the sphere of vision, the sphere of intellect, ignorance, the extinction of ignorance, old age and death, the extinction of old age and death, suffering, the cause and extinction and the path toward extinction, wisdom nor the attainment of wisdom, for there is nothing to be attained. Because the *bodhisattva* relies on the *prajñāpāramitā*, the mind is unobstructed. Because there is no obstruction, there exists no fear. Abandoning all inverted phantasies, the *bodhisattva* penetrates to *Nirvāṇa*."

Nāgārjuna (ca. A.D. 150–250), who is considered to have established the foundation of Mahāyāna Buddhism, in his version of Buddhist philosophy was able to expound and demonstrate the theory of "the excellent causal origin of things (*pratītyasamutpāda*) which is non-destructive, non-productive, non-extinguishable, non-eternal, non-uniform, non-diversified, non-coming, and non-going, and causes vain phenomena to cease."[9] The eight kinds of negative expression enumerated here, referred to as the "Eight Negations," can also be found in other Mahāyāna scriptures.[10] Nāgārjuna, his followers thought, had chosen these eight negations because they are the most important representative statement of the numerous negations needed to clarify the real aspect of the emptiness of all things.[11] Thus the ultimate reality shown by Mahāyāna Buddhists is the absolute voidness (*śūnyatā*) that is devoid of all qualifications and about which no conceptual determination can be formed.

Such negative expressions of Mahāyāna Buddhism exerted a favorable influence upon many schools including the Vedānta. "There is neither extinction nor creation, neither one who has been bound nor one who has practiced austerities, neither one who wishes emancipation nor one who obtained the emancipation. This is the highest truth[12] (*paramārthatā*)."[13] The influence of such expressions can be seen not only in Śaṁkara[14] and his followers[15] but in the schools of later Hinduism.[16]

The Jains also state similarly: "[One who has obtained enlightenment is] neither long nor short nor circular nor triangular nor square nor globular nor black nor blue nor red nor yellow nor white nor fragrant nor ill-smelling nor bitter nor pungent nor puckery nor sour nor sweet nor rough nor soft nor heavy nor light nor cold nor hot nor coarse nor smooth, he neither has a body nor departs from the body nor remains in the body, he is neither feminine nor masculine nor neuter; he has wisdom (*prajñā*) and intellect (*saṁjñā*). However, there is no simile [by which the emancipated soul can be known]. The essence of the emancipated soul has no form. One who has no word cannot speak a word. There is neither sound nor color and shape nor smell nor taste nor tactile objects."[17]

Let us compare this with the parallel case of Greek philosophy where we find the ancient idea that the universe is a circular and complete globe in itself. This theory perhaps originated in Xenophanes[18] and was advocated by Parmenides who maintained that τὸ ἔον (Being) as the fundamental principle of the world is a complete globe.[19] Pythagoras and his followers thought, "What is determinate is more excellent than what is not determinate."[20] Empedocles taught that in the beginning of the world the universe was globular when it was in chaos.[21] And this idea of the globular universe was inherited by Plato[22] and Aristotle.[23]

Greek people, who had pre-eminent skill in visual intuition and such arts as sculpture, preferred to see the clear image of all things. Therefore, that which was devoid of boundaries was considered to be indeterminate, without certitude, incomplete, and imperfect, so that even in regard to the super-sensory, they could not divorce themselves from their concrete way of thinking. Even Parmenides, who seemed to grasp the ultimate principle of Being most abstractly and negatively, discussed the fundamental principle of the world as if it were a material existence, expressing it as a spatial or extended thing. And, the fact that he thought it a globe shows us that he was influenced by the intuitive and concrete view of things which was general among Greek people. Even Plato called immaterial substance by the visual name of "idea" (or literally, figure, form).

In general, the ancient Greek people had a way of thinking concretely. Though they speculated on things rationally and conceptually they rarely ever tried to reach such vague abstractions as total voidness.[24] As I shall show later, the Chinese people, even more than the Greek people, were fond of expressing themselves concretely and intuitively. On the other hand, the Indians generally disliked grasping the Absolute or the ultimate principle concretely and intuitively. We should not maintain that our conclusion would apply to all Indian thinkers, but we can say that those who liked abstract speculation were inclined to grasp the notion of the Absolute or ultimate principle in terms of the unlimited and absolute negative.

Now the Absolute which seemed to have such negative characteristics has been expressed as a *non-personal principle* by the Indians. We can also discover such a representation of the Absolute in some of the mystics in Europe, but they did call such an impersonal Absolute by the name of "God." For instance, Scotus Eriugena maintained, "It is not unreasonable for God to be called Nothing because of His transcendent superiority." Yet he called the Absolute *"Deus"* to whom he refused to give any attribute. On the contrary, Indian philosophers regard the highest God as an inferior existence when compared with the highest principle. According to the Vedānta school, the creation of the world by the highest God was caused by illusion (*māyā*). They say, "The God that is Ātman discriminates himself with his own powers of phantasy (illusion, *māyā*)."[25] "The God that is Ātman is deceived (*saṁmohita*) by the powers of phantasy (*māyā*) of this God."[26] There is no *māyā* in God himself, but when he creates the world as a Supervisor *māyā* attaches itself to him. God is in an illusory state. And because this illusion exists, the evolution of the world is possible. Therefore it became the fundamental notion in the followers of Śaṁkara that "Supervisor (*Īśvara*) = Highest Principle (*brahman*) + Illusion (*māyā*)." This view that the Absolute causes the world to come into existence through illusion has been inherited by some sects of Hinduism.

Thus the ultimate Absolute presumed by the Indians is not a personal god but an impersonal and metaphysical Principle. Here we can see the *impersonal character* of the Absolute in Indian thought.[27]

The inclination of grasping the Absolute negatively necessarily leads (as Hegel would say) to the negation of the negative expression itself. According to some *Upaniṣad*, Bādhva, a wise man, answered with silence when he was asked the true nature of *Brahman*. Someone asked him, "Please teach me the true nature of *Brahman*." Badhva was rapt in silence. The man asked again, and still Badhva spoke nothing. When he was asked repeatedly he said, "I am teaching now, but you cannot understand it. For this *Ātman* is tranquility itself."[28] Vimalakīrti, a wise Buddhist layman, seems to have attained a more abstruse state of mind. According to the *Vimalakīrtinirdeśa*, Vimalakīrti asked thirty-two Bodhisattvas, "How can it be possible to attain the unequalled truth of Buddhism?" And he listened to their answers silently. At last they asked Mañjuśrī, a Bodhisattva, to tell his opinion. He told them, "Where there is neither word nor speech, neither revelation nor consciousness. Such a state of mind is called the attainment of the unequalled truth of Buddhism." Then Mañjuśrī called on Vimalakīrti to express his own views. But Vimalakīrti was in silence. Seeing this Mañjuśrī cried, "Well done! I have spoken of 'non-word,' but you have revealed it with your body."

In India the various religions refer to the sage and to the religious aspirant as "*Muni*," which means "he who maintains silence."[29] They believe that truth is equivalent to the state of silence. Moreover, Mahāyāna Buddhism rejects any view attached to the void, and insists that "The void too must be negated." Here we have again the logic of negation.

Attraction for the Unknown

It is a fact that the Indians tend to pay more attention to the unknown and to the undefined than to the known and the defined. This attraction for the unknown resulted in a fondness for concealing even the obvious; their way of thinking tended to prefer the dark and obscure over that which was clear. As a result the Indians like expressions in the form of a difficult riddle. In the Samhitās of the Veda we can occasionally find poems offering for conjecture a riddle. Gods were pictured as amusing themselves with a riddle.[30] Even philosophical problems are expressed in the form of a riddle; e.g.,

> "A swan never pulls up one leg when getting out of water,
> If he did pull one leg up indeed there would be neither today
> nor tomorrow,
> Also there would be neither day nor night,
> Also the light at dawn would never shine."[31]

This poem is interpreted as being an expression of the following truth: The Supreme Existence manifests itself through the world, and yet exists behind the phenomenal world and is immutable. Such forms of expression found their way into the *Upaniṣads* and later literature. This method must not be confused with the riddles that also provide amusement.

In contrast to this, from the outset Buddhism has maintained the position that it was an "open" religion. "O bhikkhus, the *dharma* and the precepts revealed by the Tathāgata send forth clear light. Never are they observed in secrecy."[32] They are as clear and evident "as the sun-disk or the moon-disk." Furthermore, "Regarding the *dharma* of the Tathāgatha, there exists no closed teacher-fist"[33]; i.e., Tathāgata as a teacher has no secret in his teaching. These passages, however, can mean only that the religion that originated with Gotama would never be hidden from any people and it would never reject any people. Even Buddhists were unable to free themselves from the Indian propensity to express their thoughts through unintelligible riddles.

> "Killing his mother and his father,
> killing two kings of the Kṣatriya tribe,
> Killing the kingdom and its subjects,
> a Brāhmin goes on without pain." (*Dhammapada,* 294)
>
> "Killing his mother and his father,
> killing two kings of the Brāhmin tribe,
> Killing a tiger as the fifth,
> a Brāhmin goes on without pain." (*Ibid.,* 295)

It would be impossible for a Buddhist, who would feel it a sin to kill only a little worm, to teach another to kill his mother and father, etc. According to the commentary of these sentences, "his mother" means "passion" (*kāma*); "his father" means "conceit"; "two kings" means "two unjust opinions," i.e., to believe that the soul perishes absolutely after one's death and to believe that the soul exists for eternity after one's death; "the kingdom" means the "twelve *Āyatanas,*" i.e., the six internal organs (eyes, ears, nose, tongue, tactile organ, intellect) and the six external objects (color and shape, sound, odor, taste, tangibles, non-sensuous objects) of which our individual existence is constituted; "its subjects" means "attachment to pleasure"; "a tiger" means "doubt" and "the tiger as the fifth" means "five kinds of obstacle," i.e. covetousness, anger, sleep, evil-doing, and doubt. We are unable to understand the meaning until we paraphrase the interpretation of the commentary. Whether or not this interpretation explains the purport of the analogy, remains a problem; however, that there exists some sort of hidden meaning within this analogy cannot be seriously doubted. We can also find many allegorical expressions in the *Kaṭha, Śvetāśvatara,* and other *Upaniṣads.*

CHAPTER 4 MINIMIZING INDIVIDUALITY AND SPECIFIC PARTICULARS

Language

To lay stress on the universal inclines the mind to disregard the individual and the particular. I have already referred to the Indian disregard for the individual and the particular in a previous chapter, so in this chapter I shall consider it from a different point of view.

It is necessary to use an article (the, a) to show where the individual is placed within a proposition. There was, however, no article in ancient Indian languages. Both the definite article and the indefinite article did exist but only in a formative state which failed to develop. So the meaning of the word *"mahān"* can be both "great," as an adjective and "a great thing or the great," as a noun. And a substantive can even enter into a compound as if it were an adjective, e.g., *hinasevā* = same, with an adjective and participle used like an adjective. An adjective can even enter into a compound as if it were a substantive, e.g., *hīnasevā* = *hinānām sevā, mahadāśrayaḥ* = *mahatsv āśrayaḥ.*[1]

In the European classical languages to say "someone's descendant" or "someone's army" is expressed by *two words,* i.e., "someone" and "descendant" or "someone" and "army"; while in Sanskrit it is often expressed by one word containing a possessive connotation and thus having a vague meaning, e.g., *māmakāḥ pāṇḍavāś ca* = υἱοὶ μου καὶ οἱ τοῦ Πανδάτα, *nostrates Pānduidaeque*[2] (*Bhag. G.*, I. 1): *Saumadattḥ* = ὁ τοῦ Σομαδάτα (*ibid.* I. 8). From these instances we may infer the following: the Indians in accord with their way of thinking indicated above, express only prescribed attributes as determined, and avoid indicating the substantive as the determined; thus they lay stress on the essentially determining character of a substance which lies in the background or cannot be seen, ignoring any concrete direct perception.

Such a characteristic way of thinking can be also found in the way they express abstract notions. Early Europeans used two different concepts to express what existed independently in each abstraction; on the other hand the Indians thought that these two conceptions really came into existence conjointly so that through the correlation of these two the more profound conception, from which these two conceptions evolved, had to be sought. In accord with this way of thinking, Indians using Sanskrit often express one of two contrary conceptions by the negative form of the other, e.g., *"lābhālabhau jayājayau"* (*Bhag. G.*, II. 38) (literally "attainment and non-attainment and victory and non-victory = good and bad fortune, victory and defeat").

The tendency to grasp abstract ideas in this way of thinking appears most prominently in the philosophy of the Mādhyamika school of Mahāyāna. The founder of that school, Nāgārjuna (c. A.D. 150–250), said, "Impurity (*aśubha*) cannot exist without depending on purity (*śubha*) so that we explain purity by impurity. Therefore purity by itself cannot be attained. Purity cannot exist without depending on impurity, so that we explain impurity by purity. Therefore impurity cannot exist by itself."[3] He did not try to grasp them separately. He thought that "purity" apart from "impurity" or "impurity" apart from "purity" cannot come into existence; "purity," however, exists by negation of "impurity" and "impurity" exists by negation of "purity"; thus they are dependent on each other. He advocated as a basic notion of causation that, "When there is this, then there is that, just as when there is shortness then there is longness."[4]

On the contrary, the ancient Greeks and Romans did not like this way of thinking. So their languages expressed two opposite conceptions by two contrary words independently, as we have seen in the example of "good and bad fortune," "victory and defeat" (καὶ τὴν ἐπιτυχίον καί ἀποτυχίον, καὶ τὴν νὶκην καὶ ἧτταν).

Because their method of thinking puts more stress on the underlying features or essence of the individual than on the particular surface qualities of the self, the Indians seem inclined to stress more the relational meaning of a thing than its fundamental uniqueness. According to the dominant way of thinking in India the nature of the individual or the particular is dependent on the universal through which the individual or the particular is supported and inferred. For instance, *"gatabhartṛkā"* means a widow whose husband (*bhartṛ*) is dead (*gata*). Such a way of expression, which was called *"bahuvrīhi"* (possessive compound, attributive compound) by Indian grammarians, has developed eminently in Indian languages; so that the word of *"bahuvrīhi"* is used as a technical term in modern comparative philology.

That the Indians are inclined to neglect the individual can be noticed in many other usages of their language. Sanskrit, the classical Indian language, has no single pronoun to represent "the same," "identical." So to express "the same" an indeclinable *"eva"* (only, just), which expresses only emphasis, is added after the demonstrative pronoun *"tad,"* so that *"tad eva"* is after all a general term for a singular object. To express "identical" an adjective *"sama"* is used in Sanskrit—this word is derived from the same etymological origin as the English "same"—but this word means also "equal" and "similar." And a noun *"sāmya"* means "equality" and "identity." Thus the Indians did not strictly distinguish between "equality," "similarity," and "identity" in their daily usage. This usage is again evidence of their tendency to disregard the individual. Therefore when they need to express "identical" or "same," they used *"abhinna"* whose literal meaning is "not different." Indian philosophers have invented such circuitous expressions as *"ekatva," "tādātmya," "aikātmya," "ekātmatā,"* etc. to denote the meaning of "identity" or "sameness."

In this connection the fact may be worth noting that ancient Sanskrit speaking-people used the singular form of *"sarva"* (all) to express "each" and "every."[5] The pronoun *"sarva"* means "all" in its plural form, and in the singular form it means "each" or "every," although when they wanted to express "each" they used the word *"ekaika"* or repetition of the same word, e.g. *vane vane* (in each forest), *dine dine* (every day), *yadā yadā* (whenever). Moreover, the dual form has remained in Sanskrit and it has never been dropped. The dual form can also be seen in ancient Greek in Homer's epics, the Gothic (ancient German language), Celtic (Irish native tongue), etc., which are called collectively Indo-European languages. The Latin language dropped the dual form in its early stage, but we can find the traces of the dual form adhering to some words. The German language lost it in the thirteenth century, but we can find its traces in colloquial Bavarian. Among Slavic languages it remains only in some meaningless colloquial phrases. Among the Ugric (Hungarian and Finnish) languages, of different descent from that of Indo-European languages, it remains only in colloquial Ostyac and Vogul whose cultures are mostly extinct, and in other languages it has been dropped already.[6]

The meaning of the dual form is not, as is usually thought, that it indicates "two things" or multiplication by two, but indeed two things in such a relation that when one of them is expressed the other is necessarily remembered. For example, the Indian god of Heaven, Varuṇa, is always connected intimately with Mitra, so "Mitrau" (the dual form of Mitra) means "Mitra and Varuṇa"; *"pitarau"* (the dual form of *pitṛ* = father) means not "two fathers" but "father and mother," i.e., "parents." The same expression remains in Finnic-Hungarian languages, where the dual form of both "father" and "mother" means "parents." As father and mother are connected intimately, such an expression by dual form becomes possible. In Finnic-Hungarian languages the dual form of both "father" and "mother" means "parents," while in the Indian language only the dual form of "father" is used. This fact shows us that in India the patriarchal system of paternal rights dates back to early times, but in the other cultures the more ancient notion was preserved.

It was an original rule that the dual form was adapted to two things which were connected intimately as pairs, e.g., two hands, two feet, pairs which exist in the natural world or which are made artificially. The Indians, however, did not limit the application of the dual form to practical use. Therefore they generally used the dual form to express two things connected to each other. It is a well-known fact that in a primitive man's mind two things connected intimately could not be separated into two units, and they were usually expressed together as one thing. Together with the advance of civilization, however, the idea of a unit became so clear that people thought it unnecessary to distinguish dual from singular and plural, so in time the dual form disappeared from the grammatical system.[7] As a concrete example of this general rule, the dual form disappeared from the colloquial Indian languages (Pāli and other Prākrits). But in India Sanskrit has been used by the intelligentsia until recently, so that the dual form has been retained in use. Thus the thought pattern of the Indian intelligentsia has been influenced to the present day by this way of thinking of a pair of things grasped and expressed in a *Gestalt* rather than each thing individually. The dual form has had only a numerical value in many cases in Indo-European languages, like the ancient Greek. This linguistic phenomenon may have had little to do with ways of thinking, but anyhow it is worth noticing as an interesting case of a linguistic habit expressing a cultural trait for a given time.

Moreover, many literate people of India liked to express the notion of number by concrete nouns which come from their historical and social life; e.g., "*ṛṣi*" (sage) is often used to express "seven" for seven *ṛṣi* are enumerated as a group in their myths, "*agni*" (fire) is "three" for three kinds of *agni* are used in a large ceremony.[8] This tendency may have some connection with the Indian tendency of fondness for poetic diction, which will be discussed later. The tendency can be seen also in ancient Egyptian and German, which express a certain quantity by a concrete noun, not by a numeral,[9] but such expressions of cardinal numerals by concrete nouns cannot be seen in other languages, especially in modern times.

Many literate people of India indeed liked to express number concretely and intuitively, although Indian logicians developed the most abstract notion of number as the class of classes, as in the case of *vyāsajya-vṛtti* in the *Navya-nyāya school.*[10]

Discussing problems about ways of thinking of ancient peoples, Max Wertheimer[11] made it clear that number and the notion of number are so very different between ancient peoples and modern Europeans—i.e., ancient peoples generally grasped concrete numbers and the abstract notion of number according to their way of thinking by laying stress on *Gestalt,* while the notion of number of modern Europeans has been reached as a result of abstracting from the process of counting by numbers in common experiences. Such a way of thinking clearly remains in the ancient Indians, e.g., 19 is expressed "subtract 1 from 20" (*ekonaviṁśati*), 597 is expressed "subtract 3 from 600."[12] The same way of expression can also be seen in the Greek language, e.g., "Now, Megasthenes says, there are '120 lacking 2' (i.e. 118) nations in India." "Ἔθνεα δὲ Ἰνδικὰ εἴκοσι ἑκατὸν τὰ πάντα λέγει Μεγασθένης δυοῖν δέοντα" (Arrianos, *Indikē* VII).

Why didn't the Indians use abstract expressions for number, in spite of their inclination, which I have mentioned on several occasions, to lay stress on the universal and to use the abstract expression? We suggest the reason for it is as follows: number is an objective form that is valid for the quantitative aspects of the objective world; and the Indians, not interested primarily in an objective study of such aspects of the external natural world, would not be too concerned with constructive reflection about the application of number. That the natural sciences did not develop as far in India as in Europe seems to have an intimate connection with their way of thinking of universals as mentioned above. And, though the Indians had an intensive consciousness of the idea of time, they had little interest in calculating, grasping, and describing time quantitatively. This fact is connected with the neglect of historical details and the temporal causes of social change by Indian thinkers who look down upon time and change as illusory.

Minimizing Individuality and Specific Particulars

The inclination of most Indians to subordinate individuality and particularity to the universal appears in many spheres of India's cultural life. In the first place, the particular details of local geography and climatology have been neglected in India. Secondly, in their ethical books and moralizing fables, there is very little attention or criticism given to the individual's feelings and conduct. Thirdly, in their essays on art and aesthetics there is a good deal of speculative discussion of the nature or essence of beauty in general, but scarcely any detailed analysis of individual works or time-honored masterpieces of the many works of art in India.

A similar tendency may be noticed in the mythological personages of India. Gods in Indian mythology have hardly any individual personality insofar as they are symbolic mainly of universal powers or virtues. For example, Indra, a thunder-god, is a very highly respected deity in the *Ṛg-Veda,* but the word "Indra" is also used as a common noun to stand for any divine being who performs the same function.[13]

The underlying idea that motivates this minimizing of the individual, as a concretely perceived being, is the Indian tendency to think that all particular beings perceived by the senses are only illusions because only the universal is real. The subsumptive judgment ("A is a B") is simply a logical step from an illusory particular to a more real universal.

It may be argued that attention to particular details of individual things characterizes the scientific literature of India, especially in the biological sciences. However, the tendency to classification in any detailed concrete fashion has been confined to Indian works of a general kind such as the *Kāmā-sūtra,* the *Artha-śāstra,* and the *Nāṭya-śāstra* of Bharata. But most of these works lack case-histories of natural phenomena, just as there is a general neglect of specific events in human history other than the court annals and family records, never as detailed as the writings of the Chinese historians.

The Buddhist logician Dharmakīrti (ca. 650 A.D.) already had investigated problems concerning analytical and synthetic judgments. For him, however, in the following inference "This is a tree, because it is a *śiṁśapā,*" the major premise "All *śiṁśapās* are trees" is an analytical judgment, and "tree" is the essence of *"śiṁśapā,"* so tree is connected to *"śiṁśapā"* by the relation of identity (*tādātmya*). Now, common sense would not identify "tree" with any of its predicates, but the Indian Buddhist logic regards the essence of the predicate to be pervasive of the subject, and in that ultimate abstract sense finds an identity between them. Dharmottara, a follower of Dharmakīrti, says:[14] " 'Identity' with the predicated fact means that (the mark) represents itself, its essence (*svabhāva*). Since (in such cases) the essence of a logical reason is contained within the predicate, it is therefore dependent on it (and invariably concomitant with it)." He then goes on to present an objection: "The question arises, if they are essentially identical, there should be no difference between the reason and the predicate, so will the argument be (a repetition or) part of the thesis?" His answer to this question is: "These two are identical with reference to the ultimately real essence (i.e., the sense datum underlying both facts). But the constructed objects (*vikalpa-viṣayas*), those (conceptions) which have been superimposed (upon reality), are not the same (in the facts constituting) the reason and the consequence."[15]

The universal or the species, upon which the particular is based, must be subsumed under the higher universal or more general species. If such a relation to higher species is pursued, then eventually ultimate existence (*sattā*) is reached, beyond which nothing exists.

As a matter of fact, Bhartṛhari (ca. A.D. 450–500) expressed just such speculative thought. He maintained that since all species are realized by ultimate existence in the final analysis, so all the meanings of words are no other than ultimate existence. Moreover, he thought, the only ultimate existence is absolute being and what gives existence to species as species is not true being; as this relation between truth and non-truth can be seen between the subsuming upper species and the subsumed lower species, so any kind of conception is non-true against the universal while it is true against the particular. He said, "Now, as it was testified in the sacred book, these two things (*bhāva*), true and non-true, are present within every thing (*bhava*); and the true thing is the species, *the individual is non-true.*"[16]

CHAPTER 5 THE CONCEPT OF THE UNITY OF ALL THINGS

As a result of their inclination to emphasize Universal Being, to which all individuals and particulars are subordinated, most Hindus concentrate on the idea of the unity of all things. They look down upon the changing manifestations of the phenomenal world as illusory. According to those Indian philosophers who were more or less Vedāntic, only Universal Being behind these manifestations is the ultimate source of reality. And the more anything is individualized, the less it shares in the essence of reality. Individuals are nothing else than limited manifestations of Universal Being. From very ancient times, the Vedāntists had a strong tendency to think of the multifarious phenomena of the world as self-realizations of the one Absolute Being. The main current of Advaita Vedāntic metaphysics has been a thoroughgoing monism imposed on pluralistic but illusory phenomena. Although there were other branches of Vedānta, such as that of Madhva who adhered to a purely realistic and pluralistic standpoint, the main emphasis was on monism. The monistic Vedānta has dominated the classical scholarship of India, which has left its impress on Indian philosophy in general. This tendency has penetrated into more popular philosophy. Even the dualistic Sāṁkhya and the Vaiśeṣika schools also finally came to make a compromise with monism.

A primitive form of this monistic view was expressed in the *Ṛg-Veda* in the hymns of the creation of the universe, and it took a more clearly defined form in the *Upaniṣads*. The *Upaniṣads* express Absolute Being in many different ways. They follow the *Vedas*, assigning the role of the primal principle to things in nature, such as Wind, Water, or Ether. Adding to those survivals of the old Vedic ideas, the *Upaniṣads* took again the primacy of Absolute Being over the principles and functions of individual being such as the Spirit, the Understanding (*vijñāna*), or the Soul (*puruṣa*). And before they named it the *Brahman* or the *Ātman*, they attempted to express Absolute Being by various notions like "the existent," "the non-existent," "that which is neither existent nor not existent," "the undeveloped," "the controller within," or "the imperishable." Though the *Upaniṣads* express the Absolute by such multiple names, we can point out one feature common to these concepts: all of them suppose the existence of the One Absolute Being, underlying the diversified phases of the phenomenal world. All of the phenomenal phases belong to it, proceed from it, depend upon it, and are controlled by it. Furthermore, in the *Upaniṣads*, they conceive that the soul in individual beings is in its ultimate nature identical with the true Self (*Brahman; Ātman*). And this metaphysical monism in the *Upaniṣads* is followed in later Hinduism.[1] It is natural, therefore, that the Indian ethics sets as its highest goal the unification and assimilation of the individual self with the Universal Self. Even when one cannot hope to attain this goal in this life, he should continue his efforts to achieve it in the next world. One of the *Upaniṣads* describes the state that a man freed from desires enters after his death as follows, "Being *Brahman*, he goes to Brahman."[2] And the sage Śāṇḍilya declares, "When I shall have departed from hence, I shall obtain it (that Self)."[3] When one has attained this final goal, he is one with the Absolute Being. There he no longer bears any personal differentiation. Uddālaka teaches as follows: "As the bees, my son, make honey by collecting the juices of distant trees, and reduce the juice into one form, and as these juices have no discrimination, so that they might say, I am the juice of this tree or that, in the same manner, my son, all these creatures, when they have become merged in the True (either in deep sleep or in death), know not that they are merged in the True."[4]

This monistic view of the *Upaniṣads* was developed further by the Vedāntic philosophers. Śaṁkara is the chief representative of the monistic philosophy of the Vedānta. "So great is the influence of the philosophy propounded by Śaṁkara and elaborated by his illustrious followers, that whenever we speak of the Vedānta philosophy we mean the philosophy that was propounded by Śaṁkara."[5] Nearly two thirds of contemporary pundits (scholars of traditional scholarship) of India belong to the school of Śaṁkara.[6]

Of course, it is wrong to say that all the Indian thinkers hold such a view of the unity of all beings. But this is the view maintained by a majority of the philosophers in India. Even the schools of Indian pluralism did not always reject monism; in the philosophy of Vallabha (1481–1533) who was a pluralistic monist, "the duality that we perceive in the world does not contradict monism; for the apparent forms and characters which are mutually different cannot contradict their metaphysical character of identity with God. So Brahman from one point of view may be regarded as without parts, and from another point of view as having parts."[7]

A monistic tendency forms the core of the theological system of the Hindu religious schools. Throughout the history of philosophy in this country, the monistic view has been accepted by a majority of its thinkers.

"The tendency of Indian philosophy, especially Hinduism, has been in the direction of monistic idealism. Almost all Indian philosophy believes that reality is *ultimately* one and *ultimately* spiritual. Some systems have seemed to espouse dualism or pluralism, but even these have been deeply permeated by a strong monistic character."[8]

The Buddhists, however, rejected the existence of any metaphysical principle as advocated in the *Upaniṣads* and in the Indian orthodox philosophical schools. And they did not engage themselves in metaphysical discussions about the unity of one with the Absolute, but they emphasized participation in the current affairs of the world for the realization of absolute virtue. They taught the importance of unity among individuals in the actual society of their fellow-beings. From its inception, the Buddhist religious movement strongly opposed class discrimination in any form. A sentence in one of their sūtras reads: "What has been designated as 'name' and 'family' in the world is only a term."[9] Within the early community of the Buddhist monks, this idea of equality of all classes was faithfully carried out. Gotama the Buddha no longer belonged to any particular caste or family (*gotra*). And whoever, having renounced the world, joins the Buddhist community (*saṁgha*) to become a Bhikṣu is called uniformly a Śākya-putra or a son of Śākyamuni the Buddha. Within the Saṁgha, everyone belongs directly to the order of the Saṁgha without any intermediary agent and he is treated as absolutely equal to others in all his qualifications. The standing order within the Saṁgha was fixed according to the number of the years elapsed since one had taken orders. So, one of their Vinaya texts describes the Saṁgha as follows: "Just, O Bhikkhus, as the great rivers—that is to say, the Gangā, the Yamunā, the Aciravatī, the Sarabhū, and the Mahī—when they have fallen into the great ocean, renounce their name and lineage and are thenceforth reckoned as the great ocean, just so, O Bhikkhus, do these four castes—the Khattiyas, the Brahmans, the Vessas, and the Suddhas—when they have gone forth from the world under the doctrine and discipline proclaimed by the Tathāgata, renounce their names and lineage, and enter into the number of the Sakyaputtiya Samaṇas."[10] In one of the *Upaniṣads,* we can find a teaching with a similar context. "Just as the flowing rivers disappear in the ocean casting off name and shape, even so the knower, freed from name and shape, attains to the divine person, higher than the high."[11] It can be said here that the metaphysical or ontological concept of the unity of all things held in the *Upaniṣads* shows itself in Buddhism only by taking the form of practical ethics.

Buddhist thought was refined remarkably in the hands of the Mahāyāna Buddhists. The idea of *Śūnyatā* or The Void admits nothing real or substantial, but even in this idea we can notice a feature of the old

Indian monism. *Śūnyatā* means absolute negation and it permits nothing differentiated. The great teacher of Mahāyāna Buddhism, Nāgārjuna, teaches: "the release (*mokṣa*) is the extinction of all action (*karman*) and of all defilement (*kleśa*). The action and the defilement arise from the differentiating notions (*vikalpa*). They come from the concept of diversity (*prapañca*). This concept of diversity, however, is terminated in the state of Voidness."[12] The release in Nāgārjuna's sense means the attainment of this state of Voidness.

For most Indians, to enter into a perfect state of tranquility where the mind is immovable and identical with the Absolute is the highest religious experience that only a man of wisdom can hope to gain. And they attach only a relative and secondary significance to other states of religious experience, considering them to be lower states only serving as intermediate means to help one attain the highest.

This tendency can also be noticed even among present-day intellectuals of India. They prefer to study the philosophy of Hegel, Bradley, or Whitehead. The philosophy of Spinoza, which is also a favorite subject for contemporary Indian philosophers, is often interpreted in the non-dualistic, monistic light of the Śaṅkaraite Vedānta; for example, the infinity of God's attributes is explained as the "absolute indeterminateness of God," which is surely a Vedāntist speaking and not Spinoza.[13]

Now, as additional evidence to show that the core of Indian thought is the idea of the unity of all things, we will proceed to study a linguistic phenomenon observed in the Indian languages. In Sanskrit, the universal class of "all the individuals or things in the universe" is designated by words in the singular like *"idaṃ sarvam," "idaṃ viśvam,* (all this) or simply *"idam"* (which means "this").

And this usage of the words in the singular number can be observed in the old *Upaniṣads,* in the Buddhist books,[14] and in many other Indian works in general.[15] In Japanese, to express "the things in the universe," we say *banyū, banshō, monomina,* all three implying the infinite diversity of the phenomenal world. In contrast to the Japanese way of thinking, the Indians tend to ignore this diversity and the differentiated phases of the phenomenal world and grasp all things as one unit. Of course, it is grammatically correct to write in the plural the Sanskrit pronoun *"sarva"* and its equivalents in other Indian languages. There are some cases of such usage in old Indian scriptures.[16] But, in those cases, we should not overlook the fact that the word *"sarva"* does not mean all things without limitation, but that it implies the whole within a certain boundary. And to mean all things without limitation, the Indians never fail to write *"sarva"* in the singular number.

This Indian usage of the words in this case presents a remarkable contrast to the Greek and the Latin usage of the equivalent words, *πάντα*, *omnia*. In Greek, though it belongs to the same language root as Sanskrit, the pronoun equivalent to "*sarva*" in the neuter plural form means "all things." There is a fine example of this Greek usage in Heraclitus' well-known proposition "all things flow (πάντα ῥεῖ)." Both Plato[17] and Aristotle[18] represent the universe as a complex body using the word πάντα in the plural number. And this usage was accepted by the Greeks for a long time up to comparatively recent times.[19] When they use the Greek equivalent of "*sarva*," in the singular number, it has the meaning of "everything" and the meaning of "all" will not be expressed accurately.[20] There is a very rare case in Greek expressing "all things in the universe" by the pronoun in the neuter singular "πᾶς."[21] But, in this case, the philosopher who used this expression took a stand very similar to the Indian monistic view of the world and its pantheism. His view was more like the Indian than like the Greek one, for such a view was rarely held by the Greeks in general. In Latin, too, they use "*omnia*," the word in the neuter plural form, to mean "all things."[22] And to mean "all things as one unit" or "the universe," the Romans have another word "*universum*" so that they have no fear of the confusion that might exist in Greek. In Greece, not only philosophers but people in general thought that the universe was a complex body consisting of innumerable individual and particular things. Greek atomists regarded the atoms as innumerable. In contrast to this Greek view, the Indian philosophers have mostly maintained that all beings in the universe are limited and particularized manifestations of the sole ultimate reality. Here, without relying upon other methods of comparative philosophy, we can maintain the foregoing conclusions through analysis of linguistic expressions.

Now, insofar as most Indians attach little significance to individual phenomena, it is natural that they should be inclined to minimize the absolute value of any individual being.

As a natural result of such a way of thinking, there appears in India the idea of the oneness of opposite pairs, of good and evil, and of beauty and ugliness. Megasthenes, referring to the features of Brahmanistic thought, writes as follows: "[According to the Brahmanists] whatever happens in human life is neither good [ἀγαθόν] nor evil [κακόν]. For if the nature of a thing or an act is fixed for good or evil, why is there any difference among men, whose notions are all more or less like a dream, of those who are pleased by a thing or act and those who are troubled by the same thing or act?"[23] In the old *Upaniṣads*, too, it is repeated that what appears good or bad to our human eyes is not so in the absolute sense and that the difference between the two is only a matter of comparison.[24] For instance, one of the *Upaniṣads* reads as follows: "[The true Self], the controller of all, the lord of all, and the ruler of all, does not become greater by good works nor smaller by evil works."[25] And in another text, it is said, "As water does not cling to a lotus leaf, so no evil deed clings to one who knows it."[26] And this idea of the oneness of opposite pairs held in the *Upaniṣads* was accepted by the Vedāntists, the most influential philosophical school in the India of later ages.[27]

To the above, of course, a counter-argument will be presented: how could the Indians have gone into such minute classification of phenomena and their division into sub-sub-types if this were really true? Also, why is it that one powerful school of philosophy has felt compelled to develop an ultimate category of differentiation (*viṣajya*) without reference to which phenomena could not be intelligible? These counter-questions are pertinent. Still the writer cannot help retaining the impression that many Indian thinkers admitted pluralism only on a secondary plane, and not in the metaphysical realm. Even if we admit the predominance of pluralism in Indian philosophy, still we cannot deny the stronger influence of monism in other cultural areas of Indian thought, such as religion.

CHAPTER 6 THE STATIC QUALITY OF UNIVERSALITY

Comprehension of This Quality Through Static Aspects of Language

It has already been suggested that most Indians incline to comprehend phenomena statically. This tendency has a close relation to their tendency to put a high value on universality. All things in this world are always changing and moving. On the other hand, the substance of these things continues as long as they exist and its nature changes little. Therefore, the tendency to prefer universality generally draws more attention to the nature or essence of things than to their manifestations which are always changing, and again this tendency stresses the static aspect of things more strongly than their dynamic functions.

Some special characteristics of this way of thinking can be found in the Indian usage of parts of speech. First, it can be said that the noun (or verbal noun) is more likely to be used than the verb in a Sanskrit sentence, because the noun expresses the more stable and unchanging aspects of the thing. Secondly, the adjective which modifies a noun is used much more frequently than the adverbial form which is seldom used in Sanskrit.

The former characteristic will be explained first. Although expression by verbs was very complicated in the sentences of the Vedas, it became very simple in classical Sanskrit. Verbal nouns came to be mainly used instead of the finite verbs in classical Sanskrit.[1] Especially in prose writings, the nominal predicate is widely used and the finite verb is seldom used. The noun which is used in Sanskrit as the predicate is in some cases a participle and in some cases a verbal noun. For example, the sentence "due to rain, the food appears" is expressed in the form of "due to rain, appearance of the food (is possible)" in Sanskrit. (*parjanyād annasaṁbhavaḥ, Bhag. G.* III, 14. = *imbre fit frugam proventus,* οι δὲ καρποὶ ἐκ τοῦ ὄμβρου.) It was the practice since ancient times to use the participial form instead of the finite verb to express the past tense, and it became a common expression in colloquial speech of the later periods.[2]

The adjectives whose quality is static are used in Sanskrit in place of the finite verbs used in the classical languages of the West. For example, the sentence "*sarvam anityam* (all things are impermanent)" is used in Sanskrit instead of the sentence "all existences change and move" (πάντα ῥεῖ).

Thus the "periphrastic form" was established in Sanskrit. Although it is seldom found in the Vedic Scripture, the periphrastic perfect, one of the periphrastic forms, can be frequently found in the literature after the Brāhmaṇas. For example, in order to express the meaning "he went," the phrase "*gamayāṁ cakāra* (he made a going)" is used. And again the form of periphrastic future is used in some cases in order to express future action.[3] For example, the word "*gantāsi* (you are the one who goes)" is used to express the meaning "you will go." (*gantāsi* = *pervenies ad* . . . ἀποστροφὴν ποιήσεις. *Bhag. G.*, II, 52.)

Again in Sanskrit, the denominative, a special form of verb, which is formed from a noun, is established. For example, *putrīyati*, a denominative which was formed from a noun *putra* (son), means "to desire to have a son," and *svāmīyati*, a denominative formed from a noun *svāmin* (master) means "to regard as a master." Generally speaking, denominative is used as the word which connotes the meaning of "to be . . . ," "to work as . . . ," "to regard as . . . ," and "to desire. . . ." Such special categories of verbs as the denominative are not found in the classical grammar of the west.

Another grammatical fact can be considered as showing a similar tendency; namely, in Sanskrit, *śakya*, an adjective, or *śakyam*, an indeclinable, is used to express the meaning "to be able to . . . ," which is expressed by using a verb or an auxiliary verb in the Western languages. (For example, "na devāsuraiḥ sarvaiḥ śakyaḥ prasahituṃ yudhi" [*Rāmāyana* II, 86, 11] = *non potest proelis superari a cunctis dis daemonibusque*.)[4]

In the Sanskrit language, it is seldom that a verb in the form of the finite verb is used; the verb is mainly used in the form of the verbal noun. Therefore, the general characteristic of Sanskrit construction is that the nominal sentence is more likely to be used than the verbal sentence. Especially in classical Sanskrit, the finite verb is seldom used.

In connection with the above fact, usage of the infinitive form of the verb is very much limited. In Sanskrit the infinitive form is never used as the subject.[5] Nor is the infinitive form ever used as the object. When it is necessary to use the infinitive verb as an object, an abstract noun formed from the root of that verb is used instead of the infinitive form of that verb. Originally, the infinitive form of a verb preserved the case ending of the verbal noun in the *Ṛg-Veda*, that is, it preserved case endings of accusative, dative, genitive, and locative cases. However, in classical Sanskrit, only one form, which ends with "—tum" (one of the above mentioned case endings), remains. Moreover, in most cases in classical Sanskrit, the infinitive form is used only when the meaning "in order to do—" which denotes an object of behavior is expressed. Even in this case, usage of the infinitive form is not necessarily the same. The infinitive form is used in both the active and passive voices.[6]

There is a remarkable difference between Sanskrit and the classical languages of the West on this point. For example, there are two kinds of infinitive, the present and the perfect, in Latin. The present infinitive expresses continuation, repetition, and process while the perfect infinitive indicates completed action. The infinitive in Latin can become subject, predicate, and also the object of a sentence as a noun, because it possesses the properties of both verb and noun.

It is quite likely that the reason why there exists such a great difference between Sanskrit and the Western languages is that the Indians did not pay as much attention to the changing and moving aspects of existence.

Another striking characteristic of Sanskrit will be considered. Sanskrit does not possess any adverbial suffix which is common to all Western languages. As a general rule, an adjective can become an adverb by adding some suffixes such as "—ως" in Greek and "—ment" in French, in the Western languages. However, there are no such adverbial suffixes in Sanskrit; so we find the accusative case of the adjective (neutral, singular) is used in Sanskrit when it is necessary to modify the verb.[7] Again accusative, ablative, and locative cases (singular) of adjective are used adverbially in some cases. In brief, the adverb is not acknowledged to be a part of speech in the system of Sanskrit grammar. And it is very common to use the adjective where the adverb is used in Western languages.

(The same disparity between the Indian way of thinking and other ways of thinking can also be found among modern Western languages. Among the modern Western languages, German tends to stress the unchanging, static, and universal aspects of phenomena. On the contrary, English attaches great importance to changing aspects of things. There exists no special suffix which can distinguish adverb from other parts of speech in German, whereas in English an adverbial suffix is added to the adjective when it modifies a verb.[8])

This tendency to comprehend things through their static aspects can also be found elsewhere. For example, a demonstrative pronoun "*sa*" is usually added to the subject when it is necessary to connect two sentences to express the meaning of "and" or "then." Namely, the demonstrative pronoun is used in Sanskrit instead of the conjunction.[9] In order to show compound events, it is often necessary to use the conjunction in Western languages. On the contrary, the Indians repeatedly mention the same subject of action which remains unchanged through a period of time.

The subject of action which influences the gerundive, which has passive meaning, or the past participle, which ends with "—ta," is expressed by the instrumental case or genitive case in Sanskrit. The following sentences are its examples: *"bhavatā* (or *bhavataḥ*) *kṛtaḥ kartavyaḥ* (you fulfilled your duty)"; *"rajñāṃ pūjitaḥ* (one was respected by kings)." Here the instrumental case is apt to express the same meaning with a participle but the genitive case is used with an adjective.[10] In the case of Western languages, the subject of action is always introduced with prepositions such as *ὑπο, ὰ,* by, *von,* or *par.* It can be concluded from the above fact that, on the whole, Western people comprehend action through its changing aspects, while Indians comprehend action attributively. That is to say, many Indians consider that action is an unchanging aspect or only an attribute of phenomenal existence.

The above-mentioned characteristic way of thinking also influenced the construction of concepts. In classical Indian languages, there was no word which corresponded to the word "to become." Although the verb formed from root *"bhū"* connotes the meaning of "to become," this word also connotes the meaning of "to exist" at the same time. Why did the ancient Indians fail to distinguish the word meaning "to become" from the word meaning "to exist" in their daily conversation? It was because "to become" was one form or aspect of "to exist" for them. A noun *"bhāva"* formed from root *"bhū"* is understood as the word which means either "being born" or "existing."[11] That is to say, "to become" is "to be born," in other words, for the Indians. Therefore, the Indians managed to produce the words *"anyathā bhavati"*[12] or *"anyathābhāva"* (being otherwise) in order to express "to become" or "to change."

For the Indians, therefore, "all the things of this world are changing and moving" is not the expression of the changing aspect of existences but is the expression of a static and unchanging state. In the sentence *"sabbe saṅkhārā aniccā* (all things are impermanent)," a common expression of the Indian Buddhists, *"aniccā"* is an adjective. Thus, change is understood statically. This adjectival form of expression is fundamentally different from the sentence "*πάντα ῥει* (all things flow)" of Western thought in which the predicate is dynamically expressed by a verb.

The Static Quality of Thought

Thus, in Indian philosophy the Absolute is generally explained as a Being beyond all temporal appearances. According to the *Upaniṣads,* the Absolute is also expressed as Imperishable (*akṣara*) in the following ways.[13]

"*Ātman* is imperishable for it cannot be destroyed. . . . It is unfettered, it does not suffer, it is not injured."[14] "This is that great unborn Self who is imperishable, incorruptible, eternal, fearless, Brahman."[15] In early Buddhism such a metaphysical principle as the Absolute is not laid down, but it is claimed that the principle of *pratītyasamutpāda,* whether the Buddha has appeared or whether he has not appeared, is unchanged and eternal. According to Mahāyāna Buddhism, *śūnyatā* or *dharmatā* (the essence of things) is the principle of *pratītyasamutpāda* that nothing can disappear or arise. As stated above, the idea of the Absolute, which Indian philosophers have conceived, is of a negative character. Accordingly, the Absolute can only be expressed as essentially static in quality in relation to all appearances of changing things.

The same kind of way of thinking is discernible concerning their concept of man. Let us compare it with the Christian concept of man. According to St. Paul, the concept of man is roughly as follows: Man is composed of two parts, i.e. body and mind, representing the external and internal aspects of man respectively. Mind is that which gives vitality to body or the source of life. He calls this mind "*psychē,*" and when he defines it as the subject of consciousness or self, especially distinguishing it from the body, he also gives the name "*pneuma*" or soul to mind. However, the term "*pneuma,*" which was employed in few cases, generally means the origin of a resurrected life in the awakened man as distinguished from the ordinary man. In other words, it denotes the generative power of the resurrective, sacred, and eternal life which comes from God or the Savior and which controls man. Accordingly, soul is identified with the Holy Spirit, which is distinctly separate from the mind of man. On the other hand, the body, which represents the external aspect of man, is supposed to be constituted by a bony substance (*sarx*). It might be acknowledged that it does not apply merely to the flesh, but to all the elements composing man-in-nature,[16] due to imagining that the sarx is the main element of all constituents of body. On the contrary, according to Indian philosophers, soul is defined as *prāṇa, ātman,* or *jīva,* and body as *śarīra* or *deha,* not as *māṃsa* or flesh. It appears that they considered the bone to be the central part of the body. *Śarīrāṇi,* the plural form of *śarīra* (body), means the bones or remains. That the bone is considered to be the fundamental component of the body, we see in the following passage of the *Dhammapada:* "Body is formed by the bones together with flesh and blood spreading on it. It contains decay, death, pride, and falsehood."[17] As seen from the above statement, the Christians in the West find the central significance of body in the dynamic element of which body is constituted; Indian philosophers in the East find it in the static element, i.e. bone.

Such being the case, generally in Indian philosophy the idea of "becoming" is not considered primary, but the idea of "being" is the central consideration. Therefore, Indian philosophers in general explain three aspects of "being," i.e. appearance, extinction, and continuance or intermediate state of "being." These three are referred to early in the Old *Upaniṣads,*[18] and they are generally accepted by the orthodox schools of Brahmanism and the Jain schools. However, the idea of "becoming" is little mentioned in these schools. *Vikāra, vikriyā, pariṇāma, vipariṇāma,* etc. are considered to be equivalent to "becoming," but they show that the simple becomes specialized into complexity, and these words rather mean evolution or development. Vārṣyāyani, philosopher of language of ancient India, set forth the theory of the sixfold aspect of being (*bhāvavikāra*)[19] in the phenomenal world, i.e. appearance, existing, changing, increasing, decreasing, and extinction, and in later ages it was accepted by the other famous Indian philosopher of language named Bhartṛhari.[20] However, Śaṁkara, the famous Vedantist, refuted this theory as meaningless, and he maintained that appearance, continuance, and extinction are recognized to be the only three aspects of "being," and that all other aspects of being might be included in these three.[21] Also in Buddhism these three aspects are designated as those of the conditioned (*saṁskāra*) or phenomenal being.[22] The Sarvāstivāda school, the most eminent of Abhidharma Buddhist schools, maintained the theory of four aspects of being by adding the fourth aspect of being or the conditioned, namely, *jarā* or decaying, which was interpreted as "changing to other" (*anyathābhāva, anyathātva*).[23] Accordingly, they show the four aspects of the conditioned as appearance, extinction, continuance, and decaying.[24] However, this theory was not accepted by all Buddhist schools.

From the point of view that the idea of "being" is considered primary, and that the idea of "becoming" is ignored, Indian thought is considerably similar to Greek thought, and departs from modern thought. As pointed out on several occasions, the central problem of ancient Greek philosophy was to investigate reality or "being," and there the truth was nothing but "being" and it was to be materialized in Existence. The truth is thus realized by insight into the *form* of reality and it denotes the discovery of the essence of "being." Accordingly, the science of geometry was the typical pattern of science in ancient times, through which the principle of the fixed forms of material bodies in space was investigated. Only Statics was developed even in the field of physical science. On the other hand, the idea of "becoming" is investigated mainly in modern thought. Kinetics has developed in the field of physics of the modern age. Mathematics has developed in the form of analytics and algebra studying variable quantities and relations. And for the first time analytical geometry was organized and studied. Indian thought is similar to Greek thought from the point of view of its difference from modern thought in which the idea of "becoming" or movement is regarded as its chief characteristic; however, compared with Greek thought, Indian thought may be said to go to extremes in expressing its ideas ontologically.

Thus, the static quality of ways of thinking of some Indian minds is distinctively far from the dynamic quality of modern thought; however, from the very point of view of its contrast with modern thought, it can offer a certain significance for modern civilization. While modern life is inclined to drive man to a disturbed or mad restlessness, the static quality of Indian thought is capable of giving peace or rest to the mind of modern people. Accordingly, Indian culture is helpful in presenting rest and a quite joy to persons today who are tired of the turbulent movement of their culture.

In introducing the life and activity of Ramakrishna (1834–1886), who was one of the most eminent religious teachers of modern India, Romain Rolland writes as follows: "He was a fruit harvester of early autum whom Europeans had rarely if ever known." And he goes on to say: "I should like to inform European people who are feverish and restless because of this arterial throbbing. I want to wet European lips with unperishable blood."[25] Even Albert Schweitzer, who is known as a devotional Christian teacher, though criticizing all Indian religions, acknowledged the following merit in them: "However, there is one significance which we European people ought to acknowledge in regard to the religious thought of India. It is that the Indian religion teaches us calmness or equanimity of mind . . . the Indian people comprehend the essential weak point in the faith of modern Christianity. We Europeans believe that Christianity is only dynamic in its religious activity. There are too few occasions when we reflect on our deeper selves. We Europeans are usually devoid of equanimity of mind."[26] In view of the contrast between Indian calm and modern activism, it is no wonder that the Indian idea of "inner peace" is so attractive to the minds of modern people.

Lack of Common-Sense Concepts of Time

The thought process which regards existence behind the phenomenal world as more important than the phenomenal world itself, naturally results in destroying the concept of time, especially the concept of differences in time necessary for expressing specific events in experience.

This thought process can be seen in the fact that mood in the Sanskrit language has gradually vanished and become simplified; various kinds of tense have disappeared, and accordingly their usages have been confused.

In the proto-Indo-European language, the difference of verb usage is mainly based on mood and, therefore, the verb of this language was based on a flimsy grasp of the concept of time. The present tense of direct speech simply indicates sustaining action, while the perfect tense denotes the state of action which was momentarily conceived regardless of duration as completed. It was somewhat later before the concept of time was emphatically introduced by the use of verbs. The old writings of the Greek language preserved a good variety of moods. It was so with the Vedic language. However, in Latin the verb is principally based on a concept of time. Even in the present Greek language the mood of the verb persists with considerable tenacity, and in the Slavic languages it is still preserved.[27] However, generally speaking, the tenses of verbs came to occupy the important place and the differentiation of tenses became developed in later ages. These trends are remarkably discernible in all modern languages.

However, though there are five kinds of tense in the Sanskrit language as in Greek,[28] they are not sharply discriminated. For example, in indicating the past tense, the following five forms are actually used almost without discrimination in usage; imperfect, perfect, past participle active, aorist, and historical present.[29] Simply concerning the frequency of each tense's use, there are differences according to periods. At the end of the period of the Brāhmaṇa writings, the aorist[30] was frequently used, and in the Pāli language a single tense denoted almost all past events. According to the famous grammarian of ancient India, Pāṇini (c. 4th century B.C.),[31] the aorist is a single tense which indicates the recent past. However, after Pāṇini, the past participle has been gradually employed as equivalent to the aorist. Finally, in classical Sanskrit there is little usage of the aorist.

Besides, the Sanskrit lacks the past perfect and future perfect tenses in either the indicative or subjunctive moods as well as the past tense in the subjunctive.[32] This fact shows that discrimination between absolute past and relative past is not made in Indian languages.

Furthermore, it is also possible to employ the present tense of Sanskrit in order to indicate recent past and future.[33] For example, in the sentence "What is the use of it? (It is of no use)," the present tense is used in the Sanskrit language, while the future tense is used in Latin: *kim karomi tena* = *quiḍ faciam eo.* Thus Indian people do not have too clear a consciousness of the discrimination of tense. There seems to be a similar linguistic phenomenon in Hindustani in which the same word—*kal,* adverb—has two meanings, namely, yesterday and tomorrow. Similarly, the term "*parsōn*" means the day after tomorrow and at the same time the day before yesterday, and the term "*atarsōn*" means three days after and before. Such being the case, the determination of the meaning of these kinds of words is dependent on the context, and so confusion can be removed.

That Indian people are not very sharply aware of the discrimination of tense denotes their unwillingness to comprehend the current of time from past to future in the form of quantitative time through which the length of time is capable of being measured. However, it does not mean that the Indian people have no concept of time, but rather the reverse. The law of transiency and its philosophical expression, i.e. their view of the uncertainty of life, sharply pointed out by the Jains and the Buddhists, can be realized only by those who understand from their heartfelt experience the changing phases of the world.

The Indian people, who have not exerted themselves to grasp the concept of time quantitatively, have rarely written historical books with accurate dates, and we have indicated that this fact signifies a characteristic feature of Indian culture. It may be said to result from the characteristic way of thinking described above. Presumably, according to the world-view of the Indian people, the universe or world and the social order remain eternal; on the other side, personal life is nothing but one of a succession of lives existing repeatedly in limitless time, and therefore finally becomes meaningless. The idea of the transition of life which the Indian people have conceived is transmigration, i.e. a perpetual wheel of rebirths. Such an idea appeared occasionally in Greek (Pythagorean) philosophy, but in India it has always been maintained by all people. So far as this way of thinking is concerned, such passing phenomena as political or social conditions, as a matter of course, do not attract people. Consequently, it is not surprising that historical descriptions have not been made with much attention to accurate dates in India.

Contemplative Attitudes

Viewing the essential universality behind and beyond the variety of concrete phenomena of our experience can be defined as a contemplative or meditative attitude. It means no more than comprehending all progressive phenomena as eternally completed. Accordingly, in describing successive events, the present participle is used only in Greek and Latin. The gerund which shows a kind of past tense is used instead in ancient Indian languages. Here are some examples: *upasamgamya* = *accedens* (*Bhag.* 1, 2); *paraṃ dṛṣtvā* = ἐπειδὴ θεωρεῖ τὸν θεόν (II, 59). (Only in this case ὁρῶν also may be used.); *pallalaṃ hitvā* = *lacum relinquens* (*Dhp.* 91) (having left a pond, the bird . . .); *maccu ādāya gacchati* = *mors prehendens abit* (*Dhp.* 46); *kumbhūpamaṃ kāyam imaṃ viditvā/naṅgarūpamaṃ cittam idaṃ ṭhapetvā/ /yojetha māraṃ paññayudhena* (*Dhp.* 40) = *Vasi simile corpus hoc agnosscens, arci similem cogitationem hanc sistens, subigat (sapiens) Māraṃ intellectus armis* (Having known that this body is a weak vessel and that the mind is like a confused thoroughfare in a city, you should battle against the Evil One with the aid of wisdom). As seen from these examples, in the Sanskrit language the main and subordinate actions are expressed in different tenses, the latter in the past tense; on the other hand, in the Greek language both are expressed in the same tense. Furthermore, in saying "by means of" for the sake of showing the instrument of action, *ādāya* or *upādāya,* the gerund form relevant to the past is used in the Sanskrit language; however, in the Greek language ἔχων or λαβῶν the present participle, is used.

Also the same characteristic is recognized in constructing compounds in the Sanskrit language. In indicating the causal relation between two notions, a compound is formed which suggests that the order of thought follows the way of tracing effect back to cause. Accordingly, the expression "effect and cause" (*phalahetu*) occurs instead of "cause and effect" as stated in other languages. Instead of the expression "the relation of cause and effect," "the relation of effect and cause" (*kāryakāraṇabhāva*)[34] is used. Likewise, the following expressions are used in the Sanskrit language: relation of the knowable and the knower (*gamyagamakabhāva*)[35]; relation of the generated and the generative (*janyajanakabhāva*); relation of the proved and the prover (*sādhyasādhakabhāva*); relation of the established and the establishing (*vyayasthāpyavyavasthāpakabhāva*)[36]; relation of one being excited to activity and the instigator (*pravartyapravartayitṛtva*)[37]; relation of that on which anything depends and that which depends on (*āśrayāśrayībhāva*).[38] These expressions of the Sanskrit language are remarkably different from those of other languages. Accordingly, when scholars translated the Indian original texts into Chinese, they changed the word order of the above expressions and they appeared as "the relation of cause and effect." The Tibetan people also translated "effect and cause" (*phalahetu*) into "*rgyu daṅ ḥbras-bu*" (cause and effect), changing its word order. The way of thinking, in which the notion of effect is first formed and that of cause is inferred and stated afterward, is retrospective, and in this regard, it is basically different from the way of thinking in which the notion of cause is first formed and then that of effect is deduced. (By the way, it is needless to say that such a way of thinking of the Indian people is basically different from the thinking process of natural science through which, with the help of inductive and deductive reasoning, the cause of an effect is investigated and is ascertained by functional correlation without giving primacy to either the cause or the effect.)

The Indian people, even if they investigate the relation of two things from cause to effect, generally do not take the view that a single effect is caused by a single active movement, but prefer to assume that various effects are produced by the combination of various causes. Therefore, most Indian thinkers do not employ the definite technical term which corresponds to efficient cause (*causa efficiens*). It seems that *nimitta-kāraṇa* is equivalent to *causa efficiens;* however, it is also used in expressing *causa occasionalis* and final cause of aim (teleological relation).

The thinking process through which the experienced action and change are immediately perceived as past matters not only restricts the thinking process of common people in India, but exerts an influence on the thinking process of Indian philosophers. The fact that the main Indian philosophies are contemplative is closely related to this thinking process. Greek philosophy is characterized as investigating overtly and speculatively the substance of matter and of watching its forms of activity, and therefore it is commonly criticized as theoretic. However, on this point, it may be rightly said that Indian philosophy has been more contemplative. Indian religious teachers have generally practiced *yoga,* by way of which they have contemplated the truth or intrinsic nature of phenomenal matter, whereas, it appears that such introspective contemplation did not predominate in Greek philosophy. It is said *theoria* is very similar to *yoga;*[39] however, *yoga* does not mean merely watching; it denotes also attaining a state transcending one's own limited self.

Passive and Forbearing Attitudes Toward Behavior

The contemplative attitude leads people usually to assume a rather passive attitude toward the objective or the natural world instead of encouraging an active attitude. They attempt to adapt themselves to nature without reconstructing nature. When assuming such an attitude, they especially tend to speak highly of the virtue of self-surrender or forbearance in its moral sense. Even in the *Upaniṣads* forbearance is mentioned as follows: "Therefore he who knows it as such, having become calm, self-controlled, withdrawn, patient and collected sees the Self in his own self, sees all in the Self."[40] In early Buddhism it is also explained as follows: "By virtue of forbearance he should suppress anger."[41] "Indeed in this world if he return evil for evil, he cannot be apart from evil. Give up his own evil and take a rest. This is eternal and unchangeable law."[42] And again, according to the Jain school, the true hero (*vīra*) is a man who has ceased hostility (*vaira-uparata*).[43] In Mahāyāna Buddhism forbearance is counted as one of six virtues (*pāramitā*). The following passage shows the predominant point of view of Indian religion: "By whom can this world be conquered? It can be conquered by the man who is truthful and patient."[44] Here, "conquest" does not denote controlling all things existing in the natural world by sheer force, but subduing one's own uncontrollable passion deserves to be called "conquest."

Accordingly, in regard to human effort in action, it is praiseworthy to hold one's desire and passion in check: "Who is the hero? He is a man who is not disturbed by the arrow of beauty's eyes."[45] The cause of our living in the illusion of becoming (*bhava*) is craving (*tṛṣṇā*).[46] We have to eliminate it in order to attain emancipation. In every Indian religion the man who eliminates all evil passions is especially extolled.[47]

Such being the case, the attitude of non-resistance by the Indian people toward outward oppression is extremely forbearing and passive. In resisting the king, Brahmins resorted to the method of fasting. It was believed in India that if a Brahmin who resorted to such a fast died of starvation, the king would sustain a dreadful injury by the force of its miraculous effect. On account of the faith in such miraculous strength, the king was obliged to submit to the resistance of Brahmins, and to grant their request. Even in India today, those who resist governmental power often resort to a hunger strike, emulating Gandhi's successful fasts against British rule.

With respect to economic morality, Indian people lay stress on the fairness of *sharing* rather than on that of *production,* because they are not inclined to have an active approach to the natural world. The plains of the Ganges, where the ancient Indian culture flourished, possesses fertile soil and the climate of this area is very hot and rainy. Accordingly, it is fit for rich farm production without much artificial effort. On the other hand, when natural violence comes, the artificial effort is wasted. As far as primitive industry is concerned, nature in India has inflicted its overwhelming power on the Indian people. In such a natural environment all production is controlled by the power of nature and only sharing it requires an artificial effort. Such being the case, the morality of sharing is invoked and taught, and the virtue of the act of giving has been emphasized. Early in the *Ṛg-veda,* there appeared about forty poems praising the act of giving (*dānastuti*), in which the Brahmin poets praised kings and lords who had offered them cows, horses, servants, etc. Since then, the virtue of the act of giving has been regarded as common in Indian society. This virtue is taught also in the *Upaniṣads.*[48] In early Buddhism, considering the extant sacred texts, the act of giving to mendicants and priests is often emphasized, however, and general charity is also taught as a virtue of social morality. The offered things are to be used efficiently and enjoyed both by oneself and by others, and the central point of giving, that one should offer what others need, is repeatedly asserted with emphasis. The sūtra condemns and rejects the notion that only those who are rich in property and full of treasures and foods live on dainty food.[49] And moreover, it teaches us that even the poor should offer what they can in the following way: "Just like a companion of a traveller proceeding on a wild plain, those who offer something in spite of being poor never perish among the dead. This is the eternal law."[50] In Jain teaching the virtue of the act of giving is alike regarded as important. In Mahāyāna Buddhism the act of giving is the first virtue which is to be practised by Buddhist followers. Accordingly, in India, guided by this thought, the act of giving things which the king and the rich offer to the poor and forsaken has become an almost fixed convention. Thus, it might be rightly said that the respect for the virtue of the act of giving is a really remarkable character of Indian morality.[51]

The extremity of the contemplative attitude finally results in praising inactivity or "absence of work as the ideal state." Jain followers set a value "on absence of work" (*akamma*),[52] and also aim at ceasing all action.[53] They aim at wiping away the dust of *karma*[54] from the past without a new *karma* or action, because good and bad actions generally produce pleasure and suffering. Also in Brahmanism inactivity or abstinence from action (*naiṣkarmya*) is regarded as an ultimate ideal. In Buddhism, though slightly different from the above teachings, the saint who has attained the highest state of quiescence has achieved what he should have sought in his practice, and there is nothing more for him to do.

However, in regard to this view, some objections have been offered by some Indian thinkers themselves. For example, Bhāskara, a scholar of the Vedānta school, says, "Properly speaking, it is impossible to do nothing at all. If emancipation could be attained by the virtue of inactivity, the religious mendicant (*parivrājaka*) would not have attained emancipation. Generally speaking, it is impossible for a living person to do nothing."[55] According to Bhāskara, it is not possible for anyone to refrain from all action, but one can and should aim at renouncing *attachment* to self-centered action. His criticism certainly applies to all. In spite of that, the majority of Indians have not thought that way, for inactivity prevails among them at least ideologically. That is the reason why so many Indians seem to lack a drive to activity.

The inactive and contemplative attitude of the Indian people has an influence even on Indian philosophy. Among the four principles, namely, efficient, material, final, and formal causes, which are ascribed to Aristotle, the cause (*causa efficiens*) corresponds to *nimitta-kāraṇa,* the material cause to *upādāna-kāraṇa,* and the final cause to *prayojana* in Indian philosophy; however, formal cause does not have its corresponding term in Indian philosophy. (Of course, it cannot be said that form has not been considered. For some Indian philosophers *śabda* is regarded as the form. However, they do not regard form as the so-called cause.) In other words, action in order to create a specific form has not been fully considered among Indian philosophers.

Some may think that the cause of such an inactive attitude on the part of Indian thought may be ascribed to the "state of despondency" arising from the influence of hot climate. It may be surely accepted as a contributory cause. However, this type of causal explanation again requires to be criticized as too one-sided.

CHAPTER 7 SUBJECTIVE COMPREHENSION OF PERSONALITY

Subjective Comprehension of Personality as Revealed in Language

When we examine the simple subject-predicate form of judgment in the Sanskrit, we find that the predicate is as a rule placed first because of the importance attached to the predicated quality or attribute; the Indians' way of thinking thus tends to emphasize qualities as subjective rather than as objective relations. This is also one of the eminent characteristics of Indian thought. We shall examine in the following passage the reflections of this way of thinking in language.

First of all, as a visible example of this tendency, in Western languages, when a person is the object of a verb, the name of the person is expressed most of the time in the accusative case, while in Sanskrit the person in question is often referred to in the nominative case. For example, in a Greek sentence: *πατέρα Ξενοφῶντα ἔκαλουν* (= They called Xenophon father), both "Xenophon" and "father" are in the accusative case. Similarly, a Latin verb "*nomino*" governs two accusatives. In Sanskrit, what is to be defined or named is expressed in the accusative case, as in Greek or Latin, but the new term to be added is expressed by a noun in the nominative case followed by an indeclinable "*iti.*" This kind of expression appears even in the oldest literature, e.g., *tám āhuḥ suprajā iti, Ṛg-Veda,* IX, 114, 1 (= they call him a man having good offspring). It may be said that in Sanskrit, importance is attached to a new term rather than to what is already known. By using this kind of syntactical form, i.e. by the use of an independent nominative case for a new term, the Indians regard a new term as the expression of an independent subjective existence different from what is named by it.

The same tendency is clearly observed in the use of the gerundive. In the cases of Greek and Latin, the object of a transitive verb is expressed in the accusative case even in gerundive construction. But in old Indian languages it is expressed in the nominative case. The Indians never use the accusative case in such a situation.

E.g. Greek: διωκιέον τοὺς πολεμίους
We should seek after the enemy.
Latin: *aeternas poenas in morte timendum est.*
We should be afraid of eternal punishment after death.
Sanskrit: *brāhmaṇo na hantavyaḥ*
A brāhmin should not be killed.
tāsmāt svādhyāyo "dhyetavyaḥ," *ŚBr.* XI, 5, 7, 3.
Therefore the daily lesson is to be practiced.

Indian languages have no form of "*accusativum cum infinitivum*" as do the Western classical languages,[1] that is, they do not use the accusative case to express the subject which takes a verb in infinitive form as the predicate. It is replaced by an instrumental.[2] This seems to reveal an Indian tendency to avoid as much as possible the use of the accusative case for expressing the subject of action.

Then what is the significance of the expression in the accusative? All noun cases except the accusative can stand for the nominal predicate of a sentence,[3] that is, among all noun cases, the accusative alone has no predicative meaning. The accusative, by definition, has an objective sense and cannot express a subjective sense. In the light of this linguistic rule and the fact mentioned above, we may be allowed to draw a conclusion that Westerners are inclined to comprehend an object of observation as an objective matter, while the Indians, disliking such a way of comprehension, try to grasp its subjective significance.

In self-reflection, the Indians did not like to comprehend themselves objectively by placing the self at a distance. In the expressions such as "to think oneself," "to call oneself," "self" is expressed in the accusative case in Latin and Greek, but it is expressed in the nominative case in ancient Sanskrit; e.g., *parābhaviṣyanti manye.* I think I shall be one who has disappeared. (*Tait. Saṃh.*, II, 5, 1, 2.) *kathaṃ so 'nuśiṣṭo bruvita.* How can he say [by himself] that he has completed his study? (*Chānd. Up.* 5, 3, 4.)[4]

The Indians did not want to reflect upon their own self objectively as the substratum of mental activities. The use of impersonal judgments in which the mental substratum, when it is influenced by sentiment, is shown in the accusative, is occasionally observed only in early Sanskrit literature.[5] But it has a fairly good number of examples in Western languages; e.g., "One should keep one's self calm." Similar contrasts between Western languages and Sanskrit are also observed in impersonal admonitions which express the idea of duty or necessity.[6] It shows that some characteristics common to the old Indo-European languages have been lost in Classical Sanskrit.

Subjective Comprehension of Personality as Revealed in Philosophy

The Indians tried to avoid comprehending mind as an external substance not only in their ordinary language but also in their philosophical thinking. The mind or soul, which is termed "νους," "*spiritus*," "*mens*," or "ψυχή" and "*anima*" by Greek and Roman philosophers, is called "*ātman*" by Indian philosophers. The term *ātman* is etymologically related to German "*atmen*" (to breathe), but is used as a reflexive pronoun in Sanskrit. In Chinese Buddhist scriptures, it is always translated into "*wo*" (I, *ich*). It was probably natural for the Indians, who thought of mind as a substance mostly in terms of subjective concepts, to use a reflexive pronoun in order to express such a concept. If a concept is named by any kind of noun, as in Western philosophy, there usually is a more or less objective comprehension about it. In Greek, there is no form like "το σεαυτόν" or "ὁ σεαυτός," and "ὁ αὐτός" means "the same," but has no sense of "the self." In modern philosophy, too, the main point of discussion was on the "I" (*das Ich*), but not so much on "the Self" (*das Selbst*) as in Indian philosophy.

One may perhaps object here that there existed a few Indian thinkers who understood the subject of mental activity in terms of the objective world; for example, the Nyāya-Vaiśeṣika school,[7] the Mīmāṁsā school, and even some Vedāntists like Bhartṛprapañca[8] held such an objective way of thinking. Indeed, these philosophers called the mind a substance, "*ātman*," but, so far as the use of such terms is concerned, it was usually in accord with the Indian mode of thought. Their natural philosophy was indeed objective, but its significance lies merely in its criticism of the general tendency of the Indian way of thinking, and they were against orthodoxy merely by way of protest. There can therefore be no objection to characterizing the Indian mode of thought in the manner indicated above.

In the main current of Indian philosophy—from the *Upaniṣads* to the Vedānta philosophy and to Hinduism—this "self," i.e. *ātman*, is regarded as identical with the Absolute, the ultimate Ego, and both are equally called *ātman*. Sometimes the latter is called *paramâtman* in contrast with the former, *jīvâtman*. Though both are different in their attributes, *parama* or *jīva*, they are included in one and the same genus of *ātman*. Thus the Indians thought of an intimate relation between the self as the substance of individuality and the reality belonging to the ultimate self. On the contrary, such an idea was hardly established among Western empiricist philosophers, for not until modern times is there an investigation of "the real self" in Western philosophy.[9]

A prominent tendency of Indian philosophy is often referred to as "pantheistic." For example, according to Śāṇḍilya, a famous Upanishadic thinker, the Absolute Brahman is said to be "that which is of true thought," "that which is of true intention," and "that whose own thought and mind is realized as they were." Also it is said that it "performs all the activities," it is "endowed with all kinds of desire," and "manifests whatever is intended by it"; therefore "it is possessed of all kinds of odor, all kinds of taste," it is limitless in its scale, "pervades everything," moves "as quick as mind," and "governs over all directions."

This kind of universality is not unique to Śāṇḍilya, and we find a similar concept of deity in the philosophy of Xenophon. However, Śāṇḍilya regarded his Absolute as being identical with the real self, whereas Xenophon did not.

One may here naturally recall the Buddhist negation of *ātman* against the orthodox *ātman*-theory, and this would raise the objection that the substantial view of *ātman* cannot be regarded as common to the Indians because a major religion such as Buddhism denies it. But did Buddhism really deny *ātman?*

According to the non-*ātman* theory expressed in the scriptures belonging to the oldest phase of early Buddhism, Buddhism denies the concept of "mine" or "my possession" (*mama*). Mendicants are first of all requested to remove their affectionate hold on the concept of "mine."[10] It means that they should not harbor the idea of possession, of "mine" vs. "others."[11] This concept of renunciation and its practice have characterized Brahmanism since ancient times. Renunciation is described in the Vedic scriptures as a kind of religious observance under the name of "*sarvamedha.*" In the earliest Upanishadic literature, a real Brahmin who realized *ātman* is said to go wandering and begging, casting off desires for sons, wealth, and the world.[12] The same idea of the rejection of the concept of "mine" is also taught in Jainism.[13] And if the so-called non-*ātman* theory means this rejection of the "mine"-concept, Jains must be said to have kept the idea of "non-*ātman*" (*nirmamatva*) until later days.[14]

Why then is the concept of "mine" to be rejected? In giving us the reason, the early Buddhist scriptures teach that whatever is regarded as one's own possession is always changeable. Therefore wealth does not belong to the self forever, and after a person's death, all the things possessed by him and all the relatives and subordinates who are regarded to be his possession will be separated from him. Therefore one should not be attached to his own possessions.[15] Thus, in early Buddhism, they taught avoidance of a wrong comprehension of non-*ātman* as a step to the real *ātman*.[16] Of things not to be identified with the self, the misunderstanding of body as *ātman* is especially strongly opposed. Foolish people comprehend their body as their own possession.[17] Even gods are captured by this sort of infatuation so that they cannot release themselves from suffering through transmigration.[18] Buddhists of early days called this mis-comprehension "the notion on account of the attachment to the existence of one's body" (*sakkāyadiṭṭhi*) and taught the abandonment of it.[19] What is therefore taught by early Buddhists is that whatever is not *ātman*, especially the body, should not be regarded as one's own. With the establishment of technical terms in Buddhist philosophy, the component elements of a body or individual thing are designated by the terms *saṁskārāḥ* (conditionings), or *pañca-skandhāḥ* (five groups), and using these terms, the scriptures explain the Non-*ātman* theory in the following way: "*pañcakkhandhā* (or *saṁkhārā*) are to be understood as different things (from *ātman*), and not as *ātman*."[20] And in the scriptures of a little later period, we find the following formulae often repeated: "Form (*rūpa* = feeling, idea, volition, consciousness) is impermanent. What is impermanent is of suffering. What is of suffering is *non-ātman*. What is *non-ātman* is not mine, nor is it I, nor is it my *ātman*." Ordinary people and philosophers superimpose the existence of *ātman*, or the soul, and are seeking it. But whichever elements, mental or physical, may compose human existence, these are not to be understood as *ātman*. These elements are always changing, and hence they are unlike *ātman* which is permanent. Also, being accompanied by suffering, they are different from *ātman*, which is the ideal perfect reality. Then what is our *ātman*? It cannot be comprehended objectively. Whichever principle or function is imagined by people to be *ātman* is in reality neither *ātman* nor that which belongs to *ātman* at all. Such is the outline of the non-*ātman* theory of Buddhism. Therefore early Buddhists never maintained the non-existence of *ātman*. They merely opposed the substantial permanence of anyone's *ātman*. As for the metaphysical question whether an absolute *ātman* exists or not, early Buddhists kept silence.

On the other hand, Buddhists admitted the self (*ātman*) as the moral agent and ground in the problem of responsibility for one's acts,[21] for example, when they say that one should perform one's own duty,[22] or one should be conscious about his "own good."[23] Here what is meant by one's own benefit (*svattha, svahita*) is neither material nor sensual but rather the realization of truth.[24] Lord Śākyamuni is said to have asked those youths who indulge themselves in amusement "to seek after the self (*ātman*)" rather than "to run after women," and advised them to become monks. Seeking after *ātman* is emphasized in the *Upaniṣads*.[25] In early Buddhism it was said that, being desirable (*priya*),[26] *ātman* was to be loved and protected.[27] This teaching corresponds to that of Yājñavalkya.[28] The Jains, too, call themselves "*ātmavādins*"[29] and teach the purification[30] and protection[31] of *ātman*.

Thus, in spite of the existence of different opinions among various religions and philosophies with regard to the essence of *ātman* as the metaphysical principle, the significance of *ātman* as the moral agent of one's actions is sure to be generally admitted among the Indians. For any religion of India, the ultimate goal of emancipation is the recovery or discovery of one's true self. In Brahmanism, attainment of self-control (*svārājyam adhigacchati*) is generally considered as the state of emancipation.[32] Hell is said to be nothing but "the state of bondage to others."[33] Buddhism specially emphasizes that "man is the master of himself."[34]

CHAPTER 8 SUPREMACY OF THE UNIVERSAL SELF OVER THE INDIVIDUAL SELF

The Unlimited Extension of the Self as Revealed in Language

From these intellectual tendencies in the culture of India, there emerges another notion, viz. the supremacy of the universal Self over the individual self. The Self which is grasped through the way of thinking described above is not identified with the numerable individual selves which are regarded as only relatively separate while they coexist on the same illusory plane of the external world. Beyond this plane of appearances the agent or subject of action transcends the opposition or gulf between the self and "other-than-self," because the transcendent agent cannot be conceived as something subjective. The qualities through which it manifests itself—that is, its qualitative phases—alone are emphasized. Here, it may be noticed that this view brings out by a striking contrast the difference in the views of the self held respectively by Indian and Western peoples. Generally it is claimed that the consciousness of self appeared at the beginning of the modern age. However, in some respects, it had appeared previously among the Western peoples of classical antiquity. The Romans of antiquity, having conceived each self as endowed with the same capacity as other selves, weighed all things respectively on the basis of their own selves. In the Latin language, the expression "*ego et tu*" (I and you) is used in order to refer to "one's self and others" at the same time.[1] In Japanese, this is a very impolite way of addressing others or one's opponent, while in Latin it is a rather usual expression. The Romans neither accepted the spiritual supremacy of another's self over one's self, not set up a distinction of social standing between one's self and another's. Even gods and superiors were addressed only by the pronoun of the second person "*tu*." This is also true in the Greek language. Hence in Western languages of ancient times honorific expressions are few. On the other hand, most Indian people are destitute of any acute awareness that the self of others is distinct from one's self. In India the tendency is not to regard another's self as an independent subject of action opposed to one's self.

This attitude of Indian thinkers is manifest in the usage of the Sanskrit language, as seen in the way they often employ a particular kind of causative mood. For example, *kārayati* (to cause to do), a causative mood of *karoti* (to do), is often used in Indian languages. However, in Western languages of ancient times there is no usage corresponding to the causative mood. When one wants to express a causal relation in the Latin language, he has to use a complicated formula, e.g. "*cogo* (*duco, permitto*) *ut* + subjunctive." Accordingly, in the Sanskrit language the causative mood is often used, in order to express a certain situation, while in the Western languages of ancient times very complicated expressions must be employed in order to show the same meaning. Here, two examples will be given: *kathaṃ sa puruṣaḥ. . . . kaṃ ghātayati hanti kam* (that man . . . how can he slay or cause to slay—whom?) (*Bhag. G.*, II, 21) = *quomodo is homo quempiam aut aliorum ministerio, aut sua manu occidat?* = πῶς οὗτος οἰηθήσεται, ὣς ἀυτὸς ἄναιρει, ἤ ἀίτιος γινεται ἀναιρεθῆναι; *naiva kurvan na kārayan* (not in the least acting nor causing to act) (*Bhag. G.*, V. 13) = *neque ipse agens, neque aliis agendi auctor* = μὴτ'ἀυτὸς πραττῶν, μῆι ἄλλοις αἴτιος γινόμενος τοῦ πράττειν.

When the expression "to cause others to . . ." is used in Greek and Latin, various attitudes of others toward one's self are taken into account, and then only after these are expressed is the causal expression used. Therefore, the causative mood "to cause someone to . . ." is formed by using various verbs according to the pattern of behavioral relations between "someone spoken to" and the speaker. In contrast with this the action of another's self is manifested as an extension of action by one's self. The Indian people, who frequently use the causative mood, are very often unconscious of the distinction between the actions of one's self as narrator, and of another self, the person addressed. Accordingly, in the Sanskrit language, there are even some cases where the meaning of the causative mood of a verb is not different from the indicative mood. For example, *dhārayati* (to cause to hold) is actually used as having the same meaning as *dharati* (he holds).

These cases become rather striking in the Pāli and Prakrit languages. Generally in these languages, the opponent, when caused to do something, is expressed by the accusative case, but when regarded as a means of action, is expressed by the instrumental case.[2] In this case, he is not regarded as possessed of intrinsic personal value, but only as an *instrument* or *means;* therefore, he may be denoted by the instrumental case, and because he is nothing but an instrument, the causative mood of a verb is actually identified with its active mood in such cases.

There is a tendency for the Indian to be concerned with an unlimited *extension of the will or volition* in place of a more finite human relation.

In such a case the subject or agent is sometimes omitted. On describing the process of personal and mental experience, the Indian people do not use a personal pronoun or a term which corresponds to "one" or "man" in English. The subject is denoted only by using a verb;[3] e.g., *gacchet* (should go) can take practically any subject (he, anyone, etc.).

In the social circumstance where the will's unrestricted extension might be materialized in another person, those who are coerced to act by this will are dependent upon that other person. This circumstance gives rise to honorific usage in addressing that person, although it has not been so highly developed in India as in Japan. However, there are some honorific words which belong to pronouns of the second person.[4] On the other hand, the Greek and Latin languages do not possess any honorific words (*bhavān* = Σὺ αὐτὸς, *tu ipse, Bhag. G.*, I, 8). We find in Indian epics that the pronoun of the second person "you" is permitted to refer to a younger person or one's contemporary but not to a senior or higher ranked person, and one is not permitted to call the latter by his real name.[5] Likewise in sacred writings of early Buddhism, it is noteworthy that those who were lower in their caste never called the Kshatriyas (members of the ruling class) by pronouns of the second person or by their real names.[6]

The Continuity of One's Self and Other Selves

Although the people of India are concerned with the unlimited extension of the self, as seen in their forms of expression, it is also undeniable that they do not ignore the personality of others; on the whole, they characteristically show a high regard for others. The early Buddhist writings and other doctrines urge everyone to pay respect to others at all times.[7] We can only suppose that they did not consider others as other selves or as opponents of one's self. In other words, they conceived the idea that other selves become one with the self as an extension of the self. The aphorism: "Buddha's identification with the self and the self's identification with the Buddha," stated in Tantric Buddhism, is based on the view of the continuity of one's self with other selves which the Indian people commonly conceive.

Here we have a striking contrast with the familiar view held by ancient as well as modern Western people who hold that other selves are hostile counterparts of one's self or stand in opposition to it. One can find any number of passages which reveal this kind of view in the writings of Western people: "War is the father of all things" (πόλεμος πατήρ πάντων—Herakleitos); "Man is a wolf to others" (*Homo homini lupus*—Plautus); "If you wish for peace, prepare for fighting" (*si vis pacem, para bellum*). Even in modern times the natural condition of human beings is comprehended as "A war of all against all" (*bellum omnium contra omnes*—Hobbes).

From ancient times, the Westerner's view of life has been rather aggressive. In Western history peace was gained largely as a result of bitter struggles. It is not a continually standing peace but the aftermath and interlude of ravages of war. On the other hand, in India, peace was eternal and the soul's tranquility the highest end. Of course, wars occurred time after time in India; however, on many occasions only lords and their mercenary soldiers fought in war, while ordinary people did not join them. In some cases, farmers near the battlefield cultivated their lands without fear and without worrying about it.[8] Hence in the agricultural districts of India, peaceful religious ceremonies and customs of a thousand years ago, or more, have been conveyed to the present time almost without sustaining any changes. Generally speaking, the character of the Indians is obedient and remarkably opposed to aggressiveness. Naturally they want and love a calm and peaceful life. As Indian history affords a proof of this view, it is difficult to find instances in which Indians invaded countries outside of India.[9]

Generally, the Indians have not cultivated the idea of hating other people. The Aryans conquered other Indian peoples and incorporated them into their community as their slaves; but they did not treat their slaves with much cruelty and did not drive them very hard. Megasthenes the Greek writes, in his record of his personal experience in India, that it is a marvellous fact that all men of India are free people and among them moral equality (ἰσότης) prevails.[10] *Śūdra,* a man of the lowest of the four castes in the ancient society of India, is commonly interpreted as "slave"; however *śūdra* denotes a kind of social standing. Accordingly, *śūdras* are not identified with the "slaves" of Western society who were treated badly and driven to hard work. It is thought that some *śūdras* were only engaged as individuals at work in some Aryan's family. Accordingly, in the eyes of a Greek, slaves did not exist in the ancient society of India.

In the ancient languages of India there is no pronoun which denotes the public or a mass of people in contrast with an individual, a pronoun which indicates the common subject, as e.g. "man" in German,[11] because the Indians did not regard the individual self in opposition to another self. Therefore, in order to indicate the common subject, generally the active voice of third person singular is used. If necessary, *sa* (he), *nara* (man), *puruṣa* (person), and *loka* (world) are substituted. Conversely, comparing the old language of India with Western languages, this fact shows that, for the sentence whose subject is *man,* the active voice of the third person singular is commonly substituted in the former language. In

India, it is common in this connection for a proposition to have a universal as its subject; it is rather exceptional that the individual is its subject. This fact exhibits a tendency to attach importance to the universal self beyond the individual self who comprehends it.

To cite an example of the ways of thinking of the Indians, people or men as subject of a sentence are, in many cases, stated in the *singular form,* and then its predicate becomes singular. For instance, *ayam pajā*[12] (whose form is singular) means "these men." In the ancient language of India, *jana* (meaning "people") is predicated in the singular form;[13] on the other hand, *people* in English takes a predicate in the plural form. In the ancient languages of the West, even though a nation or group is stated in the singular form, its predicate is expressed in the plural form.[14] This linguistic mode is inherited even in German.[15] Therefore, in the West not only modern people but also Greeks and Romans had a clear idea that the subject of action was an *aggregate* of individuals, while in India there was a strong tendency to regard the subject of action as a *group or united body.* Thus, in Western society each individual has an intrinsic value, and each individual opinion becomes the object of public attention. Such passages as "*quot homines, tot sententiae*" (there are as many thoughts as men) or "*vox populi, vox Dei*" (the voice of people is the voice of God) are characteristic of this society. The Indians, on the contrary, emphasize that as a member of the united body, i.e. of humanity, each individual is worthy of love and respect.

The distinctive feature of Indian thought that the individual self is not to be discriminated ultimately from other selves is acknowledged also by another linguistic phenomenon, the fact that the desiderative mood is often used in India. On a few occasions, an independent word which means "to desire" is used,[16] but, on the whole, the desiderative mood is preferred when the meaning "to desire to do . . ." is required. The desiderative mood is formed by a special conjugation of the verb. (As its derivative, the noun form is also used.) For instance, in order to express "he desires to live," two verbs, "to desire" and "to live," are required in the ancient languages of the West as well as in Japanese, while in the Sanskrit language a desiderative conjugation "*jujīviṣati*" is used.[17] In the latter language, "to desire" is grasped only as a case of the verb "to live," just as the future conjugation denotes only an action "to come." Therefore, in the West, the desire for action is comprehended as *different* from the action itself, since it depends upon the free will of the subject of action whether he desires to act or not, while in Indian, the desire for action is seen to be only *an annexed action* of the subject of that action.

Outside of the desiderative mood, in order to express "I hope he may. . . ." for instance, in the Latin language *"rogo ut vivat"* (= *Je veux bien qu'il vive*) (I hope he may live) is used; in the Sanskrit language, on the contrary, "*(api nāma) jīvet*" is simply used.[18]

Even in everyday practical life the idea of non-discrimination between the self and the other selves appears. According to Megasthenes, the Greek ambassador to India from Syria (c. 300 B.C.), the Indians did not ask for a bond when they lent money to others.

In brief, the Indians are not possessed of any very conscious reflection that the desires of one's self will meet with the antagonistic reaction of others. It is the *idea of non-discrimination* that underlies their attitude to all men.

About this way of thinking, Hegel says: "Intellectual substantiality (of the Indians) is the opposite of the reflection, reason, and subjective individuality of the Europeans. For us Western people, it is the important thing that, in accordance with his own nature, the individual ego desires, knows, believes, or considers something as he pleases, and on that freedom immeasurable value is subjectively placed. On the contrary, the intellect's substantiality stands on the other pole, and there the subjectivity of the self comes to lose its significance. For this subjectivity, all objective things come to be meaningless, and moreover there is neither objective truth nor duty nor right. The result is that only subjective falsehood remains."[19] Obviously, it is a misunderstanding on the part of Hegel that the Indians have no conception of either objective truth or of duty and right. The fact is that many scientific discoveries and moral conceptions were formulated in India. However, it is an obvious fact that the Indians seek their religious and moral ideal by effacing the subjectivity of the self. It is on the basis of this way of thinking that absolute unlimited devotion is emphasized in the Purāṇas of Hinduism and the Jātakas of Buddhism. It has been the ideal of the Indians to attain the state of *non-discrimination between the self and other selves.*[19a]

Consciousness of the Existence of the Self

Then would it be right to say that in India, where the idea of the continuity of one's self and others' selves is generally accepted, no attempt has been made by its thinkers to prove the existence of the self? No, on the contrary, in ancient times the thinkers of India were already engaged in the study of self-consciousness and the demonstration of its existence. But their way of conceiving the self is quite different from the more analytical methods used by modern European philosophers.

The Vaiśeṣika philosophers[20] asserted that the existence of the *ātman* or the self can be known by intuitive perception. According to Upavarṣa[21] and other Vedāntic philosophers, the existence of the *ātman* cannot be known by inference or demonstration, nor can it be accepted on the authority of scriptural statements. But the *ātman* is known to exist intuitively through the notion that every individual person entertains towards his own self. Really the *ātman* is known to exist from the very fact that "a man is conscious of his own self."[22] Because anyone can have ideas about himself, like "I get thinner" or "I perceive this," we cannot deny the existence of the *ātman* or the agent which makes him have such ideas. In a later period, the Kumārila school in the Mīmāṃsā system continued this idea of Upavarṣa, claiming immediate perception of the *ātman*. And it was on this point that this school was distinguished from the Prabhākara school of the same system.[23] In accord with what we have observed above, we can say that the assertions concerning the *ātman* by the ancient Indian thinkers are very similar to the view of the self which Western thinkers like Augustine, Descartes, Fichte, and Hegel came to hold through their study of self-consciousness.

It should be noted, however, that in India the *ātman* is generally understood to mean not only the individual ego but also the *Brahman* or the Universal Self. The Hindu thinkers were inclined to make a big leap in their reasoning; they assume that *the existence of the Universal Self is known directly from the existence of the individual self*. For instance, Śaṁkara, the prominent eighth-century Indian philosopher, makes the following statement in one of his books: "Moreover the existence of *Brahman* is known on the ground of its being the Self of everyone. For everyone is conscious of the existence of (his) Self, and never thinks 'I am not.' If the existence of the Self were not known, everyone would think 'I am not.' And this Self (of whose existence all are conscious) is *Brahman*."[24] And as to the existence of the Self (*ātman*), Śaṁkara writes as follows: "[The existence of the Self cannot be denied]; since that very person who might deny it, is the Self."[25] In another part, he gives a full explanation of the existence of the Self. "Just because it (the Self) is the Self, it is impossible for us to entertain the idea even of its being capable of refutation. For the (knowledge of the) Self is not, in any person's case, adventitious, and is not established through the so-called means of right knowledge; it is rather self-established. The Self does indeed employ perception and the other means of right knowledge for the purpose of establishing previously non-established objects of knowledge; for nobody assumes that such things as other selves can be self-established independently of the means of right knowledge. But the Self, as the abode of the mind-function that acts through the means of right knowledge, is itself established previously to that function. And to refute such a self-established entity is impossible. An adventitious thing, indeed, may be refuted, but not that which is the essential nature (of him who attempts the refutation); for it is the essential nature of him who refutes. The heat of a fire is not refuted (i.e. sublated) by the fire itself. Let us further consider the relation expressed in the following clauses: 'I know at the present moment whatever is present; I knew (at former moments) the nearer and the remoter past; I shall know (in the future) the nearer and remoter future.' Here the object of knowledge changes accordingly as it is something past or something future or something present; but the knowing agent does not change, since his nature is eternal presence. And as the nature of the Self is 'eternal presence,' it cannot undergo destruction even when the body is reduced to ashes; nay, we cannot even conceive that it ever should become something different from what it is."[26] In another part, Śaṁkara also says that the interior Self (*pratyagātman*) is "the object of the notion of the Ego (*asmaspratyayaviṣaya*)" and is well known to exist on account of its "immediate intuitive presentation (*aparokṣa*)."[27]

Apparently Śaṁkara was influenced by the idea of Upavarṣa. But, starting from the latter's standpoint, Śaṁkara developed his unique system of thought. According to him, the demonstration of the existence of the Self only proves the existence of the individual embodied self which is the agent of our consciousness, but the existence of the Highest Self or the Brahman cannot be known directly from this demonstration. The Highest Self is not the object of the notion of the ego, for it surpasses all the elements that the individual self has. What can be perceived by the individual self is limited only to the things of the phenomenal world. So Śaṁkara says: "It is only this principle of self-consciousness (*ahaṁkartṛ*), the object of the notion of the ego and the agent in all cognition, which accomplishes all actions and enjoys their results."[28] Strictly speaking, the agent that has the power to cause the notion of "the ego" is the *buddhi* within the individual self. "If the *buddhi* has the power of an agent, it must be admitted that it is also the object of self-consciousness (*ahaṁpratyaya*), since we see that everywhere activity is preceded by self-consciousness, '*I go, I come, I eat, I drink*,' etc."[29] According to Śaṁkara, it is the *buddhi* within the individual self that causes the notion of the ego and effects all action in practical existence. The Highest Self, on the other hand, shares no Ego-Consciousness that the individual self has. It is not the object of the notion of the ego, nor is it the agent that causes the notion of the ego. It surpasses all these elements. It is absolute and indivisible. It is so-called *absolute knowing*. It is beyond the perception of all ordinary people, but it reveals itself to a Yogic ascetic in the state of self-nullifying concentration (*saṁrādhana*).

"Neither from that part of the Veda which enjoins works (*vidhikāṇḍa*) nor from reasoning does anybody apprehend that the soul (*puruṣa*), different from the agent that is the object of self-consciousness, merely witnesses that which is permanent in all transitory beings; uniform; one; eternally unchanging; the Self of everything."[30] As we can observe in this quotation from Śaṁkara, the Highest Self in his sense is beyond the notion of the ego held by the individual self. We should not forget, however, that in his thought the Highest Self is understood to be identical ultimately with the individual self which is known to exist on the ground that every man has an undeniable knowledge of his own existence. Śaṁkara succeeded and relied upon Upavarṣa's idea of the Self, but he went further than his predecessor and established his own unique system of thought.

To the present day, Śaṁkara's philosophy has been accepted by most of the traditional orthodox scholars (Paṇḍits) of India. And his idea about the Self can rightly claim to be the representative view of most Indian people. Furthermore, similar views are observed in the theological assertions of modern Hinduism. The Cartesian proposition *cogito, ergo sum* was conceived in Hindu philosophy in a way quite different from the individualistic European view. The Self or the *Ātman* in the Indian concept does not simply mean that individual souls populate this phenomenal world, each one claiming itself to be distinct from others in spite of its substantial homogeneity with others. But, by the *Ātman,* Indians imply also the Self hidden behind the competing individual souls, or more properly speaking, the Absolute Self shared by every individual soul. In many Indian books of philosophy and religion, the Self means the Absolute Highest Self as well as the individual self. As the form of the word (*sol-ips-ism*) indicates to us, solipsism in the Western sense is the concept of "Only I am." On the other hand, as a result of their unique concept of the Self, the *ātmavāda* or the Indian theory of the Self-only emphasizes the oneness of all beings in the universe.

As we have seen above, Indians acknowledge the Highest Self as being the substratum of the individual soul. It is natural, therefore, that they insist on the oneness or identity of the two. The relation of the individual self and the Highest Self is one of the major problems for philosophers in India, each working out his own conclusions.

Here we shall limit ourselves to the fact that the idea of the *avatāra* or incarnation is also based on this concept of non-duality between the individual self and the Highest Self. The *avatāra* is the idea that for the salvation of living creatures the Supreme God emerges in this world in the incarnate form of man or animal. In India, this idea of incarnation is most remarkably expressed in the *Purāṇas* and subsequent works. In these works, they relate the multiple *avatāras* of Viṣṇu, though the stories of incarnation of other gods like Śiva and Indra are also abundant. The number of Viṣṇu's manifestations is said to be variously six, ten, twelve, sixteen, twenty-two or twenty-three, and is not definitely fixed. Generally the Hindu religionists count the following ten as the *avatāras* of Viṣṇu: fish, tortoise, boar, man-lion, pigmy, Rāma with the axe, the strong Rāma, Kṛṣṇa, the Buddha, and Kalki. Viṣṇu, taking those forms, subjugates evil, saves living beings and stands for Brahmanism. In Buddhism, too, the Buddhas and the Bodhisattvas are supposed to have the magical power of revealing themselves in various forms for the salvation of suffering creatures. For instance, they say that the Bodhisattva Avalokiteśvara possessed thirty-three manifestations.

In India, where people hold such a non-dualistic view, monotheism in the Western sense has never come into being. In the Upaniṣads and in the philosophical assertion of the Vedāntins, the Absolute Being is assumed to be an impersonal spiritual principle without any limiting attribute. But, because such an abstract principle is far from appropriate as an object of worship for the common people, they desired ardently to have an anthropomorphic god in place of the abstract principle. And as Hinduism supplemented its system by a religious order, one of the gods like Viṣṇu, Śiva, or Kṛṣna came to be worshipped as the Highest Absolute Being. All the gods other than the Supreme One are supposed to be His *avatāras*. Thus, the Indian worship of the One Supreme God at the same time retains a coloring of pantheism. Indians combine whole-hearted devotional faith together with mysticism of a high intellectual level. And in their religious systems, the element of refined spiritual introspection is mixed with that of primitive vulgar ritual. Indians, however, feel no sense of contradiction in this existence of antagonistic elements in one system. In their way of thinking, these elements can be embraced in one big unity. Here, it can be said that metaphysical monism in their basic way of thinking is aimed to justify this mixture of different elements.

Ethics of the Non-duality of One's Self and Other Selves

When most Indians think that each self is essentially identical with others and that the distinction of persons is merely a matter of phenomenal form, it is natural that they look upon the state of non-duality of one's self and others' selves as the ideal. In the *Upaniṣads* they teach, "All this thou art,"[31] or "I am *Brahman*."[32] And these statements form the core of their ethics. Both Brahmanism and Hinduism are founded on the basis of this view of non-dualism.

The philosophical standpoint of Buddhism was considerably different from that of Brahmanism. Buddhism adopted rather the pluralistic view. Buddhists do not acknowledge the individual soul as a metaphysical entity, so that they attach no importance to the consideration of the relation between a self and other selves. But their ethical ideal has been to remove the barriers among different ages. As we have already seen, Buddhism prescribed that men in the monastic order (*Saṁgha*) live as one body without any personal discrimination. Here, we can say that the Indian view of non-dualism between one and others takes another form of expression in Buddhism. This opinion still prevails in present-day Southern Buddhism. Reverend U. Thittila, a spiritual leader of Southern Buddhists, explaining the fundamental principle of friendliness (*mettā*), says: "It is *mettā* which attempts to break all the barriers separating one from another. There is no reason to keep aloof from others merely because they belong to another religious persuasion or nationality. The true Buddhist exercises himself with all, making no distinction whatsoever with regard to caste, color, class, or sex."[33] Mahāyāna philosophers also taught that in the ultimate state one can reach the "transformation of one's neighbor into one's ego (*parātma-parivartana*)."[34] Things being so, the union of one with others is the ideal in the practical ethics of the Mahāyāna Buddhists. In the final stage of Indian Buddhism it was claimed that everything is Buddha.[35]

According to most Indians, respect for life, which is found in any living being, can be logically deduced from non-dualism. Non-violence (*ahiṁsa*) is often described as the supreme virtue (*parama-dharma*).[36] Buddhism teaches Not-killing, and most Buddhists extend this prescription to animals. The altruistic virtues and duties have men's respect and help each other to work out their respective spiritual ideals. Every individual, every living being, thus comes to be regarded as a sacred center of potential value, deserving of respect and possessing freedom for progress toward its goal of perfection.

An Indian explanation on this point is as follows: "Insofar as the individual is a self, it is a distinct reality; its spiritual freedom is the ultimate end to which its entire life's activities should be directed. But insofar as the self is embodied, and all its activities are through the body, subtle and gross, and the body is an inseparable member and product of the world of Nature, out of which the bodies of other selves also have evolved, there is an indissoluble bond between the embodied individual and all other such individuals forming the social corpus."[37]

In Indian religious schools, a man is urged to work for "the interests of the public as well as of himself."[38] For Indians, truth (*satya*) means nothing other than the good of all living beings (*bhūtahita*).[39] They think that the good of oneself and others can be realized through one's act of love and mercy. They say, "Benevolence (*maitrī*) brings happiness and ease to people,"[40] or "Even gods make a respectful salutation to merciful (*dayā*) persons."[41] The virtue of benevolence is especially emphasized by the Buddhists. They teach that we should abandon hatred against others. "For hatred does not cease by hatred at any time: hatred ceases by love, this is an old rule."[42] And they urge us to be compassionate to others, men and all other living beings. "As a mother at the risk of her life watches over her own child, so also let everyone cultivate a boundless (friendly) mind towards all beings."[43] In another place, they teach that we should render to others a service greater than what we get from our parents and from our relatives.[44] This idea of benevolence was developed further at the time of the Mahāyāna Buddhists.

This trait of benevolence brought about an important effect on some social and economic problems. In the West capital punishment was not necessarily regarded as bad by Christians. Luther, for example, while explicitly condoning the hangman as exercising a tolerable Christian vocation, condemned the late medieval usurers and speculators.[45] Buddhists of ancient India, on the other hand, while tolerating money-lending on the basis of reasonable rate, excluded the hangman and the butcher from a list of justified vocations. (This does not hold true of Buddhism in other countries.)

The ideal of love and mercy forms one of the characteristics of Indian thought. Some Westerners recently, however, seem not to have fully realized the true nature of this Indian idea. Consciously or not, they hold biased views. And those Western views are accepted without due consideration by the Japanese. To quote Bergson as an example: "Not that Buddhism ignored charity. On the contrary it recommended it in the most exalted terms. And it joined example to precept. But it lacked warmth and glow. As a religious historian very justly puts it, it knew nothing 'of the complete and mysterious gift of self. . . .' That enthusiastic charity, that mysticism comparable to the mysticism of Christianity, we find in a Ramakrishna or a Vivekānanda, to take only the most recent examples. But Christianity, and this is just the point, have come into the world in the interval. . . . But let us suppose even that the direct action of Christianity, as a dogma, has been practically nil in India. Since it has impregnated the whole of Western civilization, one breathes it like a perfume, in everything which this civilization brings in its wake. Industrialism itself, as we shall try to prove, springs indirectly from it. And it was industrialism, it was our Western civilization, which unloosed the mysticism of a Ramakrishna or a Vivekānanada."[46]

This view of Bergson can be safely taken as one of the common views of Indian religion held among very many Westerners. But, contrary to Bergson's contention, various manuscripts and edicts of ancient India and the records of the foreigners who travelled through the country all present detailed descriptions of the political and social movements of the ancient Indians which were all based on the idea of benevolence. Bergson, either for lack of knowledge of the historical facts or because of his presumption that complete mysticism appeared only among the Christian mystics, is led to erroneous conclusions about Indian social movements.

As historical evidence reveals to us and as the historians confirm, the so-called social welfare policy or charity movement began in Asia earlier than in the Western world. Law books of the ancient Brahmanists refer to many social facilities. And the sacred books of the Buddhists of the earliest time tell us that the kings during Buddha's lifetime, under his influence, advocated a social policy for the welfare of the general public. King Aśoka (c. 250 B.C.) promoted social welfare policy on a still larger scale. He had strong faith in Buddhism and he made efforts to effect rules in conformity with the teachings of the Buddha. He taught the people that magical acts of spell and rites are useless and he persuaded them to have faith in Buddhism. He prohibited people from killing living creatures in the name of sport and from castrating animals. He built charity houses to relieve the poor and went so far as to establish hospitals even for animals. He encouraged the cultivation of medical plants. He protected the minority tribes in the remote regions. He granted amnesty to prisoners. King Aśoka's social policy, based on the teachings of the Buddha, was carried on by the Indian people of later periods, and the tradition lasted for a long time.[47]

The charity movement in the West began at a later date. In one of his historical works, Vincent A. Smith quotes Sir H. Burdett's statement as follows: "[In the West], no establishments for the relief of the sick were founded until the reign of Constantine (A.D. 306–37). Late in the fourth century Basil founded a leper hospital at Caesarea, and St. Chrysostom established a hospital at Constantinople. A law of Justinian (A.D. 527–62) included hospitals among the ecclesiastical institutions. The Maison Dieu or Hôtel Dieu of Paris is sometimes alleged to be the oldest European hospital. It dates from the seventh century."[48] In Greek philosophy, there was no element encouraging the development of social welfare services and any charity movement. The Indians are in fact the people who first established the spiritual and social tradition of public welfare service. (We should not forget, however, the fact that the social movement in India was later doomed to stagnation while the Western movement showed remarkable progress especially in the modern age. This problem will be dealt with on another occasion.)

The religious leaders in modern India have been striving to restore the spiritual tradition of their ancestors. Romain Rolland writes as follows: "Usually in European thought 'to serve' implies a feeling of voluntary debasement or humility. It is the 'Dienen, dienen' of Kundry in Parsifal.

This sentiment is completely absent from the Vedāntism of Vivekānanda. To serve, to love, is to become equal to the one served or loved. Far from abasement, Vivekānanda always regarded it as the fulfillment of life."[49] The Indian leaders of national movements emulate Ghandi whose life was in turn guided by the strong religious faith of love and service exemplified by Vivekānanda. The tradition of non-dualism of self and other selves continues to shape the attitudes of millions of Indians today.

CHAPTER 9 SUBSERVIENCE TO UNIVERSALS

Subservience to Universals as Revealed in Language

As we have seen, most Indians attach greater importance to universals than to individuals and, with respect to action, they hold the view that one's self is immersed in and identical with others. For Indians, the acts of individuals are not of great importance; they tend to emphasize the power of the universal Being which transcends individuals.

This feature of the Indian way of thinking is revealed in their language. In Sanskrit, to describe an act of a person, one is likely to write in the passive as well as in the reflexive form (*Ātmanepada*). In the Vedic language, the active form is preferred, as in Western writings. But, in the classical Sanskrit, the passive form began to be used instead, and this tendency grew stronger as time passed. In Sanskrit, even intransitive verbs have their passive forms. As a consequence, there are in Sanskrit a great number of passive sentences used impersonally;[1] e.g. *karmaṇo hy api boddhavyam* (*Bhag. G.*, IV, 16) = τὶ δ'ἐστὶ τὸ πρακτέον . . . ἐγὼ οἶδα = *tum ad opus omnino est attendum; kair mayā saha yoddhavyam* (*Bhag. G.* I, 22) = τὶ ὀὶ δὲ μοι συμπλακῆναι = *quibuscum mihi pugnandum.* These two sentences may be respectively translated into English as: "For one must understand the nature of action"; and "With whom must I fight?"

Sanskrit sentences are written impersonally in the passive mood: the subject is not stated. In the dominant Vedāntist view of the Indians, an act is not ascribed to a particular subject primarily, but is regarded as a changing phenomenon caused by many conditioning factors, and the subject of the action is only one of many factors. It can be said, therefore, that the Indian preference for propositions stated impersonally in the passive form shows a feature of their way of thinking which places importance on unrevealed and hidden power, rather than on the spontaneity of overt individual action.

The Extension of the Subject of Action

As a result of this characteristic of Indian thought which refuses to acknowledge a fixed and substantial subject of action, the moral status of the individual self became a problem, and gave rise to many ideas. The Buddhists theory of "non-self" (*anātman*) is one of the oldest of such ideas. Buddhists, as we have seen, do not necessarily deny the existence of the *Ātman* itself. But, they refuse to recognize any permanent subject of action whether it is the *Ātman* or not. The idea of "non-self" is generally supposed to be a concept unique to Buddhism, but there are in India other schools of thought having a similar view. A sentence in the *Maitrī-Upaniṣad* (3. 2.) for instance, reads as follows: "Like a bird trapped in the net, (the individual ego) binds itself thinking 'It is I (*aham*)' or 'it is Mine (*mama*).'" And it exhorts man to free himself from all bondage. The *Bhagavadgītā* (2. 71) also teaches man not to cling to one's ego saying: "The man who casts off all desires and walks without desire, with no thought of a *Mine* (*nirmama*) or of an *I* (*nirahaṅkāra*) comes unto peace."[2] A theory of "non-self" is also found in a book of the Sāṁkhya where we read that the individual soul (*puruṣa*) is delivered from attachments when it has attained "the pure and complete wisdom" that "I am not; (Nothing) is mine; and (Nothing) is I."[3] The Sāṁkhya supposes the *Puruṣa,* which is identical to the *Ātman,* to be a unique metaphysical principle. On this point, their doctrine is in essence quite different from the Buddhist theory of "non-self." However, so far as the expression of their doctrine is concerned, they are very close to the Buddhists. Bhartṛhari, in his metaphysical study of the Word, asserts a kind of "non-self" theory. According to him, the Word is the subject of cognition—the *Ātman or* the Absolute Being. And just as one projects one's image on the wall, the Word, which is the subject of cognition, projects itself objectively on the screen within itself and perceives its own image, viz. the Word as the object. This is cognition in Bhartṛhari's sense. What serves as the screen in the case of the Word is the internal organ (*antaḥkaraṇa*) which performs the apperceptive function (*buddhi*). The *Buddhi* is in reality no more than the screen reflecting the image of Absolute Being and has no active power in itself. In short, cognition is understood to be only one phase of the self-evolving process of the Absolute Being—of the Word which divides itself into two parts, one as the subjective knower and the other as the object, and unfolds itself in a process of mutual interrelation. Bhartṛhari explains action in the same way as he explains cognition.[4] This may be considered an expression of the "non-self" theory.

It is erroneous to maintain that the idea of "non-self" and ideas similar to it are popular in India apart from its metaphysical thinkers.

However, it should be noted that in no other country has the idea of "non-self" developed into such various forms as we see in India where a metaphysical way of thinking pervades the spiritual background for the growth of such ideas.

Because they were apt to suppose that the action of an individual is supervised and regulated by an invisible power so that the action, having no creative function in itself, is no more than an attribute of the self, most Indians have been inclined to take a submissive attitude toward their fate and conditions. The ideas of *Karma* and *Saṁsāra* are still deeply imbedded in the minds of most Indian people. And a man of a lowly family in India is likely to be resigned to his fate, simple expecting to be reborn under more favorable circumstances in the next life. And here it is assumed that the ultimate subject of action is not the individual but a Reality beyond and above the individual.

Because of their basic emphasis on a super-individual Being, Indians assert that the idea or action of a person is universally valid if it conforms to the True and Universal Law. And it does not matter for them whose idea or action it is.

It is not seldom in India that a book and its commentary are published at the same time; not infrequently, the two are composed by one and the same author. Indians claim that their books, which reveal the eternal truth, deserve to be handed down to posterity for ages without modification. And commentaries are necessary in order to make others understand the truth expounded in their books. For ancient Indian scholars, therefore, it was never regarded as strange to write commentaries on their own works.

In India there are many forged manuscripts, though there are, of course, many such also in China and in Western countries. But far exceeding anything like it in other countries, there exist in India a great many books claiming to be the works of ancient saints. Almost all the religious scriptures which mention the names of the authors are spurious documents. This sort of forgery is understandable in the light of the tendency of most Indians toward self-effacement and philosophical minimization of the importance of unique individuals. All the Mahāyāna texts claim unduly to be "the Buddha's discourse." They are forgeries in the sense that they were not expounded directly from the Buddha's own mouth. Even the texts of the Buddhists of earlier days, nearly all of them, were in reality completed after the Buddha's death by his followers. But all of them claim to be "the Buddha's discourse." Then, the question arises, how could the ancient Buddhists make such claims without damaging their moral conscience?

It is natural for the Buddhist devotees to assume that the Buddha's teachings are absolutely authentic. King Aśoka stated in one of his Edicts that "whatever the Buddha taught is a good teaching."[5] The Buddhists after the death of the Buddha went further and asserted that *any* idea insofar as it is good and correct is the Buddha's teaching. The *Aṅguttara-Nikāya* reads as follows:

"Imagine, O King, a great heap of grain near some village or market-town, from which country folk carry away corn on poles or in baskets, in lap or hand. And if one should approach the folk and question them saying: 'Whence bring you this corn?' how would those folk, in explaining, best explain?"

"They would best explain the matter, sir, by saying: 'We bring it from that great heap of grain.' "

"Even so, O King, *whatsoever be well spoken, all that is the word of the Exalted One, Arahant, the Fully Awakened One,* wholly based thereon is both what we and others say."[6]

The ancient Buddhists thought that *whatever is true should and must have been taught by the Buddha.* Thus, it is not surprising that most Indians were not concerned with the identity of the authors; their only concern was whether or not a certain work expounds the truth. Because the Buddha is any man who realizes the truth perfectly, any book containing the truth is rightly assumed to be the Buddha's teaching. Thus, we see why the ancient Indian Buddhists had no feeling of guilt in claiming the title of "the Buddha's discourse" for their own works.[7]

In India there are many anonymous books. The authors did not like to record their names on their own works. There is no need, they thought, to attach the name of a particular author so long as the book conveys the universal truth. In fact, the forged documents and anonymous books in India are both expressions of one basic characteristic of their way of thinking.

In India the biographies of those who expounded the truth is completely ignored. The word *buddha* is not a proper noun. It means "the enlightened one" in general. Anyone who has realized the truth is buddha. And Gotama the Buddha, the historical founder of Buddhism, is one of many enlightened ones. Since the oldest period of their history, Buddhists had faith in the Seven Buddhas of the Past—Gotama Śākyamuni and the six Buddhas preceding him.[8] In later periods, faith in the twenty-four Buddhas was cherished by them. Mahāyāna Buddhists came to think that there exist numerous Buddhas in all directions and throughout the past, present, and future. Together with this idea of the multiplicity of Buddhas, a new idea appeared which, as we see in the *Lotus Sūtra* of the Mahāyāna, asserts that the Buddha had attained enlightenment many *Kalpas* (aeons) before his awakening under the Bo-Tree of Buddha-gayā. The Jains hold a similar idea. They believe in the twenty-three saints preceding Mahāvīra. Both the Buddhists and the Jains respect Gotama and Mahāvīra as the founders of their religions; and at the same, they claim that their religions have their origin in the past long before the days of their historical founders. This attitude of the Indians toward their religions presents a remarkable contrast to the case of the unique personal God of Christianity as an historical individual.

Reverence for Universal Standards in Behavior

As a result of their inclination to submit themselves to a universal Being, Indians harbor an ardent desire to have direct relations with the Absolute and refuse to have any intermediate agent. They assert that the salvation of one's soul should be attained only by one's own efforts without relying upon others. In the philosophy of Brahmanism, regarding the emancipation of the soul, it is taught that a man who has realized the truth of the universe "gets into his own Self by dint only of his Self.[9] And Buddhists, though they do not engage in any metaphysical considera-tion of "the Self" (*Ātman*), acknowledge its moral significance as the subject of action saying that only the Self can save the Self. A passage from the *Dhammapada* reads as follows: "Sons are no help, nor a father, nor relations; there is no help from kinsfolk for one whom death has seized."[10] Jains, too, admit that all things other than one's self are useless for one's salvation saying: "They cannot help thee or protect thee."[11] They say again: "Man! Thou art thine own friend; why wishest thou for a friend beyond thyself?"[12]

In later periods the Mahāyāna Buddhists had faith in salvation through the power of the great compassion of the Buddhas and the Bodhisattvas, and the schools of Hinduism emphasize salvation by the grace of Viṣṇu or Śiva. But, it should be noted, even in such cases one confronts the absolute by pleading directly to these gods for the salvation of one's soul. And here little significance is attached to any intermediate agents between the absolute and the individual beings.

It is natural that from such views of the Indians on salvation no religious order, which is itself a limited social organization, would take active leadership as the absolute source of authority. In Europe, the monks united and formed organized communities such as the Jesuit Order which sometimes had political power equal to that of the king. In India, on the other hand, the political influence of the religious bodies was very weak. Brahmanists maintained a consanguineal cultural unity among themselves. This unity, however, served only to form their own particular exclusive class, and this body of Brahmanists did not function as a political unit.[13] What is more, they had no leader to rule over the body, and an individual

Brahmanist could behave at his own will without any check by a supervising authority. It is natural that such a loose organization had no solid financial basis like the Roman Catholic Church. Since the time of its establishment the Buddhist Saṁgha (monastic order) was also without political or economic unity. Even while the Buddha was still alive, his followers lived apart from him and no regulation was made binding all of these followers. After the death of the Buddha, they were intent only on the faithful observance of the doctrines and the disciplines set forth by their late teacher, and did not choose to have a political leader of their Saṁgha.[14]

Moreover, the Buddhist Saṁgha *did not claim to be a legislative authority* or *an authority on the interpretation of the doctrine*. This assertion can be safely made at least in respect to its attitude toward important issues. Buddhists attributed the authority of legislation exclusively to the Buddha. They considered that all the rules of the Saṁgha are authorized by claiming that they all came under the title "the Buddha's own discourse." Even the new rules established after the Buddha's death to meet the changing social situations were also attributed to the Buddha's authority. One of their books of precepts states as follows: "If a new situation arises at some time to confront the Saṁgha, not ordaining what has not been ordained, and not revoking what has been ordained, one should take it upon himself to direct himself always according to the precepts laid down. This is the resolution."[15] Interpreting the vague statements in the old texts, Buddhists attributed their own interpretation to the Buddha. And for authority they referred not to the Saṁgha but to the Buddha. This is the attitude of the Buddhists, at least the Buddhists of the early days, in their interpretation of the texts.[16]

The same features of thought discernible in the early Buddhist Saṁgha are found among the Jains. The Mahāyāna Buddhists who appeared later in history assumed the same attitude, as did the schools of Hinduism. Although some of the Indian sects—the most distinct example being the Sikhs—kept a systematic unity in their body, they were exceptional cases.

Indians, in contrast to their indifferent attitude toward social organizations like the Saṁgha, attach the greatest importance to the authority of the universal law—the law that all individuals and all social organizations should follow. And they call the law "*Dharma.*" This word comes from the root $\sqrt{\text{dhṛ}}$, which means "to hold," "to support," or "to bear." *Dharma* means "what serves as the norm to support human behavior," or in short, "the norm of action" or "the rule of conduct." They affirm that the *Dharmas* differ from other things found in the natural world. Further, *Dharma* means "usage," "customary observance," "the thing to be done," or "duty."

An old book of rites in Brahmanism prescribes the four *Dharmas* of the Brahman: to be a man of a Brahman family; to do what becomes the dignity of the Brahman; to maintain honor; and to lead the people. As to the duties that a layman should observe toward the Brahman, it mentions the four different *Dharmas:* to pay respect to the Brahman; to make offerings to the Brahman; to protect the Brahman from harm and injury; and to refrain from condemning the Brahman to death.[17]

The *Dharma,* as the norm that *guides* a man to establish and to perform moral acts, is the power that realizes "Truth" in this world. Thus, the ancient Indians understood the *Dharma* to be the truth that works as a creative power, and identified the two. "Thus the Law is what is called the true. And if a man declares what is true, they say he declares the Law; and if he declares the Law, they say he declares what is true. Thus both are the same."[18]

And in the course of time, this norm of behavior for the realization of morals was raised to the position of the Absolute. Indians came to think that the *Dharma* is the basis of the whole universe and that all things in the universe rest on the *Dharma.* "This whole universe is in the *Dharma.* Nothing is more difficult to do than the *Dharma.* On this account, they hold the *Dharma* in high esteem."[19] "The *Dharma* is the basis of the whole universe. In the world, people wish to emulate a man who keeps the *Dharma* best. They eliminate all evils by force of the *Dharma.* All beings rest in peace in the *Dharma.* On this account, they say that the *Dharma* is the highest being."[20] Furthermore, it is maintained that the *Dharma* has a form superior even to that of the creator of the universe (the Brahman).[21] In the Vaiśeṣika, it is assumed that the rise and the deliverance of the soul is attained only on the strength of the *Dharma.*[22]

Indians considered that the *Dharma* exists *eternally.* Already in an old Vedic text, a wife is required to lie down on the pyre beside her dead spouse at the cremation of her husband on the grounds that it is "the time-honored rule" (*dharmaḥ purāṇaḥ*).[23] As the following quotation tells us, the *Dharma* is allegorically identified with eternal absolute being: "He from whom the sun rises, and into whom it sets . . . Him the *Devas* (gods) made the law, he only is today, and he tomorrow also."[24]

This idea of the eternal universal law was inherited by the Jains and the Buddhists. The Jains, from their very rationalistic standpoint, assert that there exist universal laws (*dharma*) which all mankind should observe at all times and all places. For instance, one of their sacred books teaches: "All breathing, existing, living, sentient creatures, should not be slain, or treated with violence, or abused, or tormented, or driven away. This is 'the pure, unchangeable, eternal law. . . .' "[25] The founder of Jainism, Mahāvīra, set forth the philosophy and the practical morality of this religion in accord with what he believed to be the true principle or law.

Buddhists hold a similar view of the law. They consider that the law of causal origination is the unchangeable truth. "Whether there be an appearance or non-appearance of a Tathāgata, this causal law of nature, this orderly fixing of things prevails. . . ."[26] A Tathāgata is one who, having realized this law of nature, endeavors to reveal it to all sentient beings. The enlightened one is not to be considered as a mystic, inspired by a revelation, but only as a man who has fully perceived the true law of nature that exists eternally. Buddhism, or at least Buddhism in its early stage, pays special reverence to the law that is eternally valid, and assumes that the authority of the law precedes that of the Buddha. All beings, including even the gods, adore the law that the Buddha has revealed and accept it.[27] Even the gods are bound to worldly sufferings, and they have to follow the law to free themselves from the sufferings of rebirth.

Here one may find an analogue of this Buddhist idea of the law in Hugo Grotius's *jus naturale* or "natural law." His natural law is supposed to be impartial to any person or nation and unchangeable under any circumstances. Even God cannot alter this product of his reason. But it should be remembered that natural law regulates human existence. The law is valid without necessarily referring to God's authority so long as it is clear to reason as a universal principle necessary in governing the relations of human beings in this world. The Buddhist law of nature, on the other hand, is not the law regulating the relations of individual human beings, but it is the law controlling the relations between the state of ignorance (which is inevitably attached to individual human existence and behavior) and the way of deliverance from it. Though Grotius's natural law and the Buddhist law of nature are similar in form, they are quite different in essence.

As Indians put great emphasis on the universal law that stands above individuals, the significance of the individual personality is thoroughly ignored by them. And even Gotama the Buddha, the man of greatest character, is considered to be only one of many men who realized the universal law in this world. As we have pointed out in the previous section of this book, Buddhists espouse the idea of the multiplicity of Buddhas. The Jains, in a similar manner, assume the existence of twenty-three founders preceding the historical founder, Mahāvīra.[28]

In the thought of the Indians, Buddhas or the founders of religion, however deified they are as the object of worship, are human beings who are not different from ordinary people. A man can be a Buddha or a founder of religion if he has accomplished the works necessary for enlightenment. We are all in essence one and the same with the absolute

Being. This assertion is correct also in the case of Bhaktic Buddhism. The man saved by the grace of Amitābha-Buddha becomes a Buddha equal in all respects to his savior.

The concept of the eternal and universal law prevailed in Indian thought and took root among the people. King Aśoka believed in the eternal law which should be observed by all, regardless of race, religion, nationality, time or place. This law is the norm of human behavior and he called it "*dharma*" or "the time-honored rule." He stated in one of his Edicts that many kings preceding him had intended in vain to rule the people on the basis of the *Dharma*, and that the reign of the *Dharma* was first realized by him.[29] King Khāravela who ruled over South India in the second century B.C. was called "the universal monarch (Cakravartin)."[30] After Khāravela, the kings of this country sometimes claimed the title of "the king faithful to the law."[31] And all the followers of the religious sects in India were taught that to observe the law was the most precious of virtues.[32]

The Indian religion which acknowledges the authority of the eternal universal law is very rationalistic in its character and it offers a striking contrast to some less logical, personal religions of the West. Schopenhauer once said that the Indian religion which has developed from rational speculation about the world is superior to Christianity.[33] Setting aside the question of whether he is right or wrong, his remark indicates the essential difference between the Indian and Christian religions.

Moreover, there is another important question, i.e. whether this universal law was ever conceived in *specific determinate terms* as the Western notion of abstract, universal, determinate law is. A distinction should be drawn about the universality of law in the Hindu view and that in the West. Also the Hindu's distrust of any *specifically formulable* law applicable to *all* cases should be considered. Hindu laws were more flexible, and commentators on established laws allowed modifications of them in applying them to each new case. In this connection, Northrop's discussion,[34] giving specific examples to substantiate his view that the Indian is distrustful of the abstract formulation of the law and wants to consider each individual case on its own merits, should be considered relevant. However, there remain various problems for critical reflection.[35]

Perceiving the Truth: Faith and Rationalism

For Indians, it is a matter of the greatest moral and religious importance to know the Universal Law and to submit themselves to it. And this feature of Indian thought can be observed also in their concept of "faith." *Śraddhā* is the Sanskrit word that is usually translated into the Western languages as "*fides*," "*Glaube*," or "*faith*." But what Indians mean by the word is not exactly the same as the faith of Western religions. *Śraddhā* means to believe in and rely upon a man of superior wisdom and at the same time, it indicates wholehearted acceptance of the doctrines that the man professes. Indians, refusing to place faith in a particular person or saint, hope to submit themselves to the Universal Law that stands above all individuals.

In early Buddhist texts, faith in the Buddha is expressed, but this should not be understood as being a worship of a particular saint, Gotama the Buddha. Gotama is one of the Buddhas—the Enlightened Ones. Buddhist faith in the Buddha means faith in the law that makes the Enlightened One as he is. Jains hold a similar view of faith. Jains in the early stage of their history taught "not to have faith in the illusory power of god."[36] They express true faith by the word *samyagdarśana* or "right-seeing," and thus true faith in their sense is none other than to see the truth in the right way.[37]

For Indians, faith is not the worship of particular individuals and this nature of their faith can be more clearly observed in the statements of Brahmanists. Psychologically Śaṁkara defines *śraddhā* as "a particular kind of mental state (*pratyayaviśeṣa*)"[38] the nature of which is "delicate (*tanu*)."[39] As the active and practical significance of *śraddhā,* two views are given by the Brahmanists: (1) According to the Vedānta, *śraddhā* is not to put faith in a teacher, but "to accept as true the words in the *Upaniṣads* that the teacher introduces to us."[40] All other schools of Brahmanism agree with the Vedānta in the view that *śraddhā* means the acceptance of the sacred doctrine.[41] (2) As a logical consequence of the first view, *śraddhā* is applied to mean the ideology that urges people to do the things generally approved as good in the Hindu community especially to perform religious works in a broad sense of the word.[42] It is "the factor which makes all living beings do good deeds,"[43] and it is in essence "the idea of traditionalism."[44]

Since the oldest days of their history, Buddhists use the word *prasāda* to mean faith in their sense. As the Chinese translate this word by "*ch'eng ching*" (purity) or "*hsi*" (bliss), it means the calm and pure state of mind in which one feels the bliss of serenity.[45] Buddhist faith is far from fanatic worship.[46] The enthusiastic and fanatic form of reverence, which urges ardent devotion (*bhakti*) to the gods, was advocated by some Buddhist sects of later development and by the schools of Hinduism, but this kind of fanatic devotion to an individual Guru or God failed to win the heart of most Indian intellectuals of antiquity. However, we should not minimize the tremendous vogue of *Bhakti* cults among the common people of India, especially in the second millenium A.D. The most conspicuous starting-point of this trend seems to be the *Bhagavadgītā*, when Vishnu says, "If you surrender everything to Me, you will undoubtedly gain salvation." This trend still lingers in contemporary India, so that we should recognize the existence of various trends in the history of thought in India.

For Indians, the essence of faith is *to see* the truth through any means possible. Whether Buddhists, Jains, or Brahmanists, religious adherents in India all agree in their assertion that right wisdom (*samyagjñāna*) is the way to liberation.[47] They say that liberation means the awakening of mind attained by dint of right wisdom.[48] And they all pay great respect to a man of wisdom (*vivekin*).[49] They call such a man "the man who climbed the terraced heights of wisdom."[50] Thus, in India, *faith and knowledge are understood to be compatible;* consequently, the Indian religion bears a strong *tinge of philosophy*. That is why in India, such ideas "I believe it because it is absurd (*credo quia absurdum*),"[51] are rarely, if ever, held, and there is no conflict of religion and philosophy.

In fact, the Indian religion is based on philosophical contemplation and its philosophy is indistinguishable from religion. As Masson-Oursel has pointed out, in India and China religion is not antagonistic to philosophy or to science.[52] Indians are traditionally a religious and, at the same time, a philosophical people.

Transcendence of Limited Ethical Systems

TRANSCENDENCE OF NATIONAL AND RACIAL CONSCIOUSNESS

The Vedas, the oldest records in India, are collections of ritual recitations and commentaries on the rites. They are compiled chiefly for the purpose of ritualistic practices. The Vedas also preserve many legends and myths in their original forms. But for the Indo-Aryans, myths concerning the origin of their race or the legendary histories of their expansion and the lineage of their dynasties were not matters of importance. What was crucially important for them was the measure of *their direct relationship with the gods*.[53] They were religious people occupied in the consideration of the gods, or more properly speaking, of a world governed by cosmic law. On the other hand, they had a rather dim sense of national or racial consciousness. Indeed, in ancient India the aristocrats and the intellectual class took pride in their Aryan descent, which accounted for the sense of unity among them. But this unity was the result of the conviction they held in common, their faith in one superior religion, and not from their awareness of any racial oneness.

For the early Indians, universal order is the ultimate and the highest authority. They attach little significance to intermediary beings lying between the individual and universal law. It is natural then that they regard national and racial questions as secondary. We find this tendency even in their earliest history.

They regarded religion as taking precedence over such matters, so that they were thoroughly apathetic to the problems of nationality or of race. Buddhism and Jainism, arising later, continued to cultivate this outlook. They claimed the abolition of racial discrimination and preached above all things the realization of the law that is universal to all mankind—*dharma*. Even today, Indians are inclined to form religious rather than political units. In other words, their national actions are due to associations of co-religionists rather than to groups of men of common political viewpoint. And so any movement for national unification based on race is weak and bound to fail in India.

Since the oldest times in India the authority of the state and the king has been subordinated to religious authority. A story about a king illustrates the general feeling of the days before the birth of the Buddha. The king was once blamed as immoral because he placed his teacher (*purohita*) of the Vedas in a seat lower than his. But, later, having recognized his mistake, he came to take his lessons in a seat lower than that of his teacher.[54] Kings were no exceptions to the decree of Brahmanic sacred codes which stressed that "disciples are not allowed to take seats higher than that of their teacher."[55]

In the days of Buddha, kings showed absolute obedience to religious leaders who preached the supreme unchanging law that all men should follow. For instance, King Ajātaśatru of Magadha, the strongest state at the time, made a round of personal calls to the six leading philosophers of his day.[56] Another king of Magadha drove his chariot to Mt. Pāṇḍava where Buddha led a secluded life and asked for an audience.[57] There is a description in a Buddhist sūtra about a scene of a king calling on Buddha: "King Pasenadi of Śrāvastī descended from the chariot, put aside the umbrella, removed the sword, and took off his shoes. Folding his arms in token of respect, he stepped toward Buddha, threw himself to the ground, and made a bow in the most profound manner."[58] The sword, the umbrella, the crown, the brush of long white hair with jewels set in its handle, and the decorated shoes were "the five adornments of the king" that he was allowed to wear from the day of his coronation.[59] Early Buddhist texts tell us that it was an established custom of the day for kings to remove all these five precious adornments before they saw the Buddha.[60]

After the death of the Buddha, religious authority continued to hold sway. King Aśoka, who reigned over the whole land, expressed his wholehearted devotion to the three treasures of "Buddha, Dharma, and Saṁgha."[61] "King of Magadha, beloved of the gods, bows before the

Saṁgha and expresses his hope for its peaceful and healthy condition." It was the king who actually presided over and supported the religious bodies of the day. And still, as the words "beloved of the gods" indicate, Aśoka accepted the superiority of religious authority over the secular.

In the days of the Kuṣāṇa dynasty and thereafter, the religious role of the king increased remarkably, but still it was emphasized that unforeseen disasters would occur in case the king neglected to be obedient to the *Dharma.* The Indians believed in the universal law as beyond any state power. And thus religious institutions which led the people by the light of the law were assumed to be above state authority.

The state authority, therefore, seldom intervened in religious activities, and the inner organization of the religious bodies was seldom influenced by secular powers.[62] (This is still true today in India and Ceylon.) For instance, the seating arrangement within the Buddhist Saṁgha was determined solely by the length of service. Any new member, even if he were a king, had to submit to the lowest rank in the Saṁgha hierarchy.[63] This exhibits a striking contrast to the case of Japan where the men of the highest rank in the secular society, members of the royalty or nobility, always occupied the highest position even at religious functions.

Indian religious bodies, in turn, kept themselves aloof from external authorities. At the earliest stage of Buddhism, monks were already forbidden to associate with kings.[64] In one of the oldest Buddhist texts, the admonition is: "Monks, you should be mindful to keep yourselves away from state affairs."[65] Buddhists took such an attitude partly for fear of the calamities that connections with the kings might incur; but also it cannot be denied that the Buddhists of the day thought little of the kings' power. They believed that the devotee who renounced the secular world *no longer belonged to the state;* that he was *beyond state jurisdiction.*

Later on, even Mahāyāna Buddhists continued to take the aloof attitude of regarding the church above the state. Many monks deliberately tried to detach themselves from any political affairs. "Bodhisattvas do not serve the king, nor do they serve or associate with princes, ministers, and officials."[66] "A Buddhist monk should not get familiar with the king. Why so? Because the monk who associates with the king is disliked by all people and will not receive hospitable treatment. The bad monk who associates with the king is greedy for treasures, and at the court, at a village or at a crowded place, he endlessly thirsts for material gain. Even if he is not greedy for treasures, the monk who comes in contact with the king is disturbed in his meditation and in his reading. Such a monk is bound to suffer from distractions even if he tries to concentrate on the way of deliverance. These are the reasons why a Buddhist monk should not associate with the king."[67]

As already stated, the earliest Buddhist monks regarded their life as superior to that of the king. Of course, they admitted that it was significant to govern the nation well as a king. But a king was bound by the restrictions of the laity while a monk was completely free from all the restrictions of this world.[68] And it was not rare, as the following quotation from a Buddhist sūtra shows, for kings to visit Buddhist or Brahmanist monks and ask for instruction.[69] "The king made a respectful salutation and then advanced the questions: What is virtue and what is vice? What is guilt and what is not? How can one attain the beatitudes and be free from all evils? Having received the instruction, the king endeavored to realize what he was taught."[70] Although Indians placed religious authority above the king, it is true that in reality the Buddhist Saṁgha was supported and protected politically and economically by the king. But the Buddhists were too proud of their role as guardians of the *dharma* to acknowledge the king's supremacy. "The religious order forbids salutation to the king."[71]

In concert with this attitude of the Buddhists, the Brahmanists told their adherents, "There is no need for praises and salutations. Cast away any notions of good and bad, and go into the woods alone, finding things to eat on the way."[72] Another text states: "The disciples should not praise anyone, nor bow to anyone, nor worship the ancestors, but live in this ever-shifting world at will and free from all restrictions."[73]

In Greece, the religion of the *polis* required every citizen to sacrifice himself in the interest of "the thing greater than oneself—in the interest of the aggregation called *polis*." And it should be noted that this Greek self-sacrifice was done to meet the practical needs of the men in the *polis* as "a service to the fraternity."[74] The Indian religion, on the other hand, attached little importance to secular social organizations, and was primarily directed to the universal order of things. Here, the Indian religion differs essentially from the Greek religion of the gods of the city-states.

A sense of unity as a nation or a race was not nourished even among the early Indians. Alexander the Great, during his invasion of India, met resistance from some local lords but was never harassed by a defense put up by the Indian nation as a whole. To wage a war in defense of their own nation and race apparently did not appeal to the Indians of the day. King Aśoka, even after he succeeded in bringing the whole country under his control, continued to call himself "King of Magadha" and never thought of himself as the "King of India." Magadha is the place where his Maurya dynasty had its origin. In his opinion, he was a *local* king and, *as a local king of Magadha,* he guided and ruled the other localities and races in India. In some of his Edicts, he referred to the land of India as Jambudvīpa. But in this concept of a land, nothing of a racial or national superiority is implied. King Aśoka had no *racial or national consciousness* as such; he wished to think in a way that went *beyond such limitations*. He considered himself the preserver and actualizer of the *dharma,* and he was ever conscious and proud of this. All of his Edicts place emphasis on the realization of the *dharma* in this world.

After the downfall of the Maurya dynasty, India suffered many foreign invasions. But, contrary to our expectations, in the legends and myths of India there appear only a few names of national heroes who did much to defend the nation on such occasions.[75] In the epics of *Mahābhārata* and *Rāmāyaṇa,* there are legends told of many heroes. These are typical heroes of India, but they are not national heroes in the sense of any national and racial consciousness, which they, as well as their authors, lacked. Ancient Indians preached as a virtue the offering of one's property, even one's life if necessary, for the sake of others' happiness. But they were never taught self-sacrifice for a particular nation or race. The concept of the national hero in our sense did not appear in Indian history.[76]

Surprisingly, in the ancient Indian languages, there is no term equivalent to "the Indian people." *Jambudvīpa* and *Bharatavarṣa* mean only the land of India and do not connote the people living there. The Greeks called the inhabitants of this land *"Indos"* and this was adopted by the European languages in general. Indians themselves had no name to call their own nation. The Indo-Aryans, who formed the main stream of Indian civilization, called themselves *"Ārya."* It means "one who is faithful to the religion of the clan," and is the opposite of the word *"mleccha"*—barbarian or, loosely speaking, Non-Aryan. There was no word in India to include both the Aryans and the Non-Aryans together. Indians for a long time did not awaken to a sense of the unity of "the Indian peoples."

The Brahmanists thoroughly ignored state authority. The early Buddhists conceived a social contract theory for the formation of a state, while the early Jains insisted that the state power was nothing but the power of the strongest in arms. Neither the Buddhists nor the Jains found any sacred significance in the state. The ancient Indians in general believed in the rule of *dharma*—the universal law, and they assumed that state power was subordinate to the *dharma.* With such a frame of mind, there was no room for the growth of an organic theory of the state or society throughout Indian history.

For more than three thousand years, since the time of the *Ṛg-Veda* up to the present, the unity of the Indian people has come about through *common religious faiths* rather than from their awakening in national or racial consciousness. Since she gained her independence India has still been troubled with religious problems even though economic and social difficulties loom largest today. The antagonism between the Hindus and the Mohammedans has been an especially difficult political problem.[77]

THE PROBLEM OF CASTE

The caste system represents a closed and disunited social organization which was highly regarded by the Indians. Our next step is to study the idea that underlies this unique social system of India.

About 1000 B.C. the Aryan invaders advanced to the upper reaches of the Ganges and established an agricultural community. This Aryan society prevailed over the whole country and, in the course of years, went through some modifications until we find it in its present state. The members of the conquered tribes were reduced to servitude and they—the Śūdras—were strictly distinguished from the free people. Then among the Aryans themselves, new classes were formed. The priests and the warriors created their own independent classes. Their professions were transmitted through heredity and, in this process, class stratification grew rigid until finally the caste system was established. Under the major four castes of the Brāhmaṇa, the Kṣatriya, the Vaiśya and the Śūdra, many subcastes have grown.

Class rigidity in marriage and dining is universally observed among the primitive tribes of the world. But what is remarkable here is that India, which has already gone through the process of acculturation is still influenced by the caste system. Indian factory workers will share a bedroom only when they are members of the same caste. In the past when a public dining hall was planned in a large Indian city, voices would be heard that it should be constructed according to caste lines.[78]

The Buddhists completely opposed caste discrimination and preached the concept of equality among men, while the Jains compromised on it. The Buddhists were popular among the city dwellers but they failed to win the conservative rural peasants. And this is one reason why Buddhism was doomed and vanished from its birthplace. However, the concept of equality gradually seeped into the minds of the Indians and later on they began to emphasize even the Buddha's noble birth.[79]

The caste system has undergone complicated changes before taking its present form. It is not easy to explain the origin and growth of the castes in India. Many scholars have introduced various theories concerning this problem, but since it is a problem requiring separate discussion, here we can only say that the caste system cannot be explained satisfactorily simply by the study of productive means or of geographic and climatic conditions. It must be noted that a mode of thinking crystallized from ancient *mores* and ideas has a deep influence on the system.[80]

On studying the castes, we cannot overlook the influence of the Brāhmin class in Indian civilization. This priestly class has always kept the highest position in the social hierarchy and taken the intellectual leadership of India. In a country where military or political consolidation has rarely been achieved, it has done much to bring the people under one sway culturally and socially. Indeed, the civilization of India owes much to the Brāhmins, though they have strongly advocated the caste system.

Religious divinity viewed from the standpoint of Brahmanism decides the standing of a caste's social privileges. In other words, each caste shares an element of *Brāhmaṇic divinity*. Accordingly, because of the large share of divine power, the Brāhmin class enjoys the highest rank, the Kṣatriya class comes next, then the Vaiśya and the Śūdra. *Within* a caste, every member is treated with *equanimity*. This phenomenon of equality within the same caste rank is governed by the concept of eternal and universal law which functions within the differing castes and at the same time gives meaning and significance to them. The Indian social structure, therefore, is quite different from that of a consanguineal community, such as Japan, where people have a high esteem for blood-relationship, real or fictional.

Caste membership is transmitted through heredity in India too, so that blood-relationship is still significant. However, Indians consider religion as above consanguinity. If a member of a caste violates the Brāhmaṇic decrees of his caste, he is at once turned out of the caste and transferred to a lower caste. Consanguinity is *held in esteem only* insofar as the *religious divinity* serves it. Thus we see that the peculiar Indian way of thinking which submits to eternal and universal law implements and underlies the caste system.

Consciousness of Living Beings: Indian Concept of Man

When Indians speak of man, they are likely to use such terms as "*prāṇin*," "*bhūta*" "*sattva*," or "*jīva*."[81] Western scholars translate these words as "living being" or "life-force," and the meaning refers not only to man but also to beasts or any living creature.[82] In Sanskrit, there are such words as "*manuṣya*," "*puruṣa*," or "*nara*," which are equivalent to the English "human being." But Indians do not like to use these words even when they mean man in particular. They think of man more as an instance of the species of "living being" than as a member of the human race. This Indian mentality can be traced in the texts of all Indian religions,[83] according to which the subject of ethical conduct is "a living being." The moral rules that regulate human relationships are not enough. Ethics should be so extensive that it rules over all the relations among men, beasts, and other living beings. This Indian concept of man in relation to other beings is thoroughly different from the Western concept of man.[84]

From their standpoint, it is natural that Indians accentuate in ethics the idea of animal protection. Buddhists and Jains in particular both agree on this point. "All living things have deep attachment to life."[85] "They want bodily comforts. They should not be treated cruelly."[86] Brahmanists, too, preach loving care of living creatures.[87] As a matter of fact, protection of animals is emphasized in all Indian religious schools, the ideal being that not even an ant on the road should be stepped on.

There is no essential difference between man and a beast. Like a beast, man is egocentric and eager to satisfy his desires and is distressed by failures. A leading philosopher of India, Saṁkara, classed man together with the beasts: "Man's behavior is not different from that of a beast. A stimulus, such as a sound, comes to a sense organ such as the ears of a beast. The beast avoids or runs away from the sound if it feels it unpleasant, while it makes its way toward it if it feels it pleasant. When a beast sees a man swinging a club, it thinks, 'This man is going to kill me' and runs away. But when it sees a man with grass in his hands, it approaches the man. And the same can be said of man, an intelligent animal. When he recognizes a terrible-looking man threatening with a sword in hand, he runs away. But when he recognizes a man with a contrary mien, he approaches him. Thus man's actions with respect to cognitive objects and functions are shared by the beast. It is generally known that the sensations of a beast result from its confusion in not being able to distinguish between the *Ātman* and the *Non-Ātman*. Man is at many points similar to the beast in that his sensations continue to mistake the *Non-Ātman* for the *Ātman*."[88] Classifications of creatures in the ancient texts of many Indian religious schools confirm the view that there is no difference between man and beast.

The Jains hold an animistic view and maintain that everything has its proper spirit. Earth, water, fire, wind, and plant, have only tactile sensation. A worm has two sensations and an ant has three. A bee has four and only a man enjoys five sensations.[89] According to another text of Jainism, the gods, men, creatures in hell, elephants, peacocks, and fish, are said to have five sensations.[90] It seems that the Jains assume two groups among beings with five sensations, that is, those with mental faculties (*samanaska*) and those without (*asamanaska*).[91]

From the modes of birth, Jains classify living beings into three groups:

(1) Accidental (*upapāta*):	gods and creatures in hell
(2) Viviparous (*garbha*):	creatures born with placenta, without placenta, and from eggs (oviparous)
(3) Coagulative (*sammūrchana*):	creatures not included in the above-mentioned two groups[92]

The Brahmanists, on the other hand, classify beings into four groups:[93]

(1) Viviparous (*jarāyuja*):	creatures such as man
(2) Oviparous (*aṇḍaja*):	creatures such as birds
(3) Moisture-produced (*svedaja*):	creatures produced from moisture, such as the louse
(4) Germinative (*udbhijja*):	creatures produced from buds such as plants[94]

In another text, Brahmanists classify all living creatures into two; "the self-moving (*cara* or *jaṅgana*)," e.g. animals, and "those that are not self-moving (*acara* or *sthāvara*),"[95] e.g. plants.

In these Indian systems of classification, we are able to extract two common features: (1) Man corresponds to other animals as one of the viviparous creatures. This offers a sharp contrast with the Western concept of man before the Middle Ages, and possibly corresponds with the modern scientific classification. The Indian concept is not the result of scientific study of ecological phenomena, but results from their instinctive and natural way of thinking of man as belonging to the world of *living things.* (2) Indians acknowledge the spiritual factor in all living creatures. It is often stressed that not only men and beasts but even plants have souls.[96] However, the spirituality of a plant is not so remarkably developed as in a man. All this does not mean that the Indians did not, in some respects, hold that man is superior to other creatures. Man is a "thinking" animal.[97] In the text of *Āraṅyaka* of the early Brahmanists, it is stated: "The sap runs in a plant and the mind (*citta*) in an animal. And in a man, the *Ātman* is most clearly revealed because man is endowed with intelligence (*prajñāna*). He sees and tells what he cognizes, knows what tomorrow is about, distinguishes between the real and unreal worlds, and tries to attain immortality though he is mortal."[98] The Buddhists regarded highly "The rare state of being a man." One should be grateful that he is born a man for it is more difficult to be born a man than for a blind turtle to enter a hole in wood floating in the ocean.[99] The Buddhists also advocated the abolition of capital punishment. A paragraph in a Buddhist text states thus: "Be obedient to the saintly kings. Do not condemn a man to death. Why so? Because for him to come into this world as a man and as any other being is the consequence of superior factors or conditions. If you take his life, you will certainly be punished."[100] This means that man's life should be revered and no one should destroy it.[101]

In certain circumstances, man was distinguished from other creatures, being endowed with the capacity to carry out the *dharma*—ethical law. It emphasized the ethical and religious significance in human activities so that those who neglect the *dharma* are no better than beasts. In a test of the ancient *Upaniṣad,* it is stated: "Men of good deeds in this world will be reborn into the life of the Brāhmin of the Kṣatriya, or of the Vaiśya. On the contrary, men of evil doings will be reborn in the womb of a dog, of a pig, or will return as an outcast (*caṇḍāla*)."[102] The Vaiśeṣika school says: "The *Dharma* is the excellent quality of the human race (*puruṣa-guṇa*). It is the basis for man's comforts, benefits, and liberation. It is beyond human perception, and it ceases to exist when man understands correctly ultimate peace (*mokṣa*). This comes about from the unity of the human spirit and the inner faculties, for those who practise the rules of their casts and of life's stages."[103]

The *dharma,* the essential distinction between men and other beings, has continuously been emphasized throughout all Hindu thought. In fact, human life has been given the unique place, as in it alone can the soul make the effort to liberate itself from the cycle of birth and death and achieve liberation. Thus we may say in summary that many early Indian thinkers advocated the superiority of man over other living beings, on the one hand, but many people, on the other hand, considered man as equal only to beasts and worms in the whole run of living beings.

The Conservative Character of Indian Thinking

Indians, in their retrospective way of thinking, believe that an ideal state existed in the past where the norm of human behavior was faithfully carried out. But as this state is no longer ideally possible, they worship the past and admire the classics.

In the codes of Brahmanism, anything new and modern is severely criticized and rejected. In the *Laws of Manu,* it was stated: "Legends which are not based on the Scriptures (*smṛti*) and wrong concepts (*kudṛṣti*) are false and useless in bringing happiness after man's death. This is *because they are new* (*arvākkālika*)."[104]

The Buddha, who had originated a new school, scarcely thought of himself as a founder. He only thought that he had succeeded in grasping the universal law which is valid for all time. In reality he aspired to become a true Brahmin or Śramaṇa and never to build up anything new or apart from Brahmanism. The early Buddhists respected and regarded the ancient sages preceding the Buddha as men who had lived according to *Dharma.* "Verily, the *dharma* is the banner of the sages."[105] "The sages of the past were ascetics who restrained their inner passions, freed themselves from the five desires, and did what was truly good for its own sake."[106] The early Buddhists severely criticised the Brahmin priests, saying that they indulged in pleasure-seeking—storing treasures and keeping beautiful mistresses—and were no better than the secular kings.[107]

Historically speaking, however, the criticism is not true. As a matter of fact, the earliest Brahmin priests were engaged in prayers and magical rites for the general welfare of the secular. And it was rather in a late period that we find high-sounding Brahmin priests leading a secluded and ascetic life. In disregard of this historical fact, the Buddhists never ceased to set the ideal in the golden age of the past and to detest all contemporaneous things.

In the *Theragāthā,* one of the oldest texts of the early Buddhists, it is said that the monks of the day are deplorably corrupt and degraded compared with the high standard upheld in the Buddha's time. In this vein there gradually developed the Buddhist idea of the three stages [*Shō-bō* (Right Teaching), *Zō-hō* (Rote Learning), and *Map-pō* (Decay)] of the world's declining evolution, which finally took definitive form in the texts of Mahāyāna Buddhism.[108] Brahmanists on the other hand maintained the four-stage theory of world history: *Kṛta, Tretā, Dvāpara,* and *Kali.* According to this view, our present period belongs to the last one, the period of decay and termination, and is equivalent to the Buddhist *Map-pō.* Indians, assuming the ideal age to be in the past, did not accept new things or what was in existence as good and desirable.

In India, therefore, new thoughts are constantly tied in with old established authorities, from which they take on significance. For instance, the Indian national epic, *Mahābhārata,* differs from the Vedas in content and maintains that it is more important than the four Vedas,[109] and yet, it regards itself as one of the Vedas.[110] Buddhists, too, rely upon the Buddha's great authority to propagate their ideas. Many of "Buddha's Teachings" in the texts of early Buddhism and Mahāyāna Buddhism are in reality the works of scholars coming later than the Buddha but using his authority.[111]

Together with adherence to established authority, the obedience to the elders (*sthavira* or *thera*) of the Indians is really remarkable. All the religious sects in India unanimously teach the veneration of the elders and prohibit, above all things, defiance of the teachers.[112] "Those who pay due courtesy to the elders will greatly enhance their four *dharmas*—long life, knowledge, peace, and strength."[113]

Although scriptural authority was supreme, there were some materialists, and naturalists such as the followers of the Vaiśeṣika school, or logicians such as Dharmakīrti, who claimed that scriptures are not absolutely reliable because they were written by man. But these were in the minority in India. Almost all the schools of philosophy in India have accepted the words in the scriptures as the absolute authority of knowledge. Even the early rationalistic Buddhists maintained that a proposition should be verified in two ways—by logical demonstration and by confirmation through scriptural authority.[114] In India even today there still survives a tenacious and blind acceptance of the scriptures.[115]

It is true, however, that Indian obedience to the scriptures often turned out to be only nominal. In reality, the ancient Indians were not so restrained in their free thinking. Madhva and others of the Vedānta school developed a dualistic metaphysics incompatible with the monistic standpoint of the *Upaniṣads*. To resolve the contradiction, they strained their reading of the holy scriptures, and interpreted the written authority in a way that would justify their own assertions.

There was a time in early Indian history when free thinking was encouraged. This was about the time of the Buddha when materialism, skepticism, sensualism, and other kinds of very libertarian ideas flourished. At that time, many city-states were established along the banks of the Ganges. The kings of such city-states, though interested in philosophical discussions, never persecuted those who did not conform to their own opinion. But all this was a temporary phenomenon. Following the downfall of the city-states the liberal philosophical tendency in India lay dormant for a long time, so that it can be said that the Indian allegiance to orthodox authority undeniably obstructed the development of free thinking in the land.[116]

The Development of Nomothetical Learning[117]

Subservience to the universal law and neglect of individual varieties lead to "nomothetic" (universalistic) tendencies and to the lack of "idiographic" (individualistic) attitudes in the everyday living of people. Ancient Indians left few chronologies, documentary works, and personal biographies.[118] Studies of details of geography and of topography were not pursued intensively,[119] while historical and descriptive studies like natural science hardly developed. Their interests were primarily directed to the quest of the universal norm.[120]

H. Oldenberg analyzes this Indian nomothetical tendency as follows: "For Indians, history was not a true science. Generally speaking, science to their minds leads men to certain actions conforming to a system of rules. Indeed, no other nation has shown such a strong attachment to rules. Grammar handed down the rules of refined speech; philosophy adheres to the rules of release from worldly hardships, and love-poetry to the rules of true gallantry. These were the sciences that an earnest speaker, and eager Nirvāṇa-seeker, and an intent love-maker could not dispense with. Needless to say, politics, a science consisting of many rules, was acknowledged by Indians as one of the true sciences. But the task of expressing those phenomena that were not yet embodied in the rules but that could be related only in words, was transmitted naturally to a more flexible art of accomplishment and presentation, viz. literature."[121] On this point, Indians exhibit a striking contrast to the Chinese who attempted to seek universal and normative significance by the inductive means of accumulating individual cases.

Many causes are given for the lack of historical works in India. Some of them are the rather late usage of the Indian written language, the inclement weather conditions for the preservation of manuscripts, and the instability of political and military situations. But a more fundamental cause should be traced to the peculiarity of the Indian way of thinking along eternalistic rather than temporal lines.

CHAPTER 10 ALIENATION FROM THE OBJECTIVE NATURAL WORLD

Lack of the Notion of Order in the Objective Natural World

Just as the Indians made no sharp distinction between one's self and others, they had very little consciousness of the contrast between the self and its natural surroundings.

They did not, in the past, represent the regions of their native land apart from the inhabitants, so that the names of countries or districts were described using the plural form of the name of the inhabitants.[1] They showed a strong aversion to representing the land as natural surroundings existing apart from its inhabitants.

Since Indians emphasize the existence of a universal Being behind phenomena, which are limited in time and space, they tend to minimize the distinction between two kinds of existence, viz. universal reality and things in the phenomenal world, in order not to regard them as equally real. There is also a tendency to slight the distinction between things perceived directly and those perceived by means of inference and other secondary means of cognition.

This tendency of thought can be seen also in the linguistic form. For example, there is no "explicative genitive" in Sanskrit. This form, otherwise called the "definitive genitive," is used in Latin (especially in later days and in vernacular) for explaining a noun determined by it (e.g. *urbs Romae,* the city of Rome; *nomen amoris,* the name of love). The same form is observed in modern Western languages, Japanese and Tibetan, etc., while in Sanskrit, the same context is expressed by nouns in apposition. (In case an indication of determination is specially required, an indeclinable *"iti"* in the sense of "called" is used, e.g. *Pāṭaliputra iti nagaram; mṛttiketi nāmadheyam.*) When two nouns, the explaining and the one to be explained, are shown in apposition to each other, very little difference of order exists between the determining and the determined.

The expression "A as B" is also lacking in ancient Indian languages. Namely they have no term equivalent to the *as* in English or *als* in German. To express such a term, an appositional form between A and B is used. Hence the expression can be construed both ways, "A as B" and "B as A." Such a linguistic phenomenon seems to be related to the tendency already noted in the Indian way of thinking of minimizing otherness.[2]

This Indian characteristic is shown more clearly in the following grammatical construction. Sameness of content, usually shown by the subordinate clause in other languages, is expressed in apposition to a word in the principal clause in Sanskrit, in order to avoid the use of a subordinate clause, e.g. *pitā vṛddhaḥ.* = the father, when he is old. They do not like to distinguish the direct field of experience from the content of thought based upon it. They describe both as if they were in the same dimension. The sentence, "better is the birth of a daughter," is expressed in the wording: "better, a daughter, born" (*varaṃ kanyaiva janitā*). Therefore, the distinction between the principal clause and the subordinate clause is sometimes obscure. The term "*iti*" equivalent to "that" or to a quotation mark in such a sentence as "he said that . . ." or "he said: ——" is often omitted.[3] In this case, the quotation or the subordinate clause is not identifiable by its grammatical form unless we construe the meaning from the contents. Again a subordinate clause in a sentence is placed before or after the principal clause, but never in between as in most Western languages,[4] probably because of the confusion that would result due to the loose rules of Sanskrit syntax.

Indians prefer the direct narration to an indirect approach in describing an idea, opinion, thought, intention or doubt in persons other than the speaker himself. There was very little development of the indirect narration in Indian languages. In Sanskrit, it is mostly limited to the accusative *cum participio* and the indirect interrogatory sentence. A few other cases are sentences beginning with *yad* which shows the content, sentences beginning with *yad* which is equal to the infinitive, and the predicate sentences beginning with *yad* or *yathā*.[5]

The distinction between "the predicative" and "the conjunctive" as it appeared in Greek was preserved in Vedic Sanskrit, but was lost in classical Sanskrit and united in the predicative. It means that those who used classical Sanskrit vaguely thought of the same sense in the two forms originally distinguished.[6]

In modern languages, the hypothetical conditions are expressed by paraphrasing a long sentence in order to distinguish it from the description of actual matters, while in Sanskrit, there is no clear-cut syntactical distinction between the two, and the same content is expressed by shorter and simple sentences.[7]

The same characteristic style of thought is also observed in the past work in linguistics by Indians. Their studies of phonetics and grammar are incomparable in their detailed and exact analysis not only of languages in ancient countries but even in the modern world up to the 19th century. Nevertheless their linguistic studies are rather weak in the field of syntax. Indian grammar was superior to the Greeks in *analysis* of word-construction while the Greek grammar had a superiority in syntax which treats the mutual *relations* and *synthesis* of words. The Greeks, who were by no means the rival of Indians in the field of phonetics, showed a distinct superiority in the field of syntax. In regard to the reason why syntax remained undeveloped in India, it has been surmised that it is due to the extremely free sentence construction of Sanskrit.[8] Undoubtedly this is the main cause, but in a further examination, we may find that the Indians tended to be lacking in their sense of order in the objective natural world.

Again due to their way of thinking, which did not distinguish clear and direct perceptions obtained through the sense organs from knowledge obtained through fantasy or inference, Indians were poor in expressions cognizing order among phenomena. Intellectual people and scholars were able to overcome this deficiency, but there certainly was such a tendency among the common people.

First of all, this tendency can be seen again in linguistic form. Even when a change of phase is observed between two sentences according to the western concept of language, Indians describe both *plainly* without inserting the term "but" and the like. For example, "therefore the dumb can speak, but cannot hear" is expressed by the sentence: *tasmād badhiro vāca vadati na śṛṇoti.*[9] (Literally, hence a dumb one speaks, not hears.) On the other hand, Indians frequently use conjunctions to denote conclusions drawn, e.g. *tad, tasmāt, tarhi, atas.* These are used even when Westerners feel that there is no necessity to use them.[10] On this point, Indians are rather similar to the Japanese people. Speyer understood this as being in accord with the dialectical tendency of the Indian, but actually it seems to show their inadequate understanding of the relation between the grounds and conclusion in such compound sentences in spite of their strong tendency to search for and understand the logical or causal relations among phenomena.

In comparison with Westerners who make classifications of various phenomena according to their importance, Indians describe them exhaustively but without order. In the *Brāhmaṇas,* abstract concepts and concrete matters are described side by side as being in the same dimension.

Lack of the notion of order with respect to the objective world caused ancient Indians to describe the symbols of numerals in a row to be summed. For example, "163" is usually described in ancient Indian manuscripts as: 100 60 3.

The Indians are generally very fond of simple calculations of important items. This may be based upon the same tendency of thought. The *Arthaśāstra* and the *Kāmasūtra* throughout use this principle. In the philosophy of the Sāṁkhya and Nyāya schools, important principles are merely enumerated in a row and the distinctions of dimension are never indicated (viz. the 25 *tattvas* of the Sāṁkhya, the 16 *padārthas* of the Nyāya). This tendency is striking also in Buddhism, which calls those principles or terms arranged in a row 'the ordered doctrines' (e.g. *tridhātu, ratnatraya, catvāry ārya-satyāni, pañca-skandhāḥ, ṣaṭ-pāramitāḥ, dvadaśa-ṅgaḥ pratītyasamutpādaḥ, etc.*).

Thus, having no liking for summarizing or making rules of phenomena from a recognition of some order among them, Indians used *frequent repetition.* Tiresome repetition of similar sentences is commonly seen in the *Upaniṣads,* Buddhist and Jain scriptures, etc.[11]

Repetition of the same wording for each item, which makes modern readers quite tired, is said to have been used for strengthening the memory in the absence of letters. If letters had been used for description from the beginning, such repetition would have no value. Another strong reason for such repetition was the poor development and use of pronouns in ancient Indian languages. In Sanskrit the same noun is repeated where the Western classical languages would use a pronoun.

On the other hand, Indians sometimes used extremely simple expressions. This is also said to have been to help students remember content easily. If so, repetition of sentences of the same style were probably used for recitation (viz. *infra*). This explanation, however, cannot be applied to the cases of repetition of the *Upaniṣads.* (e.g. *Bṛhad. Up.*, III, 7). In the case of all Buddhist scriptures, as Oldenberg maintained (*Buddha,* 7th edition, 206–207), this probably relates to that Indian way of thinking which resorted to substituting repetition of words for recognizing objective order in nature.

Another linguistic tendency of Indians, more or less related to this way of thinking, is that synonymous words are often used side by side to express an idea or opinion. This was noticed quite early in history by the ancient Chinese people. Shih Tao-an (4th century A.D.) referred to the fact that repetitions in Buddhist scriptures were simplified and omitted when translated into Chinese, by saying: "Foreign scriptures are very detailed in their description. For example, words of admiration are repeated twice, thrice, or even four times without any concern for their tiring effect. In the present translation, these repetitions are all omitted."[12] This same criticism was also made by Japanese who said: "India is a land where people are fond of thoroughness and minuteness in everything. It is her custom to repeat synonyms in expressions of admiration. In China, people like simplicity and try to avoid repetitiousness.

Frequent use of compound words in the ancient Indian languages, and especially in Sanskrit, can also be interpreted as symptomatic of the weakness of the Indian notion of order among various phenomena or ideas. In the *Ṛg-veda,* use of long compound words was comparatively rare. After that, frequency of their use gradually increased in the course of time. In verses of *kāvya* style especially, very long compounds were welcomed and intentionally used. This same tendency can be observed in the Prakrit literature.[14] In this case, the relation among component words of a long compound is rather difficult to understand. The main purpose of the compound is not to produce an exact expression of meaning, but to originate, in the mind, the impression of the idea expressed by each word one by one without interruption. It, however, often leaves room for many interpretations of a compound and tends to make the meaning obscure and less understandable. (On this point Sanskrit resembles Chinese.) Indians, therefore, themselves tried at times to avoid the use of compounds as much as possible in scholarly works, and especially in prose. In the vernacular languages of ancient India, there is also an avoidance of long compounds. Still as a rule, there is more use of compounds in Sanskrit than in Western classical languages. Let us mention the following as an example.

Coins of Parthian kings who governed Northwest India before the Christian era have the same phrase in Greek script on one side, Indian Prakrit on the other. Words like "brother of the king" and "king of kings" are written separately in Greek while they are combined in compounds in the Indian language.[15]

The same tendency is prominently seen in popular works such as the epics. For example, in the *Bhagavadgītā,* the most famous religious work in India, many such examples can be found though the number of the compounds is comparatively less. For example: *janmabandhavinirmuktās* (II, 51) = *generationum vinculis exsoluti* = καὶ ἀπαλλαγέντες τοῦ δέσμοῦ ἧτς γεννήσεως = released from the bondage of birth (m.pl.nom.); *Kuruvṛddha* (I, 12) = *Curuidarum progenitor* = ὁ πρεσβύτερος τῶν ἐν τῇ γενεᾷ Κουροῦ = grown in Kuru; *sarvalokamaheśvaram* (acc.) (V, 29) = *universae mundi magnum dominum* = πάντων τῶν κόσμων μέγαν ἡγεμόνα = great ruler of the whole universe; *samitiṁjayaḥ* (I, 8) = *bellorum profligator* = ὁ νικητὴς ἐν πολέμῳ = victorious in battle.

In the verse (gāthā) sections of the Early Buddhist scriptures, the expressions are generally quite simple and no such complicated and artificial compounds are found as are observed in the later literature. Nevertheless, in a comparison with Latin and other Western languages, use of certain long compounds can be seen. For instance, the following examples are found in the Pāli *Dhammapada: ariyappavedite dhamme* (Dhp. 79) =

a venerandis enarrata lege = doctrines preached by venerables; *saddhammadesanā* (*Dhp.* 194) = *verae doctrinae institutio* = instruction of the true doctrine; *paradukkhūpadhānena* (*Dhp.* 291) = *aliis dolorem imponendo* = causing others' sufferings; *rājarathūpamam* (acc.), (*Dhp.* 171) = *currui regali similem* = similar to the chariot of a king; *sabbadukkhā pamuccati* (*Dhp.* 189 f.) = *ab omni dolore liberatur* = he is liberated from all sufferings.

More remarkable is the case of the Bahuvrīhi compound (possessive compound) in Sanskrit, which is very much developed and utilized frequently. A compound word of this kind requires a long sentence when translated into Western classical languages; e.g., *paṭhavīsamo* (*Dhp.* 79) = *qui terrae instar est* = one who is like the earth; *yuktasvapnāvabodhasya* (*Bhag.* VI, 17) = *qui temperans est in dormiendo ac vibilando, . . . ei* = μετρίως ἱπνοῦντι καὶ μετρίως γρηγοροῦντι = of one whose mind is in a dream as well as awake; *kapidhvajaḥ* (*Bhag.* I, 20) = *simiae effigiem in vexillo gestans* = ὁ ἔχων ἐν τῇ σημαίᾳ τὸν πίθηκα = one who is possessed of the sign of the monkey, a name for Arjuna.

Some sentences containing Bahuvrīhi compounds require sentences of an entirely different structure in translation; e.g., *manopubbaṅgamā dhammā manoseṭṭhā manomayā* (*Dhp.* 1) = *naturae a mente principium ducunt, mens est potior pars earum, e mente constant* = phenomena are governed by mind, consist mainly of mind, and are made by mind.

When the subordinate clause is required in Western modern languages, or the absolute, in the case of Western classical languages, Sanskrit expresses it often in a compound; e.g., *adharmābhibhavát* (*Bhag.*, I, 41) = *impietate gliscente* = τοῦ δὲ ἀνόμου ἐπιγενομένου = because there is arisen immorality.

Sometimes even two contrary ideas are combined in a compound; e.g., *śubhāśubham* (acc.) (*Bhag.* II, 57) = *faustum vel infaustum* = pure or impure; *puññāpāpapahīnassa* (gen.) (*Dhp.* 39) = *bono maloque vacui* = having abandoned both merit and demerit.

Successive mention of various impressive ideas in a long compound gives vast play to fantastic imagery. Therefore Indian compounds cannot be translated into Japanese or Western languages without the loss of a stylistic effect. On this point, Oldenberg said: "As our language is far less effective than Indian languages in its power of composition, we are sometimes obliged to replace one word in the Indian language by several words, which makes the final effect weak."[16]

Obscurity in the meaning of a word is also caused by omission of syllables within a word in the ancient Prakrit languages. Single consonants in particular are often omitted between two vowels. This tendency causes confusion in meaning in the early Mahārāṣṭrian lyrics. For example,

Mahārāṣṭrian "*kai*" is equivalent to either *kati* (some), *kavi* (poet), or *kapi* (monkey) in Sanskrit; in case of *uaa* (= *udaka*, Skt.), only the vowels were retained. This omission was probably due to the fact that Indian consonants are not articulated as strongly as in Western languages.[17] This omission of consonants gives the Prakrit languages a feminine impression in their pronunciation, as has already been recognized and indicated by the ancient Indians.[18] It may correspond to the feminine trend commonly observed in Indian ways of thinking. Prakrit languages are purely Indian in character, in contrast with Sanskrit, which is proto-Indo-European.

In their clear expression of order in the objective world by linguistic form, modern Western languages are far more developed than Sanskrit and classical Western languages. In the case of declarative statements, the latter maintain no distinction between subject and predicate in their grammatical form, while the former maintain it. For example, in sentences like "mountains are high," "trees are green," etc., the predicate adjective agrees with the subject in gender, number, and case, in Greek and Latin, as is also the case in Sanskrit and other ancient Indian languages. In these languages, the consciousness of assimilation or identification of both ideas contained in the subject and in the predicate is prominent. On the other hand, in modern languages the predicate adjective has no declension. (These trees are green, this tree is green.) It signifies that in modern Western languages the subject and predicate are expressed as distinct from each other in their functions, though the concordance of both parts in judgment is recognized also.

The Indian tendency to alienate the objective natural world and to live in the world of meditation also characterizes Indian art. Coomaraswamy says in effect that Indian artists never used models but resorted to imagination in making sculptures. This method, which was accepted, no doubt unconsciously at the beginning, was authorized by rules in a scripture called *Śukranītiśāstra*.[19] Indeed ancient sculptures, as seen in Sānchī (3rd–2nd century B.C.), are fairly realistic and sensual, but the character of other arts gradually changed into fantasy in the course of time.

Imagination Which Ignores Natural Law

There is a tendency among the Indians, divested in general of the concept of a perceptible objective order, not to differentiate too sharply between the actual and the ideal or between fact and imagination or fantasy. "If there were a place where the dreams of ideal existence cherished by mankind since primitive times were to be realized on earth, that place is India."[20]

To many Westerners, God is believed to exist in a high Heaven, while to the Chinese, Heaven is situated above the earth. However, the Indian Buddhists thought of Buddhas of the past, present, and future living in all corners of this universe, including worlds above and beneath the earth. In contrast to the imagination of other ethnic groups which conceived of a divinity within the limits of the visible world, the Indian imagination transcended the bounds of ordinary world concepts.

An extreme example of Indian fantasy is found in their way of conceiving numbers. A very long period of time is called a *kalpa* (eon), whose duration is beyond our ability to imagine. It is said that if a man of great longevity would rub a mountain of 40 square *yojanas* (about 3,000 square miles) with a smooth cloth once for every 100 years until the mountain were levelled, a *kalpa* would not be exhausted. Or if such a man were to take a poppy seed once in every 100 years out of the mass of seed filling a big castle of 40 square *yojanas*, a *kalpa* would not come to an end even though the seeds in the castle were exhausted.[21] They also speak of a practice lasting for 3 *mahā-asaṁkyeya-kalpas*, a period equivalent to 3 (10^{60}) *kalpas*,[22] for a man to attain Buddhahood. On the other hand, they also conceive of *kṣaṇa*, a short unit of time, which is again divided several times into smaller units.

The very rich and fanciful imagination characteristic of the Indian way of thinking leads them to ignore the common-sense limits of physical possibilities of things in space and time. This tendency is particularly marked in the Mahāyāna scriptures and the *Purāṇas*. Vimalakīrti in the *Vimalakīrti-nirdeśa* is said to have welcomed 32,000 monks to his small room by means of his supernatural power. Once when the Buddha Śākyamuni was preaching the *Saddharmapuṇḍarīka* (the Lotus Sūtra) at Mt. Gṛdhrakūṭa, it is said that a tower, which was 500 *yojanas* high and 250 sq. *yojanas* at the base, decorated with jewels, and containing the holy relics of the entire Tathāgata Prabhūta, emerged from the earth all at once, and that from it voices praising the sermon of Śākyamuni and recognizing the authority of the *Saddharmapundarīka* were heard. In dealing with these fantasies, the Indians were not concerned about the contradictions which marked such fanciful descriptions of time and space. They ignored the laws of nature and remained unperturbed. That mythology relates matters in contradiction to the natural laws of time and space is a commonplace fact in any country; however, the case of the Indians is unrivalled. They carelessly refer to such big numbers as million, billion, "as many as the number of the sands of the Gangetic river," etc. Thus the Indian mind will transcend the realm of imagination, crushing and paralyzing ordinary powers of expression.

Among the Hindu scriptures, the *Purāṇas* are particularly rich in imagery. For example, the myth of the miraculous power of the child Kṛṣṇa is typically Indian in character. The whole story is full of fantasies and the heroic Kṛṣṇa is described with qualities which are beyond most peoples' imagination. This myth corresponds exactly to the mental atmosphere created in the Indian paintings and sculptures in which we are amazed by their portrayal of fantastic and chimerical qualities. The rich and sensuous illusion that is typically Indian emerges from this myth and incites feelings of great astonishment.

Such extreme imagination often sweeps away historical facts. E. Senart, a famous French Indologist, was of the opinion that the biography of the Buddha was nothing but a kind of solar-myth. His remark bears on the difference between the Indians' fanciful mind and the Westerners' more realistic character. Indians' love of fantasy also checked the development of natural science in India. Even chemistry, which is said to have developed very early in India, inevitably changed into a kind of magic.

Furthermore, the Indians never made a conscious effort to check their extravagant development of fantasy. They are extremely sensitive. They respond immediately to all the impulses or impressions, real or illusory, brought on from the outer world, and create fantasies one after another. But they are completely passive towards such impulses or impressions, and never try to force their will on them. It may be said that they have nerves rather than muscles.

Referring to this characteristic of Indian ways of thinking, Romain Rolland once said: "Please don't compare Western 'realism' to Indian 'idealism'! There are two kinds of realism. The Indians are by nature *réalisateurs*. They find it hard to be satisfied with any abstract idea. It is through physical pleasure and alluring charm that they attain realization."[23]

Tominaga Nakamoto, a unique free-thinker in the still feudal years of 1715–1746, referring to this characteristic of Indian thought as "*gen*" or "*maboroshi*" (Japanese) = *māyā*, illusion, observed: "The Indians are habitually very fond of hallucination, which can be compared to the Chinese love of *wên* or 'culture'; he who wishes to establish a school and teach must follow its way, without which he will not be able to win the confidence of the masses."[24] He also remarked, "The learning of the Indians consists in their pursuit of hallucination without which the people will not follow."[25] Many incredible stories are narrated in the Buddhist scriptures as a sensational means designed to enlighten the masses.[26]

He quotes the following sentences as the words of a venerable personage: "Magic characterizes Buddhism. It corresponds to '*izuna*' (magic) in present-day Japan. The Indians are fond of it, and unless it is employed in preaching, there would be no followers. Therefore Śākyamuni must have been a great magician. The purpose of his six years of ascetic practices in the mountain was to learn this magic. The supernatural powers (*abhijñā*) described in the scriptures imply magic. For example, the cases of the manifestation of 3,000 worlds created by the light emitted from between the eyebrows (*ūrṇa-keśa*) or of the vast long tongue reaching the Heaven of the Brahman, or of Vimalakīrti's ability to create 84,000 seats in a small room, or of the goddess who transformed Śāriputra into a woman, are nothing but descriptions of magical powers in the realm of fantasy. Furthermore, the doctrines of transmigration, of moral causality, stories of marvelous events in previous lives, and other curious stories, were means of inducing the people to believe in the newly established doctrine. This is the Indian way of teaching, but is not the way necessarily for the Japanese."[27] If we are to follow this view, the theory of hell and paradise is nothing but a means for propagating Buddhism.[28] Criticizing this opinion, Tominaga said: "In spite of the venerable scholar's opinion, *abhijñā* is different from *izuna*. *Izuna* is merely a matter of technique, while *abhijñā* is the result of strict religious practice. Nevertheless his words stand with reason." Thus Tominaga believed that miraculous power was really attained by practice and it was this aspect which characterized Indian Buddhsim.

If we were to examine the views held by the Indian Buddhists on this matter, we find, for example, the following words of Nāgārjuna: "There is a man of evil nature, who, possessed of a jealous mind, slanderously says, 'the Buddha's wisdom is not beyond that of mortals; he misleads the world by means of magic.' The Buddha manifested the infinite divine power and infinite wisdom for the purpose of severing one from such a crooked and self-conceited state of mind."[29] Nāgārjuna further remarked, "A bird without feathers cannot fly. Likewise, the Bodhisattvas without the perfection of miraculous power cannot lead the people."[30] Thus, Nāgārjuna himself was of the opinion that the Buddhas and the Bodhisattvas were actually endowed with miraculous faculties far more powerful than those of the heretics.

Such a way of thinking naturally met with a reaction. The materialists of India strongly opposed the doctrine of miraculous power, while the natural philosophers ignored it completely.

Indian myths and legends of fantastic character were not accepted by the Greeks. Ambassador Megasthenes, who was sent by a Syrian king to the court of Indian Emperor Candragupta about 300 B.C., wrote *Ta Indika*, his report of India in those days; it was based upon his experiences, and a few fragments are preserved today. These fragments, regarded today as valuable material for the study of ancient India, record a lot of myths and legends then current in India. Modern studies show that these myths and legends are the same as those described in the *Mahābhārata* and the

Purāṇa literatures.[31] At that time, however, the Greeks who had read his report did not believe it at all.[32] Not only his report, but also descriptions of India by Deimakhos, Onesikritos, Nearkhos, and others, were generally criticized by the historian Strabo as being unfactual.[33] The Greeks thought that the myths and legends told seriously by Indians were fantastic.

The same criticism is made by modern Europeans. Hegel said: "Sensory evidence is of no value, because to the Indians, generally speaking, there is no sensory perception. Everything is reshaped into fantastic images, and any kind of dream is regarded as truth and reality."[34] Kern, a famous scholar on Buddhism, thought that when an Indian conceives an image in meditation, he seems to lose the distinction between that image and the phenomena of the objective world. "Buddhists are idealists, they maintain no clear distinction between phenomenal facts based upon observation and the products of fantasy. . . . The world is created by meditation (*dhyāna*)."[35] It may be dangerous to generalize the Buddhist way of thinking in this way, but it is true that such a tendency did exist among some Buddhists.

Among the later Vedantists, a school developed which held that by penetrating the realm of the undifferentiated by means of meditation, the world of phenomena could be eliminated; that, they believed, was the way of emancipation (*mokṣa*). This theory was called "*prapañca-vilaya-vāda*," i.e. the theory of the disappearance of phenomena. In the *Upanishads*, the frequent injunction is: "the Ātman should be conceived like this." It is a command to eliminate the realm of phenomena (*prapañca-vilaya*). In other words the dualism implied by a reality beyond and contrary to the phenomenal world constitutes "an obstacle to the realization of truth (*tattvāvabodha-pratyanīka-bhūta*)," thus, emancipation is realized only after the obstacle has been eliminated. This theory was often referred to as unorthodox in the later Vedantic works. Śaṁkara, too, denied it.[36] His criticism is as follows: "If the elimination of all phenomena means the extinction of our natural world, that is a statement of absurdity; if, on the other hand, it means the extinction of illusion which is a product of our ignorance, it is not a matter which can be realized by a 'command' but only through 'understanding.' " However, the real intent of those who maintained this theory was to "command" a series of negations and thus help one to understand that *Ātman* is devoid of character (*nirguṇa*); e.g., in the scripture, it is commanded, "conceive *Ātman* as A," "conceive *Ātman* as B," etc., in which case, by conceiving *Ātman* as A, *Ātman* is being negated as B, similarly, by conceiving *Ātman* as B, *Ātman* is being negated as A, etc. As can be seen, the theory here expressed was, more or less, similar to that held by Śaṁkara.[37] Of course, such a view was not necessarily held by the Indians in general, but it does reveal that the Indians, through one of their influential thinkers, had established a thought-pattern which can be recognized as one of their characteristic ways of thinking.

This pattern of thought is quite significant in that it provides men dwelling in darkness with light and hope for the future; but because there is no grasping of the distinction between the real and the ideal, it lacks the force of the rational recognition and control of the hard facts of reality. The Indians maintained an unlimited desire for pleasure and profit, but did not develop a system of capitalistic economy. "An unlimited desire for profit is not necessarily identical to capitalism, nor is it of the same 'spirit.' On the contrary, capitalism requires the repression of the irrational forces of desire, or at least the controlling of these forces."[38] Of course, it was not only the Indians who lacked the rationale of capitalism, but it can be reasoned that it was the fact that the Indians did not think much of controlling matters of this world that hindered their development of capitalism.

Not only is there a recognizable difference between the social and economic systems of modern India and the West, but the same is true also of their ways of thinking in the medieval periods of these two areas. Even European Scholastics who, from the viewpoint of modern men, discussed meaningless and uninteresting problems minutely, nevertheless, dealt with matters of "control" in regard to state and society (e.g. Thomas Aquinas). On the other hand, although the conservative Buddhist scholars of medieval India likewise discussed many complex problems, as indicated in the Abhidharma literature, they did not greatly concern themselves with the problems of state or social structure. They did, however, engage in long discussions pertaining to mental cultivation and sheer fantasy. Both Hīnayāna and Mahāyāna Buddhism discussed in detail the problems pertaining to the rebirth of mankind in which a cyclic process was considered the path on which to pursue the work necessary for salvation. One has the feeling that men who had indulged in the narration of this process must have lived in a world entirely different from ours.

There might be some objection to the above statement in that Mahāyāna Buddhism had dealt in considerable length with the problem of the state.[39] However, it is to be noted that Mahāyāna Buddhism cannot be considered representative of the thoughts of the Indians in general; it reveals only one characteristic aspect of Indian thought. The governing class of India supported the traditionally conservative Buddhism, and the state concept of Mahāyāna Buddhism revealed nothing more than a reaction against it. Realistic ideas of state and government were dealt with by the more secular Brahmins, while the more catholic religions of Buddhism and Jainism tended to escape from secular matters.

The Tendency to Resort to Extremes

The imagination of Indians ignores the natural limitations of time and space. It is free, boundless and extravagant, and often goes to extremes. And as they do not fully realize, in many cases, the distinction between realities and dreams, they continue to pursue their dreams even within the sphere of reality. Let me illustrate these extremes of behavior. An Indian epicurean absorbs his whole soul and body in pleasure-seeking. And an ascetic in India leads a very austere life in the woods.[40] The Buddhist advocacy of the middle path, detached from either enjoyment or self-affliction, is an exceptional case in India.[41]

The radical conservatives of the Jain monks were called "*Digambara*—the sky-clad." They went about completely naked, or in other words, "clothed in space." They said: "Our body is a cover of the *Ātman*. The garments are the outer coverings of that covered *Ātman*. To lessen the coverings of the *Ātman*, we do not wear a garment."[42] And the Jains praised as a master of the highest virtue the monk who died as the result of observing a fast. One of their sacred books gives a detailed description of how saints took to death by starvation.[43]

The Greeks set a high value on the virtue of moderation. They often quoted Solon's maxim "nothing too much" (μηδὲν ἄγαν, *ne quid nimis*). In China, too, the middle course is one of the essential virtues in their ethics. Indians, on the other hand, are likely to go to extremes. The idea of the golden mean (*aurea mediocritas*) has not developed in this land apart from the one exception of the Buddhist advocacy of *the middle path*.

As a result of this feature of their way of thinking, Indians are inclined to idealize and to consecrate great men in their history to the utmost. This offers a sharp contrast to the Western trend to avoid excessive glorification of great heroes. In India, as in other countries, there are many biographies of great men. The sagas of the saints are especially numerous. And the stories described in such books are very wild and fantastic. They are myths rather than the life stories of the heroes. In India legendary heroes like Kṛṣṇa have been deified in excessive fashion in the course of time. At first, the stories of Kṛṣṇa described the hero's birth, childhood, romances, fights, and victories in realistic style. But, as the stories were handed down among people, they were exaggerated to a fantastic extent until finally Kṛṇṣa was deified and became the object of enthusiastic savior-worship.

Fondness for Myths and Poetry

Indians are very fond of myths and poetical forms of expression, a natural result of their inclination to idealize the actual phases of human life. Indians try to beautify the hard facts of reality by contemplating them from a detached standpoint.

From the time of the *Ṛg-Veda* up to the present, for more than three thousand years, Indians have never ceased creating new myths. And many myths thus produced come from one source. The gods in the Epics of the *Mahābhārata* and the *Rāmāyaṇa* are the gods of the Vedas. The Vedic myths revived and perpetuated the legends of the Epics. The legends of the Epics are in turn assimilated in the *Purāṇas,* and the legends formed in the modern age are based on the myths transmitted in this way. Indians have always been tolerant toward the myths of older ages. Sometimes the myths of older origin are in conflict with their own, but even in that case they have included them in their mythological system.

The Chinese are much more limited in their development of mythology, while their achievements in historical works are very remarkable. Indians, on the contrary, have produced an abundance of myths, but their documents of history are quite few in number. The books of history and the sagas written in India are all embellished with mythological overtones. In their works it is difficult to distinguish the historical facts from the output of imagination.

Even in philosophical discourses, mythical explanations and metaphors are frequently used. The philosophers of India follow the rules of metaphysical and logical reasoning within their own particular circle. But in order to convey a better understanding of their theories to the common man, they are willing to resort to mythical ways of explanation. It has been recognized that the philosophers of the *Upaniṣads* resorted to this means of instruction. Uddālaka Āruṇi, for instance, explains the relation between the ultimate entity which he terms "being (*sat*)," and all other beings by resorting to various allegories.[44]

The Greeks noticed this Indian affection for myths and poems. Megasthenes observed: ". . . like Plato, they (the Brahmins) weave into the fabric of myth (*μύθος*) such (philosophical) problems as the immortality of the soul or judgment after death."[45] Thus Megasthenes found a resemblance to Plato in the figurative explanation of the philosophical issues found in the *Upaniṣads.*

The Epics, the Purāṇas, and the texts of Mahāyāna Buddhists, all resort to the allegorical method in order to explain their doctrines. The Lotus Sūtra is called "the king of all the sūtras" and is really a representative text of the Mahāyāna. And we wonder what other elements would remain in this Sūtra if we were to remove the elements of allegory and fiction explaining the past origin of present events. Indian philosophers consider allegories or illustrations (*dṛṣṭānta*) to be indispensable in explaining their thought even when they are pursuing their arguments in accordance with rules of logical reasoning.

Indians are a poetry-loving people. Since the ancient period, many poems of a high artistic standard have been composed in their country. Besides, great works in the diverse fields of religion, philosophy, politics, laws, economics, mathematics, and other sciences employ the verse form. Since ancient times, Indians have preferred to count numerically not by means of numbers but by using names—that is, common nouns; for instance, "the moon" or "the earth" stand for "one" and "the eyes" or "the wings" represent "two." And this manner of counting has grown into a very complicated one. In some extreme cases, they have forty or fifty ways of expressing a certain numerical figure by means of various nouns. It is noteworthy that they have adopted this method of counting simply to satisfy the need for a rich vocabulary for rhyming in their literature. This is distinctly one result of the Indian adherence to the verse-form even in their scientific works.

Indians are very fond of reciting verses. At present, in various parts of India, there are many "poetry-parties" where many poets gather together to read their poems before enthusiastic audiences. One of the general characteristics of today's Indian periodicals is the custom of devoting a considerable number of pages to poems.

Indians have much in common with the Western Romanticists in their way of thinking. For instance, they have in common a longing—or more properly speaking, a vague and undefined attraction—toward an infinite, distant, and supernatural Being. It is natural, therefore, that many Romanticists of the West interested themselves in Indian thought and participated in introducing this new thought to their own world. Goethe spoke in the highest terms of Kālidāsa's *Śakuntalā.* August Wilhelm von Schlegel (1765–1845) translated the *Bhagavadgītā* into Latin. Wilhelm von Humboldt read this Latin translation and extolled it as the most beautiful and most philosophical poem ever known to world literature, and was thankful for the good fortune to see the book.[46] Friedrich von Schlegel, a younger brother of Wilhelm, wrote a book which is one of the most significant works in the history of German Romanticism—*On the Language and Wisdom of the Indians* (*Über die Sprache und Weisheit der Inder,* 1808). Schopenhauer, who was influenced much by the Indian philosophy was one of the philosophers of Romanticism. A successor of his thoughts, Paul Deussen, became absorbed in the study of the philosophies of India. And Count von Keyserling, who was also deeply interested in Indian thought, once stated that "the savior of the spiritual and material disorder of the world after World War I is the ideal of the Bodhisattva."[47]

Lack of Historical Consciousness

All Indian books of history, of which there are very few, are tinged with a fantastic and legendary color. They are not products of historical science but rather works of art. Usually they are written in verse. Indians are not satisfied with the simple and naive description of facts, the language of daily use. From the artistic viewpoint, the Indians beautify the past and try to idealize it. They ignore precise figures, the sequences of events, and other prosaic details relating to the time and the place where the events took place. Furthermore, to give full play to the imagination, they exaggerate figures astronomically and stretch the truth with their magnificent and brilliant style of hyperbole. Like many of their sculptures, their historical works are far from reality, but are rather the products of their fantasy.

The *Mahāvaṁsa* is the most elaborate and reliable work of history ever produced in Ceylon. And even this book is surrounded by a mysterious and legendary atmosphere. For instance, though Mahānāman, the author of this book, lived in the fifth century—in an age not too distant from the time of King Duṭṭhagāmani's reign, his descriptions of this greatest ruler in the history of the island are full of mythical and legendary elements, and therefore, a careful distinction must be made between myth and that which is historically true. We know that the histories or "chronicles" of the monks in medieval Europe and the biographies of eminent Buddhist monks in China and Japan have a similar style. But, to an incomparably greater degree, the *Mahāvaṁsa* goes far beyond the bounds of historical truth.

Kalhaṇa's *Rājataraṅgiṇī* is the chronicle of a Kashmirian dynasty. This is one of the best historical works ever written by the Indians. In it, Kalhaṇa details the social situation of his time and the activities of the various characters in it with the accuracy that no other Indian book of history has attained. But, still, a poetic and emotional atmosphere pervades the whole of this historical work. To quote Oldenberg: "If one removes all the poetic elements from Kalhaṇa's story, and compares it with events of the time, he will find that the story is in essence on a level not higher than that of a more or less accurate article in a newspaper or a cartoon in a political comic paper. The process of formation that this story has undergone is not that of historical thinking but of poetry—poetry in the Indian sense with its brilliant quality and also with its weakness. And Kalhaṇa himself has a very distinct idea on this point; he feels himself as a poet and he is a poet."[48] And Kalhaṇa scarcely pays heed to historical or causal sequence when considering historical events. His dates are inaccurate and sometimes the products of pure imagination.

In all the Indian documents of the past, little significance has been attached to the books of history; most Indians have been much more interested in religion and poetry than in historical documentation. For the Indians, a minor error in the recitation of the Vedas has been a serious matter, but they have been thoroughly indifferent to the erroneous recording of dates or of facts in their books of history.[49] This unhistorical character of the Indian way of thinking is distinctly observable in the Buddhist attitude to the rules of their order. Buddhists in the period after the death of the Buddha had to establish new precepts for their body in order to meet the changing social conditions. As some of the rules newly established by them were not compatible with the older ones, they hesitated to include their new rules in the old and traditional books of ordination (*pāṭimokkha*), and managed to attach them to the *pāṭmokkhas* as supplements.[50] They, however, dared to claim the authority of the Buddha's own teaching even for these supplementary precepts of their own creation, completely ignoring historical evidence. *Their concern for the proper observance of the precepts and of the rites preceded and was stronger than their regard for historical accuracy.*

The Chinese derive their rules of social conduct from the examples of their ancestors as described in their books of history. The Indians, on the other hand, gain their principles of behavior from their religious books and, at the same time, *fables* and *parables* such as the *Pañcatantra* and the *Hitopadeśa* contribute toward the diffusion of practical morals into the daily life of the Indian people.[51] To quote Oldenberg again on the unhistorical character of the Indians: ". . . but, should we blame the Indians for no other reason than that they are Indians? The Indian folk-spirit would not have been what it was without the unhistorical character. For the formation of the spirit of the people, factors other than considerations of historical truth had the decisive power."[52]

The Concept of Truth

The Indian concept of *truth* is different from that of the Westerner. *Satya* is the oldest Sanskrit equivalent for truth. And as we have mentioned above, in the *Upaniṣads* of the early days *dharma* is considered to be identical with *satya*. From this fact, we become aware of the difference in the concept of *truth* as held by the ancient Indians and modern peoples. The dominant philosophical schools of ancient India did not find truth in the agreement of subjective knowledge with the objective order, nor in intersubjectively valid knowledge, but rather, they sought truth in the practice of ethics; that is in the observance of rules of conduct. In other words, they sought complete concordance or spiritual unity through ethics, and they considered this spiritual way of life to be the truth.

Later on, another word *tattva* came in use together with *satya* to mean *truth*. And, in addition to these two words, Buddhists had their unique term *tathatā* also to mean *truth*.[53] The original meaning of *tattva* is "thatness" and *tathatā*, "such-ness." Truth in the ancient Indian concept is no other than "to be that" or "to be such." They indicated truth by "that" or "such"—the terms of the simplest prescription of the object. In other words, *truth exists where all forms of discrimination have been negated.* And *satya* means "being" or "relating to being." Generally speaking, Indians are inclined to take an ontological view, and not an epistemological view, of truth. Of course, it is wrong to assume that the philosophies of India are all tinged with one color. Nevertheless, it is not incorrect to affirm that the ontological view has been dominant in this country.

In the West, on the other hand, many philosophers have found truth in the agreement of knowledge and its object. Kant, for instance, put it as follows: "If truth consists in the agreement of knowledge with its object, that object must thereby be distinguished from other objects; for knowledge is false if it does not agree with the object to which it is related, even though it contains something which may be valid for other objects."[54] Although this view of Kant was criticized by Hegel and others, we can safely say that the Kantian view of truth has been predominant in the West. And this trend can be traced back as far as the ancient Greeks. The Greek equivalent of truth is "ἀλήθεια." The original meaning of this word is "not to be hidden," "to be known as it is" or "to be noticed." It comes from the negative form of the verb "λανθάνω" which means "to escape notice," or "to be unknown." This concept of truth is based on the Greek idea of the external relationship between the subjective knower and the known object.

Non-development of Natural Sciences

In India, studies of the natural world remained underdeveloped. The ancient Greeks were aware of this fact. "As to nature (φύσις) on the other hand, the statements [of Indians] are very simple and innocent." Megasthenes goes on to say: "The reason is that they are skilled in practice (ἔργοι) rather than in argument (λόγοι), and they accept as true what is said in the myths (μύθος)."[55] Of course, it is not true to say that there was no natural science in this country. The ancient Indians developed their own astronomy chiefly in relation to the Vedic rites. In their texts of incantations and ceremonies a remarkable degree of knowledge is revealed in regard to the structure of the human body.[56] Their medical science developed into many branches of specialties, and it is said that chemistry arose in this country earlier than in any other country. In the third century B.C., and thereafter, their mathematics, astronomy, and chemistry were greatly stimulated by the introduction of the Greek sciences.[57] But the Indians ended by adopting and imitating the science of the Greeks, and there was no further development of their own in most sciences. The scientific approach to problems failed to develop in this country where thinking was much more metaphysical.

Contact with Western scientific thought began in the 19th century to encourage the study of the sciences in India.

Indians set a high value on learning. But they are not satisfied with the mere empirical knowledge of substances which are in themselves limited in time and space. They emphasize a Reality existing behind and beyond such substances—the subjective entity or Universal Being. Greek philosophy started as a study of nature (φύσις). Indian philosophy, on the other hand, from the beginning has sought the being which transcends nature. As G. Misch pointed out, Indian philosophy is *metaphysical* in marked contrast to the Greek geometrical view of the physical world.[58]

Western metaphysics has, on the whole, developed in relation to the growth and influence of physical science (*ta physika*). Western metaphysics is, or was at least up to the eighteenth century, the study of or the inquiry into ultimate principles of "being." Thus as the study of the principles attributed to "being," Western metaphysics established its own field of study clearly distinguished from that of natural science. And we can see a good example of this in the Scholastic study of "being." Most thinkers in India, however, did not and do not consider metaphysics in contradistinction to physical science. The goal of Indian philosophy (*darśana*) is to seek the ultimate principles of universal nature, and therefore, traditional Indian philosophers do not take to a positivistic philosophy of natural science. The Indians include metaphysics and natural science together as one mental activity—learning in general (*vidyā*). And they are unwilling to acknowledge natural science as an independent field of study distinguished from metaphysics. Even in the naturalistic philosophy of the Nyāya and the Vaiśeṣika, natural science held no independent position. Uddālaka and the scholars of the Vedānta, like the Greek philosophers, regarded "being" as the ultimate source of truth. But it should be noted here that there is an essential difference between the Greeks and Indians in respect to the concept of "being." For the Indians, *"being"* is *Ātman* and essentially it is *identical with the subjective knower*. "Being" as conceived by the Indians is not objective but subjective; herein lies the great difference between the Indians and Greeks.

Kautilya's *Arthaśāstra* classifies knowledge into four groups: (1) philosophy (*ānvīkṣikī*); (2) study of the Vedas (*trayī*); (3) economics (*vārttā*); (4) study of laws (*daṇḍanitī*). In his system, no independent significance is recognized for natural science. He would probably include the study equivalent to natural science, in our sense of the term, in the third group—*vārttā*—because it serves to make our lives easy and comfortable just like economics. His system of classification was accepted by many Indian philosophers of later ages.[59]

Buddhists classify knowledge into five groups: (1) study of language (*śabda-vidyā*); (2) studies of technology and the calendar (*śilpakarmasthāna-vidyā*); (3) medicine, pharmacy, and the study of magical charms (*cikitsā-vidyā*); (4) logic (*hetu-vidyā*); (5) study of the Buddhist doctrines (*adhyātma-vidyā*).[60] The second and the third groups above mentioned belong to what we call natural science. But, it should be noted that Buddhists established this system of classification only from a practical concern. They had no idea of natural science as unique and independent of other fields of studies.[61] In India of later periods, knowledge comes to be classified into more elaborate and smaller groups. And all the systems of classification follow the decrees of the Vedas and give priority to the Vedas. But no endeavor was made to establish natural science as a separate field of study.

Indian studies regarding nature developed independently of mathematics. This fact presents a great and basic difference between the Indian concept of natural science and the Western concept which, as we can see in Kant, places mathematics at the base of all natural sciences.

Indian philosophy has developed almost completely unaffected by the progress of the natural sciences. And this is one reason why epistemology in the modern sense has not made much headway in India. Generally speaking, modern Western philosophers have a different approach to the problem of knowledge from that of their predecessors in the ancient and the medieval worlds. The philosophers of the Nyāya, the Vedānta, and the Mīmāṃsā in India agree with the Western philosophers of the ancient and medieval periods in their assertion regarding truth as the agreement of knowledge with the substantial being to which it is related. However, other philosophers in India, e.g. the Buddhists, refused to acknowledge any substantial being. Both in their rejection of the concept of a self-existent substance and in their idea of the opposition of "the subjective knower" and "the object," the Buddhist view is common to the epistemological standpoint of modern (as opposed to medieval scholastic) Western philosophers. In another basic respect, however, Western epistemology differs from this ancient Indian theory of knowledge. One of the chief purposes of modern Western theories of knowledge is to supply a theoretical basis for natural sciences. And to meet this purpose, whether they are conscious of it or not, they have tried to find a theoretical basis for synthetic *a priori* judgments. It is true that the ancient Indians had a very penetrating insight into the problem of knowledge. Dharmakīrti, for instance, made a clear distinction between synthetic judgments and analytic judgments and he inquired into the functions of these two different types of judgments in actual and concrete cases of inference. But, synthetic judgments in his case are what can be acquired by experience and are not what exist *a priori*. In Dharmakīrti, there existed no factor such as the need for a foundation for rational sciences (mathematics, physics, metaphysics) which eventually led Kant into his quest for a theoretical basis for synthetic *a priori* judgments. And, though Dharmakīrti is often compared with Kant, due to the superficial similarity of their assertions, there is a distinct and essential difference between the two.

A similar characteristic can be observed in the logic of Indians. As is well known, Greek philosophy originated as a *theoria* of the order of the objective world, and it gradually formed its logic through the study of *logos*. In the case of most Indians, on the other hand, it was not the consideration of nature that led them to the study of logic. Their interest in this study arose from a different source. The need for a correct interpretation of the phrases in the Vedas led the Brahmin scholars to their study of the principles of grammar. And a close examination of the word-forms led them to an analysis of the process of thinking and subsequently, to the study of the categories and to the process of reasoning. Indeed, in contrast to the Greeks, Indians became interested in logic through their more elaborate study and analysis of language.

In India dialogue or debate developed to a great extent, but dialectics in the Platonic sense of the development of a point through conflicting and opposed points of the debate did not develop so conspicuously. In the *Upaniṣads,* the sacred books of the early Buddhists, and the codes of the Jains, discussions between a teacher and a disciple, between friends, or between a man and his wife are mentioned. In these cases, there is a sharp distinction between the one who teaches and the one who receives the teachings. The lessons were always one-sided; the teacher taught and the followers accepted his instructions with unthinking obedience. And at this stage there is hardly any interchange of ideas between the two sides. In the books of later periods, controversies between men of opposing ideas are presented. An old Buddhist sūtra *Pāyāsi-suttanta,*[62] for instance, is a story of a nihilist, Pāyāsi, who was converted to Buddhism by the refutations and persuasions of a Buddhist sage, Kumāra Kassapa. And the *Milindapañha* (Questions of King Milinda), which appeared in the second century A.D. or later in the present form bears a strong influence of the Greek "dialogue." This is a story of the conversation between Menander, a Greek king who reigned over Northern India, in the second century B.C., and a Buddhist elder, Nāgasena. It ends with the king's conversion to Buddhism out of respect for the elder. The form of dialogue employed in the *Milindapañha,* formulated under Greek influence, failed to prevail further in this country.

After the dialogue, a form of debate between two schools came to be employed. In this case, the individual elements of the representative orators were all eliminated. And they did not care who the orators were. At the end of a close and heated battle of words, the victorious party took pride in the victory while the defeated party sank into silence. But, it should be noted, the yielded party continued to adhere to the previously held view even after the defeat. Of course, there were some cases in which the defeated debater followed the opinion of the winner.[63] It is likely that the audience was converted to the winning side in an argument which, after all, is usually the case. But there were other cases in which no altering of opinion took place after the debate in either party. Indians, in their static view of things, considered truth eternal and unchangeable. And many of them failed to give deep consideration to the process of evolution or development through dialectics.

The non-development of natural science has affected the economic activities of this country. The natural science of the West with its rationalism based on mathematical calculations has made the growth of modern capitalism technologically possible in the Western world. But India has had no such foundation for its economic development.

CHAPTER 11 THE INTROSPECTIVE CHARACTER OF INDIAN THOUGHT

The Development of the Sciences of Inner Reflection

As a result of our study, we have seen that there has been a dominant trend of thought in India to emphasize the universal and to subsume the subjective and personal aspects of individuals under the universal. As a result of such tendencies in this way of thinking, material-external-objective sciences are not regarded highly and tend to stagnation. Spiritual-introspective-subjective studies, on the other hand, are greatly encouraged. Experimental physical sciences and mathematics (as a demonstrable science) failed to develop in ancient India.[1] Even later on, when theoretical Greek and technological Roman sciences were introduced into this country, these sciences did not take root among the people. On the other hand, humanistic and introspective sciences such as linguistics and reflective psychology have made noticeable advances in India; we have already acknowledged the high development of ethical and metaphysical studies in India.

Like other primitive tribes, Indians in an early phase of their history believed *language* to have the properties of objective substances, and so they identified a word—the name of an object—with the thing it indicated. In this rather primitive mode of thought, there is a magical essence in things, and language, which names objects and their properties, is endowed with mystic power. Those who know words and have a good command of them are able to control and dominate at will things and their properties. Thus they believed that *knowledge of language* constitutes power. And upon this assumption, they established the elaborate system of the Vedic rites. Some philosophers asserted that language is the ultimate principle of the universe, the master of gods, the ruler of the universe, omnipresent in the universe, and imperceptible by the senses.[2] They did not think of language as a symbolic means for communication of the will, but they acknowledged it as substantial in principle. In this regard, the Indian idea of language to some extent corresponds to the Japanese belief in the "soul of language."

The Greeks began their study of language chiefly to enhance the beauty of their language, whereas the Indians were led to the study from their belief in the mystic and sacred power of language. In India, therefore, linguistic study started first among the Brahmin scholars. At a very early stage, they concentrated their efforts on the study of the sentences in the Vedas. But, gradually they extended their study to a systematic analysis of their language, Sanskrit, which was at that time the spoken as well as the literary language. The Sanskrit grammar was first established by Pāṇini in the fourth century B.C. After the critical modifications added by Kātyāyana, this grammar was transformed into a final authoritative form by Patañjali in the second century B.C. The study of the Sanskrit grammar after Patañjali ended in the elaboration of the established doctrines, and except for some growth in the philosophical theory of language, they made no advance from the established grammar.[3]

The ancient Indians in their study of grammar were minutely empirical and analytical. They analyzed elaborately the *forms* of words. This empirical and analytical attitude of the Indian grammarians was stimulated by the fact that Sanskrit has word-forms more heterogeneous and differentiated than those of the Western classical languages. The ancient grammarians of India analyzed all words into three elements: the declensional ending, the stem, and the root. They reduced every word into what they analyzed as the corresponding root form. Not all these root forms are correct when re-examined by present methods of comparative grammar. Nevertheless, we are surprised at the thoroughness and consistency of the ancient Indians in their study of grammar. The Western grammarians adopted abstract concepts such as the stem and the root for the analysis of their languages only after the dawn of the modern age when they came into contact with the ancient grammar of India.

In the morphological study of language, the ancient Indians had their general and distinctive system of various categories. For instance, they made strict distinctions between the primary and the secondary verbal endings. Moreover, they accomplished a very elaborate system of declensions and conjugations. No other ancient nation has ever produced such a detailed system of grammar as India.

In the phonological field they also made very careful studies. They invented a very reasonable and scientific arrangement of the Sanskrit alphabet. They put the vowels first in order and then arranged the consonants. In the West, until very recently, phonology or the study of sonic elements (*τα στοιχεία, elementa*) never developed an adequate system. Although the Greeks and Romans in some measure inquired into the physiological structure of vocal sounds, they failed to achieve a clear and distinct view that equalled the system of the ancient Indians. At best, they classified the sounds into two groups: the vowels (φωνήεντα, *vocales*) and the consonants (σύμφωνα, *consonantes*), analyzing them according to degrees of vibration and their function in a syllable. It is rightly supposed that because their languages are less differentiated than Sanskrit, the Greeks and Romans fell behind the Indians in their study of linguistics.

The ancient grammarians of India arranged their texts chiefly to meet the conveniences of oral teaching and of learning by memory. They made free use of many abbreviations, rhyming words, and other efficient means which would aid memory. Naturally, their texts did not have the categories of classification which distinguish parts of phonology, morphology, and syntax in the same way as modern texts of grammar. Along with the studies of grammar, Indian scholars developed the philosophy of language to a great extent. In this field there appeared many schools.[4] The orthodox Brahmanist scholars of the Mīmāṃsā and of the Vedānta tried to establish logical theories in order to prove the permanent, unchanging nature of words. And the grammarians after Patañjali set up the doctrine of *sphoṭa* to explain metaphysically the essence of each word. Bhartṛhari (ca. 450–500 A.D.) contributed to a further development of this doctrine of words (*sphoṭa*). Generally speaking, Indian philosophy developed in close connection with linguistic speculation.[5]

Together with linguistics, *the psychology of reflection* flourished remarkably in India. The ancient Indians set a high value on introspection and they exercised the silent meditation of *Yoga* to attain serenity of mind. And at the same time, they made very careful analyses of mental processes from the religious and ethical standpoint. The *Yoga* school, as the name indicates, laid emphasis on the virtues of Yoga, and in their exercise of concentration of the mind they were engaged in the examination of its constitution. The Buddhist ascetics, too, were greatly interested in psychological problems and they arranged and expressed their views on the problems in the Abhidharmas. Maitreyanātha, Asaṅga, and Vasubandhu of Mahāyāna continued this psychological view of the Abhidharmas and systematized it into the theory of "Mind-only." Dharmapāla from his unique standpoint developed this theory further and his system of thought was brought to China, and then to Japan, to flourish in these countries as the Hossō sect. As to the psychology of "Mind-only" established chiefly by Dharmapāla, Ryō Kuroda, the Japanese psychologist, expresses the following view: "The position that the theory of 'Mind-only' deserves in the whole history of psychology remains to be determined by future studies. It is generally accepted that the Asians are excellent in the synthetic approach while their analytical ability is inferior to that of the Westerners. But, at least as far as the theory of 'Mind-only' is concerned, this general assumption is by no means true. Its sharp and minute analysis with a good command of logic (*hetu-vidyā*) exceeds the works of the Western psychologists. . . . Moreover, analysis is not the sole function of the theory of 'Mind-only.' In regard to the synthetic function as well as the analytic one, it stands unchallenged."[6] And there is the other system of Buddhist idealism which was originated by Dignāga (ca. 500 A.D.) and brought into completion by Dharmakīrti. This idealism is generally considered to be a logical and epistemological assertion rather than a psychological one. But, in reality, it contains many noteworthy suggestions from the standpoint of modern psychology.

In the West, too, as we can see in Aristotle's *De anima* and in Spinoza's *Ethica,* reflective psychology had been established long before the rise of experimental psychology, with its use of the methods of natural sciences. In a striking contrast to Indian psychology, which was deeply concerned about the ethical or practical value that the study of different types of mentalities may have, Western studies of psychology made observations of the various states of the human mind without any critical evaluation. This difference in the Western and the Indian sciences of psychology is considered to have resulted from the difference in their approach to the study of the human mind. The Westerners consider the human mind capable of being studied objectively as behavior patterns of the body, while Indians deny its objectivity and understand all mental processes as qualifying the subject experiencing them.

Indians, in their study of the volitional and the emotional mental processes, place great importance upon the ethical value that each one of these mental processes has. They evaluate the ethical and practical worth of these mental acts and, according to moral standards of judgment, classify them into three groups: good, bad, and neutral (*avyākṛta*). Furthermore, they inquire into the origin of each one of the mental states and finally go into the examination of the relation between a given mental state and the ascetic methods which will serve to check or promote it. To quote Kuroda's comment again on this point: "One of the big defects of empirical psychology is in its undue neglect of the practical or moral aspect of the problems. It is generally assumed that empirical psychology or pure psychology should confine itself to the study of the mind as it is and that the consideration of the practical significance of mental states should be left in the hands of the scholars of applied psychology and of pedagogical psychology. But, so far as psychology claims to be the study dealing with all matters touching upon the mind, psychologists should be engaged not only in observing closely individual mental phenomena and analyzing them to build a synthesis, but also should inquire into their practical value. As long as this side of the problem remains untouched, psychologists cannot claim to have done their duty properly. . . . In its powers of mental analysis, too, the theory of 'Mind-only' can match theoretical psychology which has a long history of development in the West. And with its proper regard to the practical significance of types of mentality, the theory of 'Mind-only' is akin to the idealistic system of psychology."[7]

Indians have made a very elaborate introspective examination of states of mind, especially of the emotional ones, and they have always placed special emphasis upon the practical and moral significance that such states have. These two points are the remarkable features of Indian psychology.

CHAPTER 12 THE METAPHYSICAL CHARACTER OF INDIAN THOUGHT

The Religious Character of Indian Thought

As a natural result of their ways of thinking, with their deep longing for infinity and for the unknown world, and with their deep regard for Universal Being, the Indians have imbued their civilization with a very remarkable religious coloring. The everyday life of Indians is regulated in the most minute details by their religion. In this chapter, we are to take into consideration some of the cases where their religious character is most clearly observed.

The philosophies of India are very religious. To quote Hegel: "The philosophy of India is identical with its religion; so that the interest in religion is the same as its interest in philosophy."[1] Every leading philosopher in the history of Indian thought professed faith in orthodox Brahmanism, Buddhism, or Jainism and was a member of one of the religious orders. Materialists and sceptics opposed religion, but usually their movements in India had a short duration and could not take root in the course of its history. Both Buddhism and Jainism had very philosophical systems of thought, but they grew into religious orders rather than into philosophical schools. Even logicians and scholars of natural sciences, except those who held materialistic views, all had a deep regard for mystical religious intuition. At least they acknowledged a special significance in it and believed that the release of the mind could be achieved with the aid of this intuition.

Since ancient times, philosophy with a strong religious bent held the dominant position in the Indian community. This was noticed by the Greeks. Apollonius of Tyana, a Neo-Pythagorean in the first century, wrote in his book of travel in the East that philosophy was greatly esteemed in India and that the Indians governed well under the guidance of philosophical wisdom.[2] It is clear that what Apollonius meant by the word φιλοσοφία was chiefly intellectual activity with a bent toward religion and metaphysics.

As the religious character of Indian thought is generally acknowledged, we shall simply add that the inclination toward religion is not a feature merely observed in the thought of individual philosophers, but that it had become imbedded in a deeper source—in the way of thinking of the Indian people in general. The language that they use as the means of expressing their ideas bears the unmistakable marks of the religious character of their way of thinking.

One of the religious features of the Indian languages can be clearly observed in what the Western logicians call "impersonal propositions." In the languages of the Indo-European group, the verbs expressing natural phenomena are always used impersonally in the form of the third person singular (e.g., ὕει in Greek; *pluit* in Latin; *it rains* in English; and *es regnet* in German). In the languages of ancient India, however, people preferred to use such forms of expression as "God makes the rain fall" or "God makes the thunder roll."[3] In many cases "God" is only implied and not stated clearly in words.[4] But the form of a sentence which sets "God" as the subject had been used by the Indians until recently. The ancient Greeks had similar forms of expression. In the Homeric epics, for instance, the verbs indicating the weather set Zeus as the subject.[5] In Latin, too, there were similar forms of expression, so that these ways of expression are not unique products of the Indian languages. But, the fact that these forms of expression were particularly favored by the ancient Indian people for the most part, and the fact that they had been used for centuries, indicates the religious character of the Indian people. The ancient Indians, when they thought of natural phenomena, always imagined the gods, who made the phenomena, as if they operated from behind a curtain.

The Indians developed a very elaborate idea of God, and there are numerous words which mean "god." The Sanskrit equivalent to the Greek θεός and the Latin *deus* is *deva.* These three words correspond to each other etymologically and also in their meanings. In Sanskrit, however, there are many other terms that mean god. They call the gods of lower rank *devatā,* which the Indologists translate as "divinity" or "deity." In this form of the word, *devatā* has remarkable affinities to German "Gottheit" or to the English "Godhead." But in its meaning, it is nearer to "göttliche Person" or "godlike person." *Brahman* is a neuter noun which means the ultimate principle of the universe. But when they consider this principle of the universe as the divine power, they use *brahman* as a noun of the masculine gender. Besides, they have *ātman* and *paramātman* to mean the Absolute or the innate Self.[6]

All these words indicate divine beings. But each one of them has its unique meaning and is by no means synonymous with others. In Greek such a rich vocabulary for the word "God" does not exist. Galanos in his Greek translation of the *Bhagavadgītā* managed to translate all of these words in Sanskrit by only one word θεός.[7] (Cf. Schlegel, who in his Latin translation of this Indian sacred book, gave *"deus"* for the equivalent of *deva* and *devatā; "numen"* for *brahman; "spiritus"* for *ātman; "spiritus summum locum obtinens"* for *paramātman*).

The languages of ancient India had a very rich vocabulary for conveying the idea of God, in contrast to Western classical languages. It is chiefly because the ancient Indians had a very prolific imagination concerning gods or godlike beings. But it is wrong to assume their rich vocabulary for "God" to be a result of the polytheistic system of their religion. It should be remembered that the Greek and the Roman as well as the Japanese religions were also originally polytheistic.[8]

Indians are inclined to understand every phenomenon from a religious standpoint. One of their oldest theological records explains cosmic phenomena by relating them to the parts of a beast's body in sacrifice. "Verily the dawn is the head of the horse which is fit for sacrifice, the sun its eye, the wind its breath, the mouth the Vaiśvānara fire, the year the body of the sacrificial horse. Heaven is the back, the sky the belly, the earth the chest. . . ." Similar cosmological views are expressed in the *Brāhmaṇas* and in the *Āraṇyakas*. In the North European countries and in China, there are stories equivalent to the Indian myth which explains the creation of the world by the self-splitting of the Cosmic Man,[10] but the stories which acknowledge the corresponding relation between the elements of the religious rites and natural phenomena developed exclusively in India.

In India, the Absolute is called *brahman*. Originally this word meant "the phrases in the Vedas" which were recited in the magical rites. In no other civilized countries has an idea relating to ritual, as *brahman* did, rise to the position of the Absolute.

For Brahmanists, it is a matter of great importance to attain a way of life which would permit performance of the religious rites. For them, to be born in this world is the first life; to become qualified for the performance of ceremonies is the second life; and to die to be reborn in Heaven is the third life.[11]

We referred above to the Indians' prolix style of writing, saying that it comes from their particular repugnance to arranging matters according to rules. We add here one more fundamental cause that impels them to cling to this redundant style. It is their religious concern. The ancient Indians *recited by heart* and transmitted the sacred texts of their religion by word of mouth. In the course of time, the form of recitation was established. And they came to suppose a magical power in the act of the recitation itself. To keep the magical power at work, it was conceived necessary to follow the established form obediently and to repeat it faithfully in every case of recitation. No arbitrary change of the form was allowed. Thus, the ancient Indians made neither condensations nor abridgements of the established form, however repetitive and wearisome the form might be. Every sentence in the formulae had to be recited and listened to carefully. The omission of a single word in recitation was considered a grave religious error. The ancient Indians followed obediently and patiently, without even any sense of obedience or patience in their mind, the long and dull form of recitation hardly bearable to the modern ear, and thus, for an ancient Indian ascetic in a cottage in the depths of the forest or for a monk in a dark cavern, the passage of time seemed infinite.

Indian natural sciences, too, were strongly influenced by the religious concern. The ancient Indians wrote many books of mathematics, astronomy, medicine, and other sciences, and their scientific works were stimulated further after the Greek and the Roman sciences were introduced. Here it is noteworthy that almost all these Indian books of science open with *words of admiration for and faith in the gods*. The Greek sciences made real progress only after they had shaken off the fetters of theology. The Indian sciences, on the contrary, grew as a subsidiary study to aid the study of the Vedas. Among the natural sciences, astronomy was first acknowledged as an independent field of study. From an early time, the orthodox Brahmanists regarded astronomy (*jyotiṣa*) highly as one of the six subsidiary studies for the Vedas. They needed astronomical knowledge to hold religious ceremonies on the exact dates given in the sacred codes. And for this purpose they began with the observation of the relations among the sun, the moon, and the fixed stars; thus, the study of "the twenty-eight constellations" occupied an essential part of their astronomy. It is natural that their science of the heavenly bodies had from the beginning a very strong hue of astrology and that its later development was inseparably related to this art of divination. The growth of mathematics in India was paralleled by that of astronomy. Mathematics, too, developed chiefly to meet ritualistic needs. The ancient Indians had their alchemy and this also bore a strong religious coloring.[12] The naturalistic philosophy of the Vaiśeṣika supposed "the invisible power (*adṛṣṭa*)" to explain the movements of the atoms. And with the lapse of time, they came to attach religious significance to this power.

From ancient times, all Indian scientists were pious devotees of their religions. Even at present some of the scientific research institutes in India hold religious services. This does not mean the distortion of scientific study by religion. In India, religion and science are not necessarily antithetical; rather the belief is that they exist in harmony and cooperation.

The Indian arts are also deeply connected with religion. Almost all artistic works are related to religious structures and beliefs, and according to some of the old Indian books or discourses on art, the ultimate beauty of art is understood as nothing but self-unification with the Absolute. As to their music, many of the favorite songs of Indians are religious ones. Even Indian immigrants in foreign countries retain this strong affection for their native religious songs.

Indians are a religious people. After they settled in the region of the Ganges, the ancient Indians came to conceive the idea of *Saṁsāra* (the cycle of births and rebirths), and they felt at heart that all beings including man are involved in the cycle of transmigration. Some of their verbal ways of expression tell us manifestly that the conduct of the ancient Indians in their everyday life was strongly influenced by their belief in *Saṁsāra.* For instance, the Sanskrit equivalent to English "here," *iha,* is used in many cases to mean "in this world." *The ancient Indians led their life on this side of heaven with the expectation of a life after death.* The belief in the kingdom to come after death was once very widely cherished among Western people, too. But, to a degree incomparable to that of the Western cases, the belief in rebirth permeated the mind of the Indian people and strongly influenced their daily life. It is reasonable, therefore, that the Western translators of the ancient Indian languages managed to translate *iha* only by resorting to circumlocution. E.g.: *iha* (in *Bhag.* II, 5) = ἐν τούτῳ τῷ βίῳ = *quoad vivam; idha modati pecca modati katapuñño* (in *Dhp.,* 16) = *in hoc aevo gaudet, morte obita gaudet qui bonum perfecit.*

For Indians who believe in rebirth by *Karma,* there is no eternal grace or final damnation. All conduct in this temporal world is in itself transitory and cannot be the final factor for the fate of a man in all his future lives. The fate of a man in the next world is inevitably determined by the sum of the good and evil deeds he has performed during his life in this world, and when he has lived the fate determined by his deeds in the former life, he will live a new life, and thus the transmigration by *Karma* proceeds without end.

The Tendency to Transcend This World

In India, as well as in other countries, there have been many people who have advocated indulgence in worldly pleasures.[13] Although this is one aspect of Indian thought, we find it rather difficult to find in it anything peculiarly Indian; so we pass over it in order to discuss another aspect—the sense of temporal suffering.

The Indian idea of *Saṁsāra* is based on their *view that life in this world is suffering.* This view of life is found early in the *Upaniṣads.* Yājñavalkya thought that a man is happy when he has realized the *Ātman* and that a man is in torment when he is detached from the *Ātman,* ignorant of this source of happiness. He explained the essence of the *Ātman* (the Self) saying: "This is thy Self, the ruler within, the immortal. Everything else is of evil."[14] Gotama renounced the world to seek for the way of deliverance from pain in this life. Really the first problem that Buddhism took up was the suffering pervasive of this life. Wherever he is or whatever refuge he goes to, a man cannot be free from pain. Everybody will grow old and die. "Birth is suffering, age is suffering. Grief, lamenting, suffering, sorrow, despair are suffering. Not to get what one wants, also means suffering. In short, the five *skandhas* (basic components of human life) [involve] suffering."[15] Man is exposed to the impending crisis of death.[16] "Woe upon life in this world!"[17] And the Jains proceeded further to expound the miserable state of man in this worldly existence. One of their sūtras says: "Beings torment beings. See the great danger in this world; many pains (are the lot) of creatures."[18] In another place, it says: "Having well considered it, having well looked at it, I say thus: all beings . . . (experience) individually pleasure or displeasure, pain, great terror, and unhappiness. Creatures are filled with alarm from all directions and in all directions."[19] In another place, it says: "The (living) world is afflicted, miserable, difficult to instruct, and without discrimination. In this world full of pain, suffering by their different acts, see the benighted ones caused great pain."[20]

The view that life in this world is suffering is an idea common throughout India. Mādhava, who was learned in all the philosophies of India, wrote in the fourteenth century: "That all transmigratory existence is identical with pain is the common verdict of the founders of all sects and schools; or else they would not be found so anxious to put a stop to it and engage in a method for bringing it to an end. We must, therefore, bear in mind that all is pain, and pain alone."[21] All the thinkers of India taxed their brains on this problem of suffering. Even materialists and epicureans were not excepted. They could not hold any of the optimistic views of life held by thinkers of other nations. In all the religions of India, the problem was how to find the way of emancipation from this suffering in the cycle of Saṁsāra. The way leading to peace of mind, has always been their central concern.[22]

It is natural, therefore, that Indians in the past were inclined to belittle their physical body to the extreme. The ancient Buddhists said in one of their sūtras: "After a stronghold has been made of the bones, it is covered with flesh and blood, and there dwell in it old age and death, pride and deceit."[23] Brahmanists held a similar view of their physical existence.[24] *Mokṣa* in their sense is the deliverance of the *Ātman* from the body. For Jains, deliverance means no other than "the decay of the body."[25] And we can see that Buddhists, too, in the early days of their history regarded "the cessation of the existing body" as pleasure.[26] The Indian ethic of ascetic mortification was based on these views of the physical body, far from any idea such as we see in a Chinese book of morality, *Hsiao-ching,* which reads, "We get our body, hair, and skin from the parents. To keep it from ruin and injury is the beginning of filial piety."

Indian sages refuse sensual pleasures. They teach us not to cling to the external material world. Buddhists and Jains are all in accord in teaching not to cling to things by thinking constantly "these are *my possessions* (*mama*)."[27]

Nearly every Indian religious thinker seeks to live in the bosom of nature and there to have direct communion with the Absolute. He renounces the world, lives in the depths of the forest, sits under a tree or on a rock and, keeping himself aloof from all secular affairs, concentrates his thoughts on the quest for truth. There have been a few thinkers who try to seek for truth while remaining in the secular world and living among people in the street. But, in India, such thinkers have been very few in number and not so influential. And the main current of the Indian civilization has been not in the cities but in the woods. It has been the civilization of the tranquil life in the forest.

India did not develop a city representing its entire civilization. The ancient Greeks had the center of their civilization in Athens, the ancient Romans in Rome, and the modern Europeans in London, Paris, and Berlin. But in India there was or is no city corresponding to these cities in the West. It is true that the cities of Pāṭaliputra and Kānyakubja once flourished. But the prosperity of these cities was of a short duration. There are no cities prospering throughout the whole history of India to represent its civilization.

For Indians who are inclined to transcend this world and who hold a strong longing for a future existence, it is difficult to accept a religion that sets a high value on secular mundane life.[28] More than four hundred years have passed since the Christians began their missionary work in this country, and at present (Census of 1961) there are about nine or ten million Christian adherents in India—less than one-fortieth of the whole population. Besides, as the national censuses and the reports of the Christian missions indicate, many of the converts to Christianity live in South India and consist chiefly of those expelled from the Hindu community—the Śūdras, the vagabonds, and the uncivilized people of the mountains. It is truly significant that the Christian missions have tried hard to enlighten the peoples left out of the Hindu society. But in spite of their great effort, the Christian missions have failed to capture the minds of the Hindus who are the guiding force in the Indian community. As one of the reasons for the stagnation of the Christian missionary works in India, a Japanese scholar writes as follows: "In India, a religious missionary is considered to be a man free from . . . secular desires. From the days of Śākyamuni up to the present, almost all the religious founders of India are ascetics who lead the very severe life of mortification. But, the life of a Christian missionary, who has a wife and children to accompany him, a fine house to live in, a car to drive and meat to eat, is too secular to be understood by the Hindus as the life proper for a religious man."[29]

The supermundane idea of India's religions has influenced the ethical ideas of the Indians. In India, abandoning private property is urged as a virtue. Buddhists and Jains all teach their adherents to give up the idea of "mine (*mama*)" and encourage the virtue of no-property. They teach the performance of unlimited service to others by surrendering all of one's possessions. This Indian negation of private property is very similar to the philosophy of modern socialism and communism. But, it should be noted that the Indian assertion is based on their supermundane way of thinking. In practice the socialistic reformation of Indian society is far from being accomplished.

Indians, in spite of their pessimistic view of life and of their supermundane religions, have also optimistic tendencies. This paradoxical assertion can be safely made on the basis that generally the Indian people are free from despair. Their optimism is derived from their belief that although this life is filled with suffering, once one has been united with the Absolute, one will live at ease and without fear. And the Indians never give up this hope of unification with the Absolute. This phase of their way of thinking can be observed also in their dramatic literature; they have no "tragedy." Almost all the Indian plays, after many scenes filled with thrills and suspense, end with, "They all lived happily ever after." And corresponding to this feature of the Indian way of thinking, their religion has an optimistic glow. It promises any man, however bad he is, that he will be saved if he will persevere in his earnest faith or in his practice of severe discipline.

In a striking contrast to their supermundane character, Indians have at the same time a yearning for material and sensual pleasures. But these two different trends in the Indian way of thinking possess one common trait; both tend to neglect and to transcend the rules of social organizations. Sometimes Indians venture to neglect and scorn ethical norms of behavior. In their inclination to transcend restrictive rules of institutions and in their indifference to ethical norms in pleasure-seeking there is an essential affinity with their religious passion to submit themselves to the Absolute without admitting any intermediary condition or agent between themselves and the Absolute.

The decisive factor in the idea of *Saṁsāra* is death. All the sufferings of man in this world come from death. Facing death, a man is led to the metaphysical contemplation of the problem. *And the Indian civilization has grown through meditation on the phenomenon of death.* Buddhism and Jainism both are religions arising from deep reflection on this inevitable moment of human life. A quotation from the *Dhammapada* reads as follows: "How is there laughter, how is there joy, as this world is always burning? Do you not seek a light, ye who are surrounded by darkness?"[30] Hinduism holds a similar view on the problem of death.

Megasthenes, the Greek who visited India at the end of the fourth century B.C. or thereabouts, mentioned as a remarkable inclination of the Brahmins their practice of philosophical speculation on death. He wrote: "Now, among the Brahmins, the problem of death is the issue very many times debated. Usually (they) compare the life in this world to the state of a child quickening in the mother's womb. And they hold that the true life begins verily at the moment of death in this world. And they consider this (life of truth) as the ultimate source of happiness for the philosophical (φιλοσοφήσαντες). And in order to make the mind ready for death, they urge the need of the severest asceticism (ἀσκήσις)."[31] In Japan, too, Matsumiya Kanzan (1686–1780) commented on this feature of Indian thought: "In India, . . . people are old and feeble in spirit and they like the sombre teachings of Buddhism, which is always talking about the problem of death."[32]

The artistic works of India reflect this feature of the Indian religion. Indian structures and sculptures originated from the decorative works around the *Stūpas*. A *Stūpa* is a hemispherical grave-mound built on the ashes or the remains of a sage. The *Stūpas* of the early periods were rather small in scale but after the Mauryas they began to build larger ones. The ancient Greeks called the *Stūpas* "Pyramids."[33] Gorgeous artistic works of ancient India were all carved on the gates, pillars, and railings of the *Stūpas*, and temples were first built around the *Stūpas*. The fine art of the temple architecture grew as one part of the decorative works of the *Stūpas*. It may be said that grave-worship is the origin of Indian art. But their artistic expressions, developed thus as the ornaments of the grave, bear no gloomy shade of death. On the contrary, they are bright, lively, and beautiful. This bright feature of Indian artistic works is different from the expressions of the sunny and innocent disposition of primitive or uncivilized tribes; rather, it reflects the peaceful state of mind of the religious people who challenged and conquered the fear of death. Indians seek eternity through their inner medium of meditation on death.

The Tendency of Thought to Transcend the Gods

As we have seen above, every expression of Indian thought is strongly tinged with religious coloring. It should be noted, however, that their attitude toward religion is far different from that of the Westerners. In the West, God is the center of the whole religious system. In the Indian religions, on the other hand, God does not hold such a prominent position as in the West. Indians have their own very richly and elaborately developed idea of God, but they never consider God as the Absolute Being. In the Indian concept, the gods are beings lower than the Absolute and the Absolute *stands high above the gods.*

According to the Brahmanistic point of view, the grace of the gods is the reward given in return for offerings. There is a fixed relation of cause and effect between the ritualistic service to the gods and the grace given back to man. And no free-will on the part of the gods is acknowledged to intervene in this relation. It is natural, therefore, that the idea of a personal god or of the grace given by him has been scarcely conceived among the Brahmanists. In the course of time, their attention has been focused more exclusively on the permanent law that regulates all beings including even the gods. Except for some theological assertions of Hinduism of the later periods, almost all the ancient philosophical schools of India regarded the gods as being of no great significance. Buddhists and Jains, for instance, considered the gods to be no more than beings enjoying super-human powers. And the scholars of the Vedānta school attached little importance to the God presiding over the universe; they considered him merely an incidental superior cause. In short, Indians have a higher regard for the authority of law (*dharma*) than for the gods. The gods, in their concept, are beings who follow what the law decrees. They are not the founders of the law. But, on the contrary, it is the universal and unalterable law that makes the gods what they are.

The gods in the Indian religions, especially the gods of Brahmanism, are loose in morals. Their deeds are, like the Homeric gods' pranks, not always virtuous. The *Brāhmaṇa* books tell us many stories concerning the gods' indiscreet deeds of envy, jealousy, hostility, infidelity, greed, arrogance, cowardice, and adultery. The gods of India are not different from average creatures, and are by no means the supreme authority of morality. Generally speaking, one may say that Indians who worship such gods are little awakened to any sense of morality. In the *Ṛg Veda,* only Varuṇa is the god of morality. But, as the *Brāhmaṇas* and the books of the later periods tell us, even this god gradually changed his character and lost his strict morals. It is natural, therefore, that Indians of the later ages sought the basis of their morals apart from the gods' authority. And they came to conceive that the moral law should be observed not because of the gods' authority but because of retribution according to *Karma.*[34]

Many gods of Brahmanism were adopted in the Buddhist myths and were transformed into Buddhist gods. In the Buddhist concept, these gods, though they possess super-human powers, themselves are bound to a life of ignorance and are waiting to be saved by the teachings of the Buddha. The Jains, too, refused to regard the gods as the Absolute Being. The concept of the Supreme Lord had taken a fixed form in India by the time the Christian era began. But one of the most outstanding philosophical schools of India, the Non-dualist (*advaita*) school in the Vedānta, asserted that the highest God (*Īśvara*) is no other than the Absolute, the Brahman, clouded with ignorance (*ajñāna*), and, because of this ignorance, is bound to the world of illusion like other beings. The schools of Hinduism urge us to have faith in the Supreme Lord, but, as we see in their myths relating to this Supreme Lord, he is more likely to be a human being than the Absolute Supreme Being. It is safe to generalize here and say that most Indians find the sanction of their morality in the law (*dharma*) which transcends the gods. This Indian concept stands in striking contrast to the Western idea that places the sole source of morality in the one Lord.

The ancient Greeks and Romans used their words for god (θεός and *deus,* respectively) in a rather loose way. In their thinking the philosopher-emperors, and other men of outstanding intellect who have contributed greatly to the happiness of people by delivering them from their errors and tribulations, thus leading them nearer to the divine life—such men (whether real or fictional, as it often turned out) were the godlike saviors of mankind.[35] A savior for the Indians, was not the θεὸς σῶτηρ (God-savior) of the ancient Greeks.

For Indians, on the contrary, a savior is a master of the universal law. Whether the savior is a human being or a divine being does not matter. He is a savior by the authority of the Absolute that stands higher than the gods. He is an incarnation of the Absolute, but not necessarily a god or the only son of God. The Indian concept of God has produced an idea of the savior quite different from that of Western religions.

The difference between the Western and Indian concepts of God is clearly observed also in the literary styles. The Greek writers were careful to make their gods speak in a manner appropriate to the dignity of gods, and succeeded in producing satisfactory images to that effect. But, Indian authors, for instance, the authors of the *Upaniṣads,* could not or, more properly speaking, did not care for such ways of expression. Like the Indian artists in their works of sculpture, the Indian writers scarcely attempted to idealize the gods or to describe them as being more sublime than human beings.[36]

CHAPTER 13 THE SPIRIT OF TOLERANCE AND CONCILIATION

Generally speaking, Indian people have a tendency to recognize and rationalize the fact that there exist many different world-views, philosophies, and religions in the world. For they think that these different views which seemingly conflict with each other are based on the Absolute One. Their viewpoint is based objectively on the idea that all things in the universe are one, and subjectively on the reflection that all human activities originate from a metaphysical and monistic principle.

The reflection on the fact that there are different philosophies in this world, conflicting with each other, appeared in India when Gotama the Buddha was born and when many towns thrived in the Ganges basin. Sañjaya, a sceptic, suspended judgment on any metaphysical matter. When he was asked to answer, he would speak ambiguously and offered no definite answer. It was difficult to grasp the true meaning of his answer, for it was just like attempting to grasp an eel by the hands. But Mahāvīra, founder of Jainism, tried to transcend scepticism. He advocated the relativistic theory of "*Naya*" which proved the possibility of offering varying judgments on general matters provided that the qualification "from a certain point of view" was added.

Among these philosophers of ancient India, Gotama the Buddha was the first to reflect thoroughly on this problem. He criticized the philosophers and religious leaders in endless debate as "being attached to their own views."[1] And they were said to have committed an immoral act as the result of being involved in metaphysical discussions which would never be solved. Gotama himself avoided participation in these discussions[2] and regarded them as quite useless for the attainment of Enlightenment.[3]

Gotama the Buddha was said "to have remained aloof from all discussions" and "to have taught ascetics or *bhikkhus* to transcend any *prapañca* (discussions which were useless for the attainment of the religious goal)." Gotama did not insist that his teaching was the only Absolute Truth to the exclusion of all others. Therefore, he remained in harmony with other philosophers. In this way of harmony he attained and realized the Enlightenment—tranquility of mind. Such being the case Gotama's teachings could never be compared with other teachings.[4] We cannot say that his teachings are "equal," "superior," or "inferior" to other ones. Comparison will be possible only in the case where a common standpoint is seen between two different views. Buddha's teachings differ from other doctrines in being neutral to their standpoints and conclusions. Gotama himself seems to have gone so far as to recognize the *raison d'être* of other philosophies. All philosophers, as far as they adhere to their own views, risk becoming unwisely tenacious. But there must be some reason in each opinion as long as people believe it.[5] According to Gotama, those Buddhists who want to keep aloof from the views of any type of philosophy must reflect upon themselves all the time, bearing in mind that they should not be prejudiced.

Such an attitude toward other doctrines can apparently be seen in Mahāyāna Buddhism, especially in the *Saddharmapuṇḍarīkasūtra*.[6] Even the lower doctrines, the Sūtra declares, are the *upāyas* or the means for the Buddhas to teach mankind the right way. Such a way of thinking was carried on in Vajrayāna Mysticism (Shingon Esoteric Buddhism). In Vajrayāna even heretical dogmas are regarded as a part of Buddhism. Buddhism is not a special religion which conflicts with other religions, but is, in itself, the Absolute Truth. Heretics are nothing but an offshoot-manifestation of the ultimate truth. From the absolute point of view there is in the universe only one principle called "Buddhism."

The spirit of tolerance was not totally maintained in the same manner among the later Buddhists of India. It was a natural tendency, common enough in history, for society bound by older customs to oppose the Buddhist order which had to stand against other religions and philosophies as it became an established religion and created special rites and customs. However, almost all the Buddhists in India, believing that the fundamental standpoint of Buddhism was not contradictory to other heretical views, did not intend to compete with them actively. As a result, Buddhism, in spreading over the Asian countries, caused less friction among the indigenous faiths of the peoples who had received it. Native or traditional faiths and customs were scarcely destroyed by Buddhists and could easily survive; so long as they were seen as ethical from the Buddhist point of view, they were able to remain in existence side by side with the newly-arrived Buddhism, and sometimes were absorbed in Buddhism. In later days Buddhism itself fused into one of the native religions, giving them philosophical foundations.

As for the fact that there exist many different philosophies and religions in the world, Vedānta philosophers also stated views like those of the Buddhists. Basing themselves on Absolute Monism, they regarded even heretical doctrines as having their basis in Brahman. According to them, there are many ultimate principles—elements, gods, breath, time, etc.,—

which are respectively asserted by many philosophical schools to be the Absolute Principle. And this is why there are so many schools with diversified views. From the viewpoint of Vedānta, however, none of them deserves to be regarded as the Absolute Truth. They are only assumed (*vikalpita*) to be the world-principle. The fact is that the *Ātman* is the Absolute One for the Advaita Vedāntist who believes that these philosophers misunderstood the real nature of things.

Their views, however wrong, no matter how heretical, are also included in the *Ātman*-theory of Vedānta. Vedānta philosophers thus went so far as to say that even these heretical views were manifestations of the *Ātman,* and were partly true even though they were incomplete in themselves. The standpoint of Vedānta because of its broader scope is quite different from these heretical views. In the *Māṇḍūkyakārikās* we read: "Those who admit duality, adhere to their views and are inconsistent with each other. However, (Vedāntists) are not inconsistent (with such dualists)."[7] According to Śaṁkara, this is likened to limbs that are not incompatible with their bodies.

In later Jain philosophy the same idea was also expressed. Hemacandra says: "Discussions in other schools produce jealousy because the one insists while the other opposes. But in Jainism they advocate no dogma and no discussions because they admit the teachings of 'Naya.' "[8]

Because of this way of thinking that in every heretical view some *raison d'être* exists, Indian philosophers in the medieval period tried to establish a "comprehensive system of world philosophy," or a "systematic conception of the world." These systems also show tolerance in recognizing the *raison d'être* in all others that have different views which are then reconciled into the same school. Generally speaking, we *cannot find in any Indian religion the conception of "heretic"* in the sense of Western usage.

Such a tolerant attitude is found not only in religious teachings but in the fundamental policies of administration taken by many kings and rulers throughout the history of India. King Aśoka, for example, himself an earnest Buddhist layman, never excluded other religions—Brahmanism, Jainism, Ājīvikas, etc. He "adored both monks and laymen of all religions."[9] His sincere wishes were that "everyone in every religion dwell peacefully side by side," and cooperate with one another for promoting the welfare of mankind. Though King Aśoka made Buddhism a state religion, he did not persecute the non-Buddhist religions in his territory.

King Khāravela, who gained control of the southern part of India after the collapse of the Mauryan Dynasty, was a patron of the Jaina order, but he also repaired the shrines and temples of other religions. He was called "*sarvapāṣaṇḍapūjaka* (he who adored all the sects)." King of the Kaṣāṇa Dynasty, who ruled northern India, also protected many different religions. King Kaniṣka, for example, cast many coins on which the statues of gods—of Greece, of Zoroastrianism, of Hinduism, and of Buddha—are engraved. The Gupta Dynasty in the fourth century was tolerant to all the religions.[10] Centuries later, Akbar the Great (1556–1605) ruled almost all India, and intended to establish a new religion by mixing other religions which existed before. He declared that Hindu and Mohammedan should worship the same and single God. But he was rather tolerant not only of Hinduism and Mohammedanism but also of Jainism, Parsism, and Christianity. He also admitted solar-worship. Though not complete, the principle of tolerance was retained by him in his religious policy.

Such an attitude toward other faiths is manifest in modern religious movements in India. A religious reformer in the nineteenth century, Rām Mohan Rai, organized a religious society called Brāhma-Samāj, and he made it a fundamental principle of the society for the followers to worship the same God irrespective of their race, class, nationality, and even their religion. Ramakṛṣṇa, who was the founder of the Ramakrishna Order, declared that "all religions, pursuing different ways, will finally reach the same God."[11] "All the religions that exist are true."[12] Vivekānanda, his disciple, delivered a famous address at the International Religious Conference held in Chicago on September 27, 1893, saying that: "Oh, the Sacred One, called Brahman by the Hindus, Ahura Mazdah by the Zoroastrians, Buddha by the Buddhists, Jehovah by the Hebrews, and God in heaven by the Christians! May He bestow inspiration upon us! Christians should be neither Buddhists nor Hindus. Buddhists and Hindus should never be Christians. Everyone, however, must grow up in accordance with his own religious principle, holding its individual character firmly while assimilating others' spiritual merits. . . . This Conference has proved that Holiness, Serenity, and Compassion should not be monopolized by any religious order. And it has also proved that there were no religions in the world which never produced noble and spiritual personalities. I firmly believe that we will read the following passages on the flags or banners of all the religions in the future: Help each other. Don't struggle against each other. Be reconciled with others. Don't destroy others. Keep harmony and peace. Don't compete in useless matters[13] . . . . I approve of existing of religions in the past. I adore God with them."[14]

These religious attitudes differ from those in the West. In the history of Europe we often find religious antagonisms which inevitably led to political and military conflicts. But we can hardly find many cases of religious war in India. There were, of course, in India a few rulers who adhered to some indigenous faith and oppressed some of the universal religions arising among the Indian people. But we cannot find any rulers who were Buddhists or Jainists and who persecuted other religions.

This fact would be more obvious if we compare it with the facts in the West. Christianity and Mohammedanism have both engaged in religious wars. According to the Calvinists, hatred directed against sinners or heretics is regarded as a virtue.[15] We know that religious leaders in the West were often persecuted and put to death. On the contrary, in India there were no religious wars. Neither Buddhists nor Jains ever executed heretics. What they did to heretics was only to exclude them from the orders. Religious leaders in India died peacefully attended by their disciples and followers. Toleration is the most conspicuous characteristic of Indian culture.

The Indians developed individualism in their unique way. They have preserved the attitude of religious freedom traditionally, probably more than any other country. An American professor says, "It is paradoxical that we, who put so much emphasis on individualism in economics and politics, have so little room for it in morality and religion, as compared with Indian thought."[16]

Recent questionnaires on the comparison of life-ideals show that there are many students in India who think that among many different ways of life the most noble is the recognition and understanding of the existence of varied paths. This fact shows that toleration is still alive as a way of thinking among Indian students.[17]

What, then, is the reason behind the spirit of tolerance in people's minds in India? Oldenberg enumerates the following reasons: Indian climate and circumstance, early and easy invasion of Aryan race, nonexistence of great wars, calm atmosphere in the Brahmin class, etc.[18] Wars in India were fought only by mercenary soldiers, and not by ordinary people. This fact contributed much to promote the attitude of toleration in the Indian people. Throughout the centuries of Indian history no military expedition was attempted by Indian rulers. According to Arrianos' report, "Megasthenes says that Indians never attacked other peoples outside the borders, and other peoples never attacked the Indians. Alexander was the only exception when he attacked the Indian people."[19] "Indians did not conquer other countries because of their spirit of righteousness (*dikaiotēs*)."[20]

The love of peace advocated by the philosopher of India is acknowledged by Western scholars. The word "peace" signifies in itself a willingness to recognize the claims of other views besides one's own. So the peace-loving attitude in Indian people seems to be closely related to their unique way of thinking that different philosophies and different conceptions of the world are nothing but manifestations of the Absolute One.

PART II CHINA

CHAPTER 14 INTRODUCTION

China, the largest of the Eastern countries, has a cultural tradition going back several thousand years; its influence has been widespread and taken deep root in adjacent countries. Chinese culture has even occasionally been called "the Far Eastern culture."

It is important to know to what extent the language spoken and written by the Chinese reveals the connections of its culture with its traditional ways of thinking. Many overall approaches have ended in failure. Logical studies on Chinese grammar have not sufficiently explained particular problems underlying its structure, due largely to the efforts on the part of researchers to apply the standards of Western languages to the Chinese. Their studies have not been fruitful.[1]

Other cultural aspects of the Chinese civilization will provide materials for investigating ways of thinking of the Chinese. But in this work the author will use the phenomenon of the introduction of Buddhism to China as an important clue to the problem of understanding characteristically Chinese ways of thinking.

The Chinese did not accept Buddhism in its Indian form. After it was introduced into China, it was modified under the influence of certain traditional ways of thinking of the Chinese, so that Chinese Buddhism diverged from Indian Buddhism to a very great degree. The following facts about that influence indicate the nature and extent of these divergencies:

(1) The Chinese made complete translations of the Buddhist scriptures into their own language. They did not use Sanskrit or Prakrit as the sacred language of the Buddhist church.

(2) In translating, Chinese scholars and exegetes often gave peculiarly adapted interpretations of the original. Thus the Indian texts were not always faithfully translated. Interpolations were often added. The sentences were frequently embellished with Chinese literary ornament, thus taking on the appearance of original works of Chinese literature.

(3) Later Chinese Buddhist scholars, with few exceptions, were not in a position to refer to or to understand the original Indian texts, and

sometimes they failed to understand even the meaning of earlier Chinese translations.

(4) Many texts of Chinese Buddhism developed along lines entirely different from the doctrines of Indian schools.

(5) The exegetical techniques of the Chinese Buddhists are entirely different from those of the Indians.

These differences and divergencies are understandable as occurring under the influence of the habitual and distinctive ways of thinking of the Chinese. The purpose of this section is to attempt to describe those persisting traditional ways of thinking of the Chinese by pointing out the ways in which Indian Buddhist thought was altered under their influence; we do not mean to imply that the Chinese always differed from the Indian Buddhists.

Of course, we cannot regard all people in a nation as having the same characteristics. At various times and in various regions the Chinese have engaged in diverse sorts of activities, and as in all cultures, conformity has never been 100 per cent. The opinions of learned persons may not be the same as the opinions of the masses; after all, the "characteristics" of a people are the customary ways of living and thinking of most of the population, which may or may not be reflected in or influenced by the ideas of intellectuals.

CHAPTER 15 EMPHASIS ON THE PERCEPTION OF THE CONCRETE

Graphic Character of the Writing

The results of Granet's study of the vocabulary of Chinese coincide with many of the findings of Lévy-Bruhl's study of the languages of American Indians.[1] However, there exists an important difference between Chinese and the American Indian languages. Granet says, "Whereas primitive languages are characterized by the extreme variety of verbal forms, Chinese is extremely poor on this point. It uses uninflected monosyllabic words; there is no distinction of parts of speech. However, the flavor of concreteness—provided by various forms in other languages—is shown by the extreme abundance of Chinese words which convey concrete phases of things with unparalleled power. . . ."[2]

Consequently, it is characteristic of Chinese that it is abundant in words expressing bodies and shapes, but poor in verbs expressing change and transformation. Whether this is peculiar to Chinese alone or common to primitive languages in general, is an open question. Stenzel writes:[3] "Considering the process of the establishment of syntactical forms, we can say that subjects were in origin mostly words expressing 'things,' a single word as a unit standing for a thing as a unit. When this idea of thing is applied to objects in general, appellations expressing changing phenomena come to be substantiated. This process can be perceived in German, but it is more evident in Greek. In any language, generally speaking, verbs, adjectives, pronouns, adverbs, etc. were originally nouns expressing 'things,' but they changed to become other parts of speech; losing their independent meaning, they have sometimes become affixes. This process of transformation is said to be most evident in isolated languages, especially in Chinese." No proof is offered for this statement, but it seems plausible. It seems clear, in any case, that Chinese thinking has tended to concreteness of expression.

The influence of language structure on thought can be seen in the way in which the characters are made. Chinese characters are, of course, originally hieroglyphic. The character which symbolizes the sun is derived from a drawing of a circle; another character symbolizes fire through a representation of flame. Later many phonetic characters were also devised, but these were based upon hieroglyphics. The four classic ways of constructing Chinese characters are, following Karlgren's terminology: (1) *hsiang hsing*, image shapes (pictographs); (2) *chih shih*, pointing to situations (indirect symbols); (3) *hui i*, meeting of ideas (associative compounds); (4) *hsing shêng*, picture and sound (determinative phonetics). The two modes of transference are: (1) *chuan chu*, transferable meanings (mutually interpretative symbols); (2) *chia chieh*, borrowing (phonetic loan characters).[4] Yet the hieroglyphs are fundamental to the characters developed by these six devices.

The Chinese were accustomed to these types of symbols, even when they transcribed foreign words with Chinese characters. The choice of characters for transcription was random. There was no systematic way of consistently transcribing a particular foreign sound by a particular character. Even one and the same translator often adopted different ways of transcribing one and the same sound.[5] They did not go on to invent an analytic and constructive method of consistently using an agreed set of characters equivalent to the sounds of say, Sanskrit. In choosing characters to transcribe foreign sounds, the Chinese were influenced by the appearance of the character. For example, the Pali word *bhikkhu* for "mendicant" was always transcribed *pi-ch'iu* and never as *p'i-chiu*. Characters chosen to transcribe certain key words were invariably so used, regardless of the fact that the same syllables in other words were differently transcribed.

The Concrete Expression of Concepts

On the basis of a study of the vocabulary of the *Book of Odes*, Granet observed that Chinese concepts are expressed in highly concrete form. Nearly all words express particular ideas—forms of existing things perceived in a particular state. They aim at expressing things by individualization and specification rather than by analysis. For example, in the *Book of Odes* more than three thousand words are used: this seems a very large number in proportion to the limited number of ideas expressed. These words correspond to images of ideas which are complex and particular. In the book there are 18 words which might correspond to one concept "mountain" qualified by one or more adjectives. In the same work there are 23 words which mean "horse."

On the other hand there is no one word which corresponds to a Western word expressing a general and abstract idea. Because of their synthetic and particular character Chinese words are more nearly proper nouns than the common nouns of Western languages—for example, the many words for "rivers": *ho, chiang,* etc.[5a]

The classics, including the *Odes,* were written long before Chinese philosophy appeared, and they did not propound philosophical theses. But the vocabulary of the classics has continued in use up to the present day and the observations made above thus have some application to the whole history of the expression of Chinese ideas.

The Chinese way of expressing concepts is concrete. Thus for the term "epigraphy" the Chinese use the graphically concrete expression "writing on metal and stone."

In the expression of attributive qualities they tend to use concrete numbers, thus for "a fast horse" they use *ts'ien-li-ma* "a horse good for a thousand *li*" (one *li* = 1890 feet); for a man endowed with clairvoyance they use the expression *ts'ien-li-yen* "thousand *li* vision." These numbers are not used in a simple quantitative sense but symbolize qualities which are expressed in Western languages in more abstract terms. The two characters *mao-shun* ("halberd and shield") form a compound used to mean "contradiction," and no other compound is used for expressing this concept. The association of the original meaning of these characters is not lost so that it was perfectly natural for the Chinese to create an alternative compound on the same basis, *kan-shun.*[6]

The same associative process is revealed in the case of the character *li* (reason) which is of key importance in the history of Chinese philosophy. This character originally meant "well distributed veins on minerals or precious stones." It eventually came to mean "principle" and finally "universal principle."[7] This third meaning was developed by *Ch'eng Ming-tao* (Che'eng Hao, 1032–1085) in the Sung period. Under his interpretation it became the fundamental principle which pervades and makes possible all phenomena. "The development of this abstract meaning is generally attributed to the influence of Buddhist scholars, particularly those of the *Hua-yen* sect, who set up the distinction and contrast between *li* and *shih.*[8]

The tendency to express abstract philosophical ideas in concrete images is conspicuous in Zen Buddhism. The universe or cosmos is expressed as *shan, ho, ta-ti,* "mountains, rivers, and the great earth." The basic ego of a human being is expressed as *ts'ao-yüan i-ti-shui,*[9] "a drop of water in the source," one's true nature as *pen-lai mien-mu,* "original face and eye" or as *pen-ti feng-kuang,* "the wind and light of one's native place." Words which were used as literal translations of such original Indian words as Bodhi *pen-chio* or Tathatā *chên-ju* were not well adapted to Chinese ways of thinking and they thus developed such concrete expressions as those noted above. Zen Buddhism uses highly evocative terms to create the type of concrete image which its teaching requires.

Thus for the human body the Zen term is *ch'ou-p'i-tai,* "stinking bag of skin." The Zen term for essence is *yen-mu,* "eye" or *yen-ching,* "the pupil of the eye." For a monastic community the Indian word is *saṅgha* or *gaṇa* which mean "group, conglomeration." Zen on the other hand uses the word *ts'ung-lin*[10] by which it means to suggest that the harmonious life of a monastic community is analogous to a thicket where trees and grasses grow together. The Zen term for an itinerant monk is *yün-shui,* "clouds and water" which, of course, graphically symbolizes the monks' lack of a fixed abode. This is in striking contrast to the less pictorial Indian term for medicant *parivrājaka,* "traveler."

The tendency suggested by these examples is not confined to Zen Buddhism. The founder of the San-lun sect expounded the fundamental teachings of Buddhism in concrete poetical terms of which the following is an example: "It has been a long time that the sweet drug (= the Buddha-nature) has dwelt in mountains (= the minds and bodies of individuals). A long period has elapsed since the round jewel (= the Buddha-nature) sank in water (= transmigrated). . . . May reflections be revealed in mirrors and may faces (= our proper selves) return to their proper places. Lost children (= sinful people) are those who have wandered a little from their native places."[11]

The use of concrete imagery is common not only to Buddhism but to Chinese philosophical writing in general.

Explanation by Means of Perceived Symbols

One of the most important characteristics of Chinese psychology is its reliance on sense-perception. They reluctantly dwell on that which is beyond the immediately perceived. In novels, for example, they tend to recreate the tangible world of sense-perception. Of course, there are exceptions such as the *Hsi-yu-chi* (Records of Travel in Western Regions) but works of this genre are far fewer and less influential than realistic writing.[12]

For the purposes of instruction and persuasion they resort to images that have the appeal of direct perceptions. For example, in the *Yen-shih chia-hsün* ("Family Instructions" by Yen Chih-t'ui) there is the following argument illustrative of this phenomena: "There are some who doubt the wonders and miracles accepted by the Buddhists. Such doubt is mistaken because there are things which may not lie within the field of our immediate perception but which may be perceived in the future. When I lived in South China, I could not believe that a tent existed which could cover a thousand people. But when I came to North China, I found such a tent. I, as a southerner, know very well that there are ships which can carry twenty thousand *tan* [*picul* or *tan* = 133½ lbs.] but northerners do not believe that such vessels can exist. It is the same with wonders and miracles." In conclusion Yen Chih-tui says: "What a man believes is only his ears and his eyes. Everything else is to be doubted."[13] This is an expression of a typical characteristic of Chinese thought. The Chinese in esteeming what is immediately perceptible—especially visually perceptible—seek intuitive understanding through direct perception. This tendency is reflected in the use of characters which convey concrete images to express abstract concepts; it is also revealed in the manner of elucidating philosophical doctrines. Thus, the use of diagrammatic explanation is frequently resorted to. A good example for it is the "Book of Changes" (*I-Ching*). In this work symbols are used as directly perceptible figures for a wide variety of phenomena, although they may also refer to non-perceptible concepts. Generally speaking, the Chinese have relied upon concrete perception, even in instruction or persuasion.

In Chinese perfection is often expressed as round. It is said, for example, that the heart of a sage is round.[14] In the translation of Buddhist scriptures into Chinese, the Indian word "perfect" was translated by "round and filled." The Sanskrit word *sampad*, "equipped with," was translated by the same compound. *Pariniṣpannalakṣaṇa*, the true "nature of all phenomena," was translated by Hsüan-tsang as *yüan-ch'eng shih-hsing* and in this case the word *yüan* (= round) was not expressed in the original Sanskrit term.[15] The most perfect doctrine in Buddhism was, in some systems, called "the round doctrine" (*yüan chiao*).[16] This equivalence between perfection and the circle, or the quality of roundness, was peculiar to the Chinese. It did not have such a meaning for the Indians. Roundness as used by Chinese Buddhists as a symbol of perfection—illustrating the concreteness of Chinese thought—was paralleled in the allegedly contrasting pattern of Indian thought by the wheel symbol. The wheel (*cakra*) was highly esteemed as the symbol of the perfect doctrine of the Buddha, or as an attribute of the God Vishnu. But in the figure of the Indian wheel the idea of motion was represented, while the circle is static. Moreover, the Indians regarded the absolute as without limits and therefore incapable of being represented in concrete symbols.

The Greeks regarded a sphere as the most perfect form of reality, and this attitude persisted through much of Greek philosophy.[17] But whereas the circle—symbol of perfection for the Chinese—is a plane, the Greek symbol is tri-dimensional. The Vaiśeṣika philosophy conceived an atom to be globular (*parimaṇḍala*) but the Chinese translator rendered this as *yüan t'i*, "circular."[18]

Even in expounding such an elaborate philosophical system as the *Hua-yen* its founder resorted to a visual demonstration of the close interrelationship of all phenomena by the use of ten mirrors facing inward at eight different angles and placed above and below with a Buddha figure in the middle.[19] His purpose was to elicit, through an immediate appeal to visual perception, an intuitive understanding of the nature of phenomena.

Diagramatic Explanation

In the course of the domestication of Buddhism in China there appeared a tendency to explain Buddhist doctrines by means of diagrams. *Fêng-kuei Tsung-mi* (780–841), a scholar of the *Hua-yen* sect explained the relation between the pure and the impure aspects of mind by a diagram in which the former was indicated by the sign ○ and the latter with the sign ●.

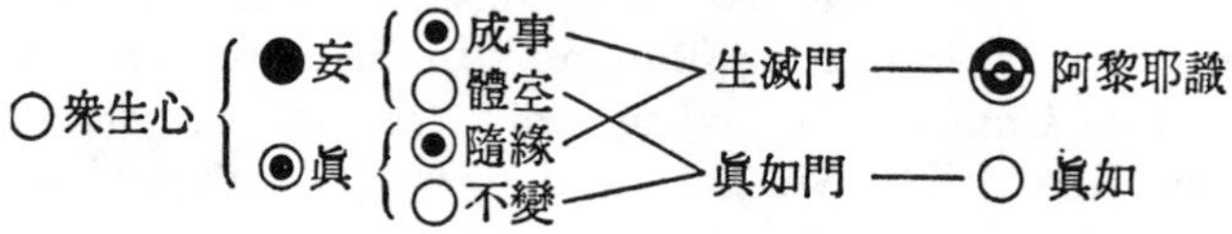

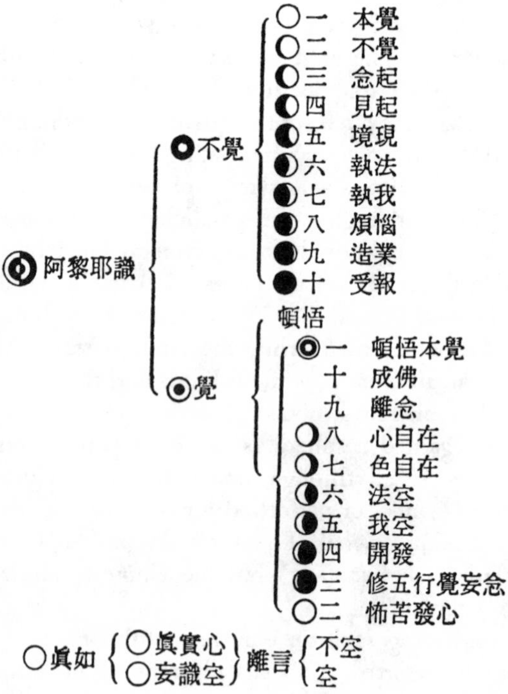

The fundamental essence of existence (*ālayavijñāna*) consists of pure and impure aspects. The process of development of a mundane creature is shown in ten stages and the means by which this existence is annulled and absorbed into reality is likewise explained in ten stages.[20]

The amalgamation of different kinds of visual arts was also characteristic of Chinese culture. For example, the Chinese custom of writing an appreciation or a panegyric on a painting did not exist in ancient Greece or in India. An example of a series of pictures accompanied with panegyrics in the Chinese Buddhist tradition is the Praises of the Mañjusrī's Diagramatic Teaching by Zen Master Fu-kuo.[21]

The same tendency manifested itself in Zen Buddhism. Tung-shan (807–869) lectured on the five stages. Behind this scheme there is a type of abstract speculation, but the disciple of this Zen master Ts'ao-shan pên-chi attempted to explain these five stages with diagrams and poems relating each stage to a hierarchical position between monarch and subject.[22] Here a set of abstract notions was explained by means of readily perceived imagery.[23] Still later this explanatory device was fused with explanations in terms of the symbols of the *I-Ching*,[24] the Book of Changes.

The tendency to explain Buddhist doctrines by diagrams came to be

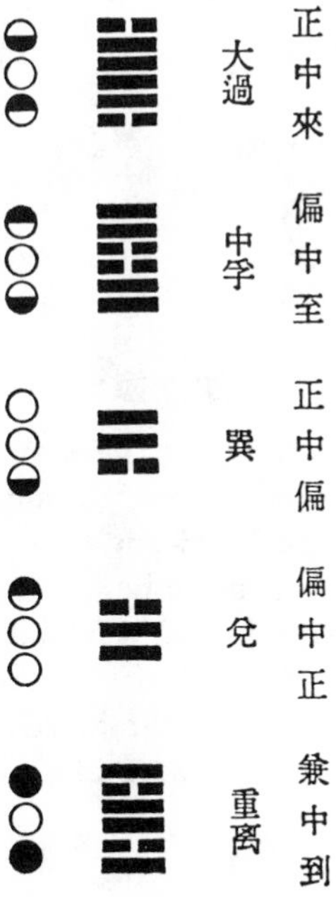

merged with traditional Chinese scholarship on the *I-Ching*. In Tung-shan's *Pao-ching San-mei-k'o* (Songs of Meditation called Jewelled Mirror), the Five Stages were explained in terms of "I-Ching" scholarship. Finally Hui-hung of the Sung period explained them with diagrams.

This tradition of diagramatic explanation exerted a great influence on Sung neo-Confucianism, and was manifested in the *"T'ai-chi-t'u"* by Chou Tun-yi (1017–1073). It has been surmised that in his diagram of the gestation of the universe he was influenced by Buddhism, although there are some scholars who doubt the influence. Anyhow, in explaining

the genesis of the universe he did not resort to abstractions of the Indian variety but introduced such concrete empirical principles as "*Yang* and *Yin*" or "man and woman."[25] It is interesting to note that the *Chou Tun-yi* (Diagram of the Supreme Ultimate) of neo-Confucianism in turn influenced Buddhism, and the theory of the five stages was modified and developed by it.[26]

In Zen Buddhism there appeared a diagram called the Poem of Reality. The twenty characters of the diagram are arranged in a circle as follows:[27]

The author advised the practitioner to meditate upon reality by means of these twenty characters. They express, or suggest, a variety of abstract notions but there is no indication of any logical connection among them.

Diagrams for explaining metaphysical theories are not found in Greece or in India where such theories were rather set forth in complicated series of sentences. The same tendency can be observed in the use of diagrammatic genealogies depicting the descent of doctrine from master to pupil,[28] while in India the same material is presented in dry prose.[29]

CHAPTER 16 NON-DEVELOPMENT OF ABSTRACT THOUGHT

Lack of Consciousness of Universals

We have seen that the Chinese esteemed the data of direct perception, especially visual perception, and that they were concerned with particular instances. This meant that they were little interested in universals which comprehend or transcend individual or particular instances. They thus seldom created a universal out of particulars.

In Chinese one finds many different words used to denote subtly shaded variations of the same thing or action. Thus, for example, the following words are used for different shadings of the action word "to carry": *tan, chih, jen, yün, pan, pao, tai, cho*. The same phenomenon can be seen in the languages of primitive peoples elsewhere. For example, in Malay there are many different words translatable simply as "carry" but which mean "to carry by hand," "to carry on a shoulder," "to carry on head," "to carry on the back," "to carry on the body, as a garment, a weapon, or an ornament," "to carry a child in the womb," etc.[1] Although one can see the residue of some such variety in Greek and English generally, such a range of variant verbs does not exist. It may be said that in these languages, unlike Malay, a high degree of universalization and abstraction has been reached.

Another example. In Chinese there is no word which corresponds to the English "old." For "sixty years or so" the Chinese word is *ch'i;* for "seventy years or more," the Chinese word is *tieh;* for "eighty or ninety years old" the Chinese character is *mao*. Similarly, different words were used to express the notions of death and to die. The term varied according to the status of the person concerned. For the Emperor it was *pêng;* for feudal lords it was *hung;* for grandees, soldiers, gentlemen, it was *pu-lu;* for the common people *ssŭ*.[2] We might draw the conclusion from such examples as these that the Chinese esteemed differences of rank more than they valued comprehending a group of related phenomena in a universal.

We do not mean that the Chinese completely lacked the concept of the universal. The existence of the concept of the universal among them is evidenced occasionally by the structure of the characters. For example, there are many words denoting different varieties of mountains, but these words include a common element *shan* which designates the universal of "mountain" or "mountainness."

The above mentioned argument is not proof that all Chinese philosophers were unconscious of a relationship between universals and particulars. Hsün-tzŭ had a rather clear notion of this.[3] He distinguished between common or general names (*kung-ming*) and particular names (*pieh-ming*). But he did not attain a full consciousness of "definition" as did Aristotle. He was not a logician by profession. Why should he have been? There was only one Aristotle! But lack of this consciousness in a Chinese philosopher so far advanced in logical thinking is symptomatic of the general lack of consciousness of *genus* and *differentia* in the abstract among the Chinese.

Of course, efforts were made to express concepts more clearly using compound words. This device aimed at making the meaning of the word clearer by defining the extent of the meaning through a second character. This is quite different from the Greek practice which aimed at making the meaning clearer by limiting the *genus* with *differentia.*

So, generally speaking, the notion of a universal and the ordering of particulars under universals are not characteristic of Chinese thought. The Chinese, on the whole, did not have a hierarchy of universals as did the Greeks and the Indians.

These phenomena may be explained by the fact that definitions and categories were formally expressed by gentlemen, not by ordinary people who had no need to indicate different meanings of "death" for differing ranks of people. These phenomena were not limited to Chinese alone, but can be noticed in Japanese also, in which educated people use more honorifics. Preference for polite diction among educated people can be seen in English also, but this feature was very common in Chinese usage in the past.

Grammatical Ambiguity of Chinese Language and Thought

The distinctive character of Chinese thought is intimately connected with the peculiarities of the Chinese language. Words corresponding to the prepositions, conjunctions, and relative pronouns of Western languages are very rare. There is no distinction between singular and plural. A single character (*jên*) can denote "a man, men, some men, or mankind." There are no fixed single terms for the expression of the tense or mood of verbs. There are no cases. One word can be noun, adjective, or verb. This kind of ambiguity explains why the exegesis of the classics has produced an immense variety of interpretations, many of which are directly opposite in sense to others.[4]

We should not expect then that the Chinese language would be as suitable as the Greek for philosophizing. If the use of plural forms were essential in philosophy, we should have to regard the Aryan languages as more suitable than the Chinese for philosophy. However, for many aspects of ethics or practical philosophy, the linguistic distinction of numbers is not necessary. But the distinction between the singular and the plural is indispensable for logical mathematical thought.

Because of this tendency toward ambiguity the Chinese had great difficulty in understanding the meaning of the Buddhist scriptures which had originally been written in an entirely different type of language. Because of the lack of number, gender, and case in Chinese pronouns, sentences in the Chinese version of Buddhist writings were misinterpretations. Misinterpretation is very often characteristic of translation from one language to another, but some of the misinterpretations thus produced were often very important in the doctrinal development of Chinese and Japanese Buddhism.

For example, the famous verse in which Nāgārjuna sets forth the concept of the middle way (*Madhyamaka śāstra,* XXIV, 18) as translated from Sanskrit runs as follows: "What do we mean by 'dependent origination' (that is, the inter-relatedness of all things)? We call it the void; that is an assumed hypothetical entity and that is the middle way." In this Nāgārjuna asserted that the four concepts—dependent origination, the void, an assumed being, the middle way—were synonymous. This verse was translated by Kumārajīva but later Chinese Buddhist scholars altered the wording of the sentences, and Hui-wen[5] explained the above verse as follows: All things have their causes. These causes are beings but not definite beings; they are devoid of all substance, and even description is not absolutely true, but hypothetical. It is this situation which is called "the middle way." The T'ien-t'ai sect explained the verse as teaching the three truths: all things have originated from causes and are destitute of individual essence, i.e. are void, but even "the void" is "hypothetical." We should not treat it as a substance; the void also should be negated. Thus this sect set up the three truths, the void, the hypothetical, and the middle way.[6] This variety of interpretations—involving possible misinterpretation—is attributable to the lack of gender, number, or case notation in the demonstrative pronoun, although this kind of misunderstanding by misinterpreting an abstract text is not confined to Chinese thought.

Because there are no plural forms of Chinese nouns, various devices are used to express the plural: adding numerals to nouns, e.g. *wu-jen, ch'ien-jen;* reduplication e.g., *jen-jen;* the addition of a character such as *chu* to nouns, e.g. *chu-jen*. Moreover the character *têng* can be used as a suffix expressing the plural, but it can mean *"et cetera."* For example, *nui-têng* may mean "oxen" or "oxen and horses and sheep." When the Chinese came in contact with Sanskrit they recognized the difference between a plural and *et cetera*. Chinese Buddhist scholars differentiated the pluralizing *têng,* namely, *hsiang-nei-têng* from the *"et cetera" têng* which they called *hsiang-wai-têng*. However, this distinction did not go beyond Buddhist scholarship. It was never used in secular thought.

Another syntactical ambiguity of Chinese is reflected in the frequency of anacolutha or change of subject within a sentence. In Sanskrit this occurs only in such ancient literature as the Brāhmaṇas,[7] whereas in Chinese it is very common because Chinese frequently omits the subject of a sentence.[8] In the Chinese versions of Buddhist scriptures anacoluthon is common even though it is rare in the Sanskrit originals from which those versions were translated. It is especially conspicuous in Kumārajīva's translations which are famous for their style—their appeal to Chinese literary taste and habitual ways of thinking.[9]

The various ambiguities described have meant that Chinese has been an awkward medium for expressing abstract thought. Although there is evidence of metaphysical speculation in the Taoist writings there is little of this in the Confucian tradition which long dominated the thinking of the ruling class. In the *Analects* of Confucius there are many separate examples of moral conduct from which certain lessons are inductively drawn. There are many aphorisms, but there is no dialectic such as one finds in Plato. This may be natural, for the *Analects* represents the beginning of philosophy in Chinese, but, even if compared with the fragments of the pre-Socratic philosophers, the sayings of Confucius (all handed down by later disciples) are less metaphysical. *I Ching* scholarship was often, in later times, united with metaphysics, but the *I Ching* itself—full of suggestive explanations of human events—did not itself aim at metaphysics. Metaphysical theory developed later. Tung Chung-shu, in the first century A.D., has metaphysics galore, although it might not be called such by some scholars. With Neo-Confucianism metaphysical speculation was brought to perfection. But even with this school, philosophizing was, as we have seen, still figurative and intuitive.

The lack of the controversial spirit of dialogue in ancient China is noteworthy, although it is still problematic whether dialectic is necessary to philosophy. The dialectic—the art of questioning and answering as a device for philosophical analysis—did not develop as it had in Greece. Western sinologues[10] often assert that the dialectic is present in the rules of discourse given by Mo-tzŭ,[11] but we have too little data on the application of these rules to establish the existence of a true dialectic.

In India it was long a custom for the assertor and the objector to argue with each other in a public assembly sponsored by a great personage. In China this practice of public debate was relatively rare. It occurred for a short period in the sixth and seventh centuries.[12] Likewise, Chinese court-procedure[13] was not characterized by the development of judicial dialogue between the accused and the accuser. The reason is that the Chinese judge was not an arbitrator between two groups, but an official who took evidence from both sides, then sent out his own underlings to examine the truth of the statements made by both sides. That is to say, Chinese court-procedure was not the same as that in the West.[14] The almost total absence of this type of phenomenon in Chinese society meant that a great deal of Indian logic, which in origin was a logic of dialogue, had no significance for the Chinese. For this reason Indian logic could not be taken over in its original form by the Chinese.

Lack of Conscious Use of General Laws

It was perhaps a result in part of the non-generalizing nominalistic characteristic of Chinese thought which we have described, that the Chinese tradition was weak in the formation of objective laws. The esteem for the individual and the concrete, a lack of interest in universals, aborted the discovery of laws which order many particulars. This parallels the lack of strict laws for linguistic expression. *Indifference to or lack of consciousness of the necessity for rules of language meant that the grammar was not developed.* Unlike the Greeks and the Indians, the ancient Chinese produced no works on grammar or syntax, although they engaged in elaborate investigations and compilations of characters, phonetics, etymology, etc. Even though some Chinese pilgrim monks became acquainted with the Indian science of grammar, they did not attempt to establish a parallel science of Chinese grammar. The science of grammar was very important in the history of Indian philosophy, whereas a scientific grammar was developed in China only after the impact of Western civilization.

In ancient times China was ahead of many other countries in the field of natural sciences. The Chinese have been most observant of religious rites and have taken utmost care in calendrical regulations.[15] It is likely that Chinese mathematics developed independently of India's although there may have been some influence from the latter.[16]

The Chinese did much with mathematics. They developed the decimal system for counting and used it in computations as early as the first century

B.C. Chinese herbals and early botanical works are oustanding. The Chinese did not develop the same sort of scientific work that the Indians and the Japanese did, but pursued the sciences in their own way. However, Chinese sciences were finally surpassed by modern ones of the West. One of the reasons may be the fact that up to a point, Chinese investigative study can be called inductive. The Chinese sought for precedents and facts but induction ceased at a certain point and deduction based on the authority of the classics then took over.[17] This is a partial explanation of the non-development of purely experimental or deductive science in China.

In Sung neo-Confucianism "ordered intuition into the essence of things" was esteemed, but this was not natural cognition nor particularly objective cognition; it was rather a quest for the essence of all things.[18] When one adopts the standpoint of "intuitionism," necessary truth is difficult to prove to others with different intuitions.

In the Chinese Buddhist tradition there is no single authoritative interpretation of a given phrase. Chinese Buddhist scholars produced different and varied interpretations of the same phase. Rather than compel a uniform belief they interpreted phrases very freely. Zen Buddhism carried this to extremes enunciating the principle "not to set up any words." Similarly, "if our mind goes astray we are ruled by the *Lotus-Sūtra*. If our mind is enlightened, we rule the *Lotus-Sūtra*."[19] "Not to set up any words" does not mean "do not resort to the use of the written word," for there were few sects which used and valued literary expression as much as the Zen sect. The term therefore means, rather, "do not set up dogmas in the form of propositions."

Zen Buddhists, with this attitude, denied the importance of the Buddhist canon. They compared the canon to fingers pointing at the moon; they also used the simile of which the Taoists were fond, and compared the Buddhist canon to fish-nets and rabbit-traps;[20] in other words, one should concentrate on the content and not place great value on the literary meaning of apprehending that content.

Chinese dislike for canonical formulae can be seen in the process of their acceptance of various Buddhist arts.[21] Although the Chinese built many Buddhist monuments and reliquaries they cannot be classified into canonical types. In the case of Buddhist images there were formulae for making images and such formulae were carefully followed in Japan, but they were not followed in China and one cannot classify surviving Chinese Buddha images according to these type-forms. For example, in China a Buddha image holding a medicine vessel is not always *Bhaiṣajyaguruta-thāgata* and his image is not always accompanied by this object. Buddha images were made arbitrarily in whatever form the artist desired. This feature is regarded as a virtue by individualistic thinkers and amateurs of art.

Acceptance of Indian Logic in a Distorted Form

Since nomothetical sciences did not develop in China, it is natural that logic which deals with the laws for the expression of thought did not develop either.

A certain degree of logical consciousness naturally existed among the Chinese, but they did not build upon that consciousness "a logical science." Some scholars assert that deductive argumentation—if not logic—was developed by the followers of Mo-tzŭ and termed *hsiao* (testing).[22] In my view, it is doubtful that this term really coincides with what is known in the West as deduction.[23]

In later times Indian logic was introduced into China, but it exerted no significant influence on the ways of thinking of the Chinese. It soon declined and disappeared as a branch of study.

In some Buddhist works translated into Chinese there are passages on logic; for example, the *Upāyahṛdaya* translated by Kiṃkara, the work translated by Paramārtha,[24] the *Nyāyamukha* of Dignāga translated by Hsüan-tsang (596–664), and the *Nyāyapraveśaka* also translated by Hsüan-tsang. The commentary upon the last work by a disciple of Hsüan-tsang, Tz'u-ên, was regarded as the highest authority in this field in China and Japan. After Hsüan-tsang at least thirty works were composed on Buddhist logic.[25]

In the history of the introduction of Buddhist logic into China we can observe several striking phenomena. First, very few logical works were translated into Chinese. If we compare that number with the vastly larger number of such works which were translated into Tibetan, we are bound to conclude that interest in Buddhist logic was very slight among the Chinese. Secondly, only logical works of the simplest kind were translated into Chinese and voluminous works intended to be systematic expositions of the whole science of logic were left untranslated. It would appear that the Chinese translated simple handbooks or compendia, the bare minimum necessary to get a rudimentary knowledge of the logical terminology of Buddhist treatises in general. Thirdly, Indian works on epistemology which attempted to develop a theory of knowledge as a basis of knowledge for logical theory were not translated. Perhaps the ultimate development of Buddhist logic in India was accomplished by Dharmakīrti. He sought the source of human knowledge in perception and reasoning. He differentiated between synthetic and analytical judgments. On this basis he established an elaborate system—a science of knowledge. His system has often been compared to that of Kant. The Tibetans translated and studied Dharmakīrti's works, whereas the Chinese Buddhists made no effort to study or to understand them. Even after Dharmakīrti the Chinese translated earlier works, mainly on discipline and ritual. For this reason it is perhaps justifiable to say that the Chinese did not seek theory for theory's sake but rather gave their attention to that which was immediately relevant to practical understanding and conduct.

Thus Indian logic was accepted only in part and even the part that was accepted was not understood in the sense of the Indian originals. Even Hsüan-tsang, who introduced Indian logic, seems not to have fully understood it. In a great assembly in India he made the inference that mind alone really exists while objects in the external world do not exist. In developing his argument he violated the rule of Indian logic which holds that the proposition "reason" should be one which is admitted by both assertor and opponent. Under this heading he set forth a proposition which was only agreed to by the assertor.[26] Tz'u-ên's work, which was regarded as the highest authority in China and Japan, contains many fallacies in philosophical and logical analysis.[27] He apparently did not understand the Indian rule that in syllogisms the middle term should be distributed by the major term. The formula of the new Buddhist logic was called the three-membered syllogism and it consisted of assertion, reason, and simile.[28] Some Chinese Buddhist scholars understood this,[29] but Tz'u-ên misunderstood it, asserting that it consisted of reason and similes of likeness and unlikeness.[30] This mistake in interpretation became henceforth authoritative in China and Japan.

In Chinese Buddhist scriptures *ratio essendi* (kāraka hetu) is translated as *sheng-yin* and *ratio cognoscendi* (jñāpaka hetu) as *liao-yin*.[31] But Tz'u-ên failed to understand the distinction and connected both concepts with the three concepts of *yen* (words), *shih* (knowledge), and *yi* (meaning).[32] In doing this he simply made a mechanical classification and his explanation is self-contradictory as well as at odds with the original meaning. His application of logical rules in elucidating the idealist philosophy (the "mind-only" theory) was utterly fallacious. This fact was pointed out even by early Japanese Buddhist scholars such as Genshin, Rinjō, and Kaijō.[33]

There is a further fundamental difference between Indian logicians and Chinese Buddhist scholars. Indian Buddhist scholars of the logical school accepted perception and reasoning as the sole sources of right knowledge; they denied independent authority to the Canon in this field whereas Chinese scholars of Buddhist logic accepted the authority of the Canon.

Even the sort of limited logical study carried on by the sect of idealism, the followers of Tz'u-ên, declined when this sect declined. It was only in the T'ang dynasty that logical studies had any vitality.

Logical studies having no basis in traditional Chinese thought never became significant and exerted very little influence on later Chinese thought. Most Chinese scholars merely accepted the authority of the Canon. This fact will probably betray a weakness in logical thinking on the part of scholars. It should be noted that this is in striking contrast to the importance and vitality of logical studies in Tibet.

The Non-Logical Character of Zen Buddhism

The non-logical character of Chinese thought is particularly conspicuous in Zen Buddhism, which is the most sinicized of Chinese Buddhist sects. Early Zen was not non-logical. The early system of explanation known as "the two enlightenments and four practices"[34] was quite logical and even later the dialogue of Hui-hai is characterized by logical consistency.[35]

However, a non-logical tendency soon manifested itself and eventually prevailed. The monk Huang-po said[36] ". . . they say that the true universal body of the Buddha is like the sky . . . but they do not understand that the universal body is sky, and sky is the universal body. The two are not different." Now the Buddha nature or the originally pure mind were often compared to the sky in India. But the Indians regarded the sky as an element or principle in the natural world, and distinguished it from the Buddha nature, whereas the Chinese lost sight of this distinction. When there is a tendency to lose sight of the function and significance of a simile, theoretical philosophy is unlikely to develop. Moreover, theoretical assertions were neither widely understood nor was their meaning developed. For example, Lin-chi's (? –867 A.D.) four alternatives are philosophically important and allow many different explanations. Their author did not, however, discuss them in an abstract speculative way. He explained them in figurative language: "(1) 'To take away man and not to take away objects'—warm days appear and brocade is laid out on the earth—baby's hairs falling are like thread. (2) 'To take away objects and not to take away man'—the king's orders are promulgated and circulate over the empire; generals take their ease outside the stronghold. (3) 'To take away both men and objects'—to live in a retreat cut off from all communication. (4) 'Not to take away either men or objects'—a king ascends to a jeweled palace and old peasants sing gaily."[37] The point in this quotation is not that figurative explanations are given but that figurative explanations alone are given. Poetical and emotional phrases take the place of logical exposition. Later explanations of these four alternatives were generally of the same sort.

The non-logical character of Zen is most evident in its dialogues. We have said that the spirit and technique of the dialogue did not develop in China, so it is important to emphasize that the so-called dialogues of Zen were utterly different from Greek dialogues. When Chao-chou (c. 850 A.D.) was asked "Does the Buddha nature exist in a dog?" he answered in the affirmative on one occasion and in the negative on another. Mo-tzŭ said on one occasion "Mind is the Buddha" and on another occasion "Neither mind nor Buddha."[38] The reasons for these contradictory answers are to be found in the concrete situations which elicited them. We may compare this to the different advice given by doctors to patients of different physical types suffering from the same disease. There is an obvious contradiction in the theoretical sense but no contradiction in the practical sense. This is an example of the aspect of expediency in Buddhist thought.

However, in the type of thought which is called expedient, there is a definite connection between the end desired and the means employed. Later Zen Buddhism gradually lost sight of that connection. For example, there is a frequently repeated question in Zen Buddhism: "For what purpose did Bodhidharma come to China?" It really means something like "What is the essence of Zen Buddhism?" To this question Zen masters give a variety of answers:[39]

"I am tired, having been sitting for a long time."

"Today and tomorrow."

"A piece of tile and a bit of stone."

"The wind blows and the sun heats."

"Frost comes upon clouds."

"An oak tree in the garden."

"In the daytime I see a mountain."

"White clouds embrace rocky stones."

"Ch'ang-an [a large city] is in the East, Lo-yang [another large city] is in the West."

"With a fan of blue silk, I feel cool enough in the wind."

"A thousand sticks of bamboo outside the gate and a piece of incense before the image of Buddha."

"There being no water during a long drought, rice plants withered in the fields."

There are said to be more than a hundred answers to this question. Since no semantic connection between the questions and the answers was required, the answers can be of infinite variety. The question and the answer are given in a moment. There is no sustained development such as characterizes Greek dialogue. The answers seem strange indeed, but it is said that many of those who heard the answers gained enlightenment. Zen masters never answered questions in the form of universal propositions.[40] They believed the philosophical problems could best be solved by evoking intuition. They gave answers in a figurative and intuitive way. This form of question and answer was more prevalent in later Zen Buddhism from the Sung period (960–1279) on.

This whole complex of ideas and practices is alien to Indian Buddhism. The *dharmas,* that is, universal religious and moral norms, were seen in China not as the content of judgments shared by other people, but as the direct experience of each individual, inexpressible in words. Yung-chia said of himself "Since my youth I was devoted to scholarship. I investigated sūtras and commentaries. Nothing but an endless discrimination of terms! It is like counting the sands in the sea. The Buddha reprimanded me saying 'What is the use of counting the treasures of others?' "[41]

Once they had given up the effort to grasp and to express truths in the form of universal propositions, the Zen Buddhists gradually fell into the habit of non-logical discourse. Chu Hsi (1130–1200) pointed out that Zen masters at first engaged in very clear dialogues but later became complacent, enmeshed in nonsensical dialogues.[42] Chu Hsi himself had this in common with the Zen masters: he never gave exact answers. The later Zen masters did not seek to give explanations in rational terms; they sought rather to give them in a figurative and intuitive way.

A commentary by Wan-sung (1166–1246) to an ancient dialogue by Bodhidharma runs as follows: (the comments are given in brackets) "Emperor Wu of the Liang inquired of Bodhidharma [he got up early and went to market without making any profit.] 'What is the ultimate reality, the sacred truth?' [now ask the second head.] Bodhidharma said 'That where there is no sacredness at all.' [He has split open the abdomen and dug out the heart.] The Emperor said 'Who is talking with me?' [We can perceive a tusk inside the nostril.] Bodhidharma said 'I don't know.' [We can see the jowls behind the brains.] The Emperor could not agree with him. [A square peg cannot go into a round hole.] Finally, Bodhidharma crossed the Yang-tse River and went to the Shao-lin temple where he practiced meditation for nine years. [If a family does not have overdue rent it cannot be rich.]"[43]

Though this dialogue itself has a hidden logic of its own, we can see from this bracketed commentary the tendency in later Zen to use explanations made up of concrete images of a suggestive kind.

CHAPTER 17 EMPHASIS ON THE PARTICULAR

Emphasis on Particular Instances

The tendency to value and to devote attention to the particular rather than to the universal is observable in many different aspects of Chinese culture.

The Five Classics, which are works of the highest authority regarded as providing the norms for human life, contain, for the most part, descriptions of particular incidents and statements of particular facts. They do not state general principles of human behavior.[1] Even the *Analects* of Confucius records mostly the actions of individuals and the dicta of Confucius on separate incidents; these dicta for the most part have a personal significance. Through the classics and their commentaries the Chinese sought valid norms of moral conduct through individual instances.

The Chinese way of esteeming concrete particulars did not let the Indian Buddhist mythology, with its fanciful creations of the imagination, stand in that form. The Chinese modified the Indian phantasmagoric myths, so remote from historical reality, so that the mythological beings were identified respectively with actual historical persons (euhemerism). Thus, for example, the Buddhist divinity Yama, King of Hell, or Yen-lo in Chinese, became identified with a Sui dynasty official who died in 592 A.D.[2]

Buddhism, which had set forth, in the Indian manner, general and universal principles, was often presented to the Chinese through concrete examples and individual instances.

Zen explanations were of this sort. The true nature of the Buddha comes not in words but only through concrete experience. Ethics is grasped on the basis of particular experiences. Universal truth is in the human being and not in a universal proposition. (By contrast, Indians mostly resorted to universal propositions.)

The most frequent example of this development is the mode of explanation developed by Zen Buddhism. "A priest asked Tung-shan: 'What is Buddha?' He replied 'Only three pounds of hemp.'" Yuan-wu of the Sung dynasty explained this as follows.[3] "Many people have given different explanations of this. Some say that Tung-shan was weighing hemp when he was asked the question. Others say that he is inclined to answer west when asked about the east [i.e., he was inclined to answer in an unexpected way]. Others say, 'Originally you yourself are Buddha whereas the questioner sought for Buddha outside himself; in order to tell him how silly he was, Tung-shan answered in an elliptical way.' Other silly people say that the three pounds of hemp themselves are nothing but Buddha. These answers have nothing to do with Tung-shan's purport." Then what is the true meaning of the answers? Yuan-wu is evasive, saying, "The true way cannot be obtained by words." In these explanations and Yuan-wu's comment we can see a distinctive feature of the Chinese way of thinking, i.e., the true way is not to be obtained by words—not through universal propositions—but only through concrete experience. Thus, one *should not regard the Buddha as something mystical and transcending ordinary life.*

Nāgārjuna had expressed a similar idea. He said that the long sequence of discussions on the essence of the Buddha did not reveal that essence. He said "The Buddha transcends all metaphysical discussions and is indestructible; yet those who discuss it fail to see the Buddha, being blinded by their own sophistication."[4] According to him, in every experience we experience Buddha. "The true essence of Buddha is nothing but that of this mundane world." This thought coincides in meaning with that of Tung-shan. But the difference between the Indian and the Chinese ways of thinking lies in the difference in the expression of that meaning. Whereas Nāgārjuna taught in the form of universal propositions, the Chinese did not do so but produced the concrete example of the three pounds of hemp.

We can see much the same contrast in the differing sorts of answers to questions about life after death. "A monk asked, 'Where did Nan-ch'ūan go after he died?' The master replied 'In an eastern house he became an ass, and in a western house he became a horse.'" This answer did not mean that he had been reborn as an ass or a horse. "The monk asked, 'What do you mean by this?' The master said, 'If he wants to ride he can ride, if he wants to get off he can get off.'"[5] This means that the deceased had attained the freedom to do what he wanted, having transcended life and death. Let us compare this with the answer to a comparable question in early Buddhism. When the Buddha was asked whether the Enlightened One existed after death, he did not give any answer to the question because, as the Sūtras say, discussion and speculation about such metaphysical problems could not lead men to enlightenment. Thus, not giving any answer is a kind of definite answer and is logically conceived. Here we can see the difference in ways of thinking between these two peoples.

Explanation on the Basis of Particular Instances

The way of thinking in which the Chinese prefer particular, concrete, and intuitive explanations may be seen in their way of explaining ideas and teaching people by the use of particular examples. To most Chinese, therefore, ethics is not understood or taught as part of a universal law, but is grasped on the basis of particular experiences, and is then utilized to realize human truth. Such a mental attitude is readily discernible in the Analects (*Lun Yü*), and especially in Zen Buddhism. Men are placed in special circumstances limited by time and space, and their experiences are changing every moment, which means that no two people can have exactly the same experience. There is a limit to collective experience. The particular situation in which the individual finds himself is called "*Chi*" by Zen Buddhism. The idea of "*Chi*" is characteristically Chinese, for we cannot find its exact equivalent in India.[6]

Next, I wish to relate, as a concrete case of a Kōan, the "Chü Chih Shu Chih"—Chü Chih's erect finger. Chü Chih was a disciple of the monk T'ien-lung. When asked about the most important matters of life and death, he would reply always by showing his finger. Later, a boy who was studying under him imitated his master's manner of showing his finger when he was asked by a stranger about his master's teaching. When Chü Chih heard of his conduct, he cut off the boy's finger. The boy went away crying, unable to endure the pain. He then called the boy back. The boy came back and saw his master unexpectedly show an erect finger. At that instant, the boy attained enlightenment. Chü Chih said at the time of his death, "I was taught Zen in a finger tip by my master, and have been unable to exhaust it all during my life-time."[6a]

I think this catechism is an admonition that one should not pretend to have attained enlightenment if one has not actually done so. I should like to make a comparison here with an Indian case. In the Vinaya-Piṭaka of Hīnayāna Buddhism, *uttari-manussa-dhamma* is thought to be one of the four terrible sins for a monk. This means that one who has not attained the superior stage, should not pretend that he has.

Indians generally liked to express the truth about human beings with a universal proposition, while the Chinese did not like to do so. The Chinese made an effort to realize the universal truth in the human being and revealed in particular instances which cannot be altered by factors of both time and space. When Fa-ch'ang, a famous monk of Zen Buddhism, gathered his disciples at his death, and finished giving his final instructions to them, they heard a flying squirrel cry out, whereupon he said, "That's it! Nothing but it! Retain this well. I am going to die soon."[7]

In Zen Buddhism, they call the particular cases "*Chi.*" It is said that an enlightened man knows "*Chi*" and utilizes expedients. It should not be called merely "Chance" or "Contingency," but should be thought of as something containing a purpose in which subject and object are in both opposition and correspondence to each other. It freely shows an adaptability to each situation. Generally speaking, it means that "one should be the master in every situation." Thus, Zen Buddhism aims at a suitable mind activity for each situation, i.e., an intuitive action "correctly manifested." Therefore, it is said that although the act of ridding oneself of mind and body is rather easy, it is difficult to express in words.[8] It is thought that we must remove deep attachments and prejudice, must be "mindless" in order to take measures suited to the occasion, and must have a "free flexibility" in order to have an adequate cognition suitable to the situation and time.

Development of Descriptive Science in Regard to the Particular

The Chinese lay stress especially on particular facts in the historical and social spheres, as the result of their emphasis on the concrete, including phenomena which are perfectly unique in time and space.

In the historical sphere, this trend may be observed in the objective and minute compilation of historical works. It is said that the ideal of the compilers of the *Erh Shih Ssu Shih* (Twenty-four Dynastic Histories up to the Manchu Dynasty) was as exhaustive an entry as possible of the incidents occurring in each dynasty. In the opinion of specialists this ideal is impossible to achieve, granted that Chinese historians were very succinct. But the fact of the existence of such a legendary ideal evidences their inclination to aim at portraying individual events in detail. Moreover, it is recognized that Chinese historians continually tried to enlarge and perfect their historical annals, and were always at work on supplements which would include materials omitted from the standard histories. Therefore, they think that the more complex the description is, the better the historical work is. Such a method of describing history is just the opposite of the method which aims at simple and concise description. Of course, we can also recognize the trend of summarization and simplification, but it was more usual to take the method of making the historical records more complex through the compilation of histories.[9] Therefore, some Westerners criticize such history books and say that they are elaborate, encyclopedic, and almost impossible to read through.[10] But even the Western scholar who believes in the superiority of Greek culture cannot help acknowledging that the Chinese history books are not only minute but also accurate and objective.

"A l'autre bout de notre continent eurasiatique, la Chine offre à notre désir d'information de prestigieuses annales, d'une objectivité hors pair, que pourrait lui jalouser notre propre culture."[11]

The Chinese made an effort to preserve the historical materials which are apt to be destroyed. They collected many kinds of epitaphs and produced such works as the *Chin Shih Ts'ui Pien* and the *Pa Ch'iung Shih Chin Shih Pu Chêng* which is a bulky work of 130 volumes. In India, we cannot find such materials as these.

Moreover, they made every effort to record climatic features and peculiarities, and produced many kinds of book catalogues like the *Ssu K'u Ch'üan Shu Tsung Mu* (The Complete Library of the Four Treasuries) in 200 volumes. So many catalogues of books have been made that we even find "catalogues of catalogues."[12]

Such phenomena are just the opposite of what holds true for India. As mentioned above, Indians wrote few historical books, and even these have contents which are largely legendary. Indians have seldom produced topographies, much less catalogues of books. The Indian paid attention chiefly to universals, neglecting historical and climatic particularities, while the Chinese, on the contrary, attached great importance to these. For this reason the descriptive sciences of particulars reached a high level of development in China. According to the philosophy of Rickert, the designation "idiographic science" is applied to that kind of descriptive science which treats non-recurring historical phenomena. If we allow this term to include peculiarities of space and climate, then it is most applicable to the studies made by the Chinese.

The Chinese way of thinking in their descriptive studies of particulars limited their acceptance of Indian Buddhism when it went contrary to Chinese attitudes. When accepting Buddhism, the Chinese did not neglect historical reflection and self-examination, and valued highly historical works on Buddhism and biographies of Buddhists, translating them into Chinese. In India also, history books and biographies were composed, though their contents were not too accurate, but these were lost because the Indians cared little for them. The *I Pu Tsung Lun Lun,* for instance, which describes the process of the formation of sects of Hīnayāna Buddhism in India was translated into Chinese three times. Besides, biographies of King Aśoka, the Buddhist philosophers, Aśvaghoṣa, Nāgārjuna, Āryadeva, Vasubandhu and others, all of which are legendary, were translated into Chinese.[13] The originals of these works have all been lost, and their translations also for the most part do not survive.[14]

As Indian historical works and biographies were few in number, the

Chinese themselves tried to write a history of Indian Buddhism. The result of these efforts is the *Fu Fa Tsang Yin Yüan Chuan* in three volumes. This is a description of the transmission of the True Teaching from the first Patriarch Mahākāśyapa to Buddhasiṁha, the twenty-third Patriarch. It is presumed that this work was completed by T'an-yao, and is based on the accounts transmitted by Kiṁkara, a monk from Central Asia, with occasional reference to the Indian "Biographies."[15] Thus, many books were produced describing the order of the transmission of the teaching from masters to disciples ranging over India and China. Sêng-hsiang, a Buddhist monk of the T'ang dynasty, compiled a Record of the Transmission of the Lotus Sūtra (*Fa Hua Ching Chuan Chi*) in 10 volumes. Similarly Fa-tsang of the T'ang dynasty wrote the *Hua Yen Ching Chuan Chi* (Record of the Transmission of the Avataṁsaka-sūtra) in five volumes, and Shih-hêng in the Sung dynasty compiled the *T'ien T'ai Chiu Tsu Chuan* (Biographies of the Nine Patriarchs of the T'ien T'ai School) in one volume; yet it was Zen Buddhists who turned out history books on the largest scale: *Ching Tê Chuan Têng Lu* (Record of the Transmission of the Lamp) in 30 volumes by Tao-yüan of the Sung dynasty, and *Fo Tsu T'ung Chi* (Record of the Genealogy of Buddhist Patriarchs) in 54 volumes by Chih-p'an of the Sung period. Besides, numerous collections of biographies of Chinese Buddhist monks were compiled from the sixth century to modern times. More than a hundred volumes of such biographical records were compiled by monks, principally by Chih-p'an, Hsieh-ch'ung (also of the Sung period) in 9 volumes, Nien-ch'ang (of the Yüan period, 1279–1367) in 22 volumes, Chiao-an (of the Ming period) in 4 volumes; also Tao-hsüan (of the T'ang period) in 30 volumes, Tsan-ning and others (of the Sung period) in 30 volumes, Ju-hsing, etc. I-tsing (of the T'ang period) in two volumes collected the lives of famous monks who went to Central Asia or India to study Buddhism, after his own travels in India and Sumatra (671–695).

The Indians, when compiling short treatises into a larger work, were apt to omit their titles and the names of their authors. Such works as the *Mahābhārata* and the *Abhidharma-mahā-vibhāṣā-śāstra* are examples of this. In China, however, each title, the authors' names and careers, etc., of the short treatises contained in the larger books were carefully preserved. Books like the *Hung Ming Chi,* the *Kuang Hung Ming Chi,* and the *Yao Pang Wên Lei* are good examples.

In this way, the Chinese, trying to understand matters historically on the basis of particular individuals, would accept even the founder Śākyamuni as a historical person. That explains the fact that Sêng-yu, a Buddhist monk of the Sung dynasty, compiled and arranged many records of biographies of the Buddha under the title *Shih Chia P'u* in 5 or 6 volumes, and Tao-hsüan, a Buddhist monk of the T'ang dynasty, edited the *Shih Chia Shih P'u* in one volume. It was a matter of great importance when, where, and to whom Śākyamuni taught the sūtras which were translated into Chinese. Therefore, they tried to relate each sūtra to a period in Śākyamuni's lifetime. The *"Wu Shih Chiao P'an"* devised by the Chinese scholar T'ien-t'ai is a typical example of this. According to modern textual criticism, we know that the sūtras were all produced in a later period, so that efforts to determine who uttered them are meaningless. Yet, Chinese Buddhist scholars at that time believed that these theories were correct. Thus the Chinese scholars at least showed their interest in particulars, more so than the Indians. We can say that the dominant object of the Chinese scholars' worship and faith was Śākyamuni, which probably was the result of their emphasis on historical matters. Even if there were some statues of Vairocana as an object of their worship, they were exceptions. They made it a rule to enshrine the statue of Amitābha in the west, Maitreya or Yao Shih Ju Lai in the east, with Śākyamuni as the central figure in the grand hall of the temple.

They usually install statues of Kāśyapa and Ānanda, the two great Arahats; but Mañjuśrī and Samantabhadra, the two great Bodhisattvas, often replace these. Śākyamuni, having these Buddhas as attendants, might be considered as a Sambhoga-kāya (a model body), i.e., a Buddha endowed with all the virtues of Buddha, by most Buddhists. Thus, we can see the tendency to regard Śākyamuni as a historical person by virtue of the fact that they enshrine the two great disciples, Kāśyapa and Ānanda. That is an important difference between Chinese and Japanese Buddhism.[16] Thus, the objects of worship in most Japanese temples, though they are not all the same, are originally Amitābha, Vairocana, Bhaiṣajyaguru, and Śākyamuni. Śākyamuni, however, had already been considered not so much a historical person as a Tathāgata (the Truth-Revealer) of Original Wisdom, namely as a Sambhoga-kāya Buddha.

There is also a tendency among the Chinese to emphasize spatial and climatic particularities. The *Fo Tsu T'ung Chi,* previously mentioned, contains two volumes on topography, entitled the *Shih Chieh Ming T'i Chih.* Records of travels written by Buddhist pilgrims who traveled to Central Asia and to India from China contain considerable geographical and climatic descriptions. The *Ta T'ang Hsi Yü Chi* (Records of the Western Regions During the T'ang Period), in 12 volumes by Hsüan Tsang is well known for its accuracy in geographical descriptions, even when compared to modern surveys. Chinese pilgrims tried to hand down detailed topographies of India although the Indians themselves did not.

Another manifestation of the tendency to emphasize particularity, as seen in the form of the acceptance of Buddhism, is the publishing of catalogues of sūtras. In the first stage, the catalogues of sūtras were only very simple lists of the sūtras found in libraries which were owned by Buddhist monks, devotees, scholars, and others. In addition, catalogues of sūtras were made to preserve the record of the achievements of Buddhist translators for posterity. Eventually, such catalogues were brought together, the many surviving catalogues of the Buddhist canon being their result. These evolved from the catalogues made for the convenience of individual scholars in their study, and included the contents of the catalogues possessed by each temple at that time. The compilers examined as carefully as possible the titles of sūtras, names of translators, dates of translation, etc., and strove to list all sūtras translated into Chinese. *Tsung Li Chung Ching Mu Lu* in one volume, which was edited by Tao-an in 374 A.D., was the first such catalogue. Fifteen kinds of catalogues were compiled by the T'ang dynasty.[17]

CHAPTER 18 CONSERVATISM EXPRESSED IN EXALTATION OF ANTIQUITY

Importance Attached to Past Events

There is a tendency in some Chinese ways of thinking to understand phenomena statically, which can be seen in certain modes of expression in the Chinese language. For example, in Chinese there is no single word capable of expressing precisely the meaning of "to become" as there is in modern European languages. The character "ch'êng" which is used by Japanese philosophers as an equivalent for "become" originally meant "accomplish," i.e. "a single phenomenon or thing is brought to a more advanced stage and this has accomplished its object," and, therefore, does not have precisely the same meaning as "become." The character "wei" is indeed used with the meaning of "to become," but it was employed as a copulative "to be" as well as "do" and "to make." Thus, it may be seen that at least ancient Chinese lacked a common verb (or auxiliary verb) meaning "to become." There is, however, a Chinese verb *kai,* "to change." This attitude of static understanding, linked with the way of thinking in some groups which emphasizes particulars, produced a trend of thinking which attaches importance to past events. The Chinese very often stress precedents, not abstract principles; whence their abundant historical allusions and set literary phrases. A people stressing particulars and concrete perception is inclined to set a basis of law in past customs and recurrent events, i.e. in previous examples as precedents. In other words, the fruit of the past experiences of people of older times arouses in the Chinese mind a sense of validity. It is only natural then that the Chinese would feel a certain uneasiness regarding the method which attempts to fix the laws governing human life solely by the abstract meditative power of the individual. The laws based on abstract thinking teach what conduct should be followed in the future, but they leave a sense of uneasiness among many Chinese who do not trust abstract thinking alone. For this reason, the conclusions reached by abstract thinking alone are not relied on to the same extent as the lived experience of the past. It is quite understandable then that with such an outlook, the Chinese try to discover in precedents the laws governing life. Thus, for the Chinese, learning implies full knowledge of the precedents of a past age, and is therefore referred to as "*Chi-ku,*" i.e. "searching out the ancient ways."

Most Chinese think it better to imitate in their writing the ways of expression used by their predecessors rather than to contrive new styles by their own efforts. Ability in writing was always closely tied to a knowledge of the classics. Therefore, classical Chinese texts consisted of a series of phrases or idioms generally taken from old texts; the foremost of these texts are the classics called the "*ching.*"

As a consequence, texts abound in literary and historical allusions, which is the result of the Chinese attachment to ways of expression based on historical particularity; for example, "*Ssu-mien Ch'u-ko*"—"to find oneself surrounded by enemies"; "*Hsien Wêi Shih*"—"to begin with oneself." In both of these instances, a phrase or a sentence denoting a single historical event is used to convey a universal, abstract concept. In the arts also, artistic effects are heightened and a powerful stimulus is given to the viewer or reader through the medium of historical allusions or quotations from the classics. Such productions as the Yüan drama (*Ch'ü-tzu*) as well as the modern *Ching-chü* are essentially a series of historical allusions and set literary phrases. Metaphors used in Chinese literature are always linked with historical facts of the past with the result that Chinese literature became very extensive and profound.[1] We can see a striking contrast, in this respect, to the Westerner's use of metaphor which is limited to his own direct experience or at least to that of the age to which he belongs. The Chinese use of metaphors contrasts also with the Indian's use of metaphors which transcend historical experience, or at least, were thought by the Indians to do so.

Chinese Buddhists did not prove to be an exception to this trend of thinking. Chinese equivalents of Sanskrit terms appearing in the Buddhist canon, when once fixed, were seldom changed thereafter. For this reason Hsüan-tsang writes, "I follow the old usage and do not translate this word anew." This traditional trend of thinking was particularly in evidence in Zen Buddhism. Particularly, the Zen sect began to use the *Kōan,* a kind of question-and-answer dialogue by a master and his disciple, with increasing frequency after the Sung dynasty. The original meaning of "*Kung-an*" (*Kōan*) is "records of cases in public office," and its meaning was changed to "pattern" or "previous example" and came to be called the "law of ancient times." Finally, in Zen Buddhism they consist of questions-and-answer dialogues, actions and anecdotes taken from the lives of famous monks as well as quotations from sūtras, among which there are not a few creative works made in a later period.

Conditioned by the above-mentioned ways of thinking, free thought along the line of individualism did not develop as prominently as it did in the West. The Spring and Autumn period (722–481 B.C.) and that of the Warring States (403–221 B.C.) may be the only exceptions.

Continuity of the Classical Way of Thinking

As long as the Chinese practiced the way of thinking described above, it is quite natural that they should have regarded the writings of their predecessors as having unquestionable authority. The thought and life of the Chinese people must always be examined in relation to the Chinese classics, for the life of the Chinese has been strongly conditioned by the classics. Since ancient times in China, the books which set the pattern of life have been fixed. They are called *Wu Ching* (the Five Classics): *I Ching* (Classic of Changes), *Shu Ching* (Classic of Documents), *Shih Ching* (Classic of Songs), *Li Chi* (Record of Rituals), *Ch'un Ch'iu* (Spring and Autumn Annals). These five classics are each nominally equal in status, and are accorded a degree of authority not possessed by any other books. According to later tradition, Confucius selected precedents which were to serve as models and compiled the works now known as the Five Classics. It seems to be true that Confucius held the *Shih* and *Li* in high esteem, and urged people to put the *Li Yüeh* of the Duke of Chou into practice. Mencius included the *Ch'un Ch'iu*. According to a legend, it was said that it was Hsün-tzŭ who finally fixed the number of classics at five. Mencius had a particularly high regard for the *Ch'un Ch'iu,* and thus strengthened the tradition of respecting precedents. Hsün-Tzŭ, who supposedly fixed the number of the classics at five and advocated respect for the doctrines of one's teacher, contributed much toward the formation of the peculiar character of classical learning in the Han dynasty afterwards.[2] Han Fei and Li Ssu, however, strongly urged replacing the laws of past emperors with the law of the new ruler. But this exceptional view held sway only during the reign of Shih-Huang-Ti of the Ch'in dynasty, and was unable to produce any change in the characteristic Chinese way of thinking.

Thus, the *Five Classics* were established as a pattern for the life of the Chinese people. It offered the precedents *par excellence,* ruling over all other precedents, so that in time the work came to be considered truth itself and perfection. It was thought that no matter how much human life might change, all the truth vital to human life was to be sought in these *Five Classics.* Another word for "*Ching*" (classics) is "*Tien*" (law) or "*Ch'ang*" (eternity), which indicate the eternal aspect of the truth embodied in the Five Classics.[3] Though dynasties in China have often changed, each dynasty has accepted the Five Classics as a supreme authority and treated them as the pattern for human life. The *Ch'un-Ch'iu Tso-Shih Chuan* tells us that this attitude towards the classics as the pattern for human life was already in existence in the time of the Chou dynasty. In the dialogue of the *Ch'un-Ch'iu Tso-Shih Chuan* we find individuals seeking authority for their own thoughts or deeds in the *Shih Ching* or the *Shu Ching*. Thus, by the middle of the Chou dynasty these two classics had to some extent enjoyed a position comparable to the one they were to have in later ages. At that time, however, the status of the *Shih Ching* and the *Shu Ching* had not yet been determined. There is a later tradition that it was Confucius who firmly established their status and laid the foundation for using the classics as the pattern for human life.[4]

Confucius' teaching did not aim at finding new truth by free speculation and originality. He tried to imitate and revive past traditions while affirming at the same time the values of the social organization and family system of his day. He had no desire to alter the system or social organization of his time. He says in his *Analects,* "I do not invent, but merely transmit; I believe in and love antiquity," and "I am not a man born wise. I favor what is ancient and strive to know it well." Therefore, he would have said that the truth in which he believed was not of his own creation, but that he was only amplifying truths handed down from ancient times. Thus, the Way of antiquity, according to Confucius, was, concretely speaking, the Way adopted by the Duke of Chou, who had laid the foundation of the political and social systems of the Chou dynasty as well as its moral principles. Confucius called the system of the Duke of Chou "the *Li* of Chou Kung," and expressed regret that it had declined and was no longer practiced completely in his days. The purpose of his teachings was the revival of the "*Li*" so that they might be practiced once more. Confucius was a teacher especially of moral ideals which do not change with time.

Respect for the classics was not limited to people of the Confucian school only; other schools also held them in high regard, although there was some difference in degree. Mo-tzŭ, for example, quotes the *Shu Ching* as a work of considerable authority. The only difference between the Confucian attitude toward the classics and the attitude of the other schools is that the former regarded following the way of the classics as indispensable.[5] The attitude of reverence toward the classics can also be seen in the Chinese translation of the Buddhistic scriptures, wherein we often come across the word "*Ching*" (classics or sūtra) in the title of a Chinese translation of a Sanskrit work, although no such word is found in the original Sanskrit text.

Many peoples besides the Chinese hold their classics in esteem and strive to make their life conform to them, without implying that their life in all its everyday details must be in complete accord with them. But in the case of China an extraordinary effort was made not only to let the classics set the patterns for life, but also to cause everyday life to conform entirely to the classics. Thus, Chinese thought was passed on from generation to generation without much change or development after its form had become fixed. As Chinese society and culture were fixed, its thought was also fixed in keeping with them. Scholars differ in their opinion as to how far fixed thought controlled the actual life of the Chinese. On this problem, Sōkichi Tsuda offers the following explanation:

"China has never had a revolution in her world of thought. The reason for this is that Chinese life itself was fixed. Yet, we should not fail to notice a secondary cause, namely, that thought had authority only as thought and did not necessarily control actual living, it was not deemed necessary to resist and reform thought which has no authority on actual life, so long as both actual society and politics, whatever the doctrines of morality or politics may be, were in effect independent of them; yet it is true that doctrine itself had an authority as doctrine in China."[6]

I think that this explanation also contains considerable truth, although China too has had great changes in the long history of her society. The degree to which ancient thought controlled the actual life of the Chinese is a question requiring further examination in the future, but at any rate, it is a peculiar feature of Chinese culture that it preserved and esteemed some forms of thought just because of their antiquity.

Once Voltaire stated that it was miraculous that there had never been any remarkable change in the legal and administrative system of the Chinese for about four thousand years, from about 2000 B.C. to his own day, and took that fact as a proof that the legal and administrative system of the Chinese was the most excellent in the world.[7] Voltaire exaggerates, but I think the reason why some ways and forms of thinking had prevailed among the Chinese for four thousand years can be attributed to the fact that they had considered the legal and administrative system devised by themselves to be the most excellent or natural, so that they dared not resist it.

People who knew China well before the Second World War would often remark that when Chinese were discussing a problem with each other, if one of them would quote a passage of the classics, the others would at once express their approval. Since China's turn to Communism, Marx, Lenin, and Mao Tse-tung have replaced the Chinese classics. Although this is a great change, we can see how deeply the way of thinking of the nation is rooted in its yielding to propaganda with little if any resistance, so long as an authority is cited from the new Communist leaders.

Influence of the Reception of Buddhism

China's classical and conservative ways of thinking modified the form of its reception of Buddhism. As we have already frequently pointed out, Chinese Buddhists, especially the priests, took over the doctrine founded and taught by Śākyamuni, and considered it their duty to exalt their interpretation of his teaching, in spite of the fact that Chinese Buddhism differs from Indian Buddhism in many respects. Therefore, they rewrote arbitrarily even the sentences of the sūtra; for instance, in spite of the original of *Fa Hua Ching* which states that "An enlightened self (*Pratyekabuddha*) opened his eyes to the Truth *without looking to his master for help* (*anācāryaka*)," the Chinese translation reads "he listened to the Buddha's law and accepted it as being true."[8] This is just the opposite of its original meaning.

The way of thinking indicated in a phrase like "I only state the truth but don't make it" dominated even Buddhist scholars in China; for instance, the venerable Hui-chao (*ca.* 714 A.D.), the second founder of the Fa Hsiang school, said that the teaching of pure consciousness, the fundamental doctrine of the Fa Hsiang school, was preached by Śākyamuni, and Vasubandhu (320–400), who expounded the doctrine of pure consciousness practically, was a mere commentator.[9] In fact, the historical Śākyamuni expounded no such teaching, but we know that Vasubandhu and other persons expounded this theory for the first time seven or eight hundred years after Śākyamuni's death; whereas, Chinese scholars thought the actual and first advocator to be the commentator. Therefore, as the venerable Chi-tsang (549–623) pointed out, in case an author of a Buddhist treatise wished to denounce the theories of other schools, he would claim that his theory was in accord with the teachings of Śākyamuni and he based his argument on the authority of the Buddha.[10] Zen Buddhists also adopted this policy (the lessons of antiquity enlighten our mind) as their fundamental attitude.[11]

Chinese Buddhists did not use historical criticism on what was claimed to have been taught by the Buddha. Buddhist sects each taught what its founder was supposed to have taught. Critical thought on such matters did not take root among Buddhists. This attitude is not true of all the intellectuals of China. The Chinese did do a considerable amount of historical criticism on their own history and classics, especially after the Chin (317–419 A.D.) dynasty.

It is true that some Chinese apologists looked at the classics from the viewpoint of historical origins or criticized them. But the situation in the modern age is different. A century and more ago the Imperial throne had a bureau of Chinese scholars prepare a critical study of each book in the Imperial library. This work has been published and is available in every good library. It represents first-rate historical criticism—as good as that in any European critical work. This includes Chinese classics, etc. Historical criticism has always been very much alive in China. The Chinese scholars include not only those who are able to harmonize contradictions in books, but those who have employed a keen sense of criticism in detection of such contradictions! Perhaps Chinese Buddhism has been more at fault logically than the Chinese classics. The Chinese as a whole have never accepted any single doctrine! So the varying interpretations of a *sūtra* represent some typical aspects of Chinese ways of thinking.

The custom of attaching importance to past events led the Chinese to a way of thinking that assumes a master is generally superior to his disciples. Then the question arose why Āryadeva, disciple of Nāgārjuna, vehemently denounced the philosophical theories of other schools in his treatise called the One Hundred Verse Treatise, although his master Nāgārjuna had never rejected other schools so explicitly; the venerable Chi-tsang explained, as the reason for this, that since Nāgārjuna had achieved world-wide fame, none of the heretics and Hīnayāna Buddhists dared argue against him, whereas they argued without restraint against Āryadeva who was only Nāgārjuna's "disciple."[12] This explanation by Chi-tsang may seem odd to a reader today.

This attitude of respect for the transmission of the master's teaching to his disciples led the Chinese Buddhists to be strict in studying the genealogy of the doctrines transmitted from a master to his disciples. The very venerable Chi-tsang, who liked arguments, examined carefully the history of schools in Indian Buddhism and the distinctions in their language.[13] The venerable Chih-i (538–597) who had completed a new Buddhist theory and founded the T'ien-t'ai sect, wrote down the transmission of the True Teaching to the disciples amounting to twenty-four Buddhist monks, from Kāśyapa, an immediate disciple of Śākyamuni's, to Buddhasiṃha in a later age.[14] As for Chinese Buddhism of that day, temples all over China belonged to the Zen schools who esteemed their master in Zen Buddhism so highly that it came to be a matter of first importance to obey the master under whom they practiced austerities and followed his teachings. Such an attitude of thinking led some to call the relation between master and disciples in question, even with respect to the age before Bodhidharma, the founder of China's Zen Buddhism, who came to China about 520 A.D.

Thus, they made up in their own way the genealogy of the twenty-eight patriarchal founders ranging from the great Kāśyapa, one of Śākyamuni's immediate disciples, to Bodhidharma.[15]

Many history books on Buddhism were composed, especially by Zen Buddhists, on the basis of the genealogy of the transmission of doctrines from master to disciples. The Indians, with their deep respect for universal law or doctrines, do not mention the transmission from master to disciples as seriously and minutely as the Chinese do.

As a result of this high esteem for the master, the Chinese Zen sects in some instances attach more importance to their founders than to Śākyamuni or the Tathāgata; they went so far as to think their respective founders' Zen Buddhism to be superior to the Tathāgata's. Consequently, in their way of thinking, the master's sayings and deeds became their golden rule, and served as clues for attaining the goal of the practice of Zen meditation; they were finally standardized in the form of many Kōan of the Zen school.

Following the former examples and ancient practices, the founder's sayings and deeds came to be regarded as more important than the sūtras of the schools of Mahāyāna Buddhism which were scanty in historical descriptions: *Kōan* depending on sūtras of the schools of Mahāyāna Buddhism are merely 5 percent of all the catechisms recorded in the *Pi Yen Lu* and the *Ts'ung Yung Lu,* and the rest, 95 percent of them, are based on the founder's sayings.[16]

Because of this high esteem for the founder's oral teachings, Zen Buddhists in later ages preferred their founder's interpretations to the Indian sūtras, and began to concentrate more and more on their many catechisms.

The origin and the significance of the Chinese manifestations of respect for elders should be dealt with separately, but I consider it to be closely related to the classical conservatism which is traditional in the Chinese. The words starting with *"Lao"* ("Elder"), *Lao Jen, Lao Tsêng,* and *Lao Han* are pronounced by Zen Buddhists in order to express a sense of respect.

Exact logical thought, which would critically examine statements in the sacred books themselves, is not an outstanding trait of those Chinese ways of thinking in which classical conservatism regards the authority of the sacred books to be absolute. This is the reason why Indian logic did not take root in China. The school of logic brought to China from India by Hsüan-tsang was the latest one (new *Hetu-vidyā*) in India of those days, which stood on a thoroughly rational standpoint and acknowledged only sense (*pratyakṣa*) and inference (*anumāna*) as the basis for forming knowledge. This Indian school considered the sacred books of religion, tradition, the sayings of great men, and so on, as unreliable sources of knowledge, and disqualified them as a basis of knowledge;[17] in this regard, it had something in common with the natural philosophy of Vaiśeṣika.

This rationalistic theory of knowledge was brought to China and taught together with Mohist formal logic, but both were not at all in tune with most Chinese who had high regard for the authority of ancient traditions. They wished to regard traditional knowledge as the solid basis of knowledge at any rate, and did not permit sense and inference as adequate substitutes for the traditional ground of knowledge in China. They insisted that the traditional sacred books are more authoritative than knowledge based upon sense and inference, and considered it natural to feel this way.[18]

Bearing in mind this characteristic attitude of Chinese Buddhists, we can easily comprehend how the problem of "forged sūtras" came about. A thought theoretically explained is not sufficient to convince the ordinary Chinese. To make the ordinary Chinese accept it, it is necessary to base it on the authority of books. Thus, many "forged sūtras" produced in China were always professed to have been made in India. If they came to be suspected of having been produced in China, they would at once be regarded as lacking truth and authority.

The Chinese popular way of thinking, which idealizes and praises the past, naturally came to consider the present and future as degraded and corrupted, so that Chinese thought is said to be pessimistic and non-futuristic; the pessimistic way of thinking that became predominant in ancient Chinese Buddhism seems to be related to this Chinese way of thinking.

Non-development of Free Thought

Of course, it cannot be said that free thought did not appear in China. It is a well-known fact that all the philosophers of the Spring and Autumn Period (722–481 B.C.), as well as the Period of the Warring States (403–222 B.C.), had been advocating their own opinions. Disputes in The Hundred Schools period died down gradually, largely because of the persecution of scholars and thinkers between 221 and 206 B.C. by the Ch'in dynasty which unified all China; it adopted the opinion of the Realists (Legalist School) who advocated: "Though certain exceptional people might be successfully ruled by kindness, the average man cannot be controlled except by law."[19] This Legalist school tended to be oppressive.

When the study of Confucianism came to be the official course of study during the Han dynasty, it became the basis for civil service examinations; i.e., the thought of intellectuals was consolidated by Confucianism. Of course, it cannot be said that all thought with the exception of Confucianism disappeared completely, but rather that no independent school of thought could exist in opposition to Confucianism. Once the authority of Confucianism was established, it prevailed in spite of some resistance to it. No questioning of its authority occurred later. Consequently, due to this kind of mentality, the Chinese felt no contradiction between their yearning for the social and administrative systems of old times and their efforts to maintain the social and administrative systems of the day. Conservatism and principles to maintain the status quo were adopted generally. It is often said that such classics as the *Four Books* and the *Five Classics* of Confucianism restrained the Chinese from thinking freely, but in fact, it is their conservative attitude and worship of the past, emphasizing the authority of the Classics, that really restrained the Chinese.

Thus, free thought was not characteristic of ancient and medieval China, except in some periods. The real cause for this seems to be connected with the fact that no urban community (apart from the Imperial capital) had developed in China. Concerning this absence of urban community, Max Weber has said the following: "In China, there had never been formed any citizens' defensive and political organization. Cities in [feudal] China did not have the characteristics of a religious service (monastic) organization or of a sworn constitutional government as in the West. Of course, there existed a prototype of civic thought. The tutelary deity of cities in ancient China was not a guardian god for civic union, but merely a guardian spirit for a region, so we might rather say that they were generally deified beings of high executives of the cities. Cities, the fortresses of the Imperial Government had, in fact, less guaranty of self-government than the village communities. Cities were permitted to have neither the right to conclude a contract nor a jurisdiction, so that they were unable to take united action. At any rate, the village communities, on the contrary, had all of those rights. Now, the reason for this type of city can be attributed to the fact that the cities in the West were formed to be trading centers, whereas in China, they were products of administrative offices. First of all, a castellated wall was constructed around a city, and then a small number of people were often forcibly brought within [for protection against robbers or by allocating land to them]. Moreover, the very name of the capital city itself or of cites in general was changed whenever one dynasty changed to the next."[20]

He added: "Cities in China were not administrative in character, and they had no administrative privilege as seen in the *polis* in Greece or modern cities in the West. It is true that there were many cases in which the whole city rose to resist the bureaucracy, but their purpose was always limited to mere opposition to a certain government official or to a given decree, especially to an imposition of a new tax, but not once did they venture to stipulate the political freedom of the city. The reason the latter could not be accomplished as it was in the West can be attributed to the fact that the Chinese could not get rid of their kinship ties. The settlers in the cities—especially the rich—had never severed their connections with their native places, or their own kinship societies, but maintained all of their ritual or individual relationships with the village communities in which they were born."[21]

In China, private property rights were established, but rights of freedom guaranteed by law did not exist.[22] It is natural, therefore, that free thinking was not encouraged, and conservative thought and respect for the past were dominant; cities did not develop as independent communities, the right to personal freedom was not recognized, and only village communities continued to maintain the same way of life as in ancient times. It was only in the earlier part of the twentieth century that revolt against tradition and anti-Confucianism started on a large scale.[23]

Traditional Character of Scholarship

Within the scope of this way of thinking, learning was apt to be mere acceptance of traditional knowledge handed down from generation to generation without change. Confucian scholarship was adopted as orthodox by the former Han dynasty. This tendency did not exclude critical scholarship. Even in Han times (first century A.D.) some extremely keen critical work was done. Chu-tzu himself was an extremely keen critic in some matters. But as a general tendency traditional scholarship was highly esteemed in the above mentioned period.

Etymologically, the Chinese word "to learn" has no other meaning but "to imitate." This is especially obvious in the Confucian teachings. The most important plea of Confucius was that man should take his norm for living from previous examples and the classics. Therefore, he regarded reading books, scarce as they were then, as most important. "The master said that once he had not taken a meal all day and stayed up all night to meditate, but he found it to be useless, and then he realized that nothing is better than learning."

In other words, our life should be guided by thorough knowledge of previous examples rather than by meditation. Therefore, Confucianist moral theory insists that the concrete contents of *Jên,* as "the way" or practical model for morality, should be taught by other persons as knowledge. However, they did not explain how the moral model given by knowledge is related to *Jên* or how *Jên* could be affected by knowledge. Also, the *Analects* of Confucius, gave no explanation of why "*Jên*" was the very core of morality itself, nor did they give any explanation of "*Yi*" or of "*T'i*" which are concrete and practical matters. Again, they did not explain definitely where the basis for morality should be placed,[24] so that, in China, "to learn" meant simply "to search for ancient ways"; consequently, "things" or "meaning" is, in fact, nothing but "things which were taught."[25] This trend then led study in the school of Confucius to become mainly the annotation of the classics. The main achievement of Chêng Hsüan (127–200), a representative scholar in the Later Han dynasty, was his explanation of the classics. Chu Hsi was the great philosopher, in the Sung dynasty, who completed Confucianism; and yet his works consist largely of annotations of the classics or his own explanations of annotations of the classics. He made no completely independent, systematic statements in his works.

This trend also dominated Buddhist scholars. Since Buddhism arose in India, Chinese Buddhist scholars were influenced by the Indian ways of thinking so that some of their statements are more systematic and inclusive, but many of them made efforts to annotate sūtras and Indian theories in order to explain their chief meaning. The venerable Chi-i (538–597) of Mount T'ien-t'ai, great Buddhist center at Chekiang, wrote an independent and systematic work in 20 volumes called *Mo Ho Chih Kuan* (On the Profound Quiescence) but most of his works consist of explanations of sūtras.

Among the works written by the venerable Chi-tsang—twenty-six sets of his works are in existence—of which only two books, i.e., *Êrh Ti I* in three volumes and *Ta Ch'eng Hsüan Lun* in five volumes, are systematic treatises; the rest of them are explanations of sūtras or of theories. As for the representative books written by the venerable Fa-tsang, who completed the doctrine of the Hua Yen school (Book on the Five Teachings of the Hua Yen School), we should mention his three-or four-volume work *Hua Yen Wu Chiao Chang,* but most of the rest of his books are explanations of sūtras or theories. Consequently, it may be correct to call Chinese Buddhism explanatory, though it is referred to as academic.

The way of thinking which emphasizes explanation brought some very extraordinary phenomena; for instance, Ch'eng-kuan, a famous scholar of the Hua Yen school in the T'ang dynasty, who wrote an explanatory work for the *Hua Yen Ching,—Ta Fang Kuang Fo Hua Yen Ching Shu,* in sixty volumes; later on, he continued his explanatory work by adding a ninety-volume study to it, called *Ta Fang Kuang Fo Hua Yen Ching Yen I Ch'ao.*

Since the sacred books of Buddhism in China were all translations from the Indian originals it may have been necessary for the Chinese to consult explanatory studies in order to grasp their meaning perfectly, so that those explanatory works themselves came to have the peculiarity of being more meaningful than the original books. The way of thinking which takes to explanations is still evidenced among the Chinese of our own day.

Once Marxism-Leninism was fixed to be a national policy, the party-leaders commented on it and lower rank leaders added explanations to the comments of the former. Such a way of thinking has been steadfastly maintained to the present day, in spite of the fact that the Chinese have often experienced revolutions.

CHAPTER 19 FONDNESS FOR COMPLEX MULTIPLICITY EXPRESSED IN CONCRETE FORM

The Concrete Character of the Artistic Imagination

The Chinese had a high regard for particulars, and presented content concretely in accordance with their way of thinking; therefore they naturally came to be fond of complex multiplicity expressed in concrete form. Their standpoint, which relied upon and clung to sensory qualities, made them especially sensitive to the complex variety of phenomena instead of the laws and abstractly conceived unity of things. Diversity rather than similarity characterizes the realm of phenomena. Consequently, the Chinese, who depend upon perceived phenomena and value particulars, are naturally sensitive to the multiplicity of things, and rarely attempt to think about the universal validity of laws which regulate this multiplicity of things.

This characteristic trait of their way of thinking has influenced the growth of various forms of Chinese art. There is a definite limit to the force of artistic imagination of the Chinese. Their attitude of observing only those things that can be concretely experienced, that are grasped specifically through sensory effects directly perceived, weakens their power of imagination. This is the reason why in China no epic has been produced, although novels and a kind of drama, which combine concreteness and reality, developed on a large scale. This is just the opposite of the Indians, who produced the *Mahābhārata,* the world's greatest epic, and the *Rāmāyaṇa,* a beautiful poem of a hero, and other similar imaginative works, but until recently, India has seldom produced novels.

The Chinese, too, under the T'ang and the Sung dynasties, produced excellent poems, but most of the ideas expressed were concrete and stayed within the natural laws of time and space. In the later T'ang dynasty, there were people like Li Chang-chi (791–817),[1] a poet who was unusually imaginative, but the basic, individual ideas contained in his poetry are not very imaginative. The Indian, on the one hand, gives abundant play to the power of his free imagination, while the Chinese, on the other hand, gives play to a different sort of imagination, hovering over the complex multiplicity which he loves so much.

Hereupon, the following question may arise: The Chinese are given to exaggeration by their artistic nature, as seen, for instance, in an expression of a poem by the famous T'ang poet Li T'ai-po (701–762): "White hair, grown 3,000 feet long on account of my sorrow." In this expression the laws of nature clearly seem to be disregarded, but, reflecting upon this example, we cannot regard it as very imaginative. Masaaki Tozaki, a Japanese scholar, offers the following explanation: "The 3,000 feet mentioned in the poem have the same meaning as thousands of feet long, i.e. unfathomably long. Expressions of 'three thousand disciples,' 'three thousand court ladies,' 'a distance of three thousand li' are similar."[2] Therefore, both the concepts of "white hair" and "three thousand" are permissible as concrete representations of human experience.

Only the combination of the words "white hair" and "3,000 feet long" ignores natural laws. This Chinese way of thinking has to be distinguished fundamentally from the Indian way of thinking, which uses huge numbers such as "hundred millions of," "hundred thousand millions of," "as many as the grains of sand in the Ganges river," which are beyond any concrete human experience and nonchalantly represent concepts outside the perceived world.

Fondness for Ornate Diction

The Chinese language consists of various kinds of rhythmical forms that appeal to the senses. The characters in sentences are often arranged in patterns of four each or seven each. For the sake of form the Chinese often sacrifice meaning, and do not reject a sentence because it is vague. This is how the euphemistically antithetic style, "*Ssu Liu P'ien Li T'i,*" originated during the Six Dynasties. It can be said that the Chinese language is an artistic one, for it aims at euphony, and that its sentences are full of elegant nuances based not upon universal and abstract concepts but rather on free usage of historical allusions and phrases.

This characteristic of the Chinese way of thinking naturally also transfigured Buddhism. The schools of Chinese Buddhism which are linked directly with the philosophical systems originating in India are abstract and speculative, while the Zen sect, a purely Chinese form of Buddhism, is very literary. I have previously indicated how this characteristic is concerned with concreteness in the Chinese way of thinking. The literary character of Zen Buddhism is especially remarkable in the verses attached to catechisms (*Kōan*) of the Zen sect, where a certain religious, metaphysical atmosphere was created by an odd array of persons and things which are concrete and appeal to the eyes. In those places, few abstract remarks can be found.

Fondness for complex multiplicity expressed in concrete form is evidenced by the efforts made by Chinese writers to fascinate people by an excessive array of similes and metaphors. In other words, the tendency is to use expressions which aim to lead people to the meaning to be conveyed by an intertwining of various representations, using complex expressions with elaborate words full of suggestions, even if the meaning is simple. Hence the habit of rhetorical devices is frequently used by the Chinese. The Japanese scholar, Tominaga Nakamoto (1715–1746) once pointed this out as follows: "The Chinese Confucian scholar likes to use ornate styles, while the Japanese is fond of using concise and pithy expressions." In other words, the Japanese prefer plain expressions and dislike exaggerations, while the learned Chinese love to use difficult passages which are hard to read.[3] He also said, "Buddhists are inclined to use passages too mysterious to understand, while Confucian philosophers like to use passages too ornate to understand. If only they would abandon this habit, they could express their true meaning."[4]

This same way of thinking appears in the Chinese fondness for discussion and eloquence. The Chinese mode of explanation is not based upon theoretical reflection. Rather the aim is to grasp the psychological state of the other person and try to convince him to agree with one's own opinion. This aim accounts for the Chinese skill in eloquence.

The Chinese themselves recognized this mental peculiarity. Tao-an (312–385), a famous Chinese monk, recognized an essential difference between the Chinese fondness for ornate diction and the writings in the Indian language. He said, "The Sanskrit sūtras lay stress on essence, but the Chinese are concerned primarily with style and strive to make the sūtras suit the taste of the people."[5] Even though there had been a gorgeous style, the so-called Kāvya style, in the ancient Indian language, it was hardly used in Buddhist sūtras. He felt that a defect of the translations of Buddhist sūtras into Chinese was the fact that the translated versions tried to please popular fancy too much by means of aesthetic effects.

Tsung-mi, another Chinese monk, felt that the sect taught the attitude of "No reliance on word or letter" in order to cure Buddhists of this bad habit. He said, "The Chinese cling to ornate styles, and harbor illusion in their minds. Because they settle for names instead of substance, Bodhidharma selected some sentences and transmitted the true meaning of Buddhism to his disciples who substituted words for substance—for instance, by practicing meditation facing the wall to break off various kinds of verbal relations with others."[6]

Yet in spite of this, it is a well known fact that Zen Buddhism eventually developed a fondness for Zen expressions and became a book religion.

China is said to have a vast literature even when no more than three percent of its population have been literate. The Chinese are fond of ornate styles and are skillful in literary composition. However, the concepts found in their writings are based on actual experiences. It is true that the Chinese are a people fond of grandiloquent styles, but such styles are no more than simple exaggeration, and it seems that there are few cases in which they overstep natural limits. The Chinese have rarely made any representations of abstract universal things themselves by enlarging on them freely, as the Indians tended to do, without any specific relation to the concrete facts of life. Since most Chinese did not indulge in abstract speculations and ignored universals, they did not try to transmit the contents of thought with logical precision, but were content to give only some suggestive impressions to the reader. Moreover, so many Chinese orators thought that the most important thing was eloquence without regard for certain logical or ethical rules concerning truth and error, good and evil. A form of Chinese sophistry at times results from such a mentality; even Confucian philosophy, which has occupied the chief position of government-supported scholarship, is sometimes prone to this sort of sophistic oratory.

Ju philosophy, which is the official name for Confucian philosophy, is a doctrine of the literati[7] who love style. As Max Weber defined it, Ju philosophy is nothing but a system of class ethics maintained by a secular and subsidized elite who have a certain literary culture.[8] However, these literati were meant to be not only intellectuals or well-read people but also moral leaders of the people in such matters as truthfulness, courtesy, etc. Successive officials in China were selected from among such literati. Although the general public could not afford to read books, fundamentally their lives centered around the lessons of the classics and the enjoyment of listening to stories.

T'ao Yüan-ming says in his work, a biography of Wu-liu: "I was fond of reading books, but I didn't always try to understand them thoroughly. Whenever I found any agreeable passage, I would often gladly forget to eat. I always enjoyed myself by composing sentences."

This was the ideal of the Chinese literati.

Exegetical and Literary Predilections of the Chinese

Chinese Buddhism was a religion for the literati in its intellectual aspect. Chinese Buddhism might be called "a religion of documents"[9] because the whole Chinese culture is characterized by an emphasis on documents. Indeed, there were many schools in Chinese Buddhism, and their variety was based upon theoretical distinctions, not upon administrative or social differences as in Japan.

We had better call them schools than sects. We can find at least seven schools which were initially formulated in India: "P'i T'an School," "Chü She School," "San Lun School," "Ssu Lun School," "Ti Lun School," "She Lun School," and the "Fa Hsiang School." These schools of Buddhism are linked directly with theories of Indian Buddhism. There are similarly seven schools of Buddhism which arose in China: "Lü School," "Nieh P'an School," "Ch'ing T'u School," "Ch'an School," "T'ien T'ai School," "Hua Yen School," and "Chen Yên School." The Lü School consists of the "Ssu Fen Lü School," the "Shih Sung Lü School," and the "Sêng Chih Lü School"; the Ch'an School is divided into five branches and seven sub-schools. The main reason why so many schools were formed is that there are basic differences among sūtras and theoretical works.[10] But these differences apply to theoretical rather than practical matters. In the Sung period a merger took place between the Pure Land School and Ch'an School, both of which are representative of the practical moral aspects of Buddhism.

Consequently, generally speaking, it can be said that Chinese Buddhism was divided into many schools along theoretic lines, but they were quite similar in their practical aspect. Chinese Buddhists were largely literati, and consequently had a deep attachment for complex styles of writing. This trend became particularly prominent during the Northern and Southern dynasties, especially during the latter. I should like to point out a few interesting examples of this. The *Sheng Man Pao K'u,* a well-known commentary, was written by Chi-tsang. He says in his comment, "I have been studying and appreciating this sūtra for many years, and have made reference to many books of all ages. I have examined many sūtras and treatises, selecting passages with profound meaning, which I have compiled into a three-volume work."[11]

As he says, we find many passages quoted from a great number of sūtras, and many explanations on each word and character. Because he cited such a wide variety of authorities, we soon become weary and bewildered when reading this work, and ironically the main meaning of the book becomes all the more vague. Fujaku (1707–1781), a Japanese monk, commented on this book thus: "We find therein very elaborate explanations. In this book, the author comments on each phrase and sentence minutely to enlarge the beginner's knowledge. There probably is no more elaborate book than this." But this commentary of Chi-tsang does not give us the main meaning of this book. That this book came to be highly prized by scholars, Fujaku observes, shows that the study of Buddhism has been degraded to mere formalism.[12] The very opposite of this may be seen in the Commentary on the Śrīmālā Sūtra (*Shōmangyōgi-sho*) written by Prince Shōtoku of Japan, which is much more concise and pertinent.

The *Chü She Lun Chi* written by Pu-kuang is said to be the most authoritative book on the *Chü She Lun* (*Abhidharma-Kośa-śāstra*), which is an important guide to the doctrines of Hīnayāna Buddhism. The book is said to include the interpretations of Sarvāstivāda scholars of Western India as related to Pu Kuang by Hsüan-tsang, which are quite accurate. However, because of his respect for tradition, Pu Kuang included the different theories found in the *Abhidharma-mahāvibhāṣā-Śāstra,* the largest explanatory work of the Sarvāstivāda School, as well as passages from the earlier translation of the *Chü She Lun* and the *Shun Chêng Li Lun* (*Nyāyānusāra-śāstra*), so that too many opinions are given and therefore it lacks conciseness.

This tendency is seen in all the commentaries on the *Fa Hua Ching* (*Saddharmapuṇḍarīka-sūtra*) produced in China, and especially the *Fa Hua Hsüan Tsan* written by K'uei-chi, which contains many ornate phrases. In general, documents written during the first part of the T'ang dynasty are hard to read, but there are few books which contain such minute and needless explanations as the *Fa Hua Ssüan Tsan*. The *Erh Ya, Kuang Ya, Shuo Wen, Yü P'ien, Ch'ieh Yün* are freely cited, but their value here is little more than decorative.[13]

Therefore, it was no easy task for Chinese Buddhist scholars to explain even the title of a sūtra or treatise. Chi-tsang explained in great detail the title of the *Madhyamaka-śāstra* (sometimes called *Chung Kuan Lun* in China) written by Nāgārjuna, on which the school of Chi-tsang was based.

As for the main point of his explanations, he says, "In short, each of these three characters of the *Chung Kuan Lun* has the meaning of *Chung,* of *Kuan* and of *Lun.*" Logically speaking, this seems utterly meaningless, and we may not be far wrong in saying that he enjoyed playing with words.[14] Judging from the next example, he must have been ignorant of the fact that a title of a book denoted a definite notion. He says, "Each of these three characters of *Chung Kuan Lun* has no definite meaning of its own and therefore, one might say *Kuan Chung Lun* or *Lun Chung Kuan.* The first one is represented by the Theorist, the second one by Insight, the third one by Theory." He added further very complicated explanations to these classifications in an effort to amplify the text.[15]

In short, it may be said that the Chinese scholars were forgetting the fact that a name indicates a certain concept. Even the scholars of Buddhistic logic, who ought to have been able to think matters through logically, took no account of this. "Ying Ming" is the Chinese equivalent for the Sanskrit word of "*hetuvidyā,*" which is translated literally "the science of reason." Nevertheless, the Chinese Buddhists forgot its original meaning and recognized only the meaning resulting from the linkage of the two characters, "Yin" and "Ming," giving arbitrary explanations. K'uei-chi says, "The character of Yin means a statement made by a debater and serves as the proposition; and the character of Ming represents the wisdom of the opponent, which illuminates meanings and words." He explains again, "It is a cause of Ming, and therefore called Ying Ming, and Ying is the original cause of a word, and Ming means a revealing cause of wisdom." All of these explanations are in error. He merely listed these absurd explanations one after another, and did not offer any conclusion, nor did he try to decide which was right. In addition, he also gave minute explanations for the title *Ying Ming Ju Chêng Li Lun* (*Nyāyapraveśaka*), listing five kinds of explanations one after another.[16]

Examples of the extremes to which Chinese commentators went when interpreting a title are not uncommon. The full title of the *Hua Yen Ching* is *Ta Fang Kuang Fo Hua Yen Ching*. Its original name is "*Mahā-vaipulya-buddha-avataṃsaka-sūtra*," and therefore, we must be careful to read it "*Ta Fang Kuang Fo Hua Yen Ching*." Nevertheless, Fa-tsang, whose teachings centered around the *Hua Yen Ching* and is recognized to be the highest authority on it, did not think that the title was composed of certain concepts, but further regarded the title merely as so many characters, and offered an explanation for each separate character: "*Ta* stands for inclusion; *Fang* for regulation; *Kuang* for a state where activity is extended universally and the mental constitution has reached its ultimate; *Fo* for a state where the effect is in perfect harmony and the enlightenment is full; *Hua* for a simile which means a state where all kinds of practices have been accomplished; *Yen* for a simile indicating the ornament of substance; *Ching* for a state where all forms of existence are linked with one another to reveal the Teaching of Buddha. Following the Law, using similes with regard to human beings, we call it *Ta Fang Kuang Fo Hua Yen Ching*."[17] It is only natural that we should grow tired of such complicated explanations, yet his predilection for explanatory expressions does not stop here. He goes on to say, "*Ta* has ten kinds of meaning," and enumerates the ten kinds of complicated explanations for this character.[18] He then says, "Next, I want to denote ten kinds of explanations of *Fa Kuang*," and enumerates ten kinds of explanations for each of the subsequent words. Fa-tsang's passion for enumerating ten kinds of explanations is due to the fact that the *Hua Yen Ching* itself has a tendency to enumerate things in groups of ten. But he does not give any conclusions about which meanings are fundamental and which of lesser importance. Also we cannot find any trace of his own reflections on these matters.

In general, when translating Buddhist sūtras into Chinese, the Chinese aimed at heightening magical and artistic effects; for instance, the Chinese equivalent for the Sanskrit *"Prajñā"* is *"Chih Hui,"* which means "Wisdom," but the Chinese chose to use their phoneme *"Pan Jo"* as the transcription of the Sanskrit word, rather than *"Chih Hui,"* in order to endow it with dignity.[19]

Such being the case, exegetical studies developed in China, but not like the scholasticism during the Middle Ages in Europe. Exegetic works lack the character of rational formalism seen in jurisprudence in the Western countries. Furthermore, it did not have the casuistic character seen in the Jesuit theologians of Catholicism, in the Talmudic Rabbis of Judaism, in the theologians of Islam, and in the Buddhist scholars studying the theory of the Abhidharma.[20]

In Chinese Buddhism, which is a religion of documents, scripture was highly esteemed, so that as a matter of course the copying of sūtras came to be regarded as an act of religious merit, of greater value than practicing the morality of Buddhism. Chih-i says, "The aim of sūtra copying lies in enforcing people to practice the Eight-fold Sacred Path so as to awaken them from delusion. There are various ways of carrying out Buddhistic practices, and therefore he who is possessed of insight into the fact that our consciousness is appearing and disappearing incessantly and is impermanent, and he who wants to practice the Eight-fold Sacred Path should copy the collection of sacred books; and he who is possessed of insight into the fact that our consciousness is capable of many kinds of false discrimination which he, the ordinary person, as well as persons of the two vehicles cannot realize, although Bodhisattvas who have eyes of the Law can perceive it, and he who wants to practice the Eight-fold Sacred Path should copy sūtras of the separate doctrines, and he who is possessed of insight into the fact that our consciousness is nothing but Buddha nature, and who wants to practice the Eight-fold Sacred Path should copy sūtras of the Middle Path."[21]

If there had been no way of thinking which emphasized sūtra-copying, such statements would never have been made. Because of this kind of thinking, stone slabs were engraved with Buddhist scriptures. The first persecution of Buddhism occurred during the reign of the Emperor Tao-wu of the Northern Wei dynasty (386–534), resulting in the destruction of Buddhist images and sūtras. A great number of monks and nuns were forced back into common society. Buddhists at that time came to have a premonition of further persecution, and therefore they engraved Buddhist sūtras in stone, on the face of cliffs, in stone pillars, in stone slabs and walls. We find the *Wei Mo Ching, Shêng Man Ching,* and *Mi Lê Ching* engraved on walls of stone caves which were polished as smooth as glass at Mt. Pei Hsiang Tang in Wu An Hsien of Honan Province. A religious vow, still extant, written by T'ang-yung, a distinguished official under the Northern Chi dynasty (550–577), tells us that he intended to engrave the entire canon on the walls of famous mountains. Under the Sui dynasty (581–617), Ching-wan, a Buddhist monk, also made a vow to engrave the canon on stone slabs. Efforts were made during five successive dynasties to have the canon incised in stone, but were at last discontinued as a result of the persecution by the T'ang Emperor Wu-tsung. Again during the Liao dynasty the work was continued with the support of the government. More than half of the entire Buddhist canon has been carved in rock.[22] It may be said that no other nation could have achieved so remarkable a feat.

In India, where Buddhism had its origins, some sūtras may have been engraved on bricks or stone slabs, but we can only find short statements of the "Twelve-linked Chain of Causality" and "the Four Noble Truths." In India, the purpose of engraving a part of a sūtra was not mere sūtra-copying, but was done for the sake of obtaining religious merit. It would be proper to say that such a difference between India and China is due to the characteristic trend of thinking of the Chinese who place such emphasis on literary style. (In this connection mention should be made of the fact that various Chinese, however, did not indulge in this custom of scripture-copying.)

CHAPTER 20 FORMAL CONFORMITY

Fondness for Formal Conformity

As mentioned before, many Chinese scholars regarded certain old classics as absolute authorities, and it was only on these that they composed their commentaries and explanations. Except for the Taoists, they never looked at the classics critically or historically, and thought it sufficient to find no contradictions among the phrases and words. That is to say, they attached great importance to formal conformity.

Cheng Hsüan (127–200), a representative scholar who commented on the Chinese classics in the Later Han dynasty, studied the Five Classics with some other classics, and composed commentaries on them as a unit. Characteristic of his style is the way in which he always referred to the other classics and tried to remove contradictions among them, because he believed that all classics stood on the same basis. In order to have uniformity in the contents of all the classics, he sometimes emended the characters because he thought some words or characters of the classics had been miscopied. This tendency continued in the San-kuo (Three Kingdoms Period, 222–280) and Liu-ch'ao dynasties.[1]

Chinese Buddhist scholars also commented on the sūtras and abhidharmas in this manner. Buddhism was first introduced into China in the time of Emperor Ming (68–75 A.D.) of the Later Han dynasty, and the translations of Buddhist scriptures first started during the time of Emperors Huan (147–167) and Ling (168–188). The basic Buddhist sūtras were translated chiefly by An Shih-Kao and the Mahāyāna sūtras by Lokarakṣa. Thus, both Hīnayāna and Mahāyāna sūtras were translated into Chinese soon after the first introductions of Buddhism. Afterwards, many sūtras were introduced and translated by many Buddhist monks such as Chi-ch'ien of the San-kuo dynasty, Dharmarakṣa of the Hsi-chin dynasty, Kumārajīva, Buddhabhadra, and Dharmarakṣa of the Tung-chin dynasty; this work was continued in later periods by other scholars. Among them, Paramārtha, who translated many abhidharma works, Hsüan-chuang, who translated many sūtras and abhidharma works, and Amoghavajra, who translated many esoteric writings, were famous. The contents of these sūtras and abhidharma works were so varied and different that Chinese Buddhists could reach no conclusion as to what the fundamental doctrine was. Therefore, Chinese Buddhist scholars selected a certain sūtra or abhidharma work as their fundamental text and classified other sūtras and abhidharma works under it. Thus they endeavored to show the mutual relations of these works, and systematized various doctrines of many sūtras under one system. This so-called "critical classification of the doctrines" was tried first in the Eastern Chin dynasty (317–420) and frequently in the later periods. It is one of the characteristics of Chinese Buddhism that the Chinese classified various doctrines of Buddhism under certain systems. Each one of the Chinese Buddhist scholars made his own classification under a certain sūtra or abhidharma work which he regarded as the highest authority. Therefore, many classifications arose in China. Among them, the classification which shows a typical way of thinking of the Chinese is the classification of "the Five Periods." The Chinese, in their high esteem of the individual man, interpreted Śākyamuni as a historical personage who preached all the sūtras. Therefore, they tried to apportion the different sūtras to certain periods—five periods of his life between the time of his enlightenment and his death. This classification of the five periods was first formed by Hui-kuan of the Liu-sung dynasty (420–479) and reorganized by Chi-i, the founder of the T'ien-t'ai sect of China. According to this classification the five periods are as follows:

(1) The first period is the period of the *Avataṁsaka Sūtra.* Just after his enlightenment, Śākyamuni preached the doctrine of the *Avataṁsaka Sūtra* at Buddhagayā under a bodhi-tree for Boddhisattvas for three weeks. The truth can immediately be realized by hearing this doctrine.

(2) The second period is the period of Deer Park. The average person could not understand the teaching of the *Avantaṁsaka Sūtra.* Therefore, Buddha expediently taught the Hīnayāna doctrine at the Deer Park near Benares in order to lead them. The length of this period is twelve years.

(3) The third period is the period of general Mahāyāna sūtras. For those who understood the teaching of the Hīnayāna doctrine, Buddha taught the doctrine of many Mahāyāna sūtras such as *Vimalakīrti-nirdeśa-sūtra, Viśeṣacintābrahma-paripṛcchā-sūtra, Suvarṇaprabhā-sottama-sūtrendrarāja-sūtra* and *Śrīmālā-siṇhanāda-sūtra.* This period continued for eight years.

(4) The fourth period is the period of the *Prajñāpāramitā-sūtras.* After the third period, Buddha taught the *Prajñāpāramitā-sūtras* for twenty-two years in order to let the people understand the doctrine of Śūnyatā (non-substantiality).

(5) The fifth period is the period of the *Saddharma-puṇḍarīka-sūtra* and the *Mahāparinirvāṇa-sūtra*. The Buddha preached the doctrines of the *Saddharmapuṇḍarīka-sūtra* in which he taught that both Hīnayāna and Mahāyāna Buddhists can realize the truth, for the last eight years of his life. At the moment of his death, he taught the *Mahāparinirvāṇa-sūtra* in order to manifest the principle of the Buddha-nature.[2]

The Chinese calculated the number of years of each period from fragmentary records concerning the duration of each preaching mentioned in the above sūtras, although most of these sūtras were composed in periods after the time of the historical Śākyamuni. Here, the characteristic of a Chinese way of thinking historically can be seen very clearly. A question of great importance was whether this sūtra came before or after that sūtra.

This division of years of each period is however most unreasonable, as the people who studied the sūtras logically were aware. For example, even though it was generally believed that the Avataṁsaka Sūtra was preached by the Buddha just after his enlightenment, there are some points in the sūtra which lead to a different conclusion, for people at the time were doubtful as to whether that sūtra was preached by the Buddha immediately after his enlightenment. It is stated in the sūtra that Śāriputra was at this preaching and listened to this sūtra with his disciples. The other sūtras, however, mention that Śāriputra lived in a remote country when Śākyamuni realized the enlightenment. Therefore, it was impossible for Śāriputra to attend the teaching of this sūtra taught by the Buddha just after his enlightenment. It is also unreasonable that the Buddha preached this sūtra in the "Hall of Truth of Universal Light,"[3] as this hall was not yet constructed at the time of Buddha's enlightenment.

Such questions from a detailed study of the text reveal its weak points. However, Chih-yen (602–668) commented on this problem as follows:

"According to the doctrine of the Avataṁsaka Sūtra, the worlds of the past, present, and future mutually interpenetrate one another and are identical. Therefore, it is not unreasonable that there are some contradictions concerning 'before and after' in this sūtra."[4]

From this statement, it appears that Chih-yen did not distinguish between time in the phenomenal world and time in the metaphysical realm. If this doctrine of Chih-yen is recognized, the criticism of the original texts cannot stand. The Chinese Buddhist scholars arranged not only the critical classifications of various doctrines, but also synthesized systematically the thought of the sūtra which they regarded as the absolute authority. It may have been the influence of the Indian way of thinking that led Chinese Buddhist scholars of the Sui and T'ang dynasties (581–907) to make systematic and methodical explanations in spite of the fact that the traditional Chinese philosopher was not fond of systematic arguments. Among the many systems of Buddhist philosophy which were organized in China, those which possessed the greatest systems are the doctrine of the T'ien-t'ai sect and the Hua-yen sect.

The sūtra upon which the T'ien-t'ai sect relies is the *Saddharma-puṇḍarīka-sūtra* from which a new philosophy was systematized. The second chapter of this sūtra in the Chinese translation states: "Only the Buddha and Buddhas can fully realize the basic truths of all existences which are in various processes thus-formed, thus-natured, thus-substantiated, thus-forced, thus-activated, thus-caused, thus-circumstanced, thus-effected, thus-rewarded, and thus-begun-ended-completed." The Chinese took the ten categories of form, nature, substance, force, activation, cause, circumstance, effect, merit, and beginning-ending-completion from this passage, and said that all existences should come under these ten categories; and this sūtra also contains the doctrine of "a moment of thought has the whole cosmos immanent in it." Based upon this doctrine, they again formed different ways of meditative practice. In such ways, the T'ien-t'ai sect developed the new doctrine based upon and summarizing the thought of the *Saddharmapuṇḍarīka-sūtra*.

The *Avataṁsaka sūtra* is a collection of sūtras of a strange kind, consisting of 60 volumes in the old translation by Buddhabhadra and 80 volumes in the new translation by Śikṣānanda. This sūtra states various philosophical ideas in an imaginary world beyond human description and ordinary thought. Therefore, it is very difficult to grasp systematically and enter into the thought itself. Chinese scholars, however, read this sūtra in detail and systematized its doctrines through their own experiences. Thus, the ten-mysteries theory of Tu-shun and six-forms theory of Chih-yen were organized. It was Fa-tsang who combined these two theories together and established the "ten-mysteries-six forms" theory.

The Chinese endeavored to systematize not only the sūtras, but also the Vinayas (disciplinary rules of monastic life). The precepts stated in various Vinaya Piṭakas (scriptures on precepts) which were conveyed from India to China were not always the same. Moreover, the views of Buddhists who practiced precepts were also different. Therefore, it was necessary for the Chinese to arrange and systematize the precepts which they actually followed in their lives. The most important personage among scholars who studied and systematized the precept-rules was Tao-hsüan. The Chinese Vinaya sect was founded by systematizing the precepts in the above manner. This sect continued to prosper for a long time in China. Although this sect was introduced into Japan, it never became popular among the people. The reason for this fact will be mentioned later. As we have seen, it was the important task of Chinese Buddhist scholars[5] to retain formal conformity by classifying, organizing, and systematizing various doctrines and precepts in sūtras and vinayas.

External Conformity

When the Chinese Buddhist scholars organized their classifications and systematizations, they did not deeply consider the logical connections of various doctrines, and only tried to retain an external and formal conformity. They were oblivious of the fact that there were many logical faults in the explanations of their commentaries. They liked to arrange all things in one diagram. A typical example of it can be seen in the theory of five natural elements. They did not investigate the essential character of each thing, but combined all things together by looking for similarities in their external appearances; namely, each one of five directions, five sounds, five forms, five tastes, five internal organs, and many other things divisible into five classes, was assigned to one of the five natural elements, each thing deriving its nature from its respective natural elements.[6] On the basis of this theory, a new doctrine was constructed, explaining the change of dynasties. This theory says that each dynasty possessed one of the natures of the five natural elements, such as wood-nature or fire-nature; therefore, a change in dynasty conformed with a change in the order of the natural elements.[7] When a dynasty would not fit satisfactorily into this system, *the sequence of the lineage of dynasties of the past periods was even reversed.*[8]

In the acceptance of Buddhism, the same kind of logic appeared. Yen Chih-t'ui (6th century) of the Northern Ch'i dynasty declared that the five precepts taught in Buddhism are the same as the five infallible instructions taught in Confucianism. And he matched each one of the five precepts to the five Confucian instructions.[9] A similar interpretation was also adopted by the Chinese Buddhist monks. For example, Tsung-mi said that the objectives of the five precepts and the five instructions were the same although their ways of being practised were different. He also identified each of the five Buddhist precepts with each of the five Confucian rules[10] even though this identification was not correct. Furthermore, Chih-i matched each one of the five precepts of Buddhism to each one of the five invariables, the five classics, and the five natural elements of Confucianism respectively.[11]

The method of classification and exposition used by each of the Chinese Buddhist scholars was to include all things in one system. A great importance was attached to their newly made systems, which tried to explain all other doctrines relative to their own basic doctrine. This tendency often went to an extreme. A typical example of this distortion of texts occurs in their version of the fourth chapter of the *Saddharma-puṇḍarīka-sūtra,* a parable in which a father sought his runaway son. The father represents the Tathāgata (a name for the Buddha, meaning "thus come") and the son stands for sentient beings. In one paragraph, the father in seeking the son arrives at a big house where there were abundant treasures and gems such as gold, silver, ruby, amber, coral, and crystal in the storehouse, and many kinds of servants, such as child servants, head-servants, the second servants, the third servants, and general servants. It is true that powerful families in the country of India possessed an abundance of treasures and servants in ancient times.

The Chinese, however, did not consider this passage merely as a parable. They thought that there must be some important meanings in this paragraph, because it was a part of the holy scripture, the *Saddharma-puṇḍarīka-sūtra.* Therefore, they tried to correlate the different kinds of servants mentioned to each step of discipline in Buddhism. According to Fa-yün's (467–529) opinion,[12] they are divided as follows:

child servants—commoners, both Buddhist and non-Buddhist, as well as novices in Buddhist study
head-servants—Bodhisattvas who are ranked higher than the eighth stage
the second servants—Bodhisattvas who are ranked between the first and seventh stages
the third servants—Pratyekabuddhas
general servants—Bodhisattvas of Ten Stage Grades

According to Chih-i's identification:[13]

child servants—Pratyekabuddhas, Śrāvakas, and Bodhisattvas of Distinct and Common Vehicles
head-servants—Boddhisattvas of Distinct and Perfect Vehicles in ten stages
the second servants—Bodhisattvas of Ten Merit-transference Grades
the third servants—Bodhisattvas of Ten Practice Grades
general servants—Bodhisattvas of Ten Stage Grades

Again, according to Chi-tsang's interpretation:[14]

child servants—non-Buddhist commoners
the third servants
and
general servants—Buddhist commoners
head-servants
and
the second servants—Bodhisattvas higher than the first stage

In the same story, the runaway son who became a laborer happened to come to his father's house and saw his father sitting on the lion's seat surrounded and respected by many Brāhmins, Kṣatriyas and capitalists (*gṛhapati*). Chinese Buddhist scholars likewise classified these people in detail. According to Fa-yün's interpretation:[15]

Brāhmins—Bodhisattvas higher than the eighth stage
Kṣatriyas—Bodhisattvas lower than the seventh stage
Capitalists—general people of Mahāyāna Buddhism

According to Chih-i's classification:[16]

Brāhmins—Bodhisattvas of enlightenment, rid of all defilement
Kṣatriyas—Bodhisattvas between the ninth and the first stages
Capitalists—Bodhisattvas of the 30 grades under the Ten Stages

According to Chi-ts'ang's interpretation:[17]

Brāhmins—Bodhisattvas higher than the eighth stage
Kṣatriyas—Bodhisattvas of the seventh stage
Capitalists—Bodhisattvas higher than the first stage

A great many of such classificational divisions and correlations can be found in the commentaries on sūtras written by Chinese scholars.

Almost all of these interpretations are unreasonable and twisted. Therefore, they are useless for comprehension of the true spirit of the *Saddharma-puṇḍarīka-sūtra*. In the philosophical and systematic doctrine of the Hua-yen Sect, all things are also frequently divided into ten categories and classified into each one of them. In this case also, the Chinese favored formal analogies rather than deductive systematic thinking.

CHAPTER 21 THE TENDENCY TOWARDS PRACTICALITY

The Anthropocentric Attitude

Since ancient times the Chinese have tended to consider all things from an anthropocentric standpoint. They tended to understand even abstract ideas in relation to man. For instance, the Indians expressed the concept of "being" by using the term "*bhāva,*" and the notion of man's "phenomenal existence" by "*bhava.*" The Chinese, however, translated both *bhāva* and *bhava* by the same term "*yu*" without distinguishing the two. "*Yu*" connotes "man has or possesses" as well as "to exist";[1] that is to say, the ancient Chinese considered all things anthropomorphically and did not consider the idea of "existence" as an abstract universal apart from man's concrete impressions of the universe.

In Chinese sentences, the subject is in many cases man (even if it does not appear in the sentence), and the object is stated in the predicate. Therefore, the Chinese can understand the meaning of the sentences in spite of the fact that case-endings are not used, the order of the words not fixed, and most of the phrases consist of the same number of characters. Therefore, there are differences in the ways of expressing ideas between the Indians and the Chinese. The Indians, sometimes, make abstract ideas the subject, while the Chinese usually make man the subject who has the ideas. For example, the Indians say, "therefore, the sufferings accompany him" (*tato naṃ dukkhaṃ anveti*),[2] while the Chinese translated the same sentence as "therefore, he endured various sufferings" (*yi tsu chung*). Thus, even when they express ideas, the Chinese are apt to consider man as the subject rather than the object of the verb. In Indo-European languages when there is no object following the transitive verb, it generally changes into a passive verb.[3] Since the Chinese did not pay much attention to the passive voice, they did not understand man objectively in spite of the fact that they considered all things anthropocentrically. Influenced by this way of considering things anthropocentrically, most Chinese were apt to be utilitarian and pragmatic. In this respect their way of thinking has been different from that of most European scholastic and idealistic philosophers.

It is a well-known fact that the habits and customs of the Chinese are usually based on practical common-sense and utilitarian ways of thinking. The philosophical traditions and studies pursued by the Chinese intelligentsia were centered on practical subjects which had direct relations with everyday living. Most of the Chinese scholars were interested in morals, politics, worldly ways of living that would lead to success. Many of the teachings of Taoism dwell on the art of self-protection, on the method of attaining success, or on the right way of governing. Confucianism, which occupied the highest position in Chinese thought, is also largely a system of ethics for the governing class and a set of precepts for governing the people.

In their characteristic mode of reasoning, the Chinese did not develop the study of logic when it had no relation to utility. The theory of the Category which was discussed by the Chinese is based on pragmatic views. The Japanese translated the word for category by "Han-chū" which is derived from the term *"Hung-fan-chiu-ch'ou"* in the *Shou Ching*. This *Hung-fan-chiu-ch'ou,* however, is not a grammatical or formal-logical category, but a political, moral, and systematic way of reasoning. Chinese historiography also is based upon this pragmatic attitude.

For example, the *Tzu-chih T'ung-chien* ("a general history written for the purpose of governing"), which is a history written by Szu-ma (Wen-kung), quoted more than two sources connected with each historical event in order to establish correct records. Whenever there are any contradictions among the records, he tried to ascertain which one was correct after a detailed documentary collation. Even if the difference was minor and did not greatly influence the event itself, he gave the collation in detail and judged which was correct. With respect to such an attitude it may be said that the style of this history is similar to the modern positive science of history.[5] The purpose of histories such as *Tzu-chih T'ung-chien* was to assist the government, as the title indicates.

Some aspects of Chinese thought can be called "realistic"[6] insofar as they are concerned only with those principles of morals and politics needed in the actual life of the people. This humanistic or anthropocentric tendency of thought also appeared at the time when Indian Buddhist thought came to be accepted by the Chinese, and when they did not accept the natural sciences and mathematics developed in India. It was an exception to the rule that Hsüan-tsang translated the *Sheng-tsung-shih-chu-i-lun* (*Vaiśeṣika-daśapadārtha-śāstra*) of the Vaiśeṣika philosophy which is a kind of natural philosophy in India. However, no one continued the studies in this book after him. In the same light, Indian logic was not accepted eagerly by the Chinese, because it lacked direct connection with practical life.

The method of keeping thoughts in close touch with objects connected with the daily life of man can be found in the expressions of Zen Buddhism which is the most typical sort of Buddhism in China. For example, Fa-tsang said at the moment of his death, "no one can stop man coming and no one can follow man going."[7] The Indian Buddhist expressed the same idea in a different way as "one must not take anything from it and must not remove anything from it. One should see truth as truth. Those who see truth are emancipated."[8] The idea which the Indian contemplated as an ontological relation between man and an object, was viewed by the Chinese in some concrete human relationship of their daily life.

This tendency has been very influential in the process of the transformation of Buddhism in China. Roughly speaking, Buddhism "from an Indian religion of non-ego, has become in China a humanistic religion,"[9] following the anthropocentric humanistic tradition of China.

Worldly Tendency in Religion

The tendency of Chinese thinking to dwell on the actual daily life of man leads to a worldly and materialistic outlook. Such a tendency appeared in various cultural spheres.

First, it can be said that there is very little mythology in Chinese writings; especially in connection with the process of how the sky, earth, sun, moon, and human beings were created. Although some mythological explanations exist in such collateral records as *Chun-nan-tzŭ* (A compilation of various schools of thought by guests of Prince Huai-nan [d. 122 B.C.]), the *Shu-i Chi* (Recorded Analysis of Different Views), and the *San-wu Li-chi* (Records of 35 Histories), this sort of explanation is scarcely found in the traditional and authoritative scriptures and records of China. The first record which is described in the *Shih-chi*, a history of ancient China written by Ssŭ-man T'an (d. 110 B.C.) and his son Ssŭ-ma-ch'ien (145–86 B.C.), is a record of five Lords who are regarded as the first human beings. Yet, supernatural and incredible stories are not mentioned in this history. From ancient times, the Chinese writers have very little use for the mythological imagination and preferred a practical and worldly realism. A typical example of this tendency can be found in the answer of Confucius when asked by people about death: "I do not know what birth is, then how can I know what death is?"[10] (The same attitude can also be found in other philosophers of China.)

Various folk religions existed in China from ancient times and exerted their influence not only on the common people, but also on intellectuals who partly followed these religions. Certain supernatural beings beyond human power were invoked. From ancient times, ancestor worship was an important ceremony in China by which the family and its prosperity were upheld. It was therefore impossible to change this sort of worship into a supernatural and metaphysical religion. There was the idea of *"T'ien"* (Heaven) which can be identified with the idea of "God" in other religions. On the one hand, they also rationalized this idea by giving it the meaning of a natural principle at the same time that they gave it the religious meaning of God. Patriarchs and sages were deified and worshipped, and even the scriptures written by them were highly respected by the people, in spite of the fact that a saint is still a human being. In the Han dynasty, Confucianists taught ways of ridding oneself of disasters and receiving good fortune, as well as many other superstitions. Lao-tzŭ was also worshipped by some people; his naturalistic doctrine was combined with a theory which insisted on the existence of immortal human beings, and which explained how one can attain immortality. Taoism was founded by organizing and systematizing the folk faiths centered on this theory of superhuman beings, and developed through Buddhist influence, but also influenced Chinese Buddhism. Consequently, the religions of China included many prayers and charms through which people wished to remove disasters and to receive good fortune. Originally, Confucianism tried to remove spells and charms from its teaching.[11] However, it could not neglect this religious tendency in the common people. It was not unusual that the teaching of morals and politics was combined with these religious teachings, because the fundamental aims of the Chinese were to satisfy the physical and material demands of human beings.[12]

Chinese Buddhism was also influenced by this worldly trend of thought. Indian Buddhism was generally a metaphysical teaching about the past and future worlds of man, but *the Buddhism which spread among the common Chinese was often a Buddhism of spells and prayers.* In the early period of Buddhism in China, most Buddhists were immigrants from Central Asia who were treated as Chinese. All the Buddhist priests who translated the sūtras into Chinese in the early period of Buddhism in China were familiar with spells and charms. For example, it is said that the Parthian prince An Chih-kao (c. 175 A.D.) mastered not only astronomy, geography, and medical science, but also the mimicry of voices of animals and birds.[13] It is also said that Dharmakāla mastered all kinds of studies and sciences;[14] and K'ang-seng-hui mastered astronomy, geography, and the art of Taoism, and worked many miracles.[15] There was Fo-t'u-ch'eng who came to China in 310 A.D. and spread Buddhism at one time among the people by performing various miracles.[16] He constructed 893 temples and pagodas during his life time. He was respected by the Emperors of the Later Ch'ao dynasty (319–352) and spread Buddhism through their political power. It was in his time that the Chinese people were openly permitted to become priests by the Emperor.[17] Most of the Chinese Buddhist priests in later periods also spread and propagated Buddhism among the people in the same way as Fo-t'u-ch'eng. As the Chinese highly esteemed the employment of spells and charms, they did not accept any sect of Buddhism which prohibited spells and charms in its doctrine. Therefore, they rejected the traditional and conservative Buddhism which prohibited spells and prayers, and called it "Hīnayāna Buddhism." On the whole, they accepted Mahāyāna Buddhism, which permitted charms and prayers to some extent.[18] In early Buddhism, any sort of charm, prayer, divination, sacrifice, or the art of devil-subjugation had been excluded as superstition. Not only priests but lay followers as well were forbidden to perform such superstitious rites in early Buddhism; this ban continued into the later periods.

Mahāyāna Buddhism, on the contrary, compromised with the faiths of the common people and adopted charms and prayers as expedient methods to teach people, for Mahāyāna Buddhism was originally founded as a religion of the common people. It was this Buddhism that was introduced later to flourish for some ten centuries or more in China until the Ming dynasty, and even later.[19] Therefore, spells and charms were clearly a part of Chinese Buddhism. For example, there is a spell in the last part of the Chinese-translated *Prajñā-pāramitā-hṛdaya-sūtra* which is the transliteration of "*gate gate pāragate pārasaṃgate bodhi svāhā*" meaning: "Gone, gone, gone to the other shore, enlightenment, gone to the other shore, so may it be!"

The Indians understood this literary phrase, while the Chinese, on the contrary, transliterated it by adopting Chinese characters which could not be understood, in order to increase the effect of the spell. Therefore, it can be said that Chinese Buddhism possessed the tendency to go in for superstitious ceremonies very strongly. Even at present, the Chinese people, when they become ill or are destitute, perform prayers to various bodhisattvas, heavenly beings and deities of Buddhism as well as to various gods of folk faiths. They also possess highly valued amulets. Buddhist schools which did not possess this tendency did not spread among the people. Even Chih-i, the founder of the T'ien-tai Sect, who was one of the philosophical and systematic Buddhist scholars, taught that "illness is in some cases caused by devils or Māras; therefore, man should chant a certain charm when he is taken ill."[20]

It was the mystical esoteric sort of Buddhism which greatly developed and taught the art of spells and charms. This Buddhism was first introduced in the T'ang dynasty (618–907) and flourished fairly well. This esoteric Buddhism was prohibited in the Ming dynasty (1368–1662) because of its harmful effects. But it has been revived in recent times, since it is suited to the traditional psychology of those Chinese who were originally very fond of ceremonies designed to insure good fortune and relieve disasters.[21]

Influenced by such a tendency among these Chinese, spells and charms came to be accepted in the doctrine of the Chinese Pure Land teachings, which, originally, did not possess magical elements. The Japanese Pure Land teachings, and in particular the Shin Sect, openly opposed such a tendency. Chinese Pure Land teachings, on the contrary, compromised with the tendency of the Chinese. When the Chinese translated the sūtras of the Pure Land teachings, they made use of the special terminology and "method of analogy" (*ko yi*) of Taoism. Moreover, they infused the thought of superhuman beings into the Pure Land teachings by adopting Taoistic words and phrases which could not be found in the original Sanskrit texts.[22] Chinese Pure Land teachings, since the time of their first introduction from India and Central Asia, have been under the influence of Taoism. Chinese Buddhism today is generally the teaching of the Pure Land sect.

At present, Chinese chant a certain spell to invite the soul of the dead before the corpse is put into the coffin. Next, the sūtra to reject hell is chanted, and finally the names of Amita Buddha, Avalokiteśvara Bodhisattva, and Kṣitigarbha Bodhisattva are called three times as a prayer for the dead, and the spell *"Oṃ maṇi padme hūṃ"* is chanted after each name.[23] Also, in the prayer which is chanted after the corpse is put into the coffin in order that the dead may be born in the Pure Land, there is a spell *"Oṃ"* at the beginning and *"Ahuṃ"* at the end.[24] The name *"O-mi-t'o Fo"* (Amita Buddha) itself, which has been in the Chinese Pure Land sects, possesses the magical element of spells or charms.

O-mi-t'o Fo is the transliteration of the Sanskrit term *Amitāyur Buddha* which connotes the meaning "Buddha who possesses infinite life." This Buddha also had another name Amitābha, which means "the one who possesses infinite light (or wisdom)." As we can see, the idea of this Buddha is very philosophical. Such a philosophical idea, however, could not spread among the illiterate people of China. Up to the Sui dynasty, the Chinese-translated name "Wu-liang-shou-fo" (Buddha of Infinite Life) was used.[25] After the T'ang dynasty, however, the Pure Land teachings spread widely, and the transliterated name *"O-mi-t'o Fo"* came to be adopted. One reason was that the tone *"Nan-wu-a-mi-ta-fo"* (Adoration to Amita Buddha!) sounded better than *"Nan-wu-wu-liang-shou-fo"* (Adoration to the Buddha who possesses the infinite life!) when chanted, and another is that the transliteration of the Sanskrit term possesses the strong power of a charm when chanted repeatedly. Moreover, the Sanskrit name which was especially sanctified and could not be understood by the Chinese was easily accepted by the Chinese Buddhists.[26] They felt an exotic and mystical connotation in the name which could not be understood. The name

"*A-mi-ta,*" however, is not the complete transliteration, because it lacks the last part, namely, *Shou* (life) or *Kuang* (light). Nevertheless, the Chinese did not pay much attention to this error. (The single name of "Amita" did not exist in India.) When the Indians say "*Amitāyur Buddha,*" it is always associated with "the Buddha whose life is infinite." On the contrary, the Chinese did not associate this name with its meaning because they transliterated it as "*A-mi-ta,*" instead of Amitāyur or Amitābha. However, the Chinese Buddhists were fascinated in chanting a word which could not be understood. Tan-luan thought that the name "*O-mi-t'o Fo*" itself was identified with the actual Buddha just as the words of Dhāraṇī cast a spell. He said that this name possessed inconceivable powers like that of a spell or charm.[27] In this sense, the Pure Land teachings which originally rejected the elements of spells and charms spread in China among the people only through their magical nature.

This tendency which gave great importance to magical power appeared in an extraordinary manner in China. For example, it was a frequent performance for a priest to cut his arm or burn his fingers in order to express his gratitude and pleasure in hearing and accepting the teachings of Buddhism from his master. When, as sometimes happened, a priest burnt himself to death in the joy of hearing the teachings, his memory was highly revered by the people.

The tendency, however, which esteemed incantation, prospered usually only so far as incantation brought worldly and material advantages, in contrast with the complicated and illusionary imagination prevalent among the Indian people.

Paramārtha, who came to China from India in 546 A.D. and translated many sūtras into Chinese, declared: "There are two kinds of felicities in China, one is that there is no devil and the other is that there is no heretical thought in this country."[28]

The Chinese thus disliked the mysterious, imaginary, and illusionary atmosphere surrounding Buddhism. Therefore, the Chinese who opposed Buddhism often attacked and criticized it at this point. In Zen Buddhism, these illusory fantasies were clearly disliked. Although it cannot be said that no mysterious tendency exists in Zen Buddhists, they acknowledge mysticism only in nature or in the events of daily life, and seldom refer to inconceivable miracles or fantastic mysteries. An example of this can be found in the following questions and answers:

A priest asked his master, "It is said that one who chants the *Prajñā-pāramitā-sūtras* can become most meritorious. Do you believe this?"

The Master answered, "I do not believe it."

Then the priest again asked, "If so, is it useless to believe in the miraculous stories mentioned in the sūtras?"

The Master then answered, "It would be useless to be dutiful to one's parents who are already dead. The sūtras consist of only words, paper, and ink. Therefore, there is no miracle in the sūtras themselves. Miracles exist only in the minds of persons who chant and believe the sūtras; namely, the divine power of the sūtra completely depends on the person who reads it. Place the sūtra on the desk. Does the sūtra possess miraculous power by itself?"[29]

According to the Zen doctrine, therefore, the divine power or the miraculous function taught in Buddhism is none other than such daily activities as "fetching water and carrying firewood."[30] In other words, they are not miraculous experiences. Furthermore, Zen Buddhism in China did not teach that one could be transported to heaven by practicing Zen meditation. The difference between heretical meditation and Buddhist meditation may be said to hinge on this point.[31] The fact that the Chinese were generally worldly does not always mean that they regarded this world as the best world from an optimistic standpoint. From ancient times, there were some thinkers in China who advocated peace of mind and also adopted a pessimistic attitude. For example, Lao-tzŭ said, "The reason why I am suffering is that I have a physical body, if I did not have this physical body, then I would not be suffering" (13th chapter of the *Lao Tzŭ*) Chuang-tzŭ also expressed a similar thought when he regarded this world as the world which should be despised, as in Buddhism. This similarity of attitude was one of the reasons why Buddhism was easily accepted by the Chinese. Nevertheless, Lao-tzŭ and Chuang-tzŭ did not consider past worlds before birth and the future world after death. The Chinese had a very simple idea concerning the destiny of man after death. They thought that death was "the separation of one's soul from the physical body." And again they believed that one's soul was always hovering over the physical body after burial in the tomb. Therefore, they thought it possible to call back the departed soul to its body by crying out and calling its name. For this reason, a religious ceremony where friends cry and weep for the dead was established over two thousand years ago, and is still performed among the common people at present in China.[32]

Chinese philosophers also were very indifferent to man's destiny after death. They thought it is useless to ask about the world after death since the present world itself cannot even be understood well. This idea is very different from the ideas of most Indian philosophers. According to the early Buddhist sūtras, Gotama Buddha was silent in answering this question about life after death. In the case of Gotama, however, he did not answer because he realized that the answer to such a question would generally perplex people. Confucius, on the contrary, would not discuss the next world because he was too concerned about moral and political problems from a worldly and utilitarian standpoint. Zen Buddhism's way of facing this problem by accepting the essential standpoint of Buddhism is strikingly Chinese. For example, Hui-hai's view can be seen in the following question and answer:

A disciple asked his master Hui-hai, "Do you know why, when, and where you were born?"

Hui-hai answered, "As I am not dead myself, it is impossible to discuss birth. If you realize that birth is identical with the essence of non-birth, then you will never assert the existence of non-birth apart from the essence of birth."[33]

In the philosophy of Chu-tzŭ (1130–1200) also, the soul and spirit are not mentioned. "Even the saint cannot explain what the soul and spirit are. It is, of course, not correct to say that the soul exists. Again it is not correct to say that the soul actually does not exist. Therefore, it is better not to mention anything about matters which man cannot actually see or clearly understand."[34]

The problem of eschatology which discusses man's destiny after death was discussed very little and hardly existed in China. According to the way of thinking of the Chinese, death is a necessary phenomenon for birth. Therefore, they faced death composedly and did not worry about life after death. That is to say, "birth is identical with death."[35] Chuang-tzŭ's attitude towards death, exemplified again and again in his work, is "one not merely of resignation nor even of acquiescence, but a lyrical, almost ecstatic acceptance."[36] Yang Hsiung (died in 18 A.D.) taught, "Those who were born will surely die. It is a natural principle that things which have a beginning must have an end."[37]

This way of thinking is very different from the conception of birth and death among the Indians. According to the view of Indians in general, man, as one of the world's living beings, has to go through repeated transmigration in cycles of birth and death. Therefore, for Indians, the ideal state of man is to be born in the heavenly world or to attain the state of absolute existence or absolute joy in the future life by accumulating good deeds and practicing various disciplines in his life. Buddhism in India was not an exception to this idea. After Buddhism was introduced into China, however, a view peculiar to the Chinese concerning the conception of birth and death appeared instead of the original view of Buddhism. For example, Chi-tsang (549–623) said at the moment of his death:

"Man cherishes birth and fears death as he does not understand the true aspect of birth and death. Death originates from birth. Therefore, man should fear birth instead of death. If I were not born, then I would surely not die. If birth, the beginning, is realized, then death, the end, will surely be known. In this sense, man has to be sad about his birth and need not fear death."[38] From this statement, we can understand why Chi-tsang, who was a great Buddhist scholar, was still actually Chinese in his way of thinking.

Such a tendency concerning the conception of birth and death can be seen most clearly in Zen Buddhism,[39] for it is widely believed that high priests who seriously practiced Zen meditation would be born in the land of death instead of in the Heaven where the Europeans and Indians believed such great recluses were born. For example, Ju-ching (1163–1228) composed the following poem at the moment of his death:

"For sixty-six years, I committed a great many sins, and now I am going to the land of death."[40]

Dōgen (1200–1253), who introduced the Sōtō Zen sect to Japan from China in 1227, also was in a similar state of mind on his death bed. In India, as in the medieval age in Europe, the thought that life in this world was a preparation for a better future world was very strong. In China, however, this thought did not arise so often, and in that sense it may be said that the Chinese did not practice deep and religious introspection; that is to say, they did not possess a deep consciousness of sin. It is often pointed out that the ideas of "original sin" and "salvation" were not taught in Confucianism. Buddhism was accepted and spread quickly in China as a religion which made good these deficiencies of the other Chinese religions, and had a great influence on Chinese culture. Chinese Buddhism, however, gradually became harmonized and mixed with popular folk religions or Taoism and again became a worldly religion. As Fung Yu-lan aptly says, we must distinguish Buddhism in China from Chinese Buddhism.

It is an undeniable fact that religion still possesses an important significance in the society of present-day China. De Groot points out in his book that those who know Chinese religions know the Chinese people because in China, as in all half-civilized societies, every activity of social life of the Chinese was greatly influenced by religious thought and religious customs which were to a great extent the basis of public morality, customs, family system, government system, and the legislation of the Chinese.[41]

In the philosophies of the Chinese religions, the deep consciousness of sin and a reliance on, or obedience to, an absolute cannot generally be found. On this point, present-day Chinese religions are greatly different from present-day Indian religions. Therefore, De Groot believes that "most of the rituals and customs which are conducted by the Chinese at present cannot be recognized by people of the world except in uncivilized areas."[42] Thus, again it can be said that some salient characteristics of the Chinese religions are their incantatory, utilitarian, and worldly features.

These same characteristics of the traditional Chinese trend of thinking, manifested in the acceptance of Buddhism, can also be found in their acceptance of Christianity. Generally speaking, the Indian Christians highly esteem the church and the faith, and they are other-worldly, transcendental, and mystical. Chinese Christians, on the contrary, are generally this-worldly, humanistic, realistic, and pragmatic. Because they are, furthermore, political and practical, they are generally indifferent to supernatural considerations concerning the transcendency of the Gospel or the relation between God and man. On the contrary, most Indian Christians believe that the practice of Christian Love is not to be sought in politics, and they exclude all worldly interests when they pray to God.[43] Thus, the same differences of ways of thinking between the Indians and the Chinese appear in the case of adopting Christianity as in the case of accepting Buddhism.

In modern times the Chinese have become increasingly worldly and more averse to accepting Indian religious thought than ever before. When Tagore—a comparatively worldly thinker for an Indian—visited China in 1924 and preached the superiority of "Eastern spirituality" over "Western materialism," he was attacked as a living symbol of the futile passivity of Eastern religions, a passivity that had reduced India to colonial and China to semi-colonial status.[44] Though "this-worldliness" is not a unique trait of the Chinese, it is especially salient as a characteristic way of thinking among them.

Non-development of Metaphysics

In connection with these tendencies, non-religious transcendental metaphysics did not develop among the Chinese out of their own habits of thinking, but only under the impact of foreign culture. In the second millennium B.C., the Chinese had the conception of "Heaven" (*T'ien*) as a place above the world where rulers, i.e. kings, generals, and ministers, went after death. Since the Supreme Ruler of the universe lived there, the term "*T'ien*" also denoted the supreme deity, who was named "the *ti*." With the passage of time, other *ti* were postulated, until there were many *ti*.

Records mentioned in the *Five Classics* (*Wu Ching*) mostly represent events connected with the actual human world, and are hardly concerned with transcendental worlds. Sometimes, we are told, *T'ien* rules all existences as well as human beings. This idea of *T'ien*, however, is not separate from the idea of *T'ien* as the visible sky above; in this sense, this idea does not transcend the empirical world.[44] Certainly with the rise of Taoism, "Heaven" became materialized.

Among the ancient Chinese philosophies, the philosophy which might be said to have a metaphysical character was Taoism. Taoists thought that the real truth (*Ta-tao*) exists in the realm where all names and ways of practices of doctrines such as benevolence and justice in Confucianism are abandoned. And the original state of the Universe was an existence of no form or name to serve as the symbol of the Truth.[45] We can recognize a germ of metaphysical character in this consideration. Taoism, however, harmonized and combined the arts of self-protection and cultivation in later periods when it renounced its metaphysical system. Aside from this idea of Taoism, there were some other metaphysical ideas in Chinese philosophies. The conception of *T'ien* in the *Five Classics,* the doctrine of *T'ai-chi* (first principle) in the *I Ching,* and the principle of *Li* (reason) taught by Chu-tzŭ, of the Southern Sung dynasty (1127–1279), are examples of such ideas. Explanations of these metaphysical principles, however, were not fully given, and clear definitions of these principles were not shown except orally. The existence of these principles was only asserted. For example, in the philosophy of Chu-tzŭ, which is the most philosophical study of all, a clear explanation of "Li" cannot be found. Chu-tzŭ declared frequently that *Li* ruled all existences in this world. However, he invariably answered the questions of his disciples as to what *Li* was as follows: "It will be realized in the near future." That is to say, he kept silent about the character of *Li* in spite of his assertion of its existence.[46]

In this manner metaphysical systems did not develop in China. Chi-tsang pointed out the fact that, in general, Chinese philosophies regarded the opposition of subjectivity and objectivity as merely relative, that is, as one that did not transcend common sense.[47] Tsung-mi also criticized this same point in the Chinese philosophies.[48] Again some Buddhist priests criticized Chinese philosophies in general because they never set forth the three worlds of the past, the present, and the future, or the six divine powers,[49] and moreover they did not understand what the soul or the spirit was.[50] These criticisms can be said to be correct evaluations of Chinese philosophies in general.

When Confucians saw the attractive aspects of metaphysics in Buddhism, they too developed a metaphysics. Neo-confucian metaphysics in the Sung Learning (*Sung-hsüeh*) owed much to Buddhist metaphysics. It is said that Chinese philosophical thought attained its summit when the *Sung-hsüeh* philosophy was completed. Nevertheless, even Chu-tzŭ, the founder of the *Sung-hsüeh* philosophy, did not state a systematic explanation of the doctrine at all.[51]

The Chinese, lacking the copula in their language, were not quite conscious of judgments of attribution. Therefore, they could not clearly distinguish the difference between the metaphysical principle of substance and derivative attributes.[52] After Buddhism was introduced into China, it was greatly influenced by the anti-metaphysical trend of thought among the Chinese. For example, the Chinese San-lun school (Three Treatises) was based upon the *Chung-lun* of Nāgārjuna and other treatises. The doctrine of Nāgārjuna states that worldly truth is the foundation of all existences, but that metaphysical truth is the essence of worldly truth and ontologically different from it. In the non-metaphysical, nominalist doctrine of the San-lun school, on the contrary, it is thought that the differences between these two truths are only differences in ways of expression. They therefore interpreted worldly truth as an explanation of what existence was and real truth as the evidence of non-substantiality.[53] In such a viewpoint a constructive metaphysics cannot be established. By this reasoning the philosophy of the *Vijñaptimātratā* (pure consciousness), which investigated the order of establishment of absolute existence, did not become influential in the world of thought in China in spite of the fact that it was introduced into China by Paramārtha in the Liang and Ch'en dynasties (6th century A.D.). This philosophy again was introduced by Hsüan-tsang in the T'ang dynasty (7th century) and was protected and supported by the Imperial Court. Nevertheless, it soon declined.[54] An analysis of psychological phenomena in the doctrine of the Abhidharma of Hīnayāna Buddhism also did not develop in China. This kind of subjective idealism was not suited to the mentality of the Chinese. Scarcely any metaphysical tendency can be found in the doctrine of Zen Buddhism. Tsung-mi acknowledged the fact that the teachings of Zen Buddhism concerning metaphysics were very simple.[55]

It may safely be said that the doctrine of the Hua-yen sect was the greatest adaptation of Mahāyāna Buddhism among the various philosophical systems organized by the Chinese. This doctrine transcends the traditional Buddhist philosophy while accepting it in modified form. Philosophical thought in Buddhism as well as in Indian metaphysics generally set forth the two ideas of absolute existence and the phenomenal world. The absolute is the idea of indeterminate non-form and non-discrimination, while the phenomenal world is known through form and discrimination. The Indian metaphysicians tried to explain the relations between them mainly by arguing about the relations between the Reality and the Appearances. The Chinese Hua-yen sect, on the contrary, insisted that all phenomena mutually interpenetrate, and moreover, each one of them possesses absolute significance in itself. In this theory, the Absolute is not the important subject while the relation between one phenomenon and another is greatly expanded. It is from this standpoint that the basic doctrines are taught that "all phenomena are interdependent without obstructions" and "one is all, and spontaneously at the same time, all is one." In these theories, the Reality is understood as something which is included in phenomena. In the Indian philosophies, the relations between individual existence and permanent existence, or the one and the many, were the central subjects. On the contrary, in the Hua-yen sect of China, the main subjects were relations between one individual being and another, or between one limited existence and another. Although this tendency can be found in the doctrines of the T'ien-t'ai sect, it is more clearly formulated in the doctrines of the Hua-yen sect; therefore, it can be said that the Hua-yen sect is a more Chinese and more developed form of Mahāyāna Buddhism. In such a philosophy, the attempt to assume metaphysical principles was completely abandoned; philosophers dwelt only in the shadow of the empirical and phenomenal worlds.

CHAPTER 22 INDIVIDUALISM

The Tendency Towards Egoism

Contrary to certain opinions current in the West, the Chinese developed an individualism of their own which goes back to ancient times.

"While property was held in common, each son had his inalienable right to inheritance. There was no individual vote guaranteed by a constitution, and yet in village meetings every male adult was a voting member by natural right. In the thirteen-century-long tradition of civil service examinations, the basis for the selection of government officials was individual merit rather than race, creed, economic status, sex, or age."[1] The significance of the individual was fully admitted in ancient Chinese philosophy: "Although the leader of three armies can be captured, the will of a common man cannot be destroyed."[2]

Confucianism, the main ideology of Chinese intellectuals, was normally and properly associated with the idea of civic participation or public service. In fact, however, there was an equally valid aspect of Confucianism, apparent in the thought of Confucius and Mencius, which justifies the individual's withdrawal from public life and official service under some conditions. Confucian eremitism was especially prevalent in the Yüan period (1271–1368). Needless to say, this tendency was strong among Buddhist recluses. In many cases they showed a voluntary eremitism in protest against political power.

Dr. Chan has recently indicated "an excess of individualism" in China:

"Actually, one of China's chief troubles in recent decades has been an excess of individualism. Everyone has his own opinion. There have been far too many individualists who think they are above society. Teamwork and cooperative enterprise have been conspicuously lacking. This is the type of thing the communists have set out to destroy. The problem is whether they will destroy the individual himself."[3]

Then, does Chinese individualism conflict with altruism? The Chinese, like other people, do not lack the spirit of altruism. Mutual helpfulness in the family and in the villages is common. There is, of course, plenty of selfishness—as there is in other cultures. Buddhist altruism helped China, but altruism was esteemed as a high virtue in China long before Buddhism arrived. The first legendary ruler is believed to have spent a good part of his life in digging watercourses for the rivers in order to stop floods, neglecting his own family in serving the public. The only difference between Chinese altruism and that of other peoples is that the Chinese consciousness of being members of the nation or state has been weak. Perhaps, that is why they were occasionally blamed as egoistic even by their countrymen, and this is what the Communist Government is striving to correct through its totalitarian indoctrination.

Chinese individualism was limited by several cultural factors, and did not develop along the same line as it did in the West. Among these factors were (as we have already seen) the traditional Chinese attitude of static understanding, their way of thinking which emphasizes concrete particulars, and the trend in their thinking which imposes upon the individual the great importance of past events and the traditional wisdom of the sage. This incubus of historical tradition differentiates clearly the concept of the individual held by the Chinese from that held by the Indians. To these limitations on Chinese individualism must be added the factor of the traditional Chinese tendency towards a "closed" society and morality. That is to say, the Chinese always regarded themselves as confined to life around such limited human relations as the family, which provides the most intimate of personal relations. In ethics, for example, moral relations among only certain individuals, such as father and son, sovereign and subject, wife and husband, were considered important, so that the Chinese people tended to pay little attention to any international principles of morality or laws valid for society in all countries (such as the *jus gentium*).

This may have been a natural way of edification. Chinese ethics was written and taught for the use of those who could read, the literate few who were the potential leaders of the people. The common people, being illiterate, were expected to follow the practices of the literate; hence if morality was taught to the literates, it would spread through the society.

The ethical doctrine of Lao-tzŭ is consequently a morality for the self-protection and safety of the individual even in the cases where altruistic virtues were taught. The Buddhists criticized Lao-tzŭ by saying that his teaching pertains only to one's own life and is useless to other people.[4] The view of Yang-tzŭ is "to complete the true nature of man and follow truth,"[5] which, he implies, is none other than to satisfy men's physical desires. Chuang-tzŭ also insisted that man should not perform good deeds for fame, should not perform evil deeds which would bring about punishment, and should behave in conformity to his physical desires, for then he would be able to realize his true nature and live a long life.[6] The theory of self-cultivation which appeared in the latter part of the *Chan-kuo* (the Age of Warring States, 403–221 B.C.) period is an art meant to protect and preserve one's physical health. The theory of seclusion also is the art of protecting one's life by keeping away from worldly and powerful positions where dangers are apt to arise. The theory of superhuman beings also stems from the desire to prolong man's life eternally and to enjoy life endlessly. All these theories can be said to foster a kind of egoism. Some scholars even regard the teaching of Mo-tzŭ (died c. 390 B.C.), who taught the way to love others, was also a form of egoism insofar as he taught that to love others is simply in order to be loved by others.[7]

The humanistic spirit of Confucianism appears in its teaching the rules of statesmanship. It, however, teaches the art of statecraft followed by the governing class. It expects that the sage will benefit all. But it does not expect the sage to teach all people, for the simple fact that illiterates could not benefit. Illiterates must be taught by ordinary Confucians, not by Confucius. For example, Tung Chung-shu (*ca.* 179–*ca.* 104 B.C.), one of the greatest Han Confucians, is said to have had over 3,000 disciples. But he never saw most of them! He taught a small coterie of intimate disciples and expected them to pass on his teaching to the others! So the ordinary Confucian was expected to be an official or a teacher.

Thus, the Confucian theory of humanism was not derived from the idea that man is saved as man and sentient beings as sentient beings. The moral practice of filial piety also possessed the tendency towards egoism. In the 13th century, Dōgen of Japan pointed out this fact very clearly in order to contrast this tendency of Confucianism with the altruism of his Buddhism. Dōgen said that the teaching that Buddhas and Bodhisattvas can appear in various forms at any place and time in order to save all living beings, cannot be found in the teachings of Confucianism.[8]

It is evident that these humanistic and individualistic tendencies in Chinese thought had a close connection with the actual conditions of life in the Chinese farm-villages. Of course, I mean pre-communist China. There was relatively little group consciousness in the Chinese farm-villages, for very seldom did farmers cultivate and irrigate the land together. Consequently, the independent government of the farmers was very conservative. These characteristics in the life of the Chinese farm-villages were naturally correlated with the Chinese way of thinking. The rural situation of present-day communist China may be different.

The Spiritual Leadership of Buddhism and Its Transformation

Chinese Buddhists criticized the self-centered attitude of other Chinese philosophers. After Buddhism was introduced into China sometime in the first century, Buddhists engaged in a great many altruistic activities in accordance with the ideal of "Compassion." Ever since Shih-lo (*ca.* 329 A.D.) of the Later Chao period, who was influenced by the teaching of Fo-t'u-ch'eng, left the education of his children to the temple, the temple possessed great importance in education. The social work of Buddhist priests was especially noticeable in its medical treatment and relief of the poor. In the Eastern Chin period (4th and 5th century A.D.), Fo-t'u-ch'eng, Fa-k'uang, K'o-lo-chieh, An-hui of Lo-yang, and Tan-tao of Lo ching-shan helped the people obtain medical treatment. The necessary offerings were also available in the temples. In the T'ang dynasty (618–907), the system of temple hospitals was established, and institutions for the poor, the sick, and the orphaned were built. In times of famine, Buddhist priests and nuns devoted themselves to the relief of the people. As the organ of monetary circulation for the common people, a pawn house called "*Wu-chin-tsang* (the limitless storehouse)" was founded in the Six Southern and Northern dynasties. Besides these activities, Buddhist priests endeavored to build bridges, plant trees, dig wells, and construct rest-houses. In the Southern and Northern dynasties, many temples were built in the center of the city. The people were charmed by the noble images of Buddhas or the ornaments of the temples which gave rise to thoughts of the Pure Land. Thus, temples became comfortable rest places for the people who became interested in and familiar with Buddhism.[9]

It appears, however, that the Chinese Buddhists were not conscious of the individual worth of others when they performed these social works, but believed that one could be identified with others by practicing these activities. From ancient times, the Tao religion taught that "the correct way of human morality is the oneness of all existence."[10] Chuang-tzŭ also esteemed "the equality of nature," and again Chang-tzŭ of the Sung philosophy said that "human beings and all other creatures are my friends."[11] In the traditional thought-system of the Chinese, it seems that the existential problem of "confrontation" of one person with another was not a relevant issue. On the contrary, in the Buddhist doctrines of the Sui and T'ang dynasties, this problem was logically resolved. According to the doctrine of the T'ien-t'ai sect, the fundamental principle which makes possible practical and altruistic activities is the "non-duality of self with the other,"[12] so that the doctrine of "helping others in conformity with their capacities" followed logically, since self-realization was the major premise. In the Hua-yen school, the doctrine that "one is all and all are one" was taught also by Zen Buddhism.[13] Philosophical arguments such as the demonstration of the existence of others, set forth by Dharmakīrti of India,[14] and the proof of the existence of the self, discussed in modern Europe, did not appear in China.

The doctrine of altruistic practice based upon the compassion of Buddhism could not completely change the Chinese tradition, which was focused on limited human relations. Buddhism was accepted and spread in China in ways which led to compromises with the thought of meditative seclusion, compromises peculiar to Chinese Buddhism and in conformity with Chinese habits of thought. Generally speaking, Chinese Buddhism was transcendent and other-worldly and apart from common society. Most of its temples were situated in forests and mountains.[15] This can be clearly found in the Chinese phrase that "to build a temple" was "to open the mountain." The famous and big temples were all built in far-off mountains far away from villages.[16] All Buddhist recluses went to these mountains and observed the precepts, practiced meditation, and furthered themselves spiritually by living together with their fellow-monks. They believed that truth could be realized only through these practices. Although the followers who chanted the name of Amida Buddha were mainly in contact with the people, many of their famous monks were confined to mountains.[17] Famous Buddhist scholars such as Tsung-mi[18] and Chih-i, the founder of the T'ien-t'ai sect, had also secluded themselves in the mountains for study and self-cultivation. It was the ideal of Zen priests to be secluded in mountains to enjoy the peaceful quiet. When Dōgen intended to return to his homeland Japan, his Chinese master, Ju-ching, instructed him as follows: "When you go back to your country, spread the doctrine of Buddhism for the benefit of both men and deities. Do not stay in the center of cities or towns. Do not be friendly with Kings and state ministers. Dwell in the deep mountains and valleys to realize the true nature of man. Do not break the tenets of our Sect!"[19]

Corresponding with this tendency among the Buddhist priests, the Chinese in general also praised and esteemed it as the pure and desirable way of life. For example, Meng-hao-jan composed the following poem to praise the hermitage and Zen practice of his teacher Yi: "Master Yi practices the quiescence of meditation and built a hermitage in the forest; a mountain is situated near it and shadows of trees cover the hermitage; when the sun sets there is perfect silence around the hermitage. Here, he realized the pure mind of man by observing the pure and beautiful lotus."

There are many poems honoring temples and priests in the *T'ang-shih-hsüan* (a collection of poems composed in the T'ang dynasty). These poems praise the fact that temples were situated in quiet places far from the villages and also praise the priests who sincerely endeavored to purify themselves and practice the Buddhist exercises in these quiet places.[20]

Such an attitude of life where one lives in a quiet place and enjoys the state of quiescence is especially prominent in Taoistic teachings. According to the Lao-tzŭ, a return to the root of existence is called quietness, and figuratively, a rebirth.[21] And again his follower, Kuan-yin, said, "one should be quiet as a mirror and response should be like an echo," and "one becomes pure by quiescence."[22] Lieh-tzŭ (third century A.D.) taught that man should abandon all discrimination and thought and should have quiescence and "emptiness."[23] T'ien-p'ien, P'eng-meng, and Shen-tao also taught that man should abandon discrimination and judgment of diversity, that is, one should reject judgments of this and that, one or the other, and should observe the oneness of all existence.[24] Such thought can also be found in the teaching of Kuan-tzŭ (Kuan Chung, *ca.* 650 B.C.).[25]

This sort of quietism also influenced Chinese Buddhism. The practice of meditation was highly esteemed in Chinese Buddhism.[26] The important practice for Chih-i (Master of the T'ien-t'ai School) was that of meditative concentration of the mind. Even the San-lun sect, which is regarded as a representative sect of philosophical Buddhism, insisted upon the importance of "concentration of mind."[27] Introspective and meditative tendency is especially prominent in Zen Buddhism, in which the mind is called "the origin of the truth or *Dharma*,"[28] and asserts that our mind is namely the Buddha itself.[29] In order to purify and attain the mind's realization, which reveals the essence of truth, one must practice the meditative posture of sitting (*zazen*).[30] Meditative rest is not merely a means to attain the final stage, but the meditative posture itself epitomizes the "fundamental or fullest essence"[31] of man. Meditation at rest is the substance of wisdom.[32]

The wisdom which is emphasized in the Ch'an (Meditation, Zen) sect is one which is absolutely separate from the confrontation of "self and others." This aim of self-realization by emancipation characterizes Buddhism in general: "The true *Dharma* (virtue) is to abandon both the mind and its objects."[33] It is when discrimination of all forms is rejected that the absolute appears: "When thought is stopped and discrimination abandoned, the Buddha spontaneously appears before one."[34] Now this state is namely the state of emancipation which can be attained only by realization of the nature of the mind in the meditative posture of sitting.[35] This state of emancipation, however, is not always a mere state of quiescence. For the enlightened priests of Ch'an (Zen) Buddhism, this state yields an awareness of life in practice. And this is called "a road of furtherance"[36] which must be realized by the man who practices it himself. Thus the technique of Zen practice became utterly Chinese; the type of meditation became occasionally diametrically opposed to Indian meditation. In Indian meditation, the mind tries to avoid the external world by ignoring outside influence; however, Chinese meditation works with the aid of external influence, operates in this world, emphasizes quick wit and insight, and aims at self-realization.[37]

The teachings of the Pure Land sect[38] were also influenced by this way of thinking advocated by Zen Buddhism, for some early Pure Land teachings of China possessed characteristics of the original teaching. For example, the Pure Land teaching of Shan-tao (613–668 A.D.) asserted that the Pure Land actually exists in the direction west of this very world. It is not surprising, therefore, to read that many people committed suicide in order to be born in the Pure Land by following the doctrine of Shan-tao who taught: "Loathe this defiled world and desire to be born in the Pure Land." The way of practicing the thinking of Buddha taught by Chih-i was to meditate and observe each one of the excellent features of Amida Buddha in one's mind.[39] The Chinese, however, who were worldly, realistic, and preferred peace of mind, changed the teachings of the Pure Land sect. They insisted that the Pure Land of Amitābha Buddha existed only in the mind of man. There is a paragraph in the Chinese translation of the *Amitāyur-dhyāna-sūtra* which states that "the Pure Land of Amitābha Buddha is situated not too far from this world, and therefore, the features of the Pure Land can be observed by meditative concentration of the mind." Zen monks interpreted this as follows: "The ignorant desire to be born in the Pure Land by calling the name of the Buddha. The enlightened one, on the contrary, purifies his own mind. The Buddha therefore, said, 'In conformity with the purity of the mind, the land of the Buddha also becomes pure.' If the mind is purified, the people of the east are sinless. If the mind is not purified, on the contrary, even the people of the west are sinful. The ignorant desire to be born in the land to the west. The lands of the east and the west, however, are situated in the same place. If the mind is pure, the Pure Land exists close to this world. On the contrary, if one awakens impure thoughts in the mind it is difficult to be born in the Pure Land even if one chants the name of the Buddha."[40]

The Zen monks then asserted the teaching which they derived from the passage of the *Vimalakīrti-nirdeśa-sūtra* that "the pure mind is identical with the Pure Land."[41] Thus, they insisted on "a mind-only doctrine"[42] and finally the teaching came to be taught that "the Pure Land of the pure mind exists in all parts of the world."[43] After the Sung dynasty, the Chinese Buddhists exclusively followed this pure-mind view, and after the Ming dynasty, no contradiction was felt in practicing simultaneously sitting and the Pure Land practice.

In Chinese Buddhism the most important practice, therefore, was to purify one's own mind so that one would need to depend exclusively upon oneself, and not rely upon any other power, not even the power of the Buddha. In this connection, Hu-hai (550–606 A.D.) said: "You should realize the fact that man saves himself, and the Buddha cannot redeem man. Practice by yourself and do not rely upon the favor of the Buddha. It is set forth in the sūtra: 'Therefore, those who look for the true *dharma* should not rely upon Buddha.' "[44]

According to this theory each individual has to face the Absolute by himself. Consequently, the authorities of the church, religious organizations, or any divine person who claimed to act as a medium between the individual and the Absolute were not recognized.

Non-formation of Religious Sects

Since priests and religious organizations as intermediaries were regarded as unnecessary in China, Chinese religions do not have the sectarian character so typical of the religions of other peoples. Confucianism, which was originally worldly, was combined with governmental officials' power. It did not, however, form a state-church organization. Neither did Taoism form a religious organization with a central state-controlled administration. The same circumstances prevailed in the case of Chinese Buddhism. There were no monks in China such as the itinerant Śramaṇas of India. All the Buddhist monks in China stayed and lived in temples, where sectarian distinctions were not recognized.[45] The individual priest had a right to live in any temple so long as he observed the Buddhist precepts.

In present-day Chinese Buddhist society, there is no organization controlling the temples and they are not interfered with politically. Mt. T'ien-t'ai is the sacred place for Chinese T'ien-t'ai priests because it was here that the founder, Chih-i, lived and founded the doctrine of this sect, so that this place became the headquarters of the Chinese T'ien-t'ai priests in various other districts, for there are no relations between an individual priest in one locality and another priest elsewhere. Similarly, the Shao-lin-ssu Temple on Mt. Sung is the place where Bodhidharma, the founder of the Zen sect, practiced meditative sitting, facing the wall for nine years, so that this temple is the most holy temple as well as the incomparable practice-ground for Zen priests. Nevertheless, it is not the headquarters of the Zen sect and there is no connection between this temple and other Zen temples although some pilgrims come to it. Zen Buddhism originally insisted on the importance of the conveyance of the teachings from teacher to disciple, and the relation between master and disciple was very important. In spite of this fact, there is no connection between various temples.[46] The temple in pre-Communist Chinese Buddhism was a mere structure to accommodate priests. Therefore, priests of various sects lived in the same temple. If the head priest of a temple was a priest of the Pure Land sect, the temple belonged to the Pure Land sect. If the head priest of a temple was a priest of the Zen sect, it was a temple of the Zen sect. For this reason, the sect of one and the same temple was always changing in accordance with the sect of the head priest.[47] In this sense, it can be said that the distinction of sects depended solely on the will of the individual priest.

In Japan, on the contrary, a temple always belongs to a certain sect, and it does not change with the sect of the head priest as in China where the sect of the temple is always changing with the change of the head priest.[48] Generally speaking, in modern times Chinese Buddhism has tried to harmonize its various Zen sects.[49] It seems to me that this tendency of Chinese Buddhism appeared in the latter part of the Ming dynasty.[50]

Therefore, Chinese became Buddhist followers only through the preaching of individual priests. Chinese temples do not have fixed followers or believers. Great land-owners who supported the temple sometimes contributed land or forests, with the income from which a temple could maintain its disciples and become prosperous. Head priests of great temples considered it a very important mission to train and foster many priests. Therefore, they requested contributions and offerings from their followers, believers or anyone with whom they had relations.[51] On the occasions of religious services and funeral rites, the Buddhist followers usually invited a certain priest to perform them. Or in some cases, they held the ceremonies at a temple they designated. In this connection, many followers of Buddhism gathered at a temple of a famous and virtuous priest whose name was widely known. Therefore, a temple was often revived or newly built through contributions and offerings which were donated to these virtuous famous priests.

What has happened to the priests and their disciples in Communist China today is not well known. Since the Communist revolution the social situation has greatly changed. But, judging from information occasionally acquired by us, the Buddhists' situation seems to remain unchanged so long as the Buddhist orders do not conflict with the policy of the government.

Universality of Tao (The Way)

Thus, Chinese Buddhists disapproved the authority of the religious organization or church as the medium between the Absolute and the individual, and they exlusively followed the *dharma* (the norm or principle) or the *tao*[52] (the way) which was considered the Absolute itself. Indian people made use of the term *dharma* in many cases but the Chinese preferred the term *tao*. The word *tao* possesses a more concrete connotation that the word *dharma*. Otherwise, the meaning of these two words was essentially the same in the eyes of Buddhists at that time. The practice of Taoists is similar to the Indian practice of Yoga with respect to seeking tranquillity of mind, longevity, miraculous powers, etc.[53]

In this sense the Chinese have been fully conscious of the universality of *tao*. They assume that even though countries differ, the same moral principles are observed and followed all over the world,[54] and that a certain thought system transcends time and possesses a universal validity true for all ages.[55] They believe that the idea of *tao*, which can be found in all religions in various forms, is also universal truth. Therefore, it is said that "*tao* is not able to realize itself, but can be realized by man. Even though there are various ways to realize it, the *tao* itself, however, does not change through the ages. That which changes in time and place is not *tao*, but men and the world. The theory of *one principle covers all* (Confucius), the idea of *non-creation* (Lao-tzŭ), and the goal of *nirvāṇa* (Śākyamuni), all point up the fact that different men taught the same truth."[56]

For some thinkers, the idea of *dharma* in Chinese Buddhism was a higher principle than that of the Buddha. The authority of the Buddha is established only insofar as it is based upon the authority of the *dharma*. "Those who realized the *dharma* are called Buddha."[57] It is said that Tan-hsia, a priest of the Zen sect, burnt a wooden image of the Buddha to admonish people who idolized the Buddha but ignored the significance of the *dharma* embodied in it. The Pure Land teachings state that one should meditate on Amitābha Buddha with all one's heart and soul. Modern Chinese interpreted this teaching as none other than to meditate on *Tathatā* (thusness).[58] Chinese Buddhists also esteemed the authority of the *dharma* more highly than filial piety, as is shown in the statement: "The obligation to ancestors covers only seven generations, while the obligation of the Buddhist teacher is so great that it covers a great many *Kalpas*."[59]

To respect a Buddhist teacher does not mean to respect the teacher himself as an individual, but it means to respect the person who realized the truth of Buddhism by himself.[60] Tsung-mi (780–841) taught that only those who were inferior in their spiritual capacities had to depend upon a teacher.[61] This point is directly contrary to the case in Japan, where devotion to or reliance on an individual teacher was and is strongly emphasized.[62]

A prominent characteristic of the Indian religions in contrast to

Chinese Buddhism appears in the fact that the idea of precepts for virtue or *dharma* was highly esteemed in both countries but was accepted in different ways. The Chinese emphasized only the concrete worldly aspect of this idea of *dharma,* so that for them the universal principle of virtue appears in different forms according to the time and place. The principle can be universal only by changing its form in different contexts. The idea of *dharma* set forth in Buddhism is not a stagnant one, and therefore, ethical principles or *dharma* naturally change and develop with the lapse of time. A characteristic of Chinese Buddhism in the later period can be seen in the greater attention given to the individual concrete form of the principle of *dharma* as interpreted by the Chinese Buddhists when compared with the attitude of most Indian Buddhists earlier.

Chinese Buddhists did not form religious organizations which governed priests and temples. Nevertheless, they did greatly esteem the observance of the precepts and believed that it was the essential basis of all good actions to keep the precepts, because they were fully conscious of the importance and sacredness of the *dharma* as the Absolute.[63] Even at present, Chinese priests observe and practice the precepts.[64] It is said that priests who violate the precepts cannot be respected by the people. The laymen as well as the priests, observe the precepts very strictly in China.[65] There is no governing religious organization in China. Therefore, Buddhist followers are not punished or expelled even if they do not observe the Buddhist precepts. Nevertheless, they follow them closely, thus differing from the Japanese Buddhist societies where the precepts are not necessarily observed by the followers in spite of the fact that these followers are strictly controlled, politically and economically, by the sectarian organization.

To keep the precepts does not merely mean to follow ascetic practices or continue a life of mortification. The great priests of China excluded ascetic practices. This can be seen in the writing of Fa-tsang (643–712) who praised the precepts of a Bodhisattva stated in the *Fang-wang-ching* (*Brahmajāla sūtra*) as follows: "If one does not observe the precepts of the Bodhisattva, he is the same as an animal or a bird even if he does undergo the ascetic practices in the mountains or eats only fruits and vegetables."[66]

In Zen Buddhism, ascetic practices were also completely excluded.[67] The observance of the precepts was esteemed only so far as it was a help in realizing the *dharma.*

In this connection, there was also no discrimination of social position or status in the monkhood and nobody was refused entrance in the Buddhist organization on this account. Thus, Chinese Buddhism in modern times came to possess a strikingly democratic character. In reaction to this tendency, members of good families or the upper class did not become priests after the time of the "Suppression of Buddhism." That is to say, people from the upper classes used to enter the priesthood in the time before the Sung period. In modern times, only people from the lower classes have entered the priesthood, and this tendency is seen in the fact that in present-day China, priests are mostly from the illiterate and ignorant classes—in particular, the farmers and common inhabitants.[68] The principle of equality in Buddhism, with regard to social position and classes, is strongly supported by many Chinese. However, it could not eliminate the idea of class morality which was traditionally and strongly rooted in Chinese society.

CHAPTER 23 ESTEEM FOR HIERARCHY

The Moral Personality

Since ancient times Chinese philosophies have respected an ethical hierarchy in human relations, and we must not forget that a salient characteristic of Chinese thought is its ethical nature.[1] The Chinese regarded ethical studies as a more important branch of learning than the sciences connected with nature. However, the contents and the significance of "ethical" in Chinese thought are clearly different from what they are in Western thought or Christianity. In the following sections, the ethical characteristic in the ways of thinking of the Chinese will be discussed.

It seems that the Chinese were not very conscious of the distinction between natural phenomena and the actions of human beings. They thought that man could exert some power over nature, when events depended upon the behavior of man, and that natural power and the power of ideas were two aspects of one and the same universe.

As a result of the humanistic trend of Chinese thought, discrimination between the individual and the human organization to which the individual belongs was not fully acknowledged. An interesting example concerning the relation between the individual and the human organization can be found in Chinese Buddhism. *Seng* is the abbreviation of *seng-chia* (the transliteration of *saṅgha*) which signifies a Buddhist organization. The individual, on the contrary, who belonged to this organization was called a *pi-ch'iu* (*bhikkhu* or *bhikṣu*). These two terms are clearly distinguished in the Buddhist sūtras. In China, however, the individual monk was also called *seng*, which originally meant the organization. In India, the individual monk was never called *saṅgha;* I-Ching, who made a pilgrimage to India, pointed out this fact,[2] which Chinese Buddhist scholars in general acknowledged. Nevertheless, they insisted that they were justified in using the term.[3] And this idea of the Chinese also was inherited by the Japanese.

The Chinese highly esteemed the cosmic hierarchy which included man, and therefore, they established a clear discrimination between human beings and other living beings. They thought that man was man only when he observed the right way of acting as a man. In this respect, Kan-t'ui-chih excluded barbarians, animals, and birds from the concept of humanity.[4] This way of thinking is remarkably different from that of the Indians. In most cases the Indians subsumed man and all other living beings under one concept which was "being" (*sattva, prāṇin,* or *dehin*), as they thought all beings suffered from the defilement and illusions of this world in the same way. Buddhism in China was at times influenced by this kind of Indian thought. According to Tsung-mi, the human being is the highest being of all existences, and is the only living being who can completely harmonize with the spirit and gods. Fa-tsang also instructed people by saying, "If an ascetic does not observe the precepts, he is exactly the same as an animal or a bird."[5] Buddhism, which originated in India, changed its way of thinking accordingly, after it went into China, so as to conform to the Chinese idea of man. That is to say, the views of the Chinese and of the Indians concerning the relation of man to other living beings were so opposed that Buddhism had to be transformed in going from India to China.

Their two different views were derived from difference in viewpoints in regard to man. As has been pointed out, the Chinese people as well as many other peoples have attached great importance to the individual or the concrete. The Indian people, on the contrary, greatly esteemed the universal or permanent. For the Chinese, social nexus attaches the most important significance to individual human beings. Man is regarded as the most significant and highest existence, and beings transcending man possess little meaning in actual human life. For the Indians, on the contrary, the life of man in this world is impermanent and mortal, with the differences between man and all other living beings being almost nil. Consequently, Chinese thought did not transcend ethics while the Indians gave ethics a subordinate place subject to discipline of a religious character. Such features in the ways of thinking are not always peculiar to a certain people, for it is also possible that a culture in time will accept different ways of thinking. The Chinese were greatly influenced by Indian thought for long periods after the introduction of Buddhism into China. For example, the idea of compassion taught in Buddhism was widely accepted in the Sung dynasty, and many compassionate acts, such as liberating living creatures, abolition of animal sacrifice, and refraining from killing living beings, were highly commended.[6]

Elegant Attitude on Sexual Matters

Generally speaking, Indians are indifferent about sexual matters. This tendency is also found in Indian Buddhism. They are plain-spoken in describing sexual affairs, and what is said is accepted by the Indians only so far as it is a description of an objective fact, and only remarks about sex which cause unpleasant reactions in one's mind are disliked. On the contrary, the Chinese, or at least Confucianists, have an aversion towards writings about sex. To be sure, some indecent literature has been written in China. It was, however, considered unworthy for wise men or gentlemen to mention such sexual affairs. Such a tendency is not peculiar only to the Chinese but to all decent people in the world as well. Nevertheless, it can be said that this tendency was one of the noteworthy characteristics of the Chinese educated people.

Buddhism was also influenced by this tendency. When the Chinese translated the Buddhist sūtras, for example, they tried to remove the plain-spoken words and phrases on sex. The Chinese version of the *Saddharma-puṇḍarīka-sūtra* (chapter "Devadatta") states that "a female dragon suddenly changed her figure to become a male dragon." This phrase is very famous as proof of enlightenment of women in China as well as in Japan. The original text, however, states that "a daughter of the dragon king in the ocean explained the fact that she became a Bodhisattva by concealing her female organ and displaying the male organ."[7] The Chinese removed or abbreviated such expressions of the Indian text when they translated it. Another example: why was it wrong to drink stimulants? This was because various evils would result. The original Pāli text says one of the defilements is that "those who drink liquor are apt to display their sexual organs." The Chinese translator turned this phrase into "those who drink liquor are apt to became angry."[8]

The Chinese version of the *Hua-yen-ching* (*Buddhāvataṁsaka-sūtra*) translated in the Chin dynasty states as follows: "Vasumitrā told Sudhanaśreṣṭhi-dāraka: 'Those who *A-li-i* me surely attain the state of Samādhi where all beings are saved, and those who *A-chung-pei* me surely attain the state of Samādhi of virtue and mystery.' "[9]

A-li-i is the transliteration of *Āliṅgana* which connotes the meaning of *embrace* while *A-chung-pei* is derived from Paricumbana which means *to kiss*. The original Sanskrit can be translated as follows: "Some people can remove all defilements only by *embracing* me and can surely attain the state of the Bodhisattva Samādhi called 'the womb which saves all beings of the world' without fail. Again some people can become rid of all defilements only by *kissing* me and can surely attain the state of the Bodhisattva Samādhi called 'the state where the womb of virtue of all beings of the world can be realized.' "[10]

As is seen in the above phrases, the Indian indifferently used terms connected with sex such as "embrace" or "kiss." On the contrary, the Chinese who taught *the correct way* (*Tao*) of a gentleman could not follow this tendency. For the Chinese, it was a terrible thing to mention sexual words in religious scriptures. They thought that indecent terms desecrated the scriptures' authority and sacredness. Buddhabhadra, therefore, who translated the *Hua-yen* sūtra, transliterated these two terms in order to conceal them.

However, in the other Chinese translation of the *Hua-yen* sūtra translated in the T'ang dynasty, these two terms *Āliṅgana* and *Paricumbana* are literally translated from the Sanskrit as embracing and kissing.[11] It is thought that Confucianism was more influential in the Chin dynasty when this sūtra was first translated than later in the T'ang dynasty.

In this connection, German scholars, among the modern Europeans, usually translated literally the sexual explanations mentioned in the Indian literatures. On the contrary, English scholars, in many cases, used the Latin or euphemistic explanations instead of the literal translation. In this respect, there seems to be a similarity between the ideal of Confucianism and that of the English gentleman.

In another part of the *Hua-yen* sūtra, there is a story of a mother and daughter whose names are Sudarśanā and Suvalitaratiprabhāsaśrī.[12] Both mother and daughter were high-class prostitutes (*agragaṇikā*). This sort of thing can also be found in modern Indian society and may be one of its characteristics. Most of this story in the Chinese T'ang dynasty version was translated literally.[13] Nevertheless, some differences can be found between the original Sanskrit text and the Chinese translation due to the influence of Confucianism. (1) According to the original text, both mother and daughter are prostitutes, and they talk about the teachings of Buddhism. From a Confucianist standpoint, such facts were not agreeable. Therefore, the word "prostitute" is removed in the Chinese translation. (2) In the original text it states that "the daughter wishes to marry the prince Tejo'dhipati." According to Confucian thought, however, marriage is none other than the wife serving her husband. Therefore, this part was translated as follows: "If possible, I wish to serve this person." (3) According to the original text, the reason why the mother had her daughter give up this love was that "we prostitutes are the pleasure instruments of all the people; therefore, you cannot become the wife of one person." On the contrary, the Chinese translation says, "We lower people are not suitable for wives of such noble people." That is to say, the reason why the daughter had to give up her love was the difference in the social position. On the contrary, the original text does not mention that the prostitute is a lower-class person. In Indian society, some prostitutes were ranked highly in society and were also very rich. Such facts, however, could not be recognized in Chinese thought.

The older Chinese version[14] of this sūtra, translated in the Chin dynasty, states that the prince instead of the daughter fell in love. This explanation is exactly opposite to the explanations of the above two—the original text and the Chinese version of the T'ang dynasty. Of these, it can safely be said that the explanation of the original Sanskrit text and the T'ang version of the Chinese are the original form since there is a contradiction in the Chinese Chin version concerning this explanation. That is to say, the Gāthā (verse) portion mentions the daughter expressing her love for the prince. Moreover, it can usually be said that the verse is older than the prose portions of the same sūtra. Therefore, it is certain that the explanation of part of the Chin version was modified in a later time. Again possibly the translator of the Chin version changed the expression of this part. Perhaps, the translator thought that if this part were translated literally, the ethics of the social position would be broken.

In connection with sexual ethics, the commentary on the *Abhidharmakośa* written by Yaśomitra states: "the man who observes the five precepts marries a wife." The Chinese version of this commentary translated by Hsüan-tsang, however, translated it as "the man who observes the five precepts takes a wife and concubines" (XVIII, 18, left). Buddhism, from its beginning, prohibited sexual relations with women except with one's own wife. Therefore, concubines were not permitted. It is true that it was permissible to have plural wives in India, as can be seen in the Brāhmin scriptures or in the Jātaka Buddhist stories (*Jātaka,* IV, 99 G). It was permissible only so far as the women were wives. China, however, permitted concubines without the sanction of marriage. Therefore, Hsüan-tsang, who translated this sūtra, added the word "concubines" when he translated this part of the sūtra. This idea was also accepted by the Japanese. For example, in the *Jū-zen-hō-go* written by Jiun of Japan, it was not forbidden to have concubines although sexual relations with wives or concubines of others are strictly prohibited. In this respect, a somewhat different ethical idea can be recognized in India on the one hand and China or Japan on the other.[15]

Buddhism seems to have had many followers among the elite; therefore, the words and phrases of the sūtras had to be translated in the above ways, at least up to the period of the T'ang dynasty. However, further investigations are necessary in this field.

Sexual relations in China were strictly prohibited if they opposed the human order based on the family system. This thought probably stemmed from the idea of the high value of the human order in the family. A love affair was regarded as physical and not spiritual. Confucianism did not recognize spiritual significance in love although some romantic poems can be found in the *Shih Ching*. This tradition also influenced Buddhism.

Esoteric Buddhism arising in the last stage of Indian Buddhism was influenced by the Śākta school, the folk-faith of that time, which included many indecent elements. Mysterious rites and ceremonies which violated public moral standards were performed under the name of Buddhism. The Chinese, however, did not accept these mysterious rites although the esoteric Buddhist doctrine itself was adopted. Among the esoteric sūtras translated into Chinese in the Sung dynasty were some which described sexual relations symbolically; yet they hardly exerted any influence. Although the Chinese accepted wholesale the magic spells of esoteric Buddhism, the indecent side connected with sex was not accepted. Therefore, no sexual esoteric image at all exists among the images of Buddhas and Bodhisattvas which were worshipped by the Chinese. A few European scholars see a similarity between the worship of Bodhisattva Avalokiteśvara and that of the Madonna, and have tried to find a latent element of Indian Śakti in Kuan-yin. Such elements, however, cannot be found in any sūtra stating the worship of Bodhisattva Avalokiteśvara. According to the Chinese view, the physical body of man is ugly and dirty, so that clothes are coverings for the ugly body.[16] Therefore, the Chinese neither accepted nor founded any religious customs such as are seen in Jainism where clothes are regarded as shackles and the naked image of the Jina is worshipped.

Formalism in Behavior

The most important thought of ancient China is the idea of *Li* (Rules governing the way of life) which Confucius gave to the whole system of political and social customs handed down from an early age. It was the ideal of moral conduct to be followed in actual life. Every duty of man, such as filial piety or obedience to an elder, had to be performed in conformity with *Li.* Therefore, the ideal of the Chinese is that every act should conform to the idea of *Li.* This doctrine was strictly observed by the Confucianists.

It has been commonly asserted that at the time of the Emperor Wu of the Han dynasty, Confucianism was accepted as the national ideology of the ruling class.[17] Thus, the idea of *Li* became the fundamental morality of literate Chinese society.

This tendency to follow rules is likely to produce formalism in behavior. Buddhism was also influenced in a manner shown above where the Chinese Buddhists at that time observed Buddhist precepts very strictly. The following story will show how rigorously (and even drastically) some of the Chinese Buddhists observed the formal precepts.

When Hui-yüan (died 416) of Lu-shan became seriously ill, his disciples asked him to drink alcohol as a cure. He refused, for it would transgress the Vinaya Rules (Piṭaka). A disciple then asked him whether he would drink rice porridge. He refused again as it was already after twelve o'clock. (In India the precepts state that the priest must not partake of food after twelve o'clock noon.) Finally, he was offered honey and told to mix it with water and drink it. Hui-yüan then told his disciples to search the Vinaya Piṭaka in order to find out whether it was admissible to drink honey with water. He died before they finished reading all the Vinaya texts."[18] Nakamoto Tominaga of Japan criticized this story saying: "One can say that he observed the precepts very strictly, since he did not break them even when he was dying. However, how eccentric it was that he did not eat the rice porridge."[19] The Vinaya sect was founded in a later period and was influenced by this kind of strictness of behavior. I-tsing even went to India at a great risk primarily to clarify the rules of the precepts. Although Zen Buddhism has become very loose today in China, the spirit of strict behavior still exists. It is said that the Pure Rules which are the precepts of Zen Buddhism were formed by Huai-hai (720–814 A.D.). It is in these Pure Rules that even the minor points of everyday life in a Zen monastery are stated. Among Zen priests in later periods, some have behaved very freely, but the tendency in which even the minor precepts are strictly observed still remains.

Esteem for Superiority in Status

The ethics of *Li* gave a high value to order of rank and social position. The ethics of Confucianism was one for the governing class, namely, for people who were ranked in high positions in society. These people were the governing class politically and the intelligentsia culturally.[20] Superiority in society and status in the govering class was the important thing. A one-sided obedience of the lower class to members of the upper class was emphasized. This phase of Confucianism was also supported by rulers of all dynasties after the Han. The fact was that Confucian morality protected the position and the power of the government and gave it justification. This line of thought was easily accepted by the Chinese, because from ancient times, Chinese society was based on an order constructed upon the discrimination of classes.

Words and expressions used commonly in every day life in China were also greatly influenced by this idea of social order. For example, there are many kinds of personal pronouns directed to others, and each of them is used according to the social class of the person addressed;[21] it is the same in the case of the person doing the talking.[22] In the universal phenomenon of death, various terms are also used according to the social status of the deceased.[23] Besides these, the Chinese classics[24] state in detail that different terms expressing the same thing should be used in accordance with the social position of the person. There are also some kinds of adverbs which express respect or humility in China.[25] Furthermore, there are gradations even among children born to the same parents. Children are called *kyōdai* in Japanese, brothers and sisters in English, and *bhaginyaś ca bhrātaraś ca* in Sanskrit. In Chinese, however, they are divided into four kinds by age—namely, *hsiung* (elder brother), *ti* (younger brother), *tzu* (elder sister), and *mei* (younger sister).

Hierarchical structure in status was, however, not a rigid one. In general, in the old-fashioned family in China, only younger generations are expected to obey their elders. But in many cases, a younger son of ability may break with the family and, especially if he attains an official position, may become much more important than his elder brother.

Buddhism, when it was introduced into Chinese society, where discrimination of standing existed and one's social position was a determining factor, was revolutionary in teaching the equality of mankind with disregard for status and class. It seemed almost impossible that Buddhism could concur or even compromise with the thought of Confucianism. Therefore, the Confucianists frequently criticized the Buddhist teaching as one which destroyed human relationships. Some Chinese Buddhists, however, asserted the superiority of the Buddhist doctrine from the standpoint of Chinese ethics. That is to say, they said that the Buddhist doctrine stemmed from Śākyamuni who was from a royal family and therefore was superior to the doctrines of Lao-tzŭ and Chuang-tzŭ, who were from the lower classes. Chih-i, the founder of the T'ien-t'ai sect, declared that "The Buddha was from a royal family in India, while Chuang-tzŭ and Lao-tzŭ were lower government officials. Therefore, one cannot compare their teachings on the same level."[26] He again stated that Tathāgata Śākyamuni turned the wheel of the *Dharma* and became the Buddha in spite of the fact that he possessed the possibility of becoming a great King of the World. Lao-tzŭ, on the other hand, did not give up his position and his land even though this mythical sage was said to be only a low official and a poor farmer; therefore, it is impossible to say that both teachings possessed the same value and significance.[27] Chi-tsang also stated this.[28] It is also said that the Buddha possessed greatness and magnificence as a spiritual king or ruler, while Lao-tzŭ and Chuang-tzŭ did not. The Chinese Buddhists finally came to the conclusion that a Buddha was expected surely to be born in the family of a King or a Brāhmin, and could not be born in a low class, or a commoner's family. Therefore, it is said that all Buddhas will never be born to the two lower classes, the Vaiśya and Śūdra, and they will surely be born to the upper two classes, the Kṣatriya and the Brāhmin.[29] Thus, we see that Chih-i and

Chi-tsang who founded the Buddhist doctrines of China could not but help compromise with the idea of class discrimination. Otherwise, they could not propagate their teachings to the general Chinese public.

The Chinese explained even philosophical ideas in the framework of class discrimination. An example of this will be shown in the following:

In the doctrine of Hīnayāna Buddhism, the function of the mind is called *caitta* (in Chinese *hsin-so*) and the central mind, *citta* (*hsin*). Hsüan-tsang, however, translated the term *citta* into *hsin-wang*, the king of the mind. After Hsüan-tsang, the Chinese scholars were fond of using this term *hsin-wang* instead of mere *hsin*. They thought that the mind could not function by itself but had to be accompanied by other actions. This character of the mind is somewhat similar to that of a king who was always accompanied by many soldiers and servants whenever he went out. (In the original Sanskrit text of the *Abhidharmakośa-śāstra;* such terms as "*citta-rāja*," which indicates the king of the mind, do not appear.)

Generally speaking, Buddhism could not be accepted by the Chinese without compromising with the idea of class discrimination.

For example, the early Buddhist texts state that both the master and his servant have duties to each other. The master had to care for his servants in the following five ways: "The task had to be given in accordance with the ability of the servant. Board and salary were necessary. Illness had to be cared for. Delicious food had to be shared. Timely rest had to be given." The servant had to serve his master in the following five ways: "He had to rise earlier and retire later than the master, receive only what he was given, work hard, and also spread the fame and praise of the master.[30]

In all ages and countries, the precept that "the servant should serve his master and the master should love his servant" has been universally taught. The early Buddhist teaching, however, states this differently in that the master should serve the servant. It can be understood that the noble religious spirit of early Buddhism can be recognized in requiring that the upper class regard the lower with a spirit of respect and service.

Such a thought, however, could not be accepted verbatim by the Chinese who thought it terrible and absurd that the master should respect and serve his servants. Therefore, the Chinese translator changed the words as follows: "The master has to *teach* his servants in five ways."[31] Only by such adaptation to traditional Chinese forms could the thought of equality in Buddhism be introduced into China.

Buddhists, therefore, could not change the idea of class status of the Chinese in spite of their acceptance of Buddhism. Although the Sung philosophy was greatly influenced by Buddhism, the ethics of Confucianism still remained. Ch'eng I-ch'uan (1032–1107) understood the philosophy of the Hua-yen Sūtra deeply and was greatly influenced by it. Nevertheless, his doctrine was based only upon the idea of harmony between noumenon and phenomenon, but he could not realize the idea of the harmony between one phenomenon and another. Perhaps he considered it harmful to the hierarchical social order for Confucian morals to teach the idea of harmony.[32]

As the result of the two revolutions in the modern period, the traditional order of status and social class is completely destroyed. However, a new class order was re-established after these two revolutions. In the Communist government, the iron rule of the party bureaucracy is supreme, and demands strict obedience from the people. In this sense, it can be said that esteem for superiority in status still persists today in China.

The High Value Placed on Patriarchal Kinship

Chinese morality was centered on the family as all-important in the life of an individual. Relations among family members provided the human basis for the moral virtues of the Chinese, and filial piety was the most important among them. The morals of Confucianism flowed from the heads of the families constituting the governing class. Family government, in other words, was applied and extended to governing the whole nation or to statesmanship.

How did this family morality of the Chinese affect Buddhism introduced from the foreign country of India? The Buddhist organization was symbolized in China by the *chia* (family or home) and was called *fo-chia* (Buddhist family).[33] Each sect of Buddhism was also called a family (*chia*). For example, priests and followers of the T'ien-tai sect called their sect "this family."[34] the rules of Zen Buddhism were generally called *chia-feng* (the customs of the family), and specially formed rules were called *chia-hsün* (the instructions of the family). These rules had to be observed and practiced because they were the customs and instructions of the Buddha, the founder of Buddhism.[35] The Chinese, furthermore, regarded people who had deep relations with Buddha as his *relatives.* For example, the Chinese regarded the five companions with whom Śākyamuni had undergone various ascetic practices before he attained enlightenment, as relatives of Śākyamuni in spite of the fact that the families and classes of these five Bhikkhus were unknown.[36]

It is a very interesting fact that the Chinese even expressed the ideas of natural science in the form of kinship relations. According to the Indian atomic theory, in ancient time, a dual-atom body is formed from the union of two atoms, and the natural world is formed by the combination of many "dual-atomic bodies." The Chinese called the simple atom a "parent atom" and the dual-atomic body a "child atom."[37] The Greeks and the Indians did not use such names in their atomic theories.

Buddhists were forced to teach filial piety to the common people in China just because the most important virtue in Confucianism was filial piety, which demanded a one-sided obedience from children, the younger people, to their parents, the venerated elders. This idea, however, did not exist in Indian Buddhism, as can be seen in the original Sanskrit texts where there is no such term corresponding to the idea of *hsiao*, filial piety, found frequently in Chinese translations of sūtras. The translators must have added this term. The virtue which corresponds to the idea of filial piety is, of course, taught in the original Buddhist sūtras, but only as one of the virtues and not as the supreme virtue.[38] The Chinese, not satisfied with the family morality taught in Indian Buddhism, composed as a last resort certain spurious sūtras such as the *Fu-mu-en-chung-ching* and the *Tai-pao-fu-mu-en-chung-ching,* which teach filial piety.[39] The great and deep obligation which all children owe to their parents was heavily emphasized. These two sūtras were diffused widely not only in China but in the neighboring countries and were frequently quoted; commentaries on them were written by famous Buddhist scholars.

The family-centered morality of China attached great importance to the ceremony of ancestor-worship which was based upon the high value of the family-line. It possesses an important social and economical significance. In India, there was the worship of *Pitṛ* (the soul of the ancestor) and of *Preta* (his ghost) which was performed in each family. China, however, gave it great importance. Ancient Israel also performed the ritual worship of the dead (*Totenkult*) which seems to have diminished in later periods with the decrease of the social and ceremonial significance of the family-line.[40] Thus, one of the remarkable characteristics of the Chinese religions is this soul and ghost worship (*chthonischer Kult,* as Max Weber calls it).[41]

After Buddhism's introduction into China, Confucianist scholars strongly criticized Buddhism as a religion which destroyed the family and its morality. As monks did not marry, they had no children, and their line becoming extinct, the ceremony of ancestor-worship was not performed for them. Chao-yüng (1011–1077 A.D.), a Confucian scholar in the Northern Sung dynasty, criticized Buddhism, saying that it was contrary to natural human relationships. "The Buddha abandoned the relationships between sovereign and subject, parents and children, wife and husband. Then how can it be said that his teaching corresponds to natural reason?"[42] Indian Brāhmanism also criticized Buddhism in the same way. The filial piety taught by the Indian Buddhists was "to respect and serve one's living parents in this world." The necessity of a memorial service for the dead parents or ancestors was not strictly taught, because the Indians believed that parents, after death, would be born either in heaven or hell according to their behavior in the past. They performed ancestor-worship only to express the feeling of gratitude to their ancestors, and the achievements or the memorial day of the individual ancestor were not contemplated as important in worship. This fact has a close relation to the tendency of Indian thought to stress universality. In this sense, it was very difficult for Buddhism to be accepted by the Chinese in its original form.

Buddhism, when transferred from India, could not, therefore, help but adopt the ancestor-worship of the Chinese. This trend is seen in the period of the Northern Wei dynasty. A good example of this amalgamation is the *Ullambana* ceremony held on July 15, the last day of the summer retreat period, for the sake of ancestors going back seven generations. On this day, people gave offerings to the monks in order to have their ancestors' sufferings cease. Although the idea existed in India that the sufferings and pains of one's dead parents could be removed by offering foods to the monks, it is not clear whether this *Ullambana* ceremony was observed in India. It was, however, greatly esteemed in China and widely performed by the Chinese from its beginning in the time of the Emperor Wu of the Liang dynasty. It is believed that one can attain the highest state of Buddhahood[43] by performing this ceremony. Its significance and method is explained in the *Ullambana-sūtra.* Many commentaries on it were written in spite of the fact that it was probably not known in India.

The concept of *karma,* in its Sinicized form, may be found in all types of literature. Before the advent of Buddhism, divine retribution was believed to fall upon families; then Buddhism introduced the idea of karmic causation, but this was on an individual basis. Finally, the two ideas were interwoven in the view that has prevailed since the Sung period, namely, that divine retribution works on a family basis but through a chain of lives.[44]

Esteem for family has a close relation with the social structure of China where the individual family could live without relationship to the prosperity of the nation. For the same reason, patriotism in the political sense did not develop well in China. Therefore, it was natural that the Chinese who esteemed only the family and relatives were surpassed in patriotic feelings by the Japanese who possessed a strong sense of nationalism in the modern period. At present social circumstances and living conditions are very different in China.

As a result of the revolutionary success of Communism, the landowner class lost its position in society. Therefore, the idea of the family has been changed drastically by the Communist Party. Present-day Chinese Communism has broken family ties; for example, children are encouraged to inform upon and even to injure their Christian parents.

Religion's Struggle Against the State and Its Defeat

The idea of respecting the Emperor is derived from the traditional Chinese esteem for order. In China, this idea was established under the name, "the theory of Heaven's command,"[45] in which Heaven was believed to have given a mandate to the Emperor. "Heaven (*t'ien*)" was believed to be the highest of all powers in the universe and to control all other powers.

The power of the Emperor ranked above various divine beings in folk-faith, and his authority was a power given by heaven. It was thought that the duty of the king was to organize a moral system and establish the social order. "Only the Emperor could discuss moral virtues and organize the system of the world" (*Chung Yung*—The Doctrine of the Mean). Thus, the Emperor was gradually deified, and after the T'ang dynasty (618–906) came to be regarded as the perfect human being. This thought cannot be found before the T'ang dynasty,[46] and it greatly influenced Chinese history subsequently. In China, however, this thought did not develop into the idea that the Emperor was a living god. His power was limited by Heaven's command. According to it, the Emperor's throne was given to him by the command of Heaven, which the people had to follow. "When the Emperor possessed little virtue and the people did not obey him, then his throne was given to the person whom the people would follow." The Chinese believed that this change of the throne was caused by a change in Heaven's command. In this respect, this theory is also called "the theory of revolution."[47] In this sense, the Emperor of China was not an absolute autocrat. High officials of the court, whenever necessary, possessed the right to advise and instruct the Emperor, who was thought to be a wise man possessing many virtues. And even the Emperor had to follow and observe the universal moral code. Though the power of the Emperor was limited by Heaven's command, in this sense, he often possessed in practice great authority and power. "The Emperor is the main trunk while the subjects are the branches."[48]

When Confucianism was ascendant, the Confucian authorities admonished the Emperor, and when Buddhism was ascendant, the Buddhist authorities did likewise! Hence it was natural that the state and the Buddhist organization should each seek to become supreme. Governmental power, however, opposed and suppressed Buddhism, the goals of which were equality and compassion for all human beings.

The most important study in Chinese ethical thought was the code for the Emperor's rule. Politics and cosmology were not separate studies as is shown in the word "*T'ien-hsia*" which connotes the meaning of the "universe" as well as of the empire.[49]

Buddhism was regarded as a teaching from the outer world, since Buddhism was introduced into China from India. After the Later Han dynasty, many Buddhist priests came from India or Central Asia to become teachers of Kings, and eventually the doctrine of Buddhism and other subjects were taught to the King as well as to state ministers and other high officials. It was natural for the Chinese, however, to attack this tendency. According to Taoists, as the Emperor is ranked the highest with the *tao* and the *t'ien,* and priests are the subjects of the Emperor, it was unreasonable that the Emperor should be taught by a low monk or to venerate monks; they were expected to respect and pay homage to the Emperor. This problem was frequently discussed in the years to come.

This problem was of great importance during the time Hui-yüan was at Lu-shan. He wrote the *Sha-men-pu-wang-che-lun* (a treatise on Buddhist priests who need not pay homage to the king) and opposed the suppression of Buddhism by Emperor Huan-hsüan who insisted that Buddhist priests should attend the Imperial ceremonies together with other government officials. This was opposed by Hui-yüan who tried to separate the Buddhist organization from governmental power. He was able to oppose the Emperor strongly because he was supported by the aristocrats of South China who cherished his opinion.

However, since the Buddhist organization flourished, it was not desirable for the state to have the Buddhists outside of its power. Thus, this attempt at independence by the Buddhists was suppressed in North China. Generally speaking, the power of the state was stronger in North China than in the South. From an early time, many people entered the priesthood in order to evade military service and payment of taxes. At times, several hundred young men would enter a temple and together become monks. The safety and prosperity of the nation was threatened by the increase of that kind of monk. As a preventive measure, examinations of monks were held often. That is to say, all those who did not possess a monk's ability were forced to return to secular life. Buddhism was finally crushed through such practices. Among the many Emperors who suppressed Buddhism, Emperor Tao-wu of the Northern Wei dynasty, Emperor Wu of the Northern Chou dynasty, King Wu of the T'ang dynasty and Emperor Shih of the Later Chou dynasty are famous.

In some cases, Buddhism was persecuted as a danger to the state's economic status in regard to metal currency. A great amount of metal and other materials was used for Buddhist arts, such as Buddha images, vases, and other temple treasures. Consequently, the economic condition of the nation became steadily worse. The state tried various measures to meet the situation, none of which were really effective in the long run.[50] The real cure was to wipe out the Buddhist organizations. In this way the Buddhist organizations were gradually taken over and controlled by the nation. A system of officials to control Buddhism was founded in the Eastern Chin dynasty (317–419): in every district and prefecture, a priestly official was appointed as a government officer to control the monk groups in the respective district or prefecture.

Because Buddhist society was completely controlled by the state, Buddhists had to compromise with the doctrine that the Emperor was deified. Fa-kuo, the first priest official in the Northern Wei dynasty (386–534), regarded Emperor Tao-wu as a living Tathāgata and said that "all monks must respect him."[51] Many other people, such as Wei Yüan-sung and Jen Tao-lin, also stated that the Emperor is a Tathāgata or Bodhisattva. Emperor Wu of the Liang dynasty was a faithful Buddhist and was called the "Bodhisattva King" or "King Bodhisattva" by his subjects, and he was called a "real Buddha" by a foreign country. A religious ceremony was held on the birthday of the Emperor beginning with the T'ang. In the Sung dynasty, a priest of Zen Buddhism prayed for the long life of the Emperor, and finally in the Yüan dynasty (1280–1367), people came to believe that the Emperor must be a Dharmakāya Buddha (the Buddha of the true body).[52]

During the Yüan dynasty, all of China was conquered by the military might of the Yüan. The Zen Buddhist organization, the representative religion of the time, showed its submissive attitude to the Yüan government by announcing: "The most important matter for man is to realize the principle of *Tao*. From ancient times, therefore, the excellent Emperors of China respected the teaching of the Buddha, the saint of the Western country, and for this reason, we Buddhist priests were treated with special hospitality by the Emperors. The Yüan government has especially treated us well. We can endeavor to realize Buddhist truth free from taxes and other worldly duties. Our obligation to the Emperor is so vast and great that it cannot be expressed by words. To return this obligation we will surely endeavor to realize the Buddha-nature and teach the holy doctrines of Buddhism to the people. We Buddhist priests will never forget his mercy and do our best."

Furthermore, a religious ceremony to honor and pray for the long life of the Emperor was provided.[53] In this respect, the attitude of Chinese Buddhists towards state power was exactly the same as the Japanese. The basic spirit of Buddhism, repeatedly taught since its original form, which was not to make friends with emperors or kings, was completely ignored.

More investigations and study are necessary to realize how this idea of Buddhism changed in the Ming and the Ch'ing dynasties. One fact is that Buddhism was supported and protected by the state. Until the establishment of the Republic of China, the authority of the Emperor ranked higher than the authority of the Buddhist organization. Although there was no king in the *Chung-hua-min-kuo,* the authority of religion was no more influential or powerful in society than it had been in the past.

In present-day Red China, religion is strongly controlled. Various opinions are expressed by people who have visited Red China recently concerning the relation between religion and state. Some people report that religious organizations are protected by the state, while others say that they are suppressed. What is common to all opinions is the power and strictness of the state. It is indeed a noteworthy fact that a strong Communist government was established in China in such a short period. However, what should be considered is that this was possible partly because the Chinese have since ancient times traditionally accepted strong state power.[54]

Racial Pride and Reverence for Lineage

The Chinese who recognized the reign of an Emperor and glorified his deification as having the highest ethical significance far above the value of individual man, insisted on the superiority and the greatness of their own nation. National pride and haughtiness made the Chinese discriminate against foreign countries, calling their own land "*Chung-kuo*" (the central state, middle kingdom, or the superior country); some even were willing to believe that other countries belonged to their country "China."

However, some people among the Chinese did not recognize the superiority of old Chinese culture, and they did not call their country the central kingdom. To the Chinese monks who traveled to India to look for the doctrines of Buddhism, China was far removed from the splendor of Indian culture. Therefore, these priests use the term "*Chung-kuo*" (the Central Country) for India.[55] However, with the spread of Buddhism in China, Chinese Buddhists also came to call their country "*Chung-hua*"[56] or "*Chung-hsia,*"[57] a tendency naturally connected with their nationalism. According to the general opinion of the non-Buddhist Chinese, Buddhism was the teaching of a foreign country and not the thought of China. They, therefore, thought that China was occupied and governed by foreign peoples for a long time because of Buddhism. For this reason, some people like Fu-i[58] insisted on the suppression of Buddhists; xenophobia in Europe was no different.

Nevertheless, the patriotic Chinese had to recognize the worth of foreign culture to some extent. Therefore, they tried another angle in order to show the superiority of their culture; namely, they claimed that all kinds of studies and true teachings were originally founded in China. When Buddhism was recognized as a teaching which stated truth, the Chinese showed the superiority of traditional Chinese thought by saying that "Buddhism was originally taught by the Chinese," instead of criticizing the doctrine of Buddhism logically. Thus, the *Lao-tzŭ-hua-hu-ching*, which was composed by the Taoists in the Western Chin dynasty, stated that Lao-tzŭ went to India and became Śākyamuni in order to teach the Indians, or again that he was the teacher of Śākyamuni. Furthermore, Fu-i of the T'ang dynasty (618–907) insisted that the Chinese Buddhists surreptitiously borrowed and used the profound terminology of Lao-tzŭ and Chuang-tzŭ in translating and interpreting the Buddhist sūtras.[59] In the Eastern Chin dynasty, many sūtras showing the relation between Taoism and Buddhism were composed by the Taoists. The Buddhists also composed many spurious sūtras concerning this problem. According to the *Ch'ing-ching-fa-hsing-ching* (The Sūtra of Pure Practice), one of the sūtras composed by the Buddhists, Buddha dispatched three disciples to China in order to teach the Chinese. It further stated that these three disciples were called "Confucius," "Yen-yüan," and "Lao-tzŭ" in China. In these arguments, doctrinal truth was not important; it was subordinated to the question of priority. The Chinese did not admit that the Indian religion originated earlier that that of China. Therefore, Chih-i, who organized a Chinese Buddhist doctrine, adopted the Chinese theory that saintliness appeared earlier in China than in India. He thought that even the devil could transform his body into a Buddha image, and heretics could show divine power; therefore, it was very possible that Lao-tzŭ taught the Indians by transforming his body into the Buddha. He further stated that the doctrines of India were not the real teaching.[60]

This way of thinking also influenced the Chinese historians of natural science. Although scholars of the Ch'ing dynasty (1644–1908) were interested in and accepted the culture of Europe to some extent, they were still proud of the superiority of Chinese culture in the same way. They accepted the astronomy of Europe, but they said that, although European astronomy had become fairly well developed, it originally came from the astronomy of China, for Chinese historians wrote that many students of astronomy went to foreign countries in order to escape war in the Chou dynasty, so that the current astronomy of Europe was developed by their descendants.[61]

As the result of this esteem for historical lineage, Chinese Buddhists came to insist that all sciences and studies were originally founded and developed by Buddhism, and that heretical people adopted these sciences and studies afterwards. Though this way of thinking can also be found in India, it can be said that it was more prominent in China than in India.[62]

Generally speaking, there may be no country which has not at some time thought that it is the "best" or "supreme" country, so that it is not surprising that this tendency remains very strong even nowadays among many Chinese leaders.

The Buddhist ideal of the Bodhisattva could be appropriated with a Chinese modification; for example, Fan Chung-yen (989–1052) pictured a Bodhisattva as "one who is first in worrying about the world's troubles and last in enjoying its pleasures." Even in modern schools this aphorism has often served as an essay topic, and has been reiterated by Chinese communists.[63]

CHAPTER 24 ESTEEM FOR NATURE

Conformity to Nature

The tendency of Chinese thought which paid attention only to concrete and phenomenal objects and considered that all things could exist only so far as they were in conformity with man, came to esteem the principle of Nature which exists in the mind of man. Since ancient times, the idea of Heaven (*T'ien*) was conceived by the Chinese in close relation with man.[1] According to a poem composed in the ancient period of the early Chou dynasty, Heaven created man, and therefore, Heaven, as the ancestor of man, handed down moral precepts which man had to observe.[2] This idea was inherited by Confucius. He recommended acknowledging the order of Heaven" which meant "one should follow the morality given to man by Heaven."[3] Some modern Europeans were deeply stirred by the fact that ancient China—where Confucianism was recognized as the national ideology, and politics was administered by its doctrine—followed laws based upon natural law. It is an undoubted fact that some similarities exist between the idea of natural law in Europe and that of ancient China.

The opinion that "man should follow his true nature" was also stated by other scholars in ancient China, and yet their meanings were different from that of Confucius. Mo-tzŭ taught that the ruler should follow what Heaven wished and not follow what it did not wish. Lao-tzŭ insisted that the correct way of man is to follow the way of Heaven; therefore, it can be said that the basis of the correct way of man is *T'ien-tao* (the Way of Heaven). Yang-chu (who lived between the time of Motzŭ and Mencius) stated, "The original nature for man desires only sex and food. Therefore, it is better for man not to have relations with others but only to satisfy his own desires." "It is a natural law that man does what he wants."[4] Mencius taught that "the true character of man is good; however, the evil mind arises by the temptation of material desires. Therefore, man should cultivate his mind himself and exhibit his own true character." An exception to Chinese thought was Hsün-tzu, who maintained that the true character of man tends to evil. Nevertheless, he recognized the possibilities in man of becoming good. Chuang-tzŭ taught that man should perfect his true character, and his followers came to teach the theory that "man should return to his true character." In the San-kuo dynasty, Wang-pi (226–249) also taught the "return to the true character."[5] This thought developed greatly in the Sung philosophy where the central theme was the concept of man's true character. The traditional current of thought in Chinese history is "to return to the true and natural character of man."

Buddhism was also influenced by this current of thought. Buddhists did not look for truth in the phenomenal world but explored the inner world by concentration of mind. In Zen Buddhism, Chinese traditional thought is expressed in a peculiarly Chinese way: "If one realizes the truth that all existences are the same, he immediately returns to his true nature."[6] Both illusion and enlightenment of man were understood to be derived from the natural character of man. "The mind is the ground and nature is the king. Where there is nature there is the king, and where there is no nature, there is no king. Where there is nature, there are the body and mind. Where no nature exists, there is neither body nor mind. Buddha is created by self-nature; therefore, one must not look for the Buddha through the body. If self-nature is an illusion, then the Buddha is namely a sentient being. If self-nature is enlightenment, then the sentient being is namely the Buddha."[7] There was, in India, no such idea of self-nature as the principle which maintains the body and mind as ignorant or enlightened. Some Chinese scholars have recognized a Taoist influence in this conception of self-nature.[8] However, this concept could have appeared from the traditional ideas of the Chinese.

Medieval Confucians said that the whole of nature is to be found in any one item, which theory seems to have originally been due to the influence of Buddhist philosophy, especially the Hua-yuen school. So Wang Yang-ming undertook to investigate a bamboo tree. After studying it in meditation for a week, with no results, he gave it up completely.

Chinese Pure Land teachings also adopted the ideas of Taoism. Chinese Buddhists had to pass through a process of complicated thought before they acknowledged a Chinese naturalism. In this connection, Chi-tsang reasoned as follows:[9] Chinese philosophical thought, especially in Lao-tzŭ and Chuang-tzŭ, regarded existence as phenomena, and voidness as a substance other than existence. Therefore, voidness was not identifiable with existence. Buddhism, on the contrary, taught that phenomena are actually the manifestation of the Absolute.[10] Therefore, the absolute significance of the phenomenal world cannot be recognized in actual life in the philosophy of Lao-tzŭ and Chuang-tzŭ. In Buddhism, however, one can accept this phenomenal world as absolute states of existence, because actual life in this world is identical with absolute existence.[11]

Although this criticism by Chi-tsang may not be correct, at least he tried to recognize a significance in life in this world. T'ien-t'ai and Hua-yen sects further expanded on this thought. According to the T'ien-t'ai sect, appearance and actuality are not different kinds of substances. Appearances are identical with reality. Therefore, they taught that "each existence in this world is the middle way." Each of the phenomenal forms of this world is a form of absolute existence. The Hua-yen sect developed this thought even further. That is to say, the theory of "mutual penetration and identification of all things with one another" is taught by this sect. The supreme meaning emerges when all phenomena are perfectly identified by their harmonious interrelationships. Therefore, nothing exists outside of phenomena and their diverse forms of manifestation.

As a result, the actual natural world was acknowledged as absolute existence. In Zen Buddhism, the following answers were given to the question "What is absolute existence?" "It is the cypress tree in the garden" or "It is three pounds of hemp." It is also seen in Su Tung-p'o's poem: "The sound of the stream is the teaching or sermon of the Buddha, and the color of the mountain is the pure and True Body (Dharmakāya) of the Buddha." This naturalistic tendency came to the conclusion that each one of the existences of this world is, just as they appear, the manifestation of truth.

Zen monks, of course, opposed and rejected mere superficial naturalism. For example, Hui-hai stated: "Ignorant people do not realize the fact that the True Body (*Dharmakāya*) manifests its form in accordance with the object although it does not possess any form originally. Therefore, they say that the green bamboo tree is none other than the True Body (*Dharmakāya*) and the chrysanthemum is identical with *Prajñā* (wisdom).[12] If the chrysanthemum is wisdom, then wisdom is the same as an insentient existence. If the green bamboo is the True Body (*Dharmakāya*), then the True Body is the same as the grass or the tree. If so, eating the bamboo-shoot carries the meaning of eating the True Body. Therefore, it is unworthy to think of such things."[13]

Nevertheless, the Chinese generally accepted the view that nature is the absolute. Finally, the T'ien-t'ai sect taught the theory that "all existences and even grass, trees, and earth can attain Buddhahood." That is to say, even physical matter existing in nature can realize enlightenment and become Buddha. Generally speaking, the tendency was to regard nature as the most beautiful and highest existence, with man on an equal plane. These were the tendencies that influenced Buddhist thought in the above manner.

Therefore, the Chinese Buddhists (especially Zen monks) tried to seek absolute significance in everyday life. "Those who wish to attain the state of the One Vehicle (Ekayāna) must not defile the six sensual objects (form, sound, smell, taste, touch, and ideas). If one does not defile the six sensual objects, then he is enlightened."[14] In other words, everyday life, just as it is, is identical wtih enlightenment. This thought is clearly found in the following questions and answers: "Chao-chou asked, 'What is Tao?' His master Nan-ch'üan answered, 'The mind in everyday life is Tao.' "[15] "The priest asked, 'What is the mind in everyday life?' His master answered, 'It is to sleep whenever necessary and to sit whenever necssary.' The priest said, 'I do not understand you.' Then the master said, 'It is to be cool when it is hot and warm when it is cold.' "[16]

The state of enlightenment is therefore none other than this actual world. A poem composed by Su-tung-p'o states that "Rain is falling at Mt. Lu and the tides are full at Che-chiang bay."[17] In other words there is a unity in nature to be enjoyed. In China many other poems exist which express nature as it is. "The moon shines and the wind blows. What shall I do in this long and beautiful night?"[18] "Various flowers bloom in the spring, the moon shines in autumn, cool wind blows in summer and snow falls in winter. How nice and pleasant the seasons are for men!"[19] "Everyday is a pleasant and good day for man."[20]

The state of enlightenment seems externally to be indistinguishable from a state of ignorance. In the following questions and answers, this is shown very clearly and impressively.

A PRIEST: "What is Buddha?"

CHAO-CHOU: "He is at Buddha's hall."

A PRIEST: "The Buddha at Buddha's hall is the Buddha image made of mud."

CHAO-CHOU: "Yes, you are right."

A PRIEST: "Then what is the true Buddha?"

CHAO-CHOU: "He is at Buddha's hall."[21]

While the external appearance is not different in the states before and after enlightenment, the spiritual condition must be completely different from the state before enlightenment. When Chih-hsien was asked "What is enlightenment?" he answered, "It is the flute behind the dead tree" or "It is the eyes behind a skeleton."[22] These things are not lifeless. Those who have realized truth can manifest the absolute light in things which seem unworthy or meaningless.[23] Zen monks, for example, expressed the state of enlightenment poetically by impressive examples.

As the result of the tendency to regard nature or actuality as absolute existence, the Chinese came to adopt the idea of optimism. Thus, they regarded this world as a good place in which to live; they finally came to believe that perfect existence must exist in this world. Here, the idea of the "*Sheng-jen*" (sage) was established. He was the perfect person such as the Chou King or Confucius. The sage is not a god but a man. However, he is in principle the ideal. In art, Wang I-chih was called "the sage of writing" and Tu Fu "the sage of poetry." They were regarded as the perfect models of principle in art.[24] In the idea of *wu* (nothingness) of the Wei and Chin dynasties, the concept of the creator or the absolute was amalgamated with the concept of the sage or the perfect human being. In this theory of nothingness, the perfect human being realizes the principle of nothingness and is able to manifest every phenomenon and give the correct way of life to every person.[25]

This way of thinking which insisted on perfect existence in this world established the thought that the perfect life existed in the past. That is to say, the Chinese made what occurred in the past the rule for governing present life. As the result, the Chinese came naturally to esteem the life in the past more highly than the life in the present. The thought which acknowledged nature's actuality was also one of the foundations for the establishment of Chinese classicism, although it was not the sufficient condition for it.

The more important fact is that the long history of China has been comparatively peaceful because the Chinese identified nature with man. Undoubtedly there were wars in China. However, Derk Bodde, an American sinologue, states that the typical hero in Chinese literature was the poor but virtuous scholar. The military genius, on the other hand, is praised and appreciated in Western literature much more than in Chinese literature, which seldom praised military heroes. The Chinese attitude is shown in the following saying: "Good iron cannot be a nail and the good man does not become a military man."[26] The harmony of all existences is necessary in order to harmonize with nature and live in peace. Thus, they asserted the idea of "moderation." As the Chinese regarded man as a part of nature or the universe, they did not regard nature as opposed to man. Since they seldom thought nature needed to be overcome by experimental manipulation in order to master her ways or laws, natural science did not develop quickly in China. This fact is perhaps the chief reason why China lagged behind other countries in the modern world. Leaders of Red China recognize this fact and are trying to improve and develop natural science.

Relationship of Interaction between Heaven and Man

In connection with their idea of nature, the Chinese elaborated an organic theory of a "reciprocal relationship between Heaven and man."

In the period of the Chan-kuo (Warring States period, 480–222 B.C.), "scholars of the positive and negative principle" advocated a kind of nature worship which was carried into the Early Han period. According to this principle, natural phenomena and man-made institutions are mutually interrelated, and therefore, if the King, who was the representative of man, governed the country well, then the phenomena of nature, such as weather, wind, and rain would be favorable to man. If the reign of the King was poor, on the other hand, then natural calamities would arise. This idea was most strongly stressed by Tung Chung-shu (c. 179–c. 104 B.C.) of the Early Han dynasty, who thought that disasters were sent from Heaven in order to admonish the King. The thought of *Ko-ming* (revolution) which means, literally, "to cut off (or take away) the mandate of Heaven from some particular ruler" played a role in checking or correcting the tyranny of autocrats.

This reciprocity between Heaven and man influenced even Chinese historians who have been well known for their accuracy in recording historical events. For example, all accounts of Confucius known to us date his birth in the year 551 B.C., whereas it actually occurred in the year 552 B.C. The reason why the date was falsified by a year is revealing. An eclipse of the sun had always been considered in China, during the last two millennia and more, as a *nefas* event, indicating the anger of the supernatural powers, especially of the supreme Chinese God, Heaven or T'ien, against some human wrong-doing. Hence, it was considered impossible that a solar eclipse could have occurred in connection with the birth of Confucius, who was early accepted as the greatest of all sages.[27]

This thought was also influential in later periods in China. Buddhism also had sūtras which stated the theory of disaster and which were highly regarded by the Chinese. A typical example of these sūtras is the *Chin-kuang-ming* (Golden Splendor) sūtra, which states in detail, in the 13th chapter, that if the King does not protect the *dharma* well, a terrible calamity will arise. That is to say, as the result of maladministration on the part of the Emperor, falsehood and struggle will increase in his country, and the ministers and subjects will rise against him. Furthermore, the deities will become angry; wars will break out; the enemy will overrun the country; family members will fight each other; nothing will be pleasant or comfortable for man. Natural phenomena will at the same time become worse.[28] Living beings will lack rigor, plagues will arise, and pestilence will sweep the land. Therefore, the Emperor should attempt his best in governing the country by the *dharma*. Now this sūtra is unusual as Buddhist sūtras seldom teach the theory that "disasters arise through poor government by the King." Yet the Chinese Buddhists highly esteemed this theory in this sūtra, as can be seen by the fact that five different Chinese translations as well as many commentaries on this sūtra were composed in China.

Naturalized Buddhist monks from India propagated Buddhism in conformity with this organismic way of Chinese thinking. Guṇavarman, for example, taught Buddhism to Emperor Wen of the Sung dynasty in the following way: "The four seas are your land and all existences are your subjects. One pleasant word and all your subjects are happy. One act in a good rule brings harmony to the people. If you only punish wrong-doers without killing and do not impose heavy taxes, then nature will harmonize with man, and fruits and crops will ripen well."[29]

More investigation is necessary to know how long this organic form of ethical thought continued in China. It can, however, be safely said that this thought of reciprocity between Heaven and human deeds is not an exclusive characteristic of Chinese ways of thinking. It was taught not only in Buddhism but also in Indian and other ethical systems that good results generally spring from good deeds and evil comes from evil deeds. Chinese Pure Land teachings also explained this ethical theory in terms of the relationship of reciprocity between Heaven and man.

CHAPTER 25 RECONCILING AND HARMONIZING TENDENCIES

The Absolute Character of Existence

If the reality of all natural phenomena is absolutely upheld, then nothing imperfect can be denied existence; this idea persisted from ancient times in China. For the Chinese, the five Confucian classics are the source of ethics. They further believed that the other classics or books are also a partial revelation of the same perfect wisdom. The Chinese believed that not only can perfection exist in this world but other existences cannot be denied in spite of the fact that they are not perfect. Thus, not even a single existence is denied, and there is perfect existence which must be absolutely affirmed.[1]

The Chinese lacked, therefore, the idea of absolute evil. Every form of human life was acknowledged as existing for some reason. It is natural that the Chinese did not explain the origin of evil because they lacked the idea of absolute evil.[2]

Chinese Buddhism was also influenced by this way of thinking, and particularly in the doctrine of the "mutual penetration of the ten worlds" of the T'ien-t'ai sect. These are the worlds of hell, hungry ghosts, beasts, fighting demons (*Asura*), man, heaven, Śrāvaka, Pratyekabuddha, Bodhisattva, and Buddha. The first six worlds belong to the illusory world and the last four to the enlightened world. Each one of these ten worlds mutually possesses all the characters of the ten worlds. Therefore, Buddhahood is possible for beings in hell, while at the same time the Buddha possesses the possibility of going into the illusory world. In such a world, there is neither an absolutely evil person nor an absolutely good person. There are neither permanent rewards nor retributions.[3]

In Chinese Zen Buddhism, this thought is explained very clearly. "The pure-nature of thusness (*tathatā*) is the actual Buddha; evil thoughts and the three kinds of defilement are the actual demons. Those who possess evil thoughts are the demons and those who have right thoughts are Buddhas. Where there are the three kinds of defilement originating from various evil thoughts, there is the king of the demons. On the contrary, where there is right thought, the demon changes its form and can attain Buddhahood."[4] Here, the demon is identical with the Buddha.

No man is absolutely evil, and everyone has the possibility of being saved. This thought greatly influenced the Pure Land teachings introduced from India. The eighteenth Vow of Amitāyus-Buddha, one which is so highly esteemed in Japanese Pure Land teachings, is as follows: "If the beings of the ten quarters—when I have attained Enlightenment (*Bodhi*)—blissfully trust in me with the most sincere mind, wish to be born in my country, and chant the name of Buddha ten times, but are not so born, may I never obtain the State of Enlightenment. Excluded, however, are those who have committed the Five Deadly Sins and who have abused the True *dharma*."

The Chinese could not understand the last part of this Vow, because they believed that all evil persons could be saved by Amitāyus-Buddha. The Five Deadly Sins are to kill one's own father, to kill one's own mother, to kill an Arhat (one who has attained enlightenment), to disturb the harmony of the Buddhist organization, and to harm Buddha's person. Shan-tao (613–681) explained the Vow as follows: "The reason why those who committed the five deadly sins or abused the *dharma* are excluded in Amitāyus-Buddha's vow is because these two transgressions are very heavy sins and if one performs them, he will surely be born in the lowest hell and stay there for a long period of time. Therefore, Tathāgata, the Perfect One, mentioned these words as a means of stopping one from committing these sins but he did not mean that he does not save evil men." He further explained why both good and evil men can be born in the Pure Land as follows: "The Amitāyus-Buddha, in compassion, took this Vow before the attainment of Buddhahood. And it is by the power of this Vow that the Five Deadly Sins and Ten Evil Deeds are cut. Therefore, those who have committed these sins can also be born in the Pure Land. Even the Icchantika (one who has no hope of being saved) who has abused the true *dharma* can be born in the Pure Land if he will turn his efforts toward the Pure Land."[5]

Religious wars or struggles over ideology, which frequently arose in Europe, did not arise in China. It is true that Buddhism was frequently suppressed, not because of Buddhist doctrine, but because the Buddhist organization menaced and weakened the nation's power politically and economically. While in Mohammedan countries fighting sometimes started on account of violations of such religious customs as eating pork, religious wars never arose in China. The emperors of China and India were similar in that they both did not regard religious differences a justification for war.

Acknowledgment of All Heretical Doctrines

The Chinese acknowledged the individual significance not only of every human being but also of each kind of philosophy as a thought possessing some degree of truth. This tolerant leniency, however, did not exist in the thought of ancient China—Confucius (or his later disciples) stated that "it is harmful to study heretical thoughts."[6] Commoners, however, thought that all writings as well as the five classics revealed truth more or less, even though they were not perfect. Study was highly esteemed in China, and it became necessary to read the classics in order to become a more perfect man.[7]

Foreign thought would not be excluded so long as the Chinese acknowledged some truth in all writings. It was not strange, therefore, that the Buddhism which was introduced into China as one great thought system was discussed and admired by the Chinese and began gradually and slowly to permeate their thought. The Chinese in the medieval period did not feel any contradiction in the fact that they followed Buddhism and also esteemed the Confucian classics as manifestations of truth at the same time.

From the very beginning, Buddhist thought was understood by the Chinese in a reconciling and harmonizing way. The method used first was *"Ko Yi"* which means to explain the meaning of Buddhist terms by analogies with the terms of another philosophy. That is to say, the doctrines of Buddhism were explained by the doctrinal writings of the Chinese philosophers. In the first stage of Chinese Buddhism, *-pāramitā-sūtras* of the *Prajñā* were translated and studied. As there were many similar points between the thought of the *Prajñāpāramitā* (Wisdom)-*sūtras* and the thought of Lao-tzŭ and Chuang-tzŭ, Buddhist scholars explained the thought of the *Prajñāpāramitā-sūtras* in conformity with these Chinese philosophies. They regarded the idea of *K'ung* (non-substantiality) of the *Prajñāpāramitā-sūtras* and the idea of *Wu* (nothingness) of the *Lao-tzŭ* and the *Chuang-tzŭ* as the same. Scholars prior to Tao-an understood Buddhism through this interpretative method of analogy.

A few Buddhist scholars started to oppose this method of interpretation. Chi-tsang, for example, rejected the interpretations made by followers of Lao-tzŭ and Chuang-tzŭ as different from Buddhism. According to his opinion, the views of Lao-tzŭ and Chuang-tzŭ were merely heretical philosophies similar to the heretical thoughts which confronted Buddhism in India.[8] Many times problems of practical morality were the issue between Confucianism and Buddhism, and gave rise to great disputes.

Chi-tsang and others, however, could not change the traditional mode of Chinese thought. A compromise between the theory of Confucianism and Buddhism was possible because both aimed at the same goal. This thought can be recognized in the *Yü-tao-lun* of Sun-ch'o (Eastern Chin dynasty) and *Chia-hsün* of Yen-chih-t'ui (531–591, Northern Ch'i dynasty). Chih-i acknowledged the authority and significance of Confucianism and identified the five permanent morals of Confucianism with the five precepts of Buddhism. He also recognized a corresponding relationship between the five precepts of Buddhism and the five sacred classics of Confucianism.[9] Again, he compared the three practices of Buddhism, *viz. Śīla* (precepts), *Samādhi* (meditation), and *Prajñā* (wisdom) with the virtues of Confucianism.[10]

The similarity of Buddhism with Taoism was noted along with that between Confucianism and Buddhism. In 467 A.D. during the Liu Sung dynasty (420–478), when Ku-huan wrote a book called "*I-hsia-lun*" in which he rejected Buddhism as Taoistic, many people opposed his opinion and insisted that Buddhism and Taoism were the same.[11] Chang-jung, a Taoist in the Southern Ch'i dynasty, is said to have passed away, with the *Lao-ching* and *Lao-tzŭ* in one hand and the Chinese version of the Wisdom Sūtra (*Prajñāpāramitā-sūtra*) and the Lotus Sūtra (*Saddharma-puṇḍarīka-sūtra*) in the other hand, on his deathbed.

A syncretism of three religions, in which Buddhism was identified with Confucianism and Taoism, finally arose from these two relations. This theory was stated by the Buddhists in the T'ang dynasty. Tsung-mi for example declared: "Confucius, Lao-tzŭ, and Śākyamuni all attained sainthood. They preached their doctrines in different ways in accordance with the time and place. However, they mutually helped and benefitted the people by their teachings." He stated, however, that Confucianism and Taoism must ultimately be rejected as they were merely expedient teachings.[12] Other Zen monks, however, at that time said these three religions were the same. When one asked whether these three religions were the same or different teachings, the master answered: "For those of great wisdom, they are the same. On the other hand, for those with little capacity they are different. Enlightenment and illusion depends solely on the capacity of man and not on the difference of teachings."[13] With this idea, Buddhists completely abandoned the idea of the superiority of Buddhism.

In the Five dynasties (907–960) and the Sung dynasty (960–1126), this theory that the three religions were the same was widely believed and supported by the general public. Many scholars of the three religions also backed this theory. Many Zen monks such as Chih-yüan, Ch'i-sung, Tsung-kao, and Shih-fan also believed in it.[14] In the Ming dynasty, many monks asserted the syncretism of Confucianism and Buddhism. Furthermore, when Mohammedanism was introduced in the Yüan dynasty, Chinese

Mohammedans identified the God of Allah with the Heaven of Confucianism.[15]

It was possible to advance such a theory because the Chinese regarded the original *tao* or principle of the Universe as one able to appear in this world in different forms, such as Buddhism and Confucianism. Therefore, they said that "Buddhism and Confucianism are not two different teachings; their origin is the same though their development is different."[16] Hui-lien (1009–1090) said: "The four seasons of Heaven nourish and further the growth of all things. In the same way the teachings of the Sages perfect and teach those under the heavens. However, the original principle or ultimate truth of these teachings is only one."[17] Ch'i-ch'ung (1007–1072) also stated "All teachings of saints are good. All the ways taught by saints are right. . . . The good and right teaching is not only Buddhism, not only Confucianism, not only this, not only that. Buddhism and Confucianism are only offshoots of the original truth."[18] That is to say that every thought-system possesses some significance. "In olden times, there were many holy saints such as Buddha, Confucius, and others. Although their teachings differed, the basic doctrine was the same. They all desired to teach people that 'man should do good.' However, this was taught in different ways. . . . The teaching of Confucianism is necessary to this world, as are also the other religions, and, therefore, Buddhism is also necessary. If one teaching vanishes, then the evil of this world will surely increase."[19] Li P'ing-shan, a Confucian scholar, also acknowledged the significance of other philosophies.[20]

Such being the case, both Buddhists and Confucianists recognized the same significance in other thought-systems as existed in their own thought-system. Of course, much opposition existed to this way of thinking. It, however, lingered on and was supported by people for a long time.

The above may not be a peculiarly Chinese feature. In Europe, too, there was the belief that all religions are the same, but among its diverse sects there was much opposition to this belief. However, in China there has been less opposition, although this may be just a difference of degree; however, it must be remembered that with regard to religion the Chinese have enjoyed freedom of belief to a very great extent. "While in traditional China the Chinese has had no personal choice in marriage, he has enjoyed absolute freedom in the choice of religion."[21]

Syncretism within Buddhism

Since the significance of all philosophical thoughts was recognized, various thoughts within a certain religion had to be harmonized. The doctrinal classification of all Buddhism by the Chinese must be considered in the light of how the different thoughts within Buddhism were regarded and harmonized.

This classification went through a complicated process of development, but what was common to all of them was the idea of expediency, which the Indians had used when different opinions existed within the same religious scripture. It can therefore be said that classification of doctrines originated from the Indian way of thinking. Such being the case, this thought also possessed the characteristics of the Indian conception of the world. For example, history is almost completely ignored. In China, however, only the doctrines within Buddhism were harmonized, and all other doctrines ignored. This syncretic attitude is common to all sects such as the T'ien-t'ai, Hua-yen, San-lun, and Fa-hsiang schools.

(It is true that the San-lun sect referred to various philosophies other than Buddhism, such as Confucianism and Taoism, because the fundamental standpoint of this sect is "the refutation of erroneous views and the elucidation of right views." However, these thoughts were only refuted as erroneous views and not acknowledged as the right views.)

The Chinese did not like to accept a belief based on only one doctrine. Therefore, the scholars' task was to criticize and classify the varieties of different thoughts within Buddhism in a harmonious arrangement. Since Buddhists, in general, did not like to bother with a complicated classification, they threw logic aside to acknowledge all sorts of thought, and thus effect an easy compromise. One example of this electicism is the theory of the "oneness of all Buddhist sects" as advocated by Tsung-mi. He deplored the fact that Buddhists insisted on the superiority of their own sect while refuting the doctrine of others,[22] and said it was useless to quarrel over the respective doctrines of the Buddhist sects. The supreme consideration, he further emphasized, was the unity of truth. "The Supreme principle is one and not two. It is unreasonable, therefore, that two types of truth should exist. The highest principle and its meaning also is not one-sided. One should not understand only a part of truth. Therefore, all Buddhist doctrines should be unified into one in order to have a perfect teaching."[23] He stated this in spite of the fact that he classified Buddhist sects into doctrinal and practical ones, and further divided them into three kinds of teachings.[24] All doctrines ultimately had to lead to the one truth.[25] Then, how were the disputes and oppositions of Buddhist scholars with one another to be reconciled in his theory? According to his opinion, disputes were not refutations but the positing of arguments on both sides, because new standpoints were established by the mutual refutation of the prejudices of each side.[26] That is to say, he wanted to acknowledge a new philosophy founded on the conclusions of the arguments among the philosophers.[27]

The way of thinking which acknowledges a significance in all Buddhist doctrines is especially striking in Zen Buddhism. For example,[28] someone asked Hui-hai: "Who is the superior? The master of precepts, the master of meditation, or the master of doctrine?" He answered: "Although the methods of presentation in accordance with ability lead to superiority in one of the three learnings, they are all ultimately one." The Zen sect, according to its followers, is not just another sect of Buddhism. "The sect founded by Bodhidharma is the essence of Buddhism."[29] Zen (meditation) is the same as the body of Buddha while it is also the essence of all meditations (Samādhis).[30] Its doctrine, therefore, neither contradicts nor opposes doctrines of other sects. One should not be overly attached to one doctrine. "One cannot understand by being confined to only one teaching, one ability, or one sentence, because the Buddha never taught any fixed doctrine. . . ."[31] "It is not difficult to realize the supreme enlightenment. One must not, however, select a fixed doctrine. If one neither likes nor dislikes a set doctrine, then enlightenment can easily be attained."[32]

Such eclecticism or syncretism can also be found in other sects. In the Sung dynasty, nobody adhered solely to the Pure Land teaching. The most famous Pure Land followers belonged to the T'ien-t'ai, Vinaya, and Zen sects. Though the Pure Land teaching especially prospered in the T'ien-t'ai sect, with the rise of the Zen sect many priests also practiced both Zen and the Pure Land practice. Yün-ch'i-chu-hung (1535–1615 A.D.), a representative Buddhist of the Ming dynasty, revived the precepts to harmonize with the Zen practice and the Pure Land practice of calling the name of Amitāyus-Buddha.

The Lotus Sūtra (*Saddharma-puṇḍarīka-sūtra*) was highly esteemed as king of all sūtras in China. It seems that this fact also was based upon a syncretic way of thinking.[33] One of the main thoughts in this sūtra is its acknowledgment of the enlightenment of those who practiced Hīnayāna. Even Devadatta, who intended to destroy the Buddhist organization, and a female dragon become enlightened in this sūtra. This spirit of tolerance and harmony nicely suited the syncretic tendency of Chinese thought.

Chinese Characteristics of Reconciling and Harmonizing

Although it seems that this way of Chinese thinking is very similar to that of the Indians, who acknowledged the authority of various thoughts in a tolerant and harmony-seeking spirit, a great difference exists between them. Most Indians acknowledged the significance of various religions and philosophies and understood them as partial manifestations of an absolute truth. Further, they considered that absolute truth was to transcend and at the same time include all religions and philosophies. They did not maintain, however, that the doctrines of these religions and philosophies could be matched and were mutually alike. The Chinese, on the contrary, simply kept asserting that the doctrines were the same. In this regard the T'ien-t'ai sect's influence was especially decisive. "The syncretism of this sect, which sought to harmonize sectarian divisions within the faith by treating them not as mutually exclusive but as forming a hierarchy of 'levels,' prepared the way for finding the truths of Buddhist metaphysics in Confucian texts as well. Several of the early T'ang Neo-Confucians were lay followers of this sect, and the influence of its metaphysics can be seen in their writings."[34]

Yen-chih-t'ui of the Northern Chai dynasty stated that the five permanent moral rules of Confucianism were the same as the five precepts of Buddhism. In the Sung dynasty as well, Ch'i-sung interpreted the ten good virtues and five precepts of Buddhism as identical with the five permanent moral rules and the idea of benevolence and justice of Confucianism.[35] Yang-kuei-shan and Hsieh-shang-ts'ai asserted the correspondence between each idea of Buddhism and each idea of Confucianism. According to their opinion, Buddhism and Confucianism were exactly the same teaching. Therefore, the founders of both teachings were the same. "The Duke of Chou and K'ung-fu-tzŭ are identical with the Buddha, and the Buddha is identical with the Duke of Chou and K'ung-fu-tzŭ at the same time. . . . The term *Buddha* is Sanskrit while the Chinese use *Chüeh* (enlightenment). Both connote the meaning of realization of truth. . . ."[36] The same statements are asserted about the oneness of Buddhism and Taoism. "Taoism is identical with Buddhism and Buddhism identical with Taoism at the same time. . . ."[37] What stands out in this sort of reasoning is a certain sort of utilitarianism and easy compromise, with cold logical consideration completely abandoned.

When the Chinese explained these theories of oneness, they used pictorial or intuitive similes. For example, they explained by the following simile that the substance of both Buddhism and Taoism was the same: "Once, a duck was flying in the sky. Someone saw it and said that it was a pigeon, while another said it was a mandarin. A duck is always a duck; however, only men distinguish things from each other."[38]

Such intuitive imagery always seems to satisfy the Chinese. Hui-sung (1007–1072) in his poem said, "Buddhism and Confucianism are like the difference between a fist and the palm. There is no difference in the respect that both the palm and the fist are the hand."[39] When Li Shih-Ch'ien was asked whether Buddhism, Confucianism, or Taoism was the superior teaching, he answered "Buddhism is the sun, Taoism the moon, and Confucianism the five stars." The questioner could not ask any more.[40] Nakamoto Tominaga (1715–1746) of Japan criticized this answer by saying: "His answer seemed excellent to the people of that time. However, this answer is meaningless. I myself cannot understand what it means. Therefore, this is not a wise and excellent answer."[41] As he pointed out, Li Shih-ch'ien's answer was not logical and yet the Chinese were satisfied. As the result of the tendency, these three teachings were harmonized without deep logical reflection.

Attempts were made to recognize one doctrine as the fundamental teaching by reinterpreting each of them, but then basic differences among the philosophical systems were overlooked. What was emphasized was which one was older historically, with the idea that anything older is more correct. For example, Taoists composed spurious ancient classics, such as *Lao-tzŭ-hua-hu-ching* (Sūtra on the Transmigration of Lao Tzŭ) and *Lao-tzŭ-hsi-sheng-ching* (Sūtra on the Western Travel of Lao Tzŭ), which stated that Sākyamuni was an incarnation of Lao-tzŭ. On the other hand, Buddhists also composed spurious sūtras such as *Ch'ing-ching-fa-hsing-ching* (Sūtra on the Advance of Buddhist Teachings) in which Śākyamuni dispatched three disciples, K'ung-fu-tzŭ (Confucius), Yen-huei, and Lao-tzŭ, to China to teach people.[42] The origins or dates of these philosophies were discussed in these cases, without any opinions as to whether any of them was more fundamental doctrinally than any other.

Although the Chinese vaguely pointed to the one way as the basis of the three religions, there were no deep metaphysical connotations. However, some Buddhists explained *tao* by a theory of two-fold truth which explained that the highest *tao* is real truth and various others are worldly manifestations of truth.[43] Or again they explained *tao* by a socially expedient theory[44] just as in the Lotus Sūtra. Again Buddhism was thought to be a metaphysical explanation, while Confucianism was a practical or secular religious teaching.[45]

The Chinese regarded these three religions not as different in teachings or thought but in ideological influence. They, therefore, did not deal with various types of thought, but with the influential power of the three religions in their society. Philosophical thoughts unpopular to the Chinese society or Indian ideas stated frequently in Buddhist sūtras were not discussed in spite of the fact they were known. Furthermore, in some cases, Indian philosophy was looked down upon. A typical example of the non-logical and political compromise tendency of the Chinese Buddhists can be found in the following sentences of Chih-i: "When the people follow the unenlightened currents of thought, evil teachings such as Sāṁkhya, Vaiśeṣika, and the 95 others arise. Again, good teachings, such as the positive-negative theory, the theory of divination, the study of the five classics, and other excellent teachings appear in accordance with the purity of the mind."[46] Why are the metaphysics of the Sāṁkhya and the natural philosophy of the Vaiśeṣika evil teachings?[47] Why are superstitions such as the theory of positive-negative and the theory of divination good teachings? The discrimination here between good and evil is not based upon any logical standard but solely upon one that is political and social. Therefore, very little philosophical criticism exists in such thought, compromising as it does with social and political powers.

Thus, it is clear that the Chinese tried to solve the problem concerning various philosophies in a frame of mind restrained by powerful conventional ideas of society. They therefore did not consider this problem of one truth from a universal standpoint, unlike the Indians who reflected on various types of philosophies with respect to their claims to truth, disputing their arguments but ignoring their practical social and political side. Materialism did not possess enough weight to become a powerful philosophical school in India. Buddhism disappeared in the 11th century in India. Nevertheless, Indian scholars with a cosmopolitan and cosmic outlook[48] always referred to it. In this respect, a great difference can be recognized between the Indian way of thinking and that of the Chinese. The study of world-concepts (*Weltanschauungslehre*) was not well established in China with the exception of the classification of doctrines that was more or less eclectic in character.

This arbitrary syncretism had a great influence on the common people, and is one of the striking characteristics of the modern Chinese religions. Typical of this compromising and syncretic attitude is that seen in a Taoist temple where many images of various deities, including a central image of Lao-tzŭ, are enshrined. A Taoistic classic mentions that Śākyamuni, Lao-tzŭ, Christ, Mohammed, and Hsiang-t'o were fellow-deities; consequently, a follower of any religion can become a Taoist without conversion. Among the various deities revered in a Taoist temple are St. John of Christianity, Chu-ko-wu-hou and Yüeh-fei,[49] images of Avalokiteśvara, and Śākyamuni, the *Prajñā-pāramitā-hṛdaya sūtra* (Wisdom of the Heart Sūtra), and *Kao-shih-kuan-yin-ching* (a Goddess of Mercy Sūtra). Taoists wrote three short classics to teach the common people, namely, the *T'ai-shang-kan-ying-p'ien*, *Wen-ch'ang-ti-chün-yin-chih-wen*, and *Kuan-sheng-ti-chün-chueh-shih-chen-ching*. The three are based upon the idea of retribution and teach that "one must not perform evil, but do good," which if followed would result in one's becoming either a heavenly superhuman being or an earthly superhuman being. This Taoist doctrine came from the ethical theory of Buddhism.

The amalgamation of Buddhism and Taoism started in the period of the Six Dynasties (222–589) and became very prominent in and after the Ch'ing dynasty. In famous large Buddhist temples today, Kuan-ti (a god of War)[50] is enshrined in most cases, with divination and fortune-telling performed. Such being the case, modern Chinese do not discriminate between Buddhism and Taoism.

The compromising and syncretic tendency is especially remarkable in the Buddhist faith of present-day Chinese. For example, in Peking, a powerful layman, who is a Pure Land devotee, enshrines not only various images of Buddhas and Bodhisattvas in his place of worship, but Tibetan Buddha images as well. No standard or fixed pattern of these images exists; for this layman, these images are neither *objets d'art* nor curios, but objects of worship to which he pays reverence and homage. In Japan, the object of worship varies according to sects. Therefore, followers of a certain sect do not worship Buddhas and Bodhisattva when they have no great importance for their sect, but merely respect them. On the other hand, the Chinese people worship any images of Buddhas and Bodhisattvas. Another example of the compromising and syncretic tendency of the Chinese is that some other equally powerful layman in Peking might be a follower of the Hung-wan religion as well as a follower of Buddhism, Confucianism, and Taoism at the same time. He sincerely believes in all of them together without the political or social reasons[51] which a Japanese would suspect him of having.

From ancient times, the Chinese governing class acknowledged Confucianism as the correct religion and tried to suppress the other religions in an attempt to maintain the superiority of their class and social position. They tried to make the teaching of Confucianism the chief fount of literary studies. Nevertheless, they failed to suppress the compromising and syncretic traditional Chinese way of thinking.

PART III TIBET

CHAPTER 26 INTRODUCTION

In Tibet, a barren highland situated a few miles above sea-level, surrounded by lofty mountains on all four sides, assailed by heavy storms, with ice and snow covering the land two-thirds of the year, its hardy people established a unique culture. Lamaism, governing the inhabitants with its great religious power, has produced many impressive religious texts and architectural structures. Describing the characteristics of Tibetan culture, Max Weber said: "Due to the existence of the military service system of the old Chinese style and of the monastic order of Lamaist priests who live side-by-side with the common men who are required to enter military services, pay taxes, and offer donations, there has been produced a culture in this land where there is, from the standpoint of capitalistic rentability, no possibility of producing great buildings because of its basically unfavorable natural conditions. The dissolution of this system would spell out an end to their traditional ways of living, practices, and beliefs."[1] Indeed, in this vast highland, of no value from the standpoint of a capitalistic economy, there flourished a unique culture.

Tibet is located to the north of India and Burma, occupying a vast plateau amounting to 625,000 square miles, an area greater than that of England, France, Germany, Spain, and Italy combined. The average altitude is almost three miles above sea-level. Throughout all seasons it is covered by snow, being surrounded by huge ranges of high mountains whose summits, some more than 18,000 feet high, tower in groups.

But nowadays Tibet is no longer a secret country. Generators and steel works have been established. In Lhasa, the capital, automobiles are running. It is only a two days' trip by truck from India, and from Peking one can get to Lhasa in ten to fourteen days. After an airport is established, Lhasa will be a short distance from Peking. When the peace of the world is established, the country will become a resort place for people of all countries, so that it is doubtful whether Tibet will be able to remain an independent cultural area in the future also. There is a report that Tibet, whose total native population is only 2,700,000 now, has had its population increased by 5,000,000 immigrants sent by the Communist Government of

China to demolish the cultural independence of Tibet. If this is true, the unique culture of Tibet will be brought to naught very soon. However, it is an undeniable fact that Tibetan culture has contributed significantly to the culture of Asia and the world.

When we talk of Tibet, we are apt to think of an uncivilized country. However, even in material respects, Tibet has left huge and magnificent things. The huge stone ramparts and simple beauty of the Potala Palace, the symbol of Lamaism, sloping inwardly in the upper part, are 900 feet high, or 70 feet higher than the golden cross on the dome of St. Peter's cathedral in Rome. It is amazing that such a huge structure was built in the wilderness.

Furthermore, this religious culture of Tibet contains an element of universality. Lamaism had some influence upon the vast inland area of Asia covering the interior of China proper, Mongolia, Manchuria, and Central Asia.[2] This fact is quite remarkable in comparison with what little influence Japanese religion has had upon foreigners despite the fact that some Japanese have been very proud of their religious heritage.

The Tibetans referred to in this work are not necessarily the inhabitants of Tibet. It is said that the total number of Tibetans in the world is four and one-half or five million, but only about two and a half million live in Tibet proper; the others live mostly in western provinces of China, although nearly all are Lamaists nonetheless.

Moreover, the regions in which Lamaism is professed are very vast. With Tibet as their center, Nepal, Sikkim, Bhutan in the south, in addition to Ladakh and Kashmir within India, outer Mongolia and the border provinces of Soviet Russia, where Briat Mongolians are Lamaists, Interior Mongolia, part of Manchuria and of Northern China in the north should be counted as Lamaist. These areas are deserts or wildernesses in terms of climate. People raise cattle, and move in search of grass. The regions to which Lamaism has spread have a similar climate.

The religious and economic phenomena of the Tibetan highlands are not easy for people of other cultures to understand. Even though the Tibetan people may be of little importance from a political, military, or economic viewpoint, so far as ways of thinking are concerned, their habits and ideas are of great significance and relevance for our study.[3]

The peculiarities of Tibetan culture are due not a little to the physical surroundings of the land. Isolation from neighboring countries by the walls of the world-famous highlands made Tibet a land of mysteries. Being a vast barren land of poor natural resources and severely cold climate, which refuses to yield food in any great quantity, the land can nourish only a limited number of people. These geographic and climatic conditions have had their influence in establishing customs characteristically Tibetan, and also in conditioning the ways in which Tibetans accepted Buddhism.

Altogether unknown to the Tibetans themselves who designate their creed "Buddha's religion" (*Saṅs-rgyas-kyi-chos*) or "the orthodox religion" (*naṅ-chos*), the term "Lamaism" is in many ways misleading, inappropriate, and undesirable.[4] However, the fact that Tibetan Buddhism is known under the current name of "Lamaism" implies that it includes various elements which cannot be found in Buddhism in general, and that fact is puzzling to outsiders. Buddhism in South Asia, China, Korea or even in Japan was never called by any name other than "Buddhism." Since the term "Lamaism" is popular, we anticipate the existence of various complicated problems or features.

According to legend Buddhism was introduced from India under the reign of King Sroṅ-btsan-sgam-po (seventh century A.D.). In the eighth century Tibet as a whole was not a Buddhist country,[5] but with the aid of its kings Buddhism gradually took root in the country, and came to the fore. However, Buddhism was severely persecuted by King Glaṅ-dar-ma, who reigned from 836 to 841 A.D., and this became a turning point in the history of Tibetan Buddhism.

Before the persecution by Glaṅ-dar-ma there was no sect in Tibetan Buddhism. The sectarian movement begins with Atīśa, the Indian monk, who came to Tibet in 1038 A.D. He is responsible for the innovation of Tibetan Buddhism—the enforced celibacy of monks—and the establishment of high moral standards; he rejected the rituals of the Bon religion which had crept into Buddhism. Then he founded the Bkaḥ-gdams-pa sect. This sect was altered slightly by Tsoṅ-kha-pa three and one-half centuries later. He demanded the strict observance of disciplines and forbade the marriage of monks against the general tendency of the order of those days, but the sect itself became more lenient with regard to the observance of disciplines, and more ritualistic. Since then this sect came to be called the Dge-lugs-pa sect. This is also called the Yellow Hat Sect in contrast to the Red Hat, or Rñiṅ-ma, sect. Moreover, the Bkaḥ-rgyud-pa sect was founded by Mar-pa in the latter half of the 11th century, and the Sa-skya sect in 1072 A.D.

Tibetan Buddhism was based upon the Tibetan Tripiṭaka (whose Peking edition comprises 3522 works), a huge collection of Tibetan translations of Buddhist texts of India. It might seem that if we compare Tibetan versions with the Indian originals very carefully and point out differences between them, we might be able to point out differences of ways of thinking of these two peoples, but this method is not so easy, for Tibetan translations adhere very literally to the Indian originals (mostly written in

Sanskrit), and distorted translations are rather rare. But we should not be disappointed, but go ahead with the task.

Although the translations are on the whole very literal and trustworthy, certain passages describing Indian life that were not understandable to Tibetans were translated with some modification. For example, the tank-pond in the Pure Land in which lotus flowers are blooming is described in the Indian original: "In these lotus-lakes there are, around all four sides, four stairs, beautiful and brilliant with the four gems—gold, silver, beryl, crystal."[6]

It is clear that in this passage the reference is to the Indian quadrangular tanks whose four sides consist of artificially made staircases. Pools of this sort are found near Hindu temples, especially, of South India, even nowadays. The author of this sūtra thought that the staircases on the four sides were made of four jewels—gold, silver, beryl and crystal—if we judge from the Sanskrit original. But Tibetans did not know that such pools were used for religious bathing. Since they could not imagine the holy bathing-places of India to be like stadiums filled with water, they translated the passage to the effect that there were four (narrow) staircases on each of the four sides, i.e. a staircase of gold, one of silver, one of beryl, and one of crystal, and so sixteen all together.

Tibetan scriptures are mostly translations of Indian texts, but there are some which were translated from Chinese, a round-about way from the original. In this respect we can discuss the additional problem of the acceptance (or refusal) of Chinese Buddhism by the Tibetans. Incidentally, the Mongolian scriptures coincide substantially with the Tibetan ones.

Modern Tibet, in the year 1931, was described by Charles Bell, the researcher of Lamaism, as follows: "Politically and socially, Tibet is in the condition of Christian Europe in the Middle Ages, but the Tibetan woman's level is, and long has been, consistently higher than what Europe could then show."[7] To be sure, Tibet had many cultural features comparable to those of mediaeval Europe, or of feudal Japan.

The brilliant culture which blossomed out in this land and the peculiar social structure which was formed with Lamaism as its center, are rapidly going to be transformed and dismembered owing to modern industrialization and communist rule. In which direction will the Tibetans develop? It is difficult to anticipate the future of Tibet. In any case, it would be impossible to ignore completely the traditional and hereditary ways of thinking of its people.

CHAPTER 27 CONSCIOUSNESS OF THE INDIVIDUAL

Weakness of Consciousness of Association among Individuals

The people of Tibet live in scattered villages and pastures connected by narrow routes. To deviate from these paths is to risk death in a mountain wilderness. Having to live under these severe conditions, the Tibetan is everywhere confronted with this physical threat to his existence so that he is constantly faced with the problem of survival. Death is a favorite subject in Tibetan poetry.

The Indian king of the dead was called *Yama* (i.e., "one who controls"), which name was introduced into China and Japan and was used without alteration. However, the Tibetans translated it as "Lord of Death" (*ḥchibdag*). This Lord of Death occurs very often as the subject of sentences in Tibetan verses.

The gloom and despair surrounding man's existence was envisaged by Mi-la-ras-pa, the religious poet (1040–1123 A.D.):

My growing old unknown to my friend;
  My sister unaware of my last illness.
If I can die in this solitude;
  This devotee will be fully content.

My death unknown to any being;
  My rotting corpse unseen by the birds.
If I can die in this solitude;
  This devotee will be fully content.

None to ask where I have gone;
  No place to point to, saying "There."
If I can die in this solitude;
  This devotee will be fully content.

May the prayer regarding the death of this beggar
  Be fulfilled for the benefit of all beings

In a rocky cave in an uninhabited country!
Then will my mind be fully content.[1]

In solitude he found deliverance:

Hail son (i.e. his master Mar-pa) of the Lord Naro and way of Deliverance!
Send the waves of grace over this beggar that he may cling to the solitude.
Keep me free from the distractions of Evil Ones and the World
Grant me advance in *samādhi* (concentration).[2]

Who would think of finding such an acute expression of profound feeling nine hundred years ago in the Tibetan plateau? Even today there are some Tibetan ascetics who practise meditation or dwell in phantasy in monasteries or caves. It is said that one of them never came down from the mountain in which he had lived for fifty years.

When the consciousness of the individual is strong and predominant, the significance of the family as a linkage of individuals tends to be weak. According to ancient inscriptions, an individual who committed a crime was punished, but his brothers, descendants, or relatives were not tried by court, nor were they punished.[3] Criminal law as practised only in modern days in other countries was already established in antiquity in Tibet.

The Tibetan family system was shrouded in curious customs that go back to prehistoric times, and became one of the most secluded institutions devised by mankind.

First of all, the Tibetan practice of polyandry must be described. If a bridegroom were to have brothers, his bride is automatically married to her brothers-in-law, and is the co-wife to all the brothers. The right to possess the co-wife is limited only to sons of the same mother. If a woman were to have a sexual relation beyond this limitation, she is regarded as an adulteress. When she bears a child, however, only the eldest husband is called the father, while the others are called uncles irrespective of who the actual father is. Such a custom seems to go against our normal sense of morality, but Tibetans think it ideal.

In Tibet one should not ask a woman who her husband is. Many Tibetan women have several husbands, so that such a question by a foreigner might be taken as an insult.

According to recent studies, details of polyandry in Tibet are as follows: "Though a large percentage of marriages are monogamous, not too negligible a percentage of polyandry is recognized among the *agricultural* Tibetans. Among the Tibetans the idea of *generation hierarchy* is feeble, but the idea of *gradation of natural age* is remarkable. Often a polyandrous wife has as her plural husbands, brothers of another clan. In fewer cases, a set of plural husbands is composed of uncle and nephew. Even paternal polyandry, in which a father and his real sons have a common wife, as long as she is not an actual mother of the sons, is reported by some travellers. These three kinds of polyandry have a common denominator. If they put importance on the difference in the ancestral hierarchy as is the case in Chinese culture, then the fraternal relationship will be quite different from the avuncular or paternal relationship in its meaning. However, if they attach more importance to the gradation of natural age, neglecting the genealogical hierarchy, then the three kinds of relationship mean only one kind of age gradation, irrespective of whether they are paternal, avuncular, or fraternal.

Among a set of plural husbands, only one is dealt with as the main husband, who can be called an *accentuated husband*. However, this status of accentuated husband is not always occupied by a certain brother or an uncle, but moves from an elder to a younger; since usually an accentuated husband coincides with a housemaster, this means that the status of housemaster also slides from an elder to a younger. The transmission of the status of housemaster usually takes place at the age of forty or so. Accordingly the system of polyandry is a device which makes it possible to charter a more able younger male kinsman as a leader in the household, avoiding friction between wives. Usually the average age of maximum ability is so young that the sons of the outgoing housemaster are too young to take leadership in the family when the ability of their father has passed the maximum.

In conclusion, polyandry is an adaptation to the principle of talent mobility, on the one hand, and an attempt to heighten the stability of a household, on the other, by trying to avoid a crisis in the household. Therefore polyandry is usually prevalent only among the agricultural Tibetans, not among the nomadic Tibetans, because the needs of property accumulation and familial cooperation are stronger in the former than in the latter."[4]

The existence of such a custom does not necessarily mean that there is sexual promiscuity among Tibetans. In Indian palace-courts there were high-class prostitutes. In an Indian drama a prostitute is mentioned by her daughter who was an actress as "a courtesan" (*ajjukā*), whereas in the Tibetan version she is mentioned as "lady-mother" (*yum*),[5] in the same way some Chinese versions avoided the term "prostitute."[6]

Why was such a system adopted in Tibet? Rev. Aoki, who had lived in Tibet for some years, once gave the following answer: (1) Being a barren land, Tibet cannot nourish so big a population. Polyandry is quite suitable to limit the increase of population. (2) Officers and merchants are often obliged to be away from home for a long time due to the difficult conditions of their journeys through the mountain wilderness. In such a case the wife stays home with the remaining brothers to whom she is married.

The *strī-rājya* (Land of Women) is often mentioned in Indian and Chinese classics, referring to a country having the custom of polyandry, but probably not Tibet.

Polygamy is also permitted. For example, the King Sroṅ-btsan-sgam-po is reported to have had five wives. Polygamy, of course, was rather a common custom among the ruling classes in the world of pre-modern periods. The peculiarity of Tibetan polygamy lies in its form—that is, one of the pre-requisites is that wives should be sisters born of the same mother. It is especially desirable for noble families that have only daughters.

Actually, however, most Tibetans adhere to monogamy: polyandry or polygamy is rather an exceptional arrangement. However, the existence of such a system seems to reveal a unique way of thinking in the Tibetan culture. That is to say, although the Tibetans do have a concrete idea of a family, they are not strongly conscious of any personal bond between man and woman.

Another example can be cited. A Tibetan re-marries immediately after the death of his or her partner, and as a result there is said to be almost no widow or widower in Tibet. In a land adhering to such a custom, marriage often means no more than a sexual relation rather than a realization of a spiritual bond. This Tibetan custom is quite the opposite of the "suttee"-custom of medieval Indians.

These customs did not change even after the introduction of Buddhism. High-priest lamas were obliged to admit this fact. Wives were once regarded as property. In Tibetan, the words for "wives" and "children" are often the same word *bu*. For example, *bu-smad* (lit. "lower child") can mean "family," "children," and "wife" (Sanskrit *kalatra*). The word *bu-chen-ma* (lit. "large child") means a "pregnant woman" (cf. the Japanese use of *ko* at the end of women's names).

Consequently, the Tibetans have no strong concept of family lineage. Ancestor-worship is hardly noticed in Tibet except in a form of a mass for the dead, similar to the Japanese *Segaki* ceremony. The term "ancestor-worship" has no equivalent in the Tibetan vocabulary. Each Tibetan home keeps the Buddha's image in a niche or altar, but unlike the Japanese and the Chinese, the Tibetans never keep ancestral tablets (Japanese *ihai*) or portraits of their ancestors on it. The Tibetans' lack of consciousness with respect to the inheritance of property, which is indirectly related to the present subject, will be discussed below.

Weakness of consciousness of association with a specific person does not mean disregard for others, but occasionally the contrary. Tibetans are well known for their hospitality. It is regarded as a virtue to be sincere to others. For this purpose, they have a strange form of greeting. They thrust their tongue out toward the guest, and show the palms of both hands. This action is the Tibetan equivalent of Western hand-shaking. That is to say, to open both hands means to show that the man is hiding no weapon; to show the tongue is relevant to the traditional Tibetan belief that the tongue of a poisoner is black. Even nowadays they send greetings by thrusting out their tongues at the driver of a fast-running automobile. However, this custom is vanishing; now Tibetan laborers prefer clapping hands and cheering when they are in groups.

Tibet was called the "Red-Face Country" in Chinese Buddhist scriptures.[7] Tibetans themselves called their country such (*gdoṅ dmar yul*), because they smeared their face with a sort of red soil. It is said that, as this strange custom was abhorred by the queen from China, King Sroṅ-btsan-sgam-po prohibited that custom for some time.[8] However, this is not essentially different from the use of cosmetics or lipstick by Western ladies, which is abhorred by South Asians, for in South Asia this custom is chiefly limited to women of dubious character. Anyhow, the custom of smearing a sort of red soil is observed in deference to others.

Social pressure by tribes upon individuals appears to have been quite strong. Among the Na-khi tribes, a group of Tibetans who live in South-Western China and practise the Bon religion, even nowadays "forced marriage between individuals who have perhaps never seen each other till the day of their marriage, and betrothal during early childhood, has caused great misery and unhappiness, and many, in order to avoid marrying people whom they have perhaps never seen or perhaps dislike, go up the mountain and commit suicide."[9]

Another example of strong social pressure appears in an interesting linguistic phenomenon. "To commit suicide" can be expressed in Tibetan with a one-syllable word: *lceb-(pa)* (to kill one's self). In English we have to use a longer expression to express this act. In Sanskrit also they used such a compound as *ātma-hatyā*. The linguistic fact that Tibetans used a short single word to denote 'committing suicide' suggests the hypothesis that it was a fairly frequent social phenomenon. In Tibetan chronicles cases of suicide are often mentioned. Killing one's self on the death of one's lord also was practiced. It seems that in these cases tribal pressure to compel one to commit suicide was strong.

Strong ethical features can be noticed in other linguistic expressions. Respect (*gaurava*) and affectionate devotion (*bhakti*), both of which are distinguished from each other in Sanskrit and other Indian languages, are both translated by one and the same word: *gus-pa* because no distinction was made between the two. Such an emotion as the anxiety of a wife about her husband or that of a devotee who worships God earnestly was not distinguished from respect in general. Affectionate devotion (*bhakti*) did not have an important religious significance in Tibet. It is likely that social and ethical elements imbuing one with respect in general overwhelmed other emotional elements (as in the case of the Japanese in feudal days).

Tribal control was strict, especially in warfare. This feature was noticed as a custom of the Tibetans by ancient Chinese.

"(Among Tibetans) order of command is strict. In battles, after the soldiers in the front rows had all died, those in the rear march forward. They esteem death in the battlefield, and dislike death by illness. A family whose members died in battles generation after generation is regarded as an excellent one. Those who were defeated in battles had tails of foxes placed on their neck in order to show everyone that their cowardice was fox-like. Being thus put to shame, they determine to die in battle next time."[10] This attitude resembles the Way of Warriors in ancient Japan.

The rule by tribal chieftains or kingly sovereignty was very strong in ancient Tibet. Ancient Chinese historians reviewed the ethics of the Tibetans who "esteemed loyalty to lords and minimized their service to parents."[11] After the unification of tribes many mausoleums of ancient monarchs were built.[12] This is in contrast to the fact that in ancient India not mausoleums of monarchs, but huge stupas of religious sages were built. Conflicts and strifes among major tribes did not cease even after the rule of Lamaism was established.

Probably due to such social pressure, Tibetans occasionally used ethical expressions more often than ancient Indians. In Sanskrit the prefix *su-* means just "good," and in this case Indians did not distinguish between "good" in the moral sense and "good" in the sensory and aesthetic sense, as in the case of Japanese. However, Tibetans distinguished between these two. For example, "a good place" (*su-gati*) was translated in Tibetan as *bde-ḥgro* (literally, "pleasure-going-place"), "a good act" (*su-kṛta*) as *legs-par-spyad-pa* ("done righteously").

Some Indian ideas were introduced with ethical connotations. The Indian word meaning "friar" was *bhikṣu,* which literally means "one who begs (food)," "one who asks for (alms)," but the Tibetans have always translated this word as "one who seeks for (morally) good" (*dge-sloṅ*). The Indian word: "one who is desirous of welfare" (*śreyaskāma*) was translated as "one who seeks for righteousness or good" (*legs-pa-ḥdod*).[13] The Indian "sage-hermit" (*ṛṣi*) was translated as "one who is straight and honest" (*draṅ-sroṅ*).

Tibetans have no fixed mythology about the origin of their race. Some of them believe that they are the descendants of the King Pāṇḍu who is spoken of in the *Mahābhārata,* the great epic of India, while others say that they are the descendants of a Rākṣasī and a monkey who lived in the Himālayas and who is believed to be the incarnation of the Bodhisattva Avalokiteśvara. These facts—the lack of a fixed mythology about their origins, and its connection to Indian mythology—seem to show that they are not quite conscious of the genealogy of their race.

The idea of a national ancestor, such as the Sun Goddess of the Japanese, is also lacking in the Tibetan consciousness. They surely venerate the three kings, Sroṅ-btsan-sgam-po, Khri-sroṅ-lde-btsan, and Dar-pa-chen, but merely as the three great ancestors who made Tibet prosperous. National consciousness, too, is lacking.

Consequently, the Tibetans do not pride themselves as a superior people or as those who live in the center of world-civilization as the Chinese did. They rather respect India as the land of the sages, and regard their country as a remote region of the world.[14]

The Gupta dynasty (320–*ca.*500 A.D.) was proud that King Candragupta, its founder, married a lady of the Licchavi clan, and this fact was mentioned in every edict (inscription) promulgated by this dynasty. In the same way, when ancient Tibetans extolled King Sroṅ-btsam-sgam-po, the virtual founder of the Tibetan Empire, inscriptions extolled him saying that he was a descendant of the Licchavi clan.[15] To extol a king for the reason that he is a descendant of a foreign clan was rather an unusual event in Asian countries. Tibetans viewed their own country's ancestry as a lineage from India.

A sort of Compendium of Buddhism written by Ḥphags-pa, a Tibetan Lama and an Imperial Preceptor of the Mongolian dynasty, and handed down in Chinese, is based upon the *Abhidharma-kośa* of Vasubandhu of India, but traces the lineage of kings from the Śākya clan through kings of India up to King Kublai Khan of the Mongolian dynasty.[16] In the Indian text only mythological monarchs were mentioned, but in the text by Ḥphags-pa and the "*Golden Annals of Mongolia*" not only mythological monarchs but also many historical kings were mentioned.

The tendency to regard India as an especially holy place is found in the impressive way in which the Indians went about compiling the whole corpus of Buddhist scriptures. The Tibetans included in the Tripiṭaka (a) the holy scriptures compiled in India and (b) the texts written by Indian scholars; (a) is called *Kangyur* and (b) *Tangyur*. Texts written by Tibetans were all placed outside of the Tripiṭaka, in contrast to the compilation of the Chinese and Japanese Tripiṭakas in which works by their own respective countrymen were included. This implies that Tibetans had a high esteem for India as a religious country.

What then is the basic idea of morality among the Tibetans, whose consciousness of association among individuals, as well as the concept of a genealogical recording of their race or nation, is not well developed? The answer lies in their unconditional submission to Lamaism.

Lamaism is the Tibetan form of Buddhism. Buddhism was officially introduced into Tibet during the rule of Sroṅ-btsan-sgam-po (in the early 7th century A.D.). The king became a devout Buddhist, welcomed Buddhist monks from India and China, and ordered them to translate the scriptures into the Tibetan language. At the same time he sent Thon-mi-saṃbhoṭa to India to study Sanskrit. On his return to Tibet, he was asked by the king to establish an official Tibetan script and to compose a Tibetan grammar. Then about a century later, Esoteric Buddhism entered Tibet during the rule of the King Khri-sroṅ-lde-btsan (755–781 A.D.), when two Indian pandits, Śāntirakṣita and Padmasaṃbhava, were said to have come to Tibet and performed miracles, quelling the curse of demons, etc., by the magical power of "mantra"-practice. Afterwards Tibet welcomed a great many Indian monks, who came to Tibet successively, and thus Esoteric Buddhism flourished in Tibet.

The uncontested predominance of Esoteric Buddhism, however, resulted in an extreme degeneration of Buddhism in Tibet. It was Tsoṅ-kha-pa (1357–1419 A.D.) who reformed this degenerate form of Buddhism. He established a religious atmosphere based upon a code of Buddhist precepts. His reformed school was called the Yellow-Caps (*shwa-ser*) in contrast to the traditional school which was called the Red-Caps (*shwa-dmar*). His first disciple, Dge-ḥdun-grub, was renowned for his virtues and regarded by the Tibetans as the incarnation of Avalokiteśvara. As the chief abbot he was endowed by the official title of *Dalai-lama,* a title which has been handed down to the present 14th Dalai-lama. The Yellow-Caps are predominant in Tibet at present, and the Dalai Lama, who resided at Mt. Potala in Lha-sa, the capital of Tibet, was the chief abbot of Lamaism and the King of Tibet as well, before his departure for India as a refugee from the Communist invaders.

Then how is Lamaism connected with ways of thinking of Tibetans in general? Details will be discussed in the following chapter.

CHAPTER 28

DISCOVERY OF THE ABSOLUTE IN MAN

In the wild and hostile climate of Tibet, people feel more dependent on each other than they do on the environment. Here we cannot expect to find that relaxed attitude that is common in Eastern Asia, where man tends emotionally and poetically to merge his being with nature around him. The Tibetans are grateful if nature lets them survive, and they respect the ability of a human being who can work with his fellow beings in order to face their harsh conditions of living. Reports of these conditions are more terrible than anyone can imagine. The *Older Tang Annals* say: "The bedrooms of Tibetans are dirty. They do not bathe or wash themselves."[1] Tibetans today who come to Buddhist temples in India appear unclean and filthy. Ancient Tibetans report that they were "mostly fond of lice which creep into their hair and clothes. When they catch these lice, they do not throw them away but put them in their mouth."[2] There is little fuel for heating purposes, and the dung of yaks is sold at a high price in the cities for fuel.

The nomadic life of the Tibetan requires active and vigorous living. The ancient Chinese described their habits as those of a people who "esteemed vigor and despised feebleness."[3] Retaining the habits of nomadic hunters, "when they treat foreign guests, they drive out the yaks, have their guests shoot them, and then treat them with the game flesh."[4]

The martial temper is extolled in the Ke-sar Saga, perhaps the oldest heroic poem of Tibet:

> "If you are powerful, come to me now.
> If you kindle a fire, it will burn you.
> . . . .
> Oh, ye three brothers, known as the foxes!
> Have you any courage? If so, arise!
> Oh, thou Sky-god of the White Tent tribe!
> If thou possessest power, display miracles!
> If the army of one hundred thousand men
> Of Hor are brave, let them come forth.

The swords of other men are made of iron;
We do not need swords; our right hands are enough.
We will split the body in the middle, and cut the side into pieces.
Other men use clubs made of wood;
We require no wood; our thumbs and forefingers are enough.
We can destroy by rubbing thrice with our fingers.
. . . .
If a skull-drum is to be sounded it should be shaken
  like this.
  (Lifting up the spy and shaking him.)
If a *dor-je* (thunderbolt-sceptre) is to be held in
  the hand, this is the proper way.
  (Holding the spy very tightly, as the *dor-je*
  should be held by a Buddhist priest.)
If a drum is to be used, this is the way to beat it.
  (Beating him.)
If a rope is to be pulled, it should be pulled like this.
If a skin is to be tanned, it should be tanned like this.
This body with eyes and head
Will be made into a hat for the King of the White Tent tribe.
I offer the heart to the war god of the white people of Ling."[5]

Tibetan dancing is orgiastic and inciting. This kind of dancing, which was introduced from Central Asia into China of the T'ang period, was rather varied and somewhat similar to that of Russian peasants in Siberia.[6]

Buddhist ethics was also accepted with its firm insistence on activity.

In the "Diamond Sūtra" the determination of the Bodhisattva is described as follows: "Not by a Bodhisattva who clings to a thing should a gift be given, nor by one who clings to any place should a gift be given. Not by one who clings to form should a gift be given, nor by one who clings to sounds, smells, tastes, touchables, or mind-objects."[7] However, the Tibetan version changed the whole structure, as follows: "A Bodhisattva should give a gift in as ardent a way as he would refuse to cling to a thing. . . . mind-objects."[8] The Indian sentences were negative and prohibitive, whereas the sentences of the Tibetan version were active, positive, and exhortative.

There are many cases in which negative expressions of the Indians were changed to positive and affirmative ones by the Tibetans. "To endeavor" was expressed by Indians as "not to be negligent" (*apramāda*), whereas Tibetans translated it with an affirmative and positive word: *"bag"* (to endeavor). The Sanskrit negative expression *anartha* (something not beneficial) as translated by the Tibetans is an affirmative expression; *gnod-pa* (something that does harm).[9] Indians used the word *amogha* (not vain), which Tibetans translated as *don yod* (significant, useful). The sentence "The result becomes not-vain" (*amoghaphalaṃ vartate*) in a Sanskrit text was translated as "The result becomes fruitful" (*don yod paḥi ḥbras bur ḥgyur ro*).[10] Early Buddhism of India taught: "One should not despise what one has acquired." (*svalābhaṃ nāvamanyeta.*) Whereas Tibetans translated it in an affirmative and positive way: "One should (plainly) accept what one has acquired." (*Raṅ gi rñed pa blaṅ bya shin.*)[11]

Pure Land Buddhism was also introduced as exhorting the practice for being born into the Pure Land.[12]

The ethics for those who have to live in difficult surroundings, facing death or life, is fundamentally different from the ethics for those who are enjoying a settled and stable life in agricultural communities. In the former situation bodily vigor matters. Deference and respect to the elderly, as found in other Asian countries, are not discernible. A Chinese classical work described this custom as follows: "(The Tibetans) do not remove bows and weapons from themselves. They esteem youth and deride the elderly. Mothers greet their children; sons conduct themselves arrogantly toward their fathers; in processions, youths go first, and old people follow them."[13]

The Tibetans were once a strong people, well-known for their bravery even after the introduction of Buddhism. Their invasion of neighboring countries lasted for about two hundred years after that. The Tibetan nation was one of the most virile ones in Eastern Asia, and overran and even conquered China more than once. But it has steadily declined in power and numbers to less than a tenth part of its former population.[14] Cultivated lands have been forsaken. Travelers often notice devastated ruins of the civilization of the past. Why has Tibet declined to such an extent? Some people ascribe it to Lamaism. It is said that in Tibet one among five persons, including women and children, is a Lama. This rate is higher than that in South Asian countries. The largest monasteries in the world were located in Tibet, one of them once accommodating nearly a hundred thousand Lamas. Such a large number of youthful men of vigor was economically unproductive, for monks were not allowed to cultivate, and they had no progeny, since most had to practice celibacy. This self-destructive system was closely connected, sociologically, with the feudal system since the medieval ages of Tibet, and, ideologically, with the predominance of medieval other-worldliness.

The tendency to live in seclusion and refrain from economical production was one of the striking features of medieval Tibet. Other-worldliness, we know, was also one of the features of the medieval period, not only in Tibet but throughout all countries in Europe as well as in India, Japan, etc.

But here in Tibet, this trait of withdrawing from the world took a very conspicuous form. However, it is an indisputable fact that the ancient Tibetans were a hardworking people, as their living descendants are. If industry and technology based upon modern sciences are introduced, Tibetans will display a new development. As can be said of Buddhism in general, Tibetan nobles did not despise commerce, quite unlike Western nobles and clergy. In this respect the development of commerce in Tibet would probably be realized without much resistance, and modernization also would be easy.

Due to the necessity of developing the wilderness to establish their material existence, the Tibetans found it natural to esteem the human body and its functions. According to the Tantric religion introduced from India to Tibet, the breath of man is understood to be articulated in three functions; i.e., breathing-in, holding the breath, and breathing-out, which are nothing but, respectively, the three holy sounds, i.e., *oṃ, āḥ* and *hūṃ*. This theory had to be religiously learnt. To carry out this theory is tantamount to repeating continually the recitation of these three holy sounds. Breathing and reciting holy formulas are not essentially different; one is supposed to continue repeating the Diamond-Recitation day and night. One practices the Diamond-Recitation twenty-one thousand six hundred times for a whole day and night.[15]

It is difficult not to believe that an extreme interpretation has been given to a natural act; while a man is breathing, he is reciting the three holy syllables: *oṃ, āḥ,* and *hūṃ,* which represent the coming, staying, and departing of the Principal Buddha. So if we retain these three syllables, we shall coincide with the ultimate truth. Accordingly, recitations of holy scriptures and holy words, worshipping images, and constructing platforms for ceremonies, etc. become useless. All these religious elements are scrapped and one returns to human nature itself again.

In Mahāyāna Buddhism, in general, it was customary to assume the three bodies of the Buddha. But the members of a certain school of Tibetan Tantric Buddhism (*Piṇḍīkṛta-sādhana*) assume a fourth body, which is called "the body in itself" (*svabhāva-kāya*). It is not a body conceived by means of abstract thinking, but the body which can be vividly felt or directly experienced. It is "the body by birth" (*sahaja-kāya*), "the body for pleasure" (*sukha-kāya*), or "the body for great enjoyment."[16] A certain scripture (*Guhyasamāja*) of Esoteric Buddhism aims at "concentration for fulfilling all desires" (*sarvakāmopabhoga-samādhi*).[17]

Therefore, Tibetan Buddhism brought a peculiar practice into existence, which is called "Non-Differentiation of Enjoyment and Voidness" (*bde-stoṅ-dbyer-med*). It is a practice based upon the thought that the State of Voidness which is the ultimate truth of Buddhism is nothing but human enjoyment (of carnal desires). (This is not the practice of Japanese Esoteric Buddhism in general.) It taught that "the Great Enjoyment," i.e., the unification of father (*yab*) and mother (*yum*) was nothing but the Enlightened State of Mind.[18] The man who has attained this state of Enlightenment experiences "the Great Enjoyment." Whatever he does is not improper, just as a lotus flower, coming out of mud, is not defiled with filth.[19] Ultimately in this sort of practice there is no need of discipline. Drinking liquor, eating meat, sexual intercourse, etc., constitute the Way of the Buddha.[20]

Of course, there was some ethical thought contrary to the above. Mi-la-ras-pa taught, "To drink wine or tea for pleasure is to drink (a brew of aconite)."[21] But such thought did not take root among common people.

Many Tantras conveyed to Tibet had to be classified in the Four Divisions. Tsoṅ-kha-pa, the Great Master of Tibetan Buddhism, showed that the way of classifying a given Tantra among one or other of the four Tantra Divisions was by four degrees of mutual attraction, or "courtship" (*anurāga*) of the male and female deities, who represent respectively "means" (*upāya*) and "insight" (*prajñā*). The four degrees are: Laughter (*rgod pa*), Looking (*lta ba*), Holding Hands (*lag bcaṅs*), and The Two United (*gñis gñis ḥkhyud*). For example, the *Vajraśekhara* has the following passage: "The goddess *Rdo-rje Ca-co-sgrogs* . . . seized the hand of the Bhagavat." Since this Tantra shows the deities attaining the third degree of mutual attraction, it is included in the third Tantra division (the *Yoga-tantra*).[22] To classify Buddhist scriptures in accordance with the degree of heightened sexual love was never dreamt of by Chinese nor by Japanese Buddhists.

According to a theory of Tantric Buddhism,[23] the "Great Pleasure" should not be worldly enjoyment. It should not be "worldly pleasure deriving from laughter, looking, holding hands, and embracing." It is the supreme and permanent pleasure transcending those mentioned above. Then, what kind of pleasure does it virtually mean? The theory of Tantric Buddhism does not clearly explain it. Bu-ston, the Buddhist scholar, explaining it, says that ultimately one should not cling to attachment, nor to non-attachment, but stay in the state of non-attachment to Nirvāṇa. He sets forth the *Great Mahāyoga-tantra* to control the desire to embrace, which is the strongest one among the above mentioned four stages of fulfilling sexual desires. He says, the vilest *Caṇḍālas* (most abject creatures) do not distinguish between things pure and things impure. They resort to all sorts of drinking and eating, and commit all sorts of vile acts, eat five kinds of meat, and five kinds of nectar (dung, urine, etc.). However, it is especially such vile people who are fittest for the *Great Yoga-tantra*. It is they who are glutted with sensuous attachments, hate, and delusion who have the possibility of attaining the Great Pleasure (the state of *Vajradhara*). In this faith in redeemability the mission of Tantric Buddhism edifies and guides lost people, knowing that they are living in defilement.[24]

Such masters as the Lamaists Dge-legs-dpal-bzaṅ-po and Tsoṅ-kha-pa say, "Human existence is a sacred (holy) existence. A man, when born, is a Buddha incarnate." The birth of a man means that "Buddha brings up Buddha's child whose essence is a Buddha, and to have a Buddha come forth."[25] Then how explain death? Death is "unification with the ultimate truth."[26]

That is how the idea of Buddha incarnate came to Tibet. Kamalaśīla, who introduced Buddhism into Tibet, has often been called "The Holy Buddha." His body was embalmed, and is still preserved in a good condition as a mummy in a monastery twenty miles north of Lhasa.[27]

Moreover, the Buddhism which admits human desires affirmatively originated in Tibet. In a practice called "the Great Practice" (*Mahāsādhana*) young daughters of dyers or dancers, say, 12 or 16 years of age, who belong to the lowest Caṇḍāla class, were chosen; their bodies were regarded as ceremonial configurations (*maṇḍala*); at each spot on their bodies a goddess was assumed to exist to be worshipped.[28] The prayer (*māntra*) for a divine being called Hayagrīva is aimed at the highest bliss with a woman (Paramānanda), because "Desires are extinguished by fulfilling desires."[29]

The concept of deliverance also changed. In order to express: "Deliverance will occur," the Indians said: "One will become free from temptations" (*nirvṛtiḥ bhaviṣyati*), whereas Tibetans said: "Mind will become pleasant" (*sems bde bar ḥgyur ro*).[30] That is to say, deliverance was beyond pleasure and suffering in the eyes of Indians, whereas it was pleasure itself in the eyes of Tibetans. In a ceremony described by Bu-ston a goddess addresses the principal Buddha of the configuration with the phrase: "May you love me!"[31]

The idea of the Pure Land also was transformed by Tibetans. According to the notion of ancient Indians there was no sexual relation between man and woman in the Pure Land of Amitābha Buddha.[32] But this was not congenial to Tibetans, who changed the passage to: "There is no adultery in the Pure Land."[33]

The religious exaltation of sexual enjoyment is one of the prominent characteristics of Tibetan Buddhism. For Buddhist mendicants, the goal is to enter the absolute state through the practice of meditation, a state which is usually expressed in a negative way. Lamaism, on the contrary, expresses its highest goal through the image of deities in sexual union as the symbol of the greatest pleasure (*mahā-sukha*). This image of coupled deities is referred to as the "Excellent Pleasure" (*bde-mchog*). This idea seems to have its origin in a Hindu image of Śiva and Kālī (-Durgā) in "*saṁyoga*" (union).[34] Also the *liṅga* (phallic symbol) is regarded as something sacred. Though there is no *liṅga* worship in Tibet, we sometimes find a scene of religious dancing there with a *liṅga* held in the hands. Even Tsoṅ-kha-pa, the reformer of Lamaism in the 14th century, could not stamp out the practices described above.

Tibetans did not accept the Buddhism of rigorous moralism whole-heartedly. Chinese Buddhists once tried to propagate their own brand of Buddhism in Tibet, but were soon expelled by the natives.[35] The strict morality of Chinese Buddhism could not take root in Tibet. What was accepted by the Tibetans was the Buddhism of worldly enjoyment which sometimes leads people to engage in sexual enjoyment, the corrupted form of Indian Esotericism.

CHAPTER 29

ABSOLUTE SUBMISSION TO A RELIGIOUSLY CHARISMATIC INDIVIDUAL

Lacking the consciousness of belonging to any such specific human nexus as a family lineage or a race, the Tibetans act on the principle of submission to the Lamas as religious preceptors. Submitting to the Lama, a person endowed with religious charisma, is then the Tibetans' way of adhering to a social order.

The attitude of absolute submission to Lamas did not appear from the beginning of the history of Tibet. As in other ancient states which first came into existence under the authority established by the "divine right of kings," Tibetan monarchs were called "sons of god" (*lha-sras*).[1] The appellation "Son of Heaven" is surmised to have been introduced from China or Khotan into Tibet.[2] In a stone pillar inscription King Khri-sroṅ-lde-btsan was extolled: "In accordance with the divine nature his power was great."[3] This king was aiming at "Tibet, the country of Law" (*chos bod yul*) in his edict,[4] and he "had Law in due consideration."[5] In this respect he aimed at relying upon universal human laws, and did not depend on the authority of any specific religious preceptor.

What Tibetan Buddhists also sought was universal laws transcending the differences of countries and peoples. The Tibetan translators went to India to learn Indian languages and Buddhist teachings; they sometimes even went as far as Burma. Their death-rate there was very high, for the climate of the tropics was deadly to those nurtured in the dry cold of Tibet. Out of a party of eight or ten, usually not more than two or three would return to their own country.[6] But the danger of death did not intimidate those anxious to seek eternal and universal laws.

However, in later days the tendency to rely upon the charismatic authority of Lamas as specific preceptors became predominant. The Tibetan attitude of absolute submission to a religiously charismatic individual is directed toward the personality of the lamas (*bla-ma*). The Tibetan term "*bla-ma*" literally means "a high (*bla*) person (*ma*)," and is identical with the Japanese concept of "*shō-nin*" in its literal sense. Actually, however, it is the Tibetan counterpart for the Sanskrit word "*guru*" (teacher), or sometimes for "*kalyāṇa-mitra*" (a friend of virtue). "*Bla-ma*" was originally an appellation for a high priest or president of a monastery, but nowadays it is used by any disciple in addressing his master. Thus, the term means "a master" or "a teacher."

The thought of extolling the charisma of a religious preceptor existed in the sects of medieval Hinduism; it was introduced to Buddhism, and was established as the Esoteric Buddhism of India.

> "One who has fallen from the summit of Mount Meru will fall down, even if he wishes not to fall.
> One who has acquired the beneficial oral tradition by grace of the Lama will attain deliverance, even if he wishes not to be delivered."[7]

This opinion became popular in Tibet.

Worship of a Lama coincides with the worship of a Buddha as a personal existence (not as an abstract principle). In Tibetan versions more honorific appellations are applied to Buddhas.[8]

A unique and important characteristic of Lamaism, which distinguishes it from other schools of Buddhism, is that the living lama is more highly revered than the Buddha or the Dharma. Bu-ston said, "A preceptor is Vajradhara himself. Without a preceptor there is no Buddha. Unless one understands this, there is no Enlightenment."[9] Mar-pa, the famous sorcerer, tested the faith of Mi-la-ras-pa, the disciple, in his *guru* (preceptor). Unless faith is complete, there can be no spiritual advance in the disciple. Bell, the British Tibetan scholar comments upon this: "We have traveled far now from the teaching of Gotama, who made but little appeal to faith. Rather we are with the form of Buddhism that has been mingled with their old Faith, and thus the more fully adapted to the needs of the great Tatar branch of humanity."[10] This is also the Tibetan equivalent of *guru* worship of Hinduism.

On this point, Lama Tada, the Japanese priest who went to Tibet, explains as follows: "There is a saying which is usually recited by Tibetan monks: 'Before the Lama there was not even the name of the Buddha. All the Buddhas of a thousand eons existed in dependence on the Lama.' It means that we can know about the existence of Buddha and his teaching only through the Lama's instruction, and only through that way can we follow the Buddhist practices; therefore Lama is the real teacher who enables us to enter the right path and leads us to enlightenment; all the Buddhas in the past, too, having received the Lama's instruction, believed in Buddhism, practiced it, and attained enlightenment. In this case the term '*lama*' seems to have kept its original meaning, i.e. 'master.'

"A more important concept is added to this term in the sense of 'one's own master who saves him.' Namely, a master is regarded by his disciples as something more venerable than the Triple Jewel. Disciples are requested to pay homage first to the Lama, then to the Buddha, Dharma, and Saṅgha, not only as a matter of concepts but also in actual practices. Therefore, for the Tibetan Buddhists, the objects of worship are the 'Four Jewels' instead of the usual 'Three Jewels.' This is the principal doctrine of Lamaism, and to take refuge in these Four Jewels is one of the characteristics which distinguish Lamaism from other schools of Buddhism. Lamaism was established and developed on the basis of such a faith.

"In a further developed form of this concept, Lama is regarded as the synthesis of the Triple Jewel. That is to say, they believe that the Jewel of the Lama is not the same as the other three, but is the unity or the substratum of them all. Lama is the substratum of all the virtues, the basis of all the paths, and the root of merits. To serve a Lama is nothing but to pay homage to the Triple Jewel. This service is to be conducted in meditation and practice, since it is not only the best way to accumulate the root of virtues but also the shortest way to acquire enlightenment. Therefore, the followers should try to satisfy their Lama materially and spiritually as well. For pursuing this duty, they are required to be prepared even to sacrifice their lives."[11]

Lamaists never speak of their master's name in front of others. They refer to their master not by name, but abstractedly or with an explanation of the meaning of his name so that hearers can judge who is the master. In case the sign of Lama's name is required for a document, etc., they do so with a preface: "though I feel it painful to scribe my master's name. . . ." Thus they hesitate even to utter the Lama's name.[12]

This religious charisma was connected with economical conditions in one respect. It was customary among Tibetan families that at least one boy take the order and be parted from his family while young. In the devout families of Ladakh in India, one son, usually one of the younger ones and occasionally the eldest or favorite one, is sent to the order to become a monk. Younger sons are not entitled to inherit property, nor can they share the same wife in common with their elder brothers. So there is no alternative but to be sent to a monastery. It is only in cases when boys do not take the order that daughters are made nuns. There are fewer nuns than monks.[13]

Before Tsoṅ-kha-pa's reformation, a kind of caste system was observed among the Lamaist priests who were actually married (although this fact was not officially recognized) and the priesthood was maintained by hereditary rights. Priests of the Yellow-caps, the reformers, practiced celibacy, and today, only the red-caps still retain this hereditary custom. Even in this case, however, the qualification to be a successor is given only to the son who is at the same time a disciple of his father. Unless he has earned the described qualification by study and practice, he cannot succeed to the priesthood. Hence, the transmission of priesthood is not always by heredity. Here, too, we can observe the way of thinking which regards the religious charisma as more important than blood.

In a society where a charisma is regarded important, we cannot expect educational training to permeate all strata of society. In Tibet, only special individuals are allowed to write books and articles.[14]

What then is the character of the Lama hierarchy? It is divided into two classes: ordinary monks and noble monks. Of these, the "noble" monks are those who had entered the order through recognition as incarnate Lamas. Their number is about thirty in each monastery and they are treated very respectfully because they are believed to be the incarnations of virtuous Lamas.[15] Thus the noble monk does not mean the monk born of the nobility, but one who is personally qualified to be treated as a noble. Contrary to the manner in which monks of noble families are accorded special treatment in Japan, the Tibetan lamas placed importance not on family origin but individual charisma.

Esteem of authority of a specific person, logically underlying Lama worship, has taken unexpectedly deep root among Tibetans, and can be noticed in various cultural phenomena.

Tantric Buddhism in India was founded by Indrabhūti (in the ninth century A.D.), and was conveyed to Tibet by Atīśa, but it has been said by tradition that many Tantric masters of India, including not only Indrabhūti but Saraha, Śabari-pa, and Nāgārjuna (tenth century A.D.), composed many works.[16] Once a specific person comes to be known as an authority, many treatises are ascribed to him in an accelerating chain reaction, and he is regarded as an authority in many fields.

Those who twisted and transformed Buddhism in Tibet did not like to be called "degenerators." In order to justify and authorize the practices adopted from the Bon religion native to Tibet, they tried to "discover" hidden revelations allegedly set forth by Padmākara, the establisher of Tibetan Buddhism. They were all spurious. But the "discoverers" of these revelations claimed that there had been twenty-five disciples of Padmākara in the past life.[17]

Mar-pa (1012–1098), the founder of the Bkaḥ-rgyud-pa sect, visited India three times, and under the pretext that he had inherited the authority of Indian Buddhism he was able to establish his own sect. The name of his sect, Bkaḥ-rgyud-pa, means "continuity of teaching," implying that the esoteric teaching was conveyed directly from master to pupil, or from father to son in the spiritual sense.

In the branches of this sect, founder-worship has prevailed. Images of the founders of respective branches of the sect have been principal objects of worship.[18]

In medieval ages a large number of biographies of high priests were composed besides various compendia of dogma and commentaries. The biography of Mi-la-ras-pa became the pattern of Lama biographies of the later Bkaḥ-rgyud-pa sect.[19]

The idea of the set of Sixteen Arhats was introduced from China (of the T'ang period) to Tibet, and finally the figure of Lha Ḥgro-baḥi mgon-po, the Chief Abbot (1186–1259), surrounded by the Sixteen Arhats, became popular and prevalent.[20]

Moreover, in Tibet religious charisma of a specific person has been closely connected with the belief in transmigration. We can trace the origin of this belief to an early date.

Tsoṅ-kha-pa, the reformer of Tibetan Buddhism, was adored so much that he was regarded as an incarnation of Avalokiteśvara or Mañjuśrī Bodhisattva; he was thought to have passed sixty-two lives before he was born Tsoṅ-kha-pa, the previous lives including those of the kings of India and Tibet and of Lamas.[21]

Here the living Lama is regarded as the Absolute. Lama is said to be the personal manifestation of the three virtues, wisdom, compassion, and power, each of which is usually held to be represented by the Bodhisattva Mañjuśrī, Avalokiteśvara, and Guhyarāja, respectively.[22] In a yoga practice called *"Biamaḥi rnal-ḥbyor,"* mendicants, sitting in front of an image of Lama, meditate upon the identity of Lama with Vajrasattva, and in accordance with this meditation, they are expected to receive a miracle by which they can get rid of all the miseries of this world. This way of thinking led finally to the belief in the Dalai Lama and Panchen Lama.

As the mountain at the southernmost edge of India in which Avalokiteśvara Bodhisattva lives is called "Potalaka," the palace of Dalai Lama in Lhasa is called the Potala Palace. The highest sovereignty of Tibet was in the hands of the Dalai Lama, while the Bkra-śis Lama (*Paṇ-chen bla-ma*) possessed merely a part of the territory. According to the religious idea commonly accepted by Tibetans, however, the Dalai Lama is believed to be the incarnation of the Bodhisattva Avalokiteśvara, while the Bkra-śis Lama is that of the Buddha Amitābha. The Dalai Lama has therefore received an honorific title of "the Holy Avalokiteśvara" (*Ḥphags-pa Spyan-ras-gzigs*). On the basis of a common belief in Indian Buddhism that Avalokiteśvara saves all living beings by means of his incarnations in thirty-three forms, the Tibetans believe that each Dalai Lama is reincarnated in this world in the form of a baby forty-nine days after his death.[23]

For the first several generations, each Dalai Lama uttered a prophecy on the name of the place where he was to be reincarnated after his death, and there was no difficulty in discovering his successor. In later days, however, a Dalai Lama passed away without such a prophecy, and the subordinates were obliged to seek his successor by means of an oracle. Since then the oracle method has become customary. The most famous place for the oracle was Nechung (Gnas-chuṅ) near the Ḥbras-phuṅ monastery, followed by the three monasteries of Bsam-yas, Dgaḥ-ldan, and Lha-mo. In each of these monasteries, there was enshrined the Protecting Deity whom the priest asked for an oracle about the successor to the Dalai Lama. The decision was made after considering the contents of the messages received from these four monasteries. Sometimes each messenger announced a different oracle. A unanimous choice among the four was hardly to be expected. Therefore, if there were more than two candidates selected by this method, the officers nourished them till the age of four or five. During this period, the candidates were examined on their abilities and behavior before the officers would render their final decision. If the final decision were still difficult to make, they would be called to Lhasa where officers selected one of them by lot. The lot-drawing was held in the public hall in the presence of high government officers, secular and ordained, and the Chinese ambassador to Tibet. In the process of lot-drawing, however, there was room for conspiracy. Sometimes the oracle was misled by corruption, sometimes by bribery of the high officials, or by collusion with the Chinese ambassador in the lot-drawing. Bribes often held the key to the final decision. "There is no social disorder because, fortunately, neither the Dalai Lama himself nor the people know that such conspiracy ever takes place."[24]

Thus the Dalai Lama, the highest sovereign in both religion and state, is determined not by hereditary right but by the commonly held belief in rebirth. Dalai Lama, the holder of the highest religious charisma, should receive a proper education deserving of his honor, and practice disciplines strictly. The rules for educating the young Dalai Lama were very strict. Needless to say, he does not drink liquor. For the first three or four years he never sees women, not even his mother, and for the rest of his life he does not associate with women.

Among the successive Dalai Lamas, the fifth and the thirteenth have been specially respected; their tombs are big. The Fifth made the Yellow Hats sect the orthodox one of Tibetan Buddhism, and constructed the Potala Palace; the Thirteenth ruled Tibet for thirty years and resisted the British Army. His corpse is shrouded with a ton of gold. So, the greatness of the Dalai Lamas is evaluated according to the measure of successful worldly achievements, but in the subjective consciousness of common people they are incarnations of Buddha through and through.

In the beginning of the twentieth century a Tibetan officer said to a

British colonel, "If the Dalai Lama told me to go to Hell, I would go there gladly. . . . Does not the proverb say? 'If told to strike a rock, strike! If told to go to Hell, go.' "[25]

The belief in rebirth also plays an important role in determining the religious charisma of common lamas. Virtuous lamas are believed to be the incarnations of certain specified lamas of ancient days. Although such beliefs in Tibet characterize the ways of thinking of its common people, those who were ambitious for worldly power must have thought in a rather different way. In previous times, a number of Lamas, and even some Dalai Lamas, are supposed to have been poisoned. There are some Tibetan medical works on poisoning. But even poisoners seem to have admitted religious charisma in the persons whom they wanted to support.

The belief in rebirth or incarnation is, needless to say, of Indian origin. It was prominent especially among Indian Mahāyānists, who believed in the doctrine that Buddhas and Bodhisattvas manifested themselves in various forms in order to save all living beings. But they had no belief, as in Tibet, that an individual of certain qualifications is the incarnation of a certain Buddha or Bodhisattva of the past. For Indians, the question was the general possibility of reincarnation, and the admission of innumerable incarnations. For Tibetans, on the contrary, the problem was limited to particular personalities of certain qualifications. Here we can observe the transformation of a thought-pattern of the Indians, who attached importance to universality, into the Tibetan way of thinking, which attached importance to individual differences. Moreover, this transformation is observed not in the form of the importance given to a mundane authority based upon blood or hierarchy as in China and Japan, but to the religious charisma of the individual, the selection of whom was based upon the belief in rebirth.

The same way of thinking exerts a great influence on the daily customs of the Tibetans. Since they attach no great importance to blood lineage, they are likely to mistreat the body of a deceased in the conduct of a funeral. "The head is tilted down between the knees, and the knees are tied firmly to the breast, making the body nothing but a solid mass of matter which is wrapped up in a dirty blanket and is placed at a corner of the room. On a fixed day, they hand it over to a carrier at early dawn. Neither relative nor pupil accompanies it. It is quite different from the elaborate funeral ceremonies observed in Japan. The Tibetans regard a body without a spirit as something like a solid lump of clay of no value. Thus the body is carried near a rocky cavern, where condors live, and is offered to them for consumption."[26]

However, in some Lamaistic areas of Nepal it is customary to throw corpses into rivers, and occasionally cremate them.[27] In the respect that they do not worship corpses their belief is in common with that of the Siamese, etc., and to have corpses eaten by vultures is a practice common with the Parsis.

The Tibetans may not be able to understand the Japanese custom of regarding the body as the Buddha's image and reciting scriptures in front of it.[28] Here is a contrast in the way of thinking between two peoples who accepted the same Esoteric Buddhism. The Japanese attaches importance to blood lineage, while Tibetans completely ignore it.

What is important for the Tibetans is the soul, the substratum of transmigration. "Generally, at the death of a Lamaist, they never offer incense and flowers for the dead, but ask the fortune-teller about the situation of the dead in the other world. If he is announced to be with Avalokiteś-vara, they make an image of the same Bodhisattva and offer incense and flowers in front of the image."[29]

There is a ceremony of the returning of the departed soul to this world observed in Lamaism. It consists of a kind of a mass for the dead similar to the Japanese *Segaki* ceremony.

To explain the reason why such an idea has occurred, climatic conditions should be taken into consideration. Chinese or Japanese who once settled in hereditary agricultural communities wish to return to home villages to die, or to bury their ashes at native places. However, nomadic Tibetans or Mongolians, being accustomed to the life of migration, do not mind forsaking corpses. What they wish is only to be born into a better world in their after life.

The way of thinking which minimizes the body and esteems the soul as the subject of human existence occasionally brings cruel practices into effect. According to the reports of Hedin and other travelers to Tibet, there is "a sage of the cave." He is reportedly said to enter a cave, enclosing himself inside it, leaving only an opening sufficient to receive food, and continues to live in this solitude and place of no light for the rest of his life. When the supplied food is found untouched, people outside recognize his entrance into *Nirvāṇa,* and open the cave in order to perform the funeral for the sage. Some sages are reported to have lived about five or six years under such conditions, while another, more than twenty years. Many sages perform this feat of asceticism and die in the conviction that it is one of the short ways to liberation.[30]

Not even the Indians observed such a harsh form of ascetic practice, which is completely different from the Zen training of Japan. Such asceticism seems possible only in the belief that the soul must be revered even at the cost of the body. This way of thinking, i.e. of attaching importance to the soul as the substratum and of ignoring the body, is also observed in the manner of keeping Buddhist discipline.

Buddhism, especially Mahāyāna Buddhism, prohibits eating meat because of its emphasis on the spirit of compassion to all living things. In Tibet, however, Buddhists could not help eating meat due to the extreme climatic and other unfavorable natural conditions. They eat boiled mutton or yak meat by cutting it into pieces with a knife. Sometimes they eat raw meat with blood dripping down. Dried meat frozen in winter is also supplied for the table. Thus Tibetan dishes are full of meat. Even today, it is reported, people often come across the sight of robed monks purchasing meat. Thus the precept which prohibited eating meat was not adhered to in Tibet.[31] The only exception is that they never eat fish because they "don't like the idea of depriving so many fish of their lives." By the same token, they do not eat birds. They interpreted the precept as follows: that to kill a big beast like a yak is not sinful because the meat of a yak can supply enough food for many, while to deprive many small animals like birds or fish of their lives for the purpose of eating is quite sinful.

Another example relevant to the problem is that in Tibet scriptures are generally written or printed upon paper, and occasionally upon silk as an excellent writing material.[32] This use of silk was forbidden in India, for silk is made by killing silkworms, and therefore regarded as unfit for holy scriptures. But it is likely that the reason why Tibetans did not mind using the silk was that the silkworms were killed by somebody else.

However, the thought that a Tibetan should not himself kill even worms interfered with their economic development. Tibetan peasants disliked the use of scythes, spades, and other metal tools for tillage, for they would cause the death of worms in the earth.

The tendency to care more for the soul than for this worldly blood relationship or personal associations also greatly influenced the economic life of the Tibetans. They have little desire to transmit their personal property to their relatives after death. The legacy of an unmarried monk is offered as a donation at his death. (In Japan such a legacy is handed over to his relatives or disciples.) In the case of a noble monk, the amount of donation at the time of his death is quite big, since he was in a position to accumulate a large amount of property. Following the monks' example laymen, too, donate one third or one fifth of their property after death. And such a habit of donation is said to make the otherwise poverty-stricken Tibetan economy run smoothly. Incidentally, donation virtually meant donation to the religious order.

The order or temples have been endowed with specially sacred significance. The Indian word "monastery" (*vihāra*) originally meant "the place where (monks and nuns) stay," whereas Tibetans translated it as "the house for sacred learning" (*gtsug-lag khaṅ*), endowing it with a special meaning.[33]

The way of thinking characterizing the importance of religious charisma can be applied to worldly affairs and political relations. For example, when the British and the Russians competed for domination of Tibet at the beginning of this century, a Mongolian lama called Dorjief, who studied in Russia, approached the Dalai Lama with a special message from the Russian Emperor and was thereby able to sway the Lhasa Government favorably to the interest of Russia. In order to arouse a pro-Russian feeling among the Tibetans, he preached "the Pure-Realm theory" and said that "the Pure Realm" meant Russia, which lay in the West, and that the Russian Emperor was actually the incarnation of the Lord Amitābha. He further interpreted Tibet as the land of Avalokiteśvara, who is virtually an incarnation of the Lord Amitābha; he added that since Russia and Tibet were but one and inseparable, therefore, Tibet should ally herself with Russia.[34] The religious charisma ascribed to a particular personality is more effective in moving the Tibetans than appealing to economic interests.

The same way of thinking, however, frequently contributes to the corruption of human morality. Because Esoteric Buddhism permitted monks to approach women, high priests of the Red Caps were allowed to have contact with many women, and a woman who bore the child of a lama and the child itself were both believed to be sacred. Such a belief and practice led the monks to indulge in promiscuity and created a vitiated atmosphere. This practice prevailed particularly in the Khams province and the provinces near Mongolia.

An extreme example in history is the life of Rwa the Translator (from the middle of the 11th century to the beginning of the 12th century). He had five Yoga Mothers (i.e., wives) for the practice of Esoteric Buddhism. When he took a girl of twelve years of age, people loudly condemned him. But he was composed, saying, "There is no Tantra which makes a Yoga Mother dispensable."[35]

Even theft is justified by faith in Lamas. "Long ago, Pliny noted that the Arabs were addicted both to robbery and to trade. And the same holds true of some Tibetan tribes, in many ways religious, whose members may trade abroad peacefully for part of the year and devote themselves to brigandage nearer home for the rest—an orderly arrangement. Even monks will go on marauding expeditions. The large monastery of Cha-trin in southeastern Tibet had on its roll many monks who did so, and not once or twice but habitually. . . . This brigand-priest was talking of coming to Lhasa to prostrate himself in worship before the Head of the Faith whose pilgrims he was plundering. But he wished to bring five hundred of his rough band with him. The Lama and his Government were quite willing that he should come, provided that he limited his escort to twenty, a manageable number. Religious devotion—and no doubt offerings—being the objective, there was no question of prohibition or punishment."[36]

When one sticks to the standpoint of esteeming the theological system of Lamaism as the absolute one, one comes to hate those who are opposed to it and to regard them as enemies. Ḥgos-khri-bzan, being a Buddhist, buried his opponents alive.[37] Even in recent times there were terrible jails attached to monasteries, and there tortures were inflicted.

The above-mentioned three tendencies are contrary to the original thought of Buddhism, and yet these evils were conducted owing to the esteem for the Lamaistic religious and social system as the absolute. While Buddhism contributed to making the mentality of the Tibetans mild and meek and to elevate their character, the charismatic authority of Lamaism, nevertheless, admitted such evils. Here we find some problems, which we shall explore below.

CHAPTER 30 ABSOLUTE ADHERENCE TO THE LAMAIST SOCIAL ORDER

The attitude of absolute submission by a collective mass of people to a religiously charismatic individual is fully exemplified by the Lamaist social order.

The historiographies of Tibet, after the establishment of Buddhism, do not often refer to wars, but concentrate on religious events. To Tibetans of the past their state did not have as much vital importance as their own religion.

Tibet is at present within the dominion of the People's Republic of China. Formerly, however, she was always an independent state, and an absolute monarchy under the rule of the Dalai Lama. The Dalai Lama was the head of Lamaism, and at the same time the political ruler of the country. Thus he was the ruler of both the religion and the state.

As a nomadic people living in a desert highland, the Tibetans were originally divided and ruled by several tribal heads. In later days, kings had arisen among these tribal heads, but they maintained no systematic political organization. It was Lamaism that organized Tibet for the first time into one political unit. The role of the Lamaist monks was important in the making of Tibet and they are sometimes compared with the Catholic priests in the age of the Germanic migration in the Western history. Till the end of the 9th century A.D., the sovereignty of Tibet was in the hands of the king, who protected the monastic order of Lamaism. Later on, however, the sovereignty was gradually transmitted to the Lamaist high priest.

The theocracy of Lamaism was established by worldly power in the thirteenth century. When Kublai Khan, the grandson of Genghis Khan, conquered Tibet, he was converted to Buddhism by the Abbot of the Sa-skya Abbey. Since this Abbot crowned the Khan as Emperor of China, he was appointed head of the nationwide order of Tibet by the Khan as a token of gratitude, and was assigned the rulership of Western Tibet. Since then, high priests of the Sa-skya sect have held the post of the Imperial Preceptor of the Yuan (Mongolian) dynasty in succession. With the help of the Mongolian kingship the Sa-skya dynasty (1270–1345) ruled Tibet.

From the fifteenth century on, virtual sovereignty was shifted to the Dalai Lama, who was at the same time the monarch of Tibet, until the invasion of the Chinese communists in recent years.

The ideas of patriotism and loyalty among the Tibetans were based upon religious faith. That is to say, Tibetan patriotism was based upon the faith that Tibet is a sacred religious country and that the Dalai Lama, the sovereign of Tibet, is an incarnation of the Bodhisattva Avalokiteśvara. Neither patriotism nor loyalty to the king could therefore exist apart from Lamaism, and to do something for the sake of the country or king was synonymous with doing something for the sake of their religion.

In Tibet there was until recently an army of armed monks called "the Golden Army." What Tibetans were most afraid of in case of an invasion by a foreign army was not the loss of their own country, but the loss of their "holy religion."

We can trace to a fairly early time the tendency of certain Tibetan families to claim the most distinguished personalities as the first who introduced Buddhism to Tibet as well as those who started the monkish tradition. Some of these families became, in the course of time, the most powerful.[1] The choice of the Dalai Lama as an individual who transmigrates could not remain a problem of one individual in the social structure of Tibet, which is made up of tribes as units. One family, from which came the eighth and twelfth Dalai Lamas, was ranked as one of the nobles. When the fourteenth Dalai Lama, the present one, was chosen, all the members of his family who formerly had been peasants were immediately appointed nobles, and were given vast areas of public lands. This treatment is in contradiction to the idea of transmigration, and yet Tibetans did not take notice of the contradiction.

As Tibet was the Lamaist kingdom, the priests played an important role both in religious and secular affairs. They were trained in the details of their religious organizations and actively participated in political matters. Tibet in the early 20th century was said to have a Central Government consisting of three premiers and four ministers who controlled both civilian and military officials in the central and provincial governments. The government was responsible to the Dalai Lama and endeavored to carry out his will politically as well as religiously. It was decreed that one of the premiers and one of the ministers must always be a monk. Such a rule was also observed among the posts occupied by sub-officials and local boards. The number of such officials was about 175 and comprised both priests and laymen. Among the local boards, the lay-officials took charge of economic affairs, while the priest-officials took care of religious and educational affairs. Lay-officials were usually in charge of judicial affairs, but sometimes the priests helped them.

In the court of the ancient Mongolian ("Yuan") dynasty there was the institution of the "Imperial Preceptor," and Lamas were especially well treated. They were very influential, although we do not exactly know to what extent they interfered with politics.

Buddhist priests in India[2] and China had seldom taken part in political matters directly as government officials. Chinese priests were concerned only with the administration of religious affairs. In Japan, even the administration of religious affairs was for most periods in the hands of secular authorities. Therefore, in the history of Buddhism it can be said that it is rather an unusual phenomenon to observe Buddhist priests taking an active part in governmental administration in their official capacity. Also it is to be observed that in most Buddhist countries a strong political consciousness or controlling force has never developed, with the inevitable result that an organized hierarchy could not be established. Tibet was an exceptional case.

What then was the relation between the Lamaist rule and the social hierarchical order in Tibet?

The hierarchy in Tibet was roughly divided into the nobility and the commoners. The latter was again divided into three: high, middle, and low, according to occupational differences. Among them the nomads constituted the largest group, followed by the peasants and merchants. The artisans were placed at the lowest level of the Tibetan hierarchy. The nobles, being descendants of feudal lords, possessed extensive lands, but did not possess the right to manage them. Their lands were governed by officials sent by the Central Government. During the reign of the fifth Dalai Lama, at which time the Central Government was established, feudal lords lost their lands. However, they obtained the right to become government officials with the status of nobility. Thus they exclusively occupied the positions of lay-officials in the government, until recently, when the posts of government officials were opened to the commoners as well. On the contrary, any priest could be a priest-official, irrespective of his origin, nobility or commoner, but he was required to be a graduate of the school of priest-officials. This fact shows the existence of a confidential belief in the religious charisma, besides the feudalistic way of thinking in Tibet.

Laws which should be applied equally were favorable to the Lamas. Laws were interpreted for the benefit of the Lamas whenever difficulties arose between clergy and laity.

Influenced probably by this idea of hierarchical order, the Tibetan language retains honorific forms to some extent. Personal pronouns differ according to the speaker's attitude towards the person spoken of. Some nouns and verbs have their honorific form besides the usual one. For example, these are pronouns of the first person singular ("I"):

ṅa	This is the most common form and can be used by everybody.
ṅed	This term seems to be preferred in elegant speech.
ṅos	This is very common in modern letter writing, at least in Western Tibet.
bdag	Originally it means "self." When speaking to superior persons, it occurs very often in books, but has disappeared from common speech, except in the province of Tsaṅ.
kho bo	Used by men in easy conversation with persons of equal rank, or to inferiors.
kho mo	Used by women.
ṅa-raṅ, *ṅa-bdag*, *ṅa-ñid*	Myself.

As pronouns of the second person singular ("you"):

khyod	Used in books in addressing even the highest persons, but in modern conversation only among equals or to inferiors.
khyed	Elegant and respectful, especially in books.
ñid-raṅ	In modern speech the usual respectful pronoun of address, like "Sie" in German.

As pronouns of the third person singular ("he," "she"):

de	Generally used in books.
kho	Seldom occurs in books.
khoṅ	Common to both the written and the spoken language, and used, at least in the latter, as respectful.
kho ma	Used in referring to ladies.
sku-shabs	(Literally, "respected; body-feet.") His Excellency.
rin-po-che	(Literally, "jewel.") His Majesty, His Holiness.

"The predilection of Eastern Asiatics for a system of ceremonials in the language is encountered also in Tibetan. There is one separate class of words, which must be used in reference to the honored person, when spoken to as well as spoken of. To this class belong, besides the pronouns *ñid raṅ, khyed, khoṅ,* all the respectful terms by which the body or soul, or parts of the same, and all things or persons pertaining to such a person, and even his actions, must be called."[3] In Sanskrit they say, "I would like to see the king" (*rājānam ahaṃ draṣṭukāmaḥ*), whereas the Tibetan translation runs literally: "I seek for seeing the face of the king." (*Bdag ni rgyal poḥi shal mthoṅ bar ḥtshal lo.*)[4]

In Tibetan, words used in addressing persons (like "Hello" in English) differ with the status of the persons addressed—"*kye*" to kings, "*ka-ye*" to be a friend, "*kva*" to an employee, and "*ba-ye*" to a servant.[5] When they address their father, they say, "Oh! God!";[6] occasionally they say, "Oh! God (*lha*)!" instead of "You!"[7] In order to show respect or to be elegant, they use nouns of different kinds, for example: *sku* (honored body) instead of *lus* (body), "(Respected) father (*yab*) and mother (*yum*)" instead of "father (*pha*) and mother (*ma*)." There is a class of verbs which show respect. A class of what might be called elegant terms is used when conversing with an honored person (or also in referring to a high person), such as "*bgyid pa*" instead of "*byed-pa*" (to do); "*mchis-pa*" instead of "*yin-pa*" (to be). For example, *lus*, the Tibetan term for "body," is replaced by *sku* when it denotes a body of a respected person; e.g., *saṅs-rgyas-kyi sku*, Buddha's Body.[8]

Due to the absolute power of Lamaism, the Tibetans accept calmly what would seem quite irrational to the eyes of modern people. For example, all the priests and monks in Tibet, more than 400,000 in number, have no tax duty. Lhasa is a tax-free area because it is a holy place. "Such an arrangement seems quite unfair to the people living outside Lhasa who are suffering from heavy taxes. But to suffer is, they believe, the result of *karma* in former births, and owing to their services to lamas in this life, they will be able to attain a happy life in the next birth in accordance with the disappearance of *karma*."[9]

Because of the unique culture of Lamaism, the Tibetans regard their country religiously and as something unique, and have therefore developed a consciousness of exclusiveness in relation to non-Tibetans.

First of all, the Tibetans call their country "the land of the lotus flower." They compare the Chos-khaṅ Palace of Lhasa to the calyx of a lotus flower, and the mountains surrounding the lands as its petals. The calyx of a lotus flower signifies the Buddha's seat or Paradise. This idea is akin to the fact that the Japanese followers of Esoteric Buddhism consider Mt. Koya the seat of the central monastery of Esoteric Buddhism in Japan, as the lotus flower with the eight petals.

The Tibetans believe that Tibet is the Pure Land of Avalokiteśvara. They say, Buddha Śākyamuni once gave prophecy to Avalokiteśvara, saying: "Beyond the Himalayas there live people to be saved. Go there instantly and save them." This prophecy is recorded in the *Mañjuśri-paramârtha-nāmasaṁgīti*.[10] Here, they think that what is meant by "the land beyond the Himalayas" is Tibet, and hence Tibet is the world entrusted to Avalokiteśvara, so that the Tibetans and Avalokiteśvara stand in the relation of people to be saved and their savior.

It was probably due to this conviction that the Tibetans have come to regard the successive Dalai Lamas, the sovereigns of Tibet, as the reincarnations of Avalokiteśvara, and called their palace in Lhasa, "*Potala,*" after the name of Avalokiteśvara's Pure Land. They are pleased to have been born in such a holy land of Avalokiteśvara and desire to be reborn in Tibet. We cannot underestimate the desire of the common Tibetan for rebirth in the Pure Land of Amitābha or in the Tuṣita Heaven of Maitreya. Generally, however, the Tibetans regard their country as an ideal world for religious reasons.

Tibetan exclusivism is the result of their idealization of their country. It is motivated by a religious idea, rather than by the thought of territorial possession as among other peoples. Although they have no idea of "the centre of the world civilization," they believe that their country is the proper land for Buddhism. They further believe that due to the Buddha's grace, this Buddhist land is secure, and even if a disaster were to occur, it would easily be removed, and everyone would be able to enjoy equally the life of peace and quietness; therefore, if foreigners entered this land, the pure Buddhist land would be instantly spoiled, the people would lose their happiness, receive the Buddha's punishment, and fall into misery forever. Such a strong belief is the basis of their exclusivism.[11]

Thus the Tibetans prohibited the entrance of foreigners into their country. When they found strange travelers, they would at once chase them out of Tibet. Some explorers were killed by them. Tibetans who tried to invite foreigners were punished in a cruel manner.

CHAPTER 31 SHAMANISTIC TENDENCIES

The Bon Religion prevailed in Tibet prior to the introduction of Buddhism. This religion is a form of Shamanism, originating somewhere in Central Asia, and was probably conveyed to Tibet in the course of tribal migration. It is animistic in character. It teaches that there exist countless free spirits in the universe, whose activities cause good or ill fortune. Through prayer, people ask these spirits to remove ill fortune and bring good fortune. These spirits reveal their will to people through mediums. At first a medium performs a ceremony in order to induce the spirit to enter his body. When the spirit transports itself into the body of the medium, the latter loses his personality, the spirit reveals itself, and utters a command or prophecy through the mouth of the medium. The belief is that the spirit sometimes performs various miracles and feats which task the imagination. Thus it cures people from illness and turns misfortune into a blessing. There was no organized doctrine in the Bon Religion.[1]

The introduction of Buddhism caused the Bon Religion to decline. But accepting Buddhist doctrines, it still lives side by side with Lamaism in the hearts of the Tibetans. The relation between the Bon Religion and Lamaism is quite similar to that between Shintoism and Buddhism in Japan. There are also similar characteristics observable in both Shintō ceremonies and those of the Bon Religion. In the Bon Religion, there is no shrine as in Japan, but the place where gods are thought to live is regarded as holy; something like a tower is built in such a sacred place, and the way to that place is adorned with sacred rope ("*shimenawa*" in Japanese). (In Shintoism, shrine construction was an art that developed at a much later period.) Sacred dance and music in Japan and in the Bon Religion are also very similar. A Lama priest who visited Japan some years back expressed his impression when he observed the *Kagura*-dance held at the Ise shrine, saying, "It is just like the sacred dance of the Bon Religion."[2] Nowadays the Bon Religion accepts Buddhist terminology, compiles scriptures, and maintains temples.

What then is the difference of the ways of thinking between the Bon Religion and Shintoism, both of which are of shamanistic origin? The answer is not a simple one. We can only compare some of the characteristics of both religions in a rather superficial manner. Respect for purity and emphasis on simplicity observed in Shintō are absolutely lacking in the Bon Religion. Not only the Bon Religion, but the Tibetans in general reveal a fondness for complexities of ornament and colors in decorating things, particularly in their paintings. Reverend Aoki, who lived in Tibet a long time, confessed that he could not understand the Tibetan characters. The virtue of love, though it is sometimes said to be lacking in Shintoism, is surely emphasized particularly in the medieval age of Japan under the name of "compassion" (*karuṇā*) due to the influence of Buddhism. But in Tibet, despite their acceptance of Buddhism, people in the mountain areas show a much more violent character. The existence of cruel penalties justifies this statement. Of course, the Tibetans, especially the educated ones, apart from the primitive mountain inhabitants, are quite gentle. Although the cruel forms of penalties which existed in the past came under a prohibition by the 13th Dalai Lama, nevertheless, the long existence of cruel forms of punishment suffices to reveal to us an aspect of Tibetan customs. The seemingly cruel behavior of the Tibetans is probably due to their habit of hunting and their nomadic life.

Buddhism, which took the place of the Bon Religion, was not entirely alien to the latter but quite compatible with it in many respects. Being of esoteric character, it was, in a sense, more shamanistic than the Bon Religion, and thus was able to replace the Bon Religion. Most scriptures translated into the Tibetan language are those concerning Esoteric Buddhism. This newly introduced Esoteric Buddhism was a developed form of Indian Tantrism, but it attached importance to the practice of ceremonies associated with alcoholic drinking, magic, and sexual enjoyment. Tsoṅ-kha-pa, in his reform program, tried to remove these elements from Lamaism, but he was not able to uproot them completely.

On the contrary, traditional, conservative Buddhism which prohibited enchantment, ceremony, magic, and divination did not find room in Tibet. In the Tibetan Tripiṭaka, there are included thirteen scriptures translated from the Pāli Canon. Out of these thirteen, nine scriptures belong to the *Parītta-saṃgaha,* i.e., the collection of scriptures and phrases which are believed, among Southern Buddhists, to be effective enough to drive out evils and invite good luck, and are equivalent to the *Mantra-piṭaka* of the Dharmākara school.[3] It seems that the Tibetans selected only passages of magical character out of the Pāli scriptures of early Buddhism.

The practice of *dhyāna*-meditation was also introduced into Tibet, but it was observed merely among the more sincere monks in monasteries, while the people in general relied upon esoteric ceremonies.[4] The people believe in the existence of the demon of ill health which invades the human body. When they fall ill, they ask a priest to tell their fortune and then, worshipping the gods and Buddhas, they offer a prayer to remove the illness. The objects of their worship are not limited to the Buddha Śākyamuni and Amitābha, but include Mahāvairocana, Mahābhaiṣajyaguru, and all the other Buddhas and Bodhisattvas of various worlds in ten directions, as well as the gods in heaven and on earth, demons and serpents. In a Lamaist temple, these objects of worship are enshrined side by side without order. Among them, the gods and demons are mostly of Bon origin. As the Tibetans absorbed Buddhism, they came to be regarded as the protectors of Buddhism.

These gods and demons are believed to take possession of selected persons, who thus become mediums or magicians. When a medium or magician is consulted on marriage, a journey, or on the fortune of a newborn child, he will be observed, with bloodshot eyes and foaming mouth, uttering words and sentences scarcely comprehensible, which are interpreted afterwards in a horoscope.

The Tibetan belief in demons exists side by side with modern technology. In their belief, there is a demon of eclipses who deprives the sun or moon of light. In order to kill the demon, they perform a ceremony against the demon, recite charms, and discharge a gun towards the eclipsed sun or moon. Unless this is done, they are convinced that the sun or the moon will lose its light and the world would become dark forever.[5]

Buddhism was accepted by the Tibetans only to the degree that it adapted itself to the Tibetan ways of thinking. Consequently, Lamaist priests were almost indifferent to the propagation of the Buddhist doctrine. They scarcely engaged in missionary work. Even in Lhasa, preaching was held only two or three times a year and the number of those who attended the sermon was not more than two or three hundred at a time. "The experience of truth is, in Lamaism, a secret, and hence, to preach to the common people is considered rather a debasement of the truth."[6]

Thus the common people[7] were almost indifferent to sermons. There were exceptional cases, however. For example, families of high position would invite an intimate lama to their home on special occasions to hear him. In Tibet, preaching did not mean propagation, but was merely a part of a ceremony. On the other hand the recitation of scriptures was very popular among the Tibetans. Every home invited lamas for this purpose.

The unique method for seeking a new Dalai Lama seems to be somehow related to the ancient shamanistic way of thinking. According to the viewpoint of the Tibetans, Lamas must be possessed of a supernatural power resulting from their perfect practice in Esoteric Buddhism which makes them immortal. Therefore their death means merely a change of body or the shift of a place for living and going from one body to another. Thus, the Tibetans seek for a newborn child at the death of a Lama, welcome him as the reincarnated Lama, and render service with a pious attitude to him as if to the former Lama. Thus a religious custom unique to the Tibetans was established.

The unification of twelve Tibetan tribes was said to have been caused in the past by magical power. When Buddhism was established in Tibet, kings decided state affairs by resorting to lottery and dreams.[8]

The same shamanistic method was used until recently even in state affairs. The state magician of the Tibetan Government, who lived in the Nechung (Gnas-chuṅ) monastery, had once influenced the course of Tibet's internal and external policy by his predictions. His greatest influence was seen when a search was conducted for a new Dalai Lama. His office was established during the reign of the fifth Dalai Lama. A very fateful part was played by one of the State Magicians in the political developments which led up to the British military expedition into Tibet in 1904. The State Oracle was consulted regarding the measures to be taken, and he suggested that a certain mountain, situated a short distance within the Sikkimese territory, should be occupied by the Tibetan troops, as this mountain, by its magical qualities, would stop further advances by the British. The move, however, did not meet with success and the Tibetan troops were easily defeated. He seems to have been still of the opinion that eventually the Tibetan army would be victorious. Therefore, the Tibetan Government refused to negotiate with the advancing British forces for a long time. This policy was reversed only after Lhasa had been captured. The Dalai Lama removed the State Magician from his office because of his false prophecies.[9]

CHAPTER 32 LOGICAL TENDENCIES

The Tibetan language belongs to the same family as the Chinese, and originally was not very suitable for the expression of abstract ideas. For example, it had no word for "size," a concept which can only be expressed in Tibetan by "big and small" (*che-chuṅ*). Under the influence of Sanskrit, however, Thon-mi-saṃbhoṭa systematized the Tibetan language and gave it, to some extent, a more logical character; this is most clearly shown in the mode of the acceptance of Buddhism by the Tibetans.

First, we shall examine this logical character as it appeared in the Tibetans' method of translating Sanskrit. If a Sanskrit word contained two ideas, they are expressed in two words in the Tibetan language. For example, the Sanskrit word *pariṇāma,* which means both the process of changing and its result, is translated into Tibetan as *yoṅs-su ḥgyur-ba* and *yoṅs-su gyur-pa,* respectively. Thus the Tibetans distinguish the result of an action from its process.

A long Sanskrit compound word that is difficult to analyze is often explained clearly in Tibetan. For example: "*Buddha-kṣetra-vyūha-ananta-praṇidhāna-prasthāna-parigṛhīta*"[1] (buddha-land-adornment-unlimited-vow-entrance-being embraced), a Bahuvrīhi-compound showing a qualification of the Bodhisattva, is translated into Tibetan in the following way: *saṅs-rgyas-kyi shiṅ-gi bkod-pa mthaḥ-yas-par smon-pa-la ḥjugs-pas yoṅs-su gzuṅ-ba.* This translation states clearly that "(a Bodhisattva who is) embraced by (the mind) enters into the vow for unlimited adornment of the Buddha's land." Thus Tibetan is indispensable for understanding Buddhist Sanskrit texts. The Indians, using Sanskrit, which is replete with technical logical terms, produced obscure expressions by using too many compounds, while the Tibetans, using a primitive and less logical language, made it possible for us to understand such expressions through their language. We cannot but acknowledge the efforts of the Tibetans, who were fairly successful in expressing the logic and the exactness of the Sanskrit words through the medium of the Tibetan language, which is generally far from having any logical clarity.[2] (The efforts of the Tibetans in this respect may suggest that the Japanese improve the structural character of their language along more logical lines.)

The same logical tendency is observed also in the Tibetans' way of accepting Buddhist ideas. The Tibetans translated a good number of Indian Buddhist works on logic (Nyāya). The Sde-dge edition of the Tibetan Tripiṭaka contains 66 works on Nyāya, some of which are quite voluminous. It is in remarkable contrast to the fact that the Chinese Tripiṭaka retains only a few Nyāya texts, e.g., the *Yin-ming chêng-li-mên-lun* (*Nyāyamukha*), the *Yin-ming-ju-chêng-li-lun* (*Nyāyapraveśaka*), all of which are simple textbooks. These Tibetan translations are indispensable for the study of Buddhist logic, in view of the fact that many Sanskrit originals are lost.[3]

The Nyāya doctrine introduced into Tibet was mainly that of Dharmakīrti, who dealt with epistemology. The Tibetans are said to have conducted a critical examination of the theory of direct perception (*pratyakṣa, mṅon-sum*) taught by him.

The Tibetans utilized the Nyāya doctrine for practical purposes. Discussions were held among student-monks in the monasteries by means of the Indian logic of dialogue in order to examine the Buddhist doctrine, a procedure which was rather different in China and Japan where logic remained merely a branch of auxiliary learning in the preparation of making a commentary on one of the Buddhist texts, but was not actually put into full practice.

The course of logic in Lamaist monasteries continues for about four years,[4] during which time students are required to learn by heart all the two thousand verses of the *Pramāṇavārttika* (Critique on knowledge), the masterpiece of Dharmakīrti.[5] This text is regarded as the basic scripture (*mūla*) on logic, and is the only text in Tibet concerning logic written by an Indian logician.[6] There are a lot of Tibetan commentaries on it, some of which present rather unique theories. The Tibetans study them by means of summaries composed by Tibetan logicians of the ten schools. Despite the existence of many commentaries by Indian writers, the Tibetans study logic only through the commentaries and summaries made by their own fellow countrymen and pay little attention to those of Indian origin.

Notable here is the fact that only the *Pramāṇavārttika* of Dharmakīrti is studied, so that all the other works by him, and by Dharmottara (who developed the Buddhist logic established by Diṅnāga and Dharmakīrti), are almost forgotten by the Tibetan logicians. Why is this so? According to Vostrikov, the Tibetans attached special importance to Chapter II of the *Pramāṇavārttika,* which discusses validity of knowledge in general, although in actuality, it is a commentary on the verses concerning the prayer to the Buddha written by Diṅnāga, and is devoted to the discussion of Mahāyāna Buddhism designed to prove that the Buddha is the Absolute, the Omniscient (*sarvajña*), and the *Manifested Knowledge* (*pramānabhūta*). In other words, in this chapter Buddhism is defended and established as a religion. Therefore, the Tibetans' attitude toward logic was basically religious; logic was merely an *"ancilla religionis,"* the handmaid of religion, so far as they were concerned. Therefore, the most suitable and acceptable section of the book was this chapter which attempted to establish a pure faith in the Omniscient and Absolute through a critical examination of the matter while Dharmakīrti's other works and those of Vasubandhu, Diṅnāga, and Dharmottara, were conceived to have taken the standpoint of agnosticism so far as their analysis of the Buddha as the Omniscient was concerned.

Although this view expressed by Vostrikov has been accepted by Stcherbatsky, it is still uncertain whether it reveals the true state of mind of the Tibetans. Two schools of thought existed in Tibet concerning the relation between logic and religion. Kun-dgaḥ-rgyal-mtshan (1182–1251, the fifth Great Lama of the Sa-skya monastery, alias Sa-skya Paṇḍita), the founder of one of the schools of logic in Tibet, was of the opinion that logic is a secular science and contains, like medical science and mathematics, not a single element of Buddhism. The same opinion was held by the famous historian, Bu-ston-Rin-po-che. On the contrary, the Dge-lugs-pa Sect (the Yellow Caps), which is the only powerful sect today, rejects this opinion and maintains that the logic of Dharmakīrti offers a firm foundation to Buddhism as a religion.[7]

Actually, however, logic did not develop very far in Tibet. Dharmakīrti's system was its final development. His relation to Tibetan logic can be compared to that of Aristotle's to European logic; and Tibetan works on logic are similar to those of Scholasticism in medieval Europe. Their main interest was in the strict definition of technical terms, establishment of scholastically detailed rules for their use, and the expression of all kinds of scientific thinking by means of syllogisms.

Logic is regarded in Tibetan monasteries as the fundamental study. School courses begin with logic. A textbook on logic used in a monastery starts with the following sentences:

> *"kha-dog yin-na dkar-po yin-pas khyab zer-na*
> *pad-ma-ra-ga kha-dog-chos-can dkar-po yin-par thal*
> *kha-dog yin-pas phyir*
> *rtags ma-grub*
> *ciḥi phyir——"*
> (If it is asked) "Must it be white if it were a color"
> Proposition: (It follows:) "A ruby possessed of color is white."

Reason: Because it is (possessed of) color.
(To this argument, the answer:) The evidence is not established.
(Questioner:) Why?

As it can be observed from the above catechism, the textbook is here going to teach an error contained in the argument with respect to general and special concepts. To our surprise, this textbook is used in Tibetan monasteries for *the exercise of children of about ten years of age.*

Tibetan lama-students often conduct a symposium in the same manner as in India, according to the manner of the Nyāya-dialogue, and the victors are awarded prizes. Thus logic is utilized in Tibet as the rule for expediting discussions.

The logical and systematical way of thinking is also evident in the way of accepting the *śūnyatā*-theory, the fundamental doctrine of Mahāyāna Buddhism. The *Prajñāpāramitā,* the principal scripture of this theory, is quite a long unsystematic one. Maitreyanātha (4th century A.D.) organized its contents and composed a commentary called the *Abhisamayālaṅkāra,* on which Haribhadra again wrote commentaries.[8] Depending solely on the commentaries of Haribhadra, the Tibetans attempt to understand the Perfection of Wisdom (*Prajñāpāramita*).

It was Nāgārjuna (2d century A.D.) who gave a philosophical basis to the theory of *śūnyatā.* However, his *Madhyamaka-kārikā* does not maintain a system in spite of the fact that it shows a sharp logical approach. Therefore, the Tibetans rather prefer the *Madhyamakāvatāra* of Candrakīrti of the Nāgārjuna school to Nāgārjuna's *Madhyamaka-kārikā* itself, because the former discusses the Mādhyamika theory in a more organized manner. Moreover, it is noteworthy that those texts liked by the Tibetans are written according to the rule of Nyāya logic. Even the texts on grammar are explained systematically by means of the Nyāyic argument.[9]

According to Reverend Tada, the subjects mainly studied in the monasteries are the Mantras, Nyāya, and Abhidharma philosophy. Works on history are not read so much, although a fairly good number of works on this subject are written by the Tibetans. Among the works concerning Hīnayāna Buddhism, the *Abhidharmakośa* is read and studied in particular. As for Vijñāna (mind-only) theory, the *Trisvabhāva-nirdeśa* is carefully studied as they believe it to be the best to lead one to emancipation, while almost no attention is paid to the *Triṁśikā* and the *Viṁśatikā* of Vasubandhu with the exception of the commentaries written on them by Tsoṅ-kha-pa. Every morning, the Dalai Lama recites the *Abhisamayālaṅkāra,* the *Madhyamakāvatāra,* and the *Pramāṇavārttika,* whose contents he knows by heart perfectly, and he reads the texts on Esoteric Buddhism in the evening.

The logical proclivities of the Tibetans made them decline Chinese Zen Buddhism, at the Council of Lhasa (792 A.D.), and accept the more logically organized system of Indian Buddhism.[10]

The Tibetans show their logical character in their critical attitudes even towards the Esoteric Buddhism introduced from India. Mahāyāna Buddhism in general formulates the theory of the Triple Body of Buddha: (1) the Absolute Body (*dharmakāya*) being the universal truth itself, (2) the Body of Bliss (*saṃbhogakāya*) being the body endowed with perfect virtues as the result of religious practice in the previous lives, and (3) the Apparitional Body (*nirmāṇakāya*) being the incarnation manifested in this world in order to preach the doctrine for the sake of living beings. Moreover it maintains that to preach the doctrine to living beings is the work of the Body of Bliss or the Apparitional Body, but not of the Absolute Body. In Esoteric Buddhism, however, the doctrine is asserted and preached by the Absolute Body (*Dharmakāya*) as the ultimate truth, and this is regarded as showing the philosophical superiority of Esoteric Buddhism over other systems. The Tibetans at the beginning accepted this theory as it was taught. (The case is the same with the Shingon school in Japan.) But the Yellow Caps, the reformers of Tibetan Buddhism, refused to accept this traditional theory, saying:

"The *Vajrasūtra* of Kālacakra of the Anuttara-yogatantra school, to which we pay our highest respect, was taught by Buddha Śākyamuni at Dhānyakaṭaka on the request of King Candrabhadra of Saṁvara State in the north. (The theory that the Dharmakāya itself preaches the doctrine) is not based on historical facts. It is fantastic and quite contrary to the facts to maintain such a theory. It is merely a product of verbal expression. Therefore we cannot accept that theory."[11]

Referring to this point, Reverend Kawaguchi commented as follows:

"If this theory (of the Yellow Caps) is acknowledged, the doctrine of the Old Sect of Shingon Esoterics of Japan will lose its ground. The preaching of the True Body (Dharmakāya) is one of the important elements with which they maintain themselves to be superior to other sects. In reality, the preaching of the True Body (Dharmakāya) is difficult to maintain unless it was preached by the Body of Bliss. As far as the Dharmakāya is regarded as the abstract truth pervading the universe, it is difficult to maintain, without encountering a contradiction, that it is endowed with the power to preach, because the all-pervading truth is one and absolute, while the activity of preaching requires such entities as the subject and object."

It was probably the spirit of pursuing logical thoroughness that caused the Tibetans to assume such a critical attitude as that shown in the doctrine of the Yellow Caps.

Not all the Tibetans can be characterized as logical, but it is at least clear that the intellectuals among them were aiming at a logical exactness in thinking and writing.

Above is an outline or a brief set of remarks concerning the characteristics of the Tibetan ways of thinking, extracted from limited sources. The author believes, however, that within these pages can be found some of the unique characteristics of the ways of thinking of the Tibetans in comparison with those of other Eastern peoples.

PART IV

JAPAN

CHAPTER 33 INTRODUCTION

It is a commonplace of the history of ideas that ideas become modified in different cultural contexts. Hence, an important clue to the peculiar features distinguishing one culture from another consists in discerning the modifications of ideas assimilated by each culture and transmitted in a new form to the other. Now Buddhism, with its moral and religious ideas for the spiritual guidance of individuals and whole peoples, became modified as it passed from India through China to Japan, where it has become an essential part of the cultural history of Japan and of the ways of thinking of its millions of people.

We are going to examine some salient features of Japanese ways of thinking in various phases of its cultural history, beginning with the influence of the older Chinese language and culture. The clearest evidence of this influence is seen in the fact that in the past Japanese thinkers expressed abstract notions as a rule through the use of the Chinese characters. That is, the Japanese, without abandoning their native language, had to resort to the Chinese script whenever they wished to convey abstract ideas in writing. The influence of the Chinese ideas embodied in the script upon Japanese patterns of thought was consequently enormous. It was through the Chinese version of the sacred scriptures (*sūtras*) of India and other philosophical writings that the Japanese first came in contact with Buddhism and Indian thought.[1]

Chinese writing was introduced into Japan about 1400 years ago. Up to the Suiko period (6th century), Chinese had been used only by a small group of specialists who had scarcely any influence on the native tongue. With the beginning of direct contact with China and the advent of the Sui and T'ang civilization (6th–9th centuries), the number of those who read and spoke Chinese increased greatly; we may well assume that Chinese words were used very often in the daily conversations of the ruling class.[2] At this early date, however, the first Chinese words adopted in Japanese were, for the most part, nouns. In the Heian period (897–1185) verbs and adverbs such as *nenzu* (meditate), *gusu* (to be equipped), *kechienni* (conspicuously), *yūni* (elegantly), *sechini* (acutely), and later *shiuneshi* (to be exquisite) and *sōzoku* (to dress oneself) came into use with Japanese inflections. The tendency to adopt Chinese words grew stronger as time passed. In the late Heian and the Kamakura period (1185–1333) which was the age of popular Buddhism, imported Chinese words were passed down orally by the monks to the common fold, and even the uneducated began using them.[3] In the Tokugawa period (1600–1867) the number of Chinese words in the spoken language increased more than ever before,[4] but it was in the period following the Meiji Restoration (1868), when the doors of Japan were opened to the rest of the world and rapid progress was made in education, that new words made by compounding Chinese characters were used more abundantly. A large number of entirely new Chinese words were coined to represent the ideas of Western sciences, techniques, and inventions.

In the world of scholarship, the most educated Japanese in ancient times, the Buddhist monks and Confucian scholars, published their works in the Chinese language. Only in the Kamakura period (c. 12th–14th century) did books on religious and philosophical thought begin to appear in the native language, and even such original 18th-century thinkers as Nakamoto Tominaga, the anti-traditionalist, and Baien Miura, the logician, left works written in Chinese. As specialists have recognized, even Japanese Buddhism, which was practically a national religion, was, "when viewed from the larger standpoint of Buddhist history, a mere branch of Buddhism growing out of the Buddhism of China."[5] Many Buddhists had formerly regarded Japanese Buddhism as identical with Chinese Buddhism, and the multifarious sects in Japan were thought to be merely offshoots of Chinese sects of Buddhism.

Buddhism in Japan, on the other hand, exercised little or no influence upon Chinese Buddhism. In 988 A.D. the Japanese Buddhist monk Eshin (Genshin) attempted with some success to introduce his doctrine into China; his book *Ōjō-Yōshū* (Compendium of Teachings Concerning Paradise and Purgatory), which called "upon all persons, believers and unbelievers alike, to join hands with the author for the purpose of attaining a rebirth in the Land of Extreme Happiness," created a temporary stir among the Buddhists of the Sung Dynasty. This, however, was one of the few instances in which the Japanese were able to have any influence on Chinese Buddhism. The Buddhism of Japan, then, grew up under the domination of Chinese Buddhism. There was always a conscious effort on the part of Japanese Buddhists to identify their religion with that of China.

How are we to explain this prevalence of Chinese culture in Japan's past? Shall we say it was the outcome of an urge to imitate slavishly the superior culture of China?

As the histories of other peoples illustrate, it is seldom the case that a backward people willingly accepts the culture derived from a more advanced people. There are generally other conditions in the recipient culture which will make acceptance of the foreign culture feasible. As we shall point out in discussing Japanese statements of reasoning and judgment, there existed a marked similarity among certain features of Japanese and Chinese ways of thinking. And we find that beside certain similarities in the social structures and economic techniques of the two countries, other conditions help explain why the ways of thinking of the Japanese at that time also favored the adoption of Chinese culture. It seems as if the similar patterns of the social life of the two peoples, accompanied by their development in a similar climate and environment, tended to produce similar ways of thinking.

Kanzan Matsumiya (1686–1780), a Japanese Confucian scholar, emphasized this environmental factor when he said, "China is not far from our land, and we see that Chinese and Japanese manners and customs do not differ greatly. Confucianism and Shintoism have therefore much in common."[6] Matsumiya in this work also speaks of the similarity of Chinese "customs and manners" as compared with those of the people of India. Although the traditional School of Japanese Classics in the feudal period was wont to stress the difference between the Japanese and Chinese mentalities and their ways of thinking, we should find in a broader perspective more points of similarity than points of difference.

In spite of its overwhelming influence, however, Chinese thought was not accepted in its pristine form by the Japanese.[7] Thus the influence of Chinese thought on the life and thought of the Japanese was quite different from its influence on the culture of the Chinese. The same can be said of Indian Buddhist thought, as it affected Chinese and Japanese culture respectively. Though Confucian scholars and Buddhist monks in Japan had a considerable reading knowledge of Chinese, their interpretations were often distortions of the original texts. Such distortions were the result either of ignorance of the Chinese language or of deliberate misrepresentation for the sake of making the texts conform to Japanese ways of thinking and living.

The Chinese language differs from the Japanese language in its origin and structure. It was a task of considerable difficulty for the Japanese to master the Chinese language, which employed as the means of expression elaborately developed characters. It appears that even the official students sent to China by the Japanese court in the Heian period (9th–12th century) were not able to understand Chinese fully.

The eight celebrated monks sent to China by the court in this period, Saichō, Kūkai, Engyō, Jōgyō, Ennin, Eun, Enchin, and Shūei, had no facilities for studying the Chinese language before their departure for China; moreover, their sojourns in China were generally too brief for them to learn to speak Chinese. They communicated with the Chinese by depending mainly on the written language. Consequently, they resorted to collecting Buddhist documents and acquiring Buddhist ceremonial articles instead of listening to lectures on Buddhist doctrine. Saichō took with him an interpreter, but others did not. They had to admit their inability to converse orally; one of them says, "I could write Chinese, but not speak it. Therefore, when I had a question to ask, I wrote it out"; and another says, "I could not speak the Chinese language, but could write it. I had a pad brought to me (whenever I wanted to ask a question) and wrote on it."[8] Hence, it is plain that the Japanese scholars had considerable difficulty in understanding the Chinese language.

It is important to note that the Japanese frequently misinterpreted the original Chinese texts. This misinterpretation of the sources for the transmission of Chinese thought is one of the most significant phenomena in the history of Japanese thought. The Japanese acquired many of the best cultural and intellectual products of Chinese thought, but it seems that they did not always feel obliged to conform strictly to the Chinese *ways* of thinking. The Japanese translators of these Chinese writings would, knowing that the Chinese language has no rigid grammar, make very free interpretations of Chinese texts, adding ideas of their own for their own purposes. It was natural that the more studious and disinterested monastic Buddhist scholars in Nara, ancient capital of Japan, and Mt. Hiei, a center of Buddhist studies, were able to read and write Chinese with accuracy because their own thought conformed to Chinese ways of thinking. This, however, was not the case with the preachers who propagated Buddhist thoughts to the Japanese people. The closer to the Japanese public the mind of the preacher was, the greater was his deviation from the Chinese source texts. For example, Shinran,[9] the great founder (1173–1262) of the Jōdo Shin sect of Buddhism, was frequently inaccurate in his reading of the original Chinese texts, a fact pointed out even by scholars today of the orthodox Jōdo Shin sect,[10] upholding the traditional doctrines. Dōgen (1200–1253),[11] the great Zen master, also put forth interpretations that betray his disregard of Chinese grammar.

More deliberate distortions recur in the popular versions of scholars like Sontoku Ninomiya who, in the early 19th century, devoted himself to preaching and working with the common masses. But we must remember that the practice of intentional misinterpretation occurred also among well-educated scholars who were sometimes even commended officially by the Imperial court, as may be seen in the Religious Debates of Ōwa

(963).[12] In all these cases, it is clear that the Chinese texts were seldom understood correctly by the Japanese.

Now, what were the factors that brought about such arbitrary modifications of the sources? It could not have been ignorance alone, for Japanese scholars well versed in Chinese were sometimes responsible for this practice. Nor could the cause have been always propagandistic since misinterpretations are found in passages not important enough strategically for propaganda purposes to require such tampering with the texts. We are obliged to believe that such cases present evidence of a distinctively Japanese cultural background with ways of thinking that did not accommodate themselves to the linguistic forms of the Chinese.

There are other cases which furnish additional discrepancies between the Chinese ways and forms of thinking and those of the Japanese Confucian and Buddhist scholars who were accomplished writers in Chinese. Where and why these discrepancies appear is one of the main concerns of this book.

Since the Chinese texts were so often modified, the elements of Buddhist and Chinese thought transmitted through these texts were not adopted in their original form. Buddhism, in particular, underwent vast changes after it was introduced into the life of Japan. Yet in the minds of many Buddhists, the doctrines held by various Japanese sects are supposed to be directly descended from those of the Buddhists of India and China, despite the evidence that Japanese Buddhism acquired a good many new and distinctive features. Were these new features merely developments of original Buddhism, as many Japanese scholars still assert? Or should they not in certain cases be regarded as a degeneration from the first form of Buddhism? What should be said of the general opinion of Japanese Buddhists that "only in Japan was the pure message of Śākyamuni (the Buddha of India) revealed?" Is this opinion merely a case of national conceit? Or did this development of Buddhism in Japan represent a more culturally significant fact of its intellectual history?

CHAPTER 34 THE ACCEPTANCE OF PHENOMENALISM

The Phenomenal World as Absolute

In the first place, we should notice that the Japanese are willing to accept the phenomenal world as Absolute because of their disposition to lay a greater emphasis upon intuitive sensible concrete events, rather than upon universals. This way of thinking with emphasis upon the fluid, arresting character of observed events regards the phenomenal world itself as Absolute and rejects the recognition of anything existing over and above the phenomenal world. What is widely known among post-Meiji philosophers in the last century as the "theory that the phenomenal is actually the real" has a deep root in Japanese tradition.

It was characteristic of the religious views of the ancient Japanese that they believed spirits to reside in all kinds of things. They personified all kinds of spirits other than those of human beings, considering them all as ancestral gods, and tending to view every spirit as a divine ghost. It is such a turn of thought that gave birth to the Shintō shrines, for in order to perform religious ceremonies the gods and spirits were fixed in certain specified places. The most primitive form of this practice consists in the invocation and worship of spirits in some specific natural object, e.g., mountain, river, forest, tree, or stone. Forms of worship of ancient times were generally of this character. Herein also lies the original significance of the "divine hedge" and "rock boundary." Even to this day there remain shrines that are merely of this type.[1]

This way of thinking runs through the subsequent history of Shintoism down to the present day. "Nowhere is there a shadow in which a god does not reside: in peaks, ridges, pines, cryptomerias, mountains, rivers, seas, villages, plains, and fields, everywhere there is a god. We can receive the constant and intimate help of these spirits in our tasks, many courtiers are passing."[2] Takasumi Senge, the priest of the Shintoism of the Great Shrine of Izumo, praised such a pantheistic point of view as follows: "There is no place in which a god does not reside, even in the wild waves' eight hundred folds or in the wild mountain's bosom."[3]

Buddhist philosophy likewise was received and assimilated on the basis of this way of thinking. To begin with, the Tendai sect in Japan is not the same as in China. The Tendai scholars in medieval Japan, using the same nomenclature as that used in continental Buddhism, arrived at a system of thought that is distinctly original. This is what is called *Honkaku Hōmon* which asserts that the appearances of things in the phenomenal world are aspects of the Buddha. The word *Honkaku* or Enlightenment appears in the Chinese translation of the *Mahāyāna-śraddhotpāda-śāstra* (*Daijyōkishinron*), a Buddhist theological work, originally composed in India. On the Asian continent, the word for enlightenment meant the ultimate comprehension of what is beyond the phenomenal world, whereas in Japan the same word was brought down to refer to understanding things within the phenomenal world. In this way, the characteristic feature of Tendai Buddhism in Japan consists in emphasis upon things rather than principles. The Japanese Tendai scholars were not very faithful to the original texts of the Chinese T'ien-t'ai, but sometimes interpreted the original texts in a rather unnatural way, their interpretation being based upon the standpoint of Absolute Phenomenalism.[4]

It is natural that the Nichiren sect, which is an outgrowth of the Japanese Tendai, also lays an emphasis upon an empirical turn of thought, Nichiren asserts that the crux of Buddha's thought is revealed in the *Jyuryōbon* chapter (Duration of Life of the Buddha) of the Lotus (Hokke) Sūtra, saying, "In the earlier half of the whole sūtra, the ten directions are called the pure land and this place is called the soiled land, while (in this Jyuryōbon part), on the contrary, this place is called the main land and the pure land in the ten directions the soiled land where Buddha has had an incarnation."[5] The Nichiren sect states that, while the Tendai sect from China onward takes the standpoint of "Action according to principles," Nichiren emphasized "Action according to things."

The way of thinking that seeks for the Absolute in the phenomenal world plays an effective role in the assimilation of the Zen sect as well. The Zen Buddhism in Dōgen seems to have been influenced by the Japanese Tendai Buddhism. This fact has often been alluded to by specialists but has not been fully explored. Here I shall point out a few examples which reveal the phenomenalist way of thinking. The Chinese translated "*dharmatā*"[6] in Sanskrit as "the real aspect of all things." This concept refers to the real aspect of all kinds of phenomena in our experience, and therefore is composed of two distinct, contradictory elements, "all things" and "the real aspect." But Tendai Buddhism gave this phrase the interpretation which emphasized that "the real aspect is all things." Dōgen meant to say that the truth which people search for is, in reality, nothing but the world of our daily experience. Thus he says, "The real aspect is all things. All things are this aspect, this character, this body, this mind, this world, this wind and this rain, this sequence of daily going, living, sitting, and lying down, this series of melancholy, joy, action, and inaction, this stick and wand, this Buddha's smile, this transmission and reception of the doctrine, this study and practice, this evergreen pine and ever unbreakable bamboo."[7]

When one asserts "all things are the real aspect," the predicate being of a larger denotation, the real aspect seems to contain something other than all things. But in the converse expression "the real aspect is all things," the meaning is that there is nothing that is not exposed to us.[8] For Dōgen, therefore, the fluid aspect of impermanence is in itself the absolute state. The changeable character of the phenomenal world is of absolute significance for Dōgen. "Impermanence is the Buddhahood. . . . [[9]] The impermanence of grass, trees, and forests is verily the Buddhahood. The impermanence of the person's body and mind is verily the Buddhahood. The impermanence of the (land) country and scenery is verily the Buddhahood."[10]

In other places, Dōgen says, "Death and life are the very life of the Buddha," and "These mountains, rivers, and earth are all the sea of the Buddhahood." In the Lotus (Hokke) Sūtra also Dōgen finds the same vein of thought. "Of the Hokke Sūtra.—The cry of a monkey is drowned in the sound of the rapid river. These are preaching this sūtra, this above all." He who attains the purport of this sūtra will discern the preaching of the doctrine even in the voices on the auction sale in the mundane world: "our Buddha's voice and form in all the sounds of the rapid river and colors of the ridge" (*Sanshō-Dōei,* Religious Poems of Umbrella-like Pine Tree).

The same vein of thought is found in the Chinese poet Su Tung-p'o's poem: "The voice of the rapid is verily the wide long tongue (of the Buddha). The color of the mountains is no other than the pure chaste body. At night we have perceived eighty-four thousand verses (of the sermon in natural phenomena). How should they be later revealed to other people?" This way of thinking is generally found in the Japanese Zen Buddhism. In the words of Mujū, "Mountains, rivers, earth, there is not a thing that is not real."[11]

Starting from such a viewpoint, Dōgen gives some phrases of the Buddhist scripture interpretations that are essentially different from the original meaning. There is a phrase in the *Mahāparinirvāṇa-sūtra*[12] that should be interpreted as "He who desires to know the meaning of the Buddhahood should survey the opportunity and conditions and wait for the occasion to come. If the opportunity comes, the Buddhahood will be revealed of itself." Thus Buddhahood is here regarded as something empirically possible and accessible. To this concept, Dōgen gives a twist, and reads the phrase "survey the opportunity and conditions" as "makes a survey in terms of opportunity and conditions" and the phrase "if the opportunity comes" as "the occasion has already come." His interpretation of the original passage becomes, in this way, something like the following: "Buddhahood is time. He who wants to know Buddhahood may know it by knowing time as it is revealed to us. And as time is something in which we are already immersed, Buddhahood also is not something that is to be sought in the future but is something that is realized where we are."[13]

In this manner, Dōgen makes an effort to free himself from the idealistic viewpoint held by some of the Mahāyāna Buddhists of India. In the Chinese *Avataṁsaka-sūtra,* there is a phrase, "In all the three worlds there is only this one mind."[14] The original Sanskrit text is as follows: "All that belongs to these three worlds is only mind. What the Buddha discriminatingly talked of as the Twelve Existence-Relations depends, in reality, solely upon the mind."[15] But Dōgen in Japan states that the meaning of "in the three worlds only mind,"[16] should be interpreted as "these three worlds are as they are regarded." He explicitly rejects its idealistic interpretation and asserts that "it is not that the three worlds are verily the mind." In another place, he makes a comment that, the mind and its object, which stand in an inseparable relation, may not be conceived in hierarchical terms as one subordinating the other. "The mind rightly interpreted is the one mind which is all things and all things which are the one mind."[17] And in another place, Dōgen says, "There is not the one mind apart from all things, and there are not all things apart from the one mind."[18]

Dōgen is critical of the Zen Buddhism of China. He chooses from the Chinese Zen Buddhism only those elements which he thinks will suit his own standpoint. The words of a Chinese Zen Buddhist, Yao-shan (751–834), contains the phrase "at a certain time." Dōgen interprets this phrase unjustifiably as "Being Time" and comments as follows: "So-called 'Being Time' means that time already is being and all being is time."[19] From this free-wheeling comment, Dōgen goes on to develop his unique philosophy of time, according to which the ever-changing, incessant temporal flux is identified with ultimate being itself.

Again and again Dōgen emphasizes that the true reality is not something static but something dynamic. "It is a heretical doctrine," Dōgen says, "to think the mind mobile and the essence of things static. It is a heretical doctrine to think that the essence is crystal clear and the appearance changeable."[20] Or again, "It is a heretical doctrine to think that in essence water does not run, and the tree does not pass through vicissitude. The Buddha's way consists in the form that exists and the condition that exists. The bloom of flowers and the fall of leaves are the conditions that exist. And yet unwise people think that in the world of essence there should be no bloom of flowers and no fall of leaves."[21]

Dōgen criticizes the Chinese Zen Buddhist Ta-hui (1089–1163) who taught that both the mind and essence are over and above birth. According to Dōgen, Ta-hui wrongly taught that "the mind is solely perception and conceptualization, and the essence is pure and tranquil."[22] Here one sees the contrast between the static way of thinking in the Chinese and the dynamic way of thinking in the Japanese. Dōgen rejects the viewpoint of the *Vimalakīrti-sūtra.* The *Vimalakīrti-sūtra* is the scripture regarded as especially important in China and Japan, nevertheless Dōgen has quite a low opinion of the significance of the silence of Vimalakīrti, which generally is highly commended.

"The reason why Vimalakīrti, a virtuous gentleman, has not yet found enlightenment and grace is because he has not entered the priesthood. Should he enter priesthood, he would have enjoyed grace. The masters of Zen of the T'ang (618–907) and Sung (960–1279) periods not having mastered the doctrine of their sect, indiscriminately recommended Vimalakīrti, whom they considered to be good in action as well as in speech. They are a despicable lot, not knowing the oral teachings of the Buddha and ignorant of the discipline of the Buddha. Among them there are even many who mistakenly conceive the ways of Vimalakīrti and the Buddha as identical. They know neither the doctrine of the Buddha, nor the way of the founder, nor do they even know or estimate Vimalakīrti. They say that Vimalakīrti's silent revelation to Bodhisattvas is identical with the silent dispositions of the Tathāgata. This proves that they do not at all know the doctrine of the Buddha and they are not competent in practice . . . . The silence of the Tathāgata and the silence of Vimalakīrti are beyond comparison." According to Dōgen mere silence or a mere expression of negation does not have any ultimate significance.

"Evil men mostly think that speech and action are temporary things which have been set up by illusions, while silence and non-action are the truth. That is not the doctrine of the Buddha. That is what is conceived by those who have heard by hearsay the teachings of the scriptures of the gods Brahma and Iśvara."[23]

The negative and static character of Indian philosophy in general is rejected here. Consequently, the Buddhism preached by Dōgen is somewhat different in its content from what was emphasized by the Indian Buddhists in general or by the Chinese Zen sects in general.

The inclination to live contentedly in this given phenomenal world appears also in modern sectarian Shintoism. The founder of the Konkō sect, for instance, teaches, "Whether alive or dead, you should regard the heaven and earth as your own habitation."[24] Jinsai Itō (1627–1705) criticizes and metamorphoses Chinese neo-Confucianism in just the same way as Dōgen criticized the Chinese Zen sect and changed the form of (or emphasized some particular ideas of) Zen thought. Itō regards heaven and earth as the evolution of great activity, where nothing but eternal development exists, *and completely denies what is called death.*

"*The Book of Change* says, 'The great virtue of heaven and earth is called life.' It means that living without ceasing is nothing but the way of heaven and earth. And in the way of heaven and earth there is no death but life, there is no divergence but convergence. Death is the end of life, and divergence is the termination of convergence. That is because the way of heaven and earth is one with life. Though the bodies of ancestors may perish, their spirits are inherited by their posterity, whose spirits are again inherited by their own posterity. When life thus evolves, without ceasing, into eternity, it may rightly be said that no one dies."[25]

According to Itō the world of reality is nothing but change and action, and action is in itself good.

"Between heaven and earth there is only one reason: motion without stillness, good without evil. Stillness is the end of motion, while evil is the change of good; and good is a kind of life, while evil is a kind of death. It is not that these two opposites are generated together, but they are all one with life."[26]

Sorai Ogyū (1666–1728), worthy rival as he was to Jinsai Itō, admires Itō's activism as "the supreme knowledge of a thousand years." He also rejects and denounces the static character of the doctrine of the School of *Li* founded by the very influential Chu Hsi (1130–1200). Most of the Japanese Confucianist scholars, even when they follow the metaphysical doctrines of Chu Hsi, never choose the dualism of *Li* and *Ch'i.* All of the characteristically Japanese scholars believe in phenomena as the fundamental mode of existence. They unanimously reject the quietism of the neo-Confucianists of the Sung period.[27]

The way of thinking that recognizes absolute significance in the phenomenal world seems to be culturally associated with the Japanese traditional love of nature. The Japanese in general love mountains, rivers, flowers, birds, grass, and trees,[28] and represent them in the patterns of their *kimono,* and they are fond of the delicacies of the season, keeping their edibles in natural forms as much as possible in cooking. Within the house, flowers are arranged in a vase and dwarf trees are placed in the alcove, flowers and birds are engraved in the transom, simple flowers and birds are also painted on the sliding screen, and in the garden miniature mountains are built and water drawn. The literature is also closely tied up with warm affection for nature. "*Makura no Sōshi*" (Pillow Books) begins with general remarks about the four seasons and then goes into the description of the scenic beauties of the seasons and human affairs.

Of essays of this kind there are many. If the poems on nature should be set aside from among the collections of Japanese poems, how few poems would be left. Seventeen-syllable short poems (*haiku*) cannot be dissociated from nature.

The love of nature, in the case of the Japanese, is tied up with their tendencies to cherish minute things and treasure delicate things. Contrast the Japanese love of individual flowers, birds, grass, and trees with the British enjoyment of the spacious view of the sea, the Dover Cliffs, and the countryside.[29] Such aesthetic preferences of various nations are culturally significant traits of their respective peoples.

The Japanese have been lovers of natural beauty since ancient days. Occasionally they sing songs in praise of grand scenic beauties. But even then the grandeur of the scenery is reduced to its miniature form. To illustrate:

> "When going forth I look far from the Shore of Tago,
> How white and glittering is
> The lofty Peak of Fuji,
> Crowned with snows!"[30]
> "As the tide flows into Waka Bay,
> The cranes, with the lagoons lost in flood,
> Go crying towards the reedy shore."[31]

They enjoy nature as it is reflected in their compact range of vision, which is particularly evident in the following poem.

> "In my garden fall the plum blossoms—
> Are they indeed snowflakes
> Whirling from the sky?"[32]
> "The nightingale sings
> Playing at the lower branches
> Lamenting the fall of the plum blossoms."[33]

In this respect the Japanese love of nature differs somewhat from the Chinese attachment to the rivers and mountains. This point may be best illustrated by the comparison of the following two poems. Dōgen writes:

> "Flowers are in Spring, Cuckoos in Summer,
> In Autumn is the moon, and in Winter,
> The pallid glimmer of snow."

The meaning of the above poem coincides with what is intended by the Chinese verse of "*Wu-men-kuan*" (Gateless Gate, by Wu-men Hui-k'ai).

> "A hundred flowers are in Spring, in Autumn is the moon,
> In Summer is the cool wind, the snow is in Winter;
> If nothing is on the mind to afflict a man,
> That is the best season for the man."

In the Chinese the word "cuckoos" of the Japanese is replaced by the "cool wind," which gives an entirely different effect. The cool wind and cuckoos are both sensible objects, but while the former gives the sense of indefinite remote boundlessness, the latter gives a limited and cosy impression.

Such a characteristically Japanese element is still better exemplified by Ryōkan, who composed the following poem on his deathbed.

> "For a memento of my existence
> What shall I leave (I need not leave anything)
> Flowers in the spring, cuckoos in the summer,
> and maple leaves
> in the autumn."

"Maple leaves" are felt to be far closer to ourselves than "the moon." Here is an illustration of the difference, amidst a common enjoyment and love of nature, between the Chinese preference of the boundless and distant and the Japanese preference of the simple and compact.

The Japanese garden typically exemplifies the Japanese attitude of expressing natural scenery in a miniature scale. In this respect, the Indians are quite different. They too love nature and construct gardens (*udyāna, ārāma*), where they plant grass and trees and lay out wells and springs, but they rarely try to imitate natural rivers and mountains on the smaller scale.

The tender love of animals traditionally runs in the vein of the Japanese, but that love is concentrated on minute lovable living things.

> "A copper pheasant warbles out.
> Listening to its voice I thought,
> Could it be the father calling?
> Could it be the mother calling?"

The image of the "copper pheasant" is very Japanese. In contrast, the peoples of India and the South Asiatic countries are fond of a fantastic story such as abandoning oneself to a hungry tiger who attacks one. But such a story, an expression of benevolence toward living things, is not quite congenial to the poetic sentiments of the Japanese, although both peoples wanted to express the idea of benevolence towards living creatures.

The Indian ascetics also composed poems in praise of nature. They enjoy and extol nature as the sanctury beyond worldly sensuous attachments, afflictions, and bondages. In their case, nature is conceived to be something opposed to human elements, and nugatory to feeling.

"Before and behind, if there be none but oneself,
That is a great tranquility for the lone dweller of the wood.
Let me now go to the forest commended by the Buddha,
Since such is the place where solitary single-minded
Ascetics take their delight.
Let me clean my arms and legs
And go alone and return alone to and from
The cool forest in full bloom
And the chilly cavern of the mountain,
When the breeze is cool and fragrant,
Sitting on the top of the mount, ignorance I shall annihilate.
At the chilly mountain slope, within the blossom-covered forest,
Let me enjoy the tranquility of deliverance
And take delight in it."[34]

In the case of the Japanese, however, priests and laymen alike are attached to nature, which is at one with human beings, and they enjoy that attachment to their hearts' content. Even when they sit on stones under trees for the purpose of getting away from the afflictions of the mind and body, they soon find flowers they enjoy and take delight in the flowers.

"Making the shades of trees
My dwelling place,
A flower gazer
I naturally become."[35]

Even Dōgen, who took a Spartan attitude toward human desires, had a tender heart for natural beauties.

"The peach blossoms begin
To bloom in the breeze of the Spring;
Not a shadow of doubt
On the branches and leaves is left."
"Though I know that I shall meet
The autumnal moon again,
How sleepless I remain,
On this moonlit night."

The Japanese esteem the sensible beauties of nature, in which they seek revelations of the absolute world.

"Cherry blossoms, falling in vain,
Remind me of the Treasure plants,
That adorn paradise."[36]

There is no inkling of a view that regards the natural world as cursed or gruesome. Dōgen says: "There are many thousands of worlds comparable to the sūtras within a single spade of dust. Within a single dust there are innumerable Buddhas. A single stalk of grass and a single tree are both the mind and body (of us and Buddhas)."[37]

Relevant to such an idea was the conception prevalent in medieval Japan that even grass and trees have spirits and consequently are eligible for salvation. The idea that even the things of "no-heart" (the objects of nature that have no spirits) can become Buddhas, based upon the Tendai doctrines, was particularly emphasized in Japan. This constituted an important theme for study in the Japanese Tendai sect, and the idea was inherited also by the Nichiren (1222–1282) sect.[38] Nichiren sought the superiority of the Hokke (Lotus) Sūtra in its recognition of the eligibility of the grass and the trees to become Buddhas. There appear time and again among the Japanese Buddhist writings the following lines: "When a Buddha, who has attained enlightenment, looks around the universe, the grass, trees, and lands, all become Buddhas."[39] In *"Noh"* songs we often come across such an idea which was taken for granted socially and religiously in those days. "The voice of Buddhahood of such a holy priest makes even the grass and trees predestined to become Buddhas . . . . Even the grass and trees have attained the effect of becoming Buddhas being led by the power that mankind is bound to be reborn into the Pure Land only if they invoke the Buddha's name and practice *nembutsu* prayer . . . . Had it not been for the teachings of Buddhahood, the spirit of the decayed willow tree which is impermanent and soulless would not have attained the Buddhahood." (*"Yugyō Yanagi."*) The "Noh" song, *"Kochō"* (Butterflies), relates the story of an insect becoming a Buddha owing to the power of the Hokke Sūtra; *"Kakitsubata"* (Iris), *"Yugyō Zakura"* (The Cherry Tree of the Itinerant), *"Fuji"* (Wisteria), and *"Bashō"* (The Banana Tree) decribe the grass and trees becoming Buddhas; and *"Sesshō Seki"* (The Stone Destroying Life) is about the stone becoming a Buddha by being given a holy robe and bowl. More recently, a *jōruri* (a ballad drama) called *"Sanjūsangendō Munagi no Yurai"* has for its main theme a story of a willow tree becoming a Buddha, based upon the religious faith of the Jōdo-shin sect.

"The Honganji Temple flourishes in the age of corruption,
The Tradition of Amitābha allows no regression;
For the coming of five hundred years,
The grass, trees, and soils all become Buddhas."[40]

The oral tradition of the medieval Tendai sect of Japan pushed the idea of the grass and trees becoming Buddhas so far as to preach "the non-becoming Buddhas of the grass and trees." According to this theory, everything is by nature a Buddha—that is to say, to attain enlightenment through ascetic practice is one and the same thing as being a Buddha without recourse to ascetic practice. Not only the grass and trees but also rivers, mountains, and the earth are themselves Buddhahood already possessed intact. There is no becoming a Buddha in the sense of coming to be something separate and different in nature. That is the reason why the non-becoming of Buddhahood was preached.[41] The logical conclusion of the idea of the acceptance of the given reality is here definitely and clearly crystallized.

Indian Buddhism also admits the spirituality of the grass and trees, along with the various schools of Indian philosophy that adopted such a view.[42] But most of the Indian philosophies maintain that all living things attain the state of deliverance through enlightened intelligence (*vidyā*), and not that the grass and trees become Buddhas in their actual state.

Such a tendency of thinking as discussed above seems to be still effective among the Japanese even in these days when the knowledge of natural science prevails. For instance, the Japanese generally use the honorific expression "o" prefixed to the names of various objects, as in the cases of "*o-cha*" (the honorific wording of tea) and "*o-mizu*" (the honorific wording of water). Probably there is no other nation on earth that uses an honorific expression prefixed to the names of everyday objects. This usage is not conceived to be anything extraordinary by the Japanese themselves. We should not regard it merely as an honorific expression, but rather consider it as a manifestation of the way of thinking that seeks a *raison d'être* and sacredness in everything that exists. According to the comments made by Westerners, "everything is Buddha" to the minds of the Japanese.

Then where do these characteristics of the Japanese to grasp the absolute in accordance with the given phenomenal world, or to love nature as it is, come from? In Japan, is it because the weather is mild, the landscape benign, and nature appears to be relatively benevolent to men, that men love nature instead of abhorring it, and feel congenial to it instead of having a grudge against it, so that nature is thought as one with men, rather than hostile to men? This seems to account only in part for the prevalence of the characteristic thought tendency of the Japanese to take the phenomenal world as absolute.

This-Worldliness

While religions of the world very often tend to regard this world as the land of impurity and the other world as the blessed land of purity where one seeks the Heaven of eternal happiness, primitive Shintoism recognizes the intrinsic value of life in this world. Each one of the Japanese people is considered a descendant of gods and goddesses. In primitive Shintoism, one can find no profound reflections either upon the soul or upon death.

The ancient Japanese called the soul "*tama*." Man's *tama* can function independently of his body, and assist in the achievement of his work. Various ideas about *tama* are nothing more than expositions of its utility in worldly enterprises. One's *tama* is supposed to remain in this world and to continue functioning after one's death, and essentially no distinction is drawn between the states of one's *tama* before and after death.[43]

In Japanese mythology, nothing is said about the future world. Indeed, there was an idea expressed that after one's death, one goes to the land of the night, a dark place supposedly located underground. When one dies, one is naturally buried underground and there is a common belief in every country that there exists a Hades. And it is also natural that death is universally abhorred. But it appears that the ancient Japanese expressed little fear of death, and rarely worried about life after death. Japanese mythology as a whole is attached to this world and makes much of this life.[44] Consequently, such a metaphysical concept as *karma* or moral law of cause and effect (i.e., post-mortem rewards for good deeds and punishment for bad ones) is lacking. They regarded death as impurity, and enjoyed solely the life of this world.

As far as this-worldliness itself is concerned, the Chinese religions of Confucianism and Taoism are also rightly called "this-worldly." Even the Zen sect is touched with its influence. In the case of the Japanese, primitive Shintoism alone was mingled with animism, Shamanism, and the tendency to attach great importance to a limited social nexus, so that this-worldliness in Japan came to assume a number of deviations and variations.

Once men became conscious of philosophical or metaphysical doubts, however, they could no longer rest assured with such easy-going religious faith. They felt an internal urge to search into some deeper truth about men. It was in an answer to such spiritual demands that Buddhism flowed into Japan. It was only natural, when Buddhism was introduced to Japan, that there were those who rejected it and those who supported it. In the first place, among those who rejected it, there was a marked predilection for the pleasures of this world.

Tabito Ōtomo sang as follows:

> This life of ours, let me enjoy;
> In the other life, I do not care,
> An insect or a bird,
> Or whatever I shall become.

This was making fun of the Buddhist theory of the transmigration of the fictitious soul. The following poem is written in an apparent mood of defiance of the Buddhist theory of the mutability of phenomenal things:

> Everything alive is said
> To be death-bound;
> If it be so, let me be happy,
> So long as I am alive.

He admired and adored the life of a hedonist and despised the Spartan life of moral austerity.

> It is better to drink
> And to weep in drunkenness,
> Than to talk like a sage;
> Ugly is the man who never drinks,
> But pretends to be wise;
> Scrutinizing his face, I've found,
> What a monkey-face he had!
> It is worse to say nothing,
> And to pretend to be wise,
> Than to drink and weep in drunkenness.

In confronting Buddhism as an imported system of culture, the traditional Japanese culture was too weak to resist it. Was it then not improbable, as Buddhism was transplanted into this country and spread among the people, that the traditional Japanese way of thinking, tending toward this-worldliness, should have completely given way to Buddhism? Buddhism, like a flood of water rushing forth from a broken dam, spread all over Japan within a very short time. It was, however, impossible for Buddhism to change completely the inclination to this-worldliness in the Japanese general public. On the contrary, it was the Japanese themselves that transformed Buddhism, which they accepted from the continent, into a religion centered upon this world.

With the advent and spread of Buddhism, the Japanese came to think seriously of life after death. But even then Buddhism was accepted as something this-worldly. All through the Nara and Heian periods, almost all the sects of Buddhism aimed at tangible rewards in this world and they mainly depended upon incantation and magic. (This point will be developed below in the chapter entitled "Problem of Shamanism.")

This stūpa in India and the great image of Buddha at Nara in Japan might be called representative edifices that symbolize the prosperity of Buddhism supported by state power in their respective countries. The stūpa is a large mound where the ashes of great men or saints were buried. The formative arts in India are embodied in the stūpa, a symbol of death, while those in Japan are concentrated in the image of Buddha, a vivid symbol of the *living* ideal man. While most Indians search for the truth of humanity through the channels of death, most Japanese try to express it intuitively through the channels of life.

The Japanese way of thinking centering upon life in this world transformed the basic Buddhist doctrines. According to the views of Indian Buddhist believers, all living things repeat their life-cycles in an infinite process of transmigration of the soul; and a life in this world is but an infinitesimal period within that eternally circulating process. Even Śākyamuni himself was able to practice religion in this world and to become a Buddha only as a reward for the multitude of good deeds accumulated in his countless lives in previous existences. Such practice as Śākyamuni had accomplished cannot be achieved by an ordinary person within one lifetime, but must be continued through many lifetimes. It was not that all the Buddhist followers in India believed thus, but the common men in India did. Buddhism, however, was at first transformed by the this-worldly Chinese, and then again it was steeped even more deeply by the Japanese in the dye of this-worldliness. There are many sects of Japanese Buddhism which emphasize the belief that even ordinary men would be able to become Buddhas, should they attain enlightenment in this world (*Sokushin Jōbutsu*).

According to the ninth-century founder of the Tendai sect in Japan, Saichō (Dengyō Daishi), in his classified comments on various doctrines of Buddhism, Hīnayāna Buddhism is a circuitous teaching, since it advocates the practice of religion through countless lives in an immensely long span of time. Some sects of the Mahāyāna Buddhism also preach that one should practice religion through similarly long periods of life, so that they were of no use to the Japanese people of Saichō's time. Mahāyāna Buddhism in general directs the way in which an ordinary man can become a Buddha in a limited time (A Direct Way). And it is the doctrine of the Hokke Sūtra that gives the fullest expression to this idea (The Great Straight Way).[45] Saichō used the phrase, "*Sokushin Jōbutsu*" (to become a Buddha alive in the human body).[46] Such an idea was as old as Buddhism itself, but the use of such a phrase seems to have been initiated by Saichō. But in the theory of "*Sokushin Jōbutsu*" preached by Saichō, the doctrine of this-worldliness was not thoroughgoing enough. It was the Japanese scholars of the Tendai sect who later pushed the idea of this-world Buddhahood, for the Tendai doctrine in China did not allow a man to become a Buddha through this life alone. Even if he did achieve Buddhahood, it was supposed to be the consequence of the ascetic practices accumulated through many lives, so that one could become a Buddha only on reaching the threshold of perfect religion. Hardly a hundred years had elapsed after the introduction by Saichō of the Tendai sect into Japan, when a Tendai scholar, Annen, began to preach not only that one could become a Buddha in this world, but also that one could become a Buddha through ascetic practice during one's life, and would be permitted to be a Buddha alive in the human body.

"At the beginning, according to a sacred priest, or according to the scriptures, learning that an affliction is nothing but an enlightenment, one achieves the Intelligence of a Buddha without overcoming one's afflictions. Learning that mundane existence is nothing but Nirvāṇa, one becomes a Buddha in the form of 'identity by name,' which is simply what the mundane existence turns out to be. That is why it is called enlightenment and also becoming a Buddha. If one's body does not become a Buddha, neither does one's mind. If one's mind has already become a Buddha, so consequently does one's body."[47]

This-worldliness was plainly expressed by Kūkai, the founder (in 816) of the Japanese Shingon (True Word) sect. According to Kūkai, the world and humanity both consist of six constituent elements; earth, water, fire, wind, sky, and intelligence. Their essence is the absolute truth (the World of the Law) and they are so perfectly interrelated as never to obstruct (or oppose) one another. It follows that mankind and Buddhas are identical in their essence. Kūkai preached that if one should follow such reasoning, then making figures with one's hands, reciting incantations, or concentrating one's mind (the three actions of man's body, mouth, and mind), would be directly identified with those of a Buddha. He specifically wrote a book called the "*Commentaries on Becoming a Buddha Alive in the Human Body*." He supports the doctrine of esoteric Buddhism: "One can attain the status of great enlightenment with the body that was born of one's parents."[48]

The doctrine of Nichiren (1222–1282), a development of the Japanese Tendai sect influenced by esoteric Buddhism, continued to stress becoming a Buddha alive in the human body. "The gate to the truth called 'Becoming a Buddha alive in the human body' ought to be studied as a matter of great importance by the scholars of the world. My own disciples in particular should keep this matter in mind above anything else. During these twenty-seven years between the fifth year of Kenchō and the third year of Kōan, I have stated in various places a great many gates to enter the truth. But all the gates lead up just to this one."[49] "Should we recite, with the sincerity of our hearts, '*Nammyō-hōrenge-kyō*' (Adoration of the Lotus Sūtra), the Perfect One in the Cosmic Body (of the *Dharma*), the eternal fundamental basis, . . . etc.—all of them would come and gather around us. That is the reason why the most devoted of the devoted followers of the true practice could become Buddhas, whether or not they take leave of their bodies."[50]

Running as a parallel to such a view in ecclesiastical doctrines, popular religions are also based upon this-worldliness. As an illustration, the religious faith in Jizō, a guardian deity of children and of the wicked (*Kṣitigarbha-bodhisattva*) became popular after the Heian period, because the common man in Japan can always look to the great benevolence of the holy person ready and willing to save him just as he is.

"*Kṣitigarbha-bodhisattva,* since he is unfathomably benevolent, does not live in the Pure Land. Since his connections with human beings are so deep, he does not call for divine death. He only makes the place of evil his own habitat, and makes friends solely with sinners."[51]

A question may be raised here. One might argue that in Japan Pure Land Buddhism was very popular, and even the Nichiren sect, under its influence, used the phrase "The Sacred Mountain which is the Pure Land."[52]

Pure Land Buddhism in Japan, however, was not always other-worldly. The Pure Land Buddhism of the Heian period, it cannot be denied, was inclined to regard practical life as worthless and to attach prime importance to a life of seclusion. But the founder of the Jōdo or Pure Land sect, Hōnen (Genkū, 1133–1212) was decidedly on the side of asserting this world. Once a warrior came and confided to Hōnen what troubled his mind: he could not reconcile his religious belief as a believer of the Jōdo sect with his duty as a *samurai* to fight on the battlefield. Hōnen answered him as follows: "The original vow of Amitābha is not concerned whether one's predisposition is good or evil, or whether the religious practice is more or less. Since it does not depend upon the purity or impurity of the body, or time, place or opportunities, the occasion of death is of no consequence. Even sinners, as sinners, are eligible for rebirth in the Pure Land, if they should invocate the name of Amitābha. This is the miracle of the original vow. As for those born into the families of warriors, who fight in war and lose their lives therein, if they only should invocate the name of Amitābha, they would be assisted by the original vow and would be welcomed by Amitābha into the Pure Land. This you should never doubt."[53]

Moreover, the Jōdo-shin sect, from the standpoint that assures anyone rebirth into the Pure Land only if one has faith in Amitābha in daily life, strives to realize absolute significance within one's life in this world. It attaches great importance to the phase of coming back to this world in contrast to the phase of going to the Pure Land. Such a standpoint gave rise to more or less distorted interpretations of phrases in the Buddhist scriptures.[54]

The point that the Jōdo sect meant to give great significance and a theoretical basis to positive action in this world has already been elaborated. But according to Pure Land Buddhism in India, this world is supposed to be the impure land smeared with dirt, where no ordinary men could ever practice religion. In order for ordinary men to attain Nirvāṇa, they must be born in the next life into the Pure Land, which is the better world, where they should, under the guidance of Amitābha, listen to the doctrine of the Buddha and practice asceticism. According to the Japanese Pure Land Buddhism, especially the Jōdo-shin sect, in contrast, to be born into the Pure Land is identical with attaining Nirvāṇa. (To be reborn into the Pure Land is nothing but Nirvāṇa.) So the upshot was that Japanese Pure Land Buddhism transposed the position of this world, which is the impure land, to the position tantamount to what was considered by the Indian followers of Pure Land Buddhism to be the delightful Pure Land. This transposition should also be attributed to the this-worldly inclination of the Japanese people.

It would be rash, however, to conclude that Pure Land Buddhism in Japan is completely this-worldly. An element of escapism cannot be denied its outlook. The attitudes of resignation and submission in every area of life were imposed upon people under the feudal regime, since, it was told, everything was predetermined as the consequence of the actions in one's previous life. Yet by comparison with the Pure Land Buddhism of India and of China, such an element of escapism from this world was relatively weak in the Pure Land Buddhism of Japan, and became even less influential toward the modern period.

The this-worldly idea of becoming a Buddha alive in the human body is also conspicuous in the Japanese Zen sect. Dōgen (1200–1253), the founder of the Sōto school, straightforwardly asserts that to attain enlightenment is not the function of the mind but *that of the body:*

"Is the Way (of liberation) achieved through the mind or through the body? The doctrinal schools speak of the identity of mind and body, and so when they speak of attaining the Way through the body, they explain it in terms of this identity. Nevertheless, this leaves one uncertain as to what 'attainment by the body' truly means. From the point of view of our school, attainment of the Way is indeed achieved through the body as well as the mind. So long as one hopes to grasp the Truth only through the mind, one will not attain it even in a thousand existences or in eons of time. Only when one lets go of the mind and ceases to seek an intellectual apprehension of the Truth is liberation attainable. Enlightenment of the mind through the sense of sight and comprehension of the Truth through the sense of hearing are truly bodily attainments. To do away with mental deliberation and cognition, and simply to go on sitting, is the method by which the Way is made an intimate part of our lives. Thus attainment of the Way becomes truly attainment through the body. That is why I put exclusive emphasis upon sitting."[55]

Dōgen recognized the uniqueness of Zen, in contrast to other doctrines, exactly on this point: to attain enlightenment with the body. In parallel with this, there is Nichiren's assertion to the effect that "The Hokke Sūtra should not only be read in the mind, but should be read in the body." Japanese Buddhism is, then, strongly imbued with an activistic behaviorism and practical tendency, which is tied up with its this-worldliness.

Toward the latest period of Mahāyāna Buddhism in India, it was maintained that the predisposition of Buddhahood (possibility of becoming an enlightened person) is constant and is not subject to change. Dōgen, linking his own view to that assertion, expounded it somewhat differently. The changing and fluctuating phases of the phenomenal world, he asserts, are themselves predispositions for a Buddha. "Grass, trees, bushes, and woods are changeable—that is, they are predispositions for a Buddha. Men, things, body, and mind are changeable—that is, they are predispositions for a Buddha. Countries, rivers, and mountains are changeable—that is, they are predispositions for a Buddha. Anuttara-Samyaksaṁbodhi (the supreme enlightenment) is changeable since it is a predisposition for a Buddha. The great perfect Nirvāṇa is a predisposition for a Buddha since it is changeable."[56]

The this-worldly character of the Zen sect is also embodied in Japanese Zen priests in later periods. Shōsan Suzuki, (1579–1655), for instance, taught the general lay believers as follows: "To pray for a happy future does not mean to pray for a world after death. It means to be delivered from afflictions here and now, and thus to attain a great comfort. Then, where do you think those afflictions come from? They spring solely from the love of your own body. Had it not been for this body of yours, from what should you suffer? To be delivered, therefore, from this body of yours is to become a Buddha."[57] His disciple, Echū, also states that Buddhism ought to be what is useful to this real world. "The law of the Buddha is supposed to serve only the future life and to be *of no use for today's affairs*. Followers, therefore, only think of their future happiness, and none of them knows how to control evils within their own minds today, and to eliminate their present afflictions. This is a great misconception."[58]

The medieval Shintoist theories adopted their terminology mainly from Buddhist scriptures. But Shintoism accepted only the *this-world* aspect which appears only in the incidental remarks at some peripheral parts of the scriptures, rejecting the *other-worldly* aspect of Buddhism. The *"Hōki-Hongi"*[59] one of the five books of Shintoism that provided the foundation for the Shintoist theology of the Ise Shrine in the Medieval period, states that if men should accomplish the supreme virtues of absolute sincerity and integrity, the result would be "living in peaceful harmony, sun and moon shining clear and bright, wind and rain coming at the right time, the nation being enriched and the people given security." Then, it goes on to say, armed force would no longer be necessary. These sentences are based upon the following part of the *"Daimuryōju-kyō* (The Larger *Sukhāvatīvyūha-sūtra*): "Wherever a Buddha goes, there is no country, town, hill, or village that is not enlightened by him. Sky and earth are in peaceful harmony, and sun and moon are clear and bright. Wind and rain come in due time and there is no calamity. The nation is enriched and people are secure and no armed forces are ever used. Virtues are respected, benevolence is promoted, and courtesy and humility are practiced in earnest." Originally, the "Daimuryōju sūtra" teaches the existence of the Pure Land and the vow of Amitābha Buddha, and the essence of its teachings is to give meaning to the activities of this world by transcending this world. The Japanese Buddhists, on the contrary, regarded the above-mentioned sentences as advocating "national defense" and laid great importance on them, while Shintoists selected only this-worldly teaching from the Pure Land scriptures.

Consequently, Shintoism and the Buddhist idea of becoming a Buddha alive in the human body were easily united.

> "The shrine of gods
> Is the body of my own,
> Inhaling breath being the Outer Shrine,
> Exhaling breath being the Inner Shrine."[60]

This-worldliness became even stronger as the nation proceeded into the Tokugawa period. The this-worldly and anti-religious tendencies were already manifest among the merchants' thoughts in the early Tokugawa period. "It is unnecessary to pray for a happy future when one is already in one's fifties. . . . It is even more unbecoming to spend days and nights at a temple on the pretext of praying for a happy future, abandoning one's family and boasting of worshipping at a temple. . . . In this life one should use one's discretion, above all else not to lose one's reputation." (The Will of Sōshitsu Shimai [1539–1615] a merchant of Hakata).[61] It is not surprising that the this-worldly tendency became especially pre-eminent during the modern period in Japan and that it even caused the emergence of materialism.

The Indian theory of the transmigration of the soul was also adopted, but even this theory sometimes underwent a transformation which led into affirming life in this world. To illustrate this point, let me quote from the famous description of Masashige Kusunoki (? –1336), at the time of his death.

"Masashige, in his seat, asked his brother Masasue: 'It is said that the good or evil of one's future life depends upon what one desires at the time of one's death. What is your wish among the nine worlds?' Masasue, laughing heartily, answered: 'It is my wish to be born as the same human being seven times in order to annihilate the Emperor's enemy.' Masashige, looking supremely delighted, said: 'A most sinful evil wish as it is, I myself also wish the same. Let us then be reborn into men and accomplish this wish of ours.' Thus pledging each other, they stabbed each other and fell upon the same pillow."[62]

According to the general view of most Indians, it is desirable *to be delivered from this world.* But here in Japan, while accepting the theory of the transmigration of the soul on one hand, most people wish, on the other hand, *to be reborn into this world.* The concept of loyalty in China was the loyalty of one's lifetime, in accordance with the Confucian theory. Chu-ko-k'ung-ming (181–234 A.D.) declares, in his "*Go Suishi-no Hyō*" (the second letter to the Emperor at the time of mobilizing the army): "I, Your Majesty's humble servant, bending myself most humbly like a ball, shall exert my best effort and shall cease only after I am dead." In contrast with this, Masashige Kusunoki states: "I wish to be reborn seven times in order to serve (the Emperor) most loyally." The idea of "Serving one's country by getting born seven times" was thereby established, and it was made most of by latter-day nationalists.

Ryōkan (Ninshō Bodhisattva, 1217–1303), famous as a reviver of the Ritsu sect during the Kamakura period, was a welfare worker who founded charity-hospitals to take care of invalids. When he was at Saidai Temple, taking pity on a leper, he repeatedly carried him on his own back to the city and begged for him whatever he wanted. Being deeply gratified with Ryōkan's deeds of benevolence, the invalid said to him on his deathbed: "I shall certainly be reborn into this world and become my master's humble servant in order to reciprocate my master's virtuous deeds. (As a mark for my master to identify me) I shall have a scar left on my face." Sure enough, in the later years of Ninshō's life, there appeared among his disciples a man with a scar on his face, who served him as an attendant. People said, we are told, that he was the leper regenerated.[63] Whereas according to the Indian Buddhist view of life and death, mankind are supposed to transmigrate through the six spheres of existence on account of their good and evil deeds, here in Japan ordinary men are acknowledged *to be reborn into this world,* should they make vows to be so.

The Japanese had been this-world-minded and optimistic long before the advent of Buddhism. It was because the mundane view of life had long remained with them that the idea of regarding this world as the strained and impure land could never take root. The theory of impurity as preached by Buddhism, therefore, was never adopted by the Japanese in its original form.

The first lesson of the ascetics of Hīnayāna Buddhism is to regard one's body as impure. Here the body is regarded as the source of all evils, and as a hindrance to the practice of the Way. Dōgen, however, revised this interpretation. According to him, contemplation should be realized in one's actions in everyday life. "So-called contemplations are everyday activities like sweeping the ground and the floor."[64] That should be conceived as exactly identical to "recognizing one's body as impure." Moreover, in that case one is expected to transcend the dichotomy of purity and impurity. "It is not a dichotomous argument of purity or impurity." Consequently, the theory of impurity emphasized by Indian Buddhism was not welcomed by the Japanese in general. "An opinion like the theory of impurity," commented Nakamoto Tominaga, "is based upon the mores of the Indians. In this land such a view is not accepted by people."[65]

Pessimism was another world view which never took a precise form in Japan. After the implantation of Buddhism into Japan, there appeared in "the *Man'yōshū*" some poems under the influence of Buddhist thoughts. But even these are no more than the lamentations of the changeability and transiency of man and things. To illustrate:

To what shall I liken this life?
It is like a boat,
Which, unmoored at morn,
Drops out of sight
And leaves nothing behind.

The fear of death, as shown in early Buddhism and Jainism, is conspicuously absent here. Let us listen to the confession of a Jain pessimist.

"Living things torture living things.
Behold, great fears of the world!

Living things abound with afflictions.
Human beings cling to lust and passion.
They go to self-destruction with their frail helpless bodies."[66]

"It is a great fear, affliction, I say.
Living beings are trembling in all directions."[67]

Such profound outcries were never heard from the Japanese. Dōgen argues even against pessimism itself.

"Mundane existence is nothing but the life of the Buddha himself. Should one loathe and try to abandon it, that is precisely to lose the life of the Buddha. Should one stay with it and cling to mundane existence, that also would mean to lose the life of the Buddha."[68]

There are innumerable poems composed in Japan to express Buddhist thought, but so far as the profound sense of pessimism is concerned, there are few expressing such a view, and they are written for a limited minority of the people. Also lacking are philosophical poems, expressing rational reflections that illuminate the nature of suffering, non-ego, and emptiness.

Japanese pessimism differs from that of Occidental people. In the West pessimism means to become wearied of existence in this world. In the case of the Japanese, by contrast, it means to be wearied only of complicated social fetters and restrictions from which they wish to be delivered. Consequently, the sense of pessimism is dispelled as soon as one comes to live close to the beauties of nature, far apart from human society. Saigyō (1118–1190), though he had escaped from the world, enjoyed contemplating the moon, hills, streams, flowers, etc., and spending the rest of his life travelling around on foot. Kamo-no-Chōmei (1151–1213), wearied as he was of this world, enjoyed nature and was contented, living a life of seclusion in his hermitage. Saint Gensei (1623–1668) of Fukakusa and, more recently, Ōtagaki Rengetsu also enjoyed nature, despite the fact that they hated to mingle in worldly affairs. Pessimism, as shown in these cases, is given its vent in the form of attachment to nature.[69]

"Changeable is this world,
So may be the cherry blossoms,
Falling in my garden."[70]

"Brief is this mortal life—
Let me go and seek the Way,
Contemplating the hills and streams undefiled![71]

Not only were they attached to nature, but they kept warm spots in their hearts for companions and never ceased to long for humanity, in the midst of their hermitage. Saigyō, in his life of a solitary traveller, enjoyed tranquility and yet in his heart he yearned for life, which he had abandoned on his own accord.

"Weary as I am
Of this world,
When autumn comes
And the moon shines serene,
I feel I should like to survive."

"Wearied of this world
Why should I be?
Those once despised by me
Today my delight turn out to be."

Even the life of Bashō (1644–1694) as a solitary wanderer was deeply imbued with a longing for companions. "What a lazy old man I am! Usually, being annoyed by visitors, I have pledged my heart not to see or to invite others. Nevertheless, on a moonlit night or on a snowy morn, how unreasonable it is of me not to long for a companion."[72] In Kenkō (1283–1350), the author of the "*Tsure-zure-gusa*" (Gleanings from Leisure Hours, or "Grasses of Idleness"), the attachment to worldly affairs is especially deep-rooted. That such a sentiment was not limited solely to some men of letters in the past is clear enough, when we look into our own minds a little deeper.

The Acceptance of Man's Natural Dispositions

I have already pointed out that the Japanese in general are inclined to search for the absolute within the phenomenal world or in what is immediately observable. Among all the natures that are most immediate to man's experience is the nature of man, so that man's natural dispositions rank highest in the average Japanese way of thinking.

Just as the Japanese are apt to accept external and objective nature as it is, so they are inclined to accept man's natural desires and sentiments as they are, and not to strive to repress or fight against them.

Love was the favorite theme of ancient Japanese poetry. Love among the ancient Japanese was sensual and unrestrained. The true meaning of life existed for them in love. In general, the expression of their sentiments was direct and open, without suppression, at least none that one can observe externally.

This tendency underwent transformations which varied according to diverse historical periods and social classes. Nevertheless, it remained as a relatively distinctive characteristic of most of the people. Japanese poetry, for instance, is rich in love poems, and seems vastly different from the poetry of the Indian or the Chinese peoples.

Norinaga Motoori (1730–1801), the great scholar of Japanese classics, recognized the distinction of the Japanese from the Chinese in this respect:

"The fact that the *Book of Poetry* (*Shih Ching*) lacks love poems reveals something of the customs of the people of that country [China]. They only make an outward show of manly appearance, concealing the womanishness of their real selves. In contrast, the abundance of love poems in our empire reveals the way to express one's genuine dispositions."[73]

In India there is an abundance of love poems. Nevertheless, the Indians in general sought an ultimate and absolute meaning beyond passions of love, which many of them were taught to annihilate. So the acceptance of natural love may be taken as a distinguishing characteristic of the Japanese compared with most of the other civilized peoples of Asia.

How does this tendency affect the Japanese way of adopting foreign cultures?

The ethical theories of Confucianism tended originally to asceticism, which was no doubt inherited by the Japanese Confucianists. Among them, however, there were those who tried to accept man's natural dispositions. *The Tale of Genji* and *The Tale of Ise* were the favorite reading of such scholars as Sorai Ogyū (1666–1728) and Keizan Hori (1688–1757). Ogyū recognized the intrinsic value of these old literary works, whose value should not be obscured by the risqué content.[74] He also maintained that since poetry expressed natural feelings, the farfetched moralizing on the poems by the Chinese critics was not relevant.[75] In this respect his attitude is in conformity with that of scholars of Japanese classics.[76]

Accepting as he does the view that the *Book of History* (*Shu Ching*), among the *Five Books*, relates the "Great Teachings and Laws of Ancient Wise Kings," he comments upon the *Book of Poetry* (*Shih Ching*) as follows:

"The *Book of Poetry* is another matter. It is composed of the language of songs, just as the later day poetry is. Confucius edited it for its wording. And the scholars studied it for wording. That is why Confucius says: 'If you do not study the *Book of Poetry*, you have nothing to say.' In the later day period, one has come to study the *Book of Poetry* in the same fashion as one reads the *Book of Writing*, and they regard the former as an exposition of the principle of punishing vice and rewarding virtue. That is why one is at one's wits' end when it comes to interpreting the lascivious poem of Cheng-wei. The moral teachings of justice are so rare in this *Book of Poetry* that they are negligible. If the neo-Confucianists' opinion be granted as true, then why should the sage have resorted to such a roundabout way (of presenting the principle of punishing vice and rewarding virtue), instead of writing directly a separate book of moral instruction? So the opinion of these Confucianists shows that they are ignorant of the essence of poetry. The preface to the *Book of Poetry* was written in the spirit of comprehending the proper meanings of poetry. . . . The later scholars, having lost the original spirit of Confucianism, wrote large and small prefaces. This is most despicable. The words of poetry touch upon all subject matters, from the government to the street, and reach also the countries of many a lord. Is there any place in the world where the difference does not exist between the noble and the low, man and woman, the wise and the foolish, the beautiful and the ugly? Through poetry, one can comprehend the changes of the world, the customs of people, their feelings, and the subtle phases of changing things. Its language is elegant and gentle, and being akin to the sentiments, its expression delicate. The subject matter of poetry can be anything, no matter how small or trivial, and thus poetry can be humbling to the spirit of pride. Herein lies, however, a key for the wise man to comprehend fools, for the brave man to understand woman, for kings to know their people, and for the age of prosperity to perceive the age of devastation."[77]

Shundai Dazai (1680–1747) called man's natural feelings the only genuine ones, which he listed as "likes and dislikes, suffering and rejoicing, anxiety and pleasure, etc." And he maintains: ". . . There is not a single human being devoid of these feelings. Either for the great or the petty, the noble or the low, there is no difference in this respect. Love of one's parents, wives, and children is also the same among the noble and the low. Since these feelings originate from an innate truthfulness, never stained with falsity, they are called genuine feelings. . . ."[78] His standpoint is pure naturalism.

"There are no double-dealings in actions that flow from natural dispositions, wherein the inside and outside are so transparent that they are one and the same thing. The natural dispositions are the innate true nature of men. Those actions done without being taught, without learning, without force but with freedom from all thoughts are the work of the natural dispositions. This is called truthfulness. And this is the significance of the golden mean."[79]

In the social realm, however, there are certain regulations of conduct, to which one should merely conform. But within one's inner self one can think whatever one pleases.

"According to the way of saints, one is said to be a man of noble character, only if one does not act against propriety but observes decorum concerning the body (regardless of), whether or not one sees a woman and imagines her lasciviously and takes delight in her beauty. That is exactly what it means to discipline one's mind through proper decorum."[80]

Apparently this is a metamorphosis of Confucianism in Japan, discarding the traditional attitude of the ancient Chinese Confucianism which refused to interpret the love poems of the *Book of Poetry* as such, and tried, instead, to interpret them as professing political and moral lessons. Dazai defiantly declared: "I would rather be a master of acrobatic feats, than a moralist."[81]

As to the proper behavior of a married couple, Chinese Confucianism taught, "one should discriminate between man and wife," according to the hierarchical order of husband and wife. Japanese Confucianists like Tōju Nakae (1608–1648), however, emphasized rather the harmony of husband and wife. "The husband should be righteous, while the wife should be obedient, and when both are in this manner in perfect harmony, that is the meaning of the way of discrimination."[82]

Atsutane Hirata (1760–1843) as a nationalist had little use for Chinese thoughts in general, but he interpreted the "Doctrine of the Mean" ("*Chung-yung*") as a doctrine of naturalism and as such he adopted it.

"Anyone knows perfectly well by nature, without borrowing others' teachings, that gods, the lords, and parents are respectable and the wife and children lovable. Teachings of the way of humanity, complex as they appear to be, do in fact originate from this simple fact. . . . The '*Chung-yung*' says, 'Whatever destiny is predetermined in Heaven is called a natural disposition. To comply with those natural dispositions is called the Way. And to practice the Way is called teaching.' Its meaning is that at the time of man's birth, man is provided with the inborn true feelings of benevolence, justice, propriety, and intelligence. . . . These are called dispositions. . . . Not to falsify or to distort them is the true way of humanity One should train and regulate the one inborn way so that no evil heart should result. To illustrate this with a near-by example, our countrymen are by nature brave, just, and straight, and that is what we call *Yamato-gokoro* (the spirit of Japan) or *Mikuni-damashii* (the soul of our country). . . . Since the True Way is as facile a matter as this, one should indeed stop acting like a sage and completely abandon the so-called mind or the way of enlightenment, and all that are affected and Buddha-ish. Let us, instead, not distort or forget this spirit of Japan, the soul of this country, but train and regulate it so that we may polish it up into a straight, just, pure, and good spirit of Japan."[83]

The naturalistic and nationalistic tendency described above represents also the Japanese mode of accepting Buddhism.

Onkō (Jiun Sonja 1718–1804), a Buddhist of the modern period, to whom credit should be given for propagating Buddhism among the common people, preached that morality means to follow man's natural dispositions.[84] Onkō accepted man's natural dispositions but also emphasized man's ability to control his lower desires and sentiments. Naturalism in this sense, however, never became popular among the Japanese in general, nor was it ever an influential guiding principle. Naturalism in the sense of satisfying man's desires and sentiments, instead, was a predominant trend in Japanese Buddhism.

The Ritsu sect with its two hundred and fifty precepts was introduced also into Japan but it never became as widespread as it was in India and China. Even the ascetic practices of the Ritsu sect (similar to those of the early Buddhist orders), which were far from being austere when compared with those of the Indian ascetics, had too many inhibitory restrictions of man's natural dispositions and instinct to be accepted by the majority of the Japanese. (These ascetic practices are still strictly observed today in Ceylon, Burma, Siam, and Cambodia.) On the whole, Japanese Buddhism inclined to hedonism. The practice of the ceremony of prayer, for instance, was an occasion to the aristocrats of the Heian period for enjoying sensory pleasure. "In front of the Prince of Spring, the fragrance of the plum blossoms wafts faintly, mingled with the scent from inside the bamboo blind, and makes one feel as though one were in the land of a living Buddha."[85] For them, a Buddhist mass in this world was already the Pure Land or Paradise. In fact, it meant merely *"to have a pleasant evening,* before having the fine-voiced chant sūtras for them."[86]

Such a tendency finally led to the repudiation of disciplines: "The Chinese monk Ganjin (Chien-chen, ca. 750 A.D.), of the Ryūkō (Lung-hsing) Temple of T'ang, propagated the Right Law of disciplines and initiated the Buddhist confirmation of that Law, which in the course of time came to be neglected. Since the medieval period, the Buddhist confirmation had become only nominal, and people gathered from various countries merely to stroll around the ordination platform of the temple. They knew nothing of the large and small disciplines, nor did they try to learn anything of the regulations about the infringement of these disciplines. Instead, they merely counted the years after taking orders, and let themselves degenerate into priests who accepted services for nothing. The observance of abstention and disciplines had thus come to an end."[87]

The repudiation of disciplines was especially popular among the followers of the Jōdo sect. "Those who practice the invocation of Amitābha alone, say that by playing the game of *go* or that of *sugoroku* (a kind of backgammon) they do not violate any of their teachings. Clandestine sexual relations or the eating of meat and flesh is no hindrance to rebirth into the Pure Land. The observance of disciplines in the age of degeneration is the tiger in the street. That ought to be dreaded; that ought to be detested. Should one be afraid of sins and shrink from evils, such a one would certainly be a man who never believes in the Buddha."[88] The Pure Realm teachings, preached by Hōnen (1133–1212), disregards the distinction between the observance and the infringement of disciplines. It lays emphasis solely upon the practice of the invocation of Amitābha. "If one who eats fish should be reborn into the Pure Land, a cormorant would certainly be the one. If one who does not eat fish should be reborn into the Pure Land, a monkey would indeed be the one. Whether or not one eats fish does not count, but it is the one who invocates Amitābha that is bound to be reborn into the Pure Land."[89]

It was Nichiren (1222–1282) who was keen enough to point out that the Jōdo sect of Japan had turned into something entirely different in practice from that of China.

"According to Zendō's (Shan-tao) *Gate to the Meditation,* it is said: 'Make a vow not to touch with your hand, nor to put into your mouth, wine, meat, and five spices. Pray that your body and mouth be attacked instantly by the venomous pox, should you breach these words.' These sentences mean that those men and women, nuns and monks, who try to practice invocation of Amitābha should abstain from wine, from fish and flesh, and from the five spices: leek, scallion, onion, garlic, ginger. Invocators who do not observe this shall be attacked by the venomous pox in this life and shall fall into the inferno. Disregarding this warning, the men and women, the nuns and monks, who practice invocation of Amitābha, drink wine and eat fish and flesh to their hearts' content. Is it not like swallowing a sword?"[90]

The tendency to ignore disciplines seemed also to be evident within the Zen sect. The *"Nomori Kagami"* (lit. "Field-watch Mirror," by Fujiwara-no-Arifusa, 1294) has the following passage rebuking the Zen sect: "By abusing the precedents of those who had attained enlightenment and by taking wine, meat, the five spices, etc., even those who have not yet attained that stage dare do the same shamelessly."[91]

It is a well-known fact that after the Meiji Restoration, practically all the sects of Buddhism broke away from the disciplines. The upshot: for the followers of the Pure Land Buddhists, it is enough to invocate Amitābha; for the followers of the Nichiren sect, to chant the title of the Lotus Sūtra; for some of the others, to chant certain sūtras and to repeat prayers (*dhāraṇīs*).

The most outstanding sample of the repudiation of the disciplines is drinking. The Indian Buddhists considered drinking a very serious religious sin. That was why "no drinking" was counted among the five disciplines and was ordained to be strictly observed not only by priests and ascetics but also by lay believers in general. In India the discipline of no drinking was well observed from the time of early Buddhism to that of the Mahāyāna Buddhism. (The late degenerate period of esoteric Buddhism was an exception.) In China also this discipline of no drinking was strictly observed. On its arrival in Japan, however, the discipline was abandoned.[92]

Hōnen, in reply to the question: "Is it a sin to drink?" answered: "In truth you ought not to drink, but drinking is after all a custom of this world."[93] Neither Shinran nor Nichiren considered drinking as necessarily evil. Nichiren preached, "Drink only with your wife, and recite *Nam-myō-hō-ren-ge-kyō* (Adoration to the Lotus Sūtra)!"[94] The Shugen sect maintained that if one inserts a slip with the following magic formula, even evil wine is transformed into good wine.

"The gods know, and
Pray gods also drink
The Pure-water wine
Of the Mimosuso River."[95]

Together with drinking, sexual relations between men and women also had their place in Buddhism in Japan. As has already been recognized in Japanese literary works, a novel such as *The Tale of Genji* (ca. 1000) describes lascivious scenes and immoral characters, considered however to be not lacking in beauty. Herein lies one of the traditions of Japanese literature, which clearly distinguishes them from the ethical views of Confucianism. Buddhism also is tinged with the same tendency. Toward the period of the degeneration of Buddhism in India, certain immoral rituals were practiced by some Buddhists, but among the Buddhists in China such a thing almost never occurred. Even esoteric Buddhism was transmitted into China in its purified form, which was then transplanted by Kōbō into Japan. The Japanese followers of the Shingon sect, which was founded by Kūkai (Kōbō Daishi, 744–835), kept their purity in their daily practice of asceticism. Toward the end of the Heian period, however, there emerged a heretical religion, in the Tachikawa group. They identified sexual intercourse with the secret meaning of becoming a Buddha alive in the human body. Such licentious secret rituals appear to be prevalent in various districts from the beginning to the middle of the Kamakura period. The decadent elements of esoteric Indian Buddhism during the era of degeneration, once almost completely purified in Chinese Buddhism, were revived once again in Japan. However limited that influence might be, such a difference in the respective characteristics of Chinese and Japanese Buddhism cannot be ignored.

A tendency similar to that of the Tachikawa sect also manifested itself in the Jōdo sect. An example of such is the so-called *Sōzoku-kaie no Ichinengi* (which assured salvation and expiation for those who observe the Doctrine of One Thought). It preaches as follows:

"What is called *ichinen* (one thought) means that two persons become united in one thought. When man and woman hold each other and both feel good, they cry out once in unison *Namu-amida-butsu;* that is exactly what the Doctrine of One Thought (*ichinengi*) means. So those who remained single, afraid that they were unable to be born into the Pure Land, sought their mates."[96]

Even Nichiren, a priest of good conduct, says: "Internal evidence reveals that the object and state of knowledge are two different things and at the same time they are one and the same thing. There are extraordinarily important Gates to the Doctrine in the meanings of the phrases: affliction is nothing but enlightenment; mundane existence is nothing but Nirvāṇa. Man and woman, in copulation, chant *Nam-myō-hō-ren-ge-kyō* (Adoration to the Lotus Sūtra)—that is exactly in line with what we call affliction as nothing but enlightenment, mundane existence as nothing but Nirvāṇa."[97] This is not what Nichiren preached in one of his books of doctrines in his serious mood, but is quoted from a passage in his letter to a certain warrior. This way of teaching, Nichiren seems to have thought, was congenial to the Japanese.

Up until now, Shōten (Gaṇeśa) and Aizen Myōō (God of Love) are widely worshipped as the objects of popular religion for the consummation of one's love. Shōten, or the God of Ecstasy, who was originally Gaṇeśa in India, was adopted and metamorphosed by the esoteric Buddhists. The images of Gaṇeśa now existent in India are by no means obscene. The religious custom of worshipping the images of the elephant-faced god and goddess in an embrace is confined perhaps to Japan and Tibet only.

It was in a similar manner that entirely different meanings were bestowed upon those phrases which originally signified the fundamental ideas of Buddhism. Monzaemon Chikamatsu, the famous playwright (1653–1724), in describing lovers on their way to committing suicide, celebrates the beauty of their last moments as follows: "Adieu to this world, adieu to the night. . . . The remaining one toll is the last sound of the bell they hear on earth; 'tranquility is comfort' is its sound."[98] "*Shinjū*" is a phenomenon peculiar to Japan and it is impossible to convey its real sentiment with such Western translations as a "lovers' double suicide" or "*Selbstmord eines Liebespaares.*" But in any case, whereas the phrase "tranquility is comfort" (*vyupaśamaḥ sukham*)[99] meant originally in both India and China the denial of worldly afflictions, it is now used in Japan for expressing the consummation of sexual love.

The various literary works of the Tokugawa period show that the words which originally stood for the sacred ideas of Buddhism came to be used cryptically to suggest scenes of lust and dissipation. Such instances of sacrilege never occurred either in India or in China. They are phenomena perhaps peculiar to Japan.

Whereas the majority of the Indians and the Chinese in general try to distinguish the world of religion from that of the lusts of the flesh, there is a latent tendency among the Japanese to identify the one with the other. In this way the *same characteristics which appeared in respect to the form of accepting Confucianism* are also said to be present in respect to that of accepting Buddhism.

Even the traditional and conservative Buddhists in India were aware of the fact that the disciplines are hard to observe strictly in their original form and that they undergo changes according to differences of time and place. "The Buddha announced to various priests, 'Although these disciplines are constituted by me, it is not necessary that you should use them all, if you find them not pure in other districts. As to disciplines that are not established by me, you should not hesitate to practice them all, if it is necessary to do so in other districts.' "[100]

In spite of these concessions made by the Buddha, the Japanese are the only Asiatic people who have forsaken almost all of the Buddhist disciplines. How should we account for this fact?

We shall later dwell upon the tendency of the Japanese to hold fast to a specific and closed social nexus. The repudiation of disciplines may seem on the surface to be incompatible with such a tendency. But these two are not necessarily in conflict. The disciplines are not always in agreement with customary morality. The eating of meat and flesh was permitted under certain circumstances by early Buddhism, whereas it was prohibited by most of Mahāyāna Buddhism. Drinking was prohibited both in Hīnayāna and Mahāyāna Buddhism. Marriage for the priest was not allowed except for the esoteric Buddhists of later periods. These are important problems from the standpoint of religion, but from the point of view of defending the interests of the closed social nexus, they do not count very much. Quite prevalent among the Japanese are the double-barreled attitudes of ignoring the disciplines on the one hand and of self-sacrificing devotion to the interests of the closed social nexus on the other. Such attitudes gave rise to their idea that the assertion of natural desires and the repudiation of the disciplines do not necessarily mean the abandonment of the moral order.

The lack of the guiding spirit is often talked about and people frequently allude to the corruption of priests. But such phenomena are more deep-rooted than the mere responsibilities of priests: they are imbedded in the traditional Japanese way of thinking.

We have reflected mainly upon the domain of religion, but similar ways of thinking seem to be prevalent in other domains also.

Emphasis on Benevolence

The tendency of the Japanese to accept the facts of life manifests itself especially in the form of the acceptance and high esteem for man's natural dispositions. Buddhist ideas are preached with frank references to matters of love, for sexual love is not considered to be incompatible with religious matters. Not only has the significance of the human body been recognized, but also the idea of taking good care of one's body has become prominent in Japanese Buddhism.[101]

"Question: The sūtra says one could not be a Bodhisattva[102] unless one serves Buddhas by burning one's own body, elbows, and fingers. What is the meaning? Answer: The burning of one's body, elbows, and fingers is metaphorically used to mean elimination of the three darknesses of the branch, the leaf, and the root. . . . If one eliminates these three darknesses, one becomes a Bodhisattva. . . . If one should try to serve the Buddhas by burning one's sensual body, would any Buddha receive it?"

Here ascetic practices actually followed among the Buddhists both in India and China were completely denied by the Japanese Buddhists.

The Japanese lay special emphasis upon the love of others. Banzan Kumazawa (1619–1691), a famous Confucianist of the Tokugawa period, calls Japan "The land of benevolence."[103] The love of others in its purified form is named "benevolence" (Sanskrit, *maitrī, karuṇā*). This idea was introduced into Japan with the advent of Buddhism, and special emphasis was laid upon it in Japanese Buddhism. Among many sects of Japanese Buddhism, the Pure Land Buddhism (Jōdo sect), a religion which typically emphasizes benevolence, enjoys great popularity. The Pure Land Buddhism preaches the benevolence of Amitābha Buddha who saves the bad man as well as the ordinary man. Most of the high priests of the sect have especially optimistic outlooks and benign attitudes.

The emphasis upon deeds of benevolence is recognizable also in other sects. The Japanese accepted the practice of the strict disciplines handed down from early Buddhism in the form of the "Ritsu sect" (Sanskrit: Vinaya sect). This 8th-century sect (one of the six Nara sects, it was introduced into Japan by Chien-chen, a Chinese missionary monk in 754) followed rather a seclusionist method of monastic rules of ascetic practice. Later, however, with its development into the Shingon-ritsu sect, a priest named Ninshō (1217–1303) launched upon such social welfare works as caring for the suffering and the sick. He dedicated his whole life to the service of others, and was even criticized by his master: "He overdid benevolence."[104] Although it was a breach of the ancient disciplines to dig ponds or wells or to give medicine and clothing to the sick or to accumulate money for them, Ninshō never let himself be deterred from doing any of these things.[105]

Needless to say, the idea of benevolence had an important significance in Chinese Buddhism. The Zen Buddhism, however, that was developed as the Chinese people's Buddhism, did not seem to emphasize the idea of benevolence too much. To confirm this, there is not a single reference made to the word "benevolence" in such well-known scriptures as *Shinjin-mei* (the Epigram of Faith), *Shōdōka* (the Songs of Enlightenment), *Sandō kai* (the Compliance with the Truth), and the *Hōkyō-zanmai* (the Precious Mirror Meditation).[106] To go back still further, nothing is said about it in what are supposed to be the teachings of Bodhidharma.

It is probably because the Chinese Zen sect, under the influence of Taoism and other traditional ideologies of China, was inclined to strict clerical seclusion and resignation, and neglected the positive approach of practicing deeds of benevolence. Such is my general impression, though a final conclusion cannot be drawn until we have made a thorough study of the general history of the Chinese Zen sect.

At the time the Zen sect was brought into Japan, however, it came to emphasize deeds of benevolence, just as the other sects in Japan did. Eisai,[107] who introduced Rinzai-zen, put the idea of benevolence first and foremost. In a reply to the question whether the Zen sect was too much obsessed by the idea of the void, he says: "To prevent by means of self-discipline evil from without and to help others with benevolence from within, this is what Zen is."[108] As for the rules for ascetics of the Zen sect, he teaches: "You should arouse the spirit of great benevolence . . . and save mankind everywhere with the pure and supreme disciplines of the Great Bodhisattva, but you ought not to seek deliverance for your own sake."[109] Soseki (Musō Kokushi), Shōsan Suzuki, Shidō Bunan, and other Zen priests represent a positive repulsion against the seclusionist and self-satisfied attitude of the traditional Zen sect. They stress, instead, the virtue of benevolence.

Dōgen (1200–1253), although he does not often use the word "benevolence" overtly, chooses for instruction the phrases "speak kindly to others" and "words of affection" from among the various Buddhist doctrines of the past. "Speaking words of affection means to generate a heart of benevolence and bestow upon others the language of affection, whenever one sees them. To speak with the heart, looking at mankind with benevolence as though they were your own children, is to utter words of affection. The virtuous should be praised, the virtueless pitied. To cause the enemy to surrender, or to make the wise yield, words of affection are most fundamental. To hear words of affection in one's presence pleases and brightens one's countenance and warms one's heart. To hear words of affection said in one's absence goes home to one's heart and soul. You should learn to know that words of affection are powerful enough to set the river on fire."[110]

In addition, he puts emphasis upon the virtues of altruism and cooperation beneath which flows the pure current of affection. The spirit of benevolence was not only preached by the Buddhists, but it also made its way into Shintoism and was tied up with one of the three divine symbols of the Japanese Imperial family. It was also popularized among the general public and came to be regarded as one of the principal virtues of the *samurai*.[111] The love of others by no means comes out of self-complacency. On the contrary, it goes with a humble reflection that I, as well as others, am an ordinary man. This had already been stressed by Prince Shōtoku at the beginning of the introduction of Buddhism into Japan.

"Forget resentment, forsake anger, do not become angry just because someone opposes you. Everyone has a mind, every mind comes to a decision, and decisions will not always be alike. If he is right, you are wrong; if you are not quite a saint, he is not quite an idiot. Both disputants are men of ordinary mind; who is decisively capable of judging an argument between them? If both are wise men or both foolish men their argument is probably a vicious circle. For this reason, if your opponent grows angry, you had better be all the more cautious lest you too should be in error. Although you might think you are quite right, it is wiser to comply with the other man."[112]

Out of this attitude emerged the spirit of tolerance, which will be discussed in the next section.

A debate once arose whether or not this tendency to benevolence is inherent in the Japanese people or came afterwards as a famous Buddhist scholar had indicated that there is no god of love in Shintoism. His criticism created a sensation among the Shintoists. They presented some counter-evidence, which seemed far from convincing. A general impression is that the spirit of benevolence was introduced into Japan probably with the advent of Buddhism and exerted a renovating influence upon the mental attitude of the Japanese. And without further speculation it may be asserted that there exists a certain element of humanism in the thinking of the common man in Japan.

The love of human beings seems to be closely tied up with the love of the beauty of nature, which is as old as humanity itself.

The Spirit of Tolerance

The Japanese are said to be distinguished for their spirit of tolerance since ancient times. Although there must have been instances of interracial conflicts in prehistoric Japan, there exists no archeological evidence that there were any very violent armed conflicts. According to the classical records also, the Japanese generally treated conquered peoples tolerantly. There are many tales of war, but there is no evidence that conquered peoples were made into slaves *in toto*. Even prisoners were not treated as slaves in the Western sense of the word. Although there remains some doubt as to whether or not there existed a slave-economy in ancient Japan, the percentage of slave-servants was very small in the whole population. It may be safely concluded, therefore, that slave labor was never used on a large scale.

Such a social condition gives rise to the tendency to stress harmony among the members of a society rather than dominance based on power. This is not to deny entirely the presence of the power relationship in Japanese society since ancient times. The social restrictions and pressures upon the individual might have been indeed stronger in Japan than in many other countries. Nevertheless in the consciousness of each individual Japanese, the spirit of conciliation and tolerance is pre-eminent.

Ancient Japanese society had a system of government by religious ritual in which the sense of harmony of the community pervaded the whole climate of social consciousness. Whereas Jehovah is the God of Jealousy, of Revenge, and of Justice, as well as of Mercy and Compassion, it is noteworthy that among the gods and goddesses worshipped in the ancient Japanese festivities, harmony and love pervade the atmosphere. The gods and goddesses called one another their "loving" ones. They are said to have "got drunk with wine and fallen asleep," or "played together for eight days and for eight nights."

The spirit of tolerance of the Japanese made it impossible to cultivate deep hatred even toward sinners. In Japan there existed hardly any cruel punishments. Since crucifixion appeared for the first time in Japanese history during the Sengoku period or Age of Civil Wars, it was presumably started after the advent of Christianity and suggested by it. Burning at the stake seems to have been practiced during the reign of Emperor Yūryaku (457–479), but it disappeared afterwards, to be revived occasionally during the modern period.[113] In the medieval West, condemnation of heretics to burning at the stake was sanctioned by church authorities. This never happened in Japan. During the Heian period (794–1185), capital punishment was not practiced for more than three hundred years until the War of Hōgen (1156) took place.[114] Although this may be attributed to the influence of Buddhism, there has hardly been any period in any other country marked by the absence of the death penalty.

For the Japanese, full of the spirit of tolerance, *eternal damnation* is absolutely inconceivable. A Catholic priest, who forsook Christianity under the persecution of the Tokugawa Government, condemned the idea of eternal damnation preached in Christianity. He said, regarding reward and punishment in the other world, if God be the Lord of Benevolence, he ought to condemn Himself rather than condemn and punish His creatures for their sins. Among the doctrines of Christianity the idea of eternal damnation was especially hard for the Japanese to comprehend. M. Anezaki commenting on this point, says that this is the outstanding line of demarcation between Christianity and Buddhism.[115] This also reveals one of the characteristic ideas long held by the Japanese.

The idea of "being beyond deliverance forever" was also hard for the Japanese to comprehend. The Hossō sect, a school of Buddhist Idealism, advocates "the difference of five predispositions." Among men there are five different types of disposition, one predisposed to become a Bodhisattva, one to become *Enkaku* (*pratyekabuddha,* one who attains self-complacent enlightenment), one to become *Shōmon* (*śrāvaka,* an ascetic of Hīnayāna Buddhism), one who is not predisposed, and one who is beyond deliverance. This idea of discriminating predispositions to salvation, like the idea of eternal damnation, was not generally accepted by the Japanese Buddhists. Generally accepted, instead, was the view, "All men are predisposed to become Buddhas."

A question may be raised here as follows. Is not the spirit of tolerance prominent among the Japanese due to the influence of Buddhism rather than an intrinsic Japanese characteristic? Before the advent of Buddhism the Japanese also resorted to atrocities. Were not Emperors Buretsu (499–506) and Yūryaku violent and ruthless? The reason why the death penalty was abandoned during the Heian period (794–1185) was that the ideal of Buddhism was realized in politics. Even in present-day Japan, statistics have proved beyond question that in the districts where *Haibutsu Kishaku* (the abolition of Buddhism by violence immediately after the Meiji Restoration) was enforced, cases of the murder of one's close relatives are high in number, whereas such cases are relatively few where Buddhism is strongly supported. Conversely, however, it is believed that because the Japanese were inherently tolerant and conciliatory, the infiltration of Buddhism into peoples' lives was rapid. It is often pointed out by cultural historians that the Chinese are no less than other people inclined to ruthlessness and cruelty, in spite of the fact that the Buddhist influence had a longer history in China than in Japan. In Tibet, despite its having been the country of Lamaism flying the banner of Buddhism, the severest of punishments were still in use.[116] Thus I am inclined to believe that the Japanese had originally possessed the spirit of tolerance and forgiveness to some extent, which was extremely strengthened by the introduction of Buddhism, and was again weakened in recent years by the aggrandizement of the secular power on the one hand and by the decline of faith in Buddhism on the other.

The fact that the Japanese manifest more of the spirit of tolerance and conciliation than the tendency to develop an intense hatred of sins also transformed Pure Land Buddhism. According to his eighteenth vow Amitābha Buddha will save the whole of mankind out of his great benevolence, excepting only "those who committed the five great sins and those who condemned the Right Law (=Buddhism)." Zendō (*Shan-t'ao*, 613–681) of China interpreted the sentence as meaning that even great sinners, under the condition that they be converted, could be reborn into the Pure Land. Introduced into Japan, these exceptions were later considered as problematic, and came to be completely ignored by Saint Hōnen (1133–1212). "This (salvation) includes all that are embraced in the great benevolence and the real vow of Amitābha, *not excluding even the ten evils and five great sins*, and those who excel in practices other than that of invocation of Amitābha are also included. Its meaning is to believe in what is revealed in the invocation of Amitābha once and also ten times."[117] "You should believe that even those who have committed the ten evils and the five heinous sins are eligible for rebirth in the Pure Land, and yet you should shrink from the slightest of all the sins."[118] As far as the surface meaning of the sentence is concerned, Hōnen is diametrically opposed to the Indian theologians who compiled the *Dai-mu-ryō-ju-kyō* (*Sukhāvatī-vyūha-sūtra*). From Hōnen's approach to the problem of redemption there evolved the so-called "view of the eligibility of evil persons for salvation" (the view that the evil are rightfully eligible for salvation by Amitābha Buddha). This view may not be what Shinran (Hōnen's disciple, 1173–1262) really meant, but the fact that such a view was generally considered to be the fundamental doctrine of the (Kōdo) Shin sect cannot be denied.

Such a way of thinking amounts to this: however evil one may be, one is always saved, provided that one is dead. The dead are called "Buddhas" by the Japanese. The dead, however heinous their earthly crimes, are completely free from all responsibility for them, and the most wicked are sometimes considered to be extraordinary spiritual entities. This gives rise to the curious result that the spirits of murderers and burglars are enshrined, and their graveyards are crowded with worshippers.

What are the rational bases for such a spirit of tolerance and conciliation? The tendency to recognize absolute significance in everything phenomenal leads to the acceptance of the justification of any view held in the mundane world, and ends up with the adaptability of any view with the spirit of tolerance and conciliation.[119]

Such a way of thinking appeared from the earliest days of the introduction of Buddhism into this country. According to Prince Shōtoku (ca. 600), the Hokke or Lotus Sūtra (*Saddharmapuṇḍarīka-sūtra*), supposed to contain the ultimate essence of Buddhism, preaches the doctrine of the One Great Vehicle and advocates the theory "that any one of myriad good acts leads to one thing, the attainment of Enlightenment."[120] According to the prince, there is no innate difference between the saint and the most stupid.[121] Everyone is primarily and equally a child of the Buddha. Prince

Shōtoku regarded secular moral teachings as the elementary gate through which to enter Buddhism. He uses the expressions "heretical doctrine" and "pagan religion" but those expressions are borrowed rather from the traditional Indian terminology. He does not mean by them the doctrines of Lao-tzŭ and Chuang-tzŭ or Confucianism.[122] His interpretation of Buddhism is characterized by its all-inclusive nature. Only through taking into consideration his philosophical background, is one able to understand the moral idea of the prince when he says, "Harmony is to be honored." [123] It was this spirit that made possible the emergence of Japan as a unified cultural state.

Prince Shōtoku's philosophical standpoint is represented by the expressions, "The One Great Vehicle" and "The Pure Great Vehicle," which are supposed to have originated in the Hokke Sūtra. Ever since Saichō (Dengyō Daishi) introduced the Tendai sect in 827 based upon the Hokke Sūtra, this Lotus Sūtra has come to constitute the backbone of Japanese Buddhism. Nichiren said: "Japan is single-heartedly the country of the Hokke Sūtra," and "For more than four hundred years since Emperor Kanmu, all the people of Japan have been single-heartedly devoted to the Hokke Sūtra."[124] These words of Nichiren are not necessarily to be regarded as a self-centered interpretation. Considering that the Pure Land Buddhism (Jōdo sect) and the Zen sect even, not to mention the Nichiren sect, are evidently under the influence of the Tendai doctrine, there is much truth in these assertions of Nichiren. Among the poems composed by various emperors on Buddhism, the subject matter is overwhelmingly concerned with the doctrines of the Hokke Sūtra. The thought-tendency characteristic of the Hokke Sūtra which tried to accept the principle of all the practices of Buddhism led to an extremely tolerant and conciliatory attitude to various ideas.

Toward the end of the Heian period, there were those among ordinary men who prayed for rebirth into the Pure Land on the sole merit of their observance of the Hokke Sūtra. "All those who act in accordance with the *Hokke*, covering themselves with the armour of forbearance and not clinging to the dew-like life of mundane existence, shall climb upon the lotus dais."[125] The idea of climbing upon the lotus dais is not to be found in the Hokke Sūtra itself. It shows rather the syncretic character of the religious faith of the period.

Kōben (1173–1232) of the Kegon sect put together various faiths of both exoteric and esoteric Buddhism. There is no unity, no central focus in his religion, whose content is mostly eclectic. "This high priest never limited himself to the teaching of one saint, but practiced in turn the religions of one saint after another." What was the reason for this? According to his own interpretation, "Each attains well-rounded enlightenment according to his customary practice. Since there is not just one customary practice (but many), well-rounded enlightenment also cannot be just one."[126] He recognized the justification of multiple religious faiths.

Owing to this spirit of tolerance and conciliation, the development of a single continuum of various sects was possible within Japanese Buddhism. In India today, there is no Buddhist tradition extant. In China uniformity was established in Buddhism, where the Zen sect, fused with the Pure Land Buddhism, was the only remaining religious sect, while the traditions of all the rest of the sects almost went out of existence. In Japan, by contrast, there still exist many traditional sects which can no longer be found in China or in India.

In spite of the highly sectarian and factional tendency of the various religious sects to keep their traditional differences intact, contempt of other sects was mutually prohibited by Japanese Buddhists. Even Rennyo (1415–1499) of the Jōdo sect, a school supposed to be inclined toward monotheism and exclusionism, warns: "You ought not make light of shrines," or "You ought not slander other sects and other teachings."[127] Shōsan Suzuki, a Zen priest, ordains: "In this monastery the right and wrong of the world or the relative merits of other sects ought not to be talked about."[128] Jiun admonishes his disciples: "The right and wrong or the high and low of the teachings of other sects should not be discussed."[129]

Such an attitude of tolerance might have been handed down from early Buddhism. It is noteworthy that, despite the sectarian and factional tendency of the Japanese, they did not want to dispute with their opponents. Realistically speaking, the accommodation of Shintoism and Buddhism might have very well been an expedient measure taken in order to avoid possible friction between the traditional religion and the incoming Buddhism, which came to be accepted as a national religion. It may also be said that it was political consideration that made Hōnen (1133–1212) and Rennyo (1415–1499) warn against rejecting sects other than their own. As far as subjective consciousness in each man is concerned, however, it is right to assert that the spirit of tolerance was the most influential factor. The most easily thought of instance of intolerance in Japan in the past is the Nichiren sect. But even this sect embraces many non-Buddhistic gods of India and of Japan and has adopted some elements of Shintoism and of popular faiths. The Jōdo sect does appear to concentrate on pure faith in Amitābha, prohibiting religious practices other than the invocation of Amitābha. Nevertheless, this sect commends the worship of such a human being as the chief abbot and other fetishistic practices.

An attitude of tolerance determined the all-inclusive and conciliatory nature of Japanese Buddhism. The ascendency of Buddhism in Japan in the course of more than ten centuries was entirely different from that of

Christianity in the West. Buddhism tolerated various primitive faiths native to Japan, but the notion of pure paganism was clearly absent in Japanese Buddhism. The gods in the native Japanese popular religion, who would have been considered pagan from the standpoint of Buddhism, were reconciled with Buddhism as "temporary manifestations" (incarnations) of the Buddha. Along this line of thought a theory, called *Honji-Suijaku-setsu,* was advanced in which the Shintoist gods were maintained as temporary incarnations of the Buddhas. Emperor Yōmei is said "to have believed in Buddhism and at the same time worshipped gods of Shintoism."[130] Precisely what Shintoism means in the above quotation needs to be clarified, since in the Nara period (710–784) the idea of the accommodation of Shintoism and Buddhism had already come to the fore. According to this school of thought, god rejoices in the Law of the Buddha and defends Buddhism, but since god is an entity in the mundane world just as other human beings are and is not free from affliction, he also seeks salvation. The Nara period saw many a shrine-temple built. The Imperial message of 767 A.D. stated that the auspicious signs appeared, thanks to the Buddhas, to the Japanese gods and goddesses of heaven and earth, and to the spirits of the various emperors.

Thereafter, during the Heian period (794–1192 A.D.), there were few shrines that did not have shrine-temples built in their confines, where Buddhist priests performed the morning and evening practices of reciting sūtras, and served shrine gods and goddesses, together with Shintoist priests. The structure of the shrines was modelled after that of Buddhist temples. At the Iwashimizu-Hachiman Shrine, whose construction was inaugurated by the priest Gyōkyō, the religious service was performed after the fashion of the Buddhist mass, and almost all the officials there in service were Buddhist priests. Simple offerings were offered, surplices and Buddhist utensils were dedicated, and the whole ritual of the shrine was very much akin to that of a temple. Later on the shrines of Gion, Kitano, and Kumano followed suit. The institution of the shrine-temple was thereby established. Its gods were named "the gods of abstinence."

Deep-rooted, however, was the belief among the common men in the native gods and goddesses, to which Buddhists had to reconcile their own ideas. The status of gods and goddesses was then enhanced to such an extent that they were entitled Bodhisattvas, and the recitation of Buddhist sūtras was performed in front of their altars. The gods and goddesses were thus exalted from the status of mankind astray to that of persons on their way toward enlightenment, or even to the status of those who save mankind. In the ninth century, priests like Saichō and Kūkai sought access to the shrines and respected them, and at the same time they tried to make their own sects prosperous by utilizing the influence of the shrine. When in 827 Saichō pioneered a Tendai sect monastery on the divine mountain of Hiei in Ōmi, near Kyoto, where the spirit of Ōyamagui-no-Mikoto had rested for ages, to construct the Enryaku temple, he enshrined therein the god of Ōmiwa, whom he named the god of Ōhiei and entitled him Sannō (the Mountain-God). Jikaku (784–864), known also as Ennin, founded the Akayama-Myōjin Shrine. Kūkai, who constructed the Kongōbu Temple at the divine place of the Nifutsu-shime Shrine, according to an old folk tale, prayed for the assistance of the deity Nifu-Myōjin in founding a Shingon sect monastery on Mt. Kōya.[131] He is also said to have made the Inari Shrine into the guardian god of the Tō Temple. These stories tell of ancient divine areas being turned into the sacred regions of Buddhism and include newly fabricated interpretations of the origins of the shrines in relation to Buddhism. The motivation for these peculiar endeavors for reconciliation, as I take it, was the building up of the security of the confines and estates of the Buddhist temple through clever manipulation of the popular faith in native gods and goddesses. During the years of Bunji (1185–1189), Chōgen (Shunjōbō) thought it an effective gesture to confine himself in the Ise Shrine and thus to appeal to the people's religious sentiments, for the realization of his great vow to solicit contributions for the reconstruction of the Tōdaiji Temple.[132]

The idea that the Japanese native gods are the temporary manifestations of Buddhas first appeared in the classical writings of the years of Kankō (1004–1012) in the middle of the Late Heian period. After the reign of Emperor Go-Sanjō (1068–1072) a question was raised as to the fundamental basis of the manifestations of those native gods and goddesses. During the period of the Civil Wars between the Genji and Heike Clans, each god or goddess was gradually allotted his or her own Buddha, whose incarnation he or she was supposed to be, until at last during the Shōkyū years (1219–1222), the idea was established that the god and the Buddha were identical in the body. "There is no difference between what is called a Buddha and what is called a god."[133] Shōgun Ashikaga Takauji (1305–1350), in his letter expressing a vow dedicated to the Shrine of Gion, says: "Although a Buddha and a god are said to be different in the body, they are the inside and outside of the selfsame thing."[134] The doctrinal organization of the theory that gods and goddesses are the temporary manifestations of Buddhas or Bodhisattvas was completed during the Kamakura period (1185–1333) and its ideological gist was kept intact up to the Meiji Restoration in 1868.

The Buddhists of the Medieval period genuinely respected Shintoist scriptures, which they studied with sincerity and piety. Almost all the representative Shintoist scriptures extant today, such as *Kojiki, Nihon-*

shoki, Kogo Shūi, and others were copied by medieval Buddhist priests and thus transmitted to posterity.[135]

What is the way of thinking that made such an accommodation of Buddhism and Shintoism possible? The influence of the traditional character of Buddhism cannot be denied, and it is particularly important to point out the influence of the idea of the One Vehicle manifested in the Hokke Sūtra. The Imperial Rescript of November of the year 836 A.D. says: "There is nothing superior to the One Vehicle to defend Shintoism."[136] It goes without saying that Nichiren, who expressed his absolute allegiance to the Hokke Sūtra, also showed his genuine loyalty to the Japanese gods and goddesses. Even the Jōdo followers, who were originally opposed to the gods and goddesses of Shintoism, tempered their oppositions in a more conciliatory attitude after Zonkaku (1290–1373). The theoretical basis for such a *rapprochement* was provided not by the triple-sūtras of the Pure Land Buddhism but by the Tendai doctrine based upon the Hokke Sūtra.

The Japanese native gods, exalted as they were as natural deities, kept their own distinctive existence intact. In this respect they differ completely from the occidental counterpart in the ancient German gods, vestiges of which remain in the form of the Christmas festivity (tree, Santa Claus, etc.) within Christianity. The Japanese never considered it necessary to repudiate their religious faith in the native gods in order to become devoted followers of Buddhism. In this manner they brought about the conception of "God-Buddhas." It is generally noticed even today that the ardent Buddhist is at the same time a pious worshipper of Shintoist gods. The majority of the Japanese pray before the shrine and at the same time pay homage to the temple, without being conscious of any contradiction.

The same relationship as exists in the mind of the Japanese between Shintoism and Buddhism also holds for the relationship between Buddhism and Confucianism. When the continental civilization was transplanted to Japan, Buddhism and Confucianism were simultaneously introduced, without any theoretical conflicts taking place in the minds of the Japanese or any ideological warfare occurring on Japanese soil. On the contrary, Okura Yamanoue (d. 733), a famous poet, took the conciliatory standpoint that despite the difference existing between Buddhism and Confucianism, they amount to the same thing: "Although their ways of guiding are two, both lead up to the one and only one attainment of enlightenment."[137]

After the dawn of the Modern era, Confucianism came to flourish with the political backing of the ruling class, and from then on a doctrine was widely advocated to assert the unity of the three religions, i.e. Shintoism, Confucianism, and Buddhism.

During the Tokugawa period (1600–1867), *Kanazōshi* (Tales in Easy

Japanese, or popular novels written in the *Kana* characters) and other similar writings were extremely popular among the common folk. Most of them were written from the Buddhist point of view, with some exceptions written from the Confucian standpoint. The most famous of those were *The Tale of Kiyomizu, The Tale of Kiyomizu Continued, The Tale of Gion, The Tale of Daibutsu,* and others, all of which were written mainly from the viewpoint of the unity of the three religions. This was in spite of the fact that the Shintoist and Buddhist priests were deeply involved in sectarian and factional conflicts. The common man reconciled and fused those religions on whose differences the priests insisted. Fujii Otoo comments as follows: "What a close union Confucianism and Buddhism came to have in the *Kanazōshi* (Tales in Easy Japanese)! Among the scholars conflicts and controversies multiplied in advocating their respective doctrines, but among common men they were made to fuse and compromise. The Japanese are by nature inclined to *rapprochement* without threshing out an issue. No one has yet taken up a noteworthy controversy between Confucianism and Buddhism, but, instead, there are already many who advocate the unity of the three religions." [138] Such a theoretical standpoint was represented in its most consistent form in the school of "Learning of the Mind" (*Sekimon Shingaku*) which exerted the greatest influence upon the comman man. Scholars like Toan Tejima, Baigan Ishida (1685–1744), Dōni Nakazawa (1735–1803), Kyūō Shibata (1783–1839) belonged to this school, from whose standpoint they were cynical about the conflicts of various sects.

Such a conciliatory attitude seems ultimately to form part of Japan's cultural heritage. When the Christian civilization penetrated into Japanese society after the Meiji Restoration, those who welcomed it were not necessarily going to become Christians. For most people in Japan there was nothing about Christianity that was incompatible with their traditional religion. That was the reason, it appears, why the Christian culture became considerably widespread despite the extremely small minority converted to the Christian religion.

Perhaps social scientists will finally furnish us with statistical verification of my suggestion that the Japanese are a tolerant people. My own impression comes, as I have shown, from the study of historical documents and personal observation.

Thanks to the spirit of tolerance, a massacre of heathens never took place in Japan. In this respect, the situation differs vastly in Japan from that of the West. As far as religion is concerned the idea of "harmony" is a foremost quality in this country's cultural history. Some apparently exceptional cases have occurred: one being an overall and thoroughgoing persecution of Christians, the second being the persecution of local Jōdo-Shin believers, and the third being a severe suppression of Nichiren and the Non-Receiving-and-Non-Giving sect[139] (one of the Nichiren sects, which has refused to receive alms from or give alms to those other than the believers of the Hokke Sūtra). These, however, were far from being religious persecutions in the Western sense of the word. These sects were suppressed and persecuted simply because the ruling class feared the subversion that might be worked by these sects upon a certain human nexus, i.e., the feudal social order maintained by the ruling class. A mere difference of religious faith was generally a matter of no consequence for the Japanese unless it was considered to be damaging to the established order of the social nexus, whereas in the West a religious difference in itself would give rise to a conflict between opposing parties.

A new problem may be introduced here. If any of the different thoughts and religions can claim its own *raison d'être,* then how can one determine their relative value, and what is the criterion of evaluation?

As has already been pointed out, the inclination to regard as absolute a limited specific human nexus naturally brings about a tendency to disregard any allegedly universal law of humanity that every man ought to observe at any place at any time. Instead, the standard of the evaluation of good and evil is identified here with the consideration of the appropriateness or inappropriateness of conduct judged solely by reference to the particular human nexus to which one happens to belong.

That Japan is the supreme country of all the countries of the world and that to defend such a country is of absolute religious significance was maintained particularly by the Shintoist thinkers: "Our Great Japan is the country of gods. Our country is founded by a heavenly ancestry; the reign of our country is transmitted forever by the Sun Goddess. Such things have happened to this country of ours that nothing is comparable to them in other countries. That is why this country is called the country of the gods."[140] These words were taken as a motto up to quite recently. According to Kanetomo Urabe (1435–1511), who advocated Shintoist Monism, "Shintoism is the root of all the teachings. Those two doctrines (Confucianism and Buddhism) are differentiations of Shintoism."[141] It goes without saying that the movements of the Shintoists and the scholars of the Japanese classical literature of the Motoori and Hirata schools had much to do with propagandizing and convincing people of such chauvinistic ideas as those just mentioned. There were some, among the Shintoists and the scholars of the Japanese classical literature themselves, who expressed their opposing opinions, but such a tendency was too weak to combat the general trend of thought.

It was not that Shintoists were completely lacking in universalistic character. That Shintoism is not the way merely of Japan but that of all nations is maintained mainly by sectarian Shintoists. The Kurozumu sect and the Misogi sect emphasize that "the four seas are brothers"; the founder of the Misogi sect teaches, "You should regard people of the world as your own parents and children"; the founder of the Revisionist sect (Kunimitsu Nitta) advocates, "You should expand this sect to all nations," and "You should treat all nations as one family and one body." The Konkō sect, in particular, worships as its principal god "the Golden God of the Universe," which has never appeared in the classics of our country, and which leads us to think that the Konkō sect itself is a world religion. "Under heaven there are no outsiders" is advocated by the founder of the Konkō sect. Shrine Shintoism in general, however, has not been inclined to universalism, except for those cases where the Buddhist idea of benevolence was adopted.[142]

What then was the attitude of the Japanese in accepting the universalistic doctrines of foreign countries? The attitude receptive to a foreign religious thought as universal and international and the attitude of looking up to Japan as absolute are by no means compatible. When the former attitude is accepted, the latter is rejected. In fact, however, the tendency to think in conformity with the limited human nexus of Japan seems to be the most prevalent.

This ambivalence and conflict of universalism and nationalism appeared in the pattern of the acceptance of Buddhism. At first Buddhism was accepted, by Prince Shōtoku and a group of bureaucrats under his control, as a universal teaching that everyone should follow. Buddhism was estimated thereby as "the terminating end of four lives (four kinds of all living creatures) and the ultimate religion of all nations," and among the Three Treasures of the Buddha, the Law, and the Brotherhood (*saṅgha*), the Law or the religious doctrine was especially esteemed. They preached, in consequence, "Why should any period or any man not reverence this law?"[143] According to Prince Shōtoku, "The Law" is "the norm" of all living creatures, "the Buddha" is in fact "the Law embodied," which "being united with Reason" becomes *saṅgha*. So, according to this way of teaching, everything converges on the one fundamental principle called "the Law."[144]

Even among the various sects of Buddhism during that characteristically Japanese period of Kamakura (1185–1333), the sense of the universality of "the Law," as preached in Buddhism, was not lost. Dōgen (1200–1253), the Zen master, says: "Because there is the Way, Buddhas and their forerunners are comprehended. Without the Way there is no comprehension. Because there is the Law, things are originated. Without the Law nothing is originated."[145] Here too the Law and the Way are used interchangeably. Shinran (1173–1262) himself quotes a sentence by Nāgārjuna: "See, enter and acquire the Law, and live in the solid Law, and don't vacillate."[146] Nichiren also esteems the Hokke Sūtra as the Truth more highly than he does the Buddha. "I am asked why I should make the prayer of the Hokke Sūtra, instead of the Buddha (Shākyamuni), the principal object of worship. I answered that. . . . while the Buddha is the originated, the Hokke Sūtra is the originator. While the Buddha is the body, the Hokke Sūtra is the spirit."[147] "The Hokke Sūtra is just as superior to a Buddha as the moon to a star and as the sun to artificial light."[148]

Among the Japanese, however, there is a strong tendency to understand such a universal law only in reference to some particular or specific phase of things. Moreover, the Japanese sought a standard for the evaluation of different thoughts by laying emphasis upon historical and topographical specificity or particularity.

In Japan, the Tendai doctrine, which laid the foundation for the doctrines of other sects of Buddhism in Japan, puts emphasis upon "Things," while in China the doctrine of the same sect regards "Reason" as most important. "Things" here mean observable *specificities or particularities* limited in time and space. Shimei (Ssu-ming, 1060–1128), a Chinese Tendai scholar, preached that the first half (*Shakumon*) of the Hokke Sūtra explains the perfect Truth in conformity with the Law of Reason (the perfect Reason), while the second half (*Honmon*) of the Sūtra exposes "the perfect Truth" in accordance with phenomena (perfect Things). Even this latter truth expresses for him the eternal Buddha. In contrast, Eshin (942–1017), a Japanese Tendai scholar, while accepting this two-fold interpretation, interpreted "the perfect Reason" to mean the comprehension of the multiplicity of the phenomenal world through the indiscriminatory Truth (*Sessō Kishō*), and "the perfect Thing" to mean the revelation of the Truth through the multiplicity of phenomena.[149]

The tendency to attach more importance to things than to reason is one of the characteristics of the Japanese Zen sect, in contrast to that of China, and the teachings of the Japanese priests like Dōgen (1200–1253) and Hakuin (1685–1768) prove it.

Based upon this pluralistic way of thinking, most of the Buddhist sects in Japan teach that doctrines should always be made "apropos of the time." Especially the idea of the age of degeneration penetrated deep into the core of the doctrines of various sects, which admitted that they were in the age of degeneration and religious doctrines ought to be made suitable to it. Each of the sects ended up claiming the superiority of their respective sūtras or doctrines, as most suited to the age of corruption. This fundamental tendency is most manifest in the teachings of Nichiren, based upon the Japanese Tendai doctrine. He lays special emphasis upon the particularity and specificity of the truth of humanity. "The learning of just one word or one phrase of the Right Law, only if it should accord with the time and the propensity of the learner, would lead him to the attainment of the Way. The mastery even of a thousand scriptures and ten thousand theories, if they should not accord with the time and the propensity of the one who masters them, would lead him nowhere."[150] Nichiren's evaluation of sectarian doctrines is called "The Five Standards of Religion." It sets five standards from which to evaluate the depth or shallowness and the superiority or inferiority of all the Buddhist doctrines originated from the Buddha, these five standards being the teaching (of the sūtra), the propensity (the spiritual endowments of the learner), the time (the demands of the age), the country (where the doctrine is practiced), and the order (before and after the propagation of the doctrine, or the preceding circumstances under which the doctrines were practiced). Nichiren concluded, judging from those five standards, that the Hokke (Lotus) Sūtra was the superior one.[151] Saichō regarded the time and the country as important factors, but he did not go so far as to establish them as basic principles. It was Nichiren (1222–1282) who presented them in a clear and distinct form, and it was Nichiren who first put forth "the circumstances" before and after the propagation of the doctrine. The tendency of the Japanese Tendai sect to lay emphasis upon actuality was brought to its extremity by Nichiren, and such a method of evaluation has hardly been found either in India or in China. Herein lies a reason why Nichirenism in the past was so easily tied up with nationalism.

Such a particularistic way of thinking as discussed above seems to be a general trend during the medieval period. The *Gukanshō,* for instance, often uses the word "reason," which by no means signifies the universal reason that applies to any country of the world, but which means each of the historical manifestations of reason peculiar to Japan. The historical manifestations, where political and religious factors are closely entangled, are not analyzed from a universal standpoint, but are classified according to the particular periods of development.

This characteristic which can be found in the process of the introduction of Buddhism also applies to the influence of Chinese thought.

The doctrine of Chu-hsi (1130–1200) was said to be established by Razan Hayashi (1583–1657) as an official doctrine in Japan, but it was by no means in its original form that he introduced it. According to Chu-hsi, *Ch'i* is the material principle that originates all physical phenomena, while "Reason" (*Li*) is the metaphysical basis. According to Razan Hayashi, however, "Reason" is nothing more than *Japanese Shintoism,* which is a characteristically Japanese interpretation of the original doctrine. "The Way of Gods is nothing but Reason (*Li*). Nothing exists outside of Reason. Reason is the truth of nature." The Way of the Gods is the *Way of Emperors* handed down from the Sun Goddess. "In our country since the

Sun Goddess, one god has been succeeded by another god, the Emperor has been succeeded by another Emperor. Why should the Way and the Way of Gods be two different things? This is what is meant by saying that Reason is identical with the Spirit."[152] He shares with Shintoists the view that "this country is the Country of Gods."[153] He denies the universal law of man as man. Instead he maintains, "I have never heard that there is anything to be called a Way other than that of the lord and the father."[154]

Such a way of thinking was not confined to Razan Hayashi, an official spokesman backed up with governmental authority, but was also recognizable in Tōju Nakae (1608–1648), an early 17th-century grass-roots scholar. He stressed that Confucianism is the absolute "Way" universally applicable to the whole world, but at the same time he considered that the manifestations of the "Way" are relative to time, space, and the hierarchical status to which each man belongs.

"Since Confucianism is originally the ancient way of gods, there is no place in the world where ships and cars can reach, where human power prevails, where the heaven overhangs, where the earth covers, where the sun and the moon shine, where the dew and the frost fall, and where the high-spirited dwell, that Confucianism is not practiced. The manners and etiquette as laid down in Confucian writings cannot be observed strictly to the letter, but it depends upon the time and the place. . . ."[155]

Nakae preached that "the manners and etiquette to associate with others" should be practiced "according to the custom of the particular country and the particular place."[156] He recommended that the Japanese follow *Japanese Shintoism* in order to observe the way of their gods in accordance with a soil-rooted primordial principle.

Banzan Kumazawa (1619–1691), his disciple, believed the same way. For him there is only One Way, namely the way of the gods of heaven and earth, the manifestations of which differ according to different countries. An unbroken line of Emperors in Japan and revolutionary changes of dynasties in China are not the reflections of differences in the way but in the national character. "In Japan naturally there are excellences peculiar to Japan."[157]

Confucian scholar that he was, he attached great importance to Shintoism as the Way of Japan. "The Way of Gods of the heaven and the earth is called the great way. In Japan there exists the way of gods in accordance with our climate." "The Japanese Way of Gods in accordance with our climate cannot be loaned to, nor borrowed from, China or barbarians."[158]

These ways of thinking of the Confucian scholars run parallel to those of Japanese Buddhists in their recognition of Japanese Shintoism. The only difference between them consists in the fact that Confucian scholars are not so strongly conscious of the historical peculiarity of the doctrine, (e.g., the idea of regarding the present period as the age of degeneration), as Buddhists are, although they make much of the topographical peculiarities of the doctrine. (This by no means applies to all the Confucianists.) Shundai Dazai's attitude of contempt toward Shintoism as a form of paganism is similar to the attitudes of the people of other races when a universal religion is introduced. So Dazai's attitude cannot be called characteristically Japanese. But the ways of thinking of the other scholars mentioned above may be rightly said to be uniquely Japanese. The tendency of Japanese Buddhism to put "Things" before "Reason," as already discussed, also appears in the formation of late Japanese Confucianism. Sorai Ogyū (1666–1728) emphasized facts rather than theories, and stressed the superiority of the former to the latter.[159]

If both Buddhists and Confucianists emphasize that in Japan there ought to be a way appropriate to Japan, and if they push that theory to its logical conclusion, will it not become meaningless for them to remain Buddhists or Confucianists? It amounts to believing that for the Japanese it is enough to observe the *Way of Japan,* even when the equally valid claims of both Confucianism and Buddhism for guiding man to the right conduct are to be taken for granted. Such a logic was presented by Masamichi Imbe, a Shintoist. He never rejects Buddhism or Confucianism as flatly as Norinaga Motoori or Atsutane Hirata does. On the contrary, he recognizes the *raison d'être* of Confucianism and Buddhism by saying that they are "both more or less different but good ways." As for Shintoism he maintains, "Shintoism is the Right Way of this country. It respects the great value of order and honors clear reason, and does not repudiate any principles as principles and never ceases to move."[160] That is to say, Shintoism, since it is the *Way of Japan,* should be relied upon. The scholars of Japanese classical literature in the Tokugawa period go so far as to reject entirely the values of Confucianism and Buddhism. Mabuchi Kamo (1697–1769) maintains that Confucianism is of no use for Japan by saying, "While the teachings of Confucius have never been put into practical use even in China, where the foundations of Confucianist teachings were laid, of what use could it be, brought to Japan?"[161] Such a view was later pushed to its extreme by the scholars of Japanese classical literature.

Those scholars who claimed to be independent of Buddhism, Confucianism, or Shintoism also followed suit. For instance, Nakamoto Tominaga (1715–1746), an Ōsaka merchant, scholar, and freethinker, advocated "the true Way" or "the Way of Ways" which he defined as "the Way that should be practiced in present-day Japan."[162] In order for the "true Way" to be realized, it should be limited both in time, i.e., "the present day," and in space, i.e., "Japan." Thus his theory evidently claims that "the Way" as the principle of human existence manifests itself in the form inevitably determined historically and geographically. He denounces as "the ways against the true Way"[163] the Shintoism advocated by his contemporary scholars of Japanese classical literature, the Confucianism taught by the Confucianists, and the Buddhism preached by the Buddhists, because, he says, all of them took no notice of the historical and topographical peculiarities of human existence.

We are now led to conclude that it was a distinctive characteristic of many Japanese scholars to use the idea of "the historically determined present-day Japan" as the measuring rod for evaluating all systems of thought.[164] This nationalistic attitude cannot be attributed to most scholars either in India or in China.

When such a way of thinking is pushed to its extreme, it ends up with its emphasis on the limited human nexus, in ethno-centricism or superna-tionalism, and with its emphasis upon the specificity of the time, in oppor-tunism, which leads to compromise in a given particular situation. It is easily turned into a tendency to neglect the universal law that ought to be observed by mankind everywhere. Any system of thought inclined to disregard the universal cannot attain a permanent place among the systems of thought of mankind. It cannot find a sympathizer among other nations. It is extremely difficult to find sincere friends among other nations so long as Japanese thought emphasizes racialism or nationalism as a basis of superiority. For that reason in the field of philosophic thought, with the exception of the development of Zen, Japan has had very little to offer to the culture of the world. In the field of art, especially of fine arts, however, Japan has contributed a great deal to the world. Take, for instance, the impressive and enduring influence that the Japanese fine arts have exerted upon those of the West.

An objection may be raised as follows. Since works of art are appreci-ated through intuition, their merits can be easily recognized by other nations, but where language is the medium of communication, however, it is difficult for one nation to understand the philosophical thought of the other. Such an objection does not hold. In spite of the fact that a consider-able number of works of Japanese thought have already been translated and contemporary Japanese philosophy has partly been introduced to for-eign countries, in some cases by the Japanese government and in some cases by government-sponsored organizations, they have exerted very little influence upon the thought of other countries. The militant attitude on the part of Japan was repulsed by other nations. In the cases of traditional Indian or Chinese philosophical thought, by contrast, no comparable efforts for introducing them abroad by the respective governments have been exerted. Nevertheless, their influence upon the thoughts of other nations is pre-eminent. The spread of Buddhism over the Eastern countries was not endorsed by any political or military force. The same is true with the propagation of Indian religions in the South Sea countries. Confucianism was not imposed upon Japan by the Chinese government, but it was voluntarily accepted by the Japanese people. The influence of Chinese thought upon the Western trends of thought of the modern Enlightenment and the contribution of Indian ideas to modern Romantic philosophy and literature have left traces too deep to be wiped out. But has Japan contributed anything of that sort to the world?

Japan failed, even before the Pacific War, in her effort to propagate Shintoism, Japan's own religion, among Asiatic countries. The cause of the failure is quite clear: since Shintoism is the tribal religion of the Japanese, it is an impossible enterprise from the very beginning to try to substitute it for the tribal religions of other peoples. The various sects of Japanese Buddhism which also sent their missionaries to other Asiatic countries were also bound to fail. Why? It was not Buddhism itself, which originally is a universal religion, but the "Japanized" Buddhism that was unanimously rejected by the people of other Asiatic countries.

The Japanese inclination to lay too much emphasis upon particular facts or specific phases amounts to the anti-intellectual standpoint of no theory or anti-theory. It ends up with the contempt of rational thinking and the worship of uncontrolled intuitionism and activism. Herein lies the intellectual cause of the failure of Japan in the past, and the danger still lies in this direction today. In order not to repeat the same failure, we ought from now on to learn to seek universal "reason" through specific "facts."

Cultural Multiplicity (Consisting of Several Strata Still Preserved) and Weakness of the Spirit of Criticism

The Japanese, owing to the tolerant and more open side of their nature, assimilated the heterogeneous cultures of foreign countries without much repercussion. They try to recognize the value of each of these different cultural elements, and at the same time they endeavor to preserve the values inherited from their own past. They seek national unity while permitting the co-existence of heterogeneous elements.

This tendency of modern Japan may be found in various fields of culture.

First, let us take up language, which is a common denominator in any nationality group. There are in Japanese a great many words of foreign origin. All the important concepts are expressed in Chinese characters. A considerable number of Western words have recently been introduced. Even the numerals, which are not easily changed in other languages, were adopted from the Chinese. Those words adopted from foreign languages are sometimes made to stand for different meanings, but on the whole the original meanings are retained. There are often cases where the archaic Japanese words are preserved in speech but they are represented by Chinese characters in writing. The absorption of so many foreign words into the system of a native language, as the Japanese have done, is quite rare among the languages of civilized nations.

The words adopted from Chinese or Western languages are on the whole nouns. By suffixing postpositions to these nouns, something similar to case-declension is effected, and also the nouns are turned into adverbs or adjectives. By adding "*su*"[165] to nouns, they are turned into verbs. These operations prove that foreign words are adopted essentially as nouns and are used as the materials of language as such. The main features of the Japanese language have undergone no considerable change, and the old form, in its syntax, has been faithfully preserved.

That is exactly the attitude of the Japanese in accepting foreign cultures. They are extremely sensitive to adopting and absorbing foreign cultures. But, in fact, a foreign culture is adopted as a constituent element of the Japanese culture. Whatever the intention and outcry of the men in charge of its adoption might be, as a social and cultural fact, foreign culture is accepted insofar as its value is recognized as a helpful means to Japan's progress. Such an attitude in the past gave rise to the conception of "the Japanese spirit and Chinese learning." Such a traditional standpoint of the Japanese is the key to understanding their cultural multiplicity.

There are various aspects of cultural multiplicity. In the field of politics in Japan, no radical revolution has really taken place since ancient times. The ruling class of one period does not end up with a complete decline. The ruling class of the past, a class whose political hegemony has already been lost, may still command the respect of the people as the preserver of the ancient cultural tradition and spiritual authority. Such a political phenomenon has never been found either in India, China, or Tibet. This tendency appears to be found somewhat among the Ural-Altaic peoples, but Japan is the most outstanding case.[166]

Multiplicity is also found in the mode of living of the Japanese, in their clothing, eating, and dwellings. In the field of arts also, unity is somewhat maintained by the juxtaposition of conflicting elements old and new. In the field of religion, different modes of belief, conflicting with one another in their respective peculiarities, not only coexist in the community, but operate at the same time within the life of the *selfsame individual person.*

It must indeed be a practical merit of the Japanese to be tolerant of individual differences and peculiarities of conflicting elements of culture, aiming at the same time to bring forth a concrete unity among them. In many cases, however, such a unity is based upon rapprochement for the sake of convenience and in the mood of opportunism. Hampered by their own inclination to accentuate the social nexus and their alogical mentality, the Japanese are often lacking in the radical spirit of confrontation and criticism.

Such a weakness shows itself in practical social behavior, as in politics and in other fields, but the weakness is most pronounced in the field of thought where logical confrontation is indispensable. As for Buddhism, the life of present-day priests and believers is completely changed from what it was before the Meiji Restoration. Consequently, there exists an abysmal gap between the old doctrine and the reality of present-day living, but few try to bridge that gap with reflective thinking. The resultant ideological chaos is most revealing as to the issues within disciplines. For instance, as long as one remains a Buddhist, drinking is absolutely prohibited, whether one is a priest or a believer. But the breach of that discipline is taken for granted in Japan.[167] Marriage would not be permitted to the priest, except for the priests of the Jōdo sect, were the strict teachings and conduct of the Japanese founders of the various sects observed as the absolute authority. The alternatives are either to follow strictly the examples of the founders or to repudiate their authority by becoming a priest under lay conditions, just as was done by some of the priests of Mahāyāna Buddhism, the priests of Nepal, Tibet, or the leaders of the Jōdo sect. Such a decision based upon thoroughgoing logical judgment is rarely thought out by the Japanese Buddhists who *very reluctantly do* any theoretical reflection upon any discrepancy between the doctrine professed and the actions performed. (Such a mental phenomenon runs parallel to the intellectual-historical fact of the lack of critical studies when Western philosophical ideas were introduced and rashly absorbed after the Meiji Restoration.)

The lack of the spirit of criticism in the theoretical field corresponds to the lack in the field of literature of any will to drive home to the reader's heart a concept or an idea, however abstract it may be. Yaichi Haga writes: "There is scarcely any inclination in the mind of the Japanese to go to extremes in getting angry with the world, in deploring, in being cynical, or in being snobbish. That is the reason why the literature of our country is simple."[168] Even the Buddhist works of literature, favored by the Japanese people, are mostly lacking in thoroughgoingness.

Even in the Medieval period, when Buddhist thought penetrated most deeply into the minds of the people, the Japanese were not serious in their religious consciousness. In the *Ryōjin Hishō,* a collection of Buddhist songs, the songs that express a gnawing consciousness of sin are extremely rare. Instead, most of them represent moods of humor and optimism.

"An insect, weaving at the Eastern Gate of the Pure Land,
Lives in the crossbeam of the Gate.
He hastily weaves a robe of prayers,
In the burning light of the Pure Land."[169]

An essay of Kamo no Chōmei (12th–13th century), known to be a representative work of Buddhist literature, also shows the lack of intensity or depth.

"In the spring the fragrant wisteria waves its blossoms like the lavender clouds that lead to the Pure Land in the west. In the summer the cuckoo brings to my mind the journey of death to the other world. The autumnal cicadas sing a melancholy song as if they were lamenting their fleeting life. In the winter I gaze in meditation at the snow, as it falls and as it melts, which reminds me of sins committed and purged. I let myself rest and relax whenever I feel too lazy to practice *nembutsu* prayers or to recite sūtras."[170]

The writer simply enjoys himself here with the changes of nature from one season to another, and there is neither any serious sense of sin and confession of sin, nor absolute devotion to the Buddha. In order to concentrate on ascetic practices the Indians made various devices to torment themselves with, such as the "five heats"—making fires burn at four sides around themselves under the burning heat of the glaring sun—or sitting on the floor where splinters are placed vertically. Such single-mindedness in the pursuit of ascetic practice has scarcely been found among the Japanese. It is utterly inconceivable for either the Chinese or for the Indians to recommend, as the Japanese do, as a representative work of Buddhist literature a confession of an idle hermit who "feels too lazy to practice *nembutsu* prayers or to recite *sūtras*." Commenting on this essay, Yoshio Yamada (1873–1958) says: "Although the author, led by the Buddhist philosophy, realized the impermanence of the phenomenal world, and thereupon escaped from this world, he neither resented Heaven nor cursed the world, but he simply secluded himself in a hermitage and found a kind of passive comfort in that state of his own. Consequently, both of his views of the impermanence of the phenomenal world and his pessimism appear to be halfhearted. Is that because the Japanese are by nature optimists?"[171]

Kenkō (1283–1350), an essayist, the author of the *Tsurezuregusa* (Gleanings from Leisure Hours), admires the ascetic practices of Buddhism, but at the same time he frankly expresses his desire for worldly pleasures. "Though I know it to be a temporary abode, a congenial dwelling place pleases me. . . . A man who does not cherish love's pleasures, however excellent he may be in thousands of other things, is extremely unstable. He is like a wine-cup which is made of precious stone but without a bottom."[172] Japanese literary men seem to have a grudge against describing a hermit who repudiates completely all of his natural desires. In this respect they are vastly different from most Indian Buddhists.

The lack of thoroughgoing theoretical reflection goes hand in hand with the humorous and comic attitude of the Japanese. We need not go into detailed discussions on this point here, since it has repeatedly been pointed out elsewhere.[173] Here it suffices to mention that even such a serious subject as Buddhism is turned into something to be laughed at.

The fact that a Buddhist priest was made into an object of a scornful mirth was as old as the *Man'yōshū* (Collection of Myriad Leaves).

"Don't tether a horse
To a stub of a whisker,
A little bit grown
On the shaven face of a monk,
Don't pull it hard,
Lest, 'ouch,' the monk may cry."[174]

Such a tendency to treat the affairs of Buddhism as the object of derision became especially pronounced in the modern period. Zen priests were then described as the heroes of comic stories. And they were supposed to write back and forth witty poems. This may be taken as a metamorphosis of the Zen catechism, but it was welcomed by the Japanese who love to make poor puns. Ikkyū is the prototype of such a priest and he is described as the hero of a series of funny stories called "Ikkyū Pieces."[175] The Zen monk Soseki, better known as the national teacher Musō (1275–1351), was also made into a comic hero. This vogue for caricature was not confined to the Zen priests, but even the austere and pious St. Gensei of the Nichiren sect was made the author of a facetious piece of literature called the *Fresco of St. Gensei,* which is an utter disgrace to such a respected man of religion. It was neither from disrespect for Gensei nor from any positive intention to defame Gensei that the real author tied up his own ludicrous stories with the honorable name of Gensei. He wanted simply to make his witticism more effective.[176]

In the same fashion, even a serious discussion is reported in a humorous frame of mind. The Zen master Hakuin (1685–1768), who spread and gave local color to the Zen teachings, preached in a quite vulgar way, though full of wit and humor.

"My name is Yūsuke Odawara, and I was an apothecary before I was born, that is, since my parents' generation. To force a sale is under the ban, I know, but pray listen to my telling you the effect of my medicine. The medicine I advertise is called the pill-of-becoming-a-Buddha-by-comprehending-one's-own-true-nature, and contains the direct heart of man. Should you use this medicine, you would get rid of tormenting sickness, and the pains of the vicissitudes of the three worlds and the sorrows of the transmigration of the soul in the six spheres would be allayed. . . . To this country, Master Senkō introduced it first, and later on twenty-four excellent apothecaries came out with it. Still later, Master Daitō at Murasakino was employed by the Emperor. At that time there appeared an apothecary who made the medicine called the pill-of-revelation and the pill-of-secrecy, that contested with the pill-of-becoming-a-Buddha for the supremacy of effectiveness. By the Imperial ordinance, Daitō debated with the apothecaries of the Mii Temple, Nara, the Mt. Hiei and their vicinities, to the victory of the former. Priest-Emperor Hanazono sent an Imperial messenger to Ibuka of Mino to call for the Master Kanzan, and honorably taking this medicine, the Priest-Emperor bestowed upon him an Imperial wine-cup as a prize. Hanazono Shop is indeed the name of my own head family. To tell you the recipe for this medicine, first we cut down with an axe the oak tree of Shao-chou, beat it in the mortar of the Sixth Patriarch, dip the Seiko water of Ma-tzu, knead it on the octagonal plate of Daitō, put on the one hand of Hakuin, make it round with the finger of Chü-ti, wrap it up with the white paper of Hsüan-sha, and on that paper we write the superscription of the pill-of-becoming-a-Buddha-by-comprehending-one's-own-true-nature, of Hanazono Shop, of the Rinzai district, of the Zen sect. Should you gulp this pill, you would vomit something called an empty intelligence and the poison remains in your body through your lifetime. If you chew it well enough and then swallow it and keep it at the bottom of your navel when you go out or come back, or when you stand up or sit down, then you will never feel happy even if you get reborn into the paradise or never feel pain even if you fall into hell. I am not to talk ill of other medicines, but the pill-of-the-six-characters (*Namu-amida-butsu*), recently on sale, may be nourishing for the ordinary man, if you take it before breakfast and after supper, but it will never, I assure you, be effective to alleviate the agony of death. It is of this kind of pill that people call the pill-of-becoming-a-Buddha for the moment of death. This kind of pill costs you three cents apiece. But as for my own pill, it costs you not a cent. Let me cut the story short, but why not try it now?"[177]

The high priests of India or China did not preach Buddhism in such a way.

In the earlier stage of the Edo period, a person called Nyoraishi wrote a book named *An Account of Hundred and Eight Chō*.[178] This book, with Buddhism as the central doctrine, asserts that each of the three doctrines, Confucianism, Taoism, and Buddhism, has one *ri* (*ri* in Japanese stands both for *reason* and *a measure of distance*). And if each of the three doctrines has one *ri*, and a *ri* stands for thirty-six *chō*, then the three doctrines together would make up one-hundred-and-eight *chō*. Thus the book was named by a play on words.[179] In this ludicrous way the unity of the three doctrines was preached and accepted by the public. Such a thing does not seem likely to take place among other peoples, but it is quite deep-rooted among the Japanese.

It is noteworthy to point out that the Japanese turn into ridicule indiscriminately a Buddha, the Seven Deities of Good Luck, or whatever else is transplanted from abroad. But they never deride their own ancestral gods.[180] Such a double-barreled wit originated, as was pointed out above, from the lack of religious consciousness on the one hand, and the confusion of the social nexus and ancestral lineage on the other.

The Japanese, with the above-mentioned characteristics, give Western observers the impression of being far less profound than the Chinese,[181] and while the Japanese themselves may boast that they have successfully synthesized the cultures of the world, actually they seem to have simply resorted to an uncritical and opportunistic attitude of compromise, leaving borrowed cultures in irrelevant juxtaposition.

CHAPTER 35 THE TENDENCY TO EMPHASIZE A LIMITED SOCIAL NEXUS

Overstressing the Social Nexus

Great importance is attached in Japan to rules of propriety based upon human relationships. This latter tendency of thought can be noticed in Japanese linguistic forms. It is to be noted that today, as a consequence of the introduction of Western thought, the uses of the passive voice and the impersonal subject occur more frequently in Japanese writing. Originally, however, with some rare exceptions, the subject of sentences was confined to human beings or living beings, especially the former, and also to animals high in the scale of intelligent creatures.[1] Furthermore, a foreign word used as a verb in Japanese would be suffixed with the native verb *"su,"* which originally indicated an action of some kind. We thus find that the operation indicated by a verb originally represented an activity of a living being rather than that of an inanimate thing.

A reply to an interrogation in Japanese is often the converse of a Western reply. The proper negative reply to the question "Aren't you going?" would be in Japanese "Yes, I am not," much the same as the Sanskrit reply *"Evam, tathā,"* ("That is so" or "Yes") in such a case. The English reply here would be "No, I am not." The Japanese reply refers to the opinion and intention of the interrogator, whereas the Western reply refers to the objective fact involved in the interrogation. In short, a Japanese replies to his interrogator, not to the fact involved. This may account for the ambiguity which the Japanese are generally accused of putting into their replies to questions.

The habit of attaching importance to human relations is manifested outwardly in their practice of the rules of propriety. Generally speaking, exchange of greetings in the West is fairly simple. Japanese greetings are, on the contrary, highly elaborate. Forms of politeness have been observed not only among strangers but even among family members of upper classes, although this tendency is now rapidly vanishing. This habit gave rise to the elaboration of honorific words and phrases in their language. It is said that if all such honorific words were taken out of Lady Murasaki's *Tale of Genji,* the book would be reduced to one half its length.

The Japanese habit of stressing proprieties is connected historically to their assimilation of Chinese thoughts. Confucianism, which was adopted with especial enthusiasm, deals largely with concepts of propriety. Proprieties are stipulated in great detail in accordance with social rank in such books as the *Book of Rites,* etc.

These Confucian concepts of propriety were much appreciated as soon as they were imported with Chinese civilization, as one may well gather from Prince Shōtoku's Injunctions (604 A.D.), Article 4 of which states that if the duty of the inferior is obedience, the duty of the superior is decorum. This does not mean, however, that the concepts of propriety were practiced in Japan simply as they were laid down by Confucianism in China. The practical rules in Japan were to differ considerably from the Chinese rules. It was as social concepts—and as a means of preserving social stability and the clan system—that Confucian proprieties were appreciated, and as social concepts the Japanese and Chinese proprieties had much in common. And it was such points of similarity that made it easy for the Japanese ruling class to enforce the rules of propriety upon the people without undue resistance and friction; Confucian precepts would not have spread so widely among the people if they had been adopted merely as counsels of government.

Stressing proprieties also had an effect on the course of the assimilation of Buddhism. We find this tendency clearly manifested in Dōgen (1200–1253), the founder of a sect (Sōtō Zen) most characteristically Japanese of all the Zen sects of this country; he laid down strict rules regarding even such minutiae of daily conduct as ablution, eating, evacuation, etc. Many of these detailed rules are considered to have been Dōgen's own creation. Now, let us compare Dōgen with his teacher Tendō Nyojō (Ju-ching, 1163–1228). We find Ju-ching saying, in the fashion of the Zen priests of the Sung Dynasty of China, things that certainly seem eccentric to contemporary readers; e.g., in the following passage: "Squatting in his private room, he gouged out the eyes of the statue of Bodhidharma. Making balls of mud, he struck people with them. In a loud voice he cried, 'Behold, the sea has dried up, the bottom can be seen. Waves rise up so high that they strike Heaven!' "[2] On the other hand, we find nothing which we may call eccentric in Dōgen's private life. Rather his daily conduct was strictly in keeping with the decorous manners of the Zen school. Many others beside Dōgen were responsible for the importation of Chinese Zen Buddhism, but the eccentricities of the Chinese Zen sects did not come into general vogue in the religious circles of Japan.

Social Relationships Take Precedence Over the Individual

Due to the stress on social proprieties in Japan another characteristic of its culture appears—the tendency of social relationships to supersede or take precedence over the individual. To lay stress upon human relationships is to place heavy stress upon the relations among many individuals rather than upon the individual as an independent entity.

The elaboration of honorifics in the Japanese language has already been mentioned as one of the phenomena ascribable to such a trait. Honorifics, it is true, are found in Korean, but not to the same great extent as in Japanese; honorifics to such an extent do not exist in other Asian or Western languages, though in the latter languages, the feeling of respect may be expressed by the uses of certain special words and the third person plural.[3] Honorifics are thus something quite peculiar to the Japanese language. Further, personal pronouns are much more complicated in Japanese than in other languages. The choice of the proper pronoun to fit the particular situation is an ever-recurring problem in speaking Japanese. Special pronouns are required for superiors, equals, inferiors, intimates, and strangers.[4] If one should confuse them, difficulties would ensue. The Japanese, therefore, must bear in mind such social relationships as rank and intimacy every time he uses a personal pronoun. Such discriminatory use of personal pronouns extends to the use of nouns and verbs as well. A distinction is made, for example, between words used in addressing persons of superior rank and those used in addressing persons of inferior rank.

This custom of using honorific words to show respect or affection for the persons addressed, or of differentiating parlance in accordance with the persons addressed, may be called a "ritual in conversation." The same sort of "ritual" is to be found in other Asian tongues under feudal reigns, but nowhere is it as pronounced as in the Japanese language.

When this type of thinking is predominant, consciousness of the individual as an entity appears always in the wider sphere of consciousness of social relationships, although the significance of the individual as an entity is still recognized; the recognition of the unique value of individuals is lessened, when he is placed in a social class.

The fact that the first person or the second person is often omitted as the subject in a Japanese sentence seems to be an indication of this type of thinking. Generally in such a case the subject is implied in the whole sentence structure, but frequently a sentence may completely lack the subject. For example, "*yuki masu*" can mean "I go" or "you go" or "he goes." Or "*yukai desune*" can mean either "I am pleasant" or "you are pleasant." The subject has to be determined according to the context. This means that the Japanese do not want to express explicitly the subject of an action, unless necessary. The Japanese rather enjoy the sort of harmonious social atmosphere of human relationship in which the speaker and the person addressed are placed. This indicates that the Japanese generally have tended not to state the subject personally, or to attribute actions to an independent individual performer of the actions.

Further, we note that number is not always made explicit in the syntax of Japanese sentences. Not always is a distinction made between the singular and plural (as also in Chinese and the languages of the South Sea Islanders),[5] and reduplication in the Japanese language (e.g., *yama-yama*–mountains, *kami-gami*–gods) cannot be said strictly to indicate plurality, as reduplication requires the individual to have signification. Thus the forms *Kuni-guni* (nation-nation) and *hito-bito* (person-person) are not strictly the equivalents of the English plural forms "nations" and "persons" or "people," but are actually like English "every nation" and "every person," or as the case may be, "several nations" and "several persons." Furthermore, not all nouns can be made plural in form. The plural suffixes *-ra, -tachi* and *-domo* cannot, as a rule, be affixed to words indicating inanimate objects, such as "book" or "stone," though the reduplicated forms *ie-ie* (house-house) and *yama-yama* (mountain-mountain) are permissible. Hence, we do not say *hon-ra* (*hon* "book"/*ra*) or *ishi-ra* (*ishi* "stone"/*ra*). Nor could we affix the plural suffixes to words meaning animals of lower orders, such as insects, fish, birds, though we sometimes hear *kemonora* (beasts) or *inudomo* (dogs). Plurals, however, become better indicated as we proceed higher from domestic animals to servants. Several kinds of plural suffixes are variously used to suit different occasions. *Domo* and *tachi* are used for persons of equal or inferior status or for intimates, as for example, *funabitodomo* or *funabitotachi* ("boatmen"), *hitotachi* ("people"), *tomodachi* ("friends"). When respect must be shown, the suffix *kata,* which originally meant place, is used, as for example, *anatagata* ("you") and *senseigata* ("teachers"). In the past, *hara,* a word for field, was used as a plural suffix; thus we have *tonobara* ("lords") and *yakkobara* ("footmen").[6] In short, the use of plural suffixes was determined by the relationship of ranks and the feeling (intimacy, hate, respect, disrespect, etc.) the speaker entertains for the persons of whom he is speaking. This clearly evidences the Japanese trait to think of things in terms of social relationships rather than as impersonal facts in the objective world. The various plurals are, therefore, not strict equivalents of Western plural forms, though in modern times owing to the influence of Western languages and science, number has come to be expressed in nearly the same way as in Western languages. (An affix: *moromorono* can be put to any word to denote plural.)

The individual, then, is not always conceived as the unit of society.

Consequently, it sometimes happens that a plural suffix attached to a noun loses its own meaning, becoming simply a blank, meaningless component of a compound, and the compound may indicate the singular number, as in the case of the word *wakaishū*, which is made up of *wakai* ("young") plus *shū* (plural suffix "people"). This word may mean both "youngsters" and "a youngster." The words *heitai* (contingent of soldiers) and *sōryo* (monks) may mean also "a soldier" and "a monk." In order to make plurality more explicit, there was created already in the Heian period such a peculiar plural form as *wakashūdomo* (young persons/plural suffix) or *kodomotachi* (child/plural suffix).[7]

The Japanese prefer, in general, not to represent number syntactically, but when two people are conversing, they are clearly aware of the distinction between singular and plural. As we have seen, one of the most distinguishing features of the Japanese language is the lack of clear indication of number. This, is not so, however, with regard to personal pronouns, particularly, the first and second person. The first and second person are clearly distinguished; the pronouns *ware* or *watakushi* ("I") could only be the first person singular, and could by no means be confused with *warera* or *watakushitachi* ("we"). It is to be noted that the plural forms here are made from the singular forms. This phenomenon in their language indicates that the Japanese who are disinclined to measure the objective world with a certain established unit are quite sensitive to the distinction between "I" and "you" in social relations. In this case the consciousness of the individual comes forward.

We note here, in passing, that in the languages of the South Sea Islanders number is rather distinctly indicated in nouns, although it is vague in other respects.

We have the converse of this in modern Western languages where number, though explicit in the case of nouns, is ambiguous in the case of personal pronouns. The second person singular, "*Sie, vous,* or *you*" are etymologically plurals. The speaker at a lecture, or the author of a book, in the West, customarily refers to himself as "we," when the actual number is singular. Speaker and audience are brought closer to each other by identification. Contemporary Japanese has a similar usage, probably due to Western influence.

This tendency in their thinking may be found also in their assimilation of Buddhism. In the course of their assimilation of Buddhism the problem of the difference between one ego and another was never given serious consideration,[8] except in cases of deep religious self-reflection, especially when the sins committed by one's self were keenly felt. The general view then held is represented by that of Master Dōgen who, in advocating identification of the self with other selves, taught that: "Oneself and others should both be benefited." Tenkei (1648–1735), his follower, said: "If you alone comprehend your own mind, then it is evident that all other beings, animate and inanimate, in all directions should partake of the wisdom of the Buddha at the same time." Ryōnin (1072–1132), the founder of the Yūzū Nembutsu sect, is said to have seen, while meditating deeply, in May 1117, Amida Buddha appear and present a poem to him, saying, "One person is all persons; all persons are one person; one meritorious deed is all meritorious deeds; all meritorious deeds are one meritorious deed. This is called deliverance to the Pure Land by the grace of Amida."

These views upheld by the Kegon sects in China and Japan have their origin in the Indian Kegon Sūtra (*Buddha-avataṁsaka-sūtra*). The Japanese mind was affected by the views of the Kegon Sūtra more than we realize. And the problem of "proving the existence of others"—a problem which Dharmakīrti, Indian logician and philosopher, was interested in—was never given attention either in China or Japan.

But while such features of the Japanese way of thinking are manifested in the linguistic phenomena of the race, good instances of their manifestation in the course of the assimilation of Buddhism cannot easily be found. Presumably, this is due to the fact that Buddhism which contained from the first the idea of identification of the self with others had little need to be influenced by traditional Japanese thought.

The lack of a clear distinction between the individual and the social group to which he belongs has, however, brought about a number of interesting phenomena. For example, individual monks training in a Buddhist order are known by the term "*sō*" (derived from the Sanskrit *saṅgha*) which is itself a term for a Buddhist order. Such a linguistic phenomenon is seen also in China. This type of thinking is apparent in Dōgen where he says: "One should be more intimate with brethren in a Buddhist order than with oneself."[9] In contrast, the primitive Buddhism of India teaches: "Sons are no help, [nor] a father, [nor] relatives; there is no help from kinsfolk for one whom death has seized"[10] and "The self is the master of the self."[11] Thus, self-reliance is taught.[12] And primitive Jainism teaches: "Friend, thou art a friend of thyself. Why seekest thou friends beside thyself?"[13] When we compare Dōgen's views with those of the Indians we cannot help being amazed by the great difference between them. Lack of individualism is common to feudal societies of all countries, but nowhere, it seems, is the sense of social affinity as predominant as in Japan.

The concept of universal law was not lacking among the Japanese, and the move to conceptualize human affairs in terms of laws and concepts which are universals has been effected by the Japanese to some extent. The concept of universal law came into existence very early in the time (ca. 600 A.D.) of Prince Shōtuku, when he said: "Sincerely revere the Three Treasures, viz., the Buddha, the Law (*Dharma*), and the Brotherhood (*Saṅgha*) which constitute the final ideal of all living beings and the ultimate foundation of all countries. Should any age or any people fail to esteem this truth? There are few men who are really vicious. They will all follow it if adequately instructed. How can the crooked ways of men be made straight unless we take refuge in the Three Treasures?"[14] Here we find the concept of a universal law which is something beyond laws based on the inductively given status of the individual in the joint family and of the family in its respective tribe or caste. But at the same time we find a strong tendency to esteem the social nexus.

Among the objective causes which might account for such a tendency in the Japanese people, is the social life peculiar to their land and climate. The primitive Indo-Europeans, being nomadic and living chiefly by hunting, were in constant contact with alien peoples. Here, human relations were marked by fierce rivalry. Peoples moved in great migrations; one race conquered another only to be conquered by still another. In such a society the struggle for existence was based not on mutual trust but on cunning and stratagem.

Japanese society, on the other hand, developed from small localized farming communities. The Japanese early gave up their nomadic life, and settled down to cultivate rice fields. People living on rice inevitably have to settle permanently in one place. In such a society *families* continue on, generation after generation. Genealogies and kinships of families through long years become so well known by its members that the society as a whole takes on the appearance of a family. In such a society individuals are closely bound to each other and they form an exclusive social nexus. Here an individual who asserts himself will hurt the feelings of others and thereby do harm to himself. The Japanese learned to adjust themselves to this type of familial society, and created forms of expression suitable to life in such a society. And here grew the worship of tutelary gods and local deities. Even today there is a strong tendency in the Japanese social structure to settle closely around such tutelary gods and local deities. This tendency is deeply rooted in the social history of the people and it has led to their stressing human relations. The Japanese have learned to attach unduly heavy importance to their social ties in disregard of the isolated individual. This question will be discussed in the next section.

Unconditional Belief in a Limited Human Nexus

On the whole (allowing always for a minority of exceptions to our generalizations), Indians regard man as the subjective performer on a metaphysical stage, while peoples of the Western Hemisphere have, from ancient times, inclined to be more empirical; in both cultures, however, men is regarded as possessing potentialities of universal significance. Most Japanese, on the other hand, tend to look upon man as a being subordinated to a specific and limited human nexus; they conceive him in terms of his relations to a circumscribed society.

Thus a human event, in this way of thinking, is not a purely personal event but an event having some value and emotional significance in a narrowly given sphere of social relations. This characteristic way of thinking seems to manifest itself in the Japanese use of an intransitive verb in the passive voice— a form expressing the subject as being indirectly affected by some event or act; for example, "*Kare wa tsuma ni shinareta*" (literally, "It happened to him that his wife died"); or, "*Kare wa kodomo ni nakareta*" (literally, "It happened to him that his child wept.") An objective event—a wife's death or a child's weeping—is here stated in its relation to one's interests and feelings. Such a statement of the event contains an entirely different significance from that contained in the Indo-European statement "His wife died," or "His child wept."

The people to whom a human nexus is important place great moral emphasis upon complete and willing dedication of the self to others in a specific human collective. This attitude, though it may be a basic moral requirement in all peoples, occupies a dominant position in Japanese social life. Self-dedication to a specific human nexus has been one of the most powerful factors in Japanese history.

In the moral sense of the early Japanese, good and evil were considered as a matter of social morality and not as a matter of fortune, as they are generally regarded in a primitive civilization. Good was not something that profits the self but something that profits others in a social group. Evil was not something that harms the self but something harmful to others or the welfare of the whole. Good and evil concern not the interests of the individual but those of others or the whole.[15] Later the highest virtue was considered to be sacrifice of the self for the sake of the sovereign, the family (especially the parents), or the community. This feudal morality assumed an extreme form after the Meiji era when it came to be expressed in the form of sacrifice of one's life for the state or the emperor. Attachment to one's native place and to neighbors from the same region are variations of this attitude.

In contrast to this we find only a few cases in which sacrifices of life were made by the Japanese for the sake of something universal, something that transcends a particular human nexus, such as academic truth or the arts. And if we exclude the persecutions of the True Pure Land sect, the Hokke sect, and Christianity, cases of dying for religious faith are exceptional phenomena. Sacrifice of all for the sake of truth, when it went contrary to the intentions of the ruler, was even regarded as evil.

Such a tendency of thinking was an influential factor in the assimilation of foreign thoughts. A good deal of Chinese thought was adopted by the Japanese, but not all of it was readily acceptable to the Japanese. Though Confucianism, which laid particular stress upon the proper order of human proprieties, was enthusiastically accepted, the liberalism of some Chinese heterodox thinkers was entirely ignored. The Taoism of Lao-Tzŭ and Chuang-Tzŭ, which valued the welfare of individuals, never spread widely among the people of Japan. Christianity, with its persistent teaching of belief in God, met the fate of persecution, and was finally uprooted by law when it came to be feared that its teachings might result in the neglect of duties to feudal lords and parents. In the Satsuma Clan the followers of the True Pure Land sect were put to death because of the fear that they would be disobedient to the clan lord.

Universal religions advocate the transcending of limited human relations. This facet of religion, however, is scarcely seen in Japanese religions. A feature common to various Japanese religions is their emphasis on group propriety. From ancient days the importance of an established, limited human nexus has been in the consciousness of the Japanese. As the psychological example parallel to it, we may cite the fact that the Japanese statement of judgment (or reasoning) is severely limited to the environment which includes the speaker and listener. Universal religions from abroad had to be transformed to suit such a tendency of thought.

In spite of the various Western modern thoughts introduced after the Meiji Restoration, the individual as a social entity has not come to be fully grasped by the general public. While the Japanese are keenly conscious of their membership in their small, closed nexus, they are hardly fully aware of themselves as individuals, or as social beings, to the extent the Western peoples are.

In the light of such a way of thinking, it is easy to understand why Japanese Buddhists have tended to disregard the Universalistic Buddhist Precepts. The traditional, conservative Precepts of Hīnayāna Buddhism, which had been observed among the clergy until the Nara period (710–784), were abandoned by Saichō (Dengyō Daishi) who adopted instead the Precepts of Māhayāna Buddhism. The so-called *Endonkai,* the Māhayāna Precepts adopted by Saichō, stipulated that Buddhist novices need not comply with the Hīnayāna Precepts. It was in this way that Buddhism came to be more readily practicable in Japan. This tendency to ignore the Precepts became stronger in Japanese Buddhist Sects, especially, in the Pure Land Buddhism. In the True Pure Land sect founded by Shinran, it was thought that even violators of the Precepts could be saved by the boundless mercy of Amitāyus Buddha. Buddhism, we note, has thus been completely transformed for the sake of practicability. Japanese society as the ground of Buddhist practice had rejected the religious practices of India and China. Japanese society was too tightly formed; the restrictive power of its secular community over religious circles was too great to permit priests to continue their imported practices.

This hardly means, however, that Japanese Buddhism was *immoral* or *amoral*. Monks and faithful alike observed assiduously the requirements of their limited human nexus; they were highly moral in this respect. They were devoted to their parents and loyal to their sovereign. They were in every respect quite different from the monks and novices of India and China. Moreover, Japanese monks were devoted workers loyal to the interests of the order to which they belonged. If the followers of one sect founder are divided into a number of different orders, monks in one of the orders become devoted to his particular order to the point of boycotting the other orders. To them the welfare of their small separate orders are their main concern and the doctrine to which they all adhere is reduced to a secondary concern. Here again they are moral in the limited sense that they are devoted to their limited human nexus. The precepts to be kept by an individual as an individual in relation to the Absolute, by an individual in relation to another individual *qua* individual tend thus to become neglected. The interests of their own small limited nexus become the factors determining their actions.

The antiquarianism so strong in the Japanese may also be said to be due to the historical, temporal aspect of their attachment to a limited human nexus. The Japanese cherish families and institutions that have a long history. One of the national prides of the Japanese people was the length of their history. Japanese poetry abounds with examples of their antiquarianism; old poetic expressions, obsolete in ordinary conversation, maintain a great role in Japanese poetry. The merits of *waka* poetry have been thought to lie in the use of the words used by poets of the past.[16] This practice continues today. In the Tokugawa period (1600–1867), writing in the archaic form was a prevalent style.

How did Japanese antiquarianism affect importations of Continental culture? Japanese antiquarianism is apparent, rather, in the fact that no liberal thoughts of the Continent took root in this country. (The question of Japanese unconditional subordination to established authorities will be discussed in detail later.) The antiquarianism of Japanese Buddhists was quite different in character from that of the Indians or Chinese. The Zen Priest Tōrei, for instance, idealizes ancient Japan in his *Shūmon Mujintō-ron* (The Inextinguishable Lamp of the Sect) and says:

"In the pure ancient age of Japan, people were honest and upright; so it was easy for them to attain to the Great Way in accordance with their ability. Gods and men were unified in the primeval chaos. What need will there be of Buddhism? In a later corrupted age, however, people gradually lost their moral sense. They were so addicted to outer (sensual) objects that they were led astray by them. They have in transmigration fallen into evil ways. Without the exquisite doctrine of the Enlightened One [the Buddha], who could be saved and freed from transmigration in these days?"

One would have thought that the Buddhists would regard pre-Buddhist Japan as a benighted nation, but here we find a Buddhist himself giving us a statement to the contrary.

Observance of Family Morals

The prevailing atmosphere in Japanese social life, we may say, is that of close intimacy and alliance, and this atmosphere of intimacy and alliance is perhaps most manifest in the family, the first and most important of their closed nexus. Under the ancient clan system, the early Japanese were devout ancestor-worshippers and diligent observers of family devotions conducted in compliance with Shintoism, their national religion. Large and small clans, related by blood, having common ancestors and occupations, set up a deity which the entire clan worshipped as their tutelary deity or *ujigami*.[17] On fixed days clan members would gather and the clan head would offer prayers of thanksgiving and petition for blessings before their protector deity. This religious custom survives today in rural districts. Festivals of tutelary deities are held today by rural villagers after a good harvest; festival charts are pulled out from the barn and travelling players come to present their plays. Thanksgiving for the good harvest will also be rendered festively. The precincts of tutelary deities were regarded as the most hallowed places, and the treasures of the clan were stored there to be guarded by all the clansmen. Thus the clan head in charge of religious affairs assumed the power of absolute dictatorship.[18]

According to the beliefs of the early Japanese, their many deities were thought to be related by blood, and these deities were also related to the Imperial ancestors. Blood-relationship, it is thus apparent, was considered to be the main force for communal unity. We must note here that a specific blood-relationship was not essential. It was not the actual ancestors who were deified for worship; it was that the deities worshipped were regarded *as their common ancestors*.[19]

Even after the collapse of the clan system, reverence for the family (although the meaning of family had changed) continued to be rooted in the social sense of the Japanese, with the family as the dominant unit of social organization. It was the family, not the individual, which was the determining factor in Japanese life of the ancient past. Yaichi Haga (1867–1927), a master of Japanese studies, for instance, says: "The unit of Western society is the individual and groups of individuals make up the

State. In Japan, the State is an aggregation of families. Therein lies the basic difference." Haga asserted that Japanese ancestor-worship and reverence for the family name are based on the following facts.[20] In ancient times, one who counterfeited a surname was made to submit to the ordeal of immersion in boiling water before the shrine of the gods. The early genealogical work *Shinsen Shōji-roku* which lists many family names, scrupulously indicates the origin of each as Imperial, divine or foreign. Then, too, there is the poem of Ōtomo-no-Yakamochi (716–785), which reads, in part: "I ponder more deeply than ever how a great office can belong to the Ōtomo clan which was served by our remote divine ancestor bearing the title 'Ōkume-nushi.' "[21] The *samurai* of the middle ages, prior to engaging in combat, would first call out his lineage. For example, "He called out, 'I am Wada Shōjirō Yoshishige, 17 years old, grandson of Miura Taisuke Yoshiaki, not far removed from a princely house, the eleventh generation from Prince Takamochi, descendant of the Emperor Kammu, let anyone come, be he general or be he retainer, I am his man.' "[22] An upstart *daimyō* would often attempt to acquire prestige by falsifying his genealogy. In the *Kyōgenki* (Medieval Comedies) we find many so-called "genealogical disputes."[23]

Hence it was natural for the religions and thought of the mainland Chinese to become assimilated by the Japanese in such a way as to fit them to their institution of ancestor-worship. In the assimilation of Confucianism it was filial piety which was most stressed. Confucian students were made to study, with especial thoroughness, the *Analects* of Confucius and the *Treatise on Filial Piety*. In the fourth month of 757 A.D. an Imperial Edict was issued which reads: "In ancient times the governing of people was generally done by means of the teaching of filial piety. Nothing is more important than this, which is the basis of all good conduct. Every house in this country should keep a copy of the *Treatise on Filial Piety*. People should study it diligently. Officials should edify them with it." The *Treatise on Filial Piety* was held to be the "book of examples for a hundred sovereigns," as it was believed that the "basic precept of a philosopher sovereign was filial piety."[24] After February 860 A.D., when the *Treatise on Filial Piety* was presented to the Emperor for his first reading of the year, it became a custom long thereafter for an Emperor to read this *Treatise* as his first book. Filial piety came to receive particular emphasis during the Tokugawa period, when Confucianism was at its height in Japan. Filial piety was given a religious color by the scholars of the idealistic Wang Yang-ming school (c. 1520); it was developed into a metaphysics by Nakae Tōju (1608–1648). The aboriginal institution of ancestor-worship was thus further solidified when it acquired from Confucianism a theoretical basis.

The Japanese, however, rejected other Chinese thoughts which ran counter to their traditional customs.

Ancestor-worship and the family system, we must remember, are not exclusively Japanese, but are the two most potent unifying factors in Chinese social organization. Here the question arises as to the difference between the Japanese and Chinese institutions of ancestor-worship and the family system. This, however, is a subject which calls for separate investigation, and can hardly be discussed here in detail. It will suffice merely to mention two or three points concerning the transformations which Chinese family morals underwent when they were introduced into Japan.

Scholars have pointed out that the Japanese family system was always patriarchal while that of China was based upon the principle of joint ownership. This point will become clearer when we compare the prescriptions of house registration of the T'ang Code with that of the Japanese Yōrō Code, which was promulgated (718 A.D.) in the Nara period. In China joint ownership of family property had since the Chou Dynasty been in wide practice; the typical family system, as stipulated by the T'ang Penal and Administrative Codes, was founded upon a basis called "joint living and joint ownership of property." Each family had its family head, assumed by the eldest patrilineal member of the family. The family head (unless he was an ancestor) had as his authority only the custody of the family property and not parental powers. The jointly-owned property of the family may be partitioned under certain circumstances. When the ancestor was the family head (this situation is called "father-children ownership") the family property was partitioned as and when he wished, and his descendants were not allowed to object to the way in which it was partitioned. In case, however, the family head were other than the ancestor, that is, if he were a patrilineal member of the family outside that of the ancestors, partitioning had to be done by him in conformity with the provisions of the Code, pending approval from the family. The Japanese Code, while based upon the T'ang Code, was altered to suit the native institutions. While the underlying principle in the T'ang Code had been fair partitioning among the brothers, the Japanese Code provides that the property, in the event of the death of the *pater familias,* shall be partitioned in a certain proportion among the legitimate and illegitimate offspring. In short, the object of partitioning was changed from jointly-owned property as defined in the T'ang Code to the property left by the head *pater familias.* The patriarchal family system was so deeply rooted in the Japanese that even the radical legislators of the time, who were bent upon imitating the Chinese system, were not able to alter it.

We may add further that one of the miscellaneous provisions of the

T'ang Code stipulates that in case a descendant sells or pawns part of the family property without the approval of the family head, the action (selling or pawning) is considered null and void. A provision to the same effect is found in the Japanese Yōrō Code. But it is interesting to note that the officially compiled annotations of the T'ang Code *Li-shu-i* uses in this case the phrase "the property of the family," while the official commentary of the Japanese Yōrō Code, *Ryō no gige* (Commentary on the Yōrō Code), uses the phrase "the property of the family head."[25]

We thus become aware of a very important difference which exists between the Japanese and Chinese family systems. It does not mean, however, that the head of the Japanese family, who was solely responsible for the custody of the family property, ruled the members with absolute authority in other family matters. Even in the days of feudalism, the power to make decisions was vested in both the head and the members. Absolute obedience of his wife and children was never enforced. This, as scholars of the civil law point out, differs considerably from the Roman patriarchal family.[26]

The Chinese moral code, which has often been said to be founded upon familism, puts great stress upon *lineage*. In Japan, on the contrary, stress was laid upon the "family" as the unifying force of a tight human nexus rather than upon lineage. Hence, adoption of an heir from a non-related family, often lower in social status, was possible. Confucianism in China, however, placed such great importance upon lineage that adoption from a family of alien stock was impossible, though recent field surveys indicate that this was sometimes done out of necessity. The professed rule, however, prohibits this even today.[27]

It was "family name" which was most highly prized in Japanese society. Non-consanguinity was not a prohibitive matter. Adoption was given approval by such Japanese Confucian scholars of the Tokugawa period as Banzan Kumazawa (1619–1691) in *Gaisho* (Foreign Papers) and Shūsai Miwa in *Yōshi-Benben* (Treatise on Family Adoption System). The views of their opponents, Keisai Asami (author of *Yōshibenshō* (Justification of Adopting Sons) and Shōsai Miyake (author of a treatise on family-naming, *Dōseiigoshōkosetsu*) did not spread widely enough to exercise restrictive power over the practice of the adoption of non-consanguineous heirs.[28]

Moreover, sociologists and ethnologists have pointed out that Japanese familism allowed elements of non-consanguineous, that is, pseudo-parent-children relations to enter into it. However, detailed investigations of such historical changes and evolution of the family in Japan, are yet to be made.[29] Nevertheless, it is true that Japanese familism is predominant in the ruler-ruled relationship, and there is actually little consciousness of opposition between the ruler and the ruled; the ruler considers the ruled as, so to speak, members of his family and the ruled also consider themselves as such. The whole Japanese nation has been regarded as an extended family; the ideal basis for society has been such familism.

Then how was Indian Buddhism to change when it was brought into such society? Buddhist Mercy, as a moral ideal, takes into consideration not only man but also even creatures of the earth, and thus applies equally to all living beings. Yet Prince Shōtoku, who first adopted and then tried systematically to introduce Buddhism to the Japanese, mostly spoke of mercy as something existing between father and child, and preached it as such. "Falsity is not employed between father and son," he said, "Precisely because there exists the relationship of father and son (between the Buddha and each living being), the Buddha can engage in the work of saving them through many, many aeons." The Mercy of the Perfect One (Nyorai, Tathāgata) is not taken here as the universal virtue of an idealized being but as a realistic, worldly virtue—the mercy of the father in the family.[30]

We have already pointed out that Japanese Buddhism placed great emphasis upon the attainment of *satori,* or spiritual awakening, through bodily experience. The body, however, having originated from one's parents, respect for one's body means respect for one's parents. The Zen priest Bankei called the absolute in the individual "the Unborn Buddhahood transmitted from parents to child." He further declared, "To change the Unborn Buddhahood transmitted from parents to us into a vile one is an extreme filial impiety." Now in Indian thought in general the body born of parents is regarded as merely the fetters of the Soul, and the world of the absolute is entered only when these fetters are discarded. But, in contrast to this, Japanese Zen Buddhists, Priest Bankei in particular, hold that the world of the absolute is attainable through one's parents. Buddhahood, in him, is identified with filial devotion. "There is nothing more gracious than the kindness of parents. They have brought us up, who are completely ignorant, till we become intelligent and hear Buddhist sermons. It is solely due to the benevolence of parents. You should respect them. This is filial piety. To follow the way of filial piety is Buddhahood. Filial piety and Buddhahood are not different."

As we have pointed out previously, Buddhism in China had to become amalgamated with the tradition of filial piety to be able to spread among the general public. Much the same situation existed in Japan. The Chinese wrote pseudo-sūtras that would preach filial piety; and the Japanese spread among the public these very sūtras with commentaries and annotations, the *Bumō-onjū-kyō* ("Sūtra of Parental Benefits") being a typical example of such.

It will be supposed from this that Buddhism, whose teachings transcend nation and family, would have to clash with the familistic morals of the Japanese. It was precisely this universal element, apparently incompatible with the familistic type of morals, that Japanese historians and Confucians took up as the target in their criticisms of Buddhism. Some Buddhists, on the other hand, asserted indeed that "true filial piety" may sometimes run contrary to the worldly morals of the family. Nichiren (1222–1282), founder of the Hokke (Lotus) Sect, declared, "Generally speaking, we should obey our parents. However, as for the way to become a Buddha, not to obey them would be the fundamental filial piety. Therefore in the Shin-ji-kwan-kyō (Sūtra on Insight into the Heart of Things), it is stated: 'To get into the Trans-mundane Way, without repaying others' kindness, is to repay it truly.' " That is, to get out of the family, without obeying the wish of one's parents and to become a Buddha is to repay their kindness truly. Even in worldly life, not to obey one's parents when they want to plot a rebellion and so on, is the true filial piety. It is stated in a Confucian canon called the *Hsiao Ching* (*The Book of Filial Piety*). When Master Tendai was practicing the meditation of the Hokke Sūtra, his parents sat on his lap and wanted to disturb his performing Buddhist practice. He said it was the Evil One in the shape of his parents who disturbed him.[31] Nichiren, as a zealous believer of the Lotus Sūtra while he unequivocally taught that one may turn his back on his parents in order to follow the Sūtras,[32] also distinguished filial piety into two kinds, "Low filial piety" and "High filial piety." *He made it plain that he upheld filial piety as an absolute virtue,* but at the same time insisted upon the validity of Buddhist universalism.

In Japanese traditional social life, the reverence for parents was the same thing as the devotion to the family. This reverence for the family affected the assimilation of all foreign religions introduced into Japan. Japanese Buddhists resembled Chinese Buddhists in that both tended to regard their religious orders as their "families."[33]

With lineage occupying so important a place in the Japanese mind, it was natural that Buddhist monks or *shukke* (literally, "those who have forsaken their worldly families"), should have instituted for themselves what we may call a "quasi-blood relation." We recall the Chinese custom in general vogue among Zen Buddhists toward the end of the Northern Sung Dynasty (976–1126) in which a document called "*Shisho*" (literally, "A document of inheritance") was issued to disciples from masters at certain stages of training. This appeared to the Japanese mind to symbolize blood succession, or establishment of blood relation, and accordingly, when this custom was adopted, the Japanese came to write this document in cinnabar ink which represented blood. Thus, it was natural, again, that Buddhist orders that approved of the secular forms of living of persons actually related by blood to the founder, should have come to be regarded with special respect. The Honganji sect, whose Temple of the Original Vow was originally the mere keeper of the grave of Shinran (1173–1262), came to receive inordinate respect and favors, and assumed the leading position in Japan, among the numerous branches of the Shin sect, simply because it had as its heads the descendants of Shinran.

Japanese Buddhism was thus able to broaden its sphere of influence as a popular religion when it linked up with the native custom of ancestor-worship. It is recorded that as early as the 2nd year of the reign of Empress Suiko (593), higher officers of the Court dedicated temples to their Empress and parents; the Rescript of Emperor Temmu (3rd month of 686 A.D.) commands: "Every family in every Province should possess a temple, and services should be conducted with the Sūtras and the image of the Buddha." This was the origin of the *butsudan,* or Buddhist shrine, found in every Japanese home. It is not known to what extent this rescript was enforced but, later, after the prohibition of Christianity, during the reign (in the early 17th century) of the Tokugawa Shogunate, Buddhist services became a family routine among the Japanese.[34] Chapels with Buddhist images have been built in homes of other Asiatic nations in the past and present, but these, unlike the case of the Japanese, have had nothing to do with ancestor-worship;[35] and we must remember that Chinese ancestor-worship was associated with Taoism rather than Buddhism. In Japan, significantly, mortuary tablets of ancestors were placed in homes with Buddhist shrines. The Japanese, thus, were made ever aware of the spirits of all their ancestors, of the immediate ones through the Buddhist mortuary tablets and of the distant ancestors through the presence of the Shintō shrine. (The family Shintō shrine, however, is connected with ancestor-worship to a much lesser degree. Shrine Shintoism does not in general practice ancestor-worship. The coexistence of the two kinds of shrines in Japanese homes cannot, therefore, be regarded merely as the result of the mixing of Shintoism and Buddhism.)

Buddhism, when brought to the Japanese soil, thus became linked with a kind of clan-consciousness. It became a vogue with aristocracies to have family temples built; the Kōfukuji, for example, was the temple of the Fujiwara clan. Headships of these temples were assumed by the members of the owner-families who had renounced secular life to become priests. (Temples similar to the Japanese family temple seem to have existed in India of the later periods.) It is interesting to note that Buddhism which had always aimed at all mankind rather than at any clan-system should come to be associated with clan-consciousness in Japan.

Amida Pure Land Buddhism, for instance, took root in the soil of Japan by virtue of a doctrine which preached, not the individual's future happiness and peace of mind, but rather the peaceful repose of the dead. The Sūtra of Infinite Life (*Sukhāvatīvyūha-sūtra*) was explained to the people at the lecture meetings held in the third year of Hakuchi (652 A.D.). Amida's Paradise came to be depicted in the mural paintings of the Hōryūji's Golden Hall, the well-known *maṇḍala* of the Taima-dera showing Paradise was completed; and all of these were expressions of the Amida Pure Land Buddhism of the time. Amida Pure Land Buddhism flourished more and more in the subsequent Nara and Heian periods.

Yet, of course, there were those who rejoiced at the Wonderful Vow of Amida and who, quite free of any customs of ancestor-worship, found individual salvation in the teachings of Amida Buddhism. Shinran (1173–1262), for example, reflected: "The vow of Amida (Amitābha) who meditated for five aeons is, when I consider it well, meant for me alone. Gracious, indeed, is the previous vow of Amida, who wanted to save me from the many fetters of *Karma*." He also said: "I have never performed invocation to Amida even once for the peaceful repose and benefit of my dead parents. Why? All living beings are parents and brothers to each other in the long process of transmigration. All should be saved and become Buddhas in future life. If I could actually accumulate some merit by my own power, I would help my dead parents by the grace of Invocation to Amida. (But it is not I who can save me, but Amida himself.) So I should give up the self-conceited attitude of hoping to save myself and others by the grace of religious practice (and I should rely on the grace of Amida). After I have been saved and become a Buddha I would save those who will come in contact with me."[36] But the Jōdo sect was not able to spread among the common people with this sort of teaching. To become the largest religious sect in Japan, as it did, it had to adopt the traditional customs of ancestor-worship. And today many who have lost the true faith of the Pure Land sect are still associated with it on the strength of this one facet of it which has to do with ancestor-worship.

The Bon Festival was instituted in the Suiko era (592–628 A.D.). Records have it that the Bon Festival was held in the third year of Emperor Saimei (657 A.D.), and in 650 A.D. the "Sūtra of Bon" was preached in temples in Kyoto as memorial services for expressing gratitude to the ancestors of the seven preceding generations. The Bon Festival, with this new meaning added, became widely practiced after this time, and is still practiced today, commonly known as "*O-bon*."

The system of memorial days and anniversaries was not a traditional feature of Buddhism. Indian Brahminism, we know, teaches a form of ancestor-worship, and the Brahmins celebrate on new moon and full moon nights what is known as Ancestor Festival, but these festivals differ widely from the memorial days and anniversaries observed in memory of any specific ancestors. Buddhism does occasionally encourage ancestor-worship, but it has never instituted a system of memorial days and anniversaries such as that devised by the Chinese. In China memorial services were held on the 49th day, 100th day, first anniversary, and third anniversary. Immediately after the introduction of this system the Japanese, of the remote past, observed the 49th day, 100th day and first anniversary, leaving out the third anniversary. Many more anniversaries, however, were added later in the Middle Ages; namely, third, seventh, 13th, 17th, 25th, 33rd, 60th, 100th, and 300th anniversaries. This was essentially the same as the system of memorial days commonly observed today, viz. 49th day, 100th day, first, third, seventh, 13th, 17th, 25th, 33rd, and 50th anniversaries.[37] Thus we may say that the system of memorial days and anniversaries was elaborated in Japan, a fact which does seem to attest to the dominance of ancestor-worship among the Japanese.

We have already made mention of funeral services. Funerals and memorial services are the two most important functions of Buddhism in Japan of today. How much will be left of the activities of the Buddhist temple, if these are taken away? "Collectivity orientations have remained a dominant part of the social environment of Japan. Such orientations are operative in a number of spheres, including the family, occupational groups, community life, and politics. The collectivity orientations are fostered in the family situation where individual goals remain largely subordinated to those of the family as a group. The traditional orientations can still be seen in many areas outside the family. The relations of the landlord and tenant in rural Japan or of the owner and worker in small and medium factories are based on simulated family ties."[38]

"The traditional pattern of the work collectivity in the framework of true or simulated kinship organization appears to remain important in spite of contractual agreements. In contemporary Japan, the traditional simulated familial ties exist in various degrees, however small or large. This factor becomes important, for it perpetuates the influence of the collectivity interest and goals over the individual. New group patterns, in many cases of activities such as we find in modern banking companies and in large factories, where the employer-employee relationship is based on a purely cash nexus, often seem to replace the older traditional scheme of organization under a simulated family system."[39]

The familistic custom of Japan undeniably appears pre-modern and even backward to the eyes of Westerners. But on the other hand, one cannot deny its socially favorable effect on present-day life. One scholar, who is a Japanese-American, recognizes in this respect its great importance for the maintenance of social stability in post-war Japan: "A Japanese individual adjusts in a social structure with strong collectivity orientations which stress ability and security and which can turn into stagnation; an American adjusts in a social environment which emphasizes self-orientation with a focus on individualism and freedom, which in excess can turn to *anomie*."[40] Concerning such a Japanese tendency, E. O. Reischauer has observed: "It injects a certain note of humanity into an otherwise ruthless exploitation of labor and keeps alive the personal factor, which we are attempting to recapture in American industry today."[41] The collectivity orientation, focused on a human nexus, serves the function of providing social security and mutual assistance within a society beset by many difficulties.[41a]

Emphasis on Rank and Social Position

As we have already seen in the section dealing with the primacy of social relations, the traditional tendency in the history of the Japanese nation shows an emphasis upon rank and the master-servant relationship, so that we may say that high esteem for the social hierarchy is one of the characteristic features of Japanese cluture. The language of the people, to begin with, reveals this tendency. The basic tenet of Buddhism—the inherent equality of all men—was modified in order to fit the Japanese way of thinking in terms of their particular social nexus.

The basic concept of social good is thought by Buddhism to be *to give* (or Sanskrit *dāna*). (This word *dāna* when translated into Chinese became *pu-shih,* or *fuse* in Japanese, meaning to serve widely.) Now, it was most difficult to find an equivalent of this word in Japanese. The Japanese words *ataeru* (to give) and *hodokosu* (to give in charity) denote an act of giving proceeding from a man of superior rank to a man of inferior rank. The words *sasageru* (to offer) and *tatematsuru* (to present), on the other hand, denote the act of giving by a person of lower rank to a person of higher rank. In short, the Japanese were able to translate what is implied in *dāna* only in relation to the social status of each party.

Anukampa, another basic concept in Sanskrit Buddhism, was also difficult to translate. *Awaremi* (pity, compassion) could perhaps be the closest Japanese equivalent, but the word also implies a downward action from one superior to another inferior. The original meaning is "to tremble in sympathy with another person." Here again, the social hierarchy of the culture, reflected in the language, prevented the proper rendering of one of the basic concepts of Buddhism.

It seems that similar instances of the Japanese emphasis on rank can be found in Japan's earliest myths. If we compare Japanese mythology with that of the Finnish people, we are struck by the great difference between them. The first outstanding feature of Finnish mythology is the equality of social status of its various characters. In the tales of *Kalevala* we find that heroes have their slaves; but kings and priests do not appear as representatives of the ruling classes; gods are treated more or less on an equal plane, and heroes appear on an equal social level. Some of these heroes are fishermen, farmers, or smiths. Japanese mythology, in contrast, is, we may say, aristocratic, for deities and heroes appearing in the *Kojiki* (Ancient Chronicle) and *Nihonshoki* (Chronicles of Japan) are rulers of the masses; classes are obviously already established.

The second feature we note in Finnish mythology is its lack of concern for lineage. The Finnish people have not, as the Japanese have, made family ancestors of their mythical gods and heroes, however much they may have looked up to them. In contrast the Japanese myths, the *Kojiki* and *Nihonshoki*, center around the Emperor, the Imperial family, and the nobility as heroes, and these myths serve only to give prestige to the lineages of these families. We may suppose that Japanese myth is only a reflection of the social behavior of the ancient Japanese.

It was thus natural enough that Confucianism, which laid stress upon a social order based on rank, should have been widely accepted by the Japanese, and it was natural also that other Chinese ideas that tended to be either individualistic or democratic should have been rejected by them.

It was probably after the time of Prince Shōtoku (c. 600 A.D.) that Japan came to have what we may call culture; and it is interesting to note that the most important tenet in Prince Shōtoku's moral views was loyalty to the Emperor and to one's parents.[42] Judging from the Edict of Emperor Kōtoku (646 A.D.), the political ideals of the Taika Reform claimed to be based largely upon Confucianism.

Before Confucianism was adopted by the ruling class of the Tokugawa period as their official philosophy, its utility as the philosophical basis of politics had already been recognized by warrior-generals of the Civil War period. We might cite, for instance, General Oda Nobunaga's moral rule issued to the citizens of Kyoto in 1573 (4th year of Genki): "Those who are diligent in Confucian study in order to rectify the affairs of the state and those who show loyalty and filial piety should be esteemed and treated in distinction to others in all important matters, through gifts and the like."[43]

Thus in this time of national upheaval, Nobunaga (1534–1582) crushed the Buddhist organization and accepted Confucianism as the guiding political philosophy. Continuing this tradition, the Tokugawa Shogunate Government publicly recognized Confucianism as the philosophical ground of centralized feudalism.

Yet, not all Confucians approved of the rank system existing in the feudal society of the Tokugawa period. Confucian Shūsai Minowa (1669–1744) of the Wang Yang-ming school, for instance, preached the complete equality of man. He said: "From the Emperor down to the petty warriors, *Eta* (pariah) and beggars, they are all men. From Sages down to men of mediocrity and outcastes, they are all men. The way of True Man is called the Way of Ancient Sage-Kings Yao and Shun." At the same time, however, it is apparent from the following remarks that he did not completely object to the existing rank system: "Even beggars who are *not fit for* the Way of Man must not be neglected," or (concerning relief work) "We will not take a single man from villages where there are many beggars and outcastes."[44] No Confucianists ever raised strong objections to the feudal rank system.

Buddhists, we find, were not different from Confucians; they kept silence on, or even were not aware of, the basic doctrine of Buddhism, i.e. equality of the castes and denial of social disparity, which had been advocated since its origin. The substance of Buddhist thought was thus transformed upon its introduction from India to suit the native custom of subordination. We note that it was in the spirit of gratitude for Imperial and parental love that Buddhism came to be observed by the Japanese of the Suiko period. The following passage from *Nihonshoki* (Chronicles of Japan) seems to confirm this fact: "The Emperor called in the Prince and the Ministers, and commanded them to promote Buddhism. Now court people and local chiefs vied with one another to erect the Houses of the Buddha, that is, temples, in order to reward the benevolence of Emperors and parents."[45] "Loyalty to the Emperor and devotion to the parents," two concepts essentially alien to Buddhism, had to be attached to Buddhism in order to make it mean something to the Japanese.

This attitude persisted down the ages. We find Nichiren saying, at the beginning of his *Kaimokusho* ("A treatise to enlighten people"), "There are three persons everybody must respect, master, teacher, parent." This, we note, is the same as the Confucian idea of piety. However, if one abides strictly by the Confucian idea of piety, he cannot at the same time fulfill to satisfaction his piety toward all three. "One who does not know the past and the future will not be able to help the future life of his father and mother, his sovereign, and his masters, and will be called an ungrateful wretch," said Nichiren, and asserted that one's piety toward the three superiors could only be accomplished by believing in the Lotus Sūtra. Here Nichiren was attempting to explain Buddhism from the standpoint of a Confucian, or native, concept.[46] Further, we find him saying, "The Second Volume of the Lotus Sūtra deals with the three important matters, the Sovereign, parents, and masters. This is the heart of the Sūtra."[47] But contrary to Nichiren's explanation, we find no mention of piety toward the three superiors in this Second Volume of the Lotus Sūtra. What is figuratively explained there is that the merciful Buddha delivers the masses of people as parents bring up their children. (Parable of carts drawn by

Sheep, Deer, and Ox; Parable of the Rich Man's Stray Son.) Neither Nichiren nor later scholars of the Nichiren sect have been able to cite exact words from the Lotus Sūtra that would serve to endorse a morality stressing class and rank distinction. What Nichiren and his followers had done was to *assume* that a book of Truth, such as the Lotus Sūtra, would advocate this kind of morality.

Now, let us take up the question of "sovereign" (*Kimi*).

As stated previously, Buddhism originally advocated caste equality, or equality of people. In books of early Buddhism little or no esteem of the sovereign, whether a feudal lord or the king of a nation, is found. As a matter of fact in a great many Buddhist writings, kings are associated with robbers that harass people through brute force. It is easy to see therefore that the concept of equality in Buddhism would not only be incompatible with, but would also threaten the very existence of the Japanese national structure based upon the class and rank system. The government of Prince Shōtoku, which made the fervent recommendation of Buddhism, not only closely guarded the class and rank system in the Injunctions, but also introduced into their version of Buddhism a class and rank morality. A new idea of respect for a sovereign was created in their annotations of the Lotus Sūtra. While Chia-hsiang Ta-shih Chi-tsang or Kajō Daishi Kichizō (Sui Dynasty), listed under the heading of "the Superiors" (in the Shōman Sūtra) master, father, elder brother and sister, Prince Shōtoku added to these categories *kimi* ("sovereign").[48]

Now what is meant by a "sovereign"? He is a ruler of subjects, or the chief of a limited, closed human nexus wherever subjugation by power prevails; he could therefore be an emperor. Reverence for a "sovereign," therefore, could at once turn into rank-consciousness in a feudal society and Emperor-worship in a nationalistic state.

The attitude of absolute devotion to the master wielded influence even upon doctrines of Japanese Buddhism. Nichiren taught that there must be only one master in a state, as in a family. Similarly, he said, there must be one sūtra which is the master of all other sūtras. His choice of the Lotus Sūtra rested upon the following reasoning: "In the world there are many who want to become powerful. But the sovereign of a country is only one. If there should be two, the land would not be peaceful. If there should be two masters in one family, it would certainly deteriorate. Concerning the complete canon of scripture, things should be the same. Only one sūtra, whatever it may be, would be the great sovereign of all the sūtras."[49]

Absolute devotion to a sovereign has constituted the basis of morality throughout Japanese history. The struggles of the Genji and Heike clans were not always motivated by hatred, or differences of interests or religious beliefs, but by devotion to the *daimyō* (clan head). In India the warrior's gallant death on the battlefield was a source of admiration only in a religious sense. Valor in the minds of Japanese warriors was different. The exemplary attitude of the warrior is given in this quotation: "Besides this bond between lord and subject, we need nothing. We will not waver at all, even on the advice of Śākyamuni, Confucius, or the Sun God of Japan (*Tenshō-Daijin*) appearing before us. Let me fall into a hell, or let me be punished by gods; we will need nothing else than to be faithful to our lord."[50] Bushidō (the Way of the Warrior) with its most important motivation in the complete subordination to the lord was, as is well-known, largely endorsed by Buddhism, particularly Zen Buddhism. The ultimate aim of Zen practice became, among the warriors, devotion to the lord.

The Buddhist idea of the transmigration of the soul was also to be revised for the sake of the Japanese stress on the master-servant relationship. The common proverb, "The parents-children relationship is good for one generation; the man-wife relationship for two generations; and the master-servant relationship for three generations" was a later creation in Japan. It was rather natural that Japanese Buddhist orders themselves came to be organized after the fashion of secular society; a complex system of rank was established in the orders. But, as already stated, early Buddhism conceived all men to be equal. These ranks of monks were determined by the number of years of service; important affairs of the order were decided by majority (*yebhuyyasikā*). To realize the great difference existing between the Buddhisms of early India and Japan, we have only to recall that, before the introduction of Western civilization into this country, such a democratic procedure as decision by majority was something entirely undreamt of in Japanese Buddhist orders.

The most significant thing about the Japanese assimilation of Buddhism, however, was the fact that original Buddhist concepts and sūtras tended to be altered, in the process of translation into simple Japanese for infiltration among the common folk, in order to satisfy the native fondness for the rank system. The Japanese word *akirameru* (to resign oneself to, to give up) was derived, so it is explained, from the form *akirakani miru* (to see clearly) under the influence of Buddhist thought. The word, however, is used when one gives up a desire that happens to run counter to the wishes of his superior. The Buddhist expression *inga wo fukumeru* (to elucidate the cause and effect of a thing) is used when one advises another to give up his desire and aspiration for the sake of his superior. What the phrase actually means is "account for the wishes of the superior." Causal relations came to be explained in terms of the rank system. This rank system, however, the Japanese accepted as a "Divine Gift," and they were aware that their society greatly differed even from the society of ancient China. We find Joken Nishikawa (1658–1724) saying: "In China customs are such that even sons of farmers and merchants can rise to government positions. They may become premier and conduct the affairs of the state. They may rule the nation in such a way that the people are made happy. There is no piety greater than this. Sons of farmers and merchants thus apply themselves diligently to studies, and aspire to obtain government positions, and rise in the world. In our country, however, things are different. Although there have been many scholars since antiquity, none has risen from the common folk, none from the common folk has managed the affairs of the state."

With such a tendency of thinking prevailing, it was natural that the individual as a free and independent agent should not have even been conceived by the Japanese till modern times. And it must be said that the retarded development of their cities was in part responsible for this. For there hardly ever arose in feudal Japan cities that were autonomous, possessing their own judicial powers. Unlike cities in China, Japanese cities were not residences of emperors; nor had they the importance of a fort city controlled by a feudal baron; they were without administrative organizations of bureaucrats. Japanese cities were rather nothing more than densely populated areas controlled by warriors. Even after the Meiji Restoration of 1868, when cities expanded rapidly, their citizens did not come to possess the self-consciousness of European citizenry. And particularly noteworthy here was the fact that there was a constant flow of farming population in and out of the cities. This farming population continued to be bound by blood relation and economy to the farming village during its residence in the city, and was free to go back to the country if subsistence in the city became difficult. This situation formed an obstacle to the growth of a general public morality as well as to an ethics for the individual in Japan.

The retarded development of cities allowed the social order, based upon feudal rank, to continue. Any movement toward equalization arising from the masses would gradually be transformed into something else by the prevailing rank system. Take for example the cult of tea. The cult of tea had its place originally in the life of the great merchants of newly-risen cities in modern times as a canon of conduct, an ideal basis of living. It aimed to create the relation of host and guest, free of the rank system in the current society, or as we find it stated, ". . . not based on rank as in ordinary life." Before long, however, the ideal of the tea cult was transformed through a series of compromises and made to conform with the prevailing pattern of feudal society. We find the following words of tea masters: "By the practice of the Tea-Ceremony, morality beginning with that between lord and subject will be naturally carried to its highest expression" or "Warriors will conform to their own ways. City people will keep their families safe. The noble and those below him will be useful (in their own positions) and they will not hate the hierarchical order."[51] (Sekishū school.)

The Zen Priest Shōsan Suzuki and his followers tried, through euphemistically publicizing anti-feudalistic views, to oppose the feudal morality based on rank, but their campaign was bound to wither away. Even the modern rationalistic thinker Baien Miura (1723–1789) had to approve feudal morality; we find him saying: "There are many vocations—warrior, farmer, artisan, and merchant. All, from the Emperor down to the masses, aim to obey and realize Divine Providence. What one aims at should be the peace of the family and the state; *what one discriminates should be the relation of noble and low, intimate and remote.*"[52] Baien's ethics was in the last analysis the ideal of the Wise Man.

It is then easy to understand why Christianity, which condemned subservience to the monarch and parents, had to confront persecution in Japan; Christianity was thought to destroy the very foundations of the social order. Christianity, or more specifically Catholicism in this case, contained within itself, no doubt, a number of elements of feudalism, being a religion that prospered during the feudal ages of Europe. But unlike Europe, where monarchs themselves were Christians of Catholic faith, feudal lords in Japan had had almost nothing to do with Catholicism or Christianity. It was the incompatibility of Christianity and the native morality of self-dedication to the clan and the Emperor which resulted in the persecution of Christianity.

In this connection we note with interest the comments on the Christian Ten Commandments by Fabian, or "Apostate Brother (*iruman*)" in his book *Hadeusu* (*Contra Deum*): He says that with the exception of the First Commandment ("I am the Lord thy God. . . . Thou shalt have no other gods before me"), the Commandments are the same as the Buddhist Five Commandments. Only the First Commandment is objectionable. For it tells one to defy one's lord and father in order to adore the Deity. It must be for the purpose of usurping our nation to spread such teachings.[53] Thus, in order to undermine Christianity, he adopts the following point of view: "If one lives in this Land of the Rising Sun, one must follow the proper way—that is, to obey the Shōgun, the ruler of the country."[54]

And we also find the following criticism of Christianity by Hakuseki Arai (1657–1725), one of the most progressive thinkers of the Tokugawa period: "It is the office of the Monarch to worship Heaven. It is therefore immoral for all people, from nobles down to the common folk, to worship Heaven, when each class has its own gods to worship."[55] Confucianism had ascended to dominance as the philosophical basis for the political structure of the society established by the warrior rulers. It was therefore natural that

Christianity, which threatened the social order based on the rank system, should meet the fate of persecution.

To the average Japanese, accustomed to stressing rank, the tests of a great religionist were his high birth and rank, not the truths he might reveal in his teachings and deeds. Modern historical research has shown that Shinran (1173–1262) was not necessarily a member of the aristocracy, but an ordinary monk at Mt. Hiei whose family origin is obscure,[56] and we detect in his writings no proud consciousness of his origin. We have come to know that it was his followers who dressed him up to be of aristocratic origin. We thus find in *Shinran Den'e* ("Illustrated Biography of Shinran"), published in 1295 A.D., 34 years after his death, the following account regarding Shinran's origin:

"His secular name was Fujiwara. He, the son of Arinori, a court minister of the Dowager Empress, who was the fifth descendant of Arikuni, a Vice-Minister, who was the sixth descendant of Duke Uchimaro, a Vice-Premier, who was the grandson of the grandson of Kamatari the Premier, who was the twenty-first descendant of Amanokoyanenomikoto. Therefore he could have grown old in the service of the court, the acme of the priestly Emperor, and lived a life of luxury. However, (he took orders . . .)." A text called *Gozokushō* (The Holy Lineage) by Rennyo (1415–1499), in which Shinran's lineage is still more exaggerated, is regularly recited at a certain "thanksgiving service" held on the anniversary of Shinran's death.

As a matter of fact most biographies of Shinran written by the followers of the Honganji sect are characterized by this tendency to glorify his birth and we are again led to believe that Shinran's religion could not have spread among the Japanese had not his followers distorted the facts of his origin in order to appeal to the peculiar tendency of Japanese thought.

A similar situation exists, in an even more pronounced form, for Nichiren. Nichiren, as he himself humbly, or to be more exact, proudly, declared that he was "the son of a *Sendara* (Sanskrit *Caṇḍāla,* despised outcast),"[57] "a son born of the lowly people living on a rocky strand of the out-of-the-way sea," "the son of a sea-diver."[58] *Nichiren was proud of his lowly birth.*[59] The Nichiren sect, however, had to fabricate a noble lineage for him in order to attract more adherents from the common folk. We thus find in Nitchō's *Nichiren Daishōnin Chūgasan*[60] (published in the early Tokugawa period) the following passage about Nichiren's lineage: "Saint Nichiren's family name is Mikuni. His father was the second son Shigetada of Nukina no Shigezane, Lord of Tōtōmi Province. The Saint was the fourth son. *He was a descendant of Emperor Shōmu.* The Saint's father was exiled from Tōtōmi Province to the lonely seashore at Kominato, village of Ichikawa, Tōjō district, Nagasa country, in the province of Awa where he became a fisherman. The Saint's mother came from the (famous noble) Family of Kiyohara." The true import of Nichiren's virtue that he was imparting the True Way in spite of his lowly birth—and this was consistent with the traditional spirit of Buddhism—was thus forever lost. Today most biographies of Nichiren we find in circulation speak of him as descending from an aristocratic family, and indeed all representative and popular religious figures have thus been made up to be sons of the aristocracy or descendants of emperors.

One may, however, explain such practice by saying: "Is it not after all, only natural that religion tries to conform to some extent to the prevailing pattern of thought? Was it not natural that these things were so, since most feudal societies do place emphasis upon lineage and hereditary rank?" But let us remember that in the feudal society of India in the Middle Ages, Āḷvārs, Hindu revolutionary religionists, were sons of the lowliest folk, and people, nevertheless, looked up to them. In India religious authority outweighed rank or lineage of secular life; the caste system was in fact based upon a traditional hierarchical social structure. Likewise, the rank system of the Lama priesthood in Tibet has nothing to do with secular rank and birth. Overstressing secular rank and lineage, therefore, is a feature, not unique to, but most pronounced, in Japanese thinking.

Problems of Ultra-Nationalism

The ultimate form in which the Japanese concept of emphasis upon a specific limited human nexus manifested itself was ultra-nationalism. Japanese ultra-nationalism did not suddenly appear in the post-Meiji period. Its beginnings can be traced to the very remote past.

The boast that Japan was the best country in the world has existed from very early times. It, no doubt, began at first in a love of the native country, pure and simple, without ambitions for expansion and conquest. Probably the earliest use of the phrase *Dai Nippon* (Great Japan) is found in some writings by Dengyō.[61] Dengyō (767–822), who had studied in China, was more keenly aware than his contemporaries of the fact that Japan's territories were smaller and her wealth and resources much more limited than China's. What Dengyō actually meant by "Great Nippon" was that Japan was a land most suitable to Mahāyāna Buddhism (Buddhism of the Greater Vehicle). Many Buddhists of later date believed that Japan was superior to all other lands, as we can see clearly in the following line from a poem by Ean (1225–1277), a Kamakura Zen monk:

> "To the end of the end of the last generation will
> This land of Ours surpass all other lands."

The notion of Japanese superiority is most boldly expressed in the concept of the Divine Nation. We find the following statement in the introductory manifesto of the *Jinnō Shōtō-ki* (Record of the Legitimate Succession of the Divine Emperors), of the 14th century, by Chikafusa Kitabatake (1293–1354), a Shintoist writer: "Our Great Nippon is a Divine Nation. Our Divine Ancestors founded it; the Sun God(dess) let her descendants reign over it for a long time. This is unique to Our Nation; no other nation has the like of it. This is the reason why Our Nation is called 'Divine Nation.'" This concept of "Divine Nation" is accepted in the Nō plays,[62] and Buddhists such as Nichiren adopted it. We find the following statements by Nichiren: "Japan is a Divine Nation,"[63] "This Nation is a Divine Nation. Deities do not respond to those lacking respect. Seven generations of Heavenly Deities, five generations of Earthly Deities, and a multitude of Good Deities support the Buddha's All-embracing Teachings."[64] A concept similar to this is found in Zen Buddhists. "Though Our Land is situated out of the Way, everlasting is its Imperial Rule, noble are its people. Thus Our Land surpasses others by far. . . . This Land of Ours is pure and divine." This shows us that Hakuin (1685–1768), the Zen master, respected Shintō concepts.

Confucianism, however, was the best system to provide a theoretical basis for the theory of ultra-nationalism. It will be remembered that Confucianism, which the Chinese had earlier adopted as their official theory of state government, was accepted by the Japanese with hardly any trouble. (The only controversial point, however, was the problem of "changing unsuitable emperors"; even this, however, caused no special friction. This point will be discussed in a section below dealing with Emperor-Worship). When Confucianism was introduced into Japan, the ruling class took to studying it so that they could "become government officials and Confucians, and serve the country."[65] This attitude toward Confucianism was to persist among the ruling classes, and in the Tokugawa period Confucianism was taught with special reference to the concept of the state (*Kokutai*) by almost all the schools and individual scholars of Confucianism including Jinsai Itō (1627–1705), Sokō Yamaga (1622–1685), Ansai Yamazaki (1618–1682), and the Mito school.

We further note that Japanese Confucianism, associated with the ultra-nationalism or the authority-consciousness of the Japanese people, asserted its own superiority over foreign systems of thought. The Confucianist Sazan Kan (1748–1827), for example, declared:

"It is only because Confucianism exists that Buddhism is practiced here. If there had been no sovereign, those saints could not have acted independently. As it is said that Buddhism avoids countries with wicked monarchs, and as it is moreover said that the Benefit of the State is one of the Four Benefits, it is obvious that it (Buddhism) could not have been founded here if it were not for the influence of Confucianism. . . . The Catholics, it is said, would willingly give their lives for their Deity. This is most outrageous. It is only because the Sovereign rules our Land that we would go through fire and water in an emergency. Besides this, there are religions of many different kinds, called by various names, in different countries and generations. They may have different names, but they are all alike in practicing the trick of setting up a master above the lord. It is most apparent that this is harmful to our political ideology."[66]

But, since the Confucian concept of the state was formulated in accordance with the needs of Chinese society, it naturally contained a number of points with which the more thorough-going of the Japanese nationalists could not agree. The state conceived by Chinese philosophers was an ideal or model state; on the other hand, the state that the Japanese nationalists had in mind was the actual Japanese state. This was the reason why Japanese nationalism, nurtured, so to speak, by Confucianism had ultimately to deny the authority of Confucianism. Shōin Yoshida (1831–1859), the most influential leader of the movement to establish the modern state of Japan, declares in his criticism of Confucius and Mencius: "It was wrong of Confucius and Mencius to have left their native states and to have served in other countries. For a sovereign and a father are essentially the same. To call one's sovereign unwise and dull, and to forsake one's native state in order to find a different sovereign in another state is like calling one's father foolish and moving from one's house to the next house to become the son of the neighbor. That Confucius and Mencius lost sight of this truth can never be justified."[67]

A similar tendency can easily be discerned in the process of the Japanese assimilation of Buddhism; Japanese Buddhists carefully picked out such doctrines as would be convenient for, or not inconsistent with, their nationalism.

The attitude which Indian Buddhism assumed toward the State was, from the time of its origination, one of cautiousness. For instance, it placed monarchs in the same category with robbers—both being thought to endanger people's welfare—and it taught people to avoid both dangers as much as possible. Indian Buddhists aimed to realize, through their concept of spiritual unity, an ideal society free of the authority of monarchs, and this was but the logical conclusion derived from their idea of Compassion. The *Saṅgha,* the collective body or brotherhood of followers, was the main agency for this cause.

Such a way of thinking was unacceptable to the Japanese, according to whose realistic, nationalistic view the Japanese state was absolute, and its sovereign, the Emperor, sacred. The traditional and conservative Buddhism of the primitive type came hence to be called the "Lesser Vehicle" (*Hīnayāna*) in Japan and looked upon with contempt; the Buddhism which came to be called the "Greater Vehicle" (*Mahāyāna*), which allowed the Japanese to pursue their religious ideals in conformity with their view of the state, was adopted by them.

Nor did the Japanese accept the view of the traditional, conservative Buddhism of the early type that the State originates in a social contract. The concept of state as held by early Buddhists was as follows:[68] Farmland was divided among individuals in remote antiquity, but there still existed individuals who encroached upon the properties of others. To prevent this sort of thing, the people elected a common head ("an equal leader") who would see to it that the people were protected, good people rewarded, evil people punished. The sovereign originated from this protective police function of the ruler. A tax was "something that was paid" to the sovereign by the people; the sovereign was "employed" by the people.[69] The sovereign thus was "the selected master of the people." This concept of sovereignty was afterwards held persistently by the traditional and conservative schools of Buddhism.

It is to be noted that scriptures of primitive Buddhism tell of the Buddha Śākyamuni praising the republic of the Vajjis as the ideal form of the state.[70] But the Japanese who accepted Buddhism on a large scale refused nevertheless to adopt its concept of the state, which to them appeared to run counter to the native idea of the "state structure" (*Kokutai*). We thus find the 14th-century Shintoist, Chikafusa Kitabatake, ready, on the one hand, to accept Buddhism in general but eager, on the other hand, to emphasize the importance of the Japanese Imperial Family in the following way: The Buddhist theory (of the state) is merely an "Indian theory"; Indian monarchs may have been "the descendants of a monarch selected for the people's welfare," but "Our Imperial Family is the only continuous and unending line of family descending from its Heavenly Ancestors."[71] Atsutane Hirata (1776–1843), on the other hand, discredits the whole Indian theory of the origin of the state as merely an explanation of the origin of "Indian chieftains."[72]

The Sūtra *Konkōmyō-kyō* (*Suvarṇaprabhāsa-sūtra*—The Golden Radiance Sūtra) and some later scriptures of Mahāyāna Buddhism, unlike those of early Buddhism, advance a theory that a monarch is "a son of divine beings" (*Tenshi, devaputra*) to whom has been given a mandate of Heaven, and whom Heaven will protect. This theory which came greatly to be cherished had had its origin in the Brahmin law-books which regulated the feudal society of medieval India. Later Buddhists came to mention this theory merely as a prevailing notion of society. It was not characteristic of Buddhism. However, this idea came especially to be stressed by the Japanese.

Buddhism was thus accepted by the Japanese as significant for the support of the state. The spread of Buddhism in this country began, as is well known, with the presentation by a Korean monarch (of Paikche) Seimei to the Japanese Emperor Kimmei in 552 of a gilded bronze image of Śākyamuni, several religious flags, umbrellas, and several volumes of the sūtras. It is particularly notable here that the adoption of Buddhism was begun in the diplomatic relations between nations, or more specifically, in the relations between the Imperial Family and a foreign country. The situation here differs widely from the acceptance of Buddhism by Later Han Emperor Ming-ti from the Yüeh-chih. In Japan a state-to-state relation brought about adoption of a universal religion. According to the *Nihonshoki* (The Chronicles of Japan), King Seimei, King of Paikche, attached to his gifts a letter, a passage from which reads as follows:

"The doctrine (of the Buddha) is the most excellent of all the various doctrines. It is difficult to comprehend and penetrate. Even the Prince of Chou and Confucius were not able to grasp it. This doctrine brings about boundless virtue and happiness, thus giving the highest salvation."

"When the Emperor learned of it, His joy was great. Summoning the Ambassador, He said: 'We have never heard to this day a doctrine as wonderful as this.'" These passages in the *Nihonshoki* are in fact, as scholars[73] have pointed out, a fabrication based upon passages from the Sūtra *Konkōmyō Saishō-ō-kyō* translated by I-Ching and the Sūtra *Konkōmyō-kyō* translated by Dharmarakṣa. I-Ching translated this Sūtra into Chinese in 703, some 151 years after the 13th year of Kimmei (552). The above-mentioned letter of Paikche's king is in fact a pure fabrication by the author of the *Nihonshoki* based upon the *Konkōmyō-kyō,* and it is quite uncertain to what degree it conveys the true content of the letter of King Seimei. What interests us here is the fact that the significance of the adoption of Buddhism was understood by the Japanese, or, at least, by such court scholars as the author of the *Nihonshoki,* in accordance with the thought expressed in the *Konkōmyō-kyō.*

The Sūtra *Konkōmyō-kyō* as distinguished from other scriptures of Mahāyāna Buddhism contains considerations for the protection of the state and references to worldly Shamanistic practices. Shamanism will be discussed later; we shall therefore examine here its ideas regarding the protection of the state. It is evident from the preceding reference to the reasons for adopting Buddhism that considerations for the protection of the state constituted a factor dominant in Japanese Buddhism from the very beginning.

The memorial tablet of the Sakas in Northwest India tells us that, in the first century B.C., the Sakas already cherished the view that Buddhism manifests its divine influence for the welfare and prosperity of a monarch or state. A certain Patika, a relative of the chieftain (*Kṣatrapa*), it is said, erected in Taxila in the heart of Northwestern India a *stūpa* (sacred burial mound of Buddhists) and a building for a religious order (*Saṅghārāma*) "for all the Buddhas, and in memory of my parents and for the long life and power of the *Kṣatrapa,* his wife and children." The lion-bearing capital discovered at Mathurā also tells us in inscription that the column is dedicated to the Three Precious Things (The Buddha, the Law, and the Priesthood), as well as to the Saka state (*Sakastana-Śakasthāna*). The inscription found on the small stūpa erected by a lady Buddhist by the name of Bhadravala, in the 134th year of the Azes era, also states: "This is dedicated to all sentient beings and to the City-State (*raṭhanikama-rāṣṭranigama*)."[74] Such a view regarding the state came to be theorized in numerous scriptures of Mahāyāna Buddhism, and it was from these that the Japanese came to have their ideas concerning state protection.

In Japan Buddhism came to be propagated as a national religion during the reign of the Empress Suiko (enthroned 592 A.D.), in accordance with Article II of Prince Shōtoku's Injunctions, which enjoins "reverence to the Three Precious Things." With political and economic aids from the state Japanese Buddhism became very active. After the Political Reform of Taika, the state's control over religions became gradually solidified. With the decline in influence of the clan aristocrats, now made bureaucrats, the government abandoned its vague protection of Buddhism as a whole and the attempt to convert it to a state religion. Instead, it adopted as a basic religious policy the positive protection of pure state Buddhism alone which would cooperate in the overall task of government. Thus the protection of Buddhism was strengthened and the government not only furnished emergency building funds, but did not hesitate even to provide vast sums for running expenses.[75]

Most Japanese monasteries in those early days were thus state-operated places of worship, as is clear in the Rescript of the Emperor Shōmu (first day of the fourth month, 749 A.D.): "Now, We, hearing that of all the various doctrines the Great Word of the Buddha is the most excellent for protecting the State. . . ."[76] Buddhism was adopted by the Court with the first regard for the protection of the State, and indeed, the most profound and difficult doctrines of Buddhism were studied for this purpose. In the Nara period (710–784), the Kegon Sect, which put forward a philosophy regarded as the highest of Buddhist philosophies, came to be given the position of a national religion. A Rescript of the Emperor Shōmu (749 A.D.) states, "We consider the Kegon Sūtra to be the most authoritative Scripture." The Tōdaiji, the Central Cathedral of the Capital, was also known as the Dai-Kegonji, or the Great Kegon Temple. Then, what in the Kegon Sect appealed so much to the Japanese to win for it the position of a state religion? According to the scriptures of the Kegon sect, each petal of the thousand-petalled lotus flower upon which the Vairocana Buddha dwells represents a universe, and in each universe there are millions of *jambūdvīpa* (buds of actual worlds). In each universe of a lotus petal is a Śākyamuni-Buddha that is a manifestation of the Vairocana Buddha, and in each of the millions of *jambūdvīpa* (buds) is a small preaching Buddha that is, in turn, a manifestation of Sākyamuni. Such symbolism was most suitable for the requirements of the State. For it was thought that the officials of the government should be manifestations of Vairocana, and the people should be manifestations of the government official, just as Small Buddhas of *jambūdvīpa* are manifestations of Śākyamuni-Buddha. As long as there is harmony among the state, the government officials, and the people, as in the cosmology of Kegon, there will be peace in the land, and the nation will be safe.[77]

The minds of the Buddhists of the time were adjusted to the government's religious policies based upon this cosmology. Zenju (723–797), a great and celebrated scholar, of the Akishino Temple in the Nara Period, asks in the Introduction of his *Hongan Yakushi-Kyō Sho* ("Commentary upon the *Bhaiṣajya-guru-vaiḍūrya-tathāgata-sūtra*"), "Unless it be by repenting one's sins with a holy heart and seeking the Commandments with sincerity, how else ought one to repay for the benevolence of the sovereign and express thanks for his goodness?" And he hopes ceremonies of repentance and reception of the commandments will be conducted in order to "abide by the Great Desire of the Sovereign, and compensate for the favors of the State." And he further hopes that through these good deeds all kinds of calamities will be eliminated; "The Imperial body will be as steady as Heaven and Earth; the Imperial life be as everlasting as the sun and moon; the Imperial Family will prosper for a thousand and myriad generations; next, peace will reign in the land; all government officials will be loyal to the throne; the people of all walks of life will be happy; all merits accumulated by sincere actions in body, speech, and mind should be converted to that end."[78] Here, beyond doubt, the first object of Buddhist prayer, i.e., "happiness of all sentient beings," has now been "supplanted" by "prosperity of the Imperial Family"; Buddhist thought has been altered to suit the rank system prevailing in Japan.

"Protection of the state," one of the most dominant concerns in the Japanese mind, was thus firmly established in religion. Buan (+840) of the Ritsu sect, a staunch believer in discipline and the precepts of Buddhism, declares: "The Precepts are the basic and most important thing which promises attainment of Nirvāṇa and Salvation." "Therefore, Precepts (*śīla*) make up a small ship for crossing the sea of sufferings; discipline (*Vinaya*) is the only vehicle for attaining the Other Side. It is clear, therefore, that discipline is most important for the protection of the State."[79]

The situation was similar in the case of the Tendai (*T'ien-t'ai* in Chinese) sect, founded by Saichō, and the Shingon (*Chên-yen* in Chinese) sect, founded in 816 by Kūkai, which are known as the Buddhism of the Heian period (9th century). Saichō (posthumously named Dengyō Daishi) of the Tendai sect, in founding the Enryakuji Monastery in 827, selected the site of Mt. Hiei which was in the Ox-Tiger direction (Northeastern direction) from the Palace. This was done with the idea of protecting the Palace. Here his efforts were exerted to the training of monks who were sincere seekers of the truth, and he called these sincere novices "treasures of the nation." His purpose in training these young Buddhist scholars was to "uphold the Buddhist Doctrine and protect the State."[80] We find in his works, say, *Kenkairon* (Elucidation of Rules of Discipline) or *Shugokok-kaishō* (Treatise for Protecting the Domain of the Country), such phrases as *Shugokokkai* (Protection of the Country), *Gokoku* (Protection of the nation), *Gokoku Rimin* (Protection of the State and benefitting people), *Kokka Yōko* (State Forever), *Kokka Annei* (Peace and prosperity for the State), etc. Kūkai (posthumously named Kōbō Daishi) (774–835), who frequently practiced prayers at the Court, said he was doing this for the benefit of the State. Kūkai, moreover, had his special names for temples; for example, *Kyō-ō Gokokuji* (The temple to teach kings how to protect the nation) for the Tōji and *Jingokokuso Shingonji* (The Temple of Esoteric Buddhism to protect the national fortune by grace of gods) for the Takaosanji.

"Protection of the State" was not the slogan only of the early Buddhist sects, a mere attempt to curry favor with the state authorities, for we find the same concern in the official documents record of the state which constitute the authoritative history of Japan. Kūkai propagated Buddhism under the slogan, "Practice virtue for the State, and thus benefit man and gods."[81] Shinnen (812–891) said that Kūkai built the Kongōbuji "to safe-guard the nation and protect the Law of Buddha."[82] In the Rescript of the Emperor Nimmyō we find it said: "The Buddhist Doctrine is the foremost and the most excellent for protecting the state and benefitting the people."[83] It was in order to "compensate for the August Goodness and protect the State" that Discipline Master Shinshō (821–873) erected the images of the Vairocana and the Buddhas of the Four Directions.[84] The *raison d'être* of the Enryaku Temple lay in the "Protection of the Imperial Family."[85] It was also to "protect the State and promote the August Throne" that the monks of the Anjō Temple adopted the *tendoku* method of reading the sūtras of various sects.[86] In his address to the Throne, Ennin or Jikaku Daishi (784–864) says, "With all our efforts we will propagate it, thereby protecting the State, benefitting the masses and repaying the favors of our teachers."[87] Discipline Master Jōan (+878) is said to have announced: "The work of copying sūtras will be done in order to protect the State."

Concerns for protection of the state are seen also in newly-risen sects of the Kamakura period. In the field of the newly imported Rinzai Zen Buddhism was Eisai (1141–1215) writing his *Kōzengokokuron* (A Treatise on Protecting the Nation by Spreading Zen Buddhism).[88] There were at that time the Six sects of Nara, and the Tendai and Shingon sects already established as state-authorized religious schools, and for any rising Zen sect it was necessary to stress its concern for protection of the state in order to be state-authorized. This motive is apparent in such works as *Nihon Bukkyō Chūkō Ganmon* (A prayer to make Japanese Buddhism prosper again) or *Kōzen Gokokuron*. The full names of the Nanzenji in Kyoto and the Kenchōji in Kamakura are respectively, *Zuiryūzan Taiheikōkoku Nanzenzenji* (A Temple to make the country peaceful and prosperous) and *Kofukusan Kenchō Kōkokuzenji*. Kōshōji in Uji which Dōgen founded upon his return from China was called *Kannon Dōri-in Kōshōgokokuji* (A Temple to protect a nation by propagating the Holy Practice).[89] Soseki (1275–1351), Buddhist priest of the Rinzai Sect, erected the Ankokujis (Temples to make the nation peaceful) in different provinces, and there are the Gokokujis (Temples to protect the nation) throughout Japan.

Now, in China, it was the rise of the Mongols that stirred state consciousness in Zen schools of the Southern Sung Dynasty (1127–1279), and this attitude of Chinese Zen schools was, no doubt, reflected in the Japanese Buddhism of the Kamakura period (1185–1333). But significant here is the fact that while in China state consciousness was soon to wither away, it persisted in Japan down to recent times.

The concern for the state, as an idea, however, did not belong logically to the doctrines of most sects. It was with the Nichiren Sect that it came to constitute an essential motive. To understand this situation we have only to observe what position it is given in Nichiren's work, *Risshō Ankokuron* (A treatise to establish righteousness and to make the country peaceful). Religion, according to Nichiren, must serve the state. He said: "Thirteen thousand thirty-seven Buddhist temples and three thousand one hundred thirty-two Shintō shrines are revered for the sake of the safety of the state."[90] To him the existence of the state was the prerequisite for the flourishing of Buddhism. He says, again: "The Nation prospers because of Buddhism; and Buddhism becomes precious because people revere it. If the Nation perish and people disappear, who will revere Buddhism? Therefore, say prayers first for thy State, then presently Buddhism will be established."

Again: "If there be no overthrow of the State and no destruction on Earth, thy body will be safe, thy mind will be at ease."[91]

Nichiren's first and last concern was Japan. In his Commentary on the Lotus Sūtra (in the fifth chapter, *yakusōyubon*), he cites the passage, "The Buddha appears in the world," and Nichiren says, "By 'world' Japan is meant." He also cites a passage which reads: "And this personage came to the world," and comments, "This personage is the Bodhisattva *Jōgyō* (*Viśiṣṭacārita*—Excellent Practice). The 'world' is Japan. . . . It is a person like Nichiren in the present." He, again, interprets the passage in the commentary by Master Myōraku (Miao-lo, 711–782). "When the son propagates the teachings of his father, it is beneficial to the world," in the following way: "By the 'son' is meant the Bodhisattvas who are said to have appeared from the earth when the Hokke Sūtra was preached. By the 'father' is meant Buddha Śākyamuni. By *'the world' is meant Japan*. The 'benefit' means becoming a Buddha."[92] Now, what Indian Buddhists meant by the "World" (or *lokadhātu*) was the area on which the light of the sun and moon shines, i.e., the four Continents around Mt. Sumeru. But Nichiren narrowed this "world"—the world that is eventually to attain salvation on the strength of the Lotus Sūtra—to Japan.

In the case of the Pure Land (Jōdo) Buddhism, however, there was comparatively less state-consciousness. Since Hōnen, for instance, was not concerned with state structure (*kokutai*), the Pure Land doctrines were therefore disapproved until recently by a group of ultra-nationalist philosophers. Indeed, the state was not a thing of great concern in the minds of Hōnen or Shinran. But as the Pure Land Buddhism broadened its sphere of influence, it became necessary, in order to protect itself from the onslaughts from outside, to compromise with the ultra-nationalists. In the sequel we shall briefly examine the case of the Pure Land (Jōdo) Buddhism.

Shinran (1173–1262), the founder of the True Pure Land (Jōdo Shin) sect, held no particular view regarding the state. His only concern was the relation between the sinful mortal, such as he regarded himself to be, and Amida Buddha the Savior. Shinran apparently had no thought of compromising with secular authority. But as the True Pure Land (Jōdo Shin) sect spread among the people through the efforts of Rennyo (1415–1499), its attitude toward the contemporary feudal authority became one of compromise. We see Rennyo saying: "Now you should in no wise neglect your duties to constables (*shugo*) of provinces or to stewards (*jitō*) of local communities on the grounds that you revere the Law of Buddha and are believers. Indeed, you should devote yourselves all the more to public affairs, so that you will be pointed out as men who know what you are about, and will be models of conduct to the *nembutsu* believer who has faith and who prays for future happiness. That is to say, you will be looked up to as men who make a point of keeping both the Law of Buddha and the Law of the Sovereign."[93] Rennyo also admonishes: "Bear in thy head the Law of the Sovereign; bear deep in thy heart the Law of the Buddha."[94] The True Pure Land (Jōdo Shin) Sect developed this idea, and brought out the dualistic theory of Truth. Originally the Buddhist *paramārtha-satya* (Japanese *shintai*) meant Absolute Truth, whereas *samvṛti-satya* (Japanese *zokutai*) meant a lower order of truth. The meaning of these terms was altered by the Shin sect, so that *shintai* represented the Law of Buddha and *zokutai* the Law of the Sovereign, thus resolving the problem of the two conflicting authorities.

In the Meiji era (after 1868), when feudal regimes had collapsed and the central authority had been established, great stress came to be placed upon the sanctity of the Emperor, and the Honganji Order came to adopt the ethics of nationalism. We find the following passage in Kōnyo's *Goikun Shōsoku* ("A Letter written by the late Chief Abbot"), dated the Fourth Year of Meiji (1871), and made public by Myōnyo in the following year:

"There is no man born in this Empire who has not benefitted from the Imperial Favor. At this time especially, when His Majesty devotes himself night and day to the furtherance of good government and the safety of his people at home and to holding his own with countries abroad, who among us, whether priest or layman, will not aid the spread of his kingly rule and cause the Imperial authority to shine with its true brilliance? What is more, since the spread of Buddhism in the world is due solely to the protection of the Sovereign and his ministers, how can the faithful Buddhist neglect the prohibitions of the Law of the Sovereign? Therefore in our sect it has already been resolved that the Law of the Sovereign should be fundamental, that benevolence and justice should be foremost, that the gods should be revered and morality observed."

Buddhist scholars, upon mentioning Shinran, are wont to argue that Shinran did have concern for the state, and they invariably cite one single passage as evidence. That is the letter that Shinran wrote to Shōshimbō:

"It would be a happy thing if all the people who recite the *nembutsu,* recite it not for the sake of their own welfare but for the Sovereign and the people. But those who are uncertain of reaching Pure Land, let them recite the *nembutsu* (name of the Buddha) for their own rebirth in Pure Land. But I think people who are certain of attaining Pure Land should bear in mind the Buddha's mercy, and, in order to repay his mercy, with all their heart recite the *nembutsu* for peace among the people and the propagation of Buddhism."

Now obviously this is not a logical piece of writing. If we were to examine it objectively, we find that the first and second sentences are really antithetical to each other in form and ironical in content. What Shinran is saying here is that happy are the people who are able to say the *nembutsu* for both the Sovereign and themselves, for their attainment of Pure Land has been assured, and so let them do so. But, he says, those who in their self-reflection are uncertain of attainment of Pure Land—that is, those who are Shinran's followers—should recite the *nembutsu* in order to attain their own salvation. I think that what Shinran is advocating here is not that the Sovereign be considered as the paramount concern but rather that faith be considered most important.[95]

Surprisingly enough, however, this passage by Shinran has hitherto been grossly misinterpreted. Japanese scholars in most cases believed that Shinran was here *teaching nationalism*. Through misinterpreting the words of the very founder, the present leaders of the sect compromised with the ultra-nationalist leaders of the military clique and were thus able to mitigate their attacks. In the case of Saint Hōnen (1133–1212), not a single reference to the state is found; this was the ground for ultra-nationalists' criticisms of Hōnen or Genkū, founder of the Jōdo or Pure Land sect.

We note here with interest that of the numerous scriptures that exist in Buddhism those which were thought to have state-protecting efficacy were especially favored, the Lotus Sūtra, the *Konkōmyō-kyō* (Golden Radiance Sūtra) and the *Ninnō hannya-kyō* (Sūtra of the Perfect Wisdom of Benign Kings) being just such. The Lotus Sūtra itself, however, embodies no thought for "state-safety"; on the contrary, it teaches that the true devotee of Buddhism "remains at a distance from monarchs and state ministers."[96] But if we were to look for the part in the Sūtra which led the Japanese to link their concern for state-safety with the Lotus Sūtra, we shall find it to be the part in which it is stated that if things are carried out in accordance with the Lotus Sūtra, there shall be peace and happiness in the world. As an example, Masashige Kusunoki (? –1336), was a believer in the Lotus Sūtra. In the colophon of a Lotus Sūtra (in the library of the Minatogawa Shrine), copied by his own hand, he says:

"The Hokke Sūtra is the essence of all the doctrines preached by the Buddha, and the heart of the One Vehicle. Therefore all spiritual leaders in the past, present, and future, regard it as the true purport of their birth, and eight kinds of divine beings regard it as the authority for the protection of the country. Especially, the capacity of this country for the fullness of the Mahāyāna doctrine is great and the solemnity of the Ise Shrine will protect us and answer our prayers. This fact is fully written down in clerical histories. I, who have been ordered by the Emperor to destroy the rebels, have made this vow; if peace comes to the world and what is in my heart be granted, one chapter of this sūtra will be read every day before the god in this shrine. So I have made a copy of it by myself and fulfilled my long-cherished desire. On the 25th of the 8th month of the 2nd year of Kemmu (1335 A.D.).

"(Signed) Kusunoki Ason Masashige, Major General of the Left Palace Guard and Governor of Kawachi."[97]

We are also told in the *Taiheiki* that Emperor Godaigo passed away "with the fifth scroll of the Lotus Sūtra in his left hand and a sword in his right."[98]

The same attitude is noticeable in the way the teachings of the *Avataṁsaka* (*Kegon*) *Sūtra* are observed by the Japanese. The Sūtra describes the ideal monarchical government. It contains, at the same time, a number of passages where monarchs and princes are admonished to forsake their states and become Buddhist ascetics.[99] Nevertheless, in Japan of the Nara period the Sūtra was considered to be a philosophy that promised the prosperity of the state. Behind the great efforts exerted for the casting of the Colossal Buddha of Nara was this understanding. And although there is clear evidence of state-consciousness in the Sūtras *Konkōmyō-kyō* and *Ninnō Hannya-kyō,* it is not an ultra-nationalistic state-consciousness. According to these Sūtras, the eternal and universal *dharma* is the only way upon which we may rely; this is the doctrine of the Perfect Wisdom (*prajñāpāramitā, Hannyaharamitsu*) which enlightens us on the right human conduct, that only through the application of the Perfect Wisdom doctrine to the activities of the state, will the state be protected and prosperous. Thus the state is not regarded as absolute. On the contrary it is emphasized that a state wherein the Law is not observed will perish. But the Japanese, inclined to nationalism, found these sūtras particularly agreeable and adaptable.

The notion that Buddhism protects the state spread eventually among the warriors and the common people. In the period 386–589, known as the Age of the Northern and Southern Dynasties, when Kyushu rose to assist Takauji Ashikaga (1305–1358), the clan of Taketoki Kikuchi (1291–1333) alone sided with the Southern Court. When Taketoki Kikuchi erected a temple in Tamana-gun, Province of Higo, and received the Zen Master Daichi as head of the temple, he presented a dedicatory address of which the following is the final part; "If the principles contained in this address are carried out, and the True Law observed with pure faith we shall receive the unseen protection of the Three Treasures and various Deities; our descendants for generations to come shall live up to the warrior ideals of our family, and be able *to protect the prosperity of our State.* I therefore shed my own blood, mix it with cinnabar ink, and present this address sealed therewith to admonish my descendants."[100]

Emphasis upon the state is noticeable even among Buddhists who were in close touch with the common folk. For example, we find in Jiun's *Regulations of the Kōki Temple* an article which enjoins "Sincerity and diligence in praying for the State."[101]

We find the case of a state assuming the character of a religious order in ancient Greece, and we also know that the religious order of Sikhism in India took on the character of a state. In Japan, however, religion was thought to constitute the foundation of the state, and the state would be protected by it. Just as Buddhism was thought to contribute to the government of the state, so, at the lower level, it was regarded as contributing to the government of the *feudal* fief. As has been frequently pointed out, the world-outlook of Zen Buddhism underlies the spirit of the so-called "Hagakure" warriors of the Sage clan in Kyūshū. The intention to assist clan politics with Buddhism is expressed in the *Gohōshijiron* (A Treatise on the Application of Buddhism to Politics) by Shōken Mori (1653–1721) of the Mito clan.

As we have pointed out before, there was hardly any political coloring or emphasis on the state, in religions in India. And in ancient China, too, it was observed that "A monk will not respect the monarch." But in the Liu Sung dynasty (420–478) monks did come to "respect the monarch." Although in the end Chinese religion became subordinated to the state, state-consciousness was never stressed by Buddhists themselves. In Japan, however, Buddhism, which is a universal religion, was adopted and spread as a religion serving the interests of the state.

We are now ready to draw some conclusions from the above examination of Japanese nationalism, and this we must do with some reservations. For religion, with which we have mainly been dealing, is merely one of many facets of culture. The outstanding features of Japanese nationalism, however, may be summed up as follows:

The Japanese people of the past dedicated a large and important part of their individual lives to their state. In this respect, the Japanese went to an extent to which no other Eastern peoples have ever gone. The great intensity of such dedication is itself the first feature of Japanese nationalism.

The second feature is that Japanese nationalism was developed from the limited exclusive concern for the particular state of Japan. Now, there are different ways in which nationalism is applied to practice. We know that nationalism has been expounded a number of times by thinkers in India and China, as well as in the West. But their nationalism was theoretically concerned with the state in general, not with their particular states. Now, nationalism tends, from its very nature, to be applied to a state in particular, but nationalism and concern for a particular state are not quite identical. In ancient India and China nationalism was rather theoretical. In Japanese nationalism, on the other hand, the particular state of Japan came to be the sole standard upon which all judgments were based. This, without doubt, has a close relation to the general tendency in Japanese thinking, especially in the past, to overlook the universal and to lay stress upon an exclusive human nexus. The natural basis for Japan's exclusive concern for herself is, I believe, the insular position of Japan, isolated from the Continent by water; there is also the historical fact that Japan has known the existence of foreign nations only indirectly, as in the cases of the Mongolian Invasion and World War II.

Certain feelings of apprehension may arise here. Some readers may ask: Is not Japanese state-consciousness already a thing of the past? Is she not being rapidly modernized? Has not the experience of defeat in World War II brought the Japanese people to consider themselves as individuals who can shape the future of their society, and participate in the sovereignty of the State, rather than be merely "subjects" of the emperor? We are, however, inclined to give only a tentative "yes" to these questions. For although it is true that changes are being made rapidly in that direction, it is also true that it is no easy task for the Japanese to do away with their traditional thinking. We must remember that the country is overflowing with people. The network of tightly-formed village communities covers the land. Many of them are rapidly becoming industrialized, and the villagers now commute to factories of heavy industry, or move to the cities. The nation's economy is such that the state must still exercise controls over a large portion of individual life. Above all, since its antiquity the nation's progress has always had its motivation in the Imperial Family, although it is now not so powerful as before. Furthermore, we may say that the Japanese sentiment toward the Imperial House has been friendly rather than hostile and, as in some foreign countries, the ruling class has often been benevolent in its dealings with the people.[102] All in all we may say that an atmosphere of family-like intimacy still pervades the country. (Such a term as "family-state," for instance, would have been rejected by Westerners, and even by the Indians, or the Chinese, as self-contradictory. The Japanese, however, felt no inconsistency in the term, but found it good and valid.) Now, after these considerations, would it really be possible to put an end to the Japanese way of thinking about the state? This is not a trait in which we can take pride before other nations, but, just as religion was the basis of the ethical thinking of the Indians, and family the basis of the practical morals of the Chinese, so the state was the basis of all thought in the Japanese. The Indians will be Indians; the Chinese will be Chinese, and we do not look down upon them or criticize them for it. The Japanese way of thinking is undergoing a change, but their thinking is an historical inheritance; it is a national cultural tradition. We feel that it is our part to see to it that this tradition never again gives rise to an inhuman ultra-nationalism.

Absolute Devotion to a Specific Individual Symbolic of the Human Nexus

The tendency to confine values to a limited human nexus reveals itself in Japan in absolute devotion to a specific individual as a concrete symbol of Japanese social values. The Japanese, unlike the Indians and Chinese, prefer not to conceive of a human nexus in an abstract way. They are apt rather to follow an individual as a living representative of that nexus. As I have previously indicated, the "family" in ancient Japan was not an abstract concept, but was embodied in the person of the living family head. There is also a tendency to identify the *shōgun* with the *bakufu* (shogunate government), the Emperor with the State. In the feudalism of the West, relations between lord and vassal were extremely complex, and the notion of contract played an important part in such relations. In feudal Japan, however, this relationship was a simple one; the vassal devoted his entire existence to his lord. This gave rise to the motto "a loyal vassal does not know two masters." This way of thinking, characteristic of Japanese society in general, manifests itself among Japanese thinkers in an attitude of absolute devotion and obedience to a specific individual.

Most Japanese thinkers of the past were either Buddhists or Confucianists. Now, of course, religion is apt to base itself upon some authority. However, Indian and Chinese thinkers do not rely on a specific individual, but tend rather to establish and follow universal laws. Japanese thinkers, on the contrary, were likely to disregard universal laws in favor of the authority of a specific individual.

For some 700 years after the adoption of Buddhism, it was customary for Buddhists to explain the doctrine and expound their theories in the Chinese language. Japanese Buddhism, therefore, was in a sense an extension of Chinese Buddhism. This does not mean, however, that the Japanese merely took over the universal teachings of Buddhism as it was practiced in China at the time of adoption. Japanese scholar-monks received their doctrines from one specific Chinese teacher, and that is precisely what they wanted to do. Saint Dengyō (767–822), for example, wished to travel to China so that he might discover the true significance of the Lotus Sūtra (*Hokke-kyō*). In his letter requesting admittance to China, he writes as follows: "I have long regretted the absence of a commentary which would explain the profound import of the Lotus Sūtra. By good fortune I have procured a copy of the excellent discourse of the T'ien t'ai sect. I have studied it a number of years, but errors and omissions in the text make it impossible to grasp the fine points. If I do not receive instruction from a master, then, even if I were to get (the meaning), I should be unable to believe in it."[103] Thus, he went to China, studied under Tao-sui (c. 800), and returned to Japan.

The attitude of absolute devotion to a specific individual became still more pronounced in Kamakura Buddhism, which is especially representative of Japanese Buddhism. The Pure Land doctrine of Hōnen (1133–1212) was based exclusively upon one master, Shan-tao (613–681). At the same time Hōnen exalted the authority of the teacher. He says, "To view the doctrine of the Pure Land without the aid of oral tradition is to lose sight of one's share in the rebirth."[104] Shinran (1173–1262), too, was absolutely devoted to his master, Hōnen. "As far as I, Shinran, am concerned, the sole reason I have faith is that a good man explained to me that in order to be saved by Amida I had only to recite the invocations (*nembutsu*). I do not know whether the *nembutsu* is actually the means to rebirth in the Pure Land, or whether perhaps it is the road to Hell. Even though I were cajoled by Saint Hōnen that I should go to Hell through the *nembutsu,* I should do so and not regret it."[105]

Wishing to establish rationally the authority of his personal interpretation of Buddhism, Shinran makes the major premise of his reasoning rest on the absolute authority of the teacher. "If the original view of Amida is true, then the teachings of Śākyamuni are true, and the commentaries of Shan-tao cannot be false; if the commentaries of Shan-tao are true, the teachings of Hōnen cannot be false; if the teachings of Hōnen are true, how would it be possible for me, Shinran, to utter a falsehood."[106]

This is cast in the form of a complex syllogism, but in each of the component syllogisms there is a hidden premise, namely, "the word of a disciple faithful to his teacher is as true as that of the teacher." Such a proposition is very questionable. The Japanese, however, consider it perfectly natural. They even pass over it in silence as not requiring overt explanation.

The watchword here is absolute docility before authority. This sort of reasoning is substantially the same as that which produced the notion, a few years back, that "the command of a superior is the command of the Emperor." Apparently this authoritarian viewpoint is also found in other oriental countries. Scholars and students of religion pretend that they have inherited the orthodox doctrine from ancient time, and cite the genealogy of their teachers to prove it. It appears, however, that in the other oriental countries these thoughts were not expressed in the form of a sorites.

At any rate, Shinran himself had not the slightest thought of originating a new sect. His proposed aim was merely to elucidate the true purport of his master Hōnen's teachings. "My master Genkū (Hōnen), being well versed in Buddhism, took pity on common people, both good and bad. He began to teach the doctrine of the true religion (*shinshū*) in the provinces, and spread the chosen original vow (of Amida) throughout this corrupt world."[107] By "true religion" Shinran refers to the Pure Land sect (*jōdo-shū*) of Hōnen, and not to the so-called True Pure Land sect (*jōdo-shinshū*).[108] The attitude of dependence upon the master was also influential among the followers of Shinran. "When I take council with myself and consider in my fumbling way the past and the present, I must regret the differences (that have sprung up) in the true faith as taught orally by our master. I fear that future students will fall into an unbroken series of errors, for, unless one is fortunate enough to be grounded upon knowledge derived from the original source, how can he possibly gain entrance to the Easy Way (*Amidian nembutsu*)? One's own insight of one's own private views should in no wise be confounded with the doctrine of Another's Strength (*tariki*).[109] Therefore I shall note down here the gist of the sayings of the late Saint Shinran, which remain in my mind. I hope thereby to dissipate the doubts of my coreligionists."[110]

This tendency is also apparent in Nichiren (1222–1282), who attacked the Pure Land teachings. At the end of the scriptures of Mahāyāna Buddhism, it is said that Śākyamuni entrusted the scriptures to various persons, but according to Nichiren the true transmission of the Lotus Sūtra depended on blood relationship.[111] Thus the true spirit of the Lotus Sūtra is revealed only by the specific person who had received its guardianship. It is for this reason that Nichiren called himself the reincarnation of the Bodhisattva Jōgyō to whom the Lotus Sūtra had been entrusted.[112]

It is especially Nichiren's conviction that he was a reincarnation of Buddha which distinguishes him from the other Chinese and Japanese who studied the Lotus Sūtra. "I, Nichiren," he says, "am like the messenger of the Bodhisattva Jōgyō. . . . Indeed I teach this doctrine. . . . I feel that I must be a reincarnation of the Bodhisattva Jōgyō."[113]

This differs considerably from the interpretation of the Lotus Sūtra by Chinese Buddhist commentators. Master T'ien-t'ai, for example, has this to say on the subject: "Thus entrusting the sūtras to innumerable Bodhisattvas of the thousand universes, he had the sūtra propagated in the sphere of the cosmic body of Buddha. Is not this teaching far superior to that which would have the sūtras spread here and there by humble mortals? May the substance of the Ten Spheres[114] penetrate the different countries of the earth, and may there be obtained the double advantage of darkness and light."[115]

Elsewhere Master Chia-hsiang (549–623), at the beginning of his interpretation of the 14th chapter of the Lotus Sūtra, says: "This chapter, like the 11th, indicates that the ensemble of the Bodhisattvas emanating from the earth, should be taken as an expression of the cosmic body of the Buddha."[116]

Whereas Chinese Buddhist commentators gave absolute value to the absolute taken as a basic principle, in Japan, Nichiren attributed this absolute authority to a specific person in certain particular circumstances.

Thus, to believe Nichiren, he himself had actually received, two thousand years before, the store of the wisdom of the Buddha, which he now in turn transmits to mankind. "On the 24th day of the second month of the eleventh year of Bunei, on Mount Ryōzen (*Gṛdhrakūṭa*) of the Pure Land, Nichiren, to whom Buddha entrusted the store of the essential verities, respectfully received priestly ordination."[117] "More than 2000 years ago Nichiren, as chief of the Bodhisattvas of the thousand worlds emerging out of the earth, received from the very mouth of the Buddha the three great secret doctrines."[118] In the Zen sect, too, Dōgen (1200–1253), for example, teaches absolute devotion to the master. "In order to embrace Buddhism, one must abandon his own judgments of good and evil. Rather must one follow the words and examples of our Buddhist predecessors, regardless of god or evil. What one regards as good, either in his own opinion or in that of other men, is not necessarily good. Therefore, heedless of the world's gaze, and oblivious of one's own opinions, one should follow the teachings of the Buddha."[119] "We recognize immediately and instinctively that such persons as Śākyamuni and Amida are Buddhas, for their features are endowed with radiance and they are remarkable for their preaching and their grace. If, however, a learned priest says that a toad or a worm is the Buddha, then one must abandon ordinary knowledge and believe that a toad or a worm is the Buddha. But if one seeks in the worm the radiance of countenance or the various virtues with which the Buddha is endowed, then one still has not modified his prejudices. One must recognize as the Buddha only that which can be seen at a given moment. Thus if one goes along modifying his prejudices in accordance with the words of the master, one will naturally reach agreement. The scholars of recent days, on the contrary, cling to their own prejudices and think that the Buddha must be such and such, according to their private opinions. If anything should differ from their opinion, they say that it cannot be so, but wonder if it may be something similar to their own preconceived notions. Thus in the main they are not devoted to the way of the Buddha."[120]

Then he explains that one should conform absolutely to the various ascetic practices, precepts and rules of the Zen sect, because they represent the continuous tradition of the past. "It is false to insist upon ascetic practice as essential, believing thereby that one may reach enlightenment, on the grounds that one should keep commandments and observe the fasts. One observes such things because they are the routine of a monk and the customs of the house of the sons of Buddha. One should not necessarily say that such things are essential because they are useful."[121]

For this reason, Dōgen planned to establish rationally each of the rules and doctrines of the Zen sect. However, he abandoned his plan before completing it, and gave precedence to authority and tradition over rational thought. For example, Buddhism recognizes four attitudes among the various daily activities of mankind, namely, walking, standing, sitting, and reclining. One speaks of "Zen," however, only in connection with the sitting position. Explaining the reason for this, Dōgen says: "It may be asked, 'Why do the priests speak of meditation and enlightenment only in connection with the sitting position?' and I answer, 'It is difficult to know the way by which all the various Buddhas achieved enlightenment. If you seek the reason, you must know that it is just because the priests employed (this way). You should not question further. Our masters before us praised sitting in meditation (*zazen*) as the gateway to bliss. This is why we know that of the four attitudes sitting is the way to bliss. What is more, it was not the practice of one or two Buddhas, but of all the Buddhas before us.' "[122]

Because of this deference to tradition, Dōgen teaches that ascetics should practice under the direction of an eminent teacher. "By practicing asceticism in a group, one attains the Way. It is like boarding a boat without knowing how to row. Since one trusts a good boatman, it makes no difference whether one knows how to row; one gets to the other side. Thus one should follow a good teacher and practice in a group. Then, since one is not relying on one's own resources, one naturally attains the Way."[123]

However, the one who decides who is an "eminent teacher" is the ascetic himself. The basis of this value judgment is the consciousness or experience of universal law within the ascetic himself. It is a rational consideration within the subjectivity of the ascetic which operates here. Thus, when we analyze Dōgen's advice to follow a good teacher without regard for any further rational considerations, one ends up in a vicious circle. Dōgen, however, never touched upon this question. He simply ordered that one was to devote himself absolutely to a venerated person.

It may be objected at this point that absolute devotion to a teacher is merely one of the social phenomena of a feudal society and that we simply have here a reflection of the feudal character in Dōgen's attitude. This is, perhaps, a plausible explanation, but I hesitate to dispose of the question so simply. One hardly finds, in the feudal societies of India or China, this advocacy of absolute devotion to a specific person. One does, to be sure, often come across the phrase "become intimate with a *zenchishiki*" in the scriptures composed in India, but here *zenchishiki* is a translation of *kalyāṇamitra* which means "good friend" or "intimate friend." In Japan, on the contrary, *zenchishiki* is taken in the sense of "religious teacher." *It is the Japanese way of thinking which we find in this socio-hierarchical interpretation.* For the Indians (and for most Chinese Buddhists) the "law" in the religious sense was not something transmitted to the pupil by the teacher as a specific individual, but rather something which *the ascetic himself mastered.* Indians would never dream of making such a statement as "I would not mind being cast into hell if I were led astray by Saint Hōnen." Thus this characteristic of the thought of Shinran and Dōgen is not attributed to traditional Indian or Chinese Buddhism, and it is, furthermore, difficult to attribute this attitude to feudalism in general.

In the case of Dōgen, one cannot say that he acquired the characteristic in question from his Chinese master Ju-ching (1163–1228). The latter, in fact, teaches the opposite of Dōgen. Ju-ching was very prone to heap scorn on authority. He called Yuima (Vimalakīrti, the wealthy gentleman) a "bandit" and Lin-chi (?–867) an "ass"; of Bodhidharma's expression "Nothing can be called holy," he says, *"He himself created it, he himself destroyed it."* He even goes so far as to say, "To practice true Zen, one does not think about the masters."[124] Moreover, in keeping with the general tendency of Chinese Zen Buddhism, he denies the authority of specific doctrines. For example, he says, "Atop Mt. Gṛdhkrakūṭa, there are no words of the Master; at the foot of Mt. Shaolin no mysteries are transmitted."[125] (Mt. Gṛdhrakūṭa is the place where the Buddha explained the Lotus Sūtra: Mt. Shaolin is the place where Bodhidharma sat for nine years in meditation, facing a wall.) Dōgen himself claims to have transmitted very faithfully the teachings of his master Ju-ching, but the fact is that Dōgen opposes him when it comes to the question of the authority of tradition.

One result of this absolute devotion to a specific person is that the faithful of the various Japanese sects are extreme in the veneration with which they acknowledge the founder of the sect and perform religious ceremonies around him as the nucleus. One has absolute faith in the master as well as in the Buddha, without feeling that there is the slightest contradiction. It is not that one pays less attention to the Buddha, but the idea is perhaps that a profound faith in the master and devotion to the Buddha have the same significance.[126]

The Japanese then exhibit an attitude of complete devotion to a specific person—the emperor, the feudal lord, the superior, the boss. In the field of religion this attitude appears in the manner we have just outlined. One may say that a similar religious attitude is present in other countries. The attitude of the medieval Catholics toward the saints or that of the Hindu toward the *guru* are two instances. In these cases, however, the religious qualities of the various saints are revered; the question of genealogy barely comes up. Japan differs from these other countries in the great importance attached to genealogy.

This attitude, aided by the Japanese tendency to emphasize blood relationship, is responsible for the veneration of the founder in the True Pure Land sect. As this sect develops, this attitude becomes more and more conspicuous. Already in the *Gaijashō* (Correction of Heresy) of Kakunyo (1270–1351), there appears the tendency to venerate a living monk as if he were Amitābha. Kakunyo himself appears to consider himself "the pure stream of Buddha's incarnation."[127] The tendency becomes still stronger when there develops an intense veneration of the chief abbot as the concrete individual leader of the Honganji order. Indeed the order maintains itself and develops around this veneration of the abbot. Intellectual comprehension of doctrine is neglected. Thus the Honganji order itself prohibited the faithful from reading the *Tannishō,* that frank and clear exposition of the essence of the True Pure Land faith. The order openly preached faith in the chief abbot as the principal consideration.

Not only is there no relation between the teachings of Shinran, as they affect the conscience of the ordinary mortal, and this devotion to the abbot which makes a specific person an absolute, but indeed the two are logically contradictory. Although Luther preached a faith very similar to that of Shinran, nobody in Germany ever thought of venerating the descendants of Luther. In Japan, however, such a religious peculiarity did develop, and this tendency, moreover, still persists in modern times. It can be seen in certain sectarian divisions of Shintoism which have flourished since the beginning of the Meiji era.

We must recognize that we are dealing with an attitude which is deeply rooted in the traditional habits of the Japanese people. This sort of socio-religious phenomenon did not appear in India or China. Sectarianism does occur in India and China, but the sects for the most part emphasize some universal law. The consciousness of the founder of the sect is often vague, and veneration of the founder hardly existed in antiquity. Needless to say, nothing comparable to the veneration of the chief abbot had ever arisen, except in sectarian Hinduism.

The attitude of absolute devotion to a specific person manifests itself as a sublimated attitude of complete devotion to the Buddha as an ideal person, and thus faith in Buddha is emphasized.

In this connection the Japanese Pure Land sect shows a remarkable development and lays much stress on the purity of faith. This sect esteems the 18th of the 48 vows of Amitābha, which, it teaches, must be *believed* with all one's heart. Hōnen did not believe with traditional Buddhism that the individual ascetic could obtain salvation through his own practices; but maintained that one would be delivered through faith in Amitābha and reliance on his vow. Among the disciples of Hōnen, Jōkakubō Kōsai (c. 1250), although regarded as a heretic for having preached the efficacy of a single utterance of the Buddha's name (*nembutsu*), placed special emphasis upon faith in Buddha. "The believer is reborn there (the Pure Land) only by virtue of the vow (of Amida), and not through his own efforts. The reason is that the sinful mortal, burdened as he is by worldly distraction, is separated by an abyss from the Pure Land. But, relying on the vow of the Buddha, he will at once succeed."[128]

Then with the evolution of the True Pure Land sect, the significance of faith came more and more to be stressed. "To be reborn in the Pure Land, one must have faith above all and not concern himself with anything else. A matter of such magnitude as rebirth in Pure Land cannot be arranged by the ordinary mortal. He must yield absolutely to the Buddha."[129]

In the Chinese T'ien t'ai sect, Buddhism was generally considered under three aspects: doctrine, practice, and illumination.[130] The Tendai sect in Japan also accepted this point of view.[131] The doctrine of the True Pure Land sect is an off-shoot of this essential Tendai doctrine. For this reason the basic scripture of the True Pure Land sect is called *Kenjōdo-shinjitsu Kyōgyōshō monrui* (abbreviated title, *Kyōgyōshinshō;*[132] *Kyōgyō-shō*-doctrine, practice, enlightenment or illumination). In the short title the *shin,* "faith," is added. That the word faith is absent from the complete title is due to the relationship with the old Tendai doctrine. However, in the book itself, faith is the principal matter considered. In Buddhism as a whole, after "faith" has been affirmed, one devotes himself to "practice"; while in the True Pure Land sect, the two are identical: faith accompanied by practice, and practice accompanied by faith. The believing heart is the "true heart." In this way faith comes to stand at the very center of Buddhism. Shinran, consequently, tends to regard a skeptic or one who relies upon his own resources as more despicable than a great sinner. Rennyo (1415–1499), who popularized the True Pure Land sect, expresses absolute devotion to Amitābha in terms which still more call to mind human relationships. The use of such expressions as "rely upon" and "help me!" seem to date from Rennyo. Such expressions appeal to popular sentiment.

That the Japanese Pure Land sect emphasizes faith and esteems the 18th of the 48 vows of Amida, i.e. the vow which exalts faith, is a peculiarly Japanese phenomenon, completely different from the case of the Pure Land sect in China. Yang Jen-shan (1837–1911), the promoter of the Buddhist revival in modern China, criticized the exclusive emphasis on the 18th vow characteristic of the Japanese True Pure Land sect. He maintains that this is an affront to Amitābha, for each and everyone of the 48 vows is true.[133]

Here a problem arises. It is natural that the Pure Land sects, which preach absolute dependence upon another's strength, should emphasize faith in a specific individual or in Buddha. However, this should not be true of the Zen sect, which maintains a contrary (doctrinal) position.

Nonetheless, Dōgen does emphasize the significance of faith just as do the partisans of Pure Land Buddhism. The very name, Dōgen, comes from Volume XIV of the Chinese translation of the *Avataṁsaka-sūtra,* which reads: "Faith is the origin of the Way (*dōgen*), the mother of virtue; it nourishes all the various good practices."[134] "Therefore it is said, 'Faith permits us to enter into the great sea of the Buddha-law.' The actuality of faith is the actuality of the Buddha himself."[135] Without faith it is difficult to achieve perfection in the practice of Buddhism. "One may teach a man who has not faith, but it is difficult for such a one to accept the teaching."[136] According to Dōgen, rather than achieve enlightenment through one's ascetic practices, one should, in the final analysis, have absolute devotion to the Buddha as an ideal person, and *be saved by him.* It is better to rely upon "another's strength" than upon one's own. "One detaches himself from his body and mind and flings himself into the house of the Buddha, there to be activated by the Buddha and follow in his footsteps. Then, without effort, physical or mental, of one's own, one escapes the cycle of rebirth and becomes a buddha."[137]

Dōgen's teaching in this regard is the exact opposite of that of the Zen sect in China (or at least of its principal representatives). Chinese Zen priests are continually pointing out that illumination is achieved through one's own efforts. Hui-hai (550–686) says: "This you should know: sentient beings save themselves; Buddha cannot save them. Strive hard! Strive hard! Perfect yourselves, and depend not upon the Buddha. In scripture it says, he who seeks the law does not seek it in the Buddha."[138] In other words, one must not rely even upon the Buddha. Nonetheless, Dōgen fervently depends upon Buddha's strength. The following is Dōgen's prayer: "Even if my past sins are piled high and there are obstacles to my enlightenment, I beg all the Buddhas and Boddhisattvas who have achieved perfection through the way of Buddha to take pity on me, deliver me from the chains of Karma, remove the impediments to my enlightenment. May their virtue fill and embrace the infinite world of the Buddha-law. May they extend to me their pity."[139]

In the Chinese Zen sect, faith is merely the portal of Buddhism. Therefore one must not become attached to the Buddha. Thus, the Chinese Zen monk Tan-hsia (?–834) in order to combat the deplorable tendency to become over-attached to an image of Buddha and regard it as the Buddha himself, burned a wooden statue of the Buddha as firewood.[140] This story is highly lauded by Chinese devotees of Zen. To the Japanese, however, it is outrageous. Dōgen teaches, "A clay, wood, or plaster image of Buddha, however poorly done, should be venerated. A scroll of scripture, no matter how battered, should be respected. A priest, even if he be a hardened sinner, should be respected for his sacerdotal character. If one respects these with faith in his heart, he is surely blessed. If one is disrespectful of a priest because he is a hardened sinner, a statue because it is poorly done, a copy of the sūtras because it is battered, then he certainly commits a sin. For according to the Buddha's teaching, the statue, the scroll of scripture, and the priest contribute to the happiness of men and gods. Therefore, one certainly profits by respecting them. One who treats them without faith is guilty of sin."[141] Yet when Dōgen is asked why Tan-hsia burned the wooden Buddha, he explains, "That was a common means of preaching the Law." Even Shōsan Suzuki (1579–1655), a Zen priest who had many ideas worthy of comparison with those of modern Western thought, condemns as "the height of immorality" the notion that "A wooden statue is nothing but wood, and an icon is merely a few strokes of the brush; there is nothing sacred in them."[142] He teaches: "Being born among men and hearing the teaching of the Buddha, one should be happy to represent the sacred form in painting and in sculpture and place them in a pagoda or temple to worship. Then, with the thought that the Buddha is actually in the world among us, we should offer our lives in homage. If our faith is not strong enough to make us willing to offer our lives, then there is no merit in it."[143]

There is also a strong emphasis on faith in the Nichiren sect. According to Nichiren, philosophical comprehension is not necessary for salvation. A robust faith is sufficient. "The Buddha, setting aside the keeping of the commandments and contemplation, addressed himself to the intelligence alone. If intelligence is lacking, faith makes up for it. The single word 'faith' is a pillar of truth. Lack of faith is the root of disrespect for the Law; faith is the cause of intelligence. . . ."[144] "For the man of superior gifts, study and contemplation are suitable. For the less gifted, faith alone is important." "He who understands the doctrines yet does not believe cannot become a buddha. He who believes, although he does not comprehend, can become a buddha."[145] "The root of the Law of Buddha is faith."[146] Thus we can say that Nichiren, in this regard, is in agreement with the views of Shinran and Dōgen. We likewise recognize here one of the characteristics which differentiates the Nichiren sect from the Tendai sect to which it owes its origin.

It is not only the new Kamakura sects which place this emphasis upon faith. The Indian or Chinese sects transplanted to Japan also preached faith in the Buddha. The Ritsu sect, for example, attempted to observe in Japan the precepts of traditional, conservative Indian Buddhism. In these precepts, there is no mention of a cult of the image of the Buddha, yet in the Ritsu temples in Japan, images of the Buddha were erected and sūtras recited before them.[147] Even the Tendai and Kegon philosophies, high points of Chinese Mahāyāna philosophy, had to accept faith as their basis, once they became acclimatized in Japan. Thus, in the Tendai sect, Ennin (792–862), emphasizing the importance of faith, says: "To enter into the sacred mysteries, one must go by the direct road of faith. He who has not faith is like a man without hands who, though he gain entry to the treasure room, can take nothing."[148] This emphasis on faith is one of the criteria by which Japanese Esoteric Tendai (*Taimitsu*) can be distinguished from the Chinese T'ien-t'ai sect. And a similar change in the concept of faith can be observed, though it is not so remarkable in this case, in the Shingon sect. Master Kōgyō (1095–1143) emphasized "the innocent acceptance of faith," saying that it is by far superior to the preparatory practice which appeals to intellectual power in order to follow what the scriptures teach.

Further, as regards the Kegon sect, Saint Myōe (alias Kōben, 1173–1232) says: "Knowledge without faith is not only not in accordance with the Law of Buddha, but is actually inimical to it. Wisdom will be founded upon faith."[149] This is a complete reversal of the rationalist position of Kegon philosophy.

In general, Indian religions and Chinese Buddhism are contemplative, focused on the vision of truth. In such religious, faith is merely the first step toward entering the innermost recesses of the religion. It is simply preparatory. However, when these sects were introduced into Japan, faith came to be recognized as the very essence of religion. Therefore, Japanese Buddhism is, above all, a Buddhism centering around faith. The Japanese emphasize purity of faith. (Even the Zen sect, in which faith is comparatively less esteemed, exhibits this trend in Japan.) This faith is of two kinds: (1) faith in a certain real person (founder, teacher); (2) faith in an ideal person (a specific Buddha or Bodhisattva). In practice, however, both appear so commingled that it is difficult to differentiate them. In either case the focus is on a specific individual.

The following criticism is offered by Enjō Inaba apropos of these differences between Chinese and Japanese Buddhism: "The defect of Chinese Buddhist thought is the acceptance, as its guiding religious principle, of an abstract 'law' such as a truth or a law divorced from the concrete 'person.' Buddhism, as a religion which is the life and strength of all men, certainly cannot center around such a law of truth. Only when this law is embodied in a person of flesh and blood can it be beneficial to us human beings. . . . It is nonsensical for a religion whose worship is directed to a law to demand religious fervor. Only by absolute devotion to a person can one savor the joy of prostrating oneself in reverent worship and of praying with all one's heart."[150]

Dr. Ryōtai Hatani (1883–) has offered the following characteristics of Japanese Buddhism: "In India and China, the speculative and practical sides of Buddhism were fully developed. However, the aspect of faith, which is the life of a religion, was never completely developed in India and China. Only in Japan has this aspect of Buddhism been fully explored. Japan had nothing particularly new to add to the speculative and practical aspects of Buddhism as developed in India and China. Japan's special contributions were in the field of faith."[151]

Japanese Buddhism does indeed exhibit the characteristics pointed out by Inaba and Hatani. However, the assertion that the "very soul of Buddhism" appears for the first time in Japan, and not in China and India, requires some further comment. Faith as it is understood by the Japanese is not a complete faith in the view of Indian Buddhists, but merely the gateway to faith. Compare, for example, the following passage of a sūtra: "Oh, good man! There are two kinds of faith. The first is 'simple faith' (reliance), the second is 'seeking.' A man may have simple faith, yet be unable to aspire; therefore his is insufficient faith. There are two further categories of faith. The first arises from hearing the teaching, the second from contemplation. A man whose faith is based on hearing the teaching and not on contemplation, has insufficient faith."[152]

The Indian concept of faith is extremely intellectual. Therefore, simple faith is of little significance, but an intelligent faith is of great value. Thus the criterion of the weight given to faith changed completely in the passage of Buddhism from India to Japan. Faith in Japanese Buddhism, then, is essentially faith in a specific person, ideal or real. In Indian Buddhism, on the contrary, it is devotion to a universal law. The traditional view of Indian Buddhism was "depend upon the law, not upon man."[153] In Japan, however, the exact opposite was followed. Related to this view is the Indian and Chinese tendency to venerate the Buddha as an embodiment of eternal law, whereas the Japanese tend to worship the Buddha as the person who achieved all the ideal virtues through his ascetic practices.

Broadly speaking, emphasis on faith appeared even in Indian Buddhism shortly before the Christian era, as it did also successively in Hinduism and Jainism in roughly the same period. Thus they developed along with the Western religion which emphasizes faith. It is a Japanese peculiarity that a specific person should be made the object of faith. With reference to this last point, there is some resemblance between Japanese faith and certain faiths in Western religion. For example, the faith of Shinran and that of Saint Paul appear very similar. In Saint Paul, however, there is an absolute distinction between God and man. Man always assumes a pious and prayerful attitude toward God, and begs his forgiveness. For Shinran, however, there is no gulf between Amida and the ordinary mortal. The sinful mortal will be saved through the mercy of Amida. If he repeats *nembutsu,* it is an expression of his joy and gratitude that he is saved by the great mercy of this Buddha. And an authentic master who understands the true meaning of *nembutsu* never utters it as a prayer. Whether it is about a secular matter or a religious one, he rejects any supplicating attitude toward him for the reason that supplication is not what this Buddha of the great vows wishes.

Generally speaking, the Japanese who devote themselves wholeheartedly to their religious teachers are inclined to assume an attitude of total submission to authority in other forms. In the first place, it can be clearly observed in their attitude to the scriptures. The Chinese Buddhists claim that it is not sufficient only to accept blindly what is said in the scriptures unless one tries to seek after truth by oneself with the help of those holy books.[154] The Japanese Buddhists, on the other hand, hold the authority of the scriptures as absolute and inviolable. And in the case of China, the number of the Kyō-shū (the sects established on the authority of specific sūtras) is almost equal to that of the Ron-shū (the sects based on particular Abhidharma treatises). But in Japan, especially after the Heian period (794–857), almost all the Buddhist sects, except for the Zen sect which claims not to rely upon any particular canon, are in the Kyō-shū in the sense that each one of them regards a particular sūtra as absolute authority.

When he introduced the doctrines of the Chinese T'ien-t'ai sect into Japan, Saint Dengyō (Saichō), whom we can properly call the first founder of Japanese Buddhism, strongly emphasized the fact that the sect pay special regard to the Lotus Sūtra. Such an emphasis on scriptural authority is one of the unique features of Dengyō that distinguished him from such Chinese teachers of the T'ien-t'ai sect as Master T'ien-t'ai or Master Miao-lo.[155]

In the Kamakura period, Shinran wrote his chief work *Kyō-gyō-shin-sho.* The full title of this work is *Ken-jōdo-shinjitsu-kyō-gyō-shō-monrui* or "an anthology of the scriptural passages teaching the true doctrine, practice, and illumination of the Pure Land." As the title of this book indicates to us, Shinran claimed authenticity for his teaching for the reason that his faith was based on the authority of the scriptural statements.

In the case of Nichiren, too, he tried in his abundant works to demonstrate theologically, on the basis of numerous scriptural statements, that the diffusion of the Lotus Sūtra in Japan at the very time that Nichiren lived is in keeping with the true intention of the Buddha. The philosophical system of Nichiren's theology is founded solely upon the Tendai doctrine of *Ichinen-sanzen* (the doctrine that teaches that all of the three thousand spheres of existence of living creatures are embraced in one thought). And as to another important doctrine of the Tendai theology which Nichiren relied upon to establish his own, "*kyō-gyō-shō*" or "doctrine, practice, and illumination," the following is asserted among his followers and is approved as authentic by the doctrinal authority of the Nichiren sect: "While the Chinese Master T'ien-t'ai and his Japanese successor Saint Dengyō both paid special regards to "practice" and "illumination" encouraging the exercise of meditation with a pacified and concentrated mind, Nichiren emphasized the importance of 'doctrine' as preceding the other two."[156] Generally speaking, the Japanese Buddhists were busy in demonstrating their authenticity on the basis of scriptural authority, and seldom sought to establish a grand philosophical system of their own creation.

Even the Zen sect, which had claimed it was originally free from any fixed traditional doctrine, was transformed in Japan into one that is sensitive to authority. It is worthy of note that Eisai, the introducer of the Rinzai Zen to Japan in 1191, thought that the inauguration of the Zen sect in Japan would cause no infringement upon the faithful observance of "the ancestral way of Mt. Hiei" or of the traditional theology of the Tendai sect.[157] In his masterpiece *Kōzen-gokoku-ron* (Treatise for the Spread of Zen and the Protection of the Country), he made many quotations from various Mahāyāna sūtras. Especially the *Yuima-kyō* (the *Vimalakīrtinirdeśa-sūtra,* on a wealthy gentleman) and the *Kongō-kyō* (the *Vajracchedikā-prajñāpāramitā-sūtra,* the Diamond Sūtra) were his favorite scriptures. In the final analysis, Eisai was not an exception. He, too, recognized scriptural statement to be the absolute authority, and for verification he went to the scriptures.

The attitude of reliance on scriptural authority is more manifestly observed in the case of Dōgen. At the time of the Sung Dynasty, almost all Chinese Buddhists were adherents of the Zen teaching. And they attached little significance to the sūtras claiming themselves not to be slaves to books. Dōgen, however, called those Chinese Buddhists "the followers of the masters who missed the right course" and denounced them. He said as follows: "Recently in Sung [China], there are many who presume to be the Ch'an-shih or the masters of Zen. . . . Those people are too stupid to take in the profound meaning of the sūtras. Ignoring their own faults, they abuse unduly the sūtras and never study them."[158] Dōgen emphasized the absolute value of the scriptures. According to him, the true intention of the Buddha can be found *only in the sūtras.* Since the earliest times, the Indian Buddhists held that the teaching of the Buddha consists of twelve portions. Following this view, Dōgen expounded it as follows: "One who sees the Doctrine of the Twelve Portions is a man who finds the Buddhist masters. One who accepts the Buddhist masters is a man who accepts the Doctrine of the Twelve Portions." Or in another part of the same work, he said, "The Three Vehicles and the Doctrine of the Twelve Portions form the core of the teaching of the Buddhist masters. Without understanding them, who can rightly call himself the descendant of the Buddhist masters? Without that understanding how can the true essence of the teaching of the Buddhist masters be properly transmitted from one master to another?"[159] It is natural that Dōgen encouraged the study of the sūtras. He said, "An ascetic, whether he is an independent ascetic or only a beginner, should never fail to keep the sūtras with the intention of becoming a son of the Buddha,"[160] or "An uninitiated ascetic, whether he has any distinct intention to follow the Buddha or not, should read and study the scriptures scrupulously."[161] The Chinese Zen monks paid so little regard to the scriptures that one of them dared to say, "The sūtras are good as toilet paper."[162] This Chinese attitude toward the scriptures presents a sharp contrast to the attitude of Dōgen.

From of old, *"kyō-ge-betsu-den"* (teaching transmitted without scriptures) is one of the fundamental principles of the Zen sect. It means that the essence of the Zen doctrine introduced to China by Bodhidharma should be transmitted intuitively from the heart of the master to that of the initiated without relying upon speech or writing. And its meaning is the same as what is signified by the expression "non-reliance on letters." Dōgen's method of teaching, as we have seen above, is undeniably inconsistent with this orthodox standpoint of the Zen sect. Since he believed in absolute obedience to traditional authority, he could not ignore the old principle of *"kyō-ge-betsu-den,"* and as a desperate measure, he made a perverted interpretation of this principle.[163] According to him, the word *"kyō* (doctrine)" designates the Buddhist teaching introduced by Kāśyapa Mātaṅga and Dharmarakṣa to China for the first time in 67 A.D. in the days of the Later Han Dynasty. And *"betsu-den* (different transmission)" means the Buddhist teaching bought newly by Bodhidharma apart from (*"ge"*) the former one. The principle originally meant the impossibility of expressing the absolute religious truth by means of speech or writing. But this old principle was thoroughly transformed in the hands of Dōgen to mean that the absolute truth is *transmissible only by oral or literal teaching* based on the authority of the authentic tradition. Thus, the principle established primarily in China of refusing acceptance of the authority of any specific doctrine was brought to Japan and changed *to mean absolute obedience to it.*

As a result of his special regard for authority, Dōgen sometimes went to extremes to repulse the rationalism that forms one of the unique characteristics of the Chinese Zen sect. One of the traditional principles of the Zen sect teaches *kenshō-jyōbutsu,* which means that a man can achieve Nirvāṇa with penetrating insight into the inner nature of his existence. Dōgen made a frontal attack upon this traditional view. He said: "The essence of Buddhism is not in *kenshō* or the intuitive grasp of innate human nature. Among the Seven Buddhas and the Twenty-eight Masters of the Zen sect in India and Central Asia, who advocated such a view? Indeed, in the *Dan-gyō* (which claims itself unduly to be the work of the sixth patriarch of the Zen Buddhism) the word *kenshō* is found. But, this work is a forgery. None of the five Indian successors of the Buddha's teaching wrote this sūtra, nor did the sixth patriarch. None of the followers of the Buddha's teaching have regarded it as a suitable authority to rely upon."[164]

While Dōgen respected the authority of the masters as well as of the scriptures, Nichiren did not pay particular regard to the authority of the masters. He was a man who concerned himself with the culling of a reliable doctrine from the various teachings of the diversified and at times contradictory Buddhist sects which existed at that time. He called himself "one who has sought the Buddha's teaching without the aid of parents or masters." What ruled his selection finally was not a philosophical consideration but his belief in *the authority of a sūtra.* Having found in the fifth volume of the Lotus Sūtra the following statement: "This Lotus Sūtra, the secret treasury of all the Buddhas and the Tathāgatas, stands the highest of all among the sūtras," Nichiren believed it and developed his unique theology on the authority of this sūtra.[165] Thus, Nichiren submitted himself unconditionally to scriptural authority. In one of his letters, he wrote: "It is of no use to try to overwhelm me with worldly authority; just show me the proper scriptural statement to verify your point."[166]

In India, many sūtras were forged with the title of "the Buddha's own teaching." The number of such spurious writings is by no means less in China. But, in Japan, few such works were made. One of the probable reasons for this is that special honor is paid in this country to the authority of the sūtras. This respect for the scriptures, however, did not necessarily lead the Japanese to the ardent study of what those sūtras teach. On the contrary, the Japanese condensed the sūtras into some simple symbolic representations and regarded these symbolic formulae as absolute and inviolable.

The obedient Japanese attitude toward the regulations that tradition imposes upon it can also be observed in the field of Japanese Buddhist art. The Chinese sculptors, disregarding the iconographic prescriptions established by the Indians, made statues of the Buddhas, by following freely their own imagination. The Japanese artists, on the other hand, adhered faithfully to the Indian prescriptions that they came to know through the books imported from China at the time of the T'ang Dynasty.

Those features that we have referred to in our study of the Japanese way of adopting Buddhism can be observed similarly in their reaction to Confucianism or Chinese thought in general. The Japanese were very much surprised to learn for the first time that the Chinese civilization was far superior to their own. Everything imported from China was an object of their admiration. They were overwhelmed by the splendor of the Chinese civilization to such a degree that they were inclined to accept all things Chinese without due criticism. Their inferior cultural standard did not allow them to assume a critical attitude toward the Chinese civilization. They believed any statement contained in Chinese books to be absolutely true, authentic, and infallible. They adopted Chinese letters and concepts and tried to interpret conditions in their own country by following these Chinese principles. They did not consider whether or not these Chinese principles would be appropriate for the explanation of the social conditions of Japan or of their own thought and life. And as a result, adopting the Chinese classification of the divinities into two groups, gods of heaven and gods of earth, the Japanese sorted out their own objects of worship, *kami*, into the same two categories. In another case, regarding their *tennō* (literally, Heaven-Emperor) in the same light as the Chinese Emperor, they borrowed from the Chinese the idea that the Imperial dignity is conferred by heaven.[167]

As a result of such a blind acceptance of Chinese civilization, it is natural that "the way of the ancient sages" played the role of absolute authority among the Japanese Confucianists. Though the critical studies of the classical works of Confucianism were started in Japan in the early years of the modern age, even the most radical mind in this field, Sorai Ogyū (1666–1718), advocated "the way of the ancient sage-kings" as the highest moral principle. In one of his books, he wrote: "To say nothing of the ancient sage-kings, those who would work for the benefit of the people and save them from miseries should also be called 'good.' For they do what the people long for. The way of the ancient sage-kings is the highest good. Under the sun, there is no principle more excellent than this one. 'The highest good' is, therefore, the word to praise the way of the ancient sage-kings."[168]

And we can find the Japanese inclination of total submission to specific masters also in the case of the Confucianists. For instance, Ansai Yamazaki (1618–1682) admired Chu-hsi (1130–1200) so enthusiastically that he tried to propagate the latter's teaching with a missionary zeal. He even went so far as to declare, "If I fall into error studying Chu Hsi, I shall be in error with Chu Hsi and shall have nothing to regret."[169] These words of Yamazaki remind us of Shinran's wholehearted devotion to Hōnen.

The attitude of absolute devotion to authority can be observed even among the nationalistic scholars of the Japanese classics who rejected both Buddhism and Confucianism. For Norinaga Motoori (1730–1801), science is nothing other than the study of "the way of the past." He said: "A scholar should confine himself in the field of study only to reveal the way. He should not try to carry it into practice at his own discretion. But, he should study well the way of the past, teach the result of his study to others, take notes of it in book form, and wait for the opportunity, though it is not known whether such an opportunity will arise five hundred years or a thousand years later, when the authorities adopt it in their ruling policies and carry it out throughout the country."[170] Though the study of the national classics in the Tokugawa period was a field of science newly risen at that time, still it was not free from the trend toward over-attachment to the authority of the specific masters. It will be enough for this account only to mention the naive devotion of Norinaga Motoori to his master Kamo Mabuchi or the case of Atsutane Hirata (1776–1842) who on every occasion claimed himself to be a disciple of Norinaga. (It is doubtful whether Hirata actually received the instruction of Motoori.)

The attitude of absolute submission to a specific person is one of the distinct features of the way of thinking that can be commonly observed among the Japanese of the past. And, as we can see in the warrior's motto "a loyal vassal does not know two masters" or in the code of "morals" even among gamblers, the actual mores of most Japanese people reflect this feature of their way of thinking. As we have seen above, this can be by no means treated simply as a social phenomenon of a feudal society.

The attitude of total submission to a specific authority is not restricted to the Japanese of the past, but can still be clearly observed among contemporary Japanese. Even in those self-styled "progressives" who are very severe toward conventional ideas, this trend is tenaciously adhered to. One reason for this is that the Japanese are always sensitive to efforts to establish compact relations among the individuals within a small closed community. This endeavor for mutual relationship serves to create a sense of unity and sympathy among the Japanese. But, at the same time, it sometimes leads them to accept blindly the principle of authority at the expense of individuality.[171]

Although not an exhaustive study, my discussion opens a way, I hope, to a deeper understanding of the great influence which leaders, especially religious leaders, have had on the Japanese people in the past and are still having in the present. The figure of the *kyōso* (founder or foundress) of modern religious movements is one instance of the fascination which a certain type of man or woman can have for the masses.

Emperor Worship

The Japanese way of thinking, which pays the highest respect to some particular living person and at the same time bows down to hierarchical distinctions of social status, culminates in ascribing absolutely divine attributes to the individual at the top of the hierarchy of Japanese society.[172] Emperor worship is thus established. Emperor worship, however, is not the only product of this tendency of thought. At times *shoguns* or their ancestors were recognized as having a claim to divine authority. For example, in the Tokugawa period, Ieyasu Tokugawa (1542–1616), the founder of the Shogunate Government, was given the appellation "*tōshō daigongen*" (literally, "great incarnate Deity of the eastern light"), and was referred to often as "*Gongen-sama*" ("The Incarnate God"). At the same time the Dutch referred to the Tokugawa Shōgun as the "Kaiser." Therefore we ought to treat Emperor worship and *Shōgun* worship as a single tendency, examining it first as ruler worship (*Kaiserkultus*) and subsequently examining it in the special sense of Emperor worship. But while an account following such a course would be logically most satisfactory, because of limitations of space we shall now merely make a few remarks about Emperor worship itself.

When the attitude of absolute loyalty to a particular person, which we have already described, is directed toward the head of the state, it becomes Emperor worship. After the Meiji Restoration and until the defeat in the recent war, the attitude of absolute self-sacrifice, which in the feudal era had been directed toward the feudal lords, was redirected toward the Emperor. "The spirit of *bushidō*, which has been developed by the warrior class over a long time,"[173] Yaichi Haga (1867–1927) said rightly in 1907, "has now come to be directed solely toward the imperial throne."

The Japanese comment has even been made that Louis XIV's remark, "*L'Etat, c'est moi*" ("I am the State"), "is a statement which could most appropriately have been uttered by the Emperor of our own country."[174] The statement, "The kingdom is nothing but the king,"[175] is found in the most famous of ancient Indian political treatises; but among the Indians no such custom as Emperor worship ever arose to any striking extent. It goes without saying that ultra-nationalism developed in close relation with the worship of the Emperor as a living god. In fact, Emperor worship has been the most influential form of belief in Japan up to 1945; and even today after the defeat, the Emperor holds his position by virtue of his significance as a symbol of the unity of the Japanese nation. The Japanese like to see in the Emperor as a living individual a condensed representation of the Japanese nation. Although this is not a phenomenon which is unknown to other nationalities, it has a special significance in Japan. In this matter Yaichi Haga has remarked: "There is a golden image of the goddess Germania at the top of a triumphal tower many feet high at the end of the Siegesallee in Berlin. The goddess was intentionally created as an imaginary person and designated 'Germania' to represent the German state. And in England in like manner an imaginary person called 'Britannia' has been fashioned, and in France one called 'Gallia.' In foreign countries where the form of government has often changed, or where one royal house frequently succeeds another, such artificial symbols are naturally devised from the need to cause people to think of their past history and to cultivate the concept of the nation. Only in our country have the soil of the nation and the Imperial House been inseparable since the age of the gods. The expressions 'for country' and 'for ruler' are to be understood as having the same meaning." Whether the Emperor is to be thought of as simply equivalent to the state, or is to be interpreted as a symbol of national unity, the Emperor-institution is a thing unique to Japan, for it must be noted that it is not to be found among other peoples. Not concerning myself here with the problem of the political and economic basis of the Emperor institution, I should like to examine the question how Emperor worship has directly molded the way of thinking of the entire Japanese people.

Such a tendency of thought did not appear suddenly after the Meiji restoration (1868); on the contrary, an incipient tendency of this kind had existed since ancient times. According to the tales of the gods in the *Kojiki* (Record of Ancient Matters), after the heavens and the earth were separated, the two divinities Izanami (Female) and Izanagi (Male) descended to the island of Onokoro, and then gave birth to the various islands of Ōyashima (i.e. the territory of Japan). After that they gave birth to various other divinities; the gods of the wind, of trees and mountains were born, and at the end the goddess (Izanami) died from burns, because she gave birth to the god of fire. Thereupon, the god (Izanagi) wanted to meet his spouse, and went to the land of night and saw her. Then, after returning to this world, when he washed the filth (of the land of death from himself), from his eyes and nose were born the three divinities Amaterasu Ōmikami (Sun Goddess), Tsukiyomi no Mikoto, and Susanō no Mikoto. It is said that this Amaterasu Ōmikami was the ancestor of the Imperial House.[176] *In this way the legend of the ancestors of the royal house is connected with the legend of the creation of the universe.* This account is without parallel among other nations. At least among other civilized people of the East these two types of legends—political and cosmogonic—generally are separated. Thus, the divine authority of the Imperial House is enhanced by the fact that its lineage is connected with the legend of the creation of heaven and earth.

Further, in the older language, the word *ōyake* ("public") originally had the sense of "the principal family,"[177] which meant the Imperial House. In contradistinction, all the people were called *koyake* (minor families). Thus the Imperial House came to be regarded as the principal ancestral family of all the Japanese.[178] Consequently, in Japan there was originally no conception corresponding to "public." Among the Japanese, public affairs consisted in nothing but relations with the Imperial Family.

It would seem that the tendency to regard the Emperor as divine has existed in Japan since very ancient times. When one looks at the many legends related in the *Kojiki* and the *Nihonshoki* (History of Japan), one finds that stories of the gods are not told for the purpose of demonstrating the greatness of the divinities believed in by the ancients; on the contrary, it is only for the purpose of showing the divine character of the Emperor that accounts are given of the gods and of the historical blood relations of these gods. To be sure, in the Occident it is a historical fact that Alexander the Great and the Roman emperors were deified, but this was a matter of the deification of these men as individuals; this is quite a different thing from a national legend rooted in the primitive faith of a people. The theory of the divine right of kings in modern Europe has as its premise the Christian conception of God, and aimed at giving a basis to the power of princes in the will of God.[179] And the theory of divine right in medieval India is to be understood in the same way. Thus, in archaic Japanese religion, the living totality of the nation is embodied symbolically in the Imperial ancestral sun-goddess and in the divine authority deriving traditionally from her. Here we find the unifying idea in the traditional stories of the historical age of the gods. Consequently, the people, united into one nation from various familial or political groups, give concrete expression to their corporate will through the Emperor or the divine Imperial ancestor who directs the government.[180] Thus, in the society of that time, bound together by ritual, the distinction between submitting to or opposing the authority of the totality of society is a distinction between submitting to or refusing to submit to the ruler who is the concrete manifestation of that authority—and this in the last analysis is reducible to submission or non-submission to the authority of the Imperial ancestor goddess. Therefore, it has been felt that the moral distinction between goodness and wickedness is nothing but the distinction between submission or non-submission to the divine authority of the corporate whole, and this means the distinction between submission and non-submission to the Emperor.[181] Therefore the Japanese people have generally felt that the rule of Japan by the Imperial House, generation after generation, has been maintained on the basis of the general will of their ancestors since antiquity.[182]

Since the Imperial House was originally conceived as having the position of ruling the entire Japanese people, the Imperial House *has no surname*. Consequently there has almost never appeared anyone aiming at becoming the highest ruler in place of the Imperial House. Of course, in Japan's long history, it is not the case that there were no persons at all who had undertaken to rebel against the Imperial House. Taira-no-Masakado (d. 940), Minamoto-no-Yoshitomo (1123–1160), and Minamoto-no-Yoshinaka (1154–1184) are generally regarded as rebels. However, even these men did not attempt to supplant the Imperial House. They desired to have some position at court, and raised rebellions through dissatisfaction at being unable to obtain it. Thus it is said that even rebels have recognized the Imperial authority. Perhaps the only exception is the case of Yuge no Dōkyō (d. 772), the Buddhist priest Prime Minister (765). Even Takauji Ashikaga (1305–1358) was able to establish his shogunate only by installing the Emperor of the northern court, at the beginning of the Muromachi Period (1338–1573).

Subsequently, also, the concept of the divinity of the Emperor became a religious tradition. In an edict issued immediately after the Taika Reforms (c. 650), the Emperor was called the "bright god" (*akitsumikami*). When the Emperor's power became stronger, there even appeared in an Imperial edict the following sentence: "We are the possessor of the wealth of the world; we are the possessor of the power of the world."[183] The divine-nation-concept and the principle of ultra-nationalism have thus a close connection with Emperor worship. In the fact that Japan has been ruled by Emperors belonging to a line unbroken for countless generations, we recognize a unique historical characteristic of the Japanese state.

Although in the past the Japanese adopted Chinese thought and culture on a large scale, still they have exercised particular care not to injure the distinctive characteristics of the Japanese state. The law codes which formed the basis of administration and justice in ancient Japan were for the most part imitations of Chinese models; however, the traditional Chinese idea of revolution was rejected.[184] In regard to the government of the state, although reference was made to the twenty-one Chinese dynastic histories, the political practices of abdication and righteous rebellion were not initiated. There is a tradition that when the book of Mencius was brought in a ship to be introduced into Japan, the ship was wrecked in a storm at sea, and consequently *The Mencius* was transmitted to Japan only with great difficulty.[185] What this means is that the notions of the ruler's abdication and righteous rebellion against the ruler, as expressed in *The Mencius,* were incompatible with the Japanese concept of the Emperor and the traditional Japanese pattern of government. The legend of the shipwreck was produced by the fear of men who did not want *The Mencius* popularized.

"Also, I have heard it said that the book of Mencius contains the following argument: at the beginning of the Chou dynasty, King Wu with one burst of anger gave response to the needs of the people; he is not to be spoken of as a subject murdering his ruler; rather he executed the villain Chou (-hsin) who was a desecrator of benevolence and righteousness. Consequently, although Chinese classics, histories, and even books of literature have all been brought over to this country, only that book of Mencius has not yet been brought to Japan; for, it is said, the ship which carries it is always sunk by a storm. If we ask why, the reason given is that, while there has been no break in the Imperial line since our country was founded and ruled by Amaterasu Ōmikami (Sun Goddess), if such a teaching were transmitted there might appear in the future an adversary who would despoil the descendants of the gods and claim to be blameless; and detesting this possibility, all the gods raise up a divine wind (*kamikaze*) and overturn the ship. Thus, even among the sage teachings of that country, there are some which are inappropriate for this land." (*Ugetsu Monogatari,* Bizarre Stories)

The introduction of Chinese Confucianism into Japan caused almost no friction or disharmony; only the doctrine of abdication and rebellion presented difficult problems. This doctrine maintains that the Emperor holds his position of Emperor so long as he receives the mandate of Heaven; if he should lose the confidence of Heaven he will inevitably lose his position; such a doctrine is under any circumstances hard to reconcile with the traditional Japanese concept of the Emperor. Therefore, this point became a problem for scholars. The following admonition to posterity is ascribed to Sugawara-no-Michizane (845–903): "The mystery of the eternal existence of our divine country is something we dare not try to understand. Although we study the Chinese classics of the three royal dynasties, of Chou King, and of Confucius, the Chinese national tendency of revolution is something we should be deeply concerned about."[186]

Thus, even Confucianism has definitely not been introduced into Japan uncritically. Tōko Fujita (1806–1855), a Confucianist of the Mito school, argued that among the doctrines of Confucianism, there are two which are "definitely not applicable" to Japan, "namely, the doctrines of abdication and of righteous rebellion. The gaining of the throne by abdication is exemplified by Shin and Yü, while the attaining of the throne by rebellion is instanced by T'ang of Yin and Wu of Chou. Since the Ch'in and Han Dynasties, those who arrogated the throne by deceiving the Emperor's orphans and widows always based their arguments on the examples of the sage-emperors Sun and Yü, while those who usurped the throne by destroying their royal houses and murdering their rulers always pretended to be following the examples of T'ang and Wu. There have been more than twenty dynasties in Chinese history, and not only have those in high and low position changed places, but even the distinction between Chinese and barbarian has been lost." In China, if the Emperor loses the virtue requisite of an Emperor, he must lose his throne; but in Japan, the Imperial throne has been for ages regarded as eternal, available only to those in the same blood lineage. Consequently, here the Emperor's possession of virtue has been irrelevant. "In our bright divine land, the unbroken Imperial succession has been transmitted without end, ever since the heavenly ancestor gave the heavenly descendants the commission to rule, the augustness of the heavenly throne is just as unsurpassable as the sun and moon. Even if there were in the world someone comparable to Shun or Yü in virtue or equal to T'ang or Wu in knowledge, still the only thing he could do would be to support the Emperor with complete devotion and assist the work of the throne. If it should chance that someone should proclaim the theory of abdication, it would be quite justifiable for any of the people of Ōyashima (Japan) to rise in indignation and attack him."[187]

Of course, most Confucianists did not express themselves so clearly. Even these were aware that there was a contradiction between the ancient Japanese form of government and Confucian theory, *but they kept silence and avoided coming to grips with this contradiction*. Once this contradiction was taken up and became a problem, there was no other course than to interpret it as did Tōko Fujita.

To be sure, among Confucianists there were people who were extremely absorbed in Chinese culture. Nevertheless, even Sorai Ogyū (1666–1728), who called himself "one of the Eastern barbarians," after all had an attitude of reverence for the throne.[188]

If we reason along the line of thinking which has been described above, we come to the conclusion that Imperial authority is not derived from abstract principles like the divine-right theory, but that his authority is regarded as inhering in his very person. For example, Banzan Kumazawa (1665–1691) emphasizes the divinity of the Japanese Emperor. "It is not to be doubted that the Japanese Emperor is the august descendant of the heavenly god." "Only in Japan has the imperial house continued without change. Even in the age of the *samurai*, a man who conquered the country could not become ruler. This is because divine authority is naturally inherent in the three sacred treasures."[189] Again, Ansai Yamazaki (1618–1682), in spite of his profound understanding of Confucianism, did not try to understand Shintō from a Confucian standpoint, but, even while using various Confucian concepts, endeavored to understand Shintō in its own terms. According to him, the god of creation is a divinity with a human body—that is to say, he is the ancestor of the Imperial family.

The phrase *shinsei* (divine sage)—as applied to this god—means that in him the divine and human are combined. He is the venerable god of the primordial universe; *he is revered as the ancestor of the Emperors, and as the source of their body and blood.* The concept of "Emperor" (*"tennō"* in Japan is different from the Chinese concept of the "son of Heaven"). "In foreign countries (*sc.* China), above the chief ruler there is the heavenly sovereign; above the edicts of the Emperor there is the mandate of high Heaven. In Japan, however, the ruler is himself this 'heavenly sovereign'; and the edicts of the Emperor must be regarded as the 'heavenly mandate' itself."[190] The Emperor is not the "son of Heaven" who receives the "mandate of Heaven," but is himself taken to be the heavenly sovereign who issues the mandate.

And so, while enthusiastic proponents of reverence for the throne study Confucian doctrines, still there are cases where they completely turn these doctrines around. It is a problem whether or not there actually is in Mencius democratic thought, but at any rate Mencius did refer to the ruler of the state as the "people's ruler" and took the position that he should be concerned with the people's living conditions. But Shōin Yoshida (1831–1859), in lecturing on Confucianism, attacked the statements in Mencius which had any democratic nuances. In considering the passage in Mencius that "The people are most valuable, the altars of the land and grain come next, and the ruler is least" (*The Book of Mencius, Chin hsin p'ien* [section on Mind] II, chapter 14), Yoshida would not accept Mencius' thought as it stood. He interpreted this passage in Mencius as meaning that "the people are most valuable from the point of view of the ruler." In this way he attacked Western democracy, and aimed at a complete overturn of Chinese thought.

"If we read this passage without understanding this meaning, we will utter, in imitation of the Western barbarians, the evil notions that the world is not the property of one man, but belongs to itself, and will come to forget the idea of state structure (*kokutai*). This is greatly to be abominated. It has recently been reported that students at Meirinkan school were asked to write an essay on the theory that the world is not the property of one man. Therefore, I reflect that, while this theory that the world does not belong to an individual appears[191] in the *Liu-tao-san-lüeh* (a work on strategy), it does not necessarily come from the classical scriptures. It is not a general notion in China. It sould seem to be held in connection with the idea of abdication and justified rebellion. But the proverb, 'throughout the world there is no land which is not the king's; throughout the world, there is no one who is not the king's subject,' clearly assumes that the world belongs to one person."[192]

The Chinese idea that "the world is not one man's" has now been changed to the contrary thesis that "the world is one man's (viz. the Emperor's)."

Hence, in spite of the widespread acceptance of Confucianism, the Chinese and Japanese forms of it have differed in their emphasis. The basis of Chinese Confucianism was the virtue of filial piety. Thus, since a basic element in their thought was the idea of the change of dynasties, the idea of loyalty to the state could not occupy the central place in their ethical scheme. However, in Japan, due to the hierarchical structure of society, the particular virtue of loyalty to the Emperor occupied the highest place among all virtues.

This difference in ways of thinking between China and Japan on the matter of the authority of the Emperor was manifested in *a difference in ways of compiling histories.* In China, the practical motivation for the compilation of most histories, especially "standard histories," was to serve as a mild check on the power of the ruler in advance, and not to let it out of control. Therefore, the official Chinese historian recorded both the good and the bad actions of the Emperor, in order to encourage the reader, whether he was the Emperor or an official, to become reflective and critical. In Japan, however, this kind of intention is lacking. If we examine the motives for the work of compiling histories in Japan, the reason for the *Kojiki* and *Nihonshoki* was to make clear "the rule of the Imperial family and the broad basis of its royal influence."[193] In other words, the intention was to record selectively, on the basis of Japan's consciousness of itself as a state distinct from the rest of the world, the facts of Japanese history, emphasizing as central the genealogy of the Imperial House. Consequently, a critical spirit was not apparent in these books.

The absence of a critical spirit based on universal human reason was too often in the past a conspicuous characteristic of the Japanese way of thinking, and this uncritical attitude appears in the way of thinking which reveres the living Emperor as divine. It is instructive to inquire into the influence exerted upon the form of adoption of Buddhism by the idea of Emperor worship, which has had such a firmly rooted existence throughout the Japanese nation since antiquity. In the case of Buddhism, in spite of the fact that it is theoretically difficult to join it to Emperor worship, in Japan a union between the two was ultimately achieved.

The idea of emphasizing the prestige and benevolence of the ruler appears in India in the Brahmanistic legal codes, but Buddhists universally rejected it. Only in a few cases, in later Mahāyāna Buddhism, has this

Brahmanistic idea been picked up. Nevertheless, the Japanese have particularly noticed these exceptional ideas in the Buddhist sacred texts. In Book Two of the *Daijō Honsō Shinji-Kan-gyō* (Sūtra of Meditation on the Real Aspect of Mind of the Mahāyāna), the "four benevolences"—of "parents," "all sentient beings," "the ruler," and "the Three Treasures"—are explained one by one. In the passage on "the benevolence of the ruler," the scripture teaches that "the happiness of the people depends on the ruler, mountains and rivers, the earth within the state, all are the possessions of the ruler. The ruler's authority is the same as that of the Buddha. He enjoys the special protection of the gods (the celestial beings of the thirty-three heavens). Therefore we ought not to try to rebel against the ruler." Such a concept of the ruler is quite exceptional in the Buddhist texts.[194] King Aśoka (3d century B.C.), who devoted himself body and soul to the realization in India's political activity of Buddhist ideals, even went so far as publicly to declare in his edicts that *the ruler receives benevolence from the people*. Yet this doctrine of four benevolences, which is exceptional in Buddhism, was regarded as especially important by the Japanese. Although in the Buddhist sacred texts these four benevolences are only dealt with together, and although the benevolence of the Three Treasures is recognized as having paramount significance, in Japan the benevolence of the ruler is especially emphasized, and is accorded the highest position. For instance, on the seventh day of the tenth month of 862, under the Emperor Seiwa, Yoshio Tomonosukune, who was Chūnagon and concurrently minister of the bureau of the populace and grand officer in the palace of the Imperial mother-in-law, submitted a memorial expressing a desire to contribute a villa near Fukakusa to a temple. In this document, after citing the doctrine of four benevolences in the *Daijō Honshō Shinji-kan-gyō,* he concluded by saying, "we ought first to repay the benevolence of the holy ruler in protecting and sustaining us, and second, to requite the virtue of the sphere of Truth for favoring us."[195] Again, in Taira no Shigemori's (1138–1179) admonitions to his father, Taira no Kiyomori, there is the passage "I have recently read in the *Shinji-kan-gyō* that the first benevolence is that of heaven and earth, the second that of the king, the third that of parents, and the fourth that of all sentient creatures. By knowing this we are human beings; by not knowing it, demons and animals. Among them the most important is the benevolence of the Emperor."[196] But the idea that the "benevolence of the Emperor" is most important is not a doctrine of the *Shinji-kan-gyō,* but is something which the Japanese have asserted using this text. Following this common point of view, later Zen masters also, for example Takuan (1573–1645), emphasized that "No one ought to slight the benevolence of the ruler."[196a]

The national Japanese idea of Emperor worship has, contrary to what one would expect, exerted an influence on Buddhists. A religionist such as Shinran, who advocated absolute devotion to the Amida Buddha, did not have at all in mind anything like Emperor worship. Nonetheless, he calls the Amida Buddha's compassionate summons of living creatures, in order to save them, an "Imperial order."[197] Nichiren also, referring to the pronouncements of the Buddha, used the phrases "edict of the Buddha" and "Imperial declaration."[198] These sectarian Buddhists preferred to use such expressions as an appropriate way to express themselves to the Japanese. (In recent years Buddhists were forbidden by the militarist government to use such expressions.)

In the case of Nichiren, in particular, the concept of Emperor worship seems to have influenced slightly the structure of his religious ideas.[199] He related that when he was young he harbored a doubt as to whether the retired Emperor at Oki or the Hōjō regent was the true ruling authority in Japan; and the same sort of doubt caused him to select the Lotus from among the many Buddhist sacred texts. "Even though when one looks about the land, one finds that each man says, I am the ruler, yet the ruler of the country is but one man. If there were two, the land would not be calm. If a family were to have two heads, that family would surely be torn apart. Isn't the Buddhist canon also just like this? Whatever Sūtra it may be, surely it is just one Sūtra that is the 'great king' of the canon! But if seven out of ten sects struggle with one another without coming to agreement, this would be as bad as if there were seven or ten kings in a country—the people would not be at peace. What could be done then?"[200] In this frame of mind he proceeded to evaluate and compare Buddhist texts, and finding in the Lotus Sūtra the statement, "This Lotus Sūtra is by far the greatest of all Sūtras," he finally declared his utter devotion to the Lotus Sūtra.

While Buddhism was being propagated in Japan, Emperor worship likewise shortly came to be generally recognized as common sense even among Buddhists. Even the Gleanings from Leisure Hours (*Tsurezuregusa*, 1331) by the priest Kenkō (1283–1350) declared: "The great position of the Emperor is awesome indeed. Even the last leaves growing in the bamboo garden (i.e. all members of the Imperial family, to the end of time) are not of the race of ordinary men; they are noble!" We have already noted the fact that Japan-minded Confucianists recognized a special excellence of the Japanese nation in the unbroken continuity of the Imperial line; but a number of Buddhists mentioned the same thing. Shiren Kokan (1278–1346), the author of the *Kenkō Shakusho* (Buddhist work written in the Genkō Era) which is the most important history of Buddhism in early Japan, recognized in the tradition of the transmission of the three sacred treasures to Japan, the reason for the superiority of the Japanese state over other countries. "Although China is called a great country and its territories are vast, still its seals of authority are all human artifacts and are not made by Heaven. Although our country is small, it was founded by gods and has been given sacred treasures by spirits. China is not even to be compared with it." (Book 17.) Again, Kōsen (1816–1892) said, "In our state there is the Way of the Emperor. This is the great way of the heavenly ancestor Gods, and is the orthodox way of the ruler. Its continuity has been endless, for divine descendants have continued in one line and have not mixed with other families. . . . Although it has been almost three thousand years since the Emperor Jimmu ('Divine Warrior') succeeded to the rule, no one yet has ever dared to usurp the heavenly throne and break the divine line of succession. The majestic virtue of the Imperial House is vast. This is why our Kingly Way is unique among all countries." (*Zenkai Ichiran,* "One wave in the sea of Zen.") These men constantly looked up to the authority of the Imperial House.

When this idea was reached, soon the theory was advanced that "The Emperor actually is the State." Tōrei (1721–1792) says, "Although heaven and earth are vast, there are only one sun and one moon. Likewise the fortunes of the state depend upon one man, the Emperor" (*Shūmon Mujintō-ron,* A treatise on the undying light of the [Zen] sect). We have already noted the tendency toward naturalism among the Japanese, and this is closely connected with the concept of esteem for lineage and with Emperor worship. Buddhists have even made the curious statement that the word "nature," in its ultimate sense, means the everlasting continuity of the Imperial line. Shiren Kokan (1278–1346) says: "Japan is an absolutely pure entity. The basis of the state is rooted in nature. No Chinese dynasty has ever been like this. That is why we praise our country. This 'nature' is the three sacred treasures. The three treasures are the sacred mirror, the sacred sword, and the sacred jewel. These three are all natural, heaven-made products. The fact that our country has one Imperial line which reaches far back in time and is unbroken over the ages is surely due to these treasures, which are natural and heaven-made. Therefore, even after countless generations, there is no danger that the throne will be menaced. Surely, these heaven-produced sacred treasures will not become the playthings of another clan or of foreign arms."

This point of view corresponds exactly to that urged by Ansai Yamazaki, mentioned earlier, but such a concept of nature is absolutely not found among Indian or Chinese Buddhists, and would perhaps seem strange to Westerners as well. Reasoning along a line identical with that just illustrated, Buddhists themselves came to advocate the thesis that the Imperial ancestor, "Amaterasu Ōmikami (Sun Goddess)" denotes the absolute. Master Tōrei (1721–1792) says, "The general meaning of '*shin*' (god, spirit) is also 'mind.' When all dirt is cleaned from the mind, and it becomes as clear as a mirror, then it is called 'spirit.' For this reason, the vehicle of spirit is symbolized by the mirror. . . . The mirror of the mind is always round and clear, and reflects all things whatsoever. This is called *'Amaterasu Ōmikami'* (*Mujintōron,* Ruzū No. 10). Here there is not the slightest trace of a conception of a pagan god. Nonetheless, Emperor worship has introduced a subtle modification and twisting of various conceptions.

Among the Five Injunctions of Buddhism there is an injunction against stealing. The original meaning of this in India was, "Do not take things that have not been given you by someone else." However, among Japanese Buddhists, a tendency appeared to interpret even this precept in connection with Emperor worship. Jiun-sonja Onkō (1718–1804), founder of the Shingon Shōhōritsu Sect, interpreted it as follows: "There are boundaries between countries just as mountains and rivers are distinct from each other. . . . the line of the Emperor of our country has been unbroken since the age of the gods. This signifies that the injunction against stealing has a natural basis. In China, the lines of Emperors are in disorder, and in the course of time even a man of lowest estate can become ruler of the world."[201]

The idea that the Emperor is divine has brought about a modification of old Buddhist conceptions regarding the relation between the "ten virtues" and the ruler. The laws which are to be especially observed by all men have since early Buddhism been called the "ten goods" or the "ten injunctions to goodness." These are the virtues which are the opposites of ten evils, namely, not killing, not stealing, non-license, not telling a lie, not breaking faith, not backbiting, not using lascivious language, not being greedy, not being angry, not holding wrong ideas. It is frequently stressed in Buddhist texts that the ruler must bring home the importance of these ten goods to the people. In regard to the true law of the ten goods which was expounded by the Buddha, the ruler ought to uphold and practice them, and by means of this law to govern the world.[202] In addition to diligently practicing the Ten Goods himself,[203] the ruler must put them into practice among all the people. "If the ruler causes (the people) to cultivate the Ten Goods, he will be called a blessed and virtuous ruler; but if he does not do so, he will be called an evil ruler."[204] "The ruler ought, like the sage king, the universal monarch (Cakravarti) of antiquity, to educate the people in the way of the Ten Goods."[205] A king under whom the youth Sudhana studied, is said to have "forever put an end to murder, robbery, and license, to have forbidden false talk, faithlessness, slander, and lascivious language, and banished avarice, anger, and wrong ideas."[206] This conception exerted a considerable influence upon the general conception of the Emperor among the Japanese. In old Japanese books, the

Emperor is often called, "master of the Ten Virtues" (*Masu Kagami, Fujigoromo*). "The ruler in whom the Ten Virtues are unlimited" (*Eiga Monogatari, Hikage no Katsura*); and the imperial throne is called "The seat of the Ten Virtues" (*Masu Kagami, Kusa-makura*), or "the imperial throne of ten thousand chariots of the ten virtues" (i.e. the throne of boundless virtue: *Heike Monogatari*); and the Emperor is regarded as one who ought to realize the Ten Virtues in human relationships. "He rules the land by putting into effect the correct law of the Ten Virtues" (*Jinnō Shōtōki*, 1).[207] Such concepts presuppose the Buddhist political theories already explained.

When these ideas came to Japan, they brought about still other interpretations. The Japanese, coming in contact with Chinese thought, identified the Japanese *tennō* (Emperor) with the *t'ien-tzŭ* (Emperor) as conceived by the Chinese, and accordingly thought of him as the "Son of Heaven"; but in Buddhist texts it is taught that all men will be born in heaven if they practice goodness; these two conceptions being combined, the Emperor came to be thought of as having kept the rules of the Ten Virtues in past existences and consequently having been born Emperor in this life because of his past merit. Thus, e.g. "By the grace of the Ten Virtues he has become Emperor (*tenshi*)." (*Jinnō Shōtōki*, 4.) The theory that the Emperor is born ruler of the land because of his practice of the Ten Virtues is probably without authority in the Buddhist sacred texts.[208] The general tendency to regard the Emperor as divine has produced this sort of conception. Although, according to Buddhism, the ruler must realize the Ten Virtues, and the true significance of the ruler is realized in just this way, in the Japanese view the Emperor has *already done this*. While according to Buddhism the divine nature of the ruler is to be realized in *the future* as a moral "ought," in the Japanese view this is reinterpreted as already given to him, and as being an accomplished fact. We can detect, in the tradition of Prince Shōtoku (573–621), a characteristic way of thinking similar to this. Prince Shōtoku, in the general conception of later Japanese, was a reincarnation of the Bodhisattva Avalokiteśvara.[209] But this sort of tradition has not appeared in India.[210] The patronage of Buddhism by King Aśoka was, with respect to its influence on world history, so great that he is not to be compared with Prince Shōtoku; but in the many traditions about King Aśoka transmitted among the Indians, he is merely thought to have acquired virtue through having presented sand playfully to the Buddha as a child in a former life. And likewise among other kings and emperors in India who have protected Buddhism, we cannot discover any such traditions. Beneath the way in which Prince Shōtoku is venerated lies the particularly Japanese tendency to Emperor worship.

The authority of the Emperor has been supposed by most Japanese to be superior to that of the Buddha. In fact Y. Haga declared: "It is a universal proverbial belief that the Buddha is of nine virtues, while the Emperor is of ten virtues." Moreover, prayers are said in Buddhist temples for the longevity and good health of the Emperor, while tablets are usually enshrined therein for the same purpose.

Since antiquity the nationalistic tendency to Emperor worship has persisted among the Japanese, and various religions in Japan have made both conscious and unconscious attempts to adapt themselves to this tendency. It is to be noticed, however, that on the part of the members of the Imperial family, efforts have been made to de-sanctify themselves. Those who became devout believers in Buddhism, in particular, were least interested in their deification. Emperor Shōmu (701–756) declared himself to be "a servant of the three treasures of Buddhism" (the Buddha, the law, and the priest). Upon finding a passage in Volume 16 of *Daijū-Kyō* (Sūtra on Great Collection) which reads: "We are allowed to take neither family nor property nor throne with us when we die. Only commandments, almsgiving, and no licentiousness are to be our companions in our present as well as in our future lives." Emperor Kazan (968–1008) left his throne and became a devout believer of Buddhism, "because he understood that even the Imperial throne and the treasures of the state were nothing but illusions."[211] He was aware of the austere fact that even the monarch must die alone, just as commoners do. Some members of the Imperial family expressed their feeling of *equality before the judgment of Hell*. They, therefore, thought it necessary to become devout believers of Buddhism in order to prepare themselves for that judgment. Emperor Daigo (885–930) is said to have composed the following thirty-one-syllable ode: "At the bottom of Hell there is no real difference whatsoever between the members of the Imperial family and slaves."[212] This is the statement of a believer in the equality of men. There are also fairly many odes to the same effect composed by other Emperors.[213] In April 1859, owing to a supplication of the Empress Dowager, three pensionaries were instituted at the Anshōji Temple. The petition reads: "Even those in Heaven cannot escape their decline, not to speak of ordinary men on the earth. Crossing the bourn before Hell, we cannot take property with us. Dragged into Yama's judgment-hall, there is no difference between the ruler and the ruled. We have come into the world alone to die alone."[214]

There are many poems composed by Emperors expressing their consciousness of wrong-doing as well as their delight in the vow of Amitābha that evil men may be saved.

> "How many might the sins of my body reflected in the mirror be, I only wish my mind to look toward the Pure Land." (Emperor Gokashiwabara, 1464–1526).

"The most sinful of all sinners are we who commit sins, knowing that we shall certainly be saved. How should Amitābha leave us out of this gracious vow!" (Emperor Gotsuchimikado, 1442–1500.)

"Afflicted as I am, I will not complain,
Since I trust the marvellous vow of Amitābha." (Emperor Tsuchimikado, 1195–1231.)

In these poems the Emperors are well aware of being ordinary men.

Motivated by such a humble consciousness, these Emperors and members of the Imperial family were led to enter the priesthood. After the death of Emperor Junwa (786–840), his bones were smashed to pieces to be scattered on the summit of Nishiyama at Ōharano (The Western Hill of the Great Field)[215] in accordance with his will. There were fairly many Emperors who stipulated in their wills not to have any tombs made for them. One of the Imperial edicts, issued in the name of Emperor Seiwa at the time of a drought, reads, "It's my fault, not the people's. My clothing and provisions should be curtailed." At the end of the Kamakura period, Ex-emperor Kameyama (1249–1305) entered the priesthood himself and prepared meals in the kitchen for those priests who visited the temple on the occasion.[216]

In these cases we cannot discern any intention on the part of the Imperial family to present themselves as living gods. Such was the general attitude of the Imperial family toward religion before the Meiji Restoration. At the time of the Meiji Restoration, Emperor worship was instituted by force under the influence of the movement of "reverence for the Emperor and expulsion of foreigners." Only in recent years did it come to be the only and absolute form of religion in Japan. It is not true, therefore, that Emperor worship was motivated by a subjective intention on the part of the Imperial family itself. On the contrary, it represents a way of thinking peculiar to the Japanese which assumed an extraordinary form of expression at a certain period of Japanese history. As has been pointed out already, this way of thinking modified the introduction and development of Buddhism in Japan. There is almost no analogue of such a tendency in India or in China. Indeed it is certain that such a form of living-god-worship is a result of neither the various conditions peculiar to Eastern societies in general nor "feudalism" for the most part. In fact, there still remain various problems to be studied in connection with Emperor worship in the ancient Orient and in the Roman Empire.

Sectarian and Factional Tendencies

In Japan there exists a strong tendency toward sectarianism and factionalism, which is another manifestation of the tendency to regard as absolute any limited and specific human nexus. It is a fact generally observed today that this tendency to clannishness is still prevalent in Japan even though it is not a phenomenon of recent origin, but has its deep roots in ancient Japanese history.

I should like to dwell upon this tendency first in reference to the constitutional make-up of the Buddhist order and the mode of worship among the believers. In Japanese Buddhism, for the most part, it is not the universal creed that is counted as most important. But rather, the emphasis has been placed upon the specific religious order itself as a limited and concrete human nexus.

In the process of the establishment of the Honganji order, which has become the largest Buddhist order in Japan, we can find historical evidence of this sectarian factionalism which is conspicuous among the Japanese. Shinran (1173–1262) himself, the founder of Jōdo-shin-shū (True Pure Land Sect), never had any thought of establishing a new sect of his own. He firmly believed, as has already been pointed out in the preceding pages, that it was his mission to follow faithfully the teachings of his master, Hōnen (1133–1212), and to reveal their true essence. Besides, Shinran recognized the universality of religious doctrine. "The teaching of the Perfect One (Buddha) is something that permeates everywhere."[217] It was just upon the basis of this belief that he could make the outright assertion that "I, Shinran, have no disciples to be called mine."[218] And he believed that "everyone of them is a disciple of the Perfect One (Buddha)" and "we are all fellow-disciples practicing religion together."[219] It was otherwise, however, with the Buddhist priests of his time. They would say, "This one is my disciple," or "That is someone else's disciple," and they vied with one another for the acquisition of more disciples of their own.[220] In spite of Shinran's strenuous effort to warn against such sectarian rivalry, it became a strong tendency even within the Shinshū order, until at last the entire group of followers of Shinshū became transformed into "those who are known to be the disciples of the Saint of the Honganji (Original Vow) Temple."[221] Since then the Honganji order has developed into a large organization on a nationwide scale, not as a free and open association of the believers, but rather as a closed order with the "pope" as its central authority. It came to be a life-and-death problem for the followers to be admitted into or expelled from the order. Rennyo (1415–1499), eighth abbot of the Honganji, in his effort to avoid an insurrection, warned the followers: "It has been rumored that the disciples are up to some evil deeds. That would be preposterous. From now on, anyone who would contrive such an intrigue should certainly be *excommunicated* forever *from the followers of the gate of the saint.*"[222] The disciples of this order, as the quotation shows, were called "*monto*" (followers of the gate), and henceforth this appellation suggested the rigidity with which the closed-door policy of the order was maintained. Each temple then came to function as "an intermediary temple" for the followers, up to the central temple.

It has been generally thought that Shinran advocated that Buddhism should be practiced under secular conditions. But "neither ecclesiastical nor secular"[223] was the way he described his standpoint, which permitted a priest to marry and raise a family. Thus he was not advocating a lay religious movement in which the priesthood would not be recognized at all. In this respect, it was not quite the same as the religious movement of the Quakers in the West, in spite of their close resemblance. The Shinshū order has centered on hereditary professional priests. It is to be admitted, however, that in its rudimentary form it resembled closely a movement for the secularization of religion. There even seemed to be no such things as temples in its earliest stage of development.[224] But in spite of this, the Shinshū order gradually acquired a pre-eminently sectarian form, and in this we can perceive a tendency of thinking characteristic of the Japanese at large.

Such exclusive tendencies are also evident among other sects of Kamakura Buddhism said to be characteristically Japanese. It is widely known that the most violently sectarian of all is the Nichiren sect, as is indicated by the four-point maxim of its founder: "Those who practice invocation to Amitābha are due to suffer continuous punishment in hell; the Zen sect is the devil; the Shingon sect is the ruiner of the country; the Ritsu (Discipline) sect is the enemy of the country." Originally the *Hokke* (Lotus) *Sūtra* taught that even the most ignorant and the stupid, should they practice Buddhism faithfully, would all attain the status of absolute perfection. That was a most generous expression of the spirit of tolerance and magnanimity, which used to be the characteristic attitude of almost all the devotees of the Hokke Scripture. When it came to Japan, however, the Nichiren sect, which took the attitude of placing absolute reliance on the Hokke Sūtra, unfailingly became sectarian and closed, and one faction of it even displayed a tendency toward extreme exclusionism. In the case of "the non-alms-giving-or-taking faction" of this sect the giving or taking of alms to or from non-believers of the Hokke Sūtra was prohibited.

If we go from Kamakura to Ashikaga, a great majority of the followers of the Jōdo sect had, not respect, but contempt for various Buddhas, Bodhisattvas, or gods and goddesses other than Amitābha.[225] This trend also came to the fore in the Jōdo-shin sect. That was precisely why Rennyo repeatedly warned his followers against showing contempt for Buddhas and gods, though they might not owe them any special obligation of respect.[226] Such a tendency is scarcely present in the Zen sect. A person like Dōgen (1200–1253), however, displayed an attitude of extreme aversion to the ideas of other sects. Being confident that he himself was the faithful propagator of the gospel of his master, Ju-ching (Nyojō, 1163–1228), he hated to adopt or compromise with ideas other than his own.[227] When we look at Ju-ching's own teachings, nevertheless, we find that he is to some extent close to the theory of the compatibility of Confucianism, Taoism, and Buddhism, which has generally been accepted in China.[228] It is correct to say, therefore, that it was Dōgen's own version of his master's teachings based upon his own method of selection, which might have very well been unconscious but which was apparently quite contrary to his avowed and conscious assertion that he was the faithful spokesman for his continental master. It amounts to this: that in Japan there has never been any official religious doctrine such as the doctrine of Three Stages, in the Sui and T'ang periods (600–907) in China, that preached the universality of the Buddha and the established religious doctrine without discrimination.

It was the Japanese tendency to emphasize the limited human nexus rather than religious faith that gave rise to the segmentation of quite a number of religious sects, each with its exclusive and closed order, in line with the general Japanese propensity for cliquism or clannishness. Among the Zen sect, as an example, it is not the difference in the religious faith or doctrine but *merely such specific factors of human relationship* as the inheritance of the master's "endowments" that account for the split of the religious school into multitudinous sects and factions.[229] The Master-and-disciple relationship has been jealously maintained. It is one of the characteristics of Japanese Buddhism to make much of the inheritance of the lineage of religious doctrines.[230] Today the communication media are so well developed that any single individual is susceptible to the influence of various ideas of many individuals. Should one insist, under such circumstances, on maintaining the absolute authority of *just one* master toward his disciples, that would inevitably foster the sectarian relationship. And nothing is farther removed from this idea than the original Buddhist stand: "Do not depend upon men, but upon the law."

The emphasis upon the inheritance of the master's endowments naturally gave rise to the system of secret and oral instruction. The Tendai sect, after being transplanted from China into Japan (c. 805), introduced later an eclectic book called *Sanjū-shichika no Hōmon* or the "Threefold-seven-point Gates to the Law" which is a secret oral instruction transmitted from the master to his disciples. It was conceived to have been established during the period before Tōyō Chūjin (1065–1138) and after Kakuchō (960–1034), and it is of great significance in Japanese Tendai theology.

"Some of the so-called orally instructed gates to the Law are," according to the Buddhist scholar and priest Daitō Shimaji (1875–1927), "unknown in respect to their origins, authors, and the date of formulation.

Nevertheless, herein lies the essence and the rudiments of the Tendai theology in medieval Japan."[231] The fact that their authors are unknown shows that their genesis was in no way connected with the authority of any particular individual, but rather that it was the Japanese esoteric way of thinking itself that was responsible for such a formulation.

This esoteric trend is also present among the Zen sect. According to the Rinzai sect, one is expected to contemplate a great number of catechetic questions for meditation, which requires the mastery of innumerable phrases and precedents, in a language other than the native tongue of the Japanese Zen priests. This meant a tremendous effort on their part. Those who were not up to the task were apt to confine themselves to the intensive reading of just one particular book out of many, and to contrive some comments of their own, which were then regarded as a "family inheritance" to be taught in secret.

This trend for emphasizing secret oral instructions became particularly distinctive among the Zen sect. *"Inka,"* the master's recognition of his disciple's attainment of enlightenment, certainly existed in China, where it meant merely a practice exercised at the moment of having attained enlightenment. In Japan, however, it came to be stressed according to the idea of inheritance. The Myōshin Temple sect reveals its inclination for secret instruction in the form of a certificate for having entered enlightenment. Moreover, all the factions of the Zen sect attached special importance to the forms of comments or footnotes given to catechetic questions for meditation and these forms were transmitted in an oral and secret way.

In any sect much is made of the relationships between the central and peripheral temples, all of which are ultimately subordinated to the head temple. Such a systematic hierarchy was also introduced into the newly-risen Buddhist sects and Shintō orders. There also existed political factors that gave rise to the split among sects. The divide-and-rule policy of the Tokugawa government was, for instance, responsible for the separation of the Hongan (Original Vow) Temple into Eastern and Western sections, whose differences in doctrine were later evolved but were of little significance.

Splits among sects in this sense of the word never occurred either in India or in China. Indeed, there were a number of different schools of Buddhism in India, which may correspond to what we call sects in Japan. But the situation was vastly different from what exists in Japan. There, distinctions among different schools stood for differences in the doctrines of respective schools. After the Maurya Dynasty (about 317–180 B.C.), each temple or monastery came to be affiliated with this or that school for the purpose of effective management. Even then the essential function of those buildings, namely "to lodge priests from all four directions," was maintained, and no priest from another school was ever refused accommodation. It often happened that people of different schools lived under the same roof. The same thing seems to have happened in China also.[232] Almost all the temples in modern China belong to the Zen sect, where the invocation of Amitābha is also practiced. Within the same temple a person may sit in religious meditation and at the same time practice invocation of Amitābha (with the hope of entering the Pure Land). The practice of meditation and that of invocation of Amitābha are considered compatible.

Contrary to those situations in India and China, a great number of sects in Japan are segregated. For illustration, the Zen school and the Jōdo school, which in China are in complete harmony without any sense of conflict, in Japan form separate sects, which are incompatible with each other.[233] (Incidentally, these two schools were not clearly distinguished from each other in India.) In Japan also, a person like Dōgen, for instance, violently disliked sect-names and refused to call his own sect the Zen sect. In reality, however, the Zen sect brought forth segmentation of factions and sub-factions.

It follows that in China, if distinction among sects is required, it is made according to the person in charge. In Japan, by contrast, each temple has its own denomination. In China, the denomination of a temple depends upon the resident priest and is consequently submitted to change from time to time, but in Japan the denomination of a temple never changes.[234]

Such denominational distinctions as exist in Buddhism in Japan, might very well be attributed to the religious policy of the Tokugawa government (1600–1867) with the situation still persisting today. But it can also be suggested that had it not been for the existence of the Japanese way of thinking to serve as a basis for the establishment of such social institutions, the enforcement of such a system would not have been possible.

Japanese Buddhist orders, with their characteristically sectarian exclusiveness, on the one hand, and the followers in general with their family system firmly established on the other, together gave rise to the system of allotting families to each temple. That system means a relationship, stabilized into an institution, between the temples and the families of their followers. The latter would entrust a particular temple with the performance of the funeral and other Buddhist services of their families and the management of their family cemeteries, and the temple leaders would take it for granted to expect, in return for those services, not only remuneration for those services but also contributions of money to cover the building, reconstructing, repairing, and other maintenance expenses of the temples. Such a system emerged voluntarily toward the end of the medieval age, and was later adopted and enforced by the Tokugawa government. Moreover, during the Tokugawa period, a system was established in which each individual's religious faith had to be guaranteed by his temple. Those who were confirmed as not pagan were registered in "the denominational census-register."

Thereupon the Japanese family, as a unit, came to be affiliated with one or another temple, and accordingly they submitted to this or that denomination. It follows that, in traditional Japan, it was not the individual but the *family* which determined religious faith. The individual faith of a person is indistinguishable from that of his or her *family*. The relationship between the temple and its parishioners was not always established according to the choice of a religious faith on the part of the parishioners. Mostly their relationship was based purely on customary habits of the family, not usually accompanied by the sense of joy accompanying individual conversion or redemption. The lack of freely chosen individual religious faith prevalent among the Japanese today has its socio-historical roots in this fact.

The attitudes of exclusiveness and closedness were the characteristics not only of the Buddhist orders. A similar situation existed among various Shintō sects, as has been admitted by the Japanese themselves. "Those who advocate Shintoism," criticized Kanzan Matsumiya, "mostly boast of their own secret teachings, occult instructions, and conceited bigotry, and do not wish to impart their knowledge to the people in general. They are all concerned only with trifles. . . ."[235] The fact that such an attitude prevails not only in Shintoism but also pervades various arts and crafts was pointed out by Nakamoto Tominaga as follows:

"The habits of Shintoism, to begin with, are occultism and secret-instruction, both being tantamount simply to hiding everything. Hiding is the beginning of lying and stealing. Witchcraft and figures of speech may be permissible as being interesting to look at and listen to. But depending on those habits alone is extremely harmful. In the old days when people were honest there must have been less harmful means for teaching and guiding them. Our age today is one of corruption by liars and robbers. So it is wrong on the part of the teachers of Shintoism to defend those evil doings. Even those ignoble businesses like *Sarugaku* [a medieval Noh-dance] and tea-ceremony, all following the example of those habits of Shintoism, fabricate secret instructions and certificates for having attained enlightenment, and even set a price on them for huge profit-making. This certainly is deplorable. When one asks why such things come about, they answer that it is because their instructions are not easily transmitted to those who are not ripe for them. That appears to be somewhat reasonable. But one needs to be reminded that a way, which is to be kept in secret, which is not to be readily transmitted, and for which a price is set for instruction, cannot in any sense be called genuine."[236]

A sectarianism not quite so closed, but still exclusive, was pushed to its extreme in Hirata Shintoism. After the Meiji Restoration (1868), sectarian Shintoism spread with enormous rapidity. In spite of the fact that state interference or guidance was no longer exerted upon Shintoism, curiously enough, there appeared symptoms almost identical to those of the Buddhist orders under the control of the Tokugawa government. Moreover, it should be noted in particular that the Honganji Temple order and the newly-emerging Shintō orders were once organized according to the prototype of the Emperor-system.

Such a tendency as exists in the religious life of the Japanese cannot be defended simply as a token of respect for the purity of faith. It is attributable rather to the social inclination of the Japanese in general toward the establishment of some form of limited and closed human nexus. To say the least, the segmentation of closed religious sects cannot be ascribed to a difference of religious convictions in these respective sects, since the Japanese in general are so markedly indifferent to religious dogmas, apart from family-affiliation to a sectarian temple and the devotion to the clan and Emperor.

Even scientists and mathematicians were not free from the tendency to form a closed society. The results of the studies by the mathematician, Yoshihiro Kurushima (died 1753), were not transmitted as his work, but were mostly mingled with those of the preceding mathematical school of Kowa Seki (1642–c. 1700), because the leaders of this school wished to credit them to be their own or their master's productions, in order to add to their fame or influence.[237] In such a secluded society Japanese mathematics developed only to a limited extent. The concepts of differential calculus and integration were found by the Japanese a century after Newton and Leibniz, but Japanese mathematics did not develop greatly till the time of the introduction of Western mathematics. "The usage of keeping inventions in secrecy must have considerably delayed the progress of science, for those to whom the secret subjects were imparted were not, and could not be, always the best minds of their times. Unfortunately, the spirit of vested interests ruled the conduct of scholars."[238]

Then a question should be raised as to why the tendency toward sectarian clannishness is conspicuous among the Japanese in general. It might be tied up with the Japanese inclination to love and enjoy the small-scaled and closed way of communal living. In search of the empirical basis of the tendency to exclusiveness among such small-scaled communities, we have to take into consideration the factor of a social mode of living adapted to the topographical elements of the environment. The density of population of the narrow island since ancient days might be taken as a proof that life here used to be comparatively easy and peaceful. On the other hand the same fact may account for the formation of the traits of exclusiveness. Such problems ought to be discussed independently. Suffice it to point out that these characteristics are distinctive of the Japanese in general, as cultural manifestations.

As pointed out in preceding sections, the Japanese attach great importance to a limited and specific human nexus, and the family, the lord-and-vassal relationship, the clan, the state (or the Emperor), and even universal world religions, once transplanted into this country, were transformed to fit their clannish propensity. Scarcely any thought has been given to any universal external law which every man should follow beyond the confines of this limited human nexus. Generally speaking, the Japanese mode of adopting a foreign religion was confined to those cases which were considered helpful to promoting and developing some concrete human relationship which the Japanese regarded as absolute. For those individuals who took religious faith seriously, it might have implied "devotion and obedience," but for the Japanese society as a whole it only meant "absorption and adoption." Consequently, although Buddhism has been the flesh and blood of Japanese culture for more than the past ten centuries, the people by and large still regard it as "an imported system of thought." In this respect, our attitude differs fundamentally from those of Western nations in regard to Christianity and from those of southern Asiatic nations in regard to Buddhism. As for those nations, universal world religions are conceived to be such integral parts of their own culture that they are linked to the formation of the respective nations themselves. But for the Japanese, in contrast, such a conception is totally absent. What is called the non-religious character of the Japanese is explicable partly by their attachment, on the one hand, to the limited concrete human nexus and partly by the conscious or unconscious indifference, on the other, to the dogmas of universal religion.

In order to interpret these cultural and social phenomena of Japan, one might refer to the deficiencies of modern bourgeois society. Indeed, that is also one of the causes. But an economic interpretation is not enough to explain away all the characteristics mentioned above. An oversimplified ascription of these phenomena to the facts of immaturity of capitalism, its unbalanced development, and the cultural lag of feudal social institutions is far from satisfactory, since those socio-economic factors are commonly shared by other Asiatic countries and are not the unique properties of Japan alone. With respect to the mode of production in agriculture also there exists a distinct similarity among Asiatic countries. In regard to religious thoughts, however, there exist some characteristics unique to Japan, which are rather absent among other Asiatic peoples.

One cannot but attribute these characteristics, therefore, to the ways of thinking arising from the historical traditions still alive in the minds of the Japanese. And without the Japanese subjecting these mental propensities to a thorough-going examination and radical criticism, and without their taking strong measures to do something about them, it would be difficult, as I see it, to predict an overall change of outlook among the Japanese in the future.

Defense of a Human Nexus by Force

The view that a specific and concrete system of human relationships is absolute tends to carry with it the notion that the defense and development of the system is also an absolute. When the existence of the system of human relationships to which one belongs is endangered, one is apt to defend it even by recourse to force. In the Japanese way of thinking, the use of force was not generally discussed as ethically good or evil, or as justified or not under various particular conditions. One is inclined, instead, to seek a sacred cause in the mere act of defending a specific human nexus. High esteem for arms had a very important place among the thought-tendencies in Japan, at least in the past.

Such a tendency was already obvious in the ancient mythology. This land was then called "the country of one thousand fine halberds," the name suggestive of the fact that the Japanese were, since ancient times, a nation of military prowess. A comparison of the Japanese myths with those of other nations reveals some characteristics of the Japanese people. For instance, Finnish mythology, as represented in the Kalevala, is said to be rather lacking in the concept of respect for military power. In Japanese mythology, however, instances of conquest by arms occur very frequently, and the concept of respect for military power is consistently followed. It is noteworthy, as archaeological remains prove to us, that no violent interracial conflicts seem to have occurred on Japanese soil. Nevertheless, on the conceptual level there is a strong tendency toward respect for military power, which constitutes a distinct characteristic of Japanese mythology.

In later periods other nations admitted and the Japanese themselves boasted that they were brave and superior in military matters. Kanzan Matsumiya (1686–1780) writes: "The Japanese are high-spirited and fond of arms. Valour and dauntlessness make up their distinctive style."[239] Atsutane Hirata (1776–1843) also comments as follows:

"The Japanese are endowed with extraordinarily courageous spirit, which one may as well call either fearlessness or heroism. Which is it? Being defeated by their enemy or having a grudge against their enemy, and yet having failed to take their revenge, they calmly commit *harakiri* without flinching. Such is the way of the Japanese who, faced with an emergency, are never afraid of death.[240]

The underlying motivation for such prowess is an absolute devotion to one's lord.

> "I will not from today
> Turn back toward home. . . .
> I who have set out to serve
> As Her Majesty's humble shield."[241]

Whether in devotion to one's feudal lord or in loyalty to the Emperor, the identical way of thinking is present. It is a vastly different matter in the case of the Indians. The Indians, indeed, also have their own epics of wars. But they always use religious teachings to encourage their heroes. Indians are taught that those brave soldiers fallen on the battlefield will be reborn in *the Heaven of Indra*[242] or that they will dwell with the god *Viṣṇu*.[243] It would be totally inconceivable to the Indians that one should march to the battlefield with the conviction that: "Into hell may I fall; punishment by the gods may be upon me. I pray nothing but to serve my lord, with utmost loyalty."[244]

A question may be raised here. We have already said that among the Japanese there is a familial inclination to affection. Is it not incompatible with the propensity for military prowess? Banzan Kumazawa (1665–1691) was already conscious of this problem: "An old friend asked: 'Japan is a land of military prowess. Why is it then that she is also said to be the land of benevolence?' I answered: 'It is exactly because she is the land of benevolence that she is the land of military prowess. Is it not obvious that the benevolent are always brave?' "

The fact that the Japanese of the past esteemed military force does not imply that they used violence merely for the sake of destruction. Insofar as they had to maintain and defend the interests of a specific system of human relationship—a feudal clan, the state, a group of gangsters, or whatever—they appealed to force. In combat they were brave. The virtue of self-sacrifice was always manifested. But if the leader of the system to which one belonged should ever order cease fire, they would stop using force at once, and instantaneously establish peace, as was seen at the end of World War II. The reason is that their objective was not to kill men and destroy things but to defend the human nexus by force.

If this way of thinking among the Japanese is once understood, it would also be possible to comprehend the fact that the dauntless generals of old Japan were at the same time refined gentlemen of gracious heart, who composed poems, appreciated the beauties of nature, were well-versed in the tea-ceremony, and were considerate to other people. In almost all the books on the way of the *samurai,* the virtue of "benevolence" is recommended. It was possible for daring brave generals and soldiers to be followers of Buddhism, which ordained against killing even a single insect without cause. Herein lies, I take it, the key to the paradox that the Japanese are in religion peaceful, but brave in combat. In order to be brave on the battlefield, soldiers were expected to get rid of their fears and worldly concerns. For that purpose, Buddhism, Zen in particular, was observed as a guiding doctrine.

The fact that among the attitudes of the Japanese as warriors such traits were pre-eminent might very well be attributed to the way of thinking common to the Japanese in general. If such had been the thinking pattern transmitted and maintained only among the *samurai*-class, it would not have been possible that among the chivalrous outlaws, coming from the common people, and among the rank-and-file soldiers after the Meiji Restoration, the same traits should appear in just the same fashion as in the *samurai* of the earlier days. These attitudes cannot be interpreted merely by means of Communistic theories of class-ethics or of the mode of production. The effort to maintain and defend the human nexus even by recourse to force naturally increased the influence of the military in Japanese society and made them the ruling class for so long a time.

Japanese society has never firmly established a class comparable to the literati in China or to the caste of Brahmin-priests in India. It cannot be said that the socio-economic situation in Japan prevented such a class from emerging. It was rather the Japanese inclination to emphasize the order of human nexus that enabled the soldiers, whose essential function was the use of force, to rise to high positions as the rulers of the society. This tendency persisted from antiquity down to very recent days. Men of letters were, generally speaking, given only minor positions as aides and advisers. These characteristics made Japan vastly different from other Asiatic countries. In reference to this point, Max Weber explains:[245] "The contrast of Japan with China came from elements intimately associated with the cultural features of feudal Japan, particularly in the following aspects. In Japan it was not the unmilitary literati but the class of professional soldiers that were most influential socially. As in the Medieval West, it was the custom and culture of the knight that regulated practical conduct, not the certificate of passing an examination or scholarly refinement as in China. It was also a this-worldly (*innerweltlich*) culture that regulated practical conduct as in the ancient classical West, not the transcendent philosophy of deliverance as in India." As far as this aspect is concerned, the comment of this German sociologist seems to be valid.

Within Japanese society a pattern of conduct had thus been established, in which the soldiers took pride in their position as soldiers, pledged loyalty under any circumstances to their lords, and readily died for them.

Readiness to defend the human nexus even by force, and the consequent dominance of the soldier, also determined modes of acculturation. In transplanting Confucianism, the Japanese ruling class equated the Confucian bureaucracy and the *samurai* class in Japan. The two, however, were essentially different; therefore, the way of the high officials was not immediately identified with the way of the *samurai*. Consequently, they had to wait until a scholar like Sokō Yamaka (1622–1685) appeared and formulated the theory of the way of *samurai* availing himself of Confucian theory. Most of the books on the way of *samurai* were written in a spirit apparently independent of Confucian theory.

What changes did Buddhism suffer in this regard? Buddhism originally abhorred control by force and aimed at the achievement of an ideal society not based upon the relationship of dominance-submission due to power. Consequently, both in India and in China, followers of Buddhism regarded benevolence and forbearance as particularly important virtues. Laymen might resort to violence, but never the clergy. In any monastic order of any world religion in past history, it would be hard to find men so far removed from military power as the Buddhist believers in India and China. Even after the advent of Buddhism to Japan, among the earliest Buddhist orders such virtues were still kept intact.

It was impossible, however, that a religious order should alone escape from the general way of thinking prevalent among the Japanese. After the Heian period, various large temples, which owned large estates, supported priest-soldiers, whose force was utilized to achieve the temples' demands. There were also armed conflicts between temples and shrines. At the time of the feud between the Genji and Heike clans, old shrine families affiliated themselves to one or the other clan and fought. The fleet of the Kumano Shrine, for instance, assisted Genji, while the head priest of the Usa Shrine belonged to Heike. Originally the ideal of shrines and temples was to stand aloof from political conflicts and to keep their estates intact, as sacred neutral zones, against invasion from all directions. But the attitude that men of religion are justified in using armed force naturally led the priests of temples and shrines to take up arms for self-defense. According to the reports of Christian missionaries in Japan, the monasteries at Negoro always supported a host of priest-soldiers and let them train themselves in military affairs. Once a giant bell was rung, it was said, 30,000 soldiers could be summoned in just three or four hours.[246] In the 15th and 16th centuries and the Age of Civil Wars, the followers of the True Pure Land sect and the Nichiren sect rose to arms against the pressure of feudal lords. At the time the chief abbot Rennyo was in Yoshizaki; he summoned the priests and their families, belonging to the central cathedral, and forced them to decide a few days in advance. "Our destiny is predetermined by the deeds in our previous lives, *so you should not be afraid of death. You should fight.*"[247]

No precedent has ever been recognized in India or in China sanctioning the use of force by a Buddhist order. In India the Sikhs, Nāga, and Śaiva ascetics were once armed but those were rather exceptional cases. In Japan, at an early stage of the modern period, there occurred a war based upon the conflict of religions in the case of the insurrection of Japanese Catholics at Shimabara. Compared with the Catholic-Protestant religious strife in the West, this insurrection is hardly worth mentioning. But it is noteworthy that such a phenomenon appeared at a considerably early date solely in Japan and not in other Asiatic countries. It was a manifestation of the effort of devotion to defend one's own religious order even when recourse to force was necessary. This is why, once the security of the religious order was assured, the order instantly ceased fighting. After national unification was brought about by Hideyoshi Toyotomi (1536–1598), all the Buddhist orders abandoned arms. Subsequently, however, the inclination to maintain and expand Buddhist orders by force persisted. This is, according to my view, mainly based upon the "sectarian-factional tendency" already discussed.

The Japanese respect for arms in the past influenced the mode of acceptance of Buddhist *thought;* the fact that the worship of Acalanātha is considerably popular among the Japanese people is an illustration. Acalanātha, wearing the features of indignation, living in the midst of blazing flame, with a sharp-edged sword in his right hand and a rope in his left hand, is the scourge of all troubles and disturbances, both internal and external, and defeats and annihilates devils. Acalanātha is a divine being who made his first appearance toward the last stage of Buddhism when esoteric Buddhism was founded and popular religion was adopted. He scarcely appears in the extant Sanskrit Buddhist Scriptures.[248] His place in Indian Buddhism was therefore dubious. In China he was hardly respected either.[249] There are five great Buddhas portrayed in the Diamond Realm (*Kongō-kai*) and Realm of the Womb (*Taizō-kai*) *maṇḍalas,* introduced by Kōbō (Kūkai, 774–835), and thereafter, in Japan, Acalanātha and other Myōōs (*Vidyārāja*) or Sage-Kings were very often represented in painting and sculpture. So in the T'ang dynasty (618–907) in China, Acalanātha and other Myōōs might at first have been worshipped. But the fact that they ceased to be worshipped later seems to be a proof that the idea of the conquest of devils with swords, which is the intrinsic virtue and merit of Acalanātha, was not congenial to the Chinese view of religion. Benevolence characterized by Avalokiteśvara Bodhisattva was the religious ideal of the Chinese. In contrast, the feature of defeating enemies and conquering devils is embodied in Acalanātha and is better suited to the minds of the Japanese. For the same reason the worship of the great commander (*Āṭavika*) was widely practiced in Japan. Even Amitābha, who is benevolence itself, was supposed to use armed force. The expression, "the sharp-edged sword of Amitābha," is often used in Japanese literature. It was originally derived from a phrase in the *Hanju Panegyric,* written by Shan-tao of the T'ang period in China; "The sharp-edged sword is another name for Amitābha. An invocation of the name absolves one from all sin." The sharp-edged sword in this case, however, is a mere figure of speech. The Japanese took it as if Amitābha had used the real sword to punish the wicked.[250] And they sought in this interpretation of Amitābha for the justification of using armed force in war.

The Japanese respect for arms is manifested in the rigor and relentlessness with which Zen priests trained their disciples. Jakurei Tsūgen (1322–1391), whose teaching was most widely inherited in the Sōtō sect, is famous for his "pit of burying-alive." When an itinerant priest came to him in order to receive training, it was said, he tested the newcomer and if he perceived in the latter any impurity of motivation, he then simply threw him down into the pit.[251] In India there were many who performed religious austerities upon themselves, but no such atrocity was perpetrated upon others. Shōsan Suzuki (1579–1655), a *samurai* by origin, advocated what is called the Zen of the Two Kings. The gist of his teaching is to practice Zen with the spirit of Two Kings, the fierce and the brave. "In these days," he preaches, "it has been overlooked that the Buddhist Law is saturated with great strength of prowess and solidity. It has come to be soft, gentle, disinterested, and goodnatured, but none has trained himself to bring forth the spirit of a vengeful Ghost. Everyone should be trained to be brave, and to become a vengeful Ghost of Buddhism."[252] He taught his followers to practice religion, face to face with high-spirited images of Buddha. "Observing the features of the construction of Buddhist images, one would see at the gate an image of Vajra Sattva, in the parlor, Twelve Divinities, Sixteen Good Gods, Eight Attendants of Vajrasatta, the Four Kings of Gods and Five Great Buddhas, all displaying their strength, dressed in suits of armour, and armed with halberds, swords, sticks, and bows and arrows. Those who do not grasp the meaning of such display would be unable to heal the six afflictions which should be regarded as enemies. Pray, observe Buddhist images well and practice religion."[253] Such a violent way of preaching as the above seems never to have occurred among Buddhist followers in either India or China. That was the way in which Buddhism, particularly the Zen sect, was made to bestow upon swordsmanship its spiritual basis. The Zen priest, Takuan (1573–1645), preached to a swordsman, Yagiu Tajima-no-Kami: "What is called the flash of striking fire with stones means to be as quick as a lightning. If one's name is called out, 'Emon!' [like 'Jack!' in English], he answers, 'Aye.' That is intelligence. But if he is called 'Emon' and asks back, 'What do you want?' after stopping to think about what the caller wants, that is an affliction characteristic of the mind of a mediocrity, which stops to be moved by things and to go astray. That is called an affliction that is prone to stay. To answer 'Aye,' at the moment he is called 'Emon!,' is the wisdom of Buddhas. Buddhas and living beings are not two different things; gods and men are not two different things. Such a mind as described above may be called either god or Buddha. Though there are many ways such as the way of Shintoism, the way of poetry, or the way of Confucianism, all amount to the lucidity of such a mind." The act of killing in combat is here justified by Buddhism. It is the distinctive feature probably of Japanese Buddhism alone to aim at the vindication of Buddhism by fighting.

Emphasis upon Human Activities

The emergent and fluid way of thinking, i.e. the way of thinking that asserts that reality is becoming or is in flux, as previously explained, is compatible with the Japanese tendency to be anchored to a particular human nexus. These two factors are combined to bring about an emphasis upon activities within a concrete social nexus. The variety of religious movements in Japan's history illustrates this social emphasis.

It is a well-known fact that primitive Shintoism was closely tied up with agricultural rituals in agrarian villages, and that Shintoist gods have been symbolized, even today, as gods of production.

Coming into contact with foreign cultures and getting acquainted with Chinese religions, the Japanese selected Confucianism in particular, although they were somewhat influenced also by the thoughts of both Lao-tsŭ and Chuang-tsŭ. In other words, out of diverse Chinese philosophies, they adopted and absorbed Confucianism, in particular, which instructs one in the way of right conduct within a concrete human nexus. The thoughts of Lao-tsŭ and Chuang-tsŭ favor a life of seclusion in which one escapes from a particular human nexus and seeks tranquility in contemplative solitude. Such a way of life was not to the taste of most Japanese. In contrast, Confucianism is essentially a doctrine whose secular concerns make it rather hard to call it a religion, for it principally determines rules of conduct according to social proprieties and political principles. In this respect, Confucianism never caused any serious conflict with the existing Japanese thinking-pattern at the time of its importation.

In the case of Buddhism, however, there arose many problems. Buddhism declares itself to be a teaching of the way to transcend worldliness.

According to Buddhist philosophy, the positive stage of "transcending worldliness" is attained by renouncing "this world." The central figures in Buddhist orders were all priests, who had freed themselves not only from their families but from any specific human nexus. In China, Buddhism was severely criticized by Confucians on the ground that by commending priesthood the Buddhists were destroying the family and civic basis of the human nexus.[254] In the same manner, Buddhism was condemned in Japan in the modern period by scholars of Japanese and Chinese classical literature. It is a well-known fact that at the time of the advent of Buddhism there arose various conflicts. Nevertheless Buddhism rushed in like a torrent and, before the Meiji Restoration, Japan appeared to be entirely a country of Buddhism. How was it then that the Japanese, who had a high esteem for a concrete worldly human nexus, accepted Buddhism, which was condemned for tending to destroy this nexus? Let us dwell a while upon this question.

In early Indian Buddhism the central figures of the orders were *bhikṣus* (monks) and *bhikṣunīs* (nuns). The lay followers assisted and protected the monks and nuns, and became devotees under their spiritual guidance and education. Not only in Buddhism but in the religious orders of the time in general, except for Brahmins, the central figures were monks (ascetics). Early Buddhism merely followed the modes of the day. The monks of early Buddhism at first formed an exclusive community, the *Saṁgha* (the ideal society), keeping themselves aloof from the impurities of the secular world; and then they tried to guide laymen with their religious and moral influence. So it is too rash to conclude that to become a monk was to destroy the human nexus. Moreover, in those days there existed good social reasons that made it necessary for a great many people to become monks.

The topographical characteristics of Japan, vastly different from those of India, required men to serve humanity within a specific human nexus. The doctrine of early Buddhism is not quite compatible with such requirements. So it came about that early Buddhism, together with traditional conservative Buddhism which inherited the former teachings, was despised and rejected under the name of "*Hīnayāna*" (Forsaken or Lesser Vehicle),[255] whereas the *Mahāyāna* (Greater Vehicle) form of Buddhism was particularly favored and adopted. Mahāyāna Buddhism was a popular religion that came to the fore after the Christian era, after the period when the *Kuṣāṇa* people were in power in Northern India. Some schools of Mahāyāna Buddhism, if not all, advocated comprehending the absolute truth *within secular life,* and in accepting Buddhism, the Japanese selected a school of just such a nature. And even in accepting those doctrines originally devoid of such a secular nature, they deliberately bestowed such a this-wordly character upon them. The phrase, "Japan is the country where *Mahāyāna* Buddhism is in practice,"[256] should be understood especially in the light of these basic facts.

This attitude of accepting Buddhism is clearly shown in the case of Prince Shōtoku. His "Commentaries upon Three Sūtras" are those upon "the *Shōman* Sūtra," "the *Yuima* Sūtra," and "the *Hokke* Sūtra." The selection of these three Sūtras out of a multitude was entirely based upon the Japanese way of thinking. "The *Shōman* Sūtra" was preached, allegedly in compliance with Buddha's command, by Shōman (Śrīmālādevī), who was a queen and a lay believer during the life-time of the Buddha. "The *Yuima* Sūtra" has a dramatic composition, in which Yuima, a lay believer, gives a sermon to *monks and ascetics,* reversing the usual order because it commends grasping the truth in secular life. And according to "the *Hokke* or Lotus Sūtra" all laymen who faithfully follow the teachings of the Buddha are expected to be delivered. The Crown Prince himself, all through his life, remained a lay believer. It is said that he called himself *"Shōman, a Child of the Buddha."*[257] The intention of Prince Shōtoku was to put emphasis upon the realization of Buddhist ideals within a concrete human nexus and to remain himself in secular life.[258]

All through the "Commentaries" by Prince Shōtoku, the author seeks an absolute significance, in each instance, of practical conduct in everyday life. He asserts: "Reality is no more than today's occurrence of cause and effect." And he interprets: "The ten thousand virtues are all contained in today's effect."[259] Such an interpretation has something in common with the doctrines of the Tendai and Kegon sects, but the particularistic expression "today's" makes it distinctly Japanese. Since it attaches great importance to action in actual human conditions, for those who have gone through Buddhist reflection, this world of impurities and sufferings in itself turns out to be a place of blessings. "Since a sage wishes to enlighten mankind, he regards life and death as a garden."[260] All the good deeds practiced in the world of life and death are eventually turned into the causes that lead men to the rank of a Buddha. *"Uncountable or myriad good deeds* equally lead to becoming a Buddha."[261] It is worth noting that the ultimate state of religion is not bestowed upon men by divine entities that transcend them, but is realized through practice within the human situation. "The result of becoming a Buddha springs from myriad deeds."[262]

Mahāyāna Buddhism stressed altruistic deeds. Prince Shōtoku put a special emphasis upon the belief that Buddhas and Bodhisattvas should serve all mankind (or living beings); this is the reason for certain distorted interpretations given by the Prince to phrases in the Buddhist scriptures.[263]

According to the "Hokke Sūtra" one is advised to sit always in religious meditation. This sentence was revised by Prince Shōtoku to read: "Do not approach a person who always sits in religious meditation."[264] The meaning is that unintermittent sitting in meditation prevents a man from practicing altruistic deeds.

A similar idea underlies the later teachings of Japanese Buddhism. According to Saichō (Saint Dengyō), both priests and laymen should achieve the self-same ideal (the consistency of priesthood and laity). According to Kūkai (Saint Kōbō), absolute reason should be realized through actuality (Reality is revealed in accordance with things).

That famous poem of the alphabet (*Iroha-uta*) is said to have been written by Kōbō, but in fact it is a Japanese version of a Chinese poem which in turn is a translation of a Sanskrit poem.

(The Japanese version:)

Although fragrant in hue,
(blossoms) are scattered
For everyone, life is impermanent.
This morning I crossed the uttermost limit
A shallow dream I will not dream, nor will I become intoxicated.

(The Chinese poem:)

Whatever is phenomenal is impermanent;
Their essential characteristic is appearance and disappearance;
When these appearances and disappearances come to repose, tranquility is comfort.

In the poetry quoted above, the Indians said, *"Peace of mind consoles"* (*Vūpasamo sukho*); the Chinese translated it: *"Tranquility is comfort."* But the Japanese, not being satisfied with these expressions that give impressions of passivity and negation, revised it: "A shallow dream I will not dream, nor will I become intoxicated." In this translation there is an expression of positive determination. (It is to be noted that while the original Indian poem contains only very abstract concepts, the Japanese revised them into concrete and intuitive symbols.)

Some people might argue that the Pure Land (Jōdo) sects advised their believers to abandon this world and induced them gladly to seek the other world. But that is a serious misconception of the essence of the Pure Land teachings. According to the Pure Land Buddhism, this world is subordinate to the other world, and the other world reveals itself in this world, the land of impurity. The practice of the most pious among the believers is to realize what is beyond this world within this very world. *"The Larger Sukhāvati Sūtra"* (*Daimuryō-ju kyō*) praises the splendor and grandeur of the heavenly world (*Sukhāvatī-lokadhātu*), and at the same time it puts emphasis upon the noble meaning of moral deeds in this world.

The maintenance of abstention and purification of one's self with sincerity and determination in this world even for a day and night would excel a hundred years of good deeds in the heavenly world. The reason is, it is taught, that this world abounds with evils and men suffer from afflictions.

The idea that he who believes in the true wish of Amitābha would be delivered even though he remained a layman, persisted all through the Heian period (794–1185) as an influential current of thought. From court nobles, warriors, and hunters, to prostitutes and robbers, they all expected, even if they remained laymen, to be born again in the Pure Land.[265] It was Hōnen (1133–1212) who gave a theoretical basis to such a tendency of thinking. And this idea of becoming a Buddha, although one was a layman, was handed down to Nichiren (1222–1282).[266]

It was Shinran (1173–1262) who pushed this secularism to its extreme. He completely denied the life of an ascetic. He advocated becoming a Buddhist as a layman, and put it into practice himself. He worshipped Prince Shōtoku, who was a layman, as "the founder of the religion of Japan." And he maintained that the absolute state commended by the Pure Land Buddhism can be attained in the secular life. Let us compare his idea with that of the Chinese Pure Land Buddhism. The Chinese Pure Land teachings attach great importance to the significance of the moment of death. According to Tao-ch'o (562–645) of China, at the moment of death, a man's whole existence is revealed by way of overall settlement of the accounts of his conduct not only in this world but also in former existences. "Should a streak of evil thought come to one's mind at the moment of death, that being by far the most evil of all evils, one should certainly fall into the road of agony (hell, the inferno of starvation, and the world of beasts), making nil all his blessings in the three worlds, i.e. carnal, material, and non-material."[267] This Chinese Buddhist's view was inherited by Hōnen.

According to Shinran, however, one puts an end to this life of delusion at the moment of the attainment of faith, and a new life begins thereupon. In his view, therefore, the moment of death does not count much. "The true believer of the Buddha, since the Buddha accepts and never abandons those genuinely devoted to *nembutsu* prayers, is to stay in the rank of those already destined to be saved. Such a person, therefore, does not need to wait until the moment of death to pray for the welcome of the Buddha. When one's faith is settled, one's birth in the Pure Land is also determined."[268] At the moment when one attains religious belief even in an everyday situation, he preaches, the cause for one to be reborn into the Pure Land has already been established.

Right along with such a point of view, Shinran, following the Taoist writings of Shan T'ao (613–681) of China, gives a somewhat different interpretation to them. Shan T'ao says in his "Praise of Birth in the Pure Land"[269] as follows: "Those who wish to be reborn into the Pure Land now ought constantly to exercise self-denial and ought not to cease to do so even for a moment till the end of their lives. Should they keep practicing *nembutsu* all through their lives, hard as it might be, if at one moment their life comes to an end, then in the next moment they will be reborn into the Pure Land. And they would receive celestial blessing that would never come to an end." These lines mean that one who practices the *nembutsu* prayer (reciting the name of Buddha) can be reborn, the moment after his death, into the Pure Land. But according to the Jōdo-shin sect, which maintains that one is saved at the time when one establishes one's belief, without waiting until the moment of death, the former moment is interpreted as the moment when one attains belief, and the latter as the moment after one is saved.[270] "What is called Rebirth in the Pure Land does *not necessarily designate the moment when life ends,* but it means that the delusive causes in the six roads, where souls are transmigrating from time without beginning, are annihilated by the power of the vow (grace) of the Buddha on which one relies by once invoking his name, '*Namu-amida-butsu.*' And it means that the true cause, which inevitably brings forth Nirvāṇa, for the first time begins to emanate. This is exactly what is to be interpreted from being reborn into the Pure Land and not regressing into the realm of the transmigration of the soul."[271]

In similar fashion, the Jōdo thought of Tao-ch'o underwent transformation when it was accepted. He says: "If one is able to be reborn into the Pure Land, the cause-and-effect linkage of the three worlds comes to its end. This is nothing but attaining the status of Nirvāṇa, without being delivered from afflictions. Why should we speculate on it?"[272] This means that after one is reborn into the Pure Land, then one is entitled to enter Nirvāṇa. Basing himself upon this sentence, Shinran asserts: "Without being delivered from afflictions, one attains Nirvāṇa."[273] According to the doctrine of the Jōdo-shin sect, to be reborn into the Pure Land is itself Nirvāṇa, to be entitled to enter Nirvāṇa is a divine favor given to one in this world.[274] Rennyo (1415–1499) is said to have declared: "When one once comes to rely upon the Buddha, one is disposed to the condition of being reborn into the Pure Land. This is the secret of rebirth into the Pure Land. This predisposition is what is called the preliminary state of getting into Nirvāṇa."[275]

The Jōdo-shin sect emphasizes not only that all living creatures are saved through their religious faith (the turning towards the Pure Land), but also that the Great Benevolence saves all those who are lost (the returning from the Pure Land).[276] Pure Land Buddhism was originally full of justifications for realistic and practical activities, which were particularly accentuated in Japan. During the Tokugawa period (1600–1867), the merchants of Ōmi province, who peddled their wares assiduously all around the country, were mostly devoted followers of the Jōdo-shin sect, and travelled around in a spirit of service to others.[277]

A similar tendency is also present in the Zen sect. Eisai (1141–1215) who inherited the Zen of the Rinzai school somewhat compromised and fused with other sects. But Dōgen (1200–1253) who inherited the Zen of the Sōtō school emphasized: "Concentrate on sitting in meditation." This concentration on sitting in meditation was spread among the people not as a method for each monk to attain tranquility of mind, but rather as a method for warriors and other laymen to acquire their mental training.

Among the Japanese advocates of Zen, in contrast to the Indian and Chinese Zen masters, there arose an opinion that even monks should perform religious practices in the midst of the tumult of secular life. A didactic poem by Myōchō (National Master Daitō, 1282–1337) says:

> "Sit in meditation, and behold the pedestrians,
> On the Shijō Bridge, on the Gojō Bridge,
> Emerging like trees on the mountain ridge."[278]

The Zen monks traditionally lived in seclusion in the steep mountains and dark valleys and concentrated upon their ascetic practices, severing their ties to the secular world. But here the poem preaches that one should attain the mental atmosphere of Zen practice in the midst of secular life, amidst the clamor of the city. It was inconceivable for the Chinese Zen priests to make such a statement.

Shōsan Suzuki (1579–1655), a Zen priest of modernistic learning, pushed this point still further, and advocated sitting in meditation just as though one had been on the battlefield. "Once I told a certain warrior that it was good to train oneself from the very beginning to sit in meditation in a whirl of business. Warriors especially ought to practice sitting in meditation, which means to be fit for action in the midst of a battlecry. It should mean fitness for sudden action amidst the clamor and tumult of the roaring of guns, the exchange of fights with spearheads and battlecries. How could the kind of sitting in meditation that is only fit for tranquility be of any use under such circumstances? However excellent a Buddhist doctrine may be, you had better leave it, if it be of no use amidst the battlecry. You should always try to live up to none other than the Two Deva kings."[279]

According to the regulations of the order of the monks of early Buddhism, the monks who have taken orders are not allowed to look upon soldiers on march to the battlefield. They may sojourn a few nights with the army, if there be some special reasons to do so, but even then their sojourn with the army ought not to be prolonged any further. While they are staying with the army, as the regulation goes, they are prohibited from viewing the lineup, arrangement, and inspection of the troops.[280] "A battle-cry sitting in meditation," as advocated by Shōsan Suzuki, is completely against the tradition of the Zen practice as handed down from early Buddhism. He approached Zen in the spirit of a warrior, and he was not satisfied with the attitude of the Chinese Zen priests. He criticized them as being halfway Zennists. "Ta-hui (1089–1163) showed that one should put the two characters, *Life* and *Death,* on the point of one's nose and should not forget about them. Po-shan (1575–1650) taught that everyone should paste on his forehead the character *Death*. These teachings do not have strength. To preach putting the words on the point of one's nose, or to paste them on one's forehead is a borrowed thought and not one's own thought. Persons like Ta-hui and Po-shan do not seem to have mastered the problems of life and death, or have felt in their own hearts the importance of these matters. What they say is too weak. On my part I would teach to hold on to these matters, making this one word *Death* the lord of your mind and placing it above everything else."[281]

Buddhist morals were also metamorphosed. The Indians considered alms-giving a virtue of principal importance for Buddhists, as something to be strictly observed. Most of the Buddhist scriptures extol the deeds of those who abandoned not only their country, castles, wives, and children, but also their own bodies and gave them most generously to other human beings (or animals).[282] Such a life of abandoning everything and possessing nothing was an ideal life for the Indian ascetics. Recourse to such a drastic measure, however, was not allowed by the Japanese, who attached more importance to the concrete human nexus. Prince Shōtoku, therefore, confined the meaning of "alms-giving" to "the abandonment of property other than one's own body."[283] In this manner, the inclination of the Indians to go beyond the ethics of mundane human relationships underwent revision when Buddhism was accepted by the Japanese.

The emphasis upon social and economic conditions runs parallel to the stress upon all the *productive activities* of men. In a country like India where the intensity of heat, the abundance of rainfall, and the fertility of the soil together bring forth a rich harvest, without much human labor exerted on the land, the ethics of distribution rather than that of production is naturally emphasized. That is a reason why alms-giving comes to be considered most important. In a country like Japan, by contrast, production is of vital importance, hence stress is placed upon the ethics of labor in various professions.

The Hokke (Lotus) Sūtra, the most important of all the Japanese Buddhist scriptures, was accepted by the Japanese as something that gives a theoretical basis for such a demand. The nineteenth chapter of the Hokke

Sūtra says as follows: If one preaches with the comprehension of the true meaning of the Lotus Sūtra, "when one preaches the laws of various teachings, they all coincide with the true meaning and nothing shall contradict the True Aspect. When one preaches the scriptures that are secularized, the words of this-worldly government, or the deeds of production, they all accord with the True Law."[284] This sentence was interpreted by the Japanese to mean that everything is true as long as it comes from a man who has once comprehended the truth of the Hokke Sūtra. The same sentence was interpreted by the Chinese, however, to mean that all activities in the fields of politics and economics were to be subjected to the Absolute One. The Chinese Buddhist Ch'ang-shui Tsu-hsüan (d. 1038) says: "The One mind, the Eternal Truth, and the aspect of appearance and disappearance are not separate things. That they are one is revealed in accordance with the fact that they are three; that they are three is discussed in accordance with the fact that they are one. Government and production, therefore, are not in contradiction with the True Aspect."[285] This idea of Ch'ang-shui came to be taken by the Japanese as the original idea of the Lotus Sūtra.[286]

Some of the Japanese Buddhists were thus led to recognize the particularly sacred significance of physical labor. And the Lotus Sūtra came to be accepted as a scripture to commend physical labor. The following poem, known to have been composed by Gyōki, says:

> "That I have attained the Lotus Sūtra
> Was possible only through
> Making firewood, gathering herbs,
> Drawing water, and laboring thus."[287]

This idea comes up in the tale of the Lotus Sūtra, which relates the story that in the past the Buddha entered priesthood and lived in seclusion, practicing asceticism with a hermit. "I followed a hermit, supplying daily necessities, gathering fruits, drawing water, picking up firewood, cooking meals, and making my own body a place of repose, but I never felt tired."[288] This story, which is only slightly touched upon in the Hokke Sūtra, appeared to Gyōki (668–749) as something very important, and gave him the impetus to carry out his meritorious works of social welfare.

It is a historically well-known fact that the Buddhists endeavored to go directly to the people through various works of social welfare. To illustrate, during the Nara period, Dōshō (629–700) spent his last years in travelling around the country, providing ferryboats, building bridges, and doing many other things for the good of the people. The social welfare works of Gyōki are said to have resulted in the construction of "six bridges, three water tanks, nine charity houses, two ferry depots, fifteen ponds, seven canals, four conduits, and one straight road."[289] It is also well known that Kūkai, early in the ninth century, had a reservoir constructed and built the university Shugei Shuchiin. After that a tremendous number of roads, harbors, and lodging places were built by priests and productive activities were carried out by them. During the Kamakura period, the Ritsu sect was particularly popular among common men and women on account of their endeavors in social welfare works. Eison (1201–1290) of the Saidai Temple and Ninshō (1218–1303) of the Gokuraku Temple had roads opened up, bridges constructed, wells dug, rice fields cultivated, bathrooms, hospitals, and homes for beggars built, not to speak of the construction of temples and towers, giving commandments to men and women ecclesiastical and secular, copying scriptures and drawing the images of Buddhas. That some Buddhists are enthusiasts in social welfare works is a phenomenon common to India and China. So it would be too rash to conclude that it is a manifestation of the characteristics only of the Japanese. It is noteworthy, however, that the Ritsu sect, which originally belonged to Hīnayāna Buddhism, should plunge into such practical and positive activities. It was particularly against the traditional disciplines that Ninshō carried out public works which were deeds of altruism. But it was not considered to be a breach of discipline either by himself or by his contemporaries. Japanese Buddhists came to maintain the view that one should repudiate traditional disciplines *in the name of disciplines for the promotion of productive activities*. According to the traditional discipline of early Buddhism, monks were not allowed to accumulate gold and silver, but on this point Tainin (d. 1786) of the Yagotozan Temple says:

"It is an infringement of discipline not to receive or accumulate gold and silver, being satisfied with small things, small deeds, and small ambitions, and coveting the fame of petty complacency. Now that you are already a priest who observes the three disciplines of the Mahāyāna Bodhisattva, you should live in the vow of boundless altruism and receive and accumulate gold and silver, in order to make the Three Precious Ones (The Buddha, Dharma, and Saṁgha) prosper and to benefit mankind."[290]

This way of thinking leads one to esteem highly the commonplace everyday life of men. It is to be expected that the Pure Land and Nichiren sects, which are closely connected with people's ways of living should be strongly imbued with such a tendency. But it is noteworthy that even Dōgen and his order are tinged with the same characteristics. Dōgen says that people commonly believe that an occult power is nothing more than exhaling water and fire from the body or absorbing water from the ocean into the pores. These may be called "small occult powers" but they are not worthy of the name of the true occult powers. The true occult powers, that is to say, "great occult powers," exist within and only within simple everyday occurrences of "drinking tea, eating rice, drawing water, and carrying faggots." This "great occult power" is called "the Buddha's occult power" or "the occult power that aspires to be a Buddha," and one who practices the Buddha's occult power will eventually become "an occult-power Buddha." "The occult power" is, therefore, nothing but what is experienced in everyday life. On the contrary, it is nothing but living righteously one's own daily life. It is the plain practical life that grows into the wonder of all wonders. If one lives up to this truly enough, one should be able to become a Buddha (an occult-power Buddha), immediately in his own mundane existence.[291]

Dōgen also thought that Buddhism could be realized within the vocational lives of the secular society. "One who thinks that mundane affairs hinder Buddhist practices only thinks that there is no Buddhist practice possible in mundane affairs, but knows not that there is no concern for mundane affairs within Buddhism (every activity is Buddhist)."[292] Being asked whether or not a man in the lay condition obsessed with daily business would be able to become a Buddha, and should practice asceticism, Dōgen replies: "In the great Sung country, there are no kings, ministers, warriors, commoners, and men and women who did not take note of the way of the ancient masters. Warriors and men of letters alike aspired to Zen practice and learning. Those who aspired mostly attained enlightenment. This naturally proves that mundane affairs are no hindrance to Buddhist laws."[293]

Thereafter Dōgen discarded this viewpoint and came to emphasize entrance into priesthood as a necessary condition for practicing Buddhism. It is noteworthy, however, that there was once a time, temporary as it was, when he held the secular view.

Tettsū Gikai (1219–1309), the third chief priest of the Eihei Temple says: "The dignity of a Buddha today lies within the daily movements of one's arms and legs. There is no natural law, no reality or profound reason without them."[294] The way is realized when and only when the chief priest and rank-and-file priests "are in one mind to perform actions."

The principle characteristic of *Eihei Shingi,* the regulations of life at the Eiheiji Temple Order (ordained by Dōgen), lies in the fact that they are not only a collection of prohibitory articles of conduct as the disciplinary regulations of Indian Buddhism (*pāṭimokkha*) are, but in the fact that they are the clear statements of the positive forms of action through which one may participate in the activities of a community.

At Zen temples, such daily jobs as cleaning, weeding, mending, and carpentry are generally called *samu* (doing service). That Buddhism should serve as the foundation for secular life was, for Nichiren, a necessary conclusion to be deduced from the theory in the Hokke Sūtra of the True

Aspect of all Existences. Nichiren says: "When the sky clears, the features of the earth are distinct. The man who knows the Hokke attains the law of this world, does he not?"[295] According to him, the secular society where men live may in itself become the Pure Land. "These days of degeneration, the place where the Hokke Sūtra lies, the place where the ascetic lives, and the place where people, lay or priestly, male or female, and rich or poor, may live—these are the very elements of what is none other than the Pure Land. Where these things are there the Pure Land is. Then could it be possible that the one who lives there should not be a Buddha?"[296]

Such a view was upheld also by the Imperial family. Emperor Hanazono writes in 1310 as follows:

"Among good deeds, not to inflict evil upon people is the most important. One should not seek the reason of Buddhism outside of this. To reign over the country and to feed the people are the acts of redemption of the warrior clan. Why should one practice the affairs of the Buddha outside of all these? It is a corrupt custom of the time to practice the affairs of the Buddha outside of the affairs of the king. On my part, I do not seek the law of the Buddha except for what is within my own mind. One should not necessarily wait for the scripture which is set forth lawfully. . . . What is called the law of the mundane world and what is called the Law of the Buddha are not separate things. The *Hokke* says that all the words of the government of the mundane world accord with the True Law. . . .[297]

Emperor Wu of Liang in China was a devoted follower of Buddhism, who endeavored to govern the country with Buddhism. Having had many temples built, he came across Bodhidharma and asked him whether such good deeds of his were meritorious. He expected praise from him. Bodhidharma's reply was contrary to his expectation. He answered that no merits could come forth therefrom. Bodhidharma is then said to have gone to the Chao-lin-ssu Temple of Sung-shan Mountain and is said to have continued sitting on the floor, facing the wall, for nine years. It is needless now to go into a discussion as to the credibility of this story. But in it we recognize the religious ideal of the Chinese Zen priests. By contrast to their ideal, Emperor Hanazono of Japan asserted, that Buddhism was nothing but practical and secular activities.

Toward the modern period there appeared a theory that if a man put his heart and soul in his own secular profession, then he was practicing nothing but the ascetic practice of Buddhism. The Zen priest, Takuan (1573–1645), teaches: "The law of the Buddha, well observed, is identical with the law of mundane existence. The law of mundane existence, well observed, is identical with the law of the Buddha. The Way is practical only. Except for being practical, there is no Way." (*Ketsujō-shū*) This point was especially stressed by the Zen priest Shōsan Suzuki, who says:

"Many are the ascetics, lay and priestly, from olden times, who are well versed only in the law of the Buddha; but there is none who advocates applying it to matters of the mundane existence. Am I the *first to advocate* this?"[298] He writes a book called *"The Significance of Everyman's Activities"* (*Banmin Tokuyō*), in which he discusses the problems of vocational ethics. He finds absolute significance in the pursuit of any profession, whether one is a warrior, a farmer, a craftsman, a merchant, a doctor, an actor, a hunter, or a priest. Because it is the essence of Buddhism, according to him, to rely upon the original self or upon "the true Buddha of one's own," and because every vocation is the function of this "one Buddha," his teaching amounts to saying that to pursue one's own vocation is to obey the Absolute One. So he preaches to farmers, "Farming is nothing but the doings of a Buddha."[299] To merchants he teaches, "Renounce desires and pursue profits wholeheartedly. But you should never enjoy merits of your own. You should, instead, work for the good of all others." Since the afflictions of this world, it is said, are predetermined in former worlds, one should torture oneself by working hard at one's own vocation, in order to redeem the sins of the past.[300] It is noteworthy that immediately after the death of Calvin, an idea similar to his appeared almost contemporaneously in Japan. The fact, however, that it never grew into a religious movement of great consequence ought to be studied in relation to the underdevelopment of modern *bourgeois* society in Japan.

Thereafter, similar ideas appeared from time to time from among the Zen sect. Hakuin (1685–1768), who revived the Rinzai-zen sect in the modern period, maintained that Zen ought to be lived even in secular life.[301] Bokuzan Nishiari (1821–1910), a high priest and superintendent priest of the Sōtō sect says as follows: "There is nothing mundane not within the practices of the Buddha. In governing a country as a ruler, in taking part in civil life as a subject, in engaging in business, in tilling the land as a farmer, and even in the falling of the rain and in the blowing of the wind, if one opens up one's eyes wide enough and sees through them, there is nothing that is not the law of the Buddha. So to say that this is a matter of the Buddhist law or that is a matter of secular life is the saying of those who have not yet attained the law of the Buddha. In the world of the Law, there is no otiose piece of furniture. Even the otiose piece of furniture is the law of the Buddha."[302]

Such a theory of religion also lends itself to religious movements outside of this particular sect. One instance of those is the Hōtoku-sha, a kind of social service activist movement of Sontoku Ninomiya (1787–1856), the main current of whose philosophical background seems to consist of the Tendai doctrine and the doctrine of Sung Neo-Confucianism. It is worth noting that, while all the monistic philosophies of the past and the present, of the East and West, tend to produce the attitude of a resigned and indifferent spectator, his philosophy of the One Round Aspect inclines to be practical and *activistic*. Sectarian Shintoisms also assume the similar tendency. The founder of the Tenri religion teaches, "Keep your heart pure, busy yourself with your vocation, and be true to the mind of God."[303] The other sectarian Shintō movements nearly all fall into a similar pattern.

A vocational ethical theory of this sort naturally transforms the concept of freedom. To use the word "freedom" and to aspire to the state of freedom are parts of the ancient tradition of Zen Buddhism. The concept of freedom, however, was metamorphosed by some of the Japanese Zen priests. Shōsan Suzuki was an admirer of P'u-hua (9th century) of China. He had something in common with P'u-hua, in respect to his aspiration to the state of freedom, rampant and unmolested. P'u-hua was a free man, and Shōsan also thought freely. The difference, however, is that P'u-hua sought the state of freedom by *delivering himself from the human nexus,* always gadding about like a madman, constantly ringing his bell; whereas Shōsan sought his "freedom" *in compliance with the human nexus,* busying himself with his secular vocation.[304]

Respect for labor in vocational life resulted in a high esteem for things produced as the fruits of labor. Reverence for foodstuff is especially manifest. Dōgen, for instance, recognizes the sacred significance of food and says that each item of foodstuff should be called with honorifics. "So-called rice-gruel (*kayu*) ought to be called honorable gruel (*o-kayu*), or you may call it morning gruel, but just gruel, never. You should say honorable offerings or you may say the time of the offering, but just offering, never. You should say, 'honorably *whiten* rice,' but 'polish rice,' never. You should say, 'honorably *purify* rice,' but 'rinse rice,' never. You ought to say, 'Honorably select something of the honorable material of an honorable side dish,' but 'choose a side-dish' never. You should say, 'Honorably prepare some honorable soup,' but 'Boil some soup,' never. You should say, 'Honorably prepare some honorable broth,' but 'Prepare broth,' never. The honorable offerings and the honorable gruel ought to be said to be most honorably taken." Indeed, Dōgen intended to "prepare offerings of steamed and grueled rice, revering them with the use of utmost politeness and supremely august wordings."[305] The regulation that one should call the names of foodstuff with honorifics has never been found in either an Indian monastery or in any Chinese temple. Menzan Zuihō (1683–1769), one of the revivers of the Sōtō theology during the Tokugawa period, wrote a book called *"Instructions on The Five Views of Receiving Food,"* in order to teach people how to take good care of food. "You should calculate and measure how much of the hard work and toil have been put into this food before it comes to you, in order to comprehend the Reason."[306]

The way of thinking which prizes all the products of labor, however trivial they may be, is also manifest among the Jōdo-shin sect, which is diametrically opposed, in other aspects, to the Zen sect. Let me refer to the following anecdote. "Rennyo, passing through the corridor, found a piece of paper thereupon. Murmuring that one should not waste a thing of the Buddha's possession, he took it into his hands and raised it above his head, etc. It was said that even such a trifling thing as a piece of paper was considered by Rennyo as a property of the Buddha, and that was why he did not waste it."[307]

The doctrine not to waste but to respect the fruits of human labor, is not necessarily confined to Japanese religions only; it seems to be common to most of the universal religions. But in India or South Asiatic countries, where men are not required to labor too hard in order to produce daily necessities, relatively little has been preached about not wasting things. The fact that it is particularly emphasized in Japan should be considered in the light of the topographical peculiarities of Japan.

Japanese Buddhism, which tends to recognize religious significance in secular professional life or rather in everyday life in general, is apt to spread among the common people. Indian Buddhism, by contrast, never was able to become a religion of the whole nation. Besides Buddhism, there was Jainism as its rival, and stronger and more deep-rooted than either of them was Brahmanism. It is also doubtful how prevalent Chinese Buddhism was among the people. Chinese Buddhism had a strong tendency to become a religion of literati and of hermits. That Buddhism penetrated into people's lives was also true in Tibet and South Asiatic countries, just as it was in Japan, but the secularization of it was something unique in Japan.

The inclination to recognize religious significance in secular life gave rise to the tendency to seek the ideal "way" in everyday arts and crafts. Hence emerged appellations such as the way of tea-ceremony, the way of flower-arrangement, the way of calligraphy, the way of painting, the way of military arts, the way of fencing, the way of *jūjutsu* (i.e., *jūdō*), the way of archery, and the way of medicine. Their origins seem to be in the 16th century between the Muromachi and Tokugawa periods. Such appellations as these do not find their correlations in the West. In this respect, there seems to be some affinity between the Japanese and the Indians, who developed the theory of art and the theory of technology with religious justification. Even then, for the Indians, art was a medium for personal deliverance, but for the Japanese it was hardly conceived as such.

The Japanese thought that to propagate Buddhism was to profit their particular human nexus. Tetsugen (1630–1682) says: "That is why it (Buddhism) turns out to be prayer for the state, service to the gods of the heaven and earth, repayment of one's debt to one's lord and father, and compensation for the subjects' services."[308] "All phenomenal things will end up with tranquility; all the doctrines will have their proper status, heaven and earth will be in their places; everything will grow; peace will reign; and heaven and earth and the order of the state will long be secured."[309]

As long as religion in Japan tends to realize itself within secular life, it will naturally lend itself to the practical and active. Among the various Buddhist sects, the Nichiren sect is the most pronounced in such a tendency. In spite of the fact that the Hokke Sūtra itself commends ascetics to live tranquilly in a life of contemplation, the Nichiren sect which subscribes to it tends towards action. Nichiren, at the inauguration of his sect, recited "*Nammyōhōrengekyō*" (Homage to the Lotus Sūtra!) sonorously toward the rising sun in the forest of Asahi on Kiyosumi Mountain. The "sun" is a favorite character of the Nichiren sect, which often uses it for priests' names. The Nichiren followers long for the effulgent sun. The religious custom of making a procession while repeating the Nichiren prayer and beating drums would never have taken shape among the Buddhist orders of India or China. (The only thing which may possibly be comparable to this is the religious movement of Caitanya in modern India.)

For a supplementary remark, the form of the acceptance of Chinese thought was also tinged with an activistic tendency in interpreting the Way of human beings. Jinsai Itō (1627–1705), in particular, understands what is called the Way as being active and as representing the principle of growth and development, and on that basis he rejects the nihilism of Lao-tzŭ. He says: "Lao-tzŭ thinks that everything emerges out of nothing. But heaven and earth cover all from time immemorial; and the sun and moon always shine from time immemorial. The four seasons constantly shift from time immemorial; what changes with form always changes with form from time immemorial, and what changes with material always changes with material from time immemorial. Things inherit and ferment one another, and things go on living endlessly. How can one see what is called emptiness?"[310] For him the universe is one big living thing, and its incessant life is what the essence of the universe actually is. And he sought the basis for such a view of looking at the universe as a living thing in the phrase, "The great virtue of heaven and earth is called life," in *The Book of Change*.[311]

In this manner Itō bestows a characteristically Japanese interpretation even upon the words of Confucius. Confucius says in the *Analects*: "On the river, the master says, 'What passes away passes thus. It never ceases day or night.'" The medieval Chinese interpreted the saying as words of lamentation that "What passes away is like the water of a river, which, once gone, never returns." According to Chu-hsi (1130–1200), they are the reflective observation of an objective spectator in which the water of the river is made to symbolize everything that is in incessant motion and flow. The Japanese Confucian scholar, Jinsai Itō however, gives these words an interpretation entirely different from the Chinese. According to him, the river stands for "the virtue of the wise man that is everyday made new, and never becomes stagnant," and the whole sentence is the expression of the exuberance of human vitality.[312] In contrast to the negative, resigned, and indifferent character of the Chinese interpretation, Itō's is positive, active, and full of hopes. He has great confidence in human activity itself.

Sorai Ogyū (1666–1728), diametrically opposed to Jinsai Itō in everything else, extols him as far as this ethics of activism is concerned. He says, "Master Itō's theory of things alive and dead is indeed the supreme wisdom of a thousand years."[313] He positively advocates activism, and rejects the static tendency of the Confucianists of the Sung period in China. "Heaven and earth are living things, and so is man. Those who regard them as though they were tied up with a rope are only snobs poisoned by useless learning."[314] Quiet sitting and having reverential love in one's heart are the methods of mental training made by most of the Confucianists of the Sung period; these are ridiculed by Ogyū: "As I look at them, even gambling appears superior to quiet sitting and having reverential love in one's heart."[315] (This corresponds to the view of Shōsan Suzuki, who, Zen priest thought he was, rejected the ascetic practice of sitting in meditation, and, instead, recommended labor in secular professional life.) A necessary conclusion drawn from such an attitude was the recommendation, as was made by Ogyū, of practical learning, useful in practical life. And such was the mental climate which nurtured the economic theory of Shundai Dazai (1680–1747) and the legal philosophy of Chikukei Miura (1689–1756) both of whom were Ogyū's disciples.

It is one of the pronounced characteristics of Japanese Confucianism to commend activist ethics, on the one hand, and to reject the thoughts of passive quietism, on the other. The most distinctively Japanese scholars stand for the monism of matter, repudiating the dualism of reason and matter. Sokō Yamaga (1622–1685), Jinsai Itō, and Ekken Kaibara (1650–1714) are all monists, believing in matter as the first principle of existence. The second characteristic, running parallel to the first, is that Japanese Confucianism directs its attention to politics, economics, and law, the practical aspects of human life. Although Chinese Confucianism surpasses the Japanese in thinking upon metaphysical problems, Japanese Confucianism is superior in practical matters.[316]

The characteristics of Japanese thinking, as revealed in the form of the acceptance of Confucianism, exactly correspond to those revealed in the form of the acceptance of Buddhism.

That Japan alone was rapid in the process of modernization in recent years, while the other Asiatic countries were generally slow in the process, may partly be attributed to the emphasis laid by the Japanese upon practical activities within the social nexus.[317]

A great danger lies, however, in the fact that the religious view of the Japanese, as discussed above, may easily degenerate into the sheer utilitarianism of profit-seeking activities, should it lose sight of the significance of the absolute, which underlies the productive life of all vocations. It is especially true with a people like the Japanese, who are not too preoccupied with religious matters. But at the same time credit should be given to the tendency to find values in the human nexus. If the religion of Japan were enhanced to such a height where religious truth might be realized in accordance with a human nexus at once universal and particular, transcending all limited social loyalties and at the same time embracing all of them, then and only then will it acquire a universal significance.

Acuteness of Moral Self-Reflection

The emphasis put upon practice within the actual human nexus and the stress laid upon the relationships among individuals rather than upon the existence of the individual person increase the sensitivity of man to his relationship with other men. First of all, given a way of thinking which emphasizes social cooperation as the basic structure and the ground of the individual's life, it becomes a matter of vital importance for a man what others in the group may think of him. We should not fail to consider, for example, the keen sense of social prestige of the Japanese. In the sixteenth century, European missionaries came to Japan and reported that the Japanese placed social prestige before wealth, a trait not so strong among Europeans.[318] What influence this tendency exerted upon Japanese Buddhism is an interesting question to pose. It would seem that the keen sense of honor of the Japanese is closely tied up, externally, with the high esteem for the hierarchical order. And internally, in some cases, it motivates the moral faculty of self-reflection. It posits before man the ideal of the infinite good that he should strive for, it induces him to reflect, by contrast, upon the sorry fact that he himself is too weak and helpless to refrain from doing evil; and thus it awakens within him the consciousness of man's sinfulness.

The Jōdo sect, introduced from China, reached the zenith of its development with Shinran (1173–1262), in whom the anguish of moral self-reflection was extremely acute.

"Truly I have come to realize, and it is deplorable, that I am an idiotic vulture, drowned in the boundless sea of carnal desires, lost in the enormous mountains of worldly ambitions, not being pleased with becoming entitled to be saved, and taking no pleasure in approaching the True Evidence. Shame on me; woe is me!"[319]

These sentences ought not be understood as owing to the fact that Shinran was a monk under the lay condition, married and eating meat, and that he therefore wished to make a confession. There are instances, in the Indian[320] as well as in the Chinese[321] Buddhist scriptures, of monks who were married and ate meat. But moral self-reflection as acute as Shinran's seems not to be indicated in the Buddhist literature of other countries. Monks who broke their vows in India appear to have held the notion that sins could be expiated by reciting magical formulae (*dhāraṇī*).[322] Little has been said about the pangs of conscience of renegade monks in China. Shinran, on the contrary, could not but face the shameful reality of man. Shinran, who looked into the deeper self of man, turned to the Buddha, the Absolute One. He was thus led to advocate "the discipline of non-discipline," which was underlined by self-reflection of great moral intensity. (It is a pity that "the discipline of non-discipline" should now come to be interpreted by most of the Shin-sect followers as doing without discipline, and that thus it should now be identified with the lack of moral self-reflection.)

The motivation for the ascetics of India and China to enter priesthood was, in most cases, the realization of the impermanence of the phenomenal world, rather than the realization of man's sinfulness. In the case of Shinran, however, little is said about the impermanence of this world. The controlling motivation for Shinran is the sense of sinfulness in man's life rather than that man is simply variable. The fundamental thing about man is that he is a sinner, obsessed with afflictions, yielding to evils. Realizing as he does that things are impermanent, he still clutches at these impermanent things. Man is so deeply immersed in sins that he could never be saved but for the miraculous power of the vow of Amitābha. That was what Shinran preached. In his writings, he reflected upon the nature of evils and went so far as to classify the categories of evil.

The Jōdo doctrine of China was transformed by these factors of moral self-reflection into the Jōdo doctrine of Shinran. The Chinese Buddhist Shan-tao (613–681), in explaining "the heart of sincerity" which the ascetic should always observe, says: "You should not assume outwardly the appearance of wisdom, goodness and religious abstinence, while embracing deceptions inwardly."[323] According to Shinran, the deceptions such as "avarice, anger, injustice, falsehood, mischief, fraudulence, and a hundred others" make for "the evil nature" of man, which is so intrinsic to man that ascetic practice even of the utmost austerity could not possibly purify him of these evils. Such a belief of Shinran led him to read Shan-tao's words differently from the way they originally stood: "You could not assume outwardly the appearance of wisdom, goodness and religious abstinence, since you embrace illusions inwardly."[324] Shinran, whose profound moral self-reflection made him cry, "There is no end of evil nature, Man's mind is as abominable as a viper";[325] could not accept the teaching of Shan-tao without the transformation of its meaning into what he himself thought fit.

Here clearly is a theory of the redeemability of man's wicked nature. Man is by nature evil, and because he is evil, according to that theory, he is entitled to be saved by the great benevolence of Amitābha. He is not expected to be saved through any other doctrine. Although this theory of the redeemability of man's evil nature is generally recognized to have been originated by Shinran, similar views were upheld by others. The book, *Verbatim notes on the Tales of the Future Life* says: "Since the so-called Original Vow of Amitābha, it ought to be remembered, exists *solely for the sake of sinners and men of evil dispositions and not for the sake of saints and sages,* it is the meaning of faith to believe, without any shadow of doubt (in the redeemability of oneself), even if one finds oneself to be of evil disposition." A statement, presumably of Saint Hōnen's, goes as follows: "Even a good man is reborn into the Pure Land, and how much more so with a wicked man![326] This is an oral instruction transmitted to me." These two instances have much in common with the following assertion of Shinran: "Even a good man is reborn into the Pure Land, and how much more so with a wicked man! But people generally think that even a wicked man is reborn into the Pure Land, and how much more so with a good man! Though this latter way of thinking appears at first sight reasonable, yet it is not in accord with the purport of the Original Vow, the faith in the Other Power."[327]

The vehement demand for the redemption of the wicked was a consistent undercurrent all through the Heian period, and the tales of death and various other stories of the period have recorded instances that heinous criminals and those who made slaughter a trade constantly practiced *nembutsu* prayers. By the latter half of the Heian period (ca. 850), at least, the idea of the salvation of the wicked was firmly established in theory, and was socially acknowledged by believers in the doctrine that *nembutsu* practice enabled one to be reborn into the Pure Land.[328] At that time the systematization of the idea was not yet complete, but such a current of thought gradually developed, with theoretical refinements, into an intrinsic part of the Jōdo-shin doctrine. This is not to say that all the Jōdo sects of Japan held to this view. But it is significant that this assertion of the right of the wicked to be reborn into the Pure Land came to be explicitly stated in Japan only. The Jōdo sects of India and China, broadly speaking, with due allowances for exceptions, took a view similar to that of Hōnen, namely, "Even sinners are reborn (into the Pure Land), and how much more so with good men!"[329]

It is noteworthy that profound religious self-reflection, based upon the Jōdo doctrine, was professed by some of the Emperors of Japan.

"Though the mind's moon shines,
To show the way to the Pure Land,
Woe be to the clouds still uncleared."

(By Emperor Gotoba, 1180–1239)

The poem means that ardent as my desire is to be reborn into the Pure Land, trusting and relying upon the vow of Amitābha, the sins I have committed weigh so heavily upon my heart that they make me haunted by doubts about the vow; and how far beyond, how far beyond comprehension, the poem laments, is the state of true salvation.

"I wish to be awakened from a dream,
Only to enter another dream;
Beyond my vision, lies the world of Reality."

That one wishes to be awakened from a dream is a proof that one is still in the dream, the poem asserts, and to be really awakened from the dream is the state that lies still far beyond one's experience.

The idea that the wicked are eligible to become Buddhas was accepted by Nichiren and was incorporated into his religious doctrine. He recognized himself to be one of "the ordinary men as idiotic, ignorant, and unenlightened,"[330] and he reflected that "we are fools and dullards unworthy to become disciples of the Buddha, who have fallen into evil deeds in the age of corruption."[331] Unworthy as a man such as himself was, he still believed man would be saved through and only through the Hokke (Lotus) sūtra. "Even he who has committed ten evils and five heavy sins, as long as he does not violate the Lotus sūtra, shall without doubt be reborn into the Pure Land and become a Buddha."[332]

Is it not true, however, that religious and moral self-reflection as profound as the above, is confined mainly to the Jōdo sect? Is it not a fact that so-called enlightenment in the Zen sect has nothing to do with moral considerations? Such questions may naturally occur to a critical reader. The question about the relationship between Zen and morality requires a chapter of its own. Suffice it to state here that the form of the Zen doctrine accepted in Japan, as in the case of Dōgen, reveals a profound moral self-reflection. He attaches great importance to the act of making a confession. "Should you confess in this manner, the assistance of the Buddha would assuredly be yours. Make a confession to the Buddha with your soul and body, and the power of the confession will eradicate all the roots of your sins."[333] He commends good deeds and preaches that one will be able to become a Buddha through one's good doings. "In order to become a Buddha, one needs only a simple way: Not to do evil deeds, not to be obsessed with the matter of life and death, but to take pity upon mankind, to revere one's superior, to be considerate to one's inferior, and to keep one's mind free from hatred, desires, afflictions and anxieties is exactly what is called being a Buddha. One should not seek Buddhahood anywhere else."[334] He emphasizes the observance of injunctions.[335] Let us compare his attitude with that of his Chinese master, Ju-ching (1163–1228). As far as the records of Ju-ching's teachings are concerned, there is no evidence of any deep consciousness in him. On the contrary, he keeps himself aloof from the distinction between good and evil, toward which he assumes an attitude of nonchalance and dispassionate regard. "I have heard that all good deeds are like a fly eyeing blood. I have heard that all wicked deeds are like a crab falling into boiling water."[336] In the records of his teaching one finds the characteristics of the later Chinese Zen priests who used to invent nonsensical phrases.

The emphasis upon introspection among Japanese priests is apparent also among laymen. Minamoto-no-Sanetomo (1192–1219) says:

"There's no way out
Of this agonizing hell,
Whose empty vault
Only flames can fill."

(A poem reflecting upon one's sins.)

"The founder of a temple,
The erector of a tower,
For their acts get credit;
But none gets merits,
So rewarding as a repentant sinner."

(A song of confession)[337]

On the whole, when and only when one reflects upon one's deeds sincerely enough is one awakened to one's own sinfulness.

(The consciousness of man's sinfulness is also a distinctive feature of Christianity, and a comparison between Christianity and Buddhism in this respect opens a new theme which cannot be dealt with here.)

It may be argued that the psychological unrest caused by the social disturbances during the medieval period, together with the introduction of Buddhism, gave rise to the consciousness of man's sinfulness; and that the Japanese were originally lacking in such a consciousness. It is true that the Japanese of antiquity regarded sin as a kind of material entity, which could easily be purged by means of a ritual of purification. (In this respect, the Japanese have much in common with the Brahmanists of ancient India.) The lack of sin-consciousness is also noticeable among present-day Japanese. It may be rightly asserted that, generally speaking, the Japanese are not at all very sin-conscious and that this fact is closely tied up with the this-worldly tendency of the Japanese, which we have pointed out in an earlier chapter. And there are features in the history of thought in Japan which disprove the points we have just made. Take, for instance, the case of the acceptance of Confucianism. Sorai Ogyū, a Confucianist with characteristically Japanese attitudes in some respects, supported the theory that the good or evil of a deed is judged by its results as against the theory, as held by the Chinese Confucianists of the Sung period (960–1126), that it is judged by the motives of the doer.[338]

Whether or not the Japanese in general were acute in religious and moral self-reflection is difficult to decide. But one thing at least is clear, that in accepting the Buddhist thought of China, such moral transformations as have been discussed above were effected by some of the Japanese Buddhists. It was also reported by the European missionaries, who came to Japan in the sixteenth century, that crimes were relatively few, and order reigned among the Japanese.[339] In any case, although they are weak in "sin-consciousness" in its religious sense, they are sensitive in "shame-consciousness" in its practical and moral sense. For the Japanese, whether or not one infringes religious disciplines is a matter of little consequence. A matter of vital importance for them traditionally has been whether or not one conforms to the mores of a particular social nexus to which one belongs. A question may be raised as to whether the presence of moral consciousness, as just mentioned, may be inconsistent with the lack of the spirit of criticism, as discussed earlier. But the inconsistency disappears when one understands "the moral consciousness" to be applicable only to those acts within one's own immediate group.

Let us now consider how the Japanese themselves think of this repudiation of Buddhist discipline in general, on the one hand, and the observation of moral practice within a particular human nexus, on the other.

Onkō (1718–1804) was the most prominent among the high priests of the Shingon sect of the past who instructed and enlightened common people without recourse to magical practices but by means of preaching only. And it was the discipline of Ten Good Vows which was ordained as follows: love and save all living creatures with a heart of benevolence; do not deprive anyone, from the highest officials down to common men, of his proper due but let him be in his proper place; observe decorum in man-woman relationships; do not utter a falsehood; do not use flowery words, which impair the virtues of adults and go against the way of heaven and earth; do not insult others, or do not put others to shame; do not use double-tongued speech; do not be avaricious; do not yield to anger, which nullifies all good deeds; do not have a "wrong view," i.e., believe in the Buddha, in the Law, and that the virtuous power of gods is not futile.[340] He wrote many books on the subject of the Ten Good Vows, and often preached about them at various places.[341] He was interested neither in the abstract thinking of Indian Buddhism nor in the doctrines contained in the labored commentaries of Chinese Buddhism, but he was mainly concerned with the direct approach of preaching practical virtues. Surprisingly erudite as he was, remarkably well versed as he was in Buddhist philosophy, and especially, forerunner though he was in the modern method of studying Sanskrit, he thought that the discipline of the ten good deeds was enough so far as the enlightenment of the common people was concerned. Those who wished to listen to Onkō's preachings—from the Emperor to the common people—were not interested in metaphysical discussions, but solely in the moral teachings that would be of immediate use in concrete acts of everyday life. (That was why only his philosophical and doctrinal dissertations were written exclusively in *Chinese*.)

Onkō followed the tradition of Indian Buddhism when he tried to realize Buddhism within everyday acts through the discipline of the Ten Good Vows. The listing of virtues after the fashion of Indian Buddhism, however, was not to the liking of the Japanese in general, who looked for the one central virtue directly posited. It is the virtue of *"honesty"* or *"truthfulness"* which was originally adopted from Buddhism, that emerged from such a demand and came to be generally recognized as the central virtue by the Japanese.

The word "honesty" has come into use since the Nara period (710–784).[342] The Imperial rescripts, issued at their several enthronements, of the Emperors Ninmei, Montoku, Seiwa, and Yōzei during the Heian period (794–857) unanimously state "an honest heart" to be the virtue that all the subjects should strive for.[343] Probably influenced by them was the doctrine of the Ise Shrine instituted by the *Five Books of Shintoism* during the Kamakura period (1185–1333), according to which the Sun Goddess was supposed to have said: "Divine protection is based upon honesty." During the Muromachi period (1336–1573), the virtue of "honesty" as the doctrine of the Ise Shrine came to prevail among the entire populace.

According to Chikafusa Kitabatake (1293–1354), the three divine treasures of the Japanese Imperial family symbolize the virtues of "honesty," "benevolence," and "wisdom" respectively.

Although a concept corresponding to the virtue of "honesty" may very well have existed since primitive Shintoism, the term itself was adopted from Buddhism. The word "honesty" may have come also from the Confucian classics,[344] but it appears in Buddhist scriptures as well.[345] It was generally recognized by the Japanese of those days that the virtue of "honesty" in later Shintoism originated from Buddhism.[346]

The Jōdo doctrine esteems, in particular, the three states of mind, namely, sincerity, belief in the efficacy of prayer, and wishing to be reborn into the Pure Land, which are requisite for rebirth in paradise. It was Shinran who made these three states of mind converge upon one, "a heart of truthfulness, not mingled with illusion; a heart of honesty, not adulterated with falsehood."[347] According to Shinran, a religious faith ultimately amounts to honesty, or being loyal and truthful. Many other Japanese priests also extol the virtue of honesty in this sense.[348]

The virtue of honesty was especially emphasized by Nichiren, who considered that it was for honesty of heart that the Hokke Sūtra preaches the Truth, and therein he recognized the ultimate significance of the Lotus Sūtra. "The Hokke Sūtra teaches one 'to be honest and to avoid trickery,' and talks about those who are 'completely truthful,' 'straightforward in nature and flexible in intention' or 'gentle and straightforward.' It is the sūtra to believe, for those who are as honest as an arrow shot straight from a bow-string, and as a string drawn straight by a carpenter."[349] Thus he traces the authentic source of the virtue "honesty" to the Hokke (Lotus) Sūtra. He then divides "honesty" into two categories, i.e., "the honesty of this world" and "the honesty beyond this world,"[350] and maintains, "Nichiren is the only individual in Japan who is honest both in this world and beyond this world."[351]

At the beginning of the Tokugawa period in the 17th century, Zen Master Shōsan Suzuki, developed a theory of professional ethics of his own in his book, *"Rules of Conduct for Every Citizen,"* in which he urged that Buddhism put into practice was nothing but the virtue of "honesty" acted upon.[352] Neither in India nor in China was an assertion made so explicit that Buddhism was nothing but honesty put into practice, although Buddhist teachings in these countries had similar implications.

Thus, both Shintoists and Buddhists in Japan attached great importance to the word "honesty," which had appeared only sporadically in Buddhist scriptures, and finally accorded it the position of the central virtue in the general scheme of Japanese ethics.[353]

The virtue of honesty seems to be in harmony with the Japanese propensity to loyalty.[354] Such a moral consciousness probably emerged from the tendencies of the Japanese to make much of limited human relationships, their fondness for fashioning a closed social nexus, and the tendency to demand complete loyalty and mutual trust among those who belong to that nexus.

These characteristics seem to be manifest also in the forms in which the Japanese accepted Chinese thought. Chinese learning was accepted by the Japanese in the past as ethical teaching. From among various Chinese types of thought, the Japanese selected, in particular, Confucianism, strongly imbued with a moral set of precepts appropriate to a closed social nexus. This Confucianism itself was then interpreted in terms of "loyalty and fidelity," by Jinsai Itō (1627–1705), who made these notions the two central virtues of his doctrine, while the virtue of "sincerity" was stressed in the Kaitokudō school; and this line of interpretation was carried out thoroughly by the Mito school.[355] All of these three schools of Japanese Confucianism aimed at "no falsehood, no deception," as their ideal. Herein lies one of the characteristics of Japanese Confucian doctrine.

A tendency such as this emphasis on loyalty and fidelity also characterizes the Japanese acceptance of Christianity. It is pointed out that Christianity during the Meiji period (1868–1912) was fundamentally ethical and cultural in nature. Different systems of thought—Buddhism, Chinese ideas, and Western religions—met with different forms of adaptation in Japan, and each of these forms has distinct significance. But at the same time the common denominators among all of these forms of adaptation ought not to be overlooked.

Those who observed the moral confusion in Japan immediately after World War II may be led to doubt the proposition that the Japanese in the past were moralistically inclined. As far as the observance of honesty within a closed social nexus is concerned, however, little difference seems to be discoverable between traditional and recent Japanese morality. The difference seems to lie rather in the fact that what was considered to be morally tenable in Japan's "closed-door" past becomes untenable under rapidly changing worldwide social and economic conditions to which Japan is adapting itself. The traditional concept of honesty as loyalty to the clan and Emperor is applicable only to the conduct of man as a member of the particular and limited human nexus to which he belongs; it is not applicable to the conduct of man as a member of human society as a whole. This shortcoming of the traditional moral concept suddenly proves to be a weakness that needs to be overcome at a time of social confusion in the rapidly changing relations of Japan to the rest of the world.

Weak Awareness of Religious Values

There was no distinct concept of god among the primitive Japanese. As to the origin of the word "*kami*" (God), there are conflicting views among scholars, and none of them has yet produced any conclusive evidence. "*Kami*" in Japanese may mean "above" "one's superior," or "hair," and the political ruler was once called "*okami*" (the one that is above us). Everything placed above one both in space or in the hierarchical order is called "*kami.*" Even if the etymological origin of each "*kami*" is different, the difference is not discernible in daily usage. For the Japanese, therefore, God was not a distinct entity complete in itself, but was diffused in all, that is, above and beyond ordinary human beings. It was the custom of Shintoism from antiquity to deify those persons who rendered distinguished services to a particular human nexus such as a family, a village, or a native community.

"I do not understand the meaning of the term *kami*. Speaking in general, however, it may be said that *kami* signifies, in the first place, the deities of heaven and earth that appear in the ancient records and also the spirits of the shrines where they are worshipped.

It is hardly necessary to say that it includes human beings. It also includes such objects as birds, beasts, trees, plants, seas, mountains, and so forth. In ancient usage, anything whatsoever which was outside the ordinary, which possessed superior power, or which was awe-inspiring, was called *kami*. Eminence here does not refer merely to the superiority of nobility, goodness, or meritorious deeds. Evil and mysterious things, if they are extraordinary and dreadful, are called *kami*. It is needless to say that among human beings who are called *kami* the successive generations of sacred emperors are all included. The fact that emperors are also called "distant *kami*" is understandable, because from the standpoint of common people, they are remote, majestic, and worthy of reverence. In a lesser degree we find, in the present as well as ancient times, human beings who are *kami*. Although they may not be accepted throughout the whole country, in each province, each village, and each family there are human beings who are *kami*, each one according to his own proper position. The *kami* of the divine age were for the most part human beings of that time and, because the people of that time were all *kami*, that era is called the Age of the Gods (*kami-yo*)."[356]

This interpretation, which is that of Norinaga Motoori, was accepted also by Atsutane Hirata.[357] As long as such a view of gods is held, the conception of God, whether transcendental or immanent, which sets down a categorical imperative, transcending the limitation of any particular human nexus, is impossible. That was why even after the introduction of Buddhism into Japan, the Japanese never discarded their traditional standard of evaluation, that of judging things in terms of a particular human nexus. They regarded as absolute the authority of ancestors, parents, lords, the state, and the Emperor, to whom religion was subjected and made to serve. It follows that a religious order in the Western sense was never firmly established in Japan. Shrine Shintoism never gave rise to a closely knit religious order and neither did Confucianism. The same was true even in the case of Buddhism, which claims to be a universal religion.

The ecclesiastical authorities of Buddhist orders and sects in Japan were subjected to the secular authorities of the state and feudal lords, and the former assumed an attitude of compromise towards the latter to the point of subservience. The Indian Buddhist tradition that "the ascetic never pays homage to the king"[358] was neither put into practice, nor even given any attention. The Buddhists in Japan regarded honor bestowed on them by the Imperial family or by feudal lords as of supreme value. Under these circumstances the Buddhist orders in Japan, even in the medieval period, never wielded a power comparable to that of the religious orders in medieval Europe.[359] They were even less respected than the Buddhist orders in South Asiatic countries.

The orders were often placed under the control of political powers. The hierarchical structure of secular society was brought directly into the orders. In India, on the contrary, the hierarchical structure of secular society never penetrated into the religious orders, and the ranking of ascetics was determined solely according to the number of years of priesthood. Even the king of a great country, one having entered priesthood, had to accept the lowest rank.[360] Such a tradition appears to have been observed also in China. Even a rich man's son, once having entered priesthood, put on a plain raiment. It was with some surprise that Dōgen recounted the story of a rich man's son in China, who, being asked why he was dressed so plainly, answered simply, "Because I have become a monk."[361] By contrast, a son of the aristocracy in Japan, after having entered priesthood, was given a privileged status. This fact is proved by the existence of a great number of temples which the "monk-princes" made their places of residence. The status of the "monk-Emperor" or of the "monk-prince" has never been recognized in any other country than Japan. If one studies from what families the successive chief abbots of the Tendai sect came, one can better understand the close interconnection established between the secular and ecclesiastical authorities. The Honganji Temple order, which originally aimed at a religion of and for people, finally acquired the privileged status of a temple of a monk-prince. The head-temples of various branches of the Jōdo-shin sect succeeded in establishing a close connection through both economic and kinship relations with the Imperial family and aristocracy. The popes of the head-temples of the various Jodo-shin sects exercised their authority as an aristocracy and as the heads of the orders over common believers. Although their status within the hierarchy of the secular aristocracy was not high, still they enjoyed the privilege of being members of the aristocracy. This is not to deny the existence of those (and their number is by no means negligible) who kept their pride as impeccable men of religion, standing aloof from worldly privileges. Dōgen, for instance, never put on the purple robe, saying that even the monkey and the stork would laugh at him, should he ever wear it.[362] The Sōtō sect, however, which continued his teachings, took to the custom of receiving the title of Zen master from the Emperor for the chief abbot of its head temples.

The transplanting of the hierarchical system of the secular world transformed the religious order into a secular community. Many of the priests of the Heian period entered temples not necessarily in order to search for the truth but in quest of worldly honors, riches, and privileges. "Gorō is a scholar and great high priest of the Tendai sect. He is a great master in Indian logic and Buddhist philosophy. He is also well-versed in the Buddhist scriptures and the canons of other schools. He has the *Abhidharmakośa* and Buddhist idealism at the tip of his tongue, and keeps the profound teaching of the Tendai doctrine at the depth of his heart. . . . No clerical position, high or low, is good enough for him. He aspires only to be chief abbot of the Tendai order."[363]

The surest way to acquire riches and honors as a priest was to become intimate with the aristocracy, who concentrated the greatest power and wealth of society in their hands. Consequently, priests availed themselves of all means and opportunities to gain access to the aristocracy.

With the decline of the power of the Fujiwara clan, an increasing number of its members entered temples and became priests, since high official positions in the secular world were no longer guaranteed to them. When the migration of the Fujiwara members into Buddhist temples took place, practically all the key positions within the temples came to be monopolized by the clan. In those days the most promising students went into temples and worked hard in order to attain high positions therein. But they were no longer able to do so, now that those positions were reserved only for the members of the Fujiwara clan. None but the clan of the Fujiwara could advance to the ranks of "*Ajari*" (ācārya, Esoteric Master) and "*Sōgō*," (Superintendent of Monks), unless one was endowed with prodigious learning and extraordinary longevity. On the other hand, even a man of mediocre ability, if he were connected to the Fujiwara family, could rise, immediately after he entered priesthood, to the rank of *"Gondaisōzu"* (Acting Chief Superintendent) at best, or to that of *"Gonshōsōzu"* (Acting Assistant Superintendent) at second best, or at least to the rank of *"Hōgen"* (Deacon).[364] For the key positions of the religious orders to be monopolized by the royal family and the members of the aristocracy would never have been possible in Buddhist countries other than Japan.

Such a sacrilege wrought by the secular powers upon the Buddhist orders up to the Heian period (794–857) seems to have its origin in the process by which those orders were instituted. The Buddhist orders of those days in Japan were not necessarily generated by any intense religious and spiritual demands of the people. On the contrary, they were instituted to meet the demands of the Imperial family and aristocracy, and developed under their protection. So it seems only natural that they were desecrated by their own originators.

The religious orders after the Kamakura period (1185–1333) stand out in contrast; they arose from genuine religious needs of the people, and developed, for the time being, independently of secular authorities. But even those orders were placed under the control of the secular authorities with the inception of the centralized government of the feudal regime at the beginning of the modern period. Even the Honganji Temple, once the stronghold of resistance against the secular power of feudalism, submitted to interference by Hideyoshi Toyotomi (1536–1598), who succeeded in unifying the country.[365] Finally the Temple was divided into the West and the East Honganji Temples by the astute policy of Ieyasu Tokugawa.

When religious orders finally yielded to the secular authority, the feudal political power established overall religious control. In the Tokugawa period, the Office of the Administration of Shrines and Temples (*Shaji Bugyō*) was established within the central government, and similar offices were established within the governments of the various *daimyō;* an Office of Issuing Orders (*huregashira*) was instituted within the central government. The function of the latter office was to convey the orders of the central government to the temples under control, and to transmit to the government petitions from the subordinate temples. To this office, priests were appointed. But the Office of the Administration of Shrines and Temples was open only to the vassals of the shogunate or to the feudal lords in hereditary vassalage to the shogunate. In medieval China also, overall religious control was set up by the government. But in medieval China, priests were appointed to the office of religious administration. In Japan, however, the secular warriors, *qua* warriors, were appointed to the office and administered religious matters. It was not a religious order itself, but the secular authority, that settled any controversy over a religious doctrine within the order. (It was the Tokugawa Government, for example, that worked out the final settlement on the controversy on the three kinds of deeds—of mind, body, and speech—the most important of all the doctrinal controversies in the Jōdo-shin sect.)

The gradual formation of the relationship between the main temple and sub-temple, based upon the principles of the lineage of teachings and of master-disciple relationship, corresponded to the development of the feudal hierarchical relationship within secular society at the beginning of the Tokugawa period. The Tokugawa Government, when it came to power, enforced this main-and-sub-temple relationship, making it a fixed system of hierarchy. It determined the control-and-submission relationships among the headquarters of main temples, and a descending order of several kinds of hierarchical sub-temples. In the religious ordinances, strict adherence to the regulations about the relations of the main-temple to the sub-temples was ordained, and it was stipulated that the infringement of the regulations would be severely punished. For those temples which did not belong to any main temple, the succession of the resident-priesthood was not allowed and the temples were even confiscated.

The history of religion in Japan shows, just as Max Weber rightly pointed out, that the state functioned not as a patron (*Schutz-patronat*) but as the religious police (*Religionspolizei*) of Buddhism.[366] And only on such a historical basis was the government after the Meiji Restoration able to attain complete religious control, and to push it to such an extreme that no parallel can be found in any other modern nation. Buddhists during the Meiji period resisted the tendency to destroy their religion with violence, by arguing that Buddhism was not in contradiction with Nipponism, and that in the West freedom of religion was guaranteed. The pressure of the state, however, was too great for them to cope with. "Freedom of religion" was at Potsdam proclaimed one of the "Four Freedoms," and it reminds us of the solitary outcries of our forebears.

Under these circumstances, religious orders in Japan have never had much authority, nor were the men of religion as highly respected as they were in the West. This lack of social status is not a phenomenon of recent origin. *The Buddhist Hymns on the Reminiscences of Grief*, by Shinran, deplores the fact as follows:

> "Tokens are these, that Buddhism they despise:
> Nuns and Monks are made their slaves,
> The names of priests are given to knaves."

Such was the situation even in the medieval period when religion was supposed to have flourished. Kenkō writes: "There are perhaps none less to be envied than monks. Lady Seishōnagon rightly says, 'People regard them as trifling as a chip.' "[367] In this, we find a man who was a priest himself deprecating the priesthood. Such attitudes were fairly typical of the Japanese in general and have continued up to the present.[368] Such attitudes would have been inconceivable to the Buddhists of either South Asia, including India, or of Eastern Asia, including China.

To illustrate this point, Yorinaga Fujiwara (1120–1156), the fighting Minister of the Left, who was exceptionally well versed for a layman in Indian logic, invited Egyō and Zōshun, priests of the Kōfuku Temple, to teach him Indian logic. The case is exactly reversed in India, where kings drove their chariots by themselves to pay homage to men of religion, and graciously asked them to teach them their teachings. In Japan, the status of the Minister of the Left was placed far above the learned priests of the time.

The reason why nuns and monks were despised may be attributed to the fact that in antiquity, even outcastes were able to become nuns and monks, and to the fact that since nuns and monks were exempted from taxes, there were many who secretly entered the priesthood, despite the laws to prohibit such a practice. But in India, where religious ascetics were highly respected, priests even of outcaste origin were never looked down upon, at least among the believers of the same sect. So we are led to conclude that this tendency to ridicule nuns and monks is associated with the Japanese inclination to lay greater emphasis upon mundane affairs.

Throughout the feudal age in Japan, the class of warriors preserved their pride and power as the ruling class, and consequently never submitted to the guidance of Buddhist priests with absolute obedience, to say nothing of Shintoist priests. Nothing like the spiritual guidance of the Guru of India ever prevailed. Although the number of Buddhist temples increased during the Tokugawa period, the social influence of Buddhism decreased. Temples degenerated into places simply for issuing certificates to their followers to prove that "they were not Christians." The ruling class did not wish to recognize in the temples any greater social significance. Since the Buddhist ideal of non-discrimination of classes was not compatible with the hierarchical order of feudal society, it was against the intention of the ruling class to have this ideal pushed too far. When the country was opened to foreign intercourse after the Meiji Restoration, the non-Christian certificates formerly issued from the temples were no longer necessary. Thenceforward funeral and memorial services came to be almost the only function of the Buddhist temples.

A salient feature of Japanese religions is that members of religious organizations were customarily not individual persons but families, and even now this feature can be noticed in many cases. "The importance of the family group orientations appears even in religion. Here the unit of worship is not the individual but the family group. Instead of being concerned with personal creed or individual salvation, the religion of Japan has traditionally supported the social system based on familial value. The basic group orientations of the Japanese were reinforced by the Buddhist Confucian doctrines; general life views differ profoundly from those of Puritan or Protestant religious teachings."[369]

It is very difficult to say whether or not the Japanese were devoted to Buddhism from the bottom of their hearts and recognized its intrinsic value. Often they simply followed it, even travestying the teaching or character of Buddha, as in such common sayings: "Not knowing is the state of Buddhahood" (Ignorance is bliss), or "Even the face of a Buddha changes (shows anger) after the third time" (There are limits to one's endurance). A Buddha is represented as something extremely close and familiar to man. Still another saying goes: "Borrowing with a *Jizō*-face, repaying with an *Emma*-face" (*Jizō* is the guardian deity of children while *Emma* [*Yama*] is the King of Hell). A children's toy (which is contrived so as to recover its upright position when thrown down) has the figure of Bodhidharma, and a lottery is named after Amitābha.[370] Buddhist terminology is quite commonly parodied in vernacular expressions of everyday language.

Degenerative as these characteristics are, Buddhists after the Meiji Restoration misconceived them as merits and virtues of Japanese Buddhism, and they emphasized the peculiarly Japanese characteristics of Buddhism, even though Buddhism is essentially a universal religion. They even went so far as to assert that the true essence of Buddhism for the first time came into actual fruition in Japan. It was within the framework of their own peculiar nationalistic standpoint and orientation that the Japanese accepted Buddhism. They were inclined to utilize it as a means and an instrument to realize a certain socio-political end. They were not converted to Buddhism. They converted Buddhism to their own tribalism.

One cannot deny, of course, that there were some contrary instances, as when the Japanese paid unqualified respect to a foreign culture and earnestly tried to accept it as it was. It is especially true of intellectuals in Japan that they are apt to become vehement admirers of foreign cultures, despising their own in every respect. It is even said to be a tradition with the Japanese completely to abandon their own tradition in their enthusiasm for a foreign culture newly adopted. The Japanese are acutely susceptible to the excellence of a foreign culture, and once inspired by it, they become extremely humble and self-effacing in learning what they believe to be fine and good. Had it not been for such an attitude, the Japanese would not have been able to absorb so quickly the diverse cultures of Asiatic countries and to cultivate them on their own soil, despite the fact that the range of actual foreign intercourse, for geographical reasons, was so limited, and the period when such intercourse was allowed, for historical reasons, was so brief.[371] Yet, so great a faculty for assimilating cultures other than their own constituted merely a subjective phenomenon in the Japanese, in the sphere of conscious choice. Objectively speaking, the Japanese never assimilated other cultures in such a way that all their values and their entire outlook might attain a completely new configuration. They always adamantly kept to their own traditional values and outlook, while assimilating some aspects of other cultures.

These facts being taken into consideration, it is easy to understand how Buddhism in its Japanized form was so quickly accepted. Modern nations like Germany, France, or England accepted Christianity in such a way that it became an acknowledged part of their own cultures. In Japan, by contrast, Buddhist thought is still an alien thought. Buddhism is so basic and prevailing a factor in Japanese culture of the past that it may very well, in many respects, be regarded as a Buddhist culture; nevertheless Buddhism, in fact, is still regarded by the Japanese as an imported religion. This is vastly different from the attitude of Westerners in regarding Christianity as their own religion. The Japanese accepted Buddhism without changing their own original standpoint an iota. That was why Buddhism spread with such speed.[372] The same seems to apply to the form of accepting Christianity after the Meiji Restoration. For most of the Japanese, Christianity as a religion was a matter of little consequence. They were more concerned with the Japanization of Christianity, just as they once succeeded in the Japanization of Buddhism.

Since the Japanese accepted Buddhism from the standpoint of Japan as a national state and of the Japanese as a people, it naturally follows that hardly any conscious attempt has been made to propagate Buddhism as a universal religion, transcending the interests of Japan as a particular nation. Even after the Meiji Restoration when the country was opened to international intercourse, no universal religious movement of any consequence ever took form in Japan. Let us compare this with the case of China, our neighbor. In China, a group was formed in 1922 under the leadership of T'ai-hsü, to establish in Wuchang "The School of World Buddhism" and to promote a "World Buddhist Movement." Their aim was to launch a Buddhist movement on an international basis, to renovate the world, and to create a new world culture. Although the realization of their intentions was blocked by internal and international wars in subsequent years, the historical significance of their movement, which inspired a great number of people inside and outside of their own country, is very great. In Japan, supposedly the vanguard of modernization in Asia, Buddhist leaders were engrossed in arguing the superiority and uniqueness of "Japanese Buddhism," in order to win the favor of the authorities, such as the Imperial family and the military clique. There was virtually no appearance of such a vision as a "World Buddhist Movement" in Japan before World War II; but the movement has been revived recently.

The weakness of the religious consciousness of the Japanese seems to have molded many Japanese into philistine materialists. They are, generally speaking, lacking in the desire for profound confession and severe compunction. Religion, in the true sense of the word, never deeply took root on Japanese soil. From this fact arises the weakness of religious orders. Thus, as religion had no strength, anti-religious movements which aim at the overthrow of religion are almost not to be found. Let us ask ourselves how many conscious atheists there were before the Meiji Restoration, apart from such people as Hantō Yamagata (1748–1821). In spite of the fact that the intellectual climate of the Japanese was extremely materialistic, atheistic materialism has never had a lucid and conscious formulation in Japan. In India, not to speak of the West, materialism developed in such a way as to rival religion. In Japan, the fact that religious thinking was not fertile kept materialism from becoming evident as a critical weapon.

The tendencies of the Japanese, as discussed above from various angles, to emphasize the human nexus, seem to be attributable to the social mode of living, peculiarly adapted to Japanese topography. Japanese mythology, for instance, clearly shows that collaboration among farmers was generally practiced in irrigation and the cultivation of the soil. To disturb cooperation in cultivation (such as "destroying the footpath between rice fields," "destroying the ditch," or "sowing the soil already sown") was a serious crime. In Indian mythology, there is no suggestion of this. The topographical conditions of India do not require such strenuous human labor as was required in Japan. In India, one can leave the crops alone and they will yield harvest. Irrigation is hardly necessary. Farmers can reap a harvest of the same kind of crops twice a year. This is vastly different from the farming conditions of Japan. In India, collaboration in farming is not practiced to such an extent as is the case in Japan. For these reasons, the Indians can afford to live in isolation and enjoy it. Since their conditions of living are mostly under the influence of nature, they tend to attach importance to magical rituals with which they believe they can influence nature. That was why Brahmanism came to exert a strong influence upon the whole society. In Japan, however, the topographical conditions are such as to require a greater human effort than in India to combat the conditions of nature; hence the social nexus is made to play an important role in agricultural labor, and consequently the pressure of the social nexus weighs heavily upon individuals. This would seem to be the origin of the principal characteristic of the Japanese, namely the high esteem of a particular social nexus, and other characteristics seem to be derived from it.

CHAPTER 36

NON-RATIONALISTIC TENDENCIES

The Tendency to Neglect Logical Rules

We have already indicated the marked tendency of the Japanese people to give special attention to those subjective and social relations and actions which form the basis of mutual understanding and loyalties to the family, clan, and nation. Upon this limited basis, there is little intention to make each man's understanding and expression universal or logical, so that, in general, the thinking of most Japanese tends to be intuitive and emotional. I should now like to discuss this aspect of Japanese ways of thinking.

As a preliminary step for discussing the main problem, we should call attention to some logical characteristics perceived in common Japanese linguistic usage which provide insight into the daily thinking of the Japanese. As is often pointed out by linguistic scholars, the expressive forms of Japanese sentences put more emphasis upon emotive factors than on cognitive factors. The forms of expression of the Japanese language are more oriented to sensitive and emotive nuances than directed toward logical exactness. The Japanese language does not tend to express precisely and accurately the various modes of being, but is satisfied merely with vague, typological expressions. As for nouns, we have no clear distinction between singular and plural, nor is there a distinction between genders, and no articles are used. For verbs, also, there are no distinctions of person and number. In these respects, Japanese resembles Chinese. But what is different from classical Chinese, giving Japanese its distinctive atmosphere, is the so-called "*te-ni-o-ha*," or the postpositional particles. This part of speech corresponds to case declensions or prepositions in other languages, and has the characteristic not only of expressing cognitive, logical relations, but also of expressing to some degree various delicate nuances of emotion. Thus this auxiliary part of speech, making its appearance amidst all kinds of words and sentences, plays the role of emphasizing some specific meanings, evoking attention to certain subjective aspects of things, distinguishing delicate variations of emotion, and leaves rich overtones of meaning just because of this ambiguity. Moreover, the abundance of auxiliary verbs and their complex usages show that the Japanese language is peculiarly sensitive in its grasp of emotion.

The original Japanese language, as clearly revealed in its classical literature, has a rich vocabulary of words denoting aesthetic or emotional states of mind. On the other hand, words denoting intellectual, inferential processes of active thought are notably lacking. In the original Japanese language, where words were for the most part concrete and intuitive, the construction of abstract nouns was lacking. Hence it is extremely difficult to express abstract concepts solely in words of the original Japanese. When Buddhism and Confucianism were later introduced to Japan and philosophical thinking developed, the vocabulary which was the means of expressing these philosophical thoughts was entirely Chinese, written the same way, but pronounced differently. Although Buddhism was so widely propagated among the people, its scriptures *were never translated* into the Japanese language. "In our country, there is no attempt to translate [Chinese versions of Buddhist scriptures]"[1] said Kokan Shiren (1278–1346), in his *Genkō Shakusho* (a History of Japanese Buddhism), and he cited this fact as a characteristic of Japanese Buddhism. Furthermore, we hardly had, before the Kamakura period (1185–1333), any original writing by Buddhists in Japanese. Even after the beginning of Kamakura, in the overwhelming majority of cases, Buddhist works were written in the Chinese language. Although the Japanese Confucians began to write some of their works in Japanese from the Tokugawa era onward (after 1600), such writings never ceased to be viewed as merely an avocation of the Confucians, and even in such works, they followed the Chinese language as far as technical terms were concerned. Now, Western philosophical ideas are widely diffused in Japan, but the linguistic means by which they are expressed are, in most cases, words coined by properly connecting two Chinese characters, which are, by convention, made to correspond to the traditional Occidental concepts. The words *gainen* and *risei,* for instance, are the present day Japanese terms for "concept" (*Begriff*) and "reason" (*Vernunft*) respectively. Sometimes such words are constructions of three or four characters. The pure original Japanese has never been able to serve as a medium for expressing philosophical concepts.

In this connection, it might be said that, as philosophical thinking gradually began to develop among the Japanese people, suddenly foreign philosophical thought came in, with the result that the opportunity to shape the Japanese language philosophically was lost; and that is why, to the present time, Japanese has been at a loss to form philosophical concepts.[2] Yet in the case of the German people, although clerics in medieval times carried on their philosophical thinking in Latin, in modern times, the Germans came to build up philosophical systems by means of the German language alone. Such attempts can even be traced back to Eckhart in the Middle Ages. On the other hand, even in very recent times, no philosophy expressed in purely original Japanese words has so far been developed in Japan. We are, therefore, forced to conclude that Japanese has not been as fit for philosophical thinking as Sanskrit or Greek was or as German seems to be.

The greatest obstacle seems to lie in the fact that the Japanese language does not have any fully established method of composing abstract nouns. The language does not have the infinitive form of the verb, the special character of which is to express abstract ideas, an indefinite situation, a "relation" itself rather than a "thing." Although we do have what is called the "nominal use" corresponding to the infinitive, this is completely identical in form with a verbal form which, in conjunction with temporal verb endings, indicates the past, or which, when joined to another verb, a noun or an adjective, forms a compound word. For example, the so-called nominal form *warai,* which is completely identical in form with the form of the verb *warau* ("to laugh") appearing in *waraitari* ("laughed"), *waraite* ("laughed and. . . ."), *waraigoto* ("laughing matter"), etc., signifies the act or fact of "laughing." Moreover, this verb form in time has tended to lose its special significance as an expression with a compounding function, and has also come to be used as a noun. For instance, *warai* has the senses both of *warau koto* (the act or fact of laughing) and of *warai to yū mono* ("laughter"); consequently the distinction between the two (as in German, "die Lache" and "das Lachen") is not made.[3]

Furthermore, the Japanese have no established method of turning adjectives into corresponding abstract nouns. As may be seen in such examples as *fukasa* ("depth"), or *fukami* ("deepness"), the suffixes *-sa* or *-mi* make abstract nouns out of adjectives to some extent. But this manner of transformation or noun-building is available for only a limited range of adjectives. In Greek, for example, Plato coined the noun *poiotes* out of the adjective *poion,* which, literally translated, means "of what sort." And Cicero, in attempting to translate the Greek, coined the abstract noun *qualitas* out of Latin *qualis,* meaning "of what sort." Both *poiotēs* and *qualitas* are invented words meaning the quality of a thing, or a thing's "of-what-sort-ness." Literally translated into Japanese, the word *dono-yo-na-sa* would give an unnatural sounding expression. This Latin translation *qualis* was current in the Middle Ages, and in modern Europe was used without change, as in the words *Qualität, quality, qualité*. But the Japanese, in translating this concept, have made use of the two Chinese characters *sei-shitsu*. This is because in the Japanese language the translation term *dono-yō-na-sa* conveys a somehow inappropriate, unnatural feeling.[4]

As the existence of too many Chinese characters in the Japanese language causes inconvenience, the Japanese are going to eliminate infrequently used Chinese characters and thus lessen the total number of Chinese characters; the language still keeps many of them,[5] and people cannot immediately get rid of the bondage of Chinese characters.

In short, the Japanese language has had, at least in the past, a structure unfit for expressing logical conceptions. Consequently, when the Japanese adopted the already highly advanced conceptual knowledge of Buddhism and Confucianism, they made no attempt to express it in the original Japanese language, but used Chinese technical terms without modification. Again, in translating the concepts of Western learning, the Japanese used Chinese characters and did not render these concepts into Japanese directly. Consequently, even today, any marked tendency to logical expression is hardly apparent in the Japanese language.

Some abstract concepts, which have been introduced from India, have been unable to take root intact among the Japanese people in general. The words *anyatara* (one between two) and *anyatama* (one among many) were translated into Chinese as *sui-i*. The ancient Japanese intellectuals used this concept in its original meaning, whereas common people since the Tokugawa period[6] have taken the word "*zuiichi*" to mean "the first" or "the most excellent." There has been no single native Japanese word representing "one between two" or "one among many."

When we pass from the realm of syntax to that of word construction, the Japanese language manifests its non-logical character all the more clearly. The language lacks the relative pronoun, "which," standing for the antecedent, that helps develop clarity of thought. The absence of such a relational word makes it inconvenient to advance closely knit thinking in Japanese.[7] It is difficult to tell what modifies what, when several adjectives or adverbs are juxtaposed. Because of these defects, Japanese presents difficulties for exact scientific expression and naturally handicaps the development of logical, scientific thinking among the Japanese people, which has actually brought about grave inconveniences in their practical lives. Indian books of Buddhistic philosophy were originally written with logical accuracy, but, as was already pointed out, Chinese versions of them became remarkably illogical. Thereafter, the Japanese continued the ambiguous and obscure interpretations of the Chinese without change, and as a result, they did not attempt to analyze them logically.

The same ambiguity can be observed in Japanese expressions of sequences or inferences made up of successively related judgments. For instance, the following is one of the well-known examples of such a loosely linked chain syllogism: "When the wind blows, it becomes dusty. If it becomes dusty, it becomes injurious to the eyes. If it becomes injurious to eyes, many people become blind, and then there appear many *samisen* (string-instrument) players. If there appear many *samisen* players, *samisens* are in great demand. If *samisens* are in great demand, cats are killed (to make the strings for this musical instrument). If cats are killed, rats increase in number. If rats increase in number, boxes are chewed, and become articles in great demand. Therefore, boxmakers become prosperous."[8]

Although special phraseologies have been worked out in legal jargon, etc., for technical considerations, to avoid ambiguity, such a practice is by no means universal.

Again, complicated expressions of Indo-European languages can hardly be translated, in corresponding forms, into Japanese. For instance, such causative passive constructions as *prāpitaś cārthaḥ*[9] ("[by some means, either a person or a thing, an individual] has been made to reach an object") can only with great difficulty be put into Japanese in like form.

In the same way, Japanese frequently omit the subject, and this too may have something to do with the inexact character of the Japanese mode of thought in general. In such a case, even though the subject is omitted, we usually find it naturally suggested or can easily infer what it is by referring to the linguistic context, or by looking at the situation in which the utterance is made. But it cannot be denied that at times, when the situation is not completely clear, the omission of the subject makes the meaning ambiguous and causes misunderstanding. This shortcoming could, of course, be overcome if the Japanese would try to make their forms of expression logical, by constructing sentences always accompanied by subjects. Nevertheless, up to the present at least, actual Japanese usage is still very inaccurate in this respect.

In connection with the omission of subjects, we must note that anacoluthon very frequently occurs in Japanese sentences. While it is to be found also in Indo-European languages, examples are few,[10] whereas the Japanese not only has abundant examples of it, but also even the fact that the subject has changed within a single sentence is not clearly noticed. For example, in literary works of the Heian period, instances of anacoluthon are very frequent. And this characteristic of the Japanese way of thinking appears also in the annotations to Chinese Buddhist texts.[11] That the Japanese people can dispense with the subject of their linguistic expression is, I think, due to the fact that the intuitive understanding of the scene referred to in their discourse is usually attained beforehand by the close personal bonds and nexus with others. Therefore, the necessity of clearly indicating the subject occurs only in those cases where some doubt about the intuitive understanding of the subject arises. (In other words, a logically correct assertion of the "obvious" sounds harsh to the Japanese people.)

Generally speaking, logical consciousness begins with consciousness of the relation between the particular and the universal; and the Japanese on the whole have not been fully aware of this relation, or have been poor in understanding a concept apart from particular instances. This exactly corresponds to the tendency, characteristic in the Japanese way of thinking, not to make a sharp contrast between subject and predicate in the expression of judgment.

Keizan Hio (1789–1859), in his two-volume work *Kunten Fukko* ("Restoration of Kunten"), criticized the usages of *kunten* (marks used in paraphrasing Chinese into Japanese) prevalent in the Tokugawa period. According to his view, for example, scholars at that time misread the Chinese passage *Yen Hui che,* which means "a man called Yen Hui i.e. Gankai," as *Gankai naru Mono,* which is an abridged form of *Gankai ni aru Mono* (strictly, "the man exemplified in Gankai").[12] In so doing, he argued, they committed an error in the indication of the meaning. However this may be, such a distinction is generally not recognized by the Japanese, and this confusion continues to the present time. Whether or not Hio's theory is right is a question to be entrusted to experts, but in any case one could say that there was no method fully established in pure Japanese for expressing universal concepts.

Therefore, the Japanese people are not inclined to present the universal concept as a predicate in a judgment, so as to make the expression of it concise. They are not usually content until they have presented a set of particular instances. Dōgen (1200–1253), who has been called one of the greatest philosophers Japan ever had, for example, wrote:

"The Acting Buddha is neither a Buddha in the perfect figure nor a transformation-Buddha. It is neither a Buddha in itself nor a Buddha in other selves. It is neither the initial enlightenment nor the ultimate enlightenment. It is neither the realization of one's own nature, nor the realization of nothing. All these Buddhas together are not equal to the Acting Buddha."[13] Where an Indian philosopher formulated an idea simply and definitely in a universal proposition, e.g., "The Three Worlds are but one Mind,"[14] Dōgen explained the thought by *enumerating various particulars.* Thus: "The mind is neither one nor two. It is neither in the Three Worlds nor beyond the Three Worlds. It is infallible. It is an enlightenment through contemplation, and it is an enlightenment without contemplation. It is walls and pebbles; it is mountains, rivers, and the earth. The mind is but the skin, flesh, bones, and marrow; the mind is but the communication of enlightenment through the Buddha's smile. There is a mind, and there is no mind. There is a mind with a body; there is a mind without a body. There is a mind prior to a body; there is a mind posterior to a body. A body is generated from the womb, the egg, moisture, or fermentation. The mind is generated from the womb, the egg, moisture, or fermentation. Blue, yellow, red, and white are nothing but the mind. Long, short, square, and round are nothing but the mind. Life and death are nothing but the mind. Years, months, days, and hours are nothing but the mind. The bubbles of water and the flames of fire are nothing but the mind. The flowers of the spring and the moon of the autumn are nothing but the mind. Confusions and dangers are nothing but the mind."[15] Although Dōgen ardently admired Bodhidarma, he never referred to the systematic doctrine of "two entrances and four practices"[16] which was the central theme of Bodhidarma's thought.

A similar way of thinking may be noticed in Japanese Confucianists. Sorai Ogyū (1666–1728), for example, did not like the sort of abstract speculation found in the Sung school; he made more of particular "things" (*wu*) than of universal "principles" (*li*): "The great sage kings of the past taught by means of 'things' and not by means of 'principles.' Those who teach by means of 'things' always have work to which they devote themselves; those who teach by means of 'principles' merely expatiate with words. In 'things' all 'principles' are brought together, hence all who have long devoted themselves to work come to have a genuine intuitive understanding of them. Why should they appeal to words?"[17] Therefore, learning consists, to him, in knowing as many particular things as possible: "Learning consists in widening one's information, absorbing extensively anything and everything one comes upon."[18] But because Ogyū ignored the science of nature, "learning" meant to amass a knowledge of particular facts, and culminated, for him, in the study of history—a preference which is closely related to the ethical character of his "learning": "Since learning is to have wide information and to have experience with realities, it culminates in history."[19]

Even the scholars of the Japanese classics, who tried to repudiate Buddhism and Confucianism, exhibited the same way of thinking. The nationalist Atsutane Hirata (1776–1843), for example, rejected the concept of abstract, universal "principles," and declared that we only had to know "actual things," or concrete particulars: "In fact, that which is called the 'true way' is given in actual things, whereas conventional scholars are erroneously inclined to think that the 'way' cannot be found out except by reading doctrinal books. For if we can appreciate actual things, doctrines are dispensed with; and it is only when actual things, in which the 'way' is given, are lacking, that doctrines arise. Therefore, doctrines are far less valuable than actual things. Lao Tzŭ recognized this fact when he said, 'When the Way decays, the doctrines of humanity and justice arise.' "[20]

As shown by the historical development of Japanese thought—although so far only several representative thinkers have been considered—the ability to think in terms of abstract universals has not fully developed among the Japanese people. They have been very poor in ordering various phenomena on the basis of a universal pattern.

[There might be a question as to how to reconcile this alleged Japanese preference for the *particular* with the commonly observed modern preference of Japanese scholarship for theoretical learning rather than concrete approaches. Among Japanese intellectuals there was, not long ago, a marked fondness for abstract German philosophy. We consider this tendency among our intellectuals not so much a preference for theoretical thinking as an attraction for things abstruse and productive of imaginative impressions upon them. Their alleged fondness for theoretical learning is not always based upon the process of induction and deduction in the logical sense.]

Of course, the Japanese do sometimes criticize themselves in such a way as to contradict what we have just said. For example, we hear it said among the Japanese themselves that "It is bad for the Japanese habitually to concern themselves with plans on paper and deal with abstract theories." Such criticism, however, confuses abstraction with fantasy (unreality), and the prevalence of such criticism in fact points up the absence in the Japanese of self-criticism in the matter of abstract thinking.

Nowadays, however, things are changing. People want to be more accurate and clear with regard to expression. This is already noticeable among novel writers.

"Writers of the present Shōwa era [1926–] who specialize in naturalism generally do not regard themselves as belonging to the writing school that follows the *kanji* style of Meiji writers or the rhetorical styles of old. Those who can read and easily digest the Chinese classical style and adopt this in their own writings belong to the older generation of Nagai, Tanizaki, and Satō. In other words, even where *kana* is concerned, the writers of the generation after Yokomitsu [1898–1947] and Kawabata [1899–] do not utilize *hentaigana* and are far removed from the refinements found in Chinese poems and classic compositions. The tendency is toward simplicity and the dialogue styles of composition. Instead of subjectivity or rhetorical flourishes, more emphasis is placed on objective delineations. It may safely be said that there is no writer after Yokomitsu and Kawabata who gladly displays in his work a knowledge of Chinese poetry and classical compositions. The Shōwa era writer, as is commonly known, depends on a healthy mode of national expression; his thoughts are conveyed as clearly and simply as possible, without sacrificing perspicuity or intelligibility. In fact, his manner in all probability reveals a deep repugnance for eccentric and ambiguous forms of expression."[21] This phenomenon noticed among novel writers will, as their influence spreads, have some effect on the ways of thinking of people who read them.

Lack of Logical Coherence

Even in ancient times, Kakinomoto-no-Hitomaro (c. 700 A.D.) composed a famous poem which said: "In our land covered with reed and rice-ears, they have not argued since the time of the gods." From such a poetic point of view, the technique of constructing universal laws reducing individuals to order was not likely to develop. Norinaga Motoori (1730–1801), a scholar who claimed to have made clear the spirit of ancient Japan, said: "In ancient times, we had no talk at all even about the Way. The classic declares that in our land covered with reed and rice-ears, they haven't argued since the time of gods. Not to argue means not to expatiate or indulge in much talk, as is the custom in foreign countries."[22]

"In ancient times in our land, even the 'Way' was not talked about at all and we had only ways directly leading to things themselves, while in foreign countries it is the custom to entertain and to talk about many different doctrines, about the principles of things, this 'Way' or that 'Way.' The Emperors' land in ancient times had no such theories or doctrines whatever, but we enjoyed peace and order then, and the descendants of the Sun-goddess have consecutively succeeded to the throne."[23]

What was the situation, then, after philosophical theories were introduced from the Chinese continent? It seems that Japanese scholars who first acquainted themselves with these theories were so hard pressed merely in learning to use Chinese ideographs that they did not get to the point of understanding and assimilating the thought expressed therein. The *Keikoku-shū* ("Anthology on the Arts of Governing the State"), which was compiled in the early Heian period, records several sets of examination questions and answers given to students around the Nara period; the questions are, e.g. "Of loyalty and filial piety which should take precedence? What is the difference between the doctrines of Confucius and those of the Taoists and Buddhists? Which of them is true? Discuss the merits and demerits of Confucianism, which declares the heaven and earth have a beginning but no end, and Buddhism, which preaches the cycle of worldly events in the order of emergence, subsistence, destruction, and emptiness." The answers entered in the work, however, are merely fraught with flowery words, and the points of arguments are so superficial and vague that consistency is hardly found. A certain answer even asserts that the two doctrines cannot be distinguished from each other, and the truth and falsity of the two cannot be judged. We are surprised at the words and the lack of logical relevance.[24]

The way of thinking on the part of the Japanese in general could not easily be changed by the introduction and dissemination of Buddhism. It is true that great efforts were made to understand and assimilate the philosophy of Buddhism as well as its artistic by-products. Those who made the efforts, however, were confined to learned monks; the Japanese in general were indifferent to philosophical argument. Since the works by the monks were nearly all written in Chinese, they made no contact with the general public. Although the founders of various Buddhistic sects which arose in the Kamakura period wrote also in the native Japanese language, their central works, which deal with the essentials of their doctrines, were all in Chinese. Some Buddhists keenly felt the necessity of disseminating Buddhistic thought among the people and produced writings in the original Japanese especially for that purpose, but such cases were remarkably few in number and small in scope.[25]

It is commonly said that Japanese Buddhism reached its maturity in the Kamakura period (1185–1333). "Kamakura Buddhism," however, did not develop much systematic philosophical thinking. As we have already learned, such prominent figures as Hōnen, Shinran, and Nichiren chiefly concentrated their efforts upon demonstrating the orthodoxy or validity of their own interpretations of Buddhist Sacred texts. To cite an extreme instance, Chishin (1239–1289), who is also called the Itinerant Sage Ippen, declared on his deathbed that the people of this world should be content with the one phrase, "Pay homage to Amitābha Buddha," (*Namu-Amida-Butsu*) and ordered his books destroyed by fire.

On the other hand, some contemporary philosophers in Japan have tried to see in Dōgen, who continued to write philosophical works throughout his lifetime, the pioneer of Japanese philosophy. Though it is doubtless true that Dōgen was a distinguished thinker as well as a high-minded spiritual leader, he was not the sort of thinker who developed a logically coherent system of thought. In spite of the fact that he cherished deep philosophical ideas which were gem-like in character, he was not inclined to elaborate his thoughts—his "*dōtoku*"—in a strictly logical system.

Dōgen commented upon a passage "Inhabitants of Ling-nan not having Buddhahood" as follows:

"This passage means neither that inhabitants of Ling-nan Peak do not possess Buddhahood nor that they possess Buddhahood. It just means inhabitants of Ling-nan not having Buddhahood."[26] Probably Dōgen thought that the judgment that they either do or do not have Buddhahood is based upon too abstract and sharp a distinction, which is foreign to Buddhahood, in which the realm of absoluteness, of All-Being (Dōgen's peculiar term) or nothing, is approached when being and non-being are transcended. Dōgen, however, did not like to expound such a principle in abstract, universal propositions, and was satisfied with the terse but obscure expression, "Inhabitants of Ling-nan not having Buddhahood."

In another place, Dōgen opined as follows, referring to the problem of life and death: "Life and death matter little because the Buddha exists therein. And one is not perplexed by life and death because the Buddha does not exist therein."[27] We have here two formally contradictory assertions about the Buddha's existence. But the gist of what he meant by the two sentences was quite the same: Be resigned!

The teacher Musō (or Soseki, 1275–1351), Buddhist priest of the Rinzai sect, declares, very clearly, that he does not aim at fixed logical coherency: "Clear-sighted masters of the Zen sect do not have a fixed doctrine as something to be cherished for all time. They present any doctrines as occasion demands, and preach as their tongues happen to dictate. They do not have a fixed source to rely upon. If one asks them what Zen is, they sometimes answer in terms of the sayings of Confucius, Mencius, Lao-Tzŭ, or Chuang-tzŭ, Non-Zen Buddhist teachers, sometimes with popular proverbs, or sometimes they explain what Zen teaches, point out a particular situation in front of them and simply swing their mace or shout in a loud voice. Or they simply raise their fingers or fists. All these are means used by the masters, and called 'the vivacious ways of the Zen sect.' "[28]

Buddhism originally embraced the idea of expediency, and among the expediencies Buddhists were allowed to use as their means of preaching, a certain system of successive ranking was thought to exist. In case of the Zen Buddhists, however, no consideration is paid to the logical relations among expediencies. Musō's saying quoted above indicates the ways of instruction employed in the Zen sect since its foundation in China, and it was through the appreciation of this aspect of it that Japan welcomed the Zen sect.

From the Tokugawa period (1600–1867), the schools of the Neo-Confucians, Chu-hsi and Wang Yang-ming, came to be energetically studied in Japan, but it is a question as to how far Japanese scholars understood them. In this connection, some examples will be given to show that Japanese Confucianists did not like metaphysical speculation.

The Chu-hsi school made a distinction between *li* (principle) or *tao* (way) which was held to be "above form" and *chi* (matter) or *ch'i* (receptacle) which was "below form." Western students of the school sometimes translate the former as "form," and the latter as "material." Roughly speaking, the world "above form" and the world "below form" as expressed in the Sung school correspond to the world of ideas and the world of phenomena respectively. This is the reason why the Japanese in modern times have translated "metaphysics" as "*keijijō-gaku*" (the study of what is above form). However, Ekken Kaibara (1650–1714), having tried to understand Confucianism from the viewpoint of Japanese practical life, did not understand the distinction between the realms "above form" and "below form." He was disposed to understand the two as belonging both to the realm of the senses and the concrete: "In my opinion," he said, "the 'form' means to be corporeal, 'over' means to be in the heavens, and 'below' to be on the earth." Referring to what the "heaven" and the "earth" are, he continues: "Those things which 'form shapes in the heaven' are simply the sun, moon, the stars and constellations."[29] "The phrase 'below form' refers to those things which form shapes on the earth, and all that have any shapes whatever, such as mountains, rivers, the ground, and men, are 'receptacles (*ch'i*).' " Thus Kaibara was never inclined to recognize the realm which transcends and underlies the natural world of the senses. Such a way of thinking quite naturally makes it impossible to develop a conception of the intelligible world, of the world of ideas. This is the reason why he could not understand the philosophical significance of the Kegon doctrine, for he often accused the Sung school of being influenced by the Kegon view of *Dharma-dhātu* (the view of the super-mundane law of the interdependence of things).

As another instance, Sorai Ogyū, who made much of the will of Heaven, could not grasp the idea of Heaven as an abstract concept. He could not conceive of it as distinct from the visible heaven of the natural world. Thus, he said: "We need not wait to understand Heaven. We all know it. When we look at Heaven, it seems blue and boundless, and beyond any means of measuring it. It embraces the sun, moon, stars and constellations, and is the source of rain, wind, and cold and hot weather. Heaven is the place where all things receive their destinies, and it is the god of gods, holy beyond any comparison, and nothing can rise to its height."[30]

In theoretically denouncing the doctrines of Christianity, most Japanese did so on the ground of no particular philosophy. Habiyan (Fabian, c. 1650), for example, became a priest of the Nichiren sect after he forsook the Christian faith, but he did not make use of the doctrine or philosophy of the Nichiren sect in criticizing his former faith. All he had to do, as he saw it, was to point out weak spots of the Christian doctrine and repudiate it in any way whatever. Hence no logical consistency can be found in his attitude. He said he had never witnessed a Christian miracle, and then praised most highly, as a genuine miracle, Nichiren's escape from death. Controversies between a Catholic Father[31] *iruman* and Razan Hayashi (1583–1657), the Confucianist, descended also to a mere exchange of contemptuous shouts, "You blighter!" and "You idiot!"[32]

Absence or neglect of theoretical and systematic thinking is equally characteristic of former scholars of Japanese classics. Norinaga Motoori, for example, had no concrete conception of method in his learning: "In final conclusion, to make strenuous efforts consecutively for long years is most essential to those who are engaged in learning, and it does not matter how they learn. The *How* is the question about which they need not worry so much."[33] Motoori exhorted all students just to be diligent in their study, and did not develop any constructive thinking about the method of learning itself.[34]

Of course, it is possible to express one's self as clearly in Japanese as in any other language, if one has the disposition as well as the logical clarity and habits of thought to do so. We must not forget the important conditioning of ways of thinking by the cultural customs ingrained in the habits of people, and according to one school of thought, such customs are more important than the temporal limitations of the language in which they are expressed. Since we do not wish to advocate any single-factor theory of cultural or historical determinism, we must admit the working of many influences that have brought it about that the aesthetic aspects of Japanese life and thought are far more dominant than any concern for exact logical modes of expression. At least, it is historically true that the neglect of logic is one of the salient features of traditional Japanese ways of thinking. Concrete intuitions are favored much more than abstract concepts devoid of any tangible connection with the humanly perceived world.

Slow Development of Logic in Japan

The logic of Buddhism, *Inmyō,* was introduced into Japan at a very early date. In 653 A.D. during the reign of Emperor Kōtoku, Dōshō went to study in China, and, together with the monk Jion (Tz'u-ên), personally studied under Hsüan-tsang the doctrine of idealism (*wei-shih, vijñaptimātratā*), which was the newest philosophy of the time, and also schooled himself in logic (*inmyō*). In 661, during the reign of Saimei, he returned to Japan and introduced Buddhist logic to Japan. After Hsüan-Tsang's round trip to India (629–645), he translated 74 Buddhist works in 1338 volumes. His *Hsi-yü chi* (Record of the Western Regions) "is the most important work of its kind" (Reischauer and Fairbanks, 146).

Since Dōshō disseminated his newly acquired knowledge at the Gangō Temple, the scholarship which he originated is generally referred to as "the tradition of the Southern Temple," and also, as "the Asuka tradition." It was only sixteen years after the Buddhistic logic was introduced to China that it was further conveyed to Japan. Later on in 716, Gembō went to China to study the Buddhistic logic under Chishū (Chih-chou), the third patriarch of the Hossō sect. After he came back to Japan, he propagated learning at the Kōfuku Temple; this is referred to as "the tradition of the Northern Temple," and also as the "tradition of Kasayama." Since that time, this system of logic came to be studied in the Hossō sect as a discipline supplementing Buddhistic idealism (vijñaptimātratāsiddhi), and the *Abhidharmakośa-śāstra.* The number of books written in Japan on Buddhistic logic amounts to a considerable figure, and even the bibliography entered at the end of the *Inmyō Zuigenki* ("*The Origin of the Buddhistic Logic*") written by Hōtan at the middle of the Tokugawa period, comprises eighty-four Japanese works of the kind.

In looking into the characteristic way in which the Buddhist logic was disseminated in Japan, we find in the first place that this logic was employed as a technique of expression in questions and answers at Buddhist meetings. Logic was then likely to be studied not as a subject matter in itself but as a technique of oral expression. At the very beginning, in places like the Yuima (*Vimalakīrti*) meetings in the Kōfuku Temple, where the essential doctrine of that sect was propounded, a "confirmer," an "assertor," and a "questioner" were designated, and argument was conducted according to the forms of Buddhist Logic (*inmyō*). Later it was employed at the Jion-meeting, where the use of logic came to be ritualized.[35] Still later, the Enryaku Temple and the Onjō Temple held regular Hokke-meetings in which the catechism of the Lotus Sūtra was discussed, and those who did not know the Buddhist logic were not allowed to join such meetings. Buddhist logic was at that time considered a common subject to be mastered by monks of any sect. Further in the Great-transmission-meetings (*Daidenbō-e*), in the Kongōbu Temple in the Muromachi period (1336–1573), the Chishakuin Temple, the Hase Temple, and other places in the Tokugawa period (1600–1867), the subjects of Commentaries were discussed according to the forms of Buddhist logic, and ultimately even the Jōdo and Zen sects came to hold such meetings. These were called "discussions" (*rongi*), and in the Zen sect, because of their special form, they were called "questions and answers" (*mondō*). In these uses the *inmyō* deteriorated to the point of extreme formalism.

In the Tendai sect the periodic examinations of state-supported student priests were conducted according to this form of argumentation. The official gazette of the Enryaku period (782–806) informs us that five questions and ten problems were put and all of them were answered aloud. This was the first step toward ritualization of logical argument. Further, it is held that this is the origin of the argument in the Noh-drama.

In this situation it goes without saying that the forms of *Inmyō,* as well as the discussion-style of *rongi,* were used, and further both questions and answers were *recited,* and moreover were accompanied by a certain gracious rhythm. Finally, outside of Buddhism, the practice of holding public discussions of lyric verse and of The Tale of Genji developed in various places; also there came into being the *utaawase,* or form of poetry discussion, in which poems were discussed with questions and answers. Moreover, the ritualized debate continues to be held at Mt. Kōya, even to this day. In this ritual, the answerers (*Rissha*), the questioners (*Monja*), the judge (*Tandai*), the stenographer (*Chūki*), and the manager (*Gyōji*) sit in pious attitude around the statue of the Buddha, according to fixed rule; Buddhist hymns are sung and the sūtras are read. Thus, in Japan, logical debate was reduced to a mere Buddhist meeting, a decorum of the most pious form. Further, the form of the ritual was extended without change to the poetic debate or *utaawase*.[36] Therefore, the meeting of debate, in which logic was applied to concrete cases, was completely transformed into a formalized ceremony, then into the arts in the manner peculiar to the Japanese culture. Surely, we may say that this phenomenon reveals the artistic, as well as non-logical, character of the Japanese educated or literary class and people influenced by them.

It is relevant that the formula of reasoning or syllogism of Indian logic was introduced into Japan in a modified form.

One of the original Indian formulae runs as follows:

(1) the conclusion:	Words are impermanent.
(2) the reason:	Because they have been made.
(3) the explanatory example:	It is a fact of experience that whatever has been made is impermanent, as are jars, etc. It is a fact of experience that whatever is permanent has not been made, as with space.[37]

In the above-mentioned formula, the conclusion was not regarded by the Japanese as an assertive sentence, but was interpreted as an exhortation for persuading others. Therefore it has been usually read in Japanese: "*Koe wa mujō naru beshi.*" (Words should be regarded as impermanent.) That is to say, Japanese logicians understood the assertion as one to be made in debating. Classical Indian logic also was essentially a logic of dialogue. The distinction between inference for one's self and inference for others was there from the beginning, and the five-membered syllogism belongs to the latter class which was used in argument and debate. But Japanese logicians of antiquity were more interested in the human relations in which debate was conducted than in abstracting the subject of the debate from the surrounding human situation. Further the statement of the example is usually read:

"Jo so tso, chien pi wu ch'ang"
"Consider whatever has been made as impermanent!"
"Consider whatever is permanent as not having been made![38]

Nevertheless the word *"chien"* which has been translated as the imperative "Consider!" does not have the meaning of imperative in the Chinese translation. Moreover, according to the Sanskrit original, it means "by experience (*dṛṣṭam*)." Therefore, the statements in question originally mean "Everything which has been made is known to be impermanent by our experience. For instance, it is similar to a thing like a vase," and "what is permanent is by experience known to be that which has not been made; for instance, it is like space."

As is seen here, the Japanese have not been interested in abstracting universally valid sentences from their social relations. As scholars of Buddhist logic always thought of meetings at which debates took place, they made much of the *practical* side of Buddhist logic, especially deliberation on fallacies. Such works as *"the Treatise on Thirty-three Fallacies"* (*Sanjūsan-kahon-sahō*) were composed. They have always been considered to be useful for discussion among scholarly clergymen.[39]

In the second place, Indian logic, ever since it was introduced from China, has been studied in a dogmatic spirit. The interpretation of logical scriptures given by Jion (Tz'u-ên, 632–682), the founder of the Fa-hsiang (Japanese, Hossō) sect, was respected as the highest and absolute authority, which should be studied with the spirit of a defender of the faith. Under Gembō (?–746 A.D.), the importer of logic, Zen-shu, of the Akishino Temple, studied various commentaries on logic and wrote his own commentary in twelve volumes, *"Inmyō Ronsho myōtōshō"* (Explanatory Lamp for the Commentary on the Introduction to Buddhist Logic). Not only was this work written in the form of an annotation to Jion's commentary, *Nisshōri-ron-sho* (Commentary on the Introduction to Buddhist Logic), but he also studied logic from Jion's viewpoint, defending his comments and denouncing those of others. This book is the best example of those books which were written with the spirit of a defender of the faith. Thus, as a whole, logic, in Japan, was traditionally studied as one of the auxiliary disciplines of the study of the idealistic doctrines of the Hossō sect. This was presumably due to the fact that the Buddhist logic was the essential preparatory discipline for understanding the texts of the Indian idealistic philosophy. The other sects of the Nara period, for example, the Kegon and Sanron sects, also studied logic. They were influenced by the Hossō sect's keen interest in it, though it was not indispensable to the understanding of their own doctrines. But this tendency did not permeate all sects of Japanese Buddhism. Dengyō (767–822) especially resisted this tendency, owing to his hostility toward the Hossō sect, the strongest enemy of his new religious movement. He declared that logic was necessary to preach the doctrine of "Three Vehicles" of the Hossō sect, but that this sect was, after all, nothing but a second-rate Buddhism. In his opinion, no system of logic has any value for the doctrine of "One Vehicle" (*eka-yāna*) of the Tendai sect, which is the highest type of Buddhism. Ever since then, the followers of Dengyō on Mt. Hiei attached no importance to logic.

Of course, there were exceptions. For example, Genshin (Eshin 942–1017), though he had the same views in all respects as Dengyō, was well-versed in logic and wrote a book to comment in detail on one of its most difficult problems, the doctrine of Four Types of Contradiction (*Shi-sō-i*). Though this was one of the most important events in the history of logic in Japan,[40] it was an exceptional phenomenon in the Tendai sect itself. In a word, the study of logic has never been extended to the whole Buddhist world of Japan. This was because of the fact that logic, defended by the Hossō sect as its essential discipline, was ignored by other sects[41] just because they, too, had this same dogmatic sectarian spirit.

In the third place, we must mention the tendency of the study of logic to become an *esoteric* tradition. This tendency was conspicuous especially at the zenith of prosperity of logic, that is, from the end of the Heian period to the middle of the Kamakura period. In Nara of those days the study of logic centered in the Kōfuku Temple of the Hossō sect, and extended to the other two big temples, Tōdai and Hōryū. The Gangō Temple, called Nan-ji (the Temple of the South), had already decayed. Only the school of the Kōfuku Temple, called Hoku-ji (the Temple of the North), prospered, because it was protected politically and financially by the Fujiwaras, the ruling clan at that period. The study of logic, however, gradually showed a tendency to decline after the middle of the Kamakura period, just as did Buddhist idealism, and counted only a few generations of students after Jōkei (1155–1213).

It is true that some of the Japanese scholars had tried to give an international and universal character to the study of logic. For example, Genshin sent his work, "Short Commentaries on the Four Types of Contradiction in Logic" (*Inmyō Ronsho Shisōi Ryakuchūshaku*) through Sung merchants to disciples of Master Hung-tao of the Tz'u-ên Temple in China, and wished "to distinguish, in detail, between right and wrong, and to enlighten them."[42] But this was an exceptional case. In Japan, logic was transmitted from a master to only one disciple, and it was forbidden to communicate it to others. For example, in the Kamakura period, when Jōkei gave his work "Short Commentary on Logic" (*Myō hon-shō*) to his disciple, Ryō-san, he wrote: "I made only one copy. But, because I cannot disappoint those two people, I gave the first half (seven volumes) to the Vicar-General of the Tōhokuin, and the second half (six volumes) to the Preceptor of the Kōmyōin. By mutual agreement each can borrow the other half and make a copy of it. While any of the two is living, *the number of copies should not be increased.* When you transmit it in the future, you must choose a person who has the same religious disposition as you." In answer to these instructions, Ryō-san pledged: "So long as I live, not even two copies, to say nothing of many, will be permitted to be made of this book. Even if a noble lord orders it, or if an influential man of the world urges it, *there will never exist many copies.* In short, other men will not be allowed to copy it. And, after my death, it will be transmitted to a man of religious disposition among my disciples, and even to such a one I will not transmit it, if he is a worldly, unlawful, or unjust man." Moreover, if he breaks this pledge, "may all of the punishments of the God Kasuga afflict me in every pore of my body." Since then, this Commentary was kept in the *secret treasury-box* of the Kasuga Shrine in the Kōfuku Temple and transmitted to chosen disciples only under very strict rules. A later document dealing with the transmission of this book (dated 25/12/1256) said that "This book should be the secret of the Temple, inaccessible to outsiders."

Also, Shinken (1145–1225) closed the postscript of his "Short Account of the Real Essence of the Predicate" (*Hōjisō-yōmonshō*) with the following words: "My disciples to whom this book will be transmitted should keep it in greatest secrecy."[43] And Ryōben (–1252) has among his writings a book the title of which is "Of the Secret Account of the Transmission of Logic" (*Inmyō Sōjō Himitsushō*). We know therefore that the Buddhist logic was transmitted secretly. On the mark-papers inserted into copies of these books, we can sometimes see the names of the people to whom the book was transmitted, and we sometimes find on these papers the warning "Absolute Secrecy." In Japan, therefore, logic was adopted as a secretly transmitted catechistic technique not to be generally disseminated. This prevented logic from becoming disseminated as a universal science.

We must pay particular attention also to the social fact that Indian logic, in Japan, had been studied only by learned Buddhist priests, not by the Japanese people in general. Even these learned priests applied logic only to the interpretation of Buddhist philosophical works. These learned priests did not use logic for other subjects. It goes without saying that the mass of the Japanese people and many Buddhist priests were unacquainted with the Buddhist logic. In short, the sacred writing of logic was reduced to an apparatus for the interpretation of scriptures.

In the fourth place, because the Japanese *inmyō* was a continuation of the Chinese version of logic, it was consequently exegetical in character, and did not have the character of formal logical inquiry. Nineteen books were written, in Japan only, to comment on the Four Types of Contradiction, working from just that part of Tz'u-ên's "Great Commentary on

Logic" (*Inmyō Daisho*)[44] which had dealt with them. None of these books, however, was a logical interpretation of this problem.[45] This was probably inevitable, because the commentary of Tz'u-ên itself did not offer a logical interpretation of the Four Types of Contradictions, and it had been respected as the highest authority by Japanese students. These commentaries on logic had, in general, fallen to the level of exegetic commentaries on words, and hundreds of commentaries, produced during more than one thousand years, had almost nothing to contribute to the development of logic. None of them has made efforts to set forth a well organized logical system based upon the author's own thinking.

In the fifth place, the study of logic in Japan, as in China, did not treat the problem of the critical study of knowledge. On this point, it was quite different from the highly rationalistic logic of Dharmakīrti and others in India. Because the Japanese studied logic only through the Chinese translation, the Indian ideas that had not been introduced into China were inaccessible to the Japanese.

Japanese scholars, like their predecessors in China, scarcely studied the logical works of Dignāga (c 400–480), founder of Buddhist logic in India. His principal work, the *Pramāṇasamuccaya,* once translated into Chinese, was lost very soon without ever being utilized. Hsüan-tsang translated a compendium by Dignāga, called the *Nyāyamukha* (A Primer of Logic), into Chinese, but few Chinese and Japanese scholars seem to have ever studied this work. The *Nyāyapraveśaka* (Introduction to Logic), which Japanese scholars looked upon as their exclusive authority, is only a poor synopsis of the *Nyāyamukha.* Tibetan Buddhists, on the other hand, continued the study of the more important and more voluminous works of Dharmakīrti, the brilliant successor of Dignāga. We owe to the Tibetans the important information about Buddhist logic in India.

Thus in Japan, just as in China, the logic of Indian Buddhism could not take root and develop. Apart from the translations and commentaries, no original books on logic were written in the native Japanese language. Cursed by secret transmission, also, a knowledge of logic could not have spread widely among the Japanese. Another point to be noted is that in Japan logic as a discipline had nothing to do with mathematics and natural sciences. Even in native Japanese mathematics, we cannot find any trace of the influence of traditional formal logic. It was not simply that logical thinking was not developed among the Japanese people; the significance of exact logic was not realized by them at all. And it was far more difficult for them to develop their own logic, independently of Indian logic. It is asserted frequently that, in the Tokugawa period, logical thinking appeared in some Japanese scholars, for example, in Baien Miura (1723–1789), but all that we can discern in him is a way of thinking similar to Hegelian dialectics.[46] Miura did not know formal logic. He had no connection with the tradition of the Indian logic.

Since the Meiji era, Western formal logic has been introduced into Japan, and included in the curriculum of junior college education. But, in Japan, the study of logic has made rather poor progress, compared with developments in other fields of culture. While an enormous number of philosophic works have been produced since the Restoration, they are mostly of the essay genre and consequently not always written with logical precision. Excellent works of formal logic written by Japanese have been very few and little philosophical thought has appeared which exhibits logical thinking in the sense of the formal structure of deductive systems.

Hopes for Development of Exact Logical Thinking in Japan

We need not despair completely, however, of the capacity of the Japanese people for logical thinking; a way of thinking of a people is simply a customary tendency and is capable of being reformed. There is evidence for this in the fact that modes of expression in the Japanese language have gradually been growing more and more strict and precise in recent years. Although it is true that the Japanese language has not been very suitable for philosophical thinking, it may improve in the future in this respect. On the other hand, it must also be remembered, that Leibniz himself chose not to compose his chief philosophical works in German. He wrote in a more logical style in Latin and French; that is to say, the German language became philosophically significant only after the efforts of a few later scholars, such as Wolff, Kant, and their followers. We cannot also forget that the middle high German poets, e.g. Wolfram von Eschenbach, had to express their ideas far more concretely, and consequently less philosophically, than the modern German poets, such as Goethe, Schiller, Novalis, and others. In other words, the German language was not fit for philosophical thinking at the beginning, but was elaborated by some eminent persons, including Meister Eckhart in the thirteenth century. Terms such as "Begriff" (concept) or "Vernunft" (reason) would never have gained their philosophical implications without the systems of German idealism. In the same way the Japanese may make progress in logical forms of expression. This hope finds support in the Japanese linguistic trend of recent years toward more and more precise expression. Japanese adaptation to Western ways of expressing thought is remarkable, although it is questionable whether it always means improvement.

The fact that Buddhist logic did not fully develop in the past can be ascribed to the poor logical character of its immediate source, the Chinese *inmyō*. In spite of this limitation there were Japanese who tried on several points to initiate a development in Japan beyond the Chinese logic. We can mention an interesting, if rather trivial, example. In the Chinese logic, the word *shūhō* (*tsung-fa, pakṣadharma*) represents the predicate of an assertive proposition (*tong*, major term, *sādhya*) as well as the predicate of a causal proposition (*yin*, middle term, *sādhana*). The Chinese technical terminology did not distinguish between the two. Even if there were at first a distinction made between the two uses through pronunciation, this distinction could not be preserved for a long time in a country using the Chinese language in which pronunciation rather frequently changed. The Japanese, distinguishing the two terms in pronunciation, read in voiceless sound *Shūhō*, in one case, where it means the predicate of an assertive proposition, and in voiced sound (*Shūbō*), in the other case, where it means the predicate of a causal proposition. Moreover, before the Meiji era, there were several scholars who had mastered[47] the Indian formal logic and had actually applied it to the study of Buddhist ideas—for example, Rinjō (1751–1810) and Kaijō (died 1805), of the Buzan school of the New Shingon sect. Surely logic can be disseminated and developed among the Japanese people, if we endeavor seriously to study it.

There are some cases of Japanese in the past who were willing to use the terms of Buddhist logic, even if with changed meanings. For example, it has been asserted that the word *"rippa"* (magnificent, splendid) is a phonetic equivalent to *"ryūha"* (assertion and refutation in a debate), and that *"mutai"* (unreasonable) also is due to Buddhist logic.[48] Although it is doubtful whether this assertion or conjecture is correct, it is an established fact that there were some men of letters who explained it that way. It means that some ideas related to logic were not alien to laymen although they were not fully aware of the exact meaning of them.

Taking these facts into consideration, we believe that logic can be disseminated and developed among the Japanese people, if studied seriously in an exact way. Logical improvement will not be impossible for the Japanese in the future, although it is fraught with many difficulties.

Intuitive and Emotional Tendencies

Although the Japanese language, as already explained, is unsuitable for logically precise expression, it is well adapted to the expression of intuition and of individual emotion. On this point, Dr. Watsuji says: "In Japanese, the expression of feeling and will comes to the foreground. And, owing to this characteristic, what man understands in his direct and practical action is extremely well preserved [in language]. One of the modes of expression conspicuous in Japanese literature, surely owes its high degree of development to this characteristic of the Japanese language. This mode consists in connecting together words and phrases which exhibit no connection of cognitive meaning, simply according to identity or similarity of pronunciation, and moreover through the connection of their emotive and affective content, achieving the expression of one complete concrete emotion. It seems to me that this characteristic is nothing more or less than a characteristic of the Japanese spirit."[49]

The Japanese themselves have been conscious of this characteristic for a long time. The *Waka* poet Yamanoue-no-Okura (660–733) called Japan "the land where the spirit of language prospers." In Japan, almost everybody is a poet, and can compose and criticize *tanka* (the verse of thirty-one syllables) or *haiku* (the verse of seventeen syllables). But between the Japanese and other peoples there is a great difference in the significance of poetic expression.

The non-logical disposition of the Japanese and their emphasis on emotional moods are revealed in the form of their poetic expression. A conspicuous difference appears when Japanese poetry is compared with that of another Eastern people, the Indians, to say nothing of poetry in Western language. In Indian poetry, the subject and the predicate of sentences are distinguished, and also the relation between the principal and subordinate clauses is clearly recognized. And these characteristics are probably due to the special character of the Sanskrit language. Accordingly, so far as the linguistic materials used in it are concerned, it is almost not different from prose, except for a flavor of poetical emotion produced by rhyme. In the Japanese *tanka,* on the contrary, the subject and the predicate are hardly ever distinguished, and the relation between the principal and the subordinate clauses is not clear. Although some *tankas* are composed with logical precision,[50] they are, in the aesthetic opinion of the Japanese, rather poor in artistic value. And in *haiku,* where the abridgment of wording is carried to an extreme, words are cut down to a still shorter form; consequently the emotional mood which is conveyed by each single word has greater importance.

In Japanese, the same judgment can have various expressions, and among these expressions there are very delicate nuances of emotional implication. And as has been pointed out, in Japanese the use of honorific expressions has become very complicated; it is an error, furthermore, to think that honorific language reflects only social status in the linguistic vestiges of a feudal hierarchy. Rather it is often used in order to lend an air of grace and courtesy to the expression. For example, miso (bean) soup is called *"o-mi-o-tsu-ke,"* and the foot *"o-mi-ashi,"* through the addition of two or three honorific particles. Furthermore, in some cases, for example, *"o-shiroi"* (face powder), and *"o-mocha"* (toy), the honorific expression merges into the word and becomes an integral part of it. On this point, Yaichi Haga (1867–1917) gives the following explanation: "Essentially, an honorific expression is not always used to show reverence. In some cases it is used to express affection, or to speak gracefully. Moreover, so long as there are honorific words available, if we do not use them, we are regarded as vulgar. Consequently, men of upper classes and men of refined manners use polite words even toward their inferiors."[51]

Owing to this way of thinking, Japanese thought did not shape itself in the form of intellectual and systematic theories; rather it was apt to be expressed in the intuitive and emotional style of the arts.

Ancient books of Japanese history written in the Japanese language, for example, *Ō-kagami* (Great Mirror), *Mizu-kagami* (Water Mirror), *Ima-kagami* (contemporary), and lastly *Masu-kagami* (Additional Mirror) are literary works rich in feeling. On this point, Japanese historiography is quite different from that of the Chinese. The Chinese interpret and criticize historical facts from moral and political standpoints. The Japanese, however, describe the historical facts with artistic feeling. And, while the Chinese word "*Chien*" (mirror), used frequently in the title of the books of Chinese history, for example, in *Tzu-chih-t'ung-chien* (A Mirror for Helping Government), means a reflection of moral and political principles, the Japanese word "*kagami*" (mirror) has no such moral connotation.

This characteristic way of thinking was revealed also in the process of the assimilation of Buddhism in Japan. When Buddhism came to Japan as a synthesis of religion, art, and philosophy, the Japanese people adopted a very peculiar emotional attitude toward it. The Japanese of those days took in only what was congenial to them. They were particularly charmed by the aesthetic impressions of the statues of the Buddha, and, above all, were struck by their solemn magnificence. Accordingly, they devoted themselves chiefly to plastic arts. Since then, in the Nara and the succeeding periods, the Japanese find religious inspiration in the arts of Buddhism. In Buddhist meetings, arts of all kinds, music, dancing, literature, etc., are apt to be used synthetically. Here, the Japanese seem enraptured in an ecstasy, as if they were in the Pure Land of Amitābha (*Gokuraku*) without taking leave of earthly existence.

Saint Myōe (Buddhist priest, 1173–1232) used the word "*sukigokoro*" to express the ecstatic yearning for the beautiful and the pure. This yearning, coming in contact with objects and driven by inspiration, expresses itself in poetry. Consequently, for him, poetry was almost Buddhism itself. "Considering the men of all ages," he said, "there exists not a single case of a vulgar and shameless double-dealer becoming a Buddhist. This fact was stated clearly by the Buddha in sūtras, and further it was expounded in treatises. Therefore, there is no doubt about it. I have never seen the books of physiognomists, but, when I judged the character of other people by their faces by surmising from the sayings of the Buddha, I was right eight or nine times out of ten. Through all ages eminent Buddhists emerge from men of taste. Although the poems both in Chinese and Japanese and the poetical dialogues in Japanese are not Buddhism in themselves, those who have taste for these things are certain to extend their taste to Buddhism and become wise and very kind men. Even if men of worldly mind succeed in having the appearance of virtuousness through their study, there remains some flavor of baseness, for they always look after their own material interests and suffer from excessive attachment to them. Buddhism should be taught to those who, from childhood, have delicate taste and truthful heart."[52]

Of course, the unity of literature and religion was protested by many traditional Buddhists. According to one of them, Dōgen, Buddhism should be practiced for its own sake and not as literature, which has no value for genuine devotees of Buddhism. "The people who pursue the Way should not read the books of doctrinaire sects and other religions. If they should like to read something, they should read the collection of sayings (*Goroku*). The other books must be put aside for the time."[53] Accordingly, he prohibited keeping any other books than those relating to Buddhism in the dormitories of Buddhist temples. "In the dormitories, the books of mundane affairs, astronomy, geography, other religions, poems and verses, should not be kept."[54] Herein we can hear the voice of the traditional spirit transmitted from the days of early Buddhism in India. But, in spite of this declaration, Dōgen was a great poet. His Chinese poems are lofty and elegant, while his *tankas* vibrate with warm sympathy for the beauties of nature.

The monk and Zen Master Shōsan Suzuki (1579–1655) defended and admired Dōgen's poetical talent. A man asks: "Dōgen wrote a *tanka* at Kitano on the night of August the fifteenth, 'Although I hope and expect to live and enjoy autumn again, I cannot sleep this night for the beauty of the moon.' Isn't this *tanka* unworthy of such an eminent devotee, for it expresses an attachment to the moon?"

Master (Suzuki) answers: "You are wrong. Dōgen diverted himself by writing *tankas*, for he was well versed in the Way of *tanka*. We should sing of the moon and flowers from the bottom of our heart. You seem to think it will do only if you say 'No delusion should be harbored; everything should be relinquished.' "[55]

It should be unnecessary to cite many more illustrations. In Japan, eminent religious men wrote Chinese poems and Japanese *tankas*. (This phenomenon contrasts with the case of Buddhist philosophers in India. For example, Nāgārjuna, Vasubandhu, and Dignāga did not leave any lyrical or pastoral poems. They only amused themselves by expressing abstract theories of their philosophy in verse.) Thus, the *tanka* is particularly important as the expression of Buddhist thought in the Japanese language, because it reveals clearly the characteristic aesthetic way of thinking of the Japanese people. Among the Buddhist *tanka,* some are nothing but an expression in thirty-one syllables emotionally equivalent to some one sentence in sūtras,[56] but most of them use intuitive and concrete modes of expression, that is, they use particular illustrations in order to express the universal, abstract ideas and general propositions of Buddhism. This fact will be shown clearly by the following examples.

"The Three Worlds are but One Mind" is transfigured in Japanese as: "The dews fall on thousands of grass leaves of every field, but they are the same dew of the same autumn."

"The Meditation on the Doctrine of the Middle Way" is transformed to: "In contemplation, the clouds clear away from the sky of my mind, and there, in its void, remains only the moon."

"Eternal time has passed since I really became the Buddha" is transposed to "By the river flowing far and long, we may know of its inexhaustible source."

"The Precept that Thou Shalt Not Steal" is illustrated by "Along the white wave-swelling (*shiranaminotatsu*) stream of Mt. Tatsuta, you should not break even a twig of a maple tree, if you are not permitted by its owner. Or else you shall have the bad name (*naga-tatsu*) of a shameless robber (*shiranami*)."

"The Precept that Thou Shalt Not Commit Adultery" is illustrated by: "You must content yourselves with enjoying the beautiful sight of a mountain spring. Do not go beyond that. Do not scoop and soil water, even if it is overflowing."

"The Identity of Mind and the Buddha" is given its emotional equivalent in: "I am floating and sinking among the waves indistinguishable from the mandarine duck or the sea gull."

The "alphabet" verse (*Iroha-uta*), commonly ascribed to Kōbō, is one of the best examples:

> Although fragrant in hue,
> (blossoms) are scattered.
> For everyone, life is impermanent.
> This morning I crossed the outermost limit,
> and I am not intoxicated.

This is the Japanese translation in verse of a hymn which had been transmitted since the days of early Buddhism in India. The original hymn means that "Whatever is phenomenal is impermanent; their essential quality is appearance and disappearance; when these (appearance and disappearance) repose, tranquility is comfort." In the Japanese "alphabet" verse, these abstract expressions were changed by emotional expressions, which use as materials colorful and pictorial images such as "gay," "hue," "crossing," "outermost limits," "dreams," "intoxicated," and merely suggest abstract theories behind them.

Thus, to interpret Buddhist ideas in poems, the Japanese people, using concrete imagery, appealed to sensuous intuition and added the flavor of emotional moods to general ideas. In the Indian versification of Buddhist doctrines, on the contrary, the contents are almost always abstract and general propositions, and the composition is systematic, with well-defined subject and predicate. It is philosophy disguised in verse-form. For example, one of the philosophers of Indian Buddhism, Nāgārjuna, in the above mentioned hymn in verse, says: "We preach that dependent causation is voidness. It is temporary, being dependent (upon something else). It is the Middle Way itself."[57] This metaphysical verse is far from anything poetic.

It has been frequently suggested that the Japanese people love purity and undefiledness,[58] and are proud of this fact. In Shintō, "purity" has been regarded as one of the most important virtues ever since ancient times. Although almost all peoples love this virtue, what the Japanese mean by "purity" differs considerably from other peoples' ideas. In Japanese, "purity" is expressed by various acts and ideas such as frequent bathing, daily sweeping and dusting, purification ceremony (*misogi*), great exorcism (*ō-harai*), image for redemption (*katashiro*), dislike of defiledness, abstinence (*monoimi*), tidiness of appearance. All of these are concrete acts, which appeal to the senses and unsophisticated sentiment. Their aim is not purity in any metaphysical or religious sense, based on a poignant consciousness of sinfulness. In this sense, the Japanese people are essentially different from the Indians. The Indians value religious and metaphysical purity more than sensuous purity. It was one of the ideals of early Buddhism that the monks who renounced the world should collect thrown-away tatters and wear them. Though in ragged clothes, they believed that they could attain spiritual purity. The clothes were called Pāṁsukūlika (*"Funzōe"* in Japanese, meaning "lavatory clothes"): "They are thrown away and not unlike lavatory clothes. And furthermore, they belong to no one. Therefore, they are called 'lavatory clothes.' "[59] To the Japanese, however, it is unbearable to wear such clothes. The Japanese clergymen kept the word *"Funzōe,"* but its meaning was changed to signify neat and tidy clothes. Dōgen emphasized the duty to clean the body.[60] And, although Buddhism has shaped one of the main currents of Japanese culture in the past, the common people are rather inclined to consider that the temples and clergymen are impure. This view is deep-rooted, perhaps owing to the fact that the Japanese people have been less apt to value spiritual and religious purity than sensuous and aesthetic refinement. And this corresponds to one of the characteristics of Japanese ways of thinking, that is, lack of consciousness of the universal.

The traditional tendency still prevails even among most advanced scientists of the present day Japan. Hideki Yukawa, a physicist, who is the only Nobel Prize winner of Japan, says that the rather extreme use of abstract concepts in physics in recent years seems to be very intimately related to the neglect of intuition for the sake of abstraction in scientific thinking. "However far we go away from the world of daily life, abstraction cannot work by itself, but is to be accompanied by intuition or imagination." He advocates that for the rejuvenation of fundamental physics a better position should be given to intuition or to "the sense of beauty."[61]

Tendency to Avoid Complex Ideas

Among the Eastern peoples, while the Indians were rather inclined to attach importance to the universal, the Japanese emphasized the individual. This difference in the way of thinking is revealed in various fields of thinking of the two peoples.

The best illustration of this fact is supplied by the poetical expression of objects. In Sanskrit, the cloud (*megha*) is often called *jalada* or *aṁbuda* (water giver), the bird *vihaṁga* (flyer in the air), the elephant *matamga* (meditative walker), the lotus *ambuja* (the flower which grows out of water). All of these are compound words, formed out of two words. And the fact that the last added word is derived from the root of a verb gives an abstract character to this compound word. The concrete and phenomenal meaning is brought about on the basis of this abstract meaning of the words from which the compound is made. As shown by these examples, the Indians loved abstract expression. But, in the Japanese language, the same things are expressed by words whose origin is obscure, at least to the consciousness of their users, and consequently, whose abstract meanings have been lost; examples are *kumo* (cloud), *tori* (bird), *zō* (elephant), *hasu* (lotus).

The Japanese language is, generally speaking, very poor in imaginative words based on abstract and universal ideas. By associating concrete and particular objects and qualities with abstract ideas, and by suffusing them with figurative suggestions of the ideas ultimately to be expressed, the Japanese writer inspires particular and emotional moods. The use of "*Makura-kotoba*" (literally, "pillow words") in *tanka* and other literary works offers revealing examples.

"With these *bows of catalpa,* we have made up our mind to *shoot* (*iru*) enemies and to expect not to return from this battle. So we write down the names of those who will certainly *join* (*iru*) the dead."

"My mother very often smoothed down my *black-as-a-crow* hair (*nubatama-no-kuro-kami*), but certainly she never dreamt that the day would come when this hair would be cut off (on my becoming a nun)."

The "association word," which is used quite often in literary works, is another example of this characteristic.

Consequently, the imaginative power of the Japanese people, ever since ancient times, has been limited to, and has rarely gone beyond the concrete and intuitive world of nature. "The ancient Japanese," says Dr. Tsuda, "are generally poor in imaginative power, the power to shape elaborate fantasy."[62] And this tendency, we may say, runs through Japanese literature to the present day. Accordingly, the Japanese people have never developed titanic myths. In this, they are like the Chinese. "Among our people, who have not formed the idea of God with a human personality, it was only natural that the stories of the Gods have not been developed."[63] In this respect, Japanese literature is less profound and not so imaginative as Indian literature.

The characteristic way of thinking pointed out here determined the form of assimilation of Buddhism, too. The Buddhist sūtras had never been translated into Japanese before the Meiji Restoration (1868). This means that the complicated Buddhist thought of the Indians has hardly penetrated as a whole into the life and thought of the Japanese people.

The lack of imagination was revealed in the process of transformation of the Jōdo religion (the sect of the Pure Land of *Amitābha*). The *nembutsu* ("Keeping the Buddha in mind") practiced by the Japanese is different from the *nembutsu* preached in India. In the latter case, for example, in early Buddhism and in the Great *Sukhāvatīvyūha-sūtra* and the *Amitāyurdhyāna-sūtra,* it chiefly consists in thinking of the Buddha, recalling his sublime features. The Amitābha, created by the imagination of the Indians, had extraordinarily gigantic features.[64]

"The body of Buddha Amitāyus is a hundred thousand million times as bright as the color of the *Jambūnada* gold of the heavenly abode of Yama; the height of that Buddha is six hundred thousand *niyutas* of *koṭis* of *yojanas* as innumerable as are the sands of the river Ganges.

"The white twist of hair between the eyebrows all turning to the right, is just like the five Sumeru Mountains. The eyes of Buddha are like the water of the four great oceans; the blue and the white are quite distinct. All the roots of hair of his body issue forth brilliant rays like the Sumeru Mountains. The halo of that Buddha is like a hundred millions of the Great Chiliocosmus; in that halo there are Buddhas miraculously created, to the number of a million of *niyutas* of *koṭis* as innumerable as the sands of the Ganges; each of these Buddhas has for attendants a great assembly of countless Bodhisattvas who are also miraculously created.

"Buddha Amitāyus has eighty-four thousand signs of perfection, each sign is possessed of eighty-four minor marks of excellence, each mark has eighty-four thousand rays, each ray extends so far as to shine over the worlds of the ten quarters, whereby Buddha embraces and protects all the beings who think upon him and does not exclude (any one of them)."

Thus, the *nembutsu* of the Indians was to contemplate these gigantic features of the Buddha by vivid imaginative power. The *nembutsu* preached by the Chinese, for example, by Master Tendai Chih-i, (538–597), had the same character. But, being transplanted onto Japanese soil, it was changed to the invocation of Amitābha following the teaching of Shan-tao of China.

Even in Japan, the clergyman Genshin (Bishop Enshin, 1072–1132), preached that the *nembutsu* consists in contemplating the features of the Buddha (*Shikisōkan.*) Genshin said: "The novice cannot practice the discipline of contemplation of the profound (esoteric). . . . The various sūtras preach the merit of (contemplation of) the features of the Buddha. Therefore, now is the time to practice this discipline." His *nembutsu,* however, went a step further toward the *nembutsu* as an invocation of Amitābha. He especially emphasized the importance of the *nembutsu* on the deathbed. "Even a man of lowest rank, if he practices *Jū-nen* which is the repetition of the name of Amitābha ten times, can be reborn in the Pure Land of Amitābha." His interpretation of *Jū-nen* differs from that of the Jōdo cult in China. According to Tao-ch'ue (562–645) in China, "To recall the whole features or the partial features of Amitābha, to contemplate them in reference to objects on that occasion, during ten moments of thought with no intervention of other ideas—this I call *Jū-nen.*" But, according to Genshin, "The so-called *Jū-nen,* although variously interpreted, is to repeat ten times, with heart and soul, 'Oh! save me, thou Amitābha!' "[65]

The *nembutsu* as an invocation of the Amitābha by oral recitation of his name acquired its absolute significance in Hōnen (1133–1212), the founder of the Jōdo sect. It was not easy for the unimaginative Japanese to contemplate, as preached by sūtras, the features of Amitābha, created by the imagination of the Indians. Hōnen perceived this difficulty. "Even if you try to contemplate the features of Amitābha, it will be difficult for you to visualize them as clearly as flowers and fruits of cherry, plum, peach, and damson."[66] Therefore, he prohibited the *nembutsu* as contemplation of the features of Amitābha. "Nowadays, the devotees should not practice contemplation. Even if you try to contemplate the features of Amitābha, it will be difficult to visualize its image as sculptured by Unkei or Kōkei (masters of sculpture)." Therefore, according to Hōnen, "The Original Vow of Birth in the Pure Land of Amitābha cannot be accomplished by such varied disciplines as, for example, image-making, tower-erecting, etc., but by the sole discipline of the repetition of the name of Amitābha, because the Original Vow is pledged to receive far and wide the whole mass of people." It was for these reasons that he turned to rely on the *nembutsu* of Shan-tao of China.

In "the Panegyric of the Birth in Pure Land" (*Ojō-Raisange*) of Shan-tao, we find the following dialogue. "Question: You do not allow contemplation, but exhort only invocation. Why, and with what intention, do you rely on such a practice?

"Answer: Now, all the people are obstructed by heavy burdens. Their mind is too coarse-grained to contemplate a subtle object (that is, Amitābha). Furthermore, their spirit is always oscillating in mid-air. Hence, sympathizing with their inability to attain their contemplation, the Great Sage (Buddha) exhorts the exclusive invocation of his name. It is owing to the easiness of invocation that the people can go to be born in the Pure Land of Amitābha only through the continuous practice of this discipline."[67]

Shinran (1173–1262) followed this standpoint of Shan-tao and Hōnen. He thought it was inconceivable for us, ordinary men, to contemplate the features of Amitābha. "O deadly sinner! Invoke Amitābha alone! He is taking hold of us. Though our eyes of flesh cannot clearly see him owing to our sins, yet is his mercy constantly present to illuminate our minds."[68]

The dancing and singing monk Ippen (1239-1289) said, "We should not try to see the Amitābha, except through invocation of him. Invocation is truly seeing Amitābha itself. The Amitābha seen by the eyes of flesh is not the true Amitābha."[69]

This difference between the Indian and the Japanese *nembutsu* illustrates how the Indian mentality, with its overflowing imagination and love of subtle introspective analysis, differs from that of the Japanese who are more inclined to depend mainly on concrete symbols.

In this sense of concreteness lies the difference between the Japanese Pure Land cult and the Indian *bhakti* religion. The first, having never been given to wanton imagination, could not develop frantic or ecstatic rituals. (Although such a tendency was not absent, it was regarded as an exceptional phenomenon and rejected by the Pure Land cult in general.)

The characteristic way of thinking, which we pointed out in the process of transformation of the Pure Land cult, can also be recognized in the case of *zazen* (*dhyāna,* to sit in contemplation). The Indians, in *samādhi,* silent meditation and abstraction of thought, kept an image or idea in mind; for example, they imagined that the universe is like space, or that it is larger than space, or that, on the contrary, it is smaller than a grain of rice, or that the soul is as large as a thumb. This type of discipline had been practiced in Buddhism as well as in Brahminism, since the days of the philosophers of the Upanishads. It was to keep the Buddha or truth in mind or to recall the Past Life. It may be called *the Zazen as contemplation of features.*[70]

In the Japanese Zen sect, however, *Zazen* aims at detachment from discursive knowledge, regardless of whether the latter is in the form of the deliberation of catechetic questions assigned by master, or in the form of endeavoring to do away with conceptualization. What Dōgen adopted as his motto was the precept: "Practice only sitting."

Japanese philosophy in the past has been influenced by this tendency to shun theoretical argument. The learning of exegesis and interpretation was enjoyed as ornamental literature in China, but the Japanese scholars endeavored to grasp only what they could utilize in that learning for practical understanding.

Examples of this characteristic inclination of concreteness can be found in the process of the Japanese assimilation of Buddhism. The commentary on sūtras by Prince Shōtoku of Japan is not pedantic at all. It is brief and to the point. But, the Chinese reference book which Prince Shōtoku made use of, the commentary of Master Chia-hsiang, Chi-tsang (549–623) of China, mentions many meanings in the interpretation of just one word. We cannot recognize, and the author does not try even to demonstrate, which of these meanings is the correct one. Therefore, so far as the purpose of clear exposition is concerned, the Commentary of Prince Shōtoku is superior, as Fujaku (1707–1781) had pointed out.[71] Of course, we cannot find this characteristic in all of the commentaries written by Japanese Buddhists. But, compared with the general tendency of the Chinese commentaries, the majority of the Japanese commentaries are rather succinct summaries. The Japanese not only studied the scholastic doctrines of the *Vijñaptimātratāsiddhi* or *Abhidharmakośa* in great detail, but also they wrote on them many commentaries which are brief and to the point.

It seems that the study of Confucianism in Japan showed the same tendency. The positivist scholars in the 18th and 19th centuries, in the Ch'ing period, who devoted their life to the exact philological study of Chinese classics, had never tried to summarize its results and to expose their essentials. But, the Japanese Confucians of the Archaist (*Kogaku*) school, inferior to the Chinese in the exactitude of their philological study, were very skilled in summarizing the results of their study and leaving them to posterity.[72]

Thus, most Japanese scholars concentrated their energies on arriving promptly at a conclusion. Their attitude may be called practical. In the past, they were, on the whole, rather weak in critical observation of nature and its logical reconstruction. One cause of this attitude may be found in the fact that the Japanese generally disliked complicated, structural thinking and valued practical things above all.

The tendency to avoid complicated, structural thinking was revealed also in the system of the Buddhist doctrines in Japan. In the critical classification of various sects according to their doctrines, the Chinese arranged them hierarchically, for example, by the five periods and the eight categories of Śākyamuni's teaching, or by the five and ten divisions of Buddhism of the Hua-yen school. The Japanese, on the contrary, simply distinguished doctrines of their own sect, on the one hand, from those of other sects, on the other. The Shingon sect calls itself the "esoteric school" and all other sects "exoteric schools." The Zen sect summarizes other sects under the name of "doctrinaire sects." The Pure Land sects contrast their own school of "the immediate salvation by faith in Amitābha" with the other ordinary schools of "the way of holiness by the process of practice." The complicated and hierarchical classification of the Chinese has never been adopted by the Japanese Buddhists. (Although a type of simple classification had already also appeared in China, we must point out that the Japanese especially prefer to classify things by simple types.)

It has been said that the Japanese people are adept in imitation and sterile in invention. They are apt not to try to understand a foreign culture through an abstract study of the general principles and structure. They import precipitately only those parts which can be put into practical use. How abundant, in fact, Japanese culture in the past was in such superficial imitations!

The originality of Japanese Buddhism has frequently been asserted by Japanese scholars. But it means chiefly that the Japanese simplified the Buddhism of the Continent and popularized it. It rarely criticized Continental Buddhism in its principles and structure.

The practical character of Japanese Buddhism is also frequently emphasized. It is true that, owing to its simplification, its disciplines could be practiced with ease by common people, and that it penetrated into their everyday life. But there was the danger of sacrificing theory for practice. For example, Dōgen said, "Buddhists should not discuss the relative merits of various doctrines or the relative profundity of various tenets. It is sufficient for them to know the truthfulness of disciplines."[73]

The Japanese people, because of their aversion to complicated, structural thinking, are inclined to reject the "doctrine of expediency," one of the most characteristic doctrines of Buddhism. Buddhism's original standpoint of "Preach according to each man's nature" permits clergymen to preach different doctrines to different persons—that is, to preach a doctrine suitable to each person. Eminent Buddhists in India were not worried about contradictions among the different doctrines adopted for "expediency." Chinese Buddhists conspicuously preserved this expedient standpoint in contrast to the Japanese Buddhists; for example, Hōnen, Shinran, and Nichiren rejected this doctrine as too complicated. They preached the same simple and consistent doctrine to all. Furthermore, Dōgen explained why he opposed the doctrine of expediency. "If a man asks about the essence of the doctrine and disciplines, certainly monks should answer by truth. They should not answer by false expediency, considering that his caliber is not sufficient, or that the truth cannot be understood by this uninitiated and unlearned man. The true meaning of the precepts of Bodhisattva is that, if the man of calibre of 'the Smaller Vehicle' asks about the Way of 'the Smaller Vehicle,' they should answer by the Way of 'the Greater Vehicle.' It is the same with the precepts for salvation, laid down by the Buddha during his life. The false doctrine of expediency is really not useful. The final (ultimate) true doctrine alone is useful. Accordingly, they should answer only by truth, without considering whether it will be understood by the questioner or not."[74]

Dōgen's rejection of expediency in the name of the one simple truth for all, can be discerned plainly in Nichiren also. All sūtras, except the Hokke Sūtra, preach the doctrine of expediency, and, therefore, must be rejected, he asserted. "In the Hokke Sūtra, it is preached in the beginning that 'the Exalted One will certainly preach the truth, after he taught the various doctrines for a long time,' and then, that 'There exist neither two doctrines nor three doctrines. The doctrine of expediency of the Buddha must be rejected.' And also that 'Rejecting expediency in earnest,' or 'Thou shalt not believe in any of the hymns of other sūtras.' Therefore, since the Good Law that 'There exists only one vehicle of the Buddha' is the Great Law which can accomplish the salvation of the mass of the people, the sūtras other than the Hokke Sūtra have no use at all."[75]

Characteristically, most Japanese Buddhists were single-minded. This may have some relation to the fact that the Japanese, as mentioned already, valued the virtue of honesty interpreted as simple truthfulness and loyalty. The special emphasis put on this virtue by Buddhists and common people in Japan, is, for one thing, associated with their aversion to complicated thinking in human relations.

Already in the Tokugawa period, Nakamoto Tominaga, defining the spiritual characteristics of the Japanese, said, borrowing the words of the *Analects* of Confucius, that they were honest, did not stick to complicated etiquette, and valued straightforwardness.[76] And Kanzan Matsumiya (1686–1780) said, "In our country, the Japanese people are simple and honest," and "The teaching of the gods" is "the doctrine of simplicity and honesty."[77]

Fondness for Simple Symbolic Expressions

Traditionally, the Japanese have been inclined to dislike fanciful, complicated expressions and to take to simple and naive expressions. The Japanese language, as pointed out already, is deficient in words expressing prolix and abstract conceptions. Consequently, even to this day, they use Chinese words, in most cases, to express abstract ideas.

In art, also, this tendency can be discerned clearly. The Japanese are very fond of the impromptu short verse, like the *haiku* and *tanka*. In the history of Japanese poetry, the long verse (*chōka*) is reduced to a short one (*tanka*), and then to a still shorter one (*haiku*). The extremely short form of artistic expression is characteristically Japanese and the like of it cannot be found elsewhere. Moreover, long verse-forms like epic poetry have never prospered in Japan. Not to mention the cases of Greek and Teutonic peoples, the Indians produced an epic of more than one hundred thousand verses, the *Mahābhārata*. Such an achievement would be hardly conceivable in the case of the Japanese. In Japanese literature, lyric poems and scenery sketches have been highly developed, but poems of grand style, with dramatic plots full of twists and turns, have made only a poor start.

Not only in poetry but also in architecture, we can recognize the characteristic love of simplicity. The Japanese imported various formative arts from Indian Buddhism, indirectly through the hands of Chinese and Koreans. As seen in the magnificent splendor of golden Buddhist altars and mural paintings of temples, the complicated sculptures of transoms, the fantastic statue of the Goddess of Mercy (Avalokiteśvara) with a thousand arms, the square diagram of figures (Maṇḍala) with its intricate and delicate composition—all of them had, in general, a very elaborate structure. But, such an art could hardly penetrate into the life of the common people. The Japanese could not abandon the simple and unpainted wooden architecture of ancient style, in many shrines as well as in the Great Shrine of Ise. And, even in the architecture of Buddhist temples, the various sects of the Kamakura period turned to a rather simple style. Also, in the Zen-influenced taste of the tea-ceremony house, we can discern a naive simplicity. The Japanese grave-marker (*sotoba*), which is a symbolic imitation of the gigantic cairn of the Indian people (*stūpa*), is nothing but a very small wooden tablet.

This simplicity, however, does not always mean the obliteration of all complexity. In some cases, especially under the influence of the Zen cult, the Japanese endeavored to infuse unlimited complexity into this simplicity. This tendency emerged especially in such arts as architecture, drawing, and poetry. For example, the void of empty spaces or of silent pauses is often not devoid, in fact, of important meaning. Even in the etiquette and conversation of everyday life, silence can be a very positive expression at times. This ideal fusion of the complex and the simple was realized by the Chinese people, who loved complicated thinking and whose spiritual life was greatly influenced by the Zen cult. When introduced into Japan, however, this, too, was altered by greater simplification.

Thus, the Japanese people, in general averse to forms of complicated thinking, have not been apt to think or imagine objects in relation to a universal structure. For example, in India, as well as in China, the worship of stars prospered, and myths and legends concerning them were numerous. The Chinese worshipped the Stars of the Cowboy (Altair) and of the Weaver (Vega). But the primitive Shintō in Japan, although it contained many and various folk religions as in the case of other peoples, did not worship stars.[78] When the Japanese imported the Chinese worship of stars, the star of the Weaver was identified with the Japanese Goddess of the Weaver (*Ame-no-tanabatahime-no-kami*), and its worship was transformed into the Festival of the Weaver (*Tanabata-matsuri*). In short, stars were not holy and austere gods for the Japanese. They were lovely and intimate heroes and heroines of familiar legends. The Japanese could not produce the sublime metaphorical expression of Kant, who wondered at both "the moral law within and the starry heavens above."

Thus, because complicated symbols were not used by the Japanese in their thinking, the philosophical theories of Indian and Chinese Buddhism were too profound, abstruse, and complicated to penetrate into the life of the common people in Japan. Consequently, they had to be simplified.

The Japanese, in assimilating Buddhism, did not depend upon its philosophical doctrines. Of course, the clergymen of large temples were engaged in philosophical debates and wrote a great number of books. The common people, however, demanded concrete and empirical clues rather than philosophical theories. Although they extolled the Lotus (Hokke) Sūtra and the *Suvarṇaprabhāṣa-sūtra* (Sūtra of Golden Splendor), they could not understand their philosophical theories. They valued only the incidental contents of sūtras, that is, their magical elements. The same attitude persists to this day.

In fact, Japanese Buddhism simplified doctrines, separating them from the study of philosophical theories, and transcended scholastic systems of doctrines. The Buddhist sects of the Nara period (710-784), which, as a whole, introduced and studied the Chinese doctrines, could not be propagated among common people. The Tendai and Shingon sects, introduced at the beginning of the Heian period (in the ninth century), followed, in the main, the doctrines of the Chinese sects of the same name. The Tendai sect, however, experienced an original development as time passed. This sect, developing the theory of the "Truth of All Beings" on the basis of the Lotus Sūtra, divided this sūtra into two parts—the first fourteen chapters (*Shakumon,* Section on Incarnation), relating to the purpose of the Buddha's earthly life and various teachings, and the following fourteen chapters (*Honmon,* Section on the Eternal Buddha), relating to the final revelation of the Buddha as the eternal one. The discipline of the contemplation of truth through these two gates (*Mon*) was called *Shikan* (the tranquility and contemplation of mind). But the new Tendai school of the Kamakura period went a step further. In its critical classification of doctrines of various sects, it relied on the fourfold criteria, and asserted that the first three criteria—(1) the doctrines delivered before the Lotus (Hokke) Sūtra (*Nizen*), (2) the doctrines delivered in *Shakumon,* (3) the doctrines delivered in *Honmon*—should be "discarded." Then, and only then, the last and the true criterion—the contemplation of the absolute truth (*Kan*)—arises. This standpoint clearly values practice based on non-discursive wisdom above complicated, theoretical wisdom.

In Japan, Pure Land Buddhism also developed in the sole direction of belief in, and reliance on Amitābha. The Pure Land Buddhism which has been prevalent in China up to this day is conflated with Zen Buddhism and other various forms of faith. In Japan, however, the faith in, and reliance on Amitābha has been preserved in a purer form.

The devotional faith in Pure Land became prevalent in the Kamakura period (1185–1333). But even before that—in fact, throughout the Heian period—the devotees of this cult were numerous.[79] But, it was Hōnen who advocated the doctrine of invocation of the Pure Land of Amitābha (*Jōdo-nembutsu*) on theoretical ground, detaching it from other doctrines. Hōnen preached that the period of degeneration and extinction of the Buddha-law (*Mappō*) has come. Men cannot attain higher perception (*Satori*) by various disciplines. They shall be given salvation only through faith in Amitābha. Renounce the spirit of self-relying disciplines; shut the gate of silent meditation and cultivation of virtues; ignore all of the devices; throw away all knowledge; and concentrate on the one discipline of invocation of the Buddha.[80] Thus, Hōnen's admonition to "renounce, shut, ignore, and throw away" is one of the most famous assertions in the history of Japanese Buddhism. Rejecting all the other doctrines, he chose the doctrine of *Jōdo-nembutsu* (The Choice of *Nembutsu* as the Original Vow of the Buddha).

The disciples of Hōnen went further in the direction of simplification of the Pure Land cult. One of them advocated the following extreme doctrine: "Saint Hōnen repeated the name of the Buddha (*nembutsu*) seventy thousand times a day, but such verbal repetition is only an external expediency. There exists a true interior meaning unknown to ordinary men. What I call true is this: If you penetrate into, and believe in, the Original Vow of Amitābha, and repeat his name only once, you can go, at once, to be born in the Pure Land of Amitābha. Thus, the practice of the Pure Land cult will be accomplished. You can go to the Pure Land, if you invoke the Buddha only once. You need not invoke his name many times. And the ultimate meaning is to penetrate into, and believe in, the Original Vow."[81] There appeared some who went so far as to say: "Those who want to repeat invocations do not, in fact, believe in the Vow of the Buddha."[82]

In the direction of simplification, Shinran, too, went further than Hōnen. According to him, invocation of the name of Amitābha, that is, "Oh, save me, thou Amitabha!" (*Namuamidabutsu*), is the essence and idol of the fundamental sūtra, *the Larger Sukhāvatīvyūha-sūtra*. To understand the words or sentences of this sūtra, is not so important. The consummation of faith consists in the invocation of Amitābha. Hōnen advocated that the name of Amitābha should be repeated sixty thousand times a day, but Shinran rejected this doctrine as meaningless. Although he inherited the terms of the pure and exclusive discipline, he changed the meaning completely. "You should believe, with an exclusive, pure, and sincere heart, in the Original Vow that we can go to be born in the Pure Land of Amitābha if we say '*Namuamidabutsu*' only once. This discipline can be called the pure and exclusive discipline."[83] "The exclusive heart referred to in the Commentary (the *Sanzengi* of Zendō) is nothing but the single heart. It states that we should not have two hearts. The exclusive discipline referred to is nothing but a single discipline. It expresses that we should not have two disciplines."[84]

Thus, the doctrine of *one-time-nembutsu* reached its climax in Shinran. Although it had been embraced by many devotees of the Pure Land cult before him, it was Shinran that gave it a theoretical expression.[85]

Since then, Ippen, the founder of the Ji sect, advocated the *nembutsu*, too. According to a legend, he, on his deathbed, "burnt down, with his own hands, the books in his possession, and said that all the holy doctrines of the whole life of the Buddha were reduced to *nembutsu*."[86] Rennyo, too, valued "the image of Amitābha more than his statue, his name more than his image."[87]

Then, in the Japanese Pure Land cult, the invocation of "*Namuamidabutsu*" had a central significance. On this point, it was quite different from the *nembutsu* practiced by the Chinese. When the Chinese Buddhist clergymen greet each other, saying, "*Amitōfo*" (Amitābha), it has only an external significance.[88]

As the Pure Land cult was simplified in the direction of *nembutsu*, the doctrine of the Tendai sect, which embraced the teaching of the Lotus

(Hokke) Sūtra, was simplified in the direction of "*Daimoku*" (the heading of the sūtra).

In the Japanese Tendai sect, it was considered difficult for common people to understand the philosophical theories of the Lotus Sūtra. Dengyō is said to have preached: "For ordinary men, who are born among the extremely inferior men of the lowest status in the period of degeneration and extinction of the Buddha-law, it is vain to endeavor to pretend to be an ascetic figure that is fresh and unobscured by nature. The men of superior disposition and wisdom should practice disciplines and acquire merits. For those of inferior disposition and wisdom, the Buddha has bequeathed the panacea that summarizes the holy teaching of all his life—the five words of *Myō-hō-ren-ge-kyō* (the Sūtra of the Lotus of the Good Law). Therefore, this heading was preached and propagated far and wide among the multitude of all spheres of existence during the last five hundred years of the period of degeneration and extinction of the Buddha-law." Thus, according to Dengyō, the panacea for salvation of the common people is not the philosophical theories of the Lotus (Hokke) Sūtra, but its heading of five words, *Myō-hō-ren-ge-kyō*. Then, before the appearance of Nichiren, in the new Tendai doctrine of the Kamakura period, it was preached that, to attain salvation, it was sufficient to practice only the invocation of the heading of the Lotus Sūtra, and not any troublesome contemplation—for example, the simultaneous contemplation from the viewpoints of "void," "fictions," and "middle," or the contemplation of the three thousand spheres in one thought. "If you repeat *Namumyōhōrengekyō* on your deathbed, you can, by virtue of the Three Powers of the Good Law, attain the state of the enlightened mind and deliver yourself from the burden of birth and death."[89] "The contemplation of the three thousand spheres in one thought, on your deathbed, is nothing but the invocation of the Sūtra of the Good Law (*Myō-hō-ren-ge-kyō*). *Myō* corresponds to one thought, *Hō* to the three thousand spheres; therefore, these two are synonymous with the three thousand spheres in one thought. On your deathbed, you should just repeat *Myō-hō-ren-ge-kyō* with your whole heart."[90] And, in fact, the devotees, who repeated only this heading, were already numerous in the Heian period.[91]

It was Nichiren, however, that pushed this doctrine to its "logical" conclusion. "In the Hokke Sūtra," he said, "you should consider that the reading of the whole eight volumes, or one volume, or one chapter, or one hymn, or one sentence can have no more value than the reading of one heading."[92] "This sūtra, I think, states that the assignment of one heading or one hymn is sufficient as a duty of the devotee, and decides that the time of its practice must be the time when you rejoice wholeheartedly in the doctrine. Generally speaking, the gigantic treasury of Buddhist scriptures of eighty thousand volumes or the vast sūtra of eight volumes (Hokke Sūtra) exists only to preach these five words. . . . Only by the repetition of *Namumyōhōrengekyō*, can you atone for all your sins and have all blessings."[93] Pushing the argument to the extreme, regardless of the historical connection of the various doctrines, we can say that the religion of Nichiren, so far as the love of simplicity is concerned, is nothing but the replacement of the name of Amitābha by the heading of the Hokke Sūtra. Nichiren said: "The saying of 'Embrace only this sūtra' (which is preached in the Hokke Sūtra), does not mean a study of the whole sūtra. It means simply that we should embrace only the heading, with no intervention of other sentences."[94] Clearly this was not the original use of the sūtra. The simplification that the invocation of the heading is sufficient for salvation has never been adopted in other countries. And, with this simplification, the sect of exclusive faith in the Hokke Sūtra was established, a phenomenon also unknown in other countries.

Thus, the devotees of *Nembutsu* as well as of the "Heading" have relied on the simple symbol of faith. Then, we must consider the case of the Zen cult. Eisai (1141–1215), who introduced the Rinzai Zen sect, brought the various cults into his Zen cult. But Dōgen (1200–1253), who introduced the Sōtō Zen sect, taught repeatedly to "endeavor exclusively to sit in meditation (*dhyāna, zazen*)." He said, "The study and practice of the doctrine of the Zen cult is the freedom from the burden of body and soul (*shin-jin-datsuraku*). Incense burning, adoration, *nembutsu*, confession, sūtra-reading are unnecessary. It is necessary only to sit in meditation."[95] Once a man asked Dōgen if the devotees of Zazen might practice the discipline of magical formulae of the Shingon sect and also that of tranquility and contemplation of mind of the Tendai sect. He answered: "When I asked my Master about the true secrets, while I was in China, he said he had never heard that the Great Masters of all ages and all countries, who had transmitted the Buddha-seal, had practiced those disciplines. In fact, if you don't concentrate yourself in one discipline, you can never attain even one wisdom."[96]

Therefore, according to Dōgen, the idle study of doctrines was meaningless. "It is the same in the case of sūtras. In spite of their immensity, we should believe in and devote ourselves to one hymn or one sentence. We cannot understand the eighty thousand (doctrines)."[97] "Erudition and extensive reading are unattainable for us. We must renounce this design resolutely. We should concentrate ourselves in one discipline only, learn the views and usages, and follow the practices of the predecessors, with no pretention of being a teacher or a leader."[98]

Dōgen preached that clergymen should themselves concentrate on only one discipline with their whole body and soul. "Even men of the world should not practice many disciplines simultaneously if they wish to be adept in any of them. Rather they should practice only one discipline so as to be more adept in it than other people. . . . If they want to practise the various disciplines of the vast Buddha-doctrine, they cannot accomplish any of them. Even when they concentrate on one discipline, its accomplishment during their life is difficult for those of poor disposition by nature. Hence, the devotees should endeavor to concentrate on one discipline exclusively."[99] When Ejō, one of his disciples, asked him what discipline among the Buddha-laws he should practice wholeheartedly, Dōgen answered: "Although it must be decided according to each man's nature and disposition, it is Contemplation that has been transmitted and practiced exclusively from ancient masters. This discipline can conform to all kinds of nature and be practiced by all sorts of dispositions." Thus, he was opposed to one of the traditional doctrines of Buddhism, the doctrine that preaching must conform to the nature of each different person (*Taiki-seppō*).

On this point the Zen cult advocated by Dōgen is diametrically opposed to that of the Chinese. In Chinese Buddhism, practically only the Zen cult prevailed after the Sung period, but it practiced various disciplines including the Pure Land cult and the esoteric cult of the Shingon sect, and occasionally the disciplines of Early Indian Buddhism (*Vinaya-piṭaka*) also. To Dōgen, however, this eclecticism was psychologically unbearable. So he simplified Buddhism in the direction of only one discipline of Contemplation.

Although Dōgen objected to the loud repetition of *nembutsu* by the multitude of the devotees of the Pure Land Buddhism, comparing it to the voice of frogs, he sympathized completely with the exclusiveness of their disciplines. Kūamidabutsu, who had been a famous scholar of the exoteric and esoteric teachings, retiring from the world and living in a hermitage on Mt. Kōya, devoted himself to *nembutsu*. When, one day, a clergyman of the esoteric school visited him and asked him about the esoteric doctrines, he said: "I have forgotten everything. I do not remember a word."[100] Dōgen admired the thoroughness of this discipline, and therefore, agreed with the devotees of the Japanese Pure Land Buddhism, with respect to reliance on simple symbolic expression.

It has been frequently pointed out that the Zen cult exerted an enormous influence on the *Bushidō* (Way of Warriors) culture of the *samurais*. The extreme simplicity and frugality of life and deeds of Zen priests might have captured the imagination of *samurais*, warriors of the upper class who risked their life on the battlefield where scholastic doctrines of Buddhism were of no use. The sincerity of the simple doctrines "we do not value words" (*Fu-ryū-mon-ji*) or "We point to the human mind directly" (*Jiki-shi-nin-shin*) appealed to them. The spiritual training of the Zen sect, which can control the human mind completely through the very simplicity of the training, could well be practiced by the *samurais*. In the Chinese Zen cult, no accounts report that Zen clergymen taught warriors readiness for death. However, such accounts abound in Japan after the simplification of the Zen cult.

Furthermore, the Zen cult exerted a great influence on various aesthetic aspects of Japanese culture, for example, in architecture, painting, the seventeen-syllable verse (*Haiku*), flower arrangement, the tea-ceremony, etc. This influence was also largely due to the fact that the Zen cult in Japan had wholly abandoned complexity and prolixity and contained an impressive significance in its relaxed silence.

The simplification of complicated doctrines can be recognized also in the various old sects of Buddhism, early introduced into Japan. The idealistic philosophy of the Hossō sect was too difficult and complicated to be understood by common people. Therefore, Jōkei (1155–1213) advocated that ignorant people, who could not understand the doctrines of idealism, should, at least, repeat always the Praise, transmitted and taught by Three Great Sages: "The devotee of the Mahāyāna contemplates that the contents of all objects are nothing but the creation of mind, and then he effaces his own views as he does with external objects. That is to say, he contemplates and understands fully that nothing exists but the content of ideas created by himself. Thus, remaining within himself, he knows that external objects are non-existent, and furthermore, that the cognizing subject is non-existent. Then he can attain, for the first time, the state of liberty, free from everything."[101] In the Kegon sect, too, Myōe (1173–1232) taught that, in the case of common believers, it was not necessary to understand the doctrines, but to repeat "Homage to the Three Jewels and the Mind of Enlightenment. May my prayer come to be realized to perfection here as well as hereafter," or "Alas, the Three Jewels! Save me in my after-life."[102]

The cult of Maitreya, which prospered in the Kamakura period, taught the same doctrines as the Pure Land Buddhism under the influence of the faith in Amitābha. "If we practice the vow of abstention only for a moment, we can have superior happiness in our after-life, and if we invoke the name of Maitreya just once, we can go to be born in his Pure Land in some life or other. Its practice is very easy and its virtue is most great. Only by virtue of the Original Vow of the Benevolent Lord we can share its merits. This pleases all the Great Sages and it is craved by all ordinary men."[103] "According to the teaching of the Ascent Sūtra, it is very easy to be born in the Paradise of Maitreya (Tuṣita). If we crave this ascent only for a moment, and if we practice invocation just once, we can attain our cherished desire."[104] And in the Heian period and thereafter, there had been many devotees who had faith in Kṣitigarbha-Bodhisattva and repeated only his name.[105] The faith in the *dhāraṇī*, especially *Kōmyō-shingon-dhāraṇī* (Spell of Splendor) or *Hōkyōin-dhāraṇī* (Spell of the Jewelled Casket Seal), was propagated among the common people. And, so far as the way of thinking is concerned, the creed of itinerant priests (*Shugen-dō*) was a development in this direction of simplification, too. "The itinerant priests, though they have En-no-Gyōja (En the Ascetic, c. 800) and Jōzō-kisho as their predecessors, are only the devotees of one *dhāraṇī*."[106] The understanding of the whole content of *Shingon-dhāraṇī* was not demanded. It was sufficient for them to repeat any of those *dhāraṇīs*.

The tendency to fondness for simple symbols appeared in the process of adoption of Buddhist ideas by Japanese Shintoists in ancient and medieval times. It has been already mentioned that the moral ideas of Shintō were influenced by Buddhism. Shintō, in the process of its development as religion, advanced from the cleanness of the body to the idea of cleanness of spirit. This "internal cleanness" was expressed by moral virtues of "sincerity" and "honesty."[107] The virtues of gods of Shintō were admired through these virtues. But we can find these terms in the Buddhist sūtras. Besides, the benevolence and wisdom, admired as virtues of gods, are, of course, Buddhist terms. Therefore, it is not too much to say that almost all of the terms of the central virtues of medieval Shintō were derived from Buddhist sūtras. It must be pointed out, however, that Shintoists never adopted the doctrines of Buddhism indiscriminately. Only the virtues, which had originally existed as germs in Shintō, were brought to definite consciousness and expression by the help of Buddhist philosophy. The Shintoists did not take in the speculative, schematized, and generalized classifications of virtues of the Indian Buddhism, such as the Four Noble Truths, the Eight Right Ways, the Twelve Nidānas, the Six Pāramitās. They took in directly those virtues which happened to appear congenial to Shintō. Consequently, they hardly endeavored to interpret the relations among these virtues systematically and speculatively.

We have tried to demonstrate that through the process of assimilation of Buddhism many Japanese people are inclined to give direction to their practice through very simple symbols. This tendency reappeared, it seems, in the introduction of Christianity from the period of the Civil Wars to the beginning of the Tokugawa period in the 17th century. The Japanese Christians devoted themselves to such simple symbols of Christianity as the cross. The trampling of the holy image (*Fumi-e*) sufficed, on this psychological ground, as a loyalty test at the time of the Christian Inquisition in Japan.

We may say that religion is always simplified when it is popularized.

In the West, Christianity was simplified, for example, by making the sign of the cross, or by repetition of abbreviated passages of the Bible. In India, too, the Bhakti sects developed the same thought. Tulsidas (c. 1550), the author of the Hindi version of Rāmāyana, went so far as to say that the name of the Lord is greater than the Lord himself. Therefore, it may be safely said that simplification is common to the popularization of all religions. The Japanese religions, however, preached that it is sufficient to rely on simple symbolic expressions. This remarkable characteristic may correspond to the fact that Buddhism was more popularized in Japan than in other countries.

This tendency of thinking persists to this day. If we look back to the trend of Japanese thought in recent years, we can realize that the complete reliance upon simple symbols has been one of the most deep-rooted attitudes of the Japanese people.

Lack of Knowledge Concerning the Objective Order

Since the Japanese people for the most part tend to make little of objects unless they are related to familiar human relations, they do not study things enough in their objective or impersonal relations.

This tendency can be discerned in linguistic expressions of the Japanese. In the first place, the original Japanese language, as already mentioned, was not adequate for exact objective statements. Of course, this does not mean that the foundation for the recognition of the objective order is totally lacking in Japanese forms of expression. As one of the foundations, which can be used as a basis for such cognition, we may mention the distinction between the noun and the adjective in Japanese. The ancient Indian and the Chinese languages did not have such a strict distinction. In these languages, therefore, we can distinguish nouns (substantives) and adjectives (attributes) only through words in phrases or through context. These languages, so far as linguistic expression is concerned, do not distinguish very clearly between the judgment of classification and that of attribution. In Japanese, however, nouns are indeclinable and are distinguished from adjectives, which are declinable words. Therefore, we can recognize at once the distinction between the individual-substantive and the universal-attributive. On this point, Japanese resembles the Western languages, and, like them, it attracts our attention to the order or laws of the objective world of nature.

The Japanese people, however, in their characteristic way of thinking, are inclined to grasp this order or law in relation to human relations rather than as a law of objective things. This tendency has been strengthened especially through the non-logical character of the Japanese language.

Consequently, the thinking of the Japanese people has not been developed in an objective and logical direction. Rather the social rank of the person addressed and the concrete description of individuality have been emphasized. From the oldest times, the spiritual life of the Japanese has been concentrated chiefly in morals and art, not in objective knowledge. While works of literature and history in Japanese are many and excellent, scientific books in Japanese until very recently have been few. In theoretical and literary matters, the Japanese people thought and wrote mostly in the Chinese language.

This neglect of objective cognition is reflected in the usage of the Japanese language. In the original Japanese language, there is no word that expresses the object as opposed to the subject. The word "*mono*" may mean a person as subject as well as a thing as object. In such a situation, it cannot be expected that the word "*shiru*" (to know) will be employed to denote the cognition of objects as existing apart from knowing subjects. In other words, the emphasis is put rather on the understanding of inner experiences and on the feelings or mutual understanding among men, as shown by the usage of "*Nasake-o-shiru*" (to understand the feeling) and of "*Hito-to-shiri-au*" (to understand each other). Chiefly directed toward the expression of human relations, the pure Japanese language has no word corresponding to impersonal or purely objective "knowledge" or "cognition."[108] Largely as the result of Western influence have the Japanese people attained any degree of scientific self-consciousness and objective perception—that is, the perception of things as distinguished from perceiving subjects.

This characteristic appears also in the syntax. In the Indo-European languages, the nominative case of a noun, in the neutral singular, takes the same form as the accusative or objective. This is explained as follows: originally, the neutral nouns were not used as subject and consequently did not have the subjective form. Then, when they came to be used as subject, the independent subjective form was not created, and the objective form was used as subject. Perhaps, in ancient times, objective things were not personified and consequently were not used as subject. And while the Indo-European languages passed this stage early, the Japanese language has not completely emerged from it yet. In Japanese sentences, the subject is, in most cases, a human being or personified subject of action. And, in customary usage, the composition of the passive voice is rare—that is, objective things or the object of action are rarely used as subject.

The Japanese people, in general, do not give objective representation to the self as the subject of action. In Japanese, "*mizukara*" (self) is not a noun, but an adverb, that is, it is not perceived as an abstract conception. The word "*onore*" (self) is often used as noun, but it is rare that it is used as subject. The Japanese have therefore never used words which mean self—for example, *"ware," "onore," "mizukara"*—as philosophical terms, as in the languages of other civilized peoples. To express the self-examination common in Buddhist philosophy, the Japanese relied on such Chinese terms as *"ga"* or *"goga"* (self), used in the Chinese version of sūtras.

Thus, the Japanese people have seldom confronted objective reality as sharply distinguished from knowing subjects. This attitude may be called their common way of thinking. It is often said that they are practical and adept in techniques of action, but that they are rather weak in studying the objective basis of their practical action because they are too anxious to accomplish the action. It is partially owing to this characteristic that they have been inclined, for centuries, to follow foreign ideas with an uncritical mind.

Although it has been mentioned already, it is worthwhile to repeat that the Japanese in general have not traditionally given enough consideration to the importance of theoretical reasoning. Owing to the neglect of abstract reasoning they have been used to depending chiefly upon the senses. Frois, who came to Japan as a Christian missionary in the sixteenth century, said that the common people in Japan "will accept nothing but the concrete demonstration which can be seen by eyes and taken by hands."[109]

In the history of technology also the Japanese people have valued and still value intuitive perception (*Kan*) more than scientific inferences based on postulational thinking. They were apt to rely on the dexterity of artisans rather than on exact calculation by machines. For example, the proper temperature of hot water in which a forged sword (*katana*) was immersed was kept in absolute secrecy by swordsmiths, who cut off the arms of men who had tried to steal this secret. Thus, this temperature has been transmitted from master to disciple, as a secret which must be understood only through intuition.

On account of this situation, the natural sciences have almost never been established on the foundation of traditional Japanese thinking. Even in Japan, some pioneers were aware of this fact. For example, Kōkan Shiba (1747–1818), who cultivated Western methods of realistic painting and precise engravings of the globe, said: "The people of this country don't like to investigate the laws of universe. . . . They are shallow-minded and shortsighted."

The natural sciences were begun in Japan only in modern times through the introduction of sciences from Holland (*Ran-gaku*). And these sciences were not understood theoretically from fundamental principles, but were introduced rather from the standpoint of utility. Moreover, the importance of natural sciences was hardly recognized. Norinaga Motoori

(1763–1828), admitting that "the learning of the country called Holland" was universal science, common to all countries, still asserted "the superiority of the Emperor's Land."

In Japan, the science of cognition of nature had no mathematical foundation. Yukichi Fukuzawa (1834–1901), who popularized modern Western ideas in Japan, said, "Comparing the Confucianism of the East with the ideas of Western civilization, we find that two things are lacking in the East. The first is, among material things, mathematics. The second is, among immaterial things, the independent spirit." What he called "mathematics" seems to be modern mathematical physics.[110] Although not limited to Japan only, the neglect of scientific method seems to have affected the way of thinking of the Japanese people for a longer period in the modern era than other peoples of the world's leading nations. The Japanese of the past for a long time were inclined to neglect the rational perception of laws of the objective world of nature.

In general, the Japanese have not studied scientifically the language which they use every day. Before 1868 (the Restoration of Meiji), they had no standard system of grammar. During the preceding Tokugawa period, the Japanese language was not included in the curriculum. In India, the case is diametrically opposite, and grammar was taught regularly. It seems that in Greece and Rome also, people received an education in the grammar of their own language, although to a lesser extent than in India.

The way of thinking used to acquire knowledge, not by objective methodology, but through human relationships, can be seen in the process of introducing Indian logic. This has been discussed already. (What has been pointed out here cursorily has been admitted by many as one of the characteristics of the ways of thinking of the Japanese. However, in the process of the introduction of Buddhist thought there seems to be no easy way of finding the causes contributing to this very feature. It seems to be due to the fact that, as Buddhist culture in China had little to do with sciences, there occurred no need to modify Indian Buddhist logic when it was imported into Japan. The relationship between Indian Buddhism and science should be investigated independently.)

CHAPTER 37 PROBLEM OF SHAMANISM

The weakness of the critical spirit of the Japanese allowed the persistence of old ideologies that should have been abolished or modified by radical social changes. Although we have seen many social changes in the course of history, these changes have not reached the remote villages. In out-of-the-way corners, therefore, there persist, or occasionally crop out anew, the most primitive ways of living and thinking, of which Shamanism is one. Shamanism, as it is well known, was prevalent in the Asiatic continent as a religious superstition which endowed certain individuals with the gift of wielding magical power and of communicating with evil spirits. Shamanism also entered into the ancient Japanese religion.

Before the introduction of modern ideas and culture from the continent, mediums occupied a central position in the Japanese religious world. Since the mediums were always descendants of powerful gods, they could, it was generally believed, exorcise evil spirits by themselves, because it was believed, they had inherited divine powers. Hence these mediums, or those families certain members of which could be qualified as mediums, were revered by the community. They belonged to a special, honorable class, and common people managed their affairs in accordance with oracles, or the advice of the mediums. In this connection, we may suppose that charms and divinations, or something of the sort, were popular among the Japanese from time immemorial.

Now let us inquire into what modification Buddhism underwent during its first introduction into Japan under the influence of such a peculiar religious form as Shamanism. Orthodox Buddhism repudiates all of these shamanistic tendencies. Early Buddhism denied the spiritual powers peculiar to the Brahmins who were in charge of exorcism and sacred rites. This ban was also placed on magic and like matters. It was furthermore urged that one must not believe in dream-reading, palmistry, horoscopes, and divination from the cries of birds and beasts.[1] On the other hand, Buddhism could not be propagated among the lower classes of the Japanese people, which preserved, without radical changes, the old shamanistic tendency. In the case of the propagation of Christianity in the Occident, the new religion brought about a great revolution in European society. In Japan, at every critical moment when the ruling classes had lost their control over the peasantry, the primitive or shamanistic trends, which lay hidden from earliest times, came to the fore.

Let us, then, consider the problem historically. First, at the time when Buddhism was introduced into Japan, it had to have, in order to be diffused among the common people, a shamanistic character, since the shamanistic religious modes were then influential. The Ritsu sect, having preserved the manners of Conservative Buddhism, had little influence over the Japanese. This sect did not meet with great favor among the people; however, some other sects of Buddhism did meet with approval among the populace, because they made concessions to the shamanistic tendency to a considerable degree.

The most striking phenomenon in Buddhism as it was introduced into Japan was that there were relatively many nuns in proportion to priests. This may have been due to the fact that great importance was attached to nuns, paralleling the importance of female mediums who had particular qualifications to serve the gods.[2]

As a new religion, Buddhism was compelled to meet the popular requirement that it should be effective in exorcism. The Japanese type of Buddhism was largely one of prayer and exorcism. It mainly aimed at praying for benefits and wealth in this world and the next, in the interest of the state as well as of individuals. Even the reading of sūtras was considered to have an exorcistic significance, so that the most philosophic Buddhist schools could not be secure in their positions unless they compromised with this tendency. Although Ekan, who came to Japan in 625 (he was born in Korea, and studied Buddhism in China), introduced the doctrine of the Sanron sect, members of which reasoned always with extreme logical accuracy, it is said that he himself prayed for rain on the occasion of a long drought, and when he obtained a heavy rain, Empress Suiko, who reigned in 593–629, appreciated very much his service and appointed him a bishop. Nevertheless, the philosophic sects of Sanron (Three Treatises) and Hossō (Idealism) were ultimately not diffused among the Japanese. Sects which sought to spread all over the country had to adopt shamanistic or magical interpretations of Buddhism.

If we look at the course of diffusion of Buddhism, we note that the new religion was, in the first place, accepted by the nobility to meet its requirements in the mid-sixth century. The nobility at that time constructed many temples for the purpose of praying for the prosperity and permanency of their aristocratic life. Prayers were addressed to Śākyamuni for recovery from sickness and long life, to Avalokiteśvara for protection from evil, and also to the other Bodhisattvas: Bhaiṣajya-guru, Maitreya,

The Four God-kings, etc. From the Suiko period on, there were erected many statues of Avalokiteśvara. As for sūtras, the *Suvarṇaprabhāṣa Sūtra* (Sūtra of Golden Splendor), the *Saddharmapuṇḍarīka* or Hokke (Lotus) Sūtra (especially the 25th Chapter on Avalokiteśvara), *Ninnō-prajñā-pāramitā Sūtra* (Sūtra of the Perfect Wisdom of Benevolent Kings), the *Bhaiṣajyaguru Sūtra,* and so on, were recited; but this was for the main purpose of supplication, for health, long life, and recovery, since the sūtras were believed to be pregnant with magical power. After the centralization of political power in Japan, there was a vigorous advocacy of the principle that Buddhism should have as its object the protection of the state, the tranquility of the Imperial Court, and the wealth of the people. This was based upon the popular belief that the State should be guarded, that people's lives should become easier by the miraculous virtue which might be given in reciting and copying sūtras and treating monks and nuns with dinners, etc.

It was almost the same in the Heian period (after 784), excepting that the esoteric school then was more popular than the earlier schools of Buddhism. About the 7th and the 8th centuries, as far as we know now, one hundred and thirty-seven scriptures of esoteric teaching were imported, including such fundamental scriptures of that type as the *Mahāvairocana-sūtra* (The Great Sun Sūtra), the *Kongōchōkyō* (The Diamond Head Sūtra), *Susiddhi-sūtra* (The Sūtra of Perfection).

Apart from Buddhas, Bodhisattvas, gods, and spirits mentioned in the above scriptures, there were, as objects of worship, the bodhisattvas of esoteric lineage: Kannon with Eleven Faces, Kannon with Nine Faces, Kannon with a Thousand Hands, Amoghapāśa, Kannon with Horse-head, Beautiful-sight Kannon, Vajragarbha (Bodhisattva), Peacock-King (*Mahāmāgurī*), five powerful Bodhisattvas, and so forth. Buddhistic morality sometimes manifested itself in the decree of liquor prohibition and in forbidding the taking of all animal life, but they were invoked only under the particular circumstances of drought, deluge, indisposition of His Majesty, and other national calamities. This was, after all, an application in the Buddhist mould of the theocratic way of thinking peculiar to Japanese antiquity. Various Buddhistic services in the Court were of the same magical significance as Shintō rituals. They bore just the same meaning as the rituals of Shintō purification in their motives and purposes.

It is noteworthy that, in Japan, the Imperial family and the nobility were closely associated with esoteric schools. The instances when the members of the Imperial family and Court nobility became devout believers are too many to be enumerated in detail. These converts believed solely in the esoteric teaching, including not only the Shingon sect but also the Tendai sect. So many instances of the conversion of the governing-class members to esoteric sects had never been seen either in India or in China. This is why we have offered the hypothesis that shamanistic and theocratic tendencies were disguised in the Buddhist forms of the time.

A characteristic of Japanese Buddhism, subsequently, was the overwhelming predominance of Shingon esoterics over the religious world, at least before the Restoration.[3] Unlike the other Buddhist schools, the esoteric schools are recognized as the ones which deal with magic and divination forbidden by orthodox Buddhism.[4] Although Shingon esotericism originated in India and then was transmitted to China, there remains little trace of it extant in these countries, whereas in Japan esoteric rituals and manners persist even now. The esoteric doctrine, though it had its source in China, was so highly developed in Japan that it came to be almost a new and nearly original one in its content. The Tendai sect, although it was in opposition to the Shingon sect, had, from the beginning, adopted the esoteric teaching,[5] whose tenets had grown rapidly upon the sect, in the 9th century, after Master Jikaku (Ennin, 784–864) and Master Chishō (Enchin, 814–891).[6] As for esoteric studies, two scholastic lineages were formed, namely, "The esoterics of the Tōji sect (*Tōmitsu*)," handed down in the Tō (Eastern) Temple of the Shingon sect, and "The esoterics of the Tendai sect (*Taimitsu*)," transmitted in the Tendai sect. The former adopted the doctrine of the Kegon sect and the latter went by the doctrine of the Tendai sect.

These two lineages were divided into the legitimate line and collateral line, respectively; and furthermore, various interpretations of esoterics arose in each legitimate line. Shingō (?–1004) and Eison (1201–1290)—these two scholars, though they had been reared in the "Tōmitsu" school, interpreted the esoterics by the idealism of the Hossō sect. Their interpretation has been called "Esoterics of the Hossō sect (*Sōmitsu*)." By the doctrine of the Kegon sect as well, Kōben (1173–1232), of the Kegon sect, gave a new interpretation of it, which is "the esoterics of the Kegon sect (*Gonmitsu*)." Moreover these esoteric schools exerted an influence upon the Zen sect. For example, Eisai (1141–1215) founded "the esoterics of the Zen sect (*Zenmitsu*)" by adopting "*Taimitsu.*" Benni (1202–1280) introduced "*Tōmitsu*" into the doctrine of the Zen sect. The esoteric rituals have been held also in the Rinzai sect. Dōgen (1200–1253) persistently repudiated all of these esoteric interpretations, but, after the time of Jōkin Keizan (the founder of Sōji Temple), the esoteric rituals were adopted by the Sōtō sect so that its order might be able to propagate the teaching all over the country. In general, the esoteric modifications of Zen by secret transmission became popular from the Muromachi period (1336–1573) onwards.

At the mid-Tokugawa period (ca. 1750) however, Hakuin (1685–1768) inaugurated reforms in the Rinzai sect so as to eliminate the esoteric elements of the teaching. Moreover, since Menzan and Manzen of the Sōtō sect advocated returning to the spirit of Dōgen, the magical factors in the teaching had been growing weaker, yet were never abolished. All things considered, the magical or esoteric factors that were in reality alien to the essence of Zen supported the Zen sect in Japan. As collateral lines of esoterics, there are two major ways of ascetic practice of *"Shugendō"*—Shingon Ascetic Practice on the part of *"Taimitsu,"* and Tendai Ascetic Practice on the part of *"Tōmitsu."* Further, there exists in Mt. Hiei a discipline, as distinguished from the above-mentioned, of making pilgrimages to sacred peaks.

The Buddhism that was popular among the common people took the same course of development. Everywhere various magical formulae were recited. In former days—during the reign of the Empress Kōken (718–770) in the Nara period—there were constructed innumerable pagodas called the "Million Pagodas" to which printed prayers (*Dhāraṇīs*) were consigned.[7] From the Kamakura period on, common people began to believe in magical formulae, to copy prayers (*Dhāraṇīs*) and consign them to "Towers for sūtras" or "Towers for the repose of souls,"[8] which were erected everywhere at that time. Especially in the Kamakura period itself, *Benzaiten* (*Sarasvatī,* Goddess of Beauty and Happiness) was evoked and deified as a god of wealth at Enoshima, Itsukushima, Chikubushima, Amakawa, Minomo, Seburiyama, and so on. "Step once in this sacred place," claims a *"Noh"* song, "and you will have inexhaustible wealth in this world, and then will you be rewarded with a secure position in the other world, which you will never lose."[9] *Dakiniten* (*Dākini*), *Daikokuten* (*Mahākāla*), and the like, who are Hindu gods of wealth, also became objects of worship, and, as is well known, the worship of *Fudō* (*Acala*) and *Shōten* (*Gaṇeśa*) is widespread even today among many Japanese believers.

Thus esoteric devotion penetrated the daily life of the Japanese people. If you read some literary works before the Restoration, you will find there that the Buddhistic conceptions are mainly esoteric.

The esoteric schools gave a primary place to prayers. In order to acquire the superior effects of these prayers, ascetic disciplines of retirement in forests were required. Gyōsom (1054–1135), an ascetic famous for prayer in the Heian period, "did not spend a night in his private room after he entered the priesthood, but stayed in the main building of the temple for several nights on end so as to pay homage to Maitreya. . . . In those days, he made his pilgrimages to all of the sacred places—the secluded places in Mt. Ōmine, Mt. Katsuragi, and so forth, which are famous for their esoteric effectiveness. Thus he devoted his life for more than fifty years."[10]

A striking feature of Japanese esoterics was their mystical account of the life of the famous priest, Kūkai (founder of the Shingon sect). Such a view had nothing with to do earlier esoterics in the continent. Kūkai died at Kongō-buji Temple at Mt. Kōya on March 21st, 835 A.D. But the believers in the Shingon sect say: "He just then *entered into meditation* (*samādhi*) looking for the time of the descent of Maitreya the Buddha. Kūkai did not die. He is still *alive* today." So, at a fixed time, a properly qualified high priest comes and changes Kūkai's gown in the inner sanctuary, where Kūkai is supposed to be still staying in meditation. What is the condition of Kūkai the great teacher of Buddhism now? It is a great secret that laity should not talk about.

Since such a mystical view has been maintained only in Japan, we cannot help thinking that it sprang solely from the way of thinking peculiar to the Japanese people who have generally made much of magical conceptions and the spiritual prestige of particular individuals, to which we have already referred.

In looking over "Kamakura Buddhism," we find in the first place that the doctrine of Nichiren preserved most of the former Buddhistic elements. Though he persistently denounced the Shingon esotericism, his teaching was much the same as it, as far as the aim of prayers was concerned. He placed great emphasis upon the superiority of prayers in terms of the Hokke sūtra over those in the other sects.[11] "If all the people will only recite 'Homage to the Sūtra of the Lotus of the Good Law' in chorus," he said, "They will see that branches won't toss about in the wind and clouds won't burst in a downpour of rain. Then there will be a return to the Golden Age. There will be revealed the Cause of immortality of man and the creation of all things. Moreover, thanks to a promise of 'peace and tranquility in this life,' they will escape an accursed misfortune and will acquire the means of prolonging life."[12]

This thought of Nichiren's had something of the very quality of the Lotus Sūtra itself that promoted esoteric ideas like this one on every page. This fact enabled his doctrine to be easily disseminated among the people used to the shamanistic oracular practice. There are many controversies among Nichiren's followers on the significance of prayers in his doctrine, but, in fact, many of them prayed, fascinated in an auto-suggested mood induced by repetitive reciting of "Adoration to the Lotus Sūtra." Besides, Nichiren identified himself with the Viśiṣṭa-cāritra Bodhisattva predicated in the Lotus (Hokke) Sūtra. This daring claim was likely to be supported by the Japanese way of thinking which is prone to grant charismatic prestige to particular individuals. Moreover, when we consider that there is no trace either in Indian or in Chinese Buddhism of such a religious custom as reciting in chorus or demonstrating by beating fan-shaped drums, we are compelled to suppose some impact of Shamanism on the doctrine of Nichiren.

On the continent, from the beginning, the Zen sect did not approve of prayers. In Japan, also, for some time after the introduction of Zen, there was no praying, except in special cases. Dōryū Rankei (1213–1278), Funei Gottan (d. 1276), Shōnen Daikyū (1215–1289), Sogen Shigen (1226–1286), and also Dōgen, scarcely offered any prayers. Even their patrons never forced the Zen priests to pray for any benefit, before the reign of Tokiyori and Tokimune Hōjō. This tradition, however, was broken down by the Japanese who were in the habit of seeking help through prayers. In the meanwhile, the Rinzai Zen sect of Eisai and his successors began to acquire a strong tinge of esotericism, including prayer. From the time of Tokiyori Hōjō (1227–1263) and Tokimune Hōjō (1215–1284) onwards, the nobility, patrons of the Zen sect, assailed priests with demands for prayers whenever they worried themselves even over trivialities. Thus the temples of the Zen sect were going to be a sort of seminary of prayers.[23] Dōgen, the introducer of the Sōtō sect, having repudiated magic or exorcism, could hardly be supported by the generality; whereas, after his death, the order of the sect became influential all over the country. This sudden change can only be explained by the fact that Jōkin Keizan (1268–1325), his spiritual descendant, adopted the esoteric ceremonies.

The Pure Land (Jōdo) teaching, as opposed to the other sects, denounced magic or exorcism originally, asserting that looking to such magical resources was against the original vow of Amitābha Buddha. There is nevertheless no denying that the Japanese teaching of the Pure Land had some coloring of magical practice. We have already pointed out that the Chinese teaching itself was likely to be partly esoteric in later periods, because its principal idol was called "Amida," which was an exotic and shortened phoneme of the original symbol "Amitābha," the "Buddha of Eternal Life."

This trend was carried over into the Japanese teaching of Buddhism. For example, the "*Nembutsu*" (to praise the name of Amitābha), prevalent among the Japanese common people, was noticeably shamanistic. In the mid-Heian period, Saint Kūya (died 972) initiated the "*Odori-Nembutsu,*" that is, dancing to the drum or going into the street and reciting "*Nembutsu*" or hymns in Japanese. The practice enjoyed general popularity at that time. By the power of "*Nembutsu,*" it was said, Kūya conquered venomous serpents and beasts and repulsed robbers. And this monk was applauded by people everywhere.[14] As evidenced in the writings of Kanezane Fujiwara (Kujō, also Enshō, 1149–1207), it was also because of Honen's magical powers that Hōnen converted Kanezane Fujiwara to his sect.[15]

The Jōdo or Pure Land sect, founded by Hōnen (Genkū, 1133–1212), itself acquired an esoteric coloring later. Shōgei (1341–1420), the founder of the Jōdo sect in the Kantō Area, worked mysteries named "mysteries to be initiated through fivefold means." Even nowadays the priests of the Jōdo sect recite their hymns in Sanskrit, saying, "the principal magical prayer of Amitābha, the Perfect One." This is the same as the prayer used in the Shingon sect. This enigmatic formula transmitted in an unintelligible transcription runs as follows: "I will devote my life to Buddha, Law, and Order. I will devote my life to the Holy Tathāgāta (The Perfect One) of Eternal Life, the honorable Enlightened One. *Om,* the Immortal, the Immortal Life, the Immortal Appearance, the Immortal Mother's Womb, the Immortal Power." After this enumeration, it concludes with the prayer: "Perish all Karmas one by one, *svāhā.*" This certainly is a magical formula. Aside from the original vow of the teaching, the sect has been considerably esoteric in its practice.

In the Kamakura period (1185–1333) there was another promoter of *"Odori-Nembutsu"* (Invocation to Amitābha Dancing). It was Saint Ippen (1239–1289), the founder of the Ji sect. *"The Mirror of Nomori"* referred to him as follows: A priest, named Ippen, misunderstood the doctrine of *Nembutsu,* taking 'dancing-ecstasy' for the high command to dance. The orthodox performance of *Nembutsu* lay for him in dancing and keeping time with the hands and feet. Furthermore, inspired by the utterance to the effect that a simple mind will enter easily the Pure Land of Amitābha, he became naked and, without a stitch of clothing upon his body, pretended that one should reject all artificiality. In a sort of mad frenzy he condemned anyone he ever hated. And yet all people, high and low, flocked to be the first ones in his audience and were loud in praise of his conduct, as in a prosperous market.

Although the episode remains to be confirmed, there can be no doubt that *"Odori-Nembutsu"* was popular with the contemporaries of Ippen. Down to the Tokugawa Shogunate a religious custom of bowl-beating was soon to be in practice. Now we have to remember that "Shaman," from which the word "Shamanism" is derived, means a dancing man. We shall, then be justified in saying that it was into such an *"Odori-Nembutsu"* (dancing to the name of Buddha) that the teaching of Pure Land was modified in terms of Shamanism in Japan.

Against these shamanistic or magical tendencies a gallant resistance was put up by the Jōdo sect. It stood by its view that no permission should be given to look to exorcism or prayers, or to choose a lucky day or lucky star.[16] Nevertheless, another form of Shamanism was sought by its believers. (The most outstanding was *Hijihōmon,* especially *Okura-monto,* of the Jōdo-shin sect.) *"Odori-Nembutsu"* was sometimes performed by some of the believers, in spite of a strict decree against it. There appeared, in the Ashikaga period (1336–1573), a heretic view that praying to Amitābha would cure any disease. It was in the same line of mystical thinking as the custom of drinking water from the Pope's bathtub.

To recognize a magical power in the human voice is common among primitive people. Indian Buddhism, especially its esotericism from the seventh and eighth centuries on, developed a similar line of thought. But, in Japan, all religious sects have been unwittingly governed by this magical thinking.

The Japanese have, since ancient times, been disposed to regard funeral services as of great importance, and nowadays a funeral is of important significance to Buddhism itself. The Japanese funeral was a surprise to Europeans who came over at the beginning of the modern era. Yet, originally, Buddhist monks were never in charge of any funeral for secular devotees. Buddhists in India expected no salvation of the dead from funeral services which were held by Brāhmins. It was a common attitude of the leaders of the original Buddhism to "jeer and scoff at the magical formulae recited by Brāhmins."[17] (The original scripture of Buddhism tells us that the Buddha himself forbade monks to participate in a funeral.) Another source says that one could go to Heaven after his death, thanks, not to a funeral, but to his virtue. At any rate, monks did not want to bother about such secular ceremonies as funeral services.

Yet, as time went on after the entrance of Buddhism into Japan, the general public believed Buddhism, because of its metaphysical character, to have a bearing upon the phenomenon of death, and have some influence on the repose of souls. Then, at some date after the Heian period, some clergymen appeared who took charge of funeral services for secular persons in order to ameliorate the financial condition of temples. Finally, the Tokugawa Shogunate bound all the people to Buddhist temples so that people might obey strictly the decree of the Prohibition of Christianity. As a consequence, every person in Japan has had a connection with the Buddhist temple, and that connection has been chiefly through funeral services. Thus a funeral comes to be taken for one of the most important of Buddhist ceremonies nowadays. (The great temples in Nara, however, stick to the old Buddhist tradition, and do not participate in funerals of laymen at present. It is the same with great Chinese temples.) So it may be a bitter irony that the actual Buddhist circles in Japan count as their most essential social function what the monks of original Buddhism jeered at as nonsense. [Such a change may have occurred in other world-religions also. The subject requires further comparative study.]

But, the change met the social needs of people, for thus the Japanese people enjoyed the magical effects of Buddhism as well. These effects are produced by reciting the sūtras in melodious classical Chinese, the meaning of which common people cannot understand. Not only the Indians but also the Chinese were able to understand the import of sūtras in their mother tongue. In Japan, however, classical Chinese, foreign to the Japanese, does not convey any meaning except to learned persons. Yet in actual Buddhist services the long words of classical Chinese fascinate all the participants by its sheer melodiousness without giving them any understanding.

The last question to be asked is whether or not there is any relation between Shamanism and Confucianism in Japan. The Japanese did not always adopt Chinese thoughts as they were. The time-honored religious modes of Japan repudiated not only the idea of change of imperial dynasty, but also the Chinese custom of religious service and Chinese ideas of the gods, including the supreme Heaven. The Japanese, however, noticed some affinities with the Chinese trichotomy of the divine (God of Heaven, gods of earth, and ghosts of men) in the *Chou Li,* and with the differentiation between prayer and retribution in the *Li Chi* (the Book of Rituals). Especially the this-worldly character of Confucianism based upon the family system met with favor among the Japanese people.[18]

The greatest foe, however, of Chinese Confucianism was the shamanistic tendency in Japan. Japanese Confucianists, although they originally denounced magic or exorcism, could not reject wholly the Japanese habit of thinking, in a way oriented towards Shamanism. Some of the Japanese Confucian scholars, for example, Sorai Ogyū modified considerably the fundamental attitude of Confucius of keeping silent about supernatural gods, when Ogyū said, "There is evidence that Confucius himself approved the existence of spiritual beings. So, whoever denies spiritual beings does not believe in Confucius."[19] We, however, find in *The Analects of Confucius* the following sentence: "The subjects on which the Master did not talk, were extraordinary things, feats of strength, disorder, and spiritual beings." According to the interpretation of the Chinese scholar, it means that Confucius did not talk about anything beyond our sensory perception. But Ogyū explained the same sentence as follows: "Confucius, though a saint, was a man as well. Presumably he could not help being interested in ghost tales. Indeed, in everyday talks, he must have referred, from time to time, to the existence of ghosts. But he did not encourage such a reference as a precept."[20]

As for studies of Chinese classics, more energy was devoted to the study of the Book of Changes than to the study of the Book of Rituals. This may have some connection with the above-mentioned tendency.

From the Heian period onwards, not only Buddhism but Shintō adopted the Chinese dualistic principle of positive and negative. It was a magical teaching by which one could master the art of divination, hydromancy, anthroposcopy, astrology, etc. It included a doctrine of the positive and the negative, and also of the five elements. In China, the teachers, having deified "T'ien-i," "T'ai-po," "God of Mt. T'aishan" and so forth, held the festivals of "One's Star," "Fatal Destiny," "Three Cycles," and, at the same time, were in charge of magical practice. Chinese Dualism, though a magical teaching, had a theoretical construction, nevertheless. Having been introduced into Japan, however, the teaching lost its coherent doctrine of the positive and the negative. With no reference to doctrinal consideration, many Japanese, high and low, monastic and secular, believed in the magical aspect of its teaching.[21] Chinese Dualism, then, was nothing but a superstition in Japan. And yet its influence upon Japanese customs can still be discerned in the popular belief in fatalism as well as in the habit of avoiding an ominous direction. Hence, while we recognize the impact of Shamanism upon Chinese thought, we must also admit that it was not so strong as its influence on Buddhism in Japan.

Such shamanistic or magical tendencies will, with the diffusion of scientific knowledge, disappear sooner or later. A fuller investigation is required concerning the problem of the post-war growth of heretical religions of this sort.

NOTES

INTRODUCTION

1 In this book the term "Eastern" refers to India, pre-Communist China and Tibet, and Japan, and their cultural satellites, though some remarks have been added concerning the communist influence in China and Tibet.

2 R. Carnap, *Philosophy and Logical Syntax* (London: 1935), 78. W. V. O. Quine, *From a Logical Point of View* (Cambridge, Massachusetts: 1953), 61; W. V. O. Quine, *Word and Object* (Cambridge, Massachusetts: 1961), 80.

3 G. Ryle, "Ordinary Language," *The Philosophical Review*, LVII (April 1953), 167–186, especially 171; L. J. Cohen, "Are Philosophical Theses Relative to Languages?" *Analysis*, IX (April 1949), 72–77. Cf. Tsu-lin Mei, "Chinese Grammar and the Linguistic Movement in Philosophy," *The Review of Metaphysics*, XIV, 3 (March 1961), 463–492.

4 This famous article is incorporated in Wilhelm von Humboldt, *Gesammelte Werke*, VI, 562f.

5 Marcel Granet, "Quelques particularitiés de la langue et de la pensée chinoise," *Revue Philosophique* (1920), 101–102.

6 Cf. Edwin O. Reischauer and John K. Fairbank, *East Asia, The Great Tradition: A History of East Asian Civilization* (Boston: Houghton Mifflin, 1958), "The Languages" (15–19): "In both East Asia and the West there is a common misconception that these linguistic differences correspond to racial divisions, but there is no more a Chinese or Japanese race than there is a French or German race. In other words, the physical differences within these linguistic groups are as great as the differences between them and their neighbors."

7 By "logic" (defined in various ways even today) Dr. Nakamura means "forms of thought" in both empirical and formal, inductive and deductive modes of thinking, and thus inseparable from socio-psychological and cultural-linguistic conditions. The latter conditions vary from time to time not only in India, China, Tibet, and Japan, but also in the history of Western thought, and are expressed in different "object-languages"; but their common or universal features, rooted in the unity of the human mind, would have to be expressed in a meta-language, the language in which we analyze the general syntax of any language. [Editor's note.]

8 Although every judgment can be expressed in the simple form "A is B," we must divide it into several kinds. The meaning of this simple judgment may be different on different occasions. Concerning this traditional problem Joseph says, "Thus we may take the proposition, and point out that in every affirmative categorical proposition there is a subject about which something is said and a predicate, or something which is said about it. This is true equally of the propositions 'A horse is an animal,' 'First-class railway tickets are white,' and '*Londre* is London.' We may, if we like, because in all propositions there is formally the same distinction of subject and predicate, take symbols which will stand for subject and predicate, whatever they are, and say that all affirmative categorical propositions are of the form 'S is P.' But when we ask for the meaning of this form, and in what sense S is P, it is clear that the meaning varies in different propositions. *Londre* is just the same as London; but a horse is not just the same as an animal; it may be said that 'animal' is an attribute of horse, and 'white' of first-class railway tickets, but animal is an attribute belonging to horses in quite a different way from that in which white belongs to first-class railway tickets; these might well be of any other color, and still entitle the holder to travel first-class by the railway; a horse could not cease to be an animal and still continue to be a horse. The meaning of the formula 'S is P' cannot possibly be fully known merely by understanding that S and P are some subject and predicate; it is necessary to understand what kind of subject and predicate they are, what the relation is between them, and in what sense one is the other; and if this sense is different in different cases, just as animal is something different in a dog and a starfish, then the thorough study of the form of thought involves the consideration of material differences in the thoughts also." H. V. B. Joseph, *An Introduction to Logic,* 2nd ed. (Oxford: 1916), 6–7. My method is slightly different from that of Joseph. My classification will be discussed on another occasion.

9 Relational judgments are illustrated by: A is similar to B, A is different from B, A is greater than B, A is to the left of B, A gives B to C, etc. Cf. A. Tarski, *Introduction to Logic* (New York: 1940), ch. V; the logic of relations was developed by C. S. Peirce. [Editor's Note.]

10 The differences displayed by Chinese, Indians, and Greeks in their employment of the chain type of reasoning was pointed out briefly by P. Masson-Oursel, "Esquisse d'une théorie comparée du sorite," *Revue de Métaphysique et de Morale* (1912), 810–824.

11 "Logic makes us realize better what the general forms of speech that we habitually use really mean, and familiarizes us with the task of examining our reasonings and looking to see whether they are conclusive." (Joseph, *op.cit.,* 11)

12 The term "comparative philosophy" was used by Masson-Oursel, *La philosophie comparée* (Paris: 1925). See also G. Misch, *Der Weg in die Philosophie;* W. Ruben, "Indische und griechische Metaphysik,"

Zeitschrift für Indologie und Iranistik, VIII, 1931, 147f. Cf. Charles A. Moore, *Philosophy: East and West* (Princeton: Princeton University Press, 1941), and the journal edited by him, *Philosophy East and West* (University of Hawaii Press), since 1951.

13 The most provocative work in this sense was F. S. C. Northrop's *The Meeting of East and West* (New York: Macmillan, 1946).

14 Laurence J. Rosán, "Are Comparisons Between the East and the West Fruitful for Comparative Philosophy?," *Philosophy East and West,* XI, 4 (January 1962), 239f.

15 Bertrand Russell, *New Hopes for a Changing World* (London: George Allen and Unwin, 1951), 18.

16 Huston Smith, "Accents of the World's Philosophies," *Philosophy East and West,* VII, 1 and 2 (April–July 1957), 7–19.

17 Hegel, *Vorlesungen über die Geschichte der Philosophie,* herausgegeben von Michelet, 135–136.

18 Max Weber, *Aufsätze zur Religionssoziologie,* II, 364–365.

19 As to the positive inquiry into the idea of "nothingness" in East Asia, cf. Kumatarō Kawada's *Mu no Shisō no Keitōronteki Kenkyū* (Systematic Study of the Thought of "Nothingness"). *Bukkyō Shisō Ronshū* (Tokyo: Sanseidō), Part 1 (Collected Works on Buddhist Thought).

20 Already in India "*śūnyatā*" was liable to be misunderstood as "nothingness" or "*nihil.*" Those who attacked the Mādhyamika school that advocated the doctrine of *śūnyatā,* identified *śūnyatā* with nothingness, and argued that the Mādhyamika school is nihilist (*nāstika*) since it advocates *nihil,* negating everything. (*Madhyamakavṛtti,* 475, line 8; 490, lines 1–2.) If we take the connotation of *śūnyatā* as nothingness, then the Mādhyamika school becomes an advocate of a doctrine that would destroy Buddhism; therefore, even within Buddhism there appeared antagonists of the doctrine of *śūnyatā.* (*Madhyamaka Śāstra,* 24, lines 1–6.) According to Candrakīrti's commentary the Mādhyamika school was viewed as "absolutely nihilist" (*atyantanāstika, op.cit.,* 159, line 4), or "one that views everything as nothing" (*sarvanāstika,* 159, line 11), or "fundamentally nihilist" (*pradhānanāstika,* 329, line 12). The Sarvāstivādins of Hīnayāna Buddhism viewed the Mādhyamika school as "one that argues that everything is nothing" (*Taishō,* XXIX, 901 b.) The Sautrāntika also denounced it saying that "one who has a middle mind" (*Madhyamakacitta*) is "one who denies the existence of the substance of all things" and since he is obsessed with "a prejudice that everything is non-existent" (*sarvanāstigrāha*), the doctrine of this school is one of the two heretical views within Buddhism, side by side with the Vātsīputrīyas who admit *pudgala* (personal identity or individuality). *Op.cit.,* XXX, 6 b. (*Abhidharmakośa,* French translation by Poussin, IX, 271, Note.) Furthermore, the Mādhyamika school is viewed by the Vijñānavādins as an "extreme view" (*ekāntavāda*) which holds that even sense-consciousness (*vijñāna*) is non-existent. (*Triṁśikā,* 15, lines 13–16; a Chinese Buddhist Commentary on the

Triṁśikā, and further commentary in *Taishō,* XLIII, 236 b-c.) It is only natural that most of the Western scholars call the *"Prajñāpāramitā Sūtra"* or the doctrine of the Mādhyamika school "nihilism" since such criticisms were already expressed in India. Against such criticisms, however, Nāgārjuna, founder of the Mādhyamika school, says, "You are ignorant of the function of *śūnyatā,* the meaning of the *śūnyatā* and *śūnyatā* itself." (*Madhyamaka Śāstra;* 24, line 7.) According to Candrakīrti's commentary, he says, "The meaning of the word 'nothing' (*abhāva*) is not that of the word '*śūnyatā,*' and yet, you denounce us assuming that the meaning of the word 'nothing' is identical to that of the word '*śūnyatā.*' Therefore, you are equally ignorant of the meaning of the word '*śūnyatā.*' " (491, line 15f; also cf. places before and after this passage.) The object of the *Madhyamaka Śāstra* is not to elucidate the nothingness of all things but *śūnyatā* itself. (*Ibid.,* 239, line 8.) Nāgārjuna states that the philosophy which considers *śūnyatā* as nothingness is false, and argues that we should not identify the *śūnyatā* doctrine with the view of nothingness (*abhāvadarśana*). (*Ibid.,* 273, line 12f; *Madhyamakāvatāra,* 77.) He also says, "We are not nihilists. We clarify the unique way which leads to the castle of Nirvāṇa by rejecting the two extreme views of 'existence' and 'non-existence.' " (*Ibid.,* 329, line 13.) Indeed *śūnyatā* and nothingness do appear to resemble each other, as the other schools contend, but those who advocated the doctrine of *śūnyatā* make a clear distinction between the two ideas.

21 Being different from Lao-tzŭ's nihilism, Śākyamuni's way transcends the four heretical prejudices (Chi-tsang's *San-lun Hsüan-i* [Profound Doctrines of the Three Treatises], 9 b), but since Lao-tzŭ "advocated the way of expounding nothingness," Chia-hsiang-tai-shih says that we must distinguish Buddhist *śūnyatā* from Lao-tzŭ's nothingness. (*Ibid.,* 12 a.)

22 Max Weber, *op.cit.,* I, 266.

23 Albert Schweitzer, *Das Christentum und die Weltreligionen,* 52.

24 Sueo Gotō, *Shina Bunka to Shinagaku no Kigen* (Chinese Culture and the Origin of Chinese Study), 418.

25 What happens if in one family there are members whose faith differs from the others? According to *"Myōkōnin-den,"* the annals and records of devout followers of Jōdo Shin Shū, there are many such cases. A woman who married a Nichiren believer became a devotee of Jōdo Shin Shū; however she continued to worship for two years the image of the Amida Buddha. One day she was discovered by her husband, who was impressed by her devotion and eventually became a devotee. A man by the name of Gozayemon who lived in the Banshū province was constantly persuading his wife to become a Buddhist, but he always met with indifference. However, by chance he succeeded in making his wife a Shinshū believer. Such ways of proselytism as these are in vivid contrast with those of the Western religions mentioned previously.

26 For example, Schweitzer, *op.cit.,* 30f.

27 Max Weber, *ov.cit.,* II, 367.

28 Concerning ethical rationalization in the contemporary world, Max Weber asserts that the East Asians are lacking in ethical character due to their habit of identifying the interests of their profession with duty. Professor Kwanji Naitō, however, positively proved by citing the Ohmi merchants that this view of Max Weber's was incorrect. "*Shūkyō to Keizairinri—Jōdo Shin Shū to Ōmishōnin*" ("Religion and Business Ethics—Jōdo Shin Sect and Merchants of Ōmi"), *Nippon Shakaigakukai Nempō*, VIII (1941), 243–286.

29 Max Weber, *op.cit.*, I, 263–264.

30 Max Weber, *Die Protestantische Ethik und der Geist des Kapitalismus;* Japanese tr. by Tsutomu Kajiyama, 143. English: *Protestant Ethics and the Spirit of Capitalism* (London: Allen and Unwin, 1930).

31 Vivekānanda, the religious reformer of modern India, visited China and Japan in 1893, and was moved by the fact that in various temples the manuscripts and epitaphs written in ancient Indian letters had been preserved, which strengthened his faith in the *spiritual unity of Asia.* (Roman Rolland, *La Vie de Vivekānanda,* I, 42.) However, this unity points to the universality of Buddhism. Therefore, the unity of Asia is to be recognized within this context, i.e., the universality of Buddhism.

32 Sōkichi Tsuda, *Shina Shisō to Nippon* (Chinese Thought and Japan).

33 *Ibid.*, 178.

34 *Ibid.*, 148.

35 *Ibid.*, 179.

36 Cf. preceding section.

37 Max Weber, *Aufsätze zur Religionssoziologie,* Einleitung.

38 "The political and moral teachings formed in ancient times (of China) have long been traditional without losing their prestige as the thought of intellectual society; such a thought, however, should not merely be a borrowed one for other nations, but it would be also very hardly understood as a thought by them." (Sōkichi Tsuda, *Chinese Thought and Japan, op.cit.*, 8).

39 M. Winternitz, *Geschichte der indischen Litteratur,* II, 226–267.

40 Bodhisattva is Budsaf in Persian, and came to be identified with Joseph, one of the saints of the Catholic Church.

41 The contents of "*Acta Sanctorum*" (published in Japanese translation in 1591), the story of St. Joseph and one of the translations in Christian literature, show a striking identity with the life story of the Buddha. Cf. Noritsugu Muraoka, *Kirishitan Bungaku-shō* (Documents of Christian Literature), 51–88; Masaharu Anesaki, *Kirishitan Dendō no Kōhai* (Fortunes of Christian Missionary Propagation), 390–391.

42 As for the influence of Chinese thought on France, cf. Sueo Gotō, *Shinabunka to Shinagaku no Kigen* (*Chinese Culture and the Rise of Chinese Studies*), 1933.

43 As for Buddhism in the West, cf. Kaikyoku Watanabe, *Ōbei no Bukkyō* (Buddhism in Western Countries). The titles of books published in

Germany for the purpose of study and propagation of Buddhism are contained in Hans Ludwig Held's *Deutsche Bibliographie des Buddhismus* (Munich: 1916), according to which the number amounts to as many as 2544. Westerners have also appeared who have renounced the world and conducted positive activities after being ordained *bhikkhus*. The British *bhikkhu*, Ānanda Metteya, and the German *bhikkhu*, Nyānatiloka, are the best known. In Germany, too, several organizations such as *Gemeinde um Buddha* were established, whose activities were suppressed by the Nazis during the last war, but now they have reportedly started again their vigorous activities.

44 Hisashi Uda, *Nippon Bunka ni Oyoboseru Jukyō no Eikyō* (*The Influence of Confucianism upon Japanese Culture*), 340ff.

45 *Bendōsho. Book of Practice of the Way* (*Tao*).

46 Rennyo, *Jōgai Ofumi* (Yūshō Tokushi, *Rennyo Shōnin Ofumi Zenshū*, 76) (*Collected Works of Saint Rennyo*).

47 *Hokkeshō. Exposition of the Lotus Sūtra.*

48 "Megasthenes, Seleukos Nikator's contemporary, clearly writes in the third chapter of his book *India*, as follows: 'Verily whatever was taught about nature by the ancient people (of Greece) was taught likewise by the philosophers of the other countries: among Indians by Brakhmana (Brahmans) and in Syria by Iudaios (Jews).' " Clemens of Alexandria, *Strom.* I, 305 D. (Cologne: 1688); quoting from *Megasthenis Indica, Fragmenta collegit commentationem et indices addidit*, ed. E. A. Schwanbeck, Fr. 42.

49 It is a well-known fact in the history of philosophy that Schopenhauer was absorbed in the *Upaniṣad* scriptures through Anquetil du Perron's Latin version of a Persian translation; under the influence of Schopenhauer Deussen wrote a history of philosophy of all the nations of the world, that is, *Allgemeine Geschichte der Philosophie*. Although Deussen falls short of describing in detail the philosophical views in China and Japan due to linguistic difficulties, he shows due concern about them. As far as the interest in comparing *Weltanschauungen* is concerned, works such as G. Misch's *Der Weg in die Philosophie* or Keyserling's *Reisetagebuch eines Philosophen* would be in the same category. Masson-Oursel's *La Philosophie Comparée* carried such studies much farther. American philosophers, as in the case of Emerson or Royce (*The World and the Individual*), have also shown a deep interest in Indian philosophy.

49a K. Okakura (1862–1913), *Ideals of the East*, 1903.

50 P. Deussen, *Die Sūtras des Vedanta* (1920). Vorrede, 5–6.

51 P. Deussen, *Allgemeine Geschichte der Philosophie*, I, 36.

52 As for the matter of comparison of Indian philosophy with Western philosophy alone, P. Deussen's *Allgemeine Geschichte der Philosophie* (2 volumes) treated it for the first time, and then S. Radhakrishnan's *Indian Philosophy* (2 volumes, 1923, 1930) often took it into account. Rudolf Otto's *West-Östliche Mystik* (Gotha: 1929) makes comparisons

of Śaṁkara's metaphysics with Eckhart's and Fichte's. The comparison also of Kant's categorical imperative with that of Prabhākara is discussed in detail by Th. Stcherbatsky in *Festgabe Hermann Jacobi* (Bonn: 1926), 369f. These researches were introduced in Yenshō Kanakura's *Indo Tetsugaku to Seiyō Shisō* (*Indian Philosophy and Western Thought*), *Risō*, No. 172 (June 1947), in which the significance of the comparative study of the thoughts of East and West is treated.

53 Kant, *Kritik der reinen Vernunft*, 866f.

54 For instance, Rickert characterized historical science as "idiographisch" and natural science, "nomothetisch." But, as we shall see, the ways of thinking of the Chinese are idiographic, while those of the Indians are nomothetic. At least as far as the etymology of these two terms, derived from Greek, is concerned, this judgment can safely be made. Therefore, if such characteristics of the ways of thinking of the East Asians are taken into account, the discussion about learning made by Rickert, and by the Germans after him, needs to be reflected upon once again.

55 The reason why I have brought out here the concept of "climatic environment" is to prevent misunderstanding by making a distinction, as a makeshift, between this and Dr. Watsuji's concept of "climate." According to his climatology, climate is by no means a mere natural phenomenon. He says: "We can also discover climatic phenomena in all the expressions of human activity, such as literature, art, religion, and manners and customs. This is a natural consequence as long as man apprehends himself in climate." Tetsuro Watsuji, *Climate: A Philosophical Study*, trans. by G. Bownas (Printing Bureau, Japanese Government, 1961), 7–8. What I am analyzing here in connection with the problem of the existential basis of different ways of thinking, however, is climate as *natural environment* in general. Therefore, I used another word for it for the sake of distinction. (Cf. H. T. Buckle, *History of Civilization* (London: 1859) for a general environmental theory of civilization.—Editor's note).

56 According to Max Weber, there is a reason, significant for spiritual history, for the fact that cities made progress in their particular fashion in the West. First, the western cities are a cooperative society formed by the pact (social contract) based on voluntary will. A city in the West was, in the beginning, created as a defensive body, the principle of which is that it should be defended by self-fortification and by the whole city *itself*. Everywhere, except in the West, a monarch's army preceded the coming into being of cities. In the West, however, the coming into existence of an army to be led under the orders of a soldier-monarch or the separation of soldiers and the means of war, was only effected in modern times, but in Asia it existed from the very beginning. Some say that the reason is that in East Asia, Egypt, West Asia, India, or China, the river-improvement problem was of grave concern for the nation; therefore a powerful monarchy and bureaucracy were bound to appear. The second reason is said to be that in East Asian societies, ec-

clesiastical institutions were established which monopolized magical tricks and exercised a ruling power.

57 Max Weber, *Aufsätze zur Religionssoziologie,* I, 252.

58 "Although the extent to which social influence under certain economical and political conditions affected religious ethics was fairly grave in some isolated cases, the characteristic of such ethics is basically given by the role of religion. Before anything else it primarily depends on the contents of a religious message or God's testament. In any religion the needs of the class which instructs the society in its teaching count greatly, and on the other hand, once the type of religion is fixed it would exercise a great influence over various types of ways of living." (Max Weber, "Die Wirtschaftsethik der Weltreligion," *Aufsätze zur Religionssoziologie,* I, 240–241.) As for the reason why the caste-system was established in India, Weber explains: "Originally the union of the creative caste-orthodoxy with the doctrine of *karma* or the *théodicée* peculiar to the Brahmins, was a direct product of the rational and ethical thinking, and it *is not that of economical 'condition' of any sort.* And it is not until this thought-product came to be unified with the traditional social order, with the thought of transmigration (*saṃsāra*) as an intermediary, that such an order emerged and ruled over the thinking and aspirations of the people in question and to produce a firm basic religious and social establishment of every low professional group and the mean classes." (*Hinduismus und Buddhismus,* 131.)

59 Tetsurō Watsuji, *Homērosu Hihan* (*Homeric Criticism*), 40.

60 Even in a language, the vocabulary, phrases, and idioms used in that language are most liable to change, whereas grammatical rules or ways of expressions are comparatively hard to change. Even when a fairly large number of foreign words are adopted, it is quite rare that the grammatical system should come to be affected by foreign countries. Accordingly, a grammar is preserved for a long time and so the vitality of tradition in grammar is comparatively strong. *Hashimoto Shinkichi Hakase Chosakushū* (*Collected Works of Hashimoto Shinkichi*), I, 348ff. *Kokugo to Dentō* (National Language and Tradition).

PART I: WAYS OF THINKING IN INDIA

Chapter 1

1 Greek translation of the *Bhagavadgītā* by Demetrios Galanos from the Sanskrit (Athens: 1848): *Γιὰά ἤ, Θεσπέσιον μέλος, μεταφρασθεῖσα ἐκ τοῦ βραχμανικου.*

Latin translation: *Bhagavad-Gītā, textum recensuit adnotationes criticus et interpretationem Latinam adiecit,* Aug. Guil. von Schlegel. Editio altera auctior et emendatior cura Christiani Lasseni (Bonn: 1846).

Latin translation of the Pali *Dhammapada* by V. Fausböll: *Dhammapadam, ex tribus codicibus hauniensibus Palice edidit, Latine vertit, excerptis ex commentario Palico notisque illustravit* (Hauniae: 1855).

In the following I shall often use these two books, which are so representative of Indian thought and culture, as a key to the comparative study of ways of thinking.

2 I quoted from the text edited by Yenshō Kanakura in his *Indo Seishin Bunka no Kenkyū* (*Study of the Spirit of Indian Culture*), 297ff. The collection seems to have been written in its original form by a Buddhist before the 10th century. Its content was so excellent that other religions plundered whole sentences from it and each maintained respectively that it had been written by someone belonging to his own religion. The book, which was inherited by Brahmanic schools, contains later additions, so that the small books of Buddhists and Jains are worth studying.

3 The same sentences can be seen in early Buddhist canons, early Jain canons, the Mahābhārata, and Brahmanic sacred books, hence may be seen as pan-Indian thought. But sometimes they have been influenced by the common cultural pattern of the age in which they were written, so that we must be careful to compare them with various thoughts in later ages.

Chapter 2

1 In modern English, the adjective modifier is called "predicative", e.g., "He grows *old.*" "He goes *mad.*" "The dream will come *true.*" Cf. O. Jespersen, *The Philosophy of Grammar* (New York: 1924), 131–132. In Sanskrit this predicative is often expressed by an abstract noun.

2 To denote "as ———" the instrumental is used generally, but sometimes the dative and the locative are used in Sanskrit; e.g., *"vṛtavān mitratvāya uṛpo nṛpam."* (*Kathās.*, 38, 153) (The king chose a king as his friend.), *"patitve vṛtaḥ." Nala,* 5, 16 (chosen as a groom.) J. S. Speyer, *Vedische und Sanskrit-Syntax* (Strassburg: 1896), 36. What is expressed by the dative and locative seems to have a purpose-idea. Speyer, *op.cit.*, sec. 24.

3 Cf. "The Small *Sukhāvatīvyūha,*" ed. by Ryōsaburō Sakaki in his *Bongogaku* ("Sanskrit Grammar"), 251.

4 When we discuss the problem of "the individual," we should keep in mind that the term "individual" is not always clear, and very often logical confusion occurs. When we say: "Socrates is human," the subject term denotes a particular individual and the predicate term designates some property the individual is asserted to have. In this case the term "individual" means "an individual human being," whereas the logical meaning of the term is fairly different. "It should be made clear . . . that the word 'individual' is used to refer not only to persons, but to any *thing*—such as a country, a city, or in fact to anything of which a property can be meaningfully predicated." Irving M. Copi, *Introduction to Logic,* second edition. (New York: Macmillan, 1961), 303–304. This is the meaning of the term "individual" in the logical sense.

5 The literal meaning of *antya-viśeṣa* is "the final or ultimate particular." *The Vaiśeṣika Philosophy, According to the Daśapadārthaśāstra,* trans-

lated into English by H. Ui and edited by F. W. Thomas. (London: Royal Asiatic Society, 1917), 37, 67.

6 Gaurinath Sastri, *The Philosophy of Word and Meaning* (Calcutta: Sanskrit College, 1959), 136–140. However, even in classic Western logic the singular or the individual was not always discussed. "A simple example is found in the customary illustration that is given of the Aristotelian syllogism: All men are mortal; Socrates is a man; therefore, Socrates is mortal. I do not believe a single instance can be found in genuine Aristotelian writings in which a singular (which by its nature is an instance of severalty) appears as the minor premise in a rationally demonstrative syllogism." John Dewey, *Logic, The Theory of Inquiry* (New York: Holt, Rinehart and Winston, 1960), 95.

7 *Tarka-saṁgraha of Annaṃbhaṭṭa,* edited by Y. V. Athalye (Poona: The Bhandarkar Oriental Research Institute, 1930), 76.

8 D. M. Datta in *Philosophy and Culture: East and West,* edited by Charles A. Moore, (Honolulu: University of Hawaii Press, 1962), 571.

9 Th. Stcherbatsky, *Buddhist Logic,* I (photomechanical reprint), (The Hague: Mouton & Co., 1958), 79f; II (1958), 34–35; cf. 40, 267. In the West also we find a similar concept: *hacceitas* (*thisness*) in the philosophy of Duns Scotus.

10 *Ibid.,* I, 204f., 554f. Dharmakīrti's assertion is not a strange one. In contemporary America also we find a similar theory: "In actual experience, there is never any such isolated singular object or event; an object or event is always a special part, phase, or aspect, of an environing experienced world—a situation. The singular object stands out conspicuously because of its especially focal and crucial position at a given time in determination of some problem of use or enjoyment which the *total* complex environment presents." Dewey, *op.cit.,* 67. An individual situation is indivisible and unduplicable. Distinctions and relations are instituted within a situation; they are recurrent and repeatable in different situations. (*Ibid.,* 68.)

11 "Such qualities as are designated by 'distressing,' 'cheerful,' etc. are *general,* while the quality of distress and cheer that marks an existent situation is not general but is unique and inexpressible in words." (*Ibid.,* 70.)

12 *Cf.* also John Dewey's distinction between "having" and "knowing." *Experience and Nature* (Open Court, Lasalle, Illinois, Carus Lectures, 1925). [Dewey asserted that *knowing* requires more than *having* an immediate experience, against British sensationalists or Cartesian intuitionists. According to him, having an experience may indicate *that* a thing exists, but does not give us knowledge of what exists. Later we come to know *what* it is by experimental thinking, not by *a priori* reasoning. "Knowledge by acquaintance" is distinguished from "knowledge by description" by William James who himself shows an almost mystical preference for immediacy. But Dewey differed from James in this respect.—Editor's note.] The similarity between the thought

of Dharmakīrti and that of Kant was already pointed out by Stcherbatsky, *op.cit.*, *passim.*

13 This point is still problematic. "Indian philosophers had a whole category of inherence (*samavāya*) and the Indian logicians continuously distinguished between a judgment of inherence and a judgment of relation." (Comment by Dr. Daya Krishna.)

14 Naoshiro Tsuji, *Veda oyobi Burāhumana no Shisō* (Thoughts in the Vedas and Brāhmaṇas), *Iwanami Kōza Tōyō Shisō* (Iwanami Lectures on Oriental Thought), 61.

15 *Bṛhad. Up.*, VI, 2, 1–16, translated by Robert E. Hume (Oxford University Press, 2d ed., 1931), 263; *Chānd. Up.* V, 3–10; *Jaim. Br.* 1, 45–46. Thanks are especially due to Dr. Walter H. Maurer for his scholarly help in translating this obscure passage.

16 Schayer, *Ausgewählte Kapitel aus dem Prasannapadā*, Einleitung, p. XXII. W. Ruben, *Indische und Griechische Metaphysik*, 56ff. Cf. *Zeitschrift fur Indologie und Iranistik* (Leipzig: 1931), VIII, 147–227.

17 Hegel, *Vorlesungen über die Geschichte der Philosophie*, herausgegeben von Michelet, 162.

Chapter 3

1 *pamāda* = *socordia, appamāda* = *vigilantia, Dhp.*, 21f.: *vera* = *iracundia, avera* = *placabilitas, Dhp.*, 5.

2 *Yoga-sūtra* II, 30. This is taken up in the *Kūrma-purāṇa.* It is also adopted by Vivekānanda as one of the "rājayoga" practices. Cf. Romain Rolland, *La vie de Vivekananda* II, 66.

3 In Pali, *"pāṇātipātā veramaṇī, adinnadānā veramaṇī, kāmesu micchācārā veramaṇī, musāvādā veramaṇī."* In Buddhist Sanskrit, *"prāṇātipātād viratiḥ, adattādānād viratiḥ, kāmamithyācārād viratiḥ, musāvādāt prativiratiḥ."* (*Mahāvyutpatti*, XCII). The Jains say, *"hiṃsā-anṛta-steya-abrahma-parigrahebhyo viratir vratam"* ("Refraining from violence, falsehood, stealing, non-chastity, and possessions is the Vow"). (*Tatvārthādhigamasūtra*, VII, 1).

4 *Ṛg-veda*, X, 129.

5 *Bṛhad. Up.*, IV, 5, 15.

6 *Ibid.*, III, 8, 8.

7 *Kāṭhaka Up.*, V, 14. Cf. *Śvet. Up.*, VI, 14; *Muṇḍ. Up.*, II, 2, 10; *Bhag. G.*, XV, 6.

8 *Udāna*, I, 10, 9.

9 This salutation verse of the *Madhyamaka-kārikā*; cf. *Madhyamaka-vṛtti*, ed. by Louis de la Vallée Poussin, 3–4. Such an expression can also be found in the *Saddharmapuṇḍarīka-sūtra*, "He (who enters into the awakening of faith) finds that all Dharmas are non-destructive, non-productive, non-restrictive, non-resolutive, non-gloomy, and non-bright." (Edited by Wogihara and Tsuchida, 127, line 10.) Cf. *Madhyamaka-kārikā*, XVI, 5; *Mahāyāna-sūtrālaṅkāra*, VI, I.

10 Cf. *Taishō*, XXIV, 1018 c; VI, 380 b; V, 888 b; VI, 170 b; 569 b, 505 b,

987 c; XXV, 579–580 a. *Śālistamba-sūtra* (Poussin, *Théorie des douze causes*, 75); *Madhyamaka-vṛtti*, 569, etc.

11 Candrakīrti says, "*As to Pratītyasamutpāda*, though we can express endless negative predicates, here we adopt only eight negations, because these eight can reject all objections." (*Madhyamaka-vṛtti*, 11, 4f). Piṅgala also gives the same meaning. *Taishō*, XXX, 1 c.

12 "*Paramārtha*" is translated as "*shêng-i*" ("surpassing all things") in the Chinese translation of the Buddhist canon.

13 *Māṇḍūkya-kārikā*, II, 32. This verse is often quoted in many books. *Amṛtabindu-Up.*, 10; *Tripurātāpinī-Up.*, 10; *Avadhūta-Up.*, 8; *Ātma-Up.*, 31; *Vidvanmanorañjanī on Vedāntasāra*, ed. by Jacob, 135: *Sāṁkhyapravacanabhāṣya*, ed. by R. Garbe, 22, line 6; 28, line 11; 122, line 7; 159, line 8.

14 "If the oneness of *Ātman* were grasped, all expressions (*vyavahāra*) like 'bondage,' 'emancipation' and so on would come to the end." (Śaṁkara; *Brahma-sūtra-bhāṣya*, 1, 2, 6. I, 181, line 4. *AnSS*.)

15 "As to this a learned man says, 'I am the faculty of seeing, purity, unchangeable essence. In me there is no bondage and no emancipation.' " (*Vedāntasāra*, § 210, ed. by Böhtlingk) cf. *Vivekacūḍāmaṇi*, 503.

16 baddho mukta iti vyākhyā guṇato me, na vastutaḥ, guṇasya māyāmūlatvān na me mokṣo na bandhanam. (*Bhāgavatapurāṇa*, XI, 11, 1) na bandho 'sti na mokṣo 'sti nābandho 'sti na bandhanam, aprabodhād idaṃ duḥkhaṃ prabodhāt pravilīyate. (*Yogavāsiṣṭha*, IV, 38, 22.)

17 *Āyāraṅga*, 1, 5, 6, 4.

18 E. Zeller, *Die Philosophie der Griechen*, I, 661; P. Deussen, *Allgemeine Geschichte der Philosophie*, II, 1, p. 74.

19 *Ibid.*, I, 1, p. 695; Deussen, *op.cit.*, II, 1, p. 83.

20 Zeller, *op.cit.*, I, 1, p. 458; cf. p. 521

21 *Ibid.*, I, 2, p. 973; Deussen, *op.cit.*, II, 1, p. 117.

22 Zeller, *op.cit.*, II, 1, p. 808; Deussen, *op.cit.*, II, 1, p. 278.

23 Zeller, *op.cit.*, II, 2, p. 448; Deussen, *op.cit.*, II, 1, p. 354.

24 Takashi Ide, *Shijin Tetsugakusha* (Poet-Philosophers), 238, 244. [The Eleatics, of course, did discuss Non-Being, but only in order to reject it.—Editor's note.]

25 *Māṇḍūkya-kārikā*, II, 12.

26 *Ibid.*, II, 19; *nirguṇo 'pi hy ajo 'vyakto bhagavān prakṛteḥ paraḥ, svamāyāguṇam āviśya bādhyabādhakatāṃ gataḥ—Bhāgavatapurāṇa*, VII, 1, 6 (ed. by Burnouf).

27 Parallel passages showing the attitude of grasping the absolute negatively can be found in works of different religions. Examples are abundantly shown, for example, in Vidhushekhara Bhattacharyya, *The Āgamaśāstra of Gauḍapāda* (University of Calcutta, 1943). [Cf. Maimonides' view (*Moreh Nebuchim*) that we can say only what God is not.—Editor's note.]

28 This story is quoted by Śaṁkara in his *Brahma-sūtra-bhāsya*, III, 2, 17. Its origin seems to be certain Upaniṣads which have been lost.

29 *Dhp.*, 268.
30 M. Winternitz, *A History of Indian Literature* (University of Calcutta, 1927), I, 184.
31 *Atharva-veda*, XI, 4, 21.
32 *Aṅguttara-nikāya*, III, 129; I, 282.
33 *Saṁyutta-nikāya*, V, 153.

Chapter 4

1 Speyer, *Vedische und Sanskrit-Syntax*, § 2.
2 Greek translation of *Bhag. G.* by Dēmētrios Galanos, and Latin translation of *Bhag. G.* by A. W. von Schlegel; cf. fn. 1 to ch. I, above.
3 *Madhyamaka-kārikā*, XXIII, 10–11.
4 *Madhyamaka-vṛtti*, 10, line 7.
5 E.g., *sarvaḥ sarvaṃ na jānāti sarvajño nāsti kaścana.* (*Nala*, 20, 6) (Not everybody does know everything, nobody is omniscient.) *naiva sarva iva yaśaḥ śaknoti saṃyaṃtum.* (*Śatapatha-Brāhmaṇa*, XIV, I, 1, 6); cf. Śaṃkara, *BS.*, I, 28, lines 4–5; 275, line 2; 604, line 1. (ĀnSS).
6 Izuru Shimmura, *Gengogaku Josetsu* (Introduction to Linguistics), 48–149.
7 The same phenomenon and process can be seen in Semitic languages, descendants of Arabian languages. Such pronouns show that the numbers for three or four things in South-Asian and Polynesian languages are inclined to change into the plural form of the numerals three or four. cf. Shimmura, *op.cit.*, 150.
8 Cf. G. Bühler. *Indische Paläographie*, 80f.
9 Brugsch Pascha, *Aus dem Morgenlande*, Reclam 3151. In ancient times one-half of a certain amount of corn was called "Malter," one-24th was called "Scheffel" and one-384th was called "Metze." Cf. M. Wertheimer, Über das Denken der Naturvolker, I. Zahlen und Zahlgebilde. *Drei Abhandlungen zur Gestalttheorie*, 133.
10 Such properties as two-ness, three-ness, etc. correspond to classes of classes in modern logic. Cf. Daniel H. H. Ingalls, *Materials for the Study of Navya-Nyāya Logic*. Harvard Oriental Series, vol. 40 (Harvard University Press, 1951), 77f; S. Bhattacharya in *Philosophy: East and West* (October 1961).
11 Wertheimer, *op.cit.*, 106f.
12 Gauḍapāda on Sāṁkhya-kārikā, verse 2.
13 Śaṁkara, *Brahma-sūtra-bhāṣya* 1, 3, 28; cf. Richard Garbe, *The Philosophy of Ancient India* (Chicago: The Open Court), 36.
14 *Nyāyabindu*, II 17. *Śiṁśapā* is the name of a tree.
15 *Nyāyabindu-ṭikā*, 26, lines 12ff.
16 *Vākyapadīya*, III, 1, 32.

Chapter 5

1 The monistic view that the Highest Self appears in manifold forms is held also by the Viṣṇu sect of Hinduism. They teach that "Nārāyaṇa,

who is the highest Self and the Self of all, reveals himself in multiple ways." ātmanā 'tmānam anekadhā vyūhyāvasthitaḥ, Śaṁkara on *Brahmasūtra*, II, 2, 42; *SBE*, XXXIV, 440.

2 *Bṛhad. Up.*, IV, 4, 6; *The Principal Upaniṣads*, edited by S. Radhakrishnan (London: 1953), 273.

3 *Chānd. Up.*, III, 14, 4; (*SBE*), *Sacred Books of the East* I, 48.

4 *Chānd. Up.*, VI, 9, 1–2; *SBE*, I, 101; cf. *Maitri-Up.*, VI, 22.

5 Surendranath Dasgupta, *A History of Indian Philosophy* (Cambridge University Press, 1932), I, 429.

6 Moritz Winternitz, *Geschichte der indischen Litteratur*, Bd. III.

7 Surendranath Dasgupta, *A History of Indian Philosophy*, IV, *Indian Pluralism* (Cambridge University Press, 1949), 362.

8 *A Source Book in Indian Philosophy*. Edited by Sarvepalli Radhakrishnan and Charles A. Moore (Princeton: Princeton University Press, 1957), p. xxv.

9 *Suttanipāta*, 648; *SBE*, X, pt. II, p. 115; cf. *Suttanipāta*, 610; 611.

10 *Vinaya, Culla-vagga*, IX, 1, 4; *SBE*, XX, 304.

11 *Muṇḍ. Up.*, III, 2, 8; Radhakrishnaṇ. *Op.cit.*, 691.

12 *Madhyamaka-Kārikā*, 18, 5.

13 Harold E. McCarthy's review of Rama Kanta Tripathi, *Spinoza in the Light of the Vedānta* (Banaras: Banaras Hindu University, 1957), in *Philosophy East and West*, XI, 4 (January 1962), 261–265.

14 E.g., vinābhāvasantam ev' idaṃ, (*Suttanipāta*, 805); cf. sabbaṃ idaṃ calaṃ iti pekkhāmano, (*Theragāthā*, 1110); idaṃ sarvaṃ vijñāptimātrakam, (*Triṁśikā*, v. 17).

15 E.g., sarvam idam, (*Bhag. G.*, II, 17; VII, 7); idam, (*Bhag. G.*, III, 38). Schlegel translates the word "idam" by "universum." svapnādivac cedaṃ draṣṭavyam, (Śaṅkara ad *BS*. II, 2, 28).

16 E.g., tāṇi sarvāṇi, (*Bhag. G.* IV, 5, hosce universos). Cf. sabbe, (*Dhammapada*, 129; 130).

17 *πάντα χωρεῖ καὶ οὐδὲν μένει*. Plato, *Crat*. 402 A.

18 *ὢs ἀπάντων τῶν αἰσθητῶν ἀεὶ ῥεοντων*. Aristotle, *Metaph.*, I, 6. 987 a 33.

19 *τὰ πανθ' ὁρᾶ θεός, αὐτὸs οὐχ ὁρῶμενοs*. (God sees all things, himself unseen.) As this Greek quotation shows, it is commonly observed in some of the Indo-European languages that a subject in the nominative neuter plural form takes the verb in the singular. In the *Ṛg-Veda*, we can find some cases of this usage. See Harushige Kōzu, *Hikaku Gengogaku* (Comparative Linguistics), 261–262. As to this usage in the Classical Sanskrit, see Speyer, *Vedische und Sanskrit-Syntax*, 75, § 243, Anm. 1. In Prakṛit, "atthi" (= Sanskrit *asti*) can follow the subject of any gender and number and "āsī" (= Sanskrit *āsīt*), the subject of either the singular or the plural number. See Woolner, *Introduction to Prākṛit*, 53.

20 *ἐν πάντι εὐχαριστεῖτε*. (In everything give thanks.)

21 *Εν τὸ ὂν καὶ πὰν ... Ξενοφάνην ... ὑποτίθεσθαι φήσιν ὁ θέοsφράστοs*. ("Xenophanes thought that Being is one and all," it is said by Theophrastus.) Simplicius ad. *Phys*. 22, 26D.

22 E.g., *Omnia, quae sunt, vel in se, vel in alio sunt.* (Everything exists either in itself or in other things.) Spinoza, *Ethica,* Axiomata I.
23 Megasthenes, *Fragments,* 41.
24 See *Kauṣ. Up.,* I, 4; *Bṛhad. Up.,* IV, 3, 22; IV, 4, 23; *Tait. Up.,* II, 9.
25 *Bṛhad. Up.,* IV, 4, 22; Radhakrishnan, *op.cit.,* 279; cf. *Kauṣ. Up.,* III, 8.
26 *Chānd. Up.,* IV, 14, 3; *SBE,* I, 67.
27 See *Brahmasūtra,* IV, 1, 13–15.

Chapter 6

1 It has been the practice since the *Ṛg-Veda* to use the past participle instead of the finite verb. Even in the oldest Gāthās of the Jain Scripture, this tendency is found. (H. Jacobi, *Sacred Books of the East* (*SBE*), XXII, 72n.)
2 In the Apabhraṁśa language, perfect, imperfect, and aorist are seldom found and the past tense is expressed by a past participle.
3 However, there is no such example in the *Ṛg-Veda.* It can be first found in the Brāhmaṇas. Delbrück, *Altindische Syntax,* 295.
4 Speyer, *Vedische und Sanskrit-Syntax* (Strassburg: 1896), 67.
5 The sentence which begins with "yad" corresponds to such an infinitive form. Speyer, *op.cit.,* 87, § 279, b.
6 *"vṛṣala, upālabdhuṃ, tarhi vayam āhūtāḥ."* (*Mudrārākṣasa,* III [127, 6]) = "_____, so bin ich hier befohlen, um gescholten zu werden." Speyer, *op.cit.,* 67.
7 Cf. *"ekā prasūyate mātā dvitīyā vāk prasūyate."* (Pañcatantra, ed. Jīvānananda Vidyāsāgara [Calcutta: 1872], IV, 6.) In the case when the word *īdṛśa* (such) modifies adjective, this remains as an adjective. Speyer, *op.cit.,* § 148, Anm. cf. § 132.
8 Stenzel states, in his *Die Philosophie der Sprache,* 74f., that such a difference is based upon the difference of emphasis upon the subject and predicate.
9 Speyer, *op.cit.,* 82–83.
10 Speyer, *op.cit.,* § 69.
11 *"bhāva utpattiḥ sattā vā.* (*Ratnaprabhā ad Brahmasūtra,* II, 2, 3)
12 For example: Śaṁkara ad *BS.,* II, 16, line 9. (*ĀnSS.*); *Chung-lun* (Treatise on the "Middle" Doctrine) 15, 5; cf. Commentaries by Candrakīrti on the 13, 3 & 5; 15, 8 of Chung-lun.
13 *Bṛhad. Up.,* III, 8, 8–11.
14 *Bṛhad. Up.,* III, 9, 26; IV, 2, 4; IV, 4, 22; IV, 5, 15, cf. II, 3, 6.
15 *Bṛhad. Up.,* IV, 4, 25.
16 Seiichi Hatano, *Kirisutokyō no Kigen* (The Origin of Christianity), 199–200.
17 *Dhammapada,* 150.
18 *Tait. Up.,* III, 1; *Tattvārthādhigama-sūtra,* V, 29.
19 ṣaḍbhāvavikārā bhavantīti Vārṣyāyaniḥ, jāyate'sti vipariṇamate vardhate' *prakṣīyate vinaśyatīti.* (*Nirukta,* I, 2. p. 29, edited by L. Sarup.)

20 *Vākyap.*, III, 1, 36.

21 Śaṁkara *BS.*, I, 1, 2.

22 In the seventh chapter of the *Madhyamaka-Kārikā*, the theory which claims *utpāda-sthiti-bhaṅga* is refuted. Formerly, in the '*Tsêng-i-a-han*' (Chinese version of the *Ekottarāgama-sūtra* in the Tripiṭaka) XII (*Taishō*, II, 607 c), it is explained that there are three characteristics by which the conditioned elements are formed, namely, appearance, change, and elimination. The *Abhidharma-jñāna-prasthāna*, vol. 3 (*Taishō*, XXVI, 780 c) also explains the same theory.

23 *Madhyamaka-kārikā*, XV, 5. Also see the commentary of Candrakīrti upon *MK.*, XIII, 3, 5, XV, 8.

24 This is explained in the *Mahāvibhāṣā*, 39, the *Nyayānusāra*, 13, the *Abhidharma-kośa*, 5 (the Chinese translation by Hsüan-tsang), etc.

25 Romain Rolland, *La vie de Ramakrishna*, 22–24.

26 Albert Schweitzer, *Das Christentum und die Weltreligionen* (Munich: 1925), 34. Translated by Joanna Powers, *Christianity and the Religions of the World* (New York: Henry Holt, 1939).

27 Harushige Kōzu, *Hikaku Gengogaku* (Comparative Linguistics), 256–257.

28 *praesens, imperfectum, futurum, perfectum, aoristum.* In the Latin language *aoristum* is lacking, but *plusquamperfectum* and *futurum exactum* are added.

29 Speyer, *op.cit.*, 53–55.

30 It is improper to say that aorist should be interpreted as indefinite past tense. See Kōzu, *op.cit.*, 263, note 1.

31 Pāṇinī, III, 3, 135.

32 In order to make up for it, the following three combinations are usually used: past participle passive + *asa* (*abhūt*), past participle passive + *bhaviṣyati*, and past participle passive + *bhavet*. Speyer, *op.cit.*, 62. In order to show the meaning of past perfect, one may use perfect, imperfect, or past participle active. *Ibid.*, § 181.

33 *Ibid.*, 51.

34 E.g., *Nyāyabinduṭīkā*, 24, line 11. Śaṁkara on the Brahma-sūtra, I, 604, line 10 (Anandrāśma Sanskrit Series).

35 *Ibid.*, 25, line 11.

36 *Ibid.*, 15. We do not minimize the fact that there are some exceptions, e.g., *viśeṣaṇa-viśeṣya-bhāva* (*Vedāntasāra*, 168 f).

37 Śaṁkara, *op.cit.*, I, 603, line 3.

38 *Ibid.*, I, 604, line 8.

39 In the Greek translation of the *Bhagavat-gītā* by Demetrios Galanos, *yoga* is translated as *theoria*.

40 *Bṛhad. Up.*, IV, 4, 23.

41 *Dhammapada*, 223. Also see *ibid.*, XVII Kodhavagga (Chapter on Anger).

42 *Ibid.*, 5.

43 *Āyāraṅga*, I, 3: 1, 2.

44 *Praśnottararatnamālikā,* 20.
45 *Ibid.,* 7.
46 *Ibid.,* 6. Such thought is found in the theory of twelve links of causality explained in Buddhism.
47 *Ibid.,* 14.
48 *Bṛhad. Up.,* V, 2. Such a thought process is noticed in the explanation of the theory of "two paths and five fire-offerings" that those who are devotional to Brahma with offerings of religious service and pure practice, are able to proceed to the *pitṛ-yāna* or the path leading to heaven.
49 *Suttanipāta,* 102.
50 *Saṁyutta-Nikāya,* I, 18 Gāthā.
51 *Praśnottararatnamālikā,* 13, 16, 17, 26.
52 *Āyāraṅga,* I, 2: 2, 1.
53 *Ibid.,* I, 6: 3, 2.
54 *Ibid.,* I, 4: 4, 1.
55 Bhāskara, *Brahmasūtrabhāṣya,* 206, 209.

Chapter 7

1 Speyer, *Vedische und Sanskrit-Syntax,* 67.
2 *Ibid.,* 66.
3 *Ibid.,* 75, 243, Anm. 3.
4 *Ibid.,* 63.
5 *Ibid.,* 74.
6 *na tvaṃ śocituṃ arhasi* (*Bhag. G.,* II, 27) = *no te lugere oportet* = You need not be sad.

Here the subject "you" is expressed in the nominative case in the sense of *kartṛ* (agent), while it is expressed in the objective case in Greek and Latin.

7 In the Vaiśeṣika philosophy, *ātman* is counted as one of the substances (*dravya*). There is no passage in the *Nyāyasūtra* where *ātman* is defined as a substance (*dravya*). But as it often refers to the qualities (*guṇa*) which are inherent (*samavāya*) in *ātman,* it may be understood that the perception of *ātman* as a substance is recognized by the Sūtra itself.
8 According to Śaṁkara's description, Bhartṛprapañca was of the following opinion about *ātman:* The substance *ātman* has two characteristics, viz. oneness (*ekatva*) and manifoldness (*nānātva*). For example, oxen have identity through their essence (*go-dravyatā*), and at the same time are distinct from each other through different characteristics such as hanging flesh of neck, etc. Just as there is oneness and diversity within a large visible thing, similarly it should be known that in an indivisible, formless substance like space, there exist oneness and manyness side by side. Because, this (rule) is experienced everywhere without exception, the case is the same with *ātman,* which involves differentiation as in

seeing, etc., on the one hand, and identity on the other hand. Śaṁkara on *Bṛhad. Up.*, IV, 3, 24–30; *AnSS.*, 622.

This opinion is summarized in a syllogism by Ānandajñāna:

"(Proposition) What is discussed here (*ātman*) is differentiated and undifferentiated at the same time.

(Reason) Because it is a substance (*vastu*).

(Example) As in the case of the ox."

Ānandajñāna on Śaṁkara's *Bṛhad. Up. Bhāṣya,* 622.

This syllogism can be applied to Brahman, too, and hence Brahman is concluded to be one and the same, though it is differentiated and undifferentiated at the same time. [The Indian syllogism in three or five members is based on analogy and induction as well as on deduction.—Editor's note.]

9 The intention of the author is not to assert that the investigation of the "real self" was not launched in Western philosophy. Kant admitted the existence of the real self (*das eigentliche Selbst*). In the visible world, according to Kant, it is nothing but the intellect (*Intelligenz*), and human beings are merely its phenomena (*Erscheinungen*). *Grundlegung zur Metaphysik der Sitten,* herausgegeben von Karl Vorländer, 88. Also he distinguishes "the real self" from simple phenomena in the thought of its being the will (*Wille*) of the intellect. *Ibid.*, 91. However, the concept of *"das eigentliche Selbst"* had no further development in Kant's philosophy. As for the comparatively less frequent discussions on the self as a philosophical concept in Western philosophies, see Eisler, *Wörterbuch der philosophischen Begriffe,* s. v. Selbst. Also see Hegel, *Enzyklopädie,* § 405 Zusatz, § 408. [Fichte, Schelling, and Schopenhauer show the influence of Indian philosophy in their concern for the transcendental Ego and Will.—Editor's note.]

10 *Suttanipāta,* 225, 367, 466, 469, 777, 809, 922. *Dhammapada,* 367, *Theragāthā,* 717.

11 "One who has no idea of 'mine' and 'others'—he has no suffering from the notion: 'I do not have this or that,' because of the absence of 'mineness' (*mamatta*) with him." *SN.* 951; cf. 809.

12 Especially, cf. *Bṛhad. Up.*, iii, 5: 1; iv, 4, 22.

13 *Mamāiya-maiṃ jahāi = mamāyita-matiṃ jahāti.* (*Āyāraṅga,* I, 2: 6, 2)

14 *Pravacanasāra,* II, 108; Yenshō Kanakura, *Indo Seishin-bunka no Kenkyū* (Studies on the Mind and Culture of India). 287.

15 *Suttanipāta,* 805, 806.

16 "People in the world, including deities, think what is non-*ātman* as *ātman,* and are attached to its name and form." *anatani attamānam—niviṭṭhaṃ nāmarūpasmiṇ, Suttanipāta,* 231, 761.

17 *Theragāthā,* 575, 1150; cf. 766.

18 *Saṁyutta-Nikāya,* III, 86 G; *AN.* II, 34 G; *SN.* I, 200 G.

19 *SN.*, I, 13 G; cf. *Suttanipāta,* 231; 761.

20 *Theragāthā,* 1160, 1161.

21 *Ibid.*, 497.
22 *Attano kiccakārī, Theragāthā*, 729.
23 *Theragāthā*, 249, 250, 289, 587, 1097. *SN.*, I, 34 G, 55 G, 57 G, 70 G, 102 G.
24 *Attānaṃ gaveseti, Vinaya*, Mahāvagga, I, 13: p. 23. cf. *attaññū*, *AN.*, IV, 113; *DN.*, III, 252.
25 *Chānd. Up.*, VIII, 1, 1. cf. *Mahānārāyaṇa-Up.* X, 7.
26 *SN.* I, 6 G.
27 *AN.* II, 21 G; *SN.* I, 71ff; 57 G; 89; 154 G; *Dhammapada*, 66, 157, 327, 355, 379, 653; *Theragāthā*, 141, 1005.
28 "O indeed, (a wife) loves her husband not because she loves him, but because she loves *ātman*. (A husband) loves his wife not because he loves her, but because he loves *ātman*." *Bṛhad. Up.*, II, 4; IV, 5.
29 *Āyāraṅga*, 25, line 27. cf. 13, line 12; 20, line 20f. (herausgegeben von W. Schubring).
30 *Ibid.*, 44, line 20.
31 *Ibid.*, 13, line 26; 15, line 25; 34, line 30.
32 E.g. *Manusmṛti*, XII, 19.
33 *Praśnottaramālikā*, XXI.
34 *Dhammapada*, 160.

Chapter 8

1 As an exceptional case, the expression, *"ego et rex meus"* (I and my lord), which Cardinal Wolsey always used in official documents, seems arrogant.
2 For example, *tām śvabhiḥ khādayed rājā.* (The king may cause dogs to bite that woman.) In Buddhist writings some examples can be found, e.g. *tadrūpān yajñān na svayaṃ yajati na parair yājayati.* (*Bodhisattvabhūmi*, 118, line 4)
3 Mrs. Rhys Davids, *The Will to Peace*, 85.
4 Generally, *bhavān, tatrabhavān, bhagavān* are used as honorific words. *Deva* is used for a king, *ārya* for an honorable trader and others, *āryā* for a lady, *āryaputra* for an honorable husband, *āyuṣman* for a master by his driver, etc. Speyer, *Sanskrit Syntax*, 195–196.
5 *Tvaṃkāraṃ nāmadheyaṃ ca jyeṣṭhānāṃ parivarjayet. MBh.* XII (1932), 25. W. Hopkins, "The social and military position of the ruling caste in ancient India," *Journal of the American Oriental Society*, XIII (1888), 75n.
6 Fick, *Die soziale Gliederung im nordöstlichen Indien zu Buddha's Zeit*, 54.
7 For instance, see *Suttanipāta*, 206.
8 See *Fragments of Megasthenes*, 33.
9 The Indians of the Maurya Dynasty had an idea that the Indian people had neither been invaded by other people, nor had assailed the latter, except that they had been invaded by Herakles, Dionysos, and the

Macedonians. *Fragments of Megasthenes,* 46. [The recent invasion of Goa by India shocked many Easterners as well as Westerners.—Editor's note].

10 According to Megasthenes there was no slave in India (δοῦλός) in those days. "In India's land there are the following noticeable facts: All Indians are free people; none of them are slaves; among Lacedemonians, Helots are slaves and do work as slaves; on the contrary, among the Indian people other nations are not slaves, to say nothing of the slaves of Indians themselves." Arrianon, *Indike,* 10 = fr. XXVI. "He (Megasthenes) states that no Indian hires slaves. Onesikritos explains that it is peculiar to the Indians who live in Mousikanos." Athenaeus, IV, 153 = fr. XXVIII.

11 Speyer, *Vedische und Sanskrit-Syntax,* 75, sec. 246.

12 *Udāna,* VI, 6.

13 For instance, *vippaḍiveei appaṇam; "kiṃ esa jaṇo karissai? esa se paraārāme, jāo logammi itthio"* (*Sūyagaḍaṃga,* I, 5: 4, 4). I observe for myself, "What do these men do? In this world women are the best pleasure."

14 For instance, *dṛṣṭvemaṃ svajanaṃ . . . yuyutsuṃ samupasthitaṃ* (seeing my own kinsfolk here . . . that have drawn near eager to fight) (*Bhag. G.,* I, 28) = *visa ista cognatorum turba, qui proeliabundi hoc progressi sunt,*

15 *Eine Menge Menschen sind getötet.* (Many people are killed.) *Ein Heer Soldaten marschierten nach Frankreich.* (A group of soldiers marched on France.) But, the following expressions are also used: *Das Heer ist versammelt; es war viel Volk da,* etc.

16 For instance, *etān na hantum icchāmi* (*Bhag. G.,* I, 35); *kāmakāmī* (II, 70); *yuddhakāmān* (I, 22).

17 To cite some examples, *yān eva hatvā na jijīviṣāmaḥ* (*Bhag. G.,* II, 6) = *quibus caesis vivere nos non invat* = οὓς γάρ ἡμεῖς ἀνελόντες οὐκ ἐφιέμεθα ζωῆς; *cikīrṣur lokasaṁgraham* (III, 25) = *procurans generis humani commodum* = βουλόμενος ὑπόδειγμα γενέσθαι τῶ κοσμῳ; *mumukṣubhiḥ* (IV. 15) = *emancipationem affectantibus* = φίλοι τῇ ἀπαδεία; *yogasya jijñāsuḥ,* (VI, 44) = *devotionem cognoscendi studiosus,* ὁ μὲν νὺν φιλῶν κτήσα καὶ τὴν θερίαν.

18 If one addresses himself to another, he may also use the expression "*icchāmi jīvet bhavān*" ("I hope you may live"). (Speyer, *Sanskrit Syntax,* 263; cf. Pāṇini 3:3, 160).

19 Hegel, *Vorlesungen über die Geschichte der Philosophie,* edited by Michelet, 162–163.

19a Cf. H. Nakamura, "The Vedānta as Noticed in Medieval Jain Literature," *Indological Studies in Honor of W. Norman Brown* (New Haven: American Oriental Society, 1962), 186–194. The Jains illustrate the pluralistic tendencies of a minority of Indian thinkers.

20 *Vaiśeṣika-sūtra,* 3:2, 14f.

21 Jayanta, a Nyāya scholar (*ca.* 900 A.D.), quotes the following verse to express the idea of the Self held by the Upavarṣa school:

tatra pratyakṣam ātmānam Aupavarṣāḥ prapedire
ahaṃpratyayagamyatvāt svayūthyā api kecana

"Now, the men of the Upavarṣa school understand the Self by immediate perception. For the Self can be known by the notion of the ego. Some men of our school hold the same view." Then, Jayanta proceeds to explain the notion of the ego (*ahaṃpratyaya*) as follows: "This notion of the ego is within us. Some kinds of notion of the ego are in close connection (*adhikaraṇa*) with the body; e.g. 'I get fat' or 'I get thin.' And some other kinds of it are in close connection with the knowing agent (*jñātṛ*); 'I know' or 'I remember.' " Jayanta's *Nyāya-māñjarī*, Vizianagram Sanskrit Series, X, 429.

22 Śaṁkara, *Brahma-sūtra-bhāṣya,* I, 1, 1 (Ānandāśrama Sanskrit Series, I, 11, line 9; 28, line 1f.); *SBE* (*Sacred Books of the East*), edited by Friedrich Max Müller (Oxford), XXXIV, 5, 14. *Ibid.*, I, line 4; I, 75, line 9; 69, line 10; 75, line 10f.); 37; 34; 37. II, 3, 7. II, 15–16. XXXVIII, 14–15. II, 3, 38. XXXVIII, 51.

23 *Sarvasiddhāntasaṁgraha,* VIII, 37; A. B. Keith, *The Karma-Mimāṁsā,* 71.

24 Śaṁkara on *BS.*, I, 1, 1 (ĀnSS. I, 28, line 1f.); *SBE.*, XXXIV, 14.

25 ĀnSS., I, 14, 75, line 9; *SBE.*, XXXIV, 37.

26 ĀnSS., II, 3, 7, 15–16; *SBE.*, XXXVIII, 14–15. cf. III, 2, 22; II, 224, line 9).

27 ĀnSS., I, 1, line 1; I, 11, line 1; SBE., XXXIV, 5.

28 ĀnSS., I, 1, 4, I, 69, line 10; *SBE.*, XXXIV, 34.

29 ĀnSS., II, 3, 38; *SBE.*, XXXVIII, 51.

30 ĀnSS., I, 1, 4, 75, line 1 of.); *SBE.*, XXXIV, 37.

31 *Kauṣ. Up.*, I, 6; *SBE.* I, 279.

32 *Kaus. Up.*, I, 2; ĀnSS., I, 275.

33 Kenneth W. Morgan (ed.), *The Path of the Buddha: Buddhism Interpreted by Buddhists* (New York: Ronald Press, 1956), 95.

34 Maurice Winternitz, *A History of Indian Literature* (University of Calcutta, 1933), II, 373.

35 William Theodore de Bary (ed.), *Sources of Indian Tradition* (Columbia University Press, 1959), 199ff.

36 *Mahābhārata,* Anuśāsana-parvan, 116, 38.

37 D. M. Datta, *op.cit.*, 572.

38 *Praśnottararatnamālikā,* 5.

39 *Ibid.*, 12.

40 *Ibid.*, 14, 18; *"karuṇā," "dākṣiṇya,"* and *"maitrī"* are taught as the most desirable things.

41 *Ibid.*, 21.

42 *Dhammapada,* 5; *SBE,* 10, pt. I, 5.

43 *Suttanipāta,* 149; *SBE,* 10, pt. II, 25.

44 *Dhammapada,* 43; *SBE,* 10, pt. I, 15.

45 Huston Smith, *The Religions of Man* (New York: Mentor Book, The New American Library, 1961), 116.

46 Henri Bergson, *The Two Sources of Morality and Religion,* translated by R. Ashley Audra and Cloudesley Brereton (New York: Doubleday Anchor Books, 1954), 225–226.

47 According to *Kōsō Hokken Den* (Record of Travel of High Priest Fa-hien), a Chinese pilgrim to India at the time of Candragupta of the Gupta dynasty, the tradition of the social policy based on the Buddha's teaching of benevolence was still surviving, in the country of Magadha. [The Hebrew "rachmunis" (mercy and kindness) antedates Christian mercy and charity.—Editor's Note.]

48 Vincent A. Smith, *Early History of India* (Oxford: 1924), 313n. 1.

49 Romain Rolland, *Prophets of the New India,* translated by E. F. Malcolm-Smith, (London: 1930), 453.

Chapter 9

1 Speyer, *Vedische und Sanskrit-Syntax,* 75; § 169.

2 *Bhagavadgītā: or The Lord's Song,* translated by L. D. Barnett, (London: 1905), 96.

3 *Sāṁkhya-Kārikā,* No. 64. Cf. Deussen, *Allgemeine Geschichte der Philosophie,* I, 3, p. 462.

4 Cf. *Vākyapadiya,* I, 52, 125, 128; Puṇyarāja's *Comm. ad ibid.*

5 *Calcutta-Bairāt Edict.*

6 *Aṅguttara-Nikāya,* IV, 163; Pāli Text Society (*PTS*): ed., *The Books of the Gradual Sayings,* IV, 111.

7 A Japanese Buddhist scholar, Kai-jyō (1750–1805), who held a critical view of the Mahāyāna Buddhism, though he himself was a Mahāyāna Buddhist, pointed out the pretension of "the Buddha's discourse" made by the Indian Buddhists saying: "The so-called 'the Buddha's discourse' is not what Śākyamuni taught directly, but nevertheless, it is the teaching of the enlightened one. All of the Buddha's teaching is on morals and it is not on the art of recording. The ancient followers of the enlightened one called what they understood by their own studies 'the Buddha's saying.' 'The Buddha's saying' in this case means what was intended to be taught by the Buddha. Because it is in compliance with the Buddha's intention, they label their own works 'the Buddha's saying' or 'the Buddha's discourse.'" Kaijō, *Gokyōshō Chōhiroku* (Personal *Annotations* on the *Treatise on Five Doctrines*), quoted in Senshō Murakami, *Daijo Bussetsuron Hihan* (Criticism of the claim that the Mahāyāna is the authentic teaching of the Buddha), 116f.

8 The idea of *Buddhas in the past* appears in the Gāthās of the *Suttanipāta.* And as we can tell from the *Nigālī-Sāgar Edict,* King Aśoka twice enlarged the Stūpa of Konakāmana, one of the Seven Buddhas in the Past.

9 *ātmanā 'tmānam abhi saṁviveśa* (*Vāj. Saṃh.,* XXXII, 11); cf. *para-*

mātmānam adhisaṁviveśa praviśati brahmaiva bhavatīty arthaḥ (Mahīdhara's *Comm.* on *ibid.*); *saṁviśaty ātmanā 'tmānam* (*Māṇḍūkya-Up.*, 12); cf. *ātmaiva saṁviśaty ātmanā svenaiva svaṃ pāramārthikam ātmānam,* (Śaṁkara's *Comm.* on *ibid.*)

10 *Dhammapada,* 288; *SBE* (*Sacred Books of the East*), X, pt. I, 70.

11 *Āyāraṅga,* I, 2: 1, 2; *SBE,* XXII, 16.

12 *Ibid.,* I, 3: 3, 4. (Schubring, 16, line 11.); XXII, 33.

13 There are many sects and schools within Brahmanism. But among the members of a sect or of a school no sufficient sense of unity prevails, for members of the sect or the school seldom act as a unit.

14 According to the stories written in Ceylon, the first compilation of the Buddhist texts was made at Rājagṛha just after the death of the Buddha. At that time, the texts of precepts were compiled chiefly by Upāli. And from him the collection of the books of precepts (Vinaya-piṭaka) was transmitted in turn through the hands of Dāsaka, Soṇaka, Siggava, and Moggaliputta Tissa until the time of King Aśoka. Each one of those five transmitters was said to be the head of the Saṁgha of his days. The story corresponding to this one in the legends of Ceylon can be found in some of the Chinese translations of the Buddhist texts. But, it should be noted, those five men were only the masters of precepts, and they did not take part in the handing down of the Buddhist doctrines. Besides, they were not the heads to rule over all the Buddhist Saṁghas. They were no more than the heads of the Vibhajya-vādin Saṁgha in the Theravāda school.

15 *Vinaya,* Cullavagga, XI, 1, 9; *SBE,* XX, 378. At the time of the compilation of the Buddhist texts held at Vaiśālī, the Vajjians promulgated the ten new theses. But their theses were judged unlawful and rejected. Cf. *Ibid.,* Cullavagga XII.

16 Hakuju Ui, *Indo-tetsugaku Kenkyū* (Studies in Indian philosophy), II, 185f.

17 Cf. *Śatapathabrāhmaṇa,* XI, 5, 7, 1.

18 *Bṛhad. Up.,* I, 4, 14; *SBE,* XV, 89. There are many cases of the identification of *satya* and *dharma.* Cf. *Chānd. Up.,* VII, 2, 1; VII, 7, 1; *Tait. Up.,* I, 11, 1.

19 *Mahānārāyaṇa-Up.,* XXI, 2.

20 *Ibid.,* XXII, 1.

21 *śreyorūpa* (*Bṛhad. Up.,* 1, 4, 14).

22 Cf. *Vaiśeṣika-Sūtra,* I, 2. The Vaiśeṣika asserted: As there are good evidences in the Vedas, a man can reach the celestial sphere and receive blessings by the faithful performance of the religious works. (*Ibid.,* I, 1, 3; X, 2, 9). But, at this stage, the deliverance of his soul is not yet attained. "(It) results from the knowledge of the essence (*tattva-jñāna*) of the Predicables, Substance, Attribute, Action, Genus, Species, and Combination by their resemblances and differences." (*Ibid.,* I, 1, 4; *The Sacred Books of the Hindus,* VI, 9.) Ascension of the soul is produced by one kind of *Dharma* (*dharmaviśeṣa*), the low

Dharma (*aparo dharmaḥ*), and the deliverance of the soul is produced by another kind of *Dharma*, the high *Dharma* (*paro dharmaḥ*); cf. Candrakānta's *Comm.* on *ibid.* I, 1, 2. The Vaiśeṣika called the whole system of their doctrines "the *Dharma*" and they made their quest of truth in this system. (*Ibid.*, I, 1, 1.)

23 *Atharva-Veda*, XVIII, 3, 1.

24 *Bṛhad.-Up.*; I, 5, 23; *SBE*, XV, 98.

25 *dhamme suddhe nitie sāsae* (Āyāraṅga I, 4, 1, 1); *SBE*, XXII, 36.

26 *AN.* I, 286; *PTS.*: *The Books of the Gradual Sayings*, I, 264; cf. The Chinese version of the *Saṁyuktāgama*, vol. 30.

27 E.g. *S.N.*, *Mahāpadānasutta.*

28 Cf. *supra.*

29 *The Pillar Edict*, VII.

30 *King Khāravela Inscriptions.* A "*Cakravartin*" means in the political context the ruler who has conquered all enemies around his nation.

31 It can be learned from the words inscribed on the coins issued by those kings.

32 *pathyatara* (*Praśnottararatnamālikā*, 4).

33 Quoted in Albert Schweitzer, *Das Christentum und die Weltreligionen* (1924), 29.

34 F. S. C. Northrop, *The Taming of the Nations* (New York: Macmillan, 1953).

35 [One of the most important problems from the standpoint of improving mutual understanding and communication between Indian and Western thought is the status of logic as a universal science, rather than as a peculiar feature of Western "postulational thinking" as Northrop puts it, in sharp contrast with the "undifferentiated aesthetic continuum" of the whole Oriental way of thinking. It is true that the indeterminate nature of Absolute Being in that school—only one of many in India—that scorns the principle of contradiction, can lead only to a kind of mysticism which, though not absent from Western thought, is attractive to so many Indian thinkers. Have they despaired of the possibility of solving the enormous social and cultural problems of their vast country with its many peoples, and languages, poverty, illiteracy, internal and external political relations, etc. by means of intelligence and scientific methods? In any case, it is logically possible to discuss the principle of contradiction as a linguistic syntactical rule rather than as an ontological law (as Aristotle did) without lapsing into a mystical renunciation of all logic. Cf. J. F. Staal, "Negation and the Law of Contradiction in Indian Thought: A Comparative Study," *Bulletin of the School of Oriental and African Studies*, University of London, XXV, pt. 1 (1962), 52–71. Agreeing with Staal's conclusion that "no language can function without a logical structure which is implicit in it" (71), I should think that the problem for comparative East-West studies is to do the research that will make explicit the logical structures of the diverse languages and compare them in a meta-language. Such a research

project calls for the collaboration of philosophical linguists and logicians. —Editor's note.]

36 *divaṁ māyaṁ na saddahe*, Āyāraṅga, I, 8, 8, 24; (edited by Schubring), 40, line 5.

37 *Tattvārthaśraddhānaṃ samyagdarśanam, Tattvārthādhigama-sūtra*, I, 2; cf. *Yogaśāstra* I, 17; *Sarvadarśana-saṁgraha* III, line 155f.

38 *Brahmasūtra-bhāsya*, II, 143, line 9. (*ĀnSS.*) But this definition is the word of the *pūrvapakṣin*. In another place, Śaṁkara states: "the mental conception (*pratyaya*) called faith (*śraddhā*) is the attribute (*dharma*) of the mind (*manas*) or soul." Cf. *ibid.*, II, 144, line 4. And it should be noted that in some cases Śaṁkara uses *pratyaya* to mean confidence or trust; e.g. *aśraddadhānāḥ* = *apratyayavanto*, (Śaṁkara's Commentary on *Praśna-Up.*, II, 3).

39 *Brahmasūtra-bhāṣya*, II, 144, line 8.

40 *Vedāntasāra*, 23.

41 The faithful observance of the doctrines given by the teachers of the school is called *śraddhā;* cf. Śaṁkara on *BS.*, I, 524, line 6.

42 *śraddhā-pūrvakarma*, Śaṁkara on *BS.*, II, 144, line 10; religious works (sacrifices, etc.) which depend on faith, *SBE.*, XXXVIII, 108.

43 Śaṁkara on *Praśna-Up.*, VI, 4.

44 *āstikyabuddhi*, *ibid.*, I, 2.

45 It is difficult to find in the Western languages the terms exactly equivalent to *prasāda*. Cf. *pasanno buddhasāsane* (*Dhp.*, 368).

> *Buddhae praeceptis sedatus* (Fausbøll's translation).
>
> Who is calm in the doctrine of Buddha (Max Müller's translation).

Both Fausbøll's and Müller's translations fail to convey the full meaning of *prasāda.*

46 In the *Theragāthā*, 370, the man who puts faith in his teacher's words is called *bhattimā*. This is the only case of the reference to *bhakti* that can be found in all the Gāthās of the Buddhist scriptures of the early days.

47 Cf. *Praśnottararatnamālikā*, 3.

48 Cf. *ibid.*, 10.

49 Cf. *ibid.*, 4.

50 *Dhammapada*, 28; *SBE*, X, pt. I, 10. Cf. *Mahābhārata*, 12. 151. 11.

51 This problem still needs consideration. "The question is: Is there really anything in India which is regarded as ultimately and genuinely absurd?" I refer to a people that continuously emphasized the manifoldness of truth and evolved in Jain logic the doctrine of sevenfold judgment (*Saptabhaṅgīnaya*). See in this connection P. T. Raju's article on the four-fold negation, *Review of Metaphysics*, VII, 4 (June 1954), 694–713. Archie J. Bahm in *Philosophy East and West*, VII, Nos. 3 and 4 (October 1957 and January 1958), 127–130. [Dr. Daya Krishna's comment.]

52 Masson-Oursel, *La Philosophie Comparée*, 40.

53 The cases in Japan are in marked contrast to those in India. In the *Kojiki* and the *Nihonshoki,* both prominent models of ancient Japanese chronicles, the history of the Emperor's dynasty was the central concern and many myths and legends were told to strengthen its authenticity.

54 *Chavaka-Jātaka,* III, 27f.

55 *Āpastamba-Dharma-Sūtra,* 1. 2. 8. 8; *Gautama-Dharma-Sūtra,* 2. 21; *Viṣṇu-smṛti,* 28. 12; *The Laws of Manu,* 2. 198.

56 *Sāmañña-phala-suttanta* in the *Dīrgha-Nikāya* and in the Chinese version of the *Dīrgha-Nikāya.*

57 It is about King Bimbisāra of Magadha. Cf. *Suttanipāta,* 409 f.

58 *Taishō,* IV, 582 b-c.

59 *Taishō* I, 497 b and 795 c; II, 808 c.

60 *Taishō,* I, 497 b, 795 c; also 108 a, 279 a; II, 609 b, 624 a, 679 b; XXIV, 237 a.

61 Cf. *Calcutta-Bairāt Edict.*

62 It is true that ancient Indian religious bodies did not have political influence upon the outside world as did the bodies of Christianity and Mohammedanism. But their independent authority was by no means submissive to external power.

63 King Bālāditya of the Gupta dynasty was dissatisfied with his low position in the Buddhist Saṁgha. But the Buddhists dared not violate the old rule of the Saṁgha to make an exception in his favor.

64 Cf. *Vinaya, suttavibhaṅga,* IV, 159–160; *Aṅguttara-Nikāya,* V, 81–83; *Taishō,* XXIV, 786 c.

65 *Taishō,* II, 777 a-b.

66 *The Lotus Sūtra,* Chapter of *Sukha-vihāra-parivarta,* U. Wogiwara and K. Tsuchida, ed., 235.

67 *Taishō,* XVII, 294 c–295 a.

68 Cf. *Buddhacarita,* 9. 19f; *Taishō,* III, 749 a.

69 "Every fifteenth and last day of a month, the king (of Kucha) discusses national affairs with the ministers, consults the learned priests and then promulgates the decrees." Travel Records of Hsüan-Tsang, vol. I.

70 *Taishō,* XXXI, 858 a-c. Cf. Also *Taishō,* X, 714 b.

71 The *Brahmajāla-sūtra,* pt. 2. *Taishō,* XXIV, 1008 c.

72 *Mahābhārata,* 12. 242. 9.

73 *Māṇḍūkya-Kārikā,* 2. 37. Cf. *Paramahaṃsa-Upaniṣad; Paramahaṃsa-parivrājaka-Upaniṣad.*

74 Tetsurō Watsuji, *Homērosu-hihan* (Textual Criticism of Homer), 41–42; Tetsurō Watsuji, "*Polisu-no-keisei* (Formation of the Polis)" in *Jo-setsu,* I, 26f. The Indian religion also differs from the Japanese insofar as the Japanese stress individual ethical organizations rather than the universal law.

75 The founder of the Maurya dynasty, King Candragupta, who beat back the Greek forces from northwest India, is often referred to in later Indian books. But these do not praise him as the hero who defended the nation against foreign invasions.

76 In India, there remain many records of donations inscribed on monuments. Judging from these, few donations were made to secular state powers while many were made to religious bodies. The Indian idea of the nation differs a great deal from the Japanese notion and also from the Roman idea of "*patria.*"

77 [The Chinese Communists' invasion of India in the fall of 1962 had the temporary value of uniting the Hindus with the Mohammedans of Pakistan for a common defense.—Editor's note.]

78 [Increased urbanization in time is likely to produce profound changes in India's caste system.—Editor's note.]

79 "I place strong faith in the pure Enlightened One who is born of pure stock." The opening part of the *Mahāvaṁsa.*

80 Max Weber treated this problem by introducing the concept of "*Gentilcharisma*" ("prestige of gentility"). His study is worthy of praise, but this concept is not enough to explain the relationship between the way of thinking of a people and the rise of a caste system in India. Cf. Max Weber, *Aufsätze zur Religionssoziologie,* I, 268; Max Weber, *Hinduismus und Buddhismus,* 129.

81 In the oldest Gāthās of the early Buddhists, the holy scriptures of the Jains and the *Aśoka Edicts,* "*pāṇa* (*prāṇa*)" is used to mean "living being."

82 V. Fausbøll, in his Latin translation of the *Dhammapada,* translated these words as "*animans*" or "*animalis.*"

83 Cf. *Praśnottararatnamālikā,* 22; the *Aśoka Edicts.*

84 In the West, too, some philosophers have held that the subject of ethical conduct is not to be limited to man. But, as we see in Kant's idea of man's rational essence ("*vernünftige Wesen*"), they in fact focussed attention on the problem of man and ignored the consideration of living beings. Cf. Kant, *Grundlegung zur Metaphysik der Sitten, herausgegeben von Karl Vorländer,* 28f; 52f. (Kant's *Metaphysics of Morals*).

85 *Dhammapada,* 130; *Āyāraṅga,* 1. 2. 3. 4.

86 *Dhammapada,* 132 and 405, *Āyāraṅga,* 16 and 35.

87 *Mahābhārata,* 13. 113. 6. The great rites, as recorded in the ancient Vedas, required animal sacrifice. On this account, Buddhists and Jains deplored the feats of Brahmanism. The idea of animal protection appears in the Brāhmaṇic texts of the last stage of the Vedic age. In the *Upaniṣads,* it is stated that "non-harming" is to be praised just as much as offering to the priests. And in another text, it is decreed not to kill a living being at the place other than the site of rites. Cf. *Chāndogya-Upaniṣad,* 3. 17. 4; 8. 15.

88 *Brahma-sūtra-bhāṣya,* 1. 1. 1.

89 *Tattvārthādhigamasūtra,* II, 23–24. The problem of classifying creatures is dealt with fully in Śāntisūri's; *Jīvaviyāra.* (Cf. Winternitz, *A History of Indian Literature,* II [Calcutta: 1933], 354.)

90 Hemacandra, *Adhidhānacintāmaṇi,* 21–22.

91 *Davvasaṁgaha,* 12; *Sarvārthasiddhi.*

92 *Tattvārthādhigamasūtra,* II, 32f.

93 Cf. *Aitareya-Upaniṣad,* 5. 13; *Brahma-sūtra,* 3. 1. 21; *Mahābhārata,* 12, 312. 5; *The Laws of Manu,* 1. 43–46. In the *Chāndogya-Upaniṣad,* creatures are classified into three groups—viviparous, oviparous, and germinative; while there is no reference to beings produced out of moisture. The *Brahma-sūtra* interprets this assertion by saying that these latter beings are included in the group of germinative beings.

94 Cf. many commentary works on the *Brahma-sūtra,* 3. 1. 21. In a medical book, *Suśruta-saṁhitā,* these four groups are recognized for the classification of animals (*jaṅgama*) and, as examples, germinative beings, frogs, and fireflies are mentioned. (Cf. Guha, *Jīvātman,* 55.)

95 *Brahma-sūtra,* 2. 3. 16.

96 *Mahābhārata,* 12. 184. 17.

97 Sanskrit "*manuṣya,*" like English "man," is etymologically connected with the root of "*man*"—to think.

98 *Aitareya-Āraṇyaka,* 2. 3. 2.

99 *Majjhima-Nikāya,* 129.

100 *Butsui-shōkō-tenshi-setsu-ōbō-kyō* (A sūtra expounding the kingly laws of Buddhism), *Taishō,* XV, 125 b-c.

101 The Jains, too, teach that man's life is very precious and that it is highly significant to be born a man. Cf. Winternitz, *op.cit.,* II, 466.

102 *Chāndogya-Upaniṣad,* 5. 10. 7–8.

103 Praśastapāda, *Padārthadharmasaṁgraha,* § 39, *dharmalkṣaṇa.*

104 *The Laws of Manu,* 12. 95. 96.

105 *Aṅguttara-Nikāya,* II, 51 G.

106 *Suttanipāta,* 284.

107 Cf. *ibid.,* 299.

108 The Lotus Sūtra and the *Larger Sukhāvatī-vyūha* hold that their teachings are proper for the period of *Mappō*—the days of decadence. Cf. The Lotus Sūtra, chapter of *Sukha-vihāra-parivartaḥ; larger Sukhāvatī-vyūha, finis.*

109 *Mahābhārata,* 1. 1. 269.

110 *Ibid.,* 1. 1. 256.

111 The ancient Indians, too, knew full well of this perversion. To a question why *The Laws of Manu* has, contrary to the fact, the name of Manu as the author, an interpreter answered: "Every teacher consciously makes use of this measure to present his own ideas, that is, in the guise of the teachings of the great predecessors." Cf. *Kullūkabhaṭṭa on Manu,* I, 4.

112 *Dhammapada,* 260; *The Laws of Manu,* 2. 156; *Praśnottaratnamālikā,* 4.

113 *The Laws of Manu,* 2. 121. Cf. *Dhammapada,* 109.

114 Cf. Paramārtha's *Commentary on the Mahāyāna-saṁparigraha. Taishō,* XXXI, 157 b. Vasubandhu's translation does not contain a sentence which corresponds to this part. This sentence therefore was probably added by Paramārtha, the translator.

115 Indians are by no means unskilled in logic; they have developed mathematics and grammar and other studies based on scientific methods. How-

ever, still it cannot be denied that the blind acceptance of the authority of the scriptures forms a dominant character of traditional Indian ways of thinking.

116 City-states as developed in the West did not appear in India. The Indian cities could not act unitedly as a political organization, either to make treaties with other cities or to exercise proper jurisdiction over the inhabitants. This condition of the Indian cities is another reason for the slow emergence of liberal thought in India.

117 The word "nomothetical" here does not imply the meaning of laws of natural science, as in the philosophy of Heinrich Rickert, but simply universalistic.

118 Biographical details are minimal even in the cases of religious leaders who died relatively recently. Ten years or so after their death, they are treated as incarnations of the gods. In pamphlets commemorating their founders published by the religious schools established in the nineteenth and the twentieth centuries, no dates of birth and death are mentioned.

119 There are some works of topography in the Purāṇa texts.

120 "The religious tendency of the Indian districts where Buddhism spread and secured a strong footing shows a very remarkable bent toward the impersonal and the universal, of alienation from the visible and the tangible, and of submergence and dissolution into the infinite." H. Oldenberg, *Aus dem alten Indien*, 14–15.

121 *Ibid.*, 99.

Chapter 10

1 *Aṅgāḥ Kaliṅgāḥ, Pañcālā ramaṇīyāḥ* (*Kāśikā* on Pāṇini, I, 2, 52).

2 When a clear expression of "A as B" is required, they express B in the instrumental case, e.g. *"dautyena gacchati."* (He goes as a messenger.) (dautya < dūta) Mostly, however, the instrumental case is shown by *"-tvena"* (*-tva,* a suffix making the abstract noun).

3 *Kathaṃ so 'nuśiṣṭo bruvīta* (*Chānd. Up.*, V, 3, 4) = "wie könnte er sagen, er wäre ausgelernt." Cf. Speyer, *Vedische und Sanskrit-Syntax*, 56, § 186, 94, § 293.

4 Speyer, *op.cit.*, 84, § 271.

5 Sometimes a sentence starts with an indirect narration but changes into direct narration on the way. Sometimes both kinds of narration are used side by side. Such examples are observed in the *Mahābhārata* and the *Rāmāyaṇa*. Speyer, *op.cit.*, 92, § 288.

6 On this point, Latin is similar to Sanskrit.

7 For example, *"evaṃ mā kanīyāṃsam eva vadhāt kṛtvā"* (*Ś. Br.* III, 6, 3, 8) is translated by Speyer into "nachdem er mich kleiner gemacht hatte, als dass ich getroffen werden könnte."

8 Harushige Kōzu, *Hikaku-gengo-gaku* (*Comparative Linguistics*), 308, n. 1.

9 *Maitrāyaṇī-Saṁhitā* 2, 3, 6; Delbrück, *Altindische Syntax*, 41; Speyer, *op.cit.*, § 258.

10 Speyer, *op.cit.*, 81–82.
11 Speyer: *op.cit.*, § 66; M. Winternitz, *A History of Indian Literature,* II, 52; H. Oldenberg, *Buddha,* 211.
12 *Ch'u-san-tsang-chi-chi-hsü,* VIII (Preface to the Selections from the *Mahāprajñāpāramitāsūtra*). He also says: "(In Indian scriptures) when a subject has been described and another subject is going to be explained, they repeat the same sentences used for the previous subject before entering into the new subject. While (in China) the whole (repetition) is omitted." (*Ibid.*)
13 Kōgatsuin Jinrei, *Kyōgyōshinshō Kōgi* (Lectures on Shinran's Teachings, Practice, Faith, and Attainment) (Bukkyo Taikei Edition), 367.
14 This tendency is prominent in Jain scriptures of a little later date such as "Ovavaiya," and in inscriptions of c. 2nd century A.D. kept in Buddhist cave temples.
15 Coins of Spalirises, a Parthian king, have the following inscriptions: "βασιλεῶς ἀδελφοῦ Σπαλιρισου" on one side, and "*maharajabhrata dhramiasa Śpaliriśasa*" on the other. Sten Konow, *Kharoshṭhī Inscriptions,* Introduction, xli. Likewise, some coins of the King Azēs have the following inscription: "βασιλέως βασιλέων μεγάλου 'Άζου;" "*maharajasa* (or *rajatirajasa*) *mahatasa Ayasa.*" Sten Konow, *op.cit.*, xxxix. Coins of King Maues are of a similar inscription to those of Azēs. Rapson, *Indian Coins,* Plate I, no. 15.
16 H. Oldenberg, *Die Lehre der Upanishaden und die Anfänge des Buddhismus,* 49, *Anm.*
17 A. C. Woolner, *Introduction to Prakrit,* 12.
18 At the beginning of the *Karpūramañjarī,* a stage-director asks his assistant why Prakrit and not Sanskrit is used in the drama, and receives the following answer: "Sanskrit verses sound stiff, but Prakrit verses sound smooth. The difference between both languages is like the difference between a man and a woman."
19 Ananda K. Coomaraswamy, *History of Indian and Indonesian Art;* Japanese translation by Chikyō Yamamoto, *Indo oyobi Tōnan Ajiya Bijutsu-shi,* 40.
20 Romain Rolland, *La vie de Ramakrishna* (Paris: 1929), 31.
21 *Ta-chih-tu-lun* (*Mahāprajñāpāramitā-śātra*), (Commentary on the Supreme Wisdom), V.
22 *Hua-yen-wu-chiao-chang* of Fa-tsang (Kwannō Edition), Part b–2, 48 b. (Treatise on the Five Doctrines of the Hua-yen school).
23 Rolland, *op.cit.*, 56.
24 Tominaga Nakamoto, *Shutsujō-kōgo* (Discourse After Meditation), Pt. 1, Chapter 8, *Jinzū* (Miraculous Power).
25 *Ibid.*
26 "Heretics of those days, too, preached doctrines by means of fantasy." "In the Tripiṭaka, there are lots of illustrations of fantasy. It is because Indians have many experiences of fantasy in their life and they are fond of it." "Heretics called it illusion (*māyā*), while Buddhists called

it miraculous faculty (*abhijñā*). In reality, both are one and the same." "Illustrations such as a poppy-seed and Mt. Sumeru, the net of Indra are also beloved by the people." *Ibid.*, Chapter 8.

27 *Okina-no-fumi* (Letters of an Old Man) in *ibid.*, Ch. 14.

28 "And those doctrines of moral causality, of Hell and Paradise, were originally from other religions (outside of Buddhism). They were beloved by Indians." *Ibid.*, Chapter 8.

29 *Ta-chih-tu-lun, op.cit.*, I (*Taishō*, XXV, 58 b).

30 *Ibid.*, XCIV (*Taishō*, XXV, 717 b); cf. XXXVII (*Taishō*, XXV. 332 a).

31 Cf. "Megasthenes" (by O. Stein), in Pauly-Wissowa's *Realenzyklopädie.*

32 J. W. McCrindle, *Ancient India*, Introduction, 18–21.

33 *Ibid.*, 20.

34 Hegel, *Vorlesungen über die Geschichte der Philosophie,* hrsg. von Michelet, 154.

35 Kern, *Manual of Indian Buddhism,* 57.

36 Śaṁkara on *BS.*, III, 2, 21 (II, 217, lines 5ff).

37 Cf. Hiriyanna, "*Prapañcavilayavāda,* a Doctrine of Pre-Śaṁkara Vedānta," *Journal of Oriental Research Madras,* I (1927), 109ff.

38 Max Weber, *Aufsätze zur Religionssoziologie,* I, Vorbemerkung, 4.

39 The *Pao-hang-wang-chêng-lun* (*Ratnāvali*) (A Treatise on the Proper Conduct of a King) attributed to Nāgārjuna is typical.

40 An ascetic of the Yoga lies on a floor covered with projecting nails, and by such exercise, tries to accomplish the subjugation of the body to the control of his will. As for the control of the mind, we find it stated: "With the indefatigable effort required to drain off the ocean by scooping up its water with the cusp of a leaf, the control of the mind should be accomplished." *Māṇḍūkyā-Kārikā,* III, 41.

41 Judging from the old *gāthās,* Buddhists too in the earliest period of their history encouraged their followers to lead an austere life of mortification.

42 *Sarvasiddhāntasaṁgraha,* III, 12.

43 M. Winternitz, *A History of Indian Literature,* II, 452.

44 Cf. *Chāndogya-Up.*, VI.

45 Megasthenes, *The Fragments,* 41.

46 Cf. M. Winternitz, *op.cit.*, I, 16; 17; 366.

47 Cf. H. Keyserling, *Reisetagebuch eines Philosophen, finis.*

48 Cf. H. Oldenberg, *Aus dem alten Indien,* 93.

49 In India, there is no uniform system of marking historical eras. Their method of determining historical periods differs according to time and place. According to one historian, there are more than twenty ways of marking eras in India. This fact presents a great contrast to the uniform adoption in the West of the Christian era. Cf. V. A. Smith, *The Early History of India* (1957), 20.

50 H. Oldenberg, *Buddha,* 385.

51 Cf. *Pañcatantra, Hitopadeśa* and Buddhist *Jātaka* tales. Jains also have what they call *Jātakas.*

52 H. Oldenberg, *Aus dem alten Indien,* 107.

53 Cf. Hsüan-tsang's translation of *tattva* as *Bodhisattvabhūmi,* 212, line 12; 37, 39. *Tattva* is used also to mean the order of nature. Cf. *Vākyapadīya* III, 3, 3; *Nala* XVI, 38 (*tattvena hi mamācakṣva*); *Saura-Purāṇa,* a. 4 (in Gonda, *Sanskrit Reader,* 65, line 3), *brūhi me tattvataḥ.*

54 *Immanuel Kant's Critique of Pure Reason,* translated by Norman Kemp Smith, 97.

55 Megasthenes, *The Fragments,* 41.

56 Cf. Winternitz, *op.cit.,* III, 542.

57 The influence of the Greek sciences upon Indian sciences remains to be clarified by future studies.

58 Cf. G. Misch, *Der Weg in die Philosophie, passim.*

59 Cf. *Yājñavalkya-smṛti,* I, 310. The scholars of the Nyāya also accepted as true Kauṭilya's system of classification. Cf. Jacobi, *Sitzungsberichte der Preussischen Akademie* (1911), 733.

60 Sūtra on the Stages of Bodhisattvahood, III; Sūtra on the Moral Precepts of Bodhisattvahood, IV; Treatise on the Stages of the Yogācārin, XV, XXXVIII; Records on the Western Lands in the T'ang Period, II.

61 It should be remembered here that the Chinese Buddhists in some cases managed to translate these Sanskrit terms as "art of language," "art of logic," "art of internal doctrines" or the like. In their practical way of thinking, Buddhists understand learning as one of the arts. Cf. Hakuju Ui, *Indo-tetsugaku Kenkyū* (Study of Indian Philosophy), IV, 46 a f.

62 *Pāyāsi-suttanta,* in Dīghanikāya No. 23. The same story can be found in the Jain Sūtra, *Rāyapaseṇaijja;* cf. Winternitz, *A History of Indian Literature,* II, 455f.

63 For example, there is a famous classic story about the debate between Śaṁkara and Maṇḍanamiśra where the latter's conversion is supposed to have taken place after defeat in the debate. Also, Śaṁkara is supposed to have spread Vedānta in the four corners of India by defeating his adversaries in open debate. (*Śaṁkara-digvijaya, etc.*)

Chapter 11

1 The ancient Indians had advanced skill in numerical calculation, but they made no effort toward a theoretical understanding of the logical problems of mathematics. They gave no demonstrations. For instance, the Pythagorean theorem was understood by the intuitive grasp of the figure without resorting to demonstration, in contrast to the Greeks.

2 Cf. *Ṛg-Veda,* 10. 71; 10. 125.

3 In the field of the Prakrit, however, there emerged many grammarians, one after another.

4 Gaurinath Sastri, *The Philosophy of Word and Meaning* (Calcutta: Sanskrit College, 1959); David Seyfert Ruegg, *Contribution à l'histoire de la Philosophie Linguistique Indienne* (Paris: É. de Boccard, 1959).

5 Cf. D. H. H. Ingalls, "The Comparison of Indian and Western Philosophy," *Journal of Oriental Research* (Madras: 1954), XXII, 1–11.

6 Ryō Kuroda, *Yuishiki Shinrigaku* (Psychology of "Mind-only") (1944), Introduction.

7 *Ibid.*, 253.

Chapter 12

1 Hegel, *Vorlesungen über die Geschichte der Philosophie,* edited by Michelet, 144.

2 F. C. Conybeare, *Philostratus, the Life of Apollonius of Tyana* (London: 1917), I, 196–197.

3 There are the examples also in the Pāli books, e.g.: *atha ce patthayasī, pavassa deva* (*Suttanipāta* 18–19); *devo ca vassati, devo ca galagalāyati* (*Theragāthā,* 189); *deve vassante katamena udakam gaccheya* (*Milindapañha,* 57).

4 E.g., *Manu,* IV, 38; *kāle caivaṃ pravarṣati* (*Suvarṇaprabhāsa* XII, v. 61).

5 ". . . alors que chaque phénomène naturel était tenu pour le résultat de l'activité de quelque génie, ὕει signifiait 'le dieu, le génie pleut'; en fait, Homère n'a pas ὕει seulement mais deux fois ὗει δ'ἄρα Ζεύς. Le latin a *Jove tonnate,* etc. L'expression védique *vāto vāti,* 'le vent vente,' est plus caractéristique encore. Ce ne sont donc pas des impersonnels qui expriment les phénomènes naturels, mais troisième personnes dont le sujet, qui est un génie plus ou moins vaguement conçu, n'est pas indiqué avec précision." (A. Meillet, *Introduction à l'étude comparative des langues indo-européennes,* 212–213.) Cf. Shinkichi Sudo, *Ronrigaku Kōyō* (Outlines of Logic), 154.

6 Cf. *supra,* Chapter 7, section on Subjective Comprehension of Personality as Revealed in Philosophy.

7 When Galanos means Absolute Being, he writes θεός with capitals.

8 From ancient times, many Indians take the names of such gods as Śaṁkara or Viṣṇu as their family or personal names. This custom of naming people after gods is hardly found either in the West or in China or Japan.

9 *Bṛhad. Up.*, I, 1, 1; *SBE,* XV, 74.

10 Cf. Ideishi, *Jōdai Shina ni okeru Shinwa oyobi Setsuwa* (Myths and Legends in Ancient China) in Iwanami Kōza, *Tōyō Shichō* (Eastern Thoughts), 21.

11 H. Oldenberg, *Die Lehre der Upanishaden und die Anfänge des Buddhismus,* 25.

12 Cf. Mādhava, *Sarvadarśana-saṁgraha,* Chapter on Raseśvara.

13 Huston Smith, *The Religions of Man* (New York: The New American Library, 1961), 25f.; Heinrich Zimmer, *The Philosophies of India* (New York: Pantheon Books, 1951).

14 *Bṛhad. Up.*, III, 7; *SBE,* XV, 136.

15 Cf. *Dhammapada,* 189. There is an elaborate study on this familiar expression of Indian Buddhism in Hakuju Ui, *Indo-tetsugaku Kenkyū, op.cit.*, III, 353.

16 E.g. *Dhammapada*, 286–287.
17 *Suttanipāta*, 440; *SBE*, X, pt. II, 70.
18 *Āyāraṅga*, herausgegeben von W. Schubring, 27, 1. 28; *SBE*, XXII, 54.
19 *Ibid.*, 11.
20 *Ibid.*, 3.
21 *Mādhava*, The *Sarva-Darśana-Saṁgraha* or *Review of the Different Systems of Hindu Philosophy*, translated by E. B. Cowell, 22. Especially in Buddhism they assume that "all is pain and pain (*sarvam duhkham*)." Cf. *ibid.*, 15.
22 *Praśnottararatnamālikā*, 3.
23 *Dhammapada*, 150; *SBE*, X, pt. I, 42.
24 *The Laws of Manu*, 6. 761.
25 *Kāyassa viavāa* (=*vyavapāda*), *Āyāraṅga*, 32, line 20; *dehabheya* (= °_____ *bheda*), *ibid.*, 40, line 2. Cf. *ibid.*, 37, line 18.
26 Sakkāyass' *uparodhana* (*Suttanipāta*, 761); *sakkāyass' nirodha* (*SN*. III, 86G).
27 Cf. *Āyāraṅga*, 12; *Suttanipāta*, 220, 367, 466, 469, 494, 777, 922; *Theragāthā*, 717.
28 In contrast to the Chinese Christians, the Indian Christians have a strong inclination to transcend secular affairs. But this will be treated in later chapters.
29 Jinnosuke Sano, *Indo oyobi Indojin* (India and Indians), 253.
30 *Dhammapada*, 146; *SBE*, X, pt. I, 41.
31 Megasthenes, *The Fragments*, 41.
32 *Sankyō Yōron* (Essentials of the Three Schools: Confucianism, Taoism, Buddhism), in *Nihon Jurin Sōsho* (Series on Japanese Confucianism), Kaisetsubu, II, 7.
33 Pauly-Wissowa, *Realenzyklopädie*, s. v. Megasthenes, 319–320.

The Chinese word "*t'a*" has its etymological origin in *thūpa* or *thuba*, the Prakrit forms of *stūpa*. And what the Japanese mean by "*tō*" (tower) at present refers to the modified forms of the original Indian *Stūpas*.
34 In the Epics, especially in the *Bhagavadgītā*, or in the Mahāyāna texts, there are passages which show that some philosophers disregarded the system of rewards and punishments of *Karma* and sought to value goodness for its own sake, thus encouraging the observance of morality in order to realize absolute goodness in this life. This ethic of inherent goodness assumes intrinsic values of conduct that are not necessarily dependent on the concept of God.
35 Seiichi Hatano, *Kirisutokyō no Kigen* (Origin of Christianity), 214.
36 Cf. H. Oldenberg, *Die Lehre der Upanishaden und die Anfänge des Buddhismus*, 146.

Chapter 13

1 *Sutta-nipāta*, 891.
2 *Ibid.*, 844–845.

3 *Ibid.*, 837, 845.
4 *Ibid.*, 842f., 855, 860.
5 *Ibid.*, 880–881, 905–906.
6 E.g. Ta-sa-che-ni-ch'in-tzu-so-shu-ching; Ta-p'an-nie-p'an-ching; Chinese versions of the *Mahāparinirvāṇa-sūtra.*
7 *Māṇḍūkyakārikā,* 3–17.
8 *Vītarāgastuti,* 30 (*Sarvadarśana-saṁgraha,* III, line 409).
9 *Rock Edict,* Chapter 12.
10 Rama Shankar Tripathi, "Religious toleration under the Imperial Guptas," *Indian Historical Quarterly,* 1939, 1–12.
11 Romain Rolland, *La vie de Ramakrishna,* 93.
12 *Ibid.*, 186.
13 Romain Rolland, *La vie de Vivekānanda,* I, 47–48.
14 *Ibid.*, II, 110.
15 Max Weber, *Die protestantische Ethik und der Geist des Kapitalismus,* 121.
16 Abraham Kaplan, *The New World of Philosophy* (New York: Random House, 1961), 207.
17 Charles Morris, "Comparative Strength of Life-Ideals in Eastern and Western Cultures," *Essays in East-West Philosophy,* edited by Charles A. Moore (Honolulu; University of Hawaii Press, 1951), 353–370.
18 H. Oldenberg, *Die Lehre der Upanishaden und die Anfänge des Buddhismus,* 3.
19 *Arrianos,* V, 4, 7.
20 *Ibid.*, IX, 12.

Chapter 14

1 Tsu-lin Mei, "Chinese Grammar and the Linguistic Movement in Philosophy," *Review of Metaphysics,* XIV, 3 (March 1961), 463–492. The relations of Chinese language and thought are discussed in the following: T. Watters, *Essays on the Chinese Language* (Shanghai: 1899); M. Granet, "Quelques Particularités de la Langue et de la Pensée Chinoises," *Revue Philosophique* (1920); Derk Bodde, "Types of Chinese Categorical Thinking," *Journal of American Oriental Society,* LIX (1939), 200f.

Chapter 15

1 Lévy-Bruhl, *Les fonctions mentales dans les sociétés inférieures,* ch. V, 187ff.
2 M. Granet, "Quelques particularités de la langue et de la pensée chinoises," *Revue philosophique* (1920), 126. Cf. also Granet, *La penśee chinoise* (Paris: 1934).
3 Stenzel, *Die Philosophie der Sprache,* 50–51.
4 Cf. B. Karlgren, *Philology and Ancient China* (Oslo: 1926). [Editor's note.]
5 Many Chinese mystical chants (*dhāraṇis*) were attempts to repeat the

sounds of the original Sanskrit texts (cf. e.g., *chien-chih-fan-tsan* = Gaṇḍīstotra), but there was no consistent way of doing this, especially with different Chinese dialects.

5a M. Granet, *op.cit.*, 103–104.

6 Cf. *San-lun-hsüan-i* (Profound Doctrines of the San-lun Sect), edited by Y. Kanakura in Iwanami Bunko edition, 19; in other edition, *yü-shun* instead of *kan-shun.*

7 Yoshio Takeuchi, *Shina Shisō-shi* (Intellectual History of China), 263. Arthur F. Wright, *Buddhism in Chinese History* (Stanford, 1959), 47.

8 Takeuchi, *op.cit.*, 264.

9 E.g., *Jen-t'ien-yen-mu* (Giving Men and Gods the Eyes for Seeing the Truth), IV. (*Taishō* XLVIII, 323 c.)

10 A passage in the *Ta-chih-tu-lun* (*Mahā-prajñāpāramitā-śāstra*) (A Chinese Translation of Nāgārjuna's Treatise on the Supreme Wisdom,) III, is often mentioned as the source. But such an expression was not usual in India.

11 *Ta-ch'eng-hsüan-lun,* III. (*Taishō,* XLV, 35 b). [Chinese Commentary on Mahāyāna's Profound Doctrines.]

12 Kōjiro Yoshikawa, *Shinajin no Koten to sono Seikatsu* (The Classics of the Chinese and Their Way of Life), 201.

13 *Chia-hsün-kuei-hsin-pien* (Chapter on Taking One's Mind Back to the Original Principles of Family Instruction) by Yen Chih-tui, in *Kuang-hung-ming-chi* (Collection of Works on Diffusion of Knowledge, Philosophical and Religious, i.e. Buddhist, Confucian, and Taoist), III.

14 K. Yoshikawa, *op.cit.*, 32.

15 So *Chên-ti San-tsang* (Chinese name of the Indian monk Paramārtha) translated "truth" and "reality" by the same word.

16 In the system of *San Chiao,* the third division in the system of Three Divisions delivered by Kuang-tung (Vinaya Master of the Wei dynasty), the fourth in the System of Four Divisions of the T'ien-t'ai Buddhist sect, and the fifth in the System of Five Divisions of Buddhism of the Hua-yen Buddhist sect, all three are called the "Perfectly Rounded Doctrine."

17 E. Zeller, *Die Philosophie der Griechen,* I, Abt. 1: 661, 695, 458, 521, 973; II, Abt. 1: 808; II, Abt. 2, 448. Paul Deussen, *Allgemeine Geschichte der Philosophie,* II, Abt. 1: 74, 83, 117, 278, 354.

18 Maticandra, *Daśapadārthaśastra,* translated into Chinese by Hsüan-tsang. Here *"t'i"* does not mean "body" but a Sanskrit suffix *"-tva,"* designating a universal or abstract quality.

19 *Sung-kao-seng-chuan* (Biographies of the High Priests of the Sung Period), V: (*Taishō,* L, 732 a.)

20 Cf. *Ch'an-yüan-chu-chüan-chi-tu-hsü* (An Introduction to an Anthology on the Rise of Zen) edited by H. Ui, 136f.

21 *Taishō,* XLV, 793 c.

22 *Fu-chou-tsao-shan-yüan-cheng-ch'an-shih-yü-lu* (Recorded Sayings of Zen

Master *Fu-chou-tsao-shan-yüan-cheng*) (*Taishō*, XLVII, 527 a); *Jen-t'ien-yen-mu*, III (*Taishō*, XLVIII, 316 b).

23 *Loc.cit.*

24 *Yün-chou-tung-shan-wu-pen-ch'an-shih-yü-lu* (Recorded Sayings of Zen Master *Yün-chou-tung-shan-wu-pen*), (*Taishō*, XLVII, 515 a); *Jen-t'ien-yen-mu*, III (*Taishō*, XLVIII, 321 a); *Ho-ku-ch'ê* (Unified Records of Zen Schools) I, Second series, XVI, fasc. 2.

25 Although the words "man and woman," (yang and yin), cannot be taken in a literal sense, yet the author preferred them.

26 *Tung-shang-ku-ch'ê* (Records of the Tung School) I. Manji edition of Tripiṭika, Second series, XVI, fasc. 2.

27 *Jen-t'ien-yen-mu* (Giving Men and Gods the Eyes for Seeing the Truth), VI.

28 *Chung-hua-chuan-hsin-ti-ch'an-mên-shih-tzu-ch'eng-hsi-t'u* (Diagram of Transmission of the Heart of Zen Doctrines in China), edited by H. Ui, 188f.

29 For example, cf. genealogies transmitted in the monasteries of the Vedānta schools.

Chapter 16

1 Stenzel, *Die Philosophie der Sprache*, 76. "The Chinese are not interested in 'carrying,' since 'carrying' is not something that gentlemen do. Chinese writing is not done by laborers, but only by gentlemen!" —Comment by Dr. Homer H. Dubs.

2 *Li Chi* (Book of Rites), Part 1 and Part 2.

3 *Hsün-tzŭ*, Chapter on "Rectification of Names"; cf. Yoshio Takeuchi, *Shina Shisō-shi* (Intellectual History of China), 12. Cf. H. H. Dubs, translation of *The Works of Hsüntze*. (London: 1928).

4 Cf. Kōjirō Yoshikawa, *Shinajin no Koten to sono Seikatsu* (Chinese Classics and Way of Life), 73–81.

5 Chi-tsang, *Ėrh-ti-i* (Theory of Double Truth), I (*Taishō*, XLV, 82 c, 83 b); *Chung-lun-shu* (Summary of the Middle Doctrine Treatise), *Taishō*, XLV, 49 a, 973; *Fo-tsu-tung-chi* (Genealogy of the Buddhist Patriarchs), VI. (*Taishō*, XLIX, 178 c.)

6 Especially in the works of *Chih-i* (538–597), founder of the T'ien-t'ai school.

7 J. S. Speyer, *Vedische und Sanskrit-Syntax*, 91.

8 "But it is difficult to determine what in Chinese is a 'sentence,' since there is no punctuation in classical Chinese. Do not English 'sentences' change their subjects in compound sentences?"—Comment by Dr. Homer H. Dubs.

9 Cf. Giei Honda, *Hokekyō Ron* (Essays on the Lotus Sūtra), 287–288.

10 H. Maspero, "Notes sur la Logique de Mo-tseu et de son École," *Toung-Pao* (1927), 29. Maspero says that the school of Mo-tzŭ had a true dialectic. But we have too little information about the school of Mo-

tzŭ, and it did not last long enough to leave any discernible influence on Chinese thought.

11 Mo-tzŭ, No. 45. Mo-tzŭ (ca. 479–381 B.C.) was the founder of the Mohist school, famous for its logic and critical social philosophy. Cf. Fung Yu-lan, *A History of Chinese Philosophy,* translated by Derk Bodde (Princeton: 1953), 11, 12, 53, 147, 150, 160–1, 203, 220, 409, 492, 495–6, 518, 613, 614, 651, 693.

12 *Hsü-kao-tsêng-chuan* (Further Biographies of Buddhist High Priests), 24; *ibid.,* 11. Cf. Hiroshi Yamazaki, *Shina Chūsei Bukkyō no Tenkai.* (The Development of Chinese Buddhism in the Medieval Period), 721ff, 727.

13 Max Weber, *Gesammelte Aufssätze zur Religionssoziologie,* I, 416.

14 The author and editor are indebted to Dr. Homer H. Dubs for his helpful critical comments here as well as in other parts of this revised edition.

15 Yoshio Mikami, *The Development of Mathematics in China and Japan* (New York: Chelsea Publishing Company, 1913), *passim.*

16 *Ibid.,* 56–61. Cf. also Joseph Needham's recent work on the history of Chinese Sciences. [Editor's note.]

17 Cf. Yoshikawa, *op.cit.,* 136–141.

18 Takeuchi, *op.cit.,* 292.

19 *Liu-tsu-tan-ching* (Platform Sūtra of the Sixth Zen Patriarch).

20 *Ching-tê-chuan-têng-lu* (Records of the Transmission of the Lamp of Enlightenment), XXVIII. (*Taishō,* LI, 443 c.)

21 Daijō Tokiwa, *Shina Bukkyō-no Kenkyū* (A Study on Chinese Buddhism), III, 109–110.

22 Henri Maspero, "Notes sur la logique de Mo-tseu et de son école," *Toung-Pao* (1927), 12.

23 Hu Shih, *The Development of the Logical Method in Ancient China* (Shanghai: 1922), 83, 95.

24 Cf. Hakuju Ui, *Indo Tetsugaku Kenkyū* (Studies in Indian Philosophy), VI, 72ff, 94ff.

25 Cf. Shoko Watanabe, *Inmyō Ronsho Myōtōshō Kaidai* (Exposition of the Commentary on Indian Logic) in the series Kokuyaku Issaikyō, *Ronshobu,* XVIII.

26 *Taishō,* XLIV, 115 b; LXXI, 451f. Cf. Hakuju Ui, *Bukkyō Ronri Gaku* (Buddhist Logic), 321, 323; *Indo Tetsugaku Kenkyū* (Studies on Indian Philosophy), V, 104ff; Kōyō Sakaino, *Bukkyō Ronri Gaku* (Buddist Logic).

27 Cf. his explanation about *sapakṣe sattvam* "the determinate characteristics of being in similar cases," (in his Commentary on the *Nyāyapraveśaka*), I. (*Taishō,* XLIV, 105 a).

28 Cf. Hakuju Ui, *Bukkyō Ronri Gaku* (Buddhist Logic), 365.

29 Ting Pin was one of them. (Cf. Shōkō Watanabe, *op.cit.,* XVIII, 4).

30 "Proof consists of one reason and two illustrations." (Commentary on the *Nyāyapraveśaka, op.cit.,* 106 c).

31 Hakuju Ui, *Indo Tetsugaku Kenkyū*, II, 478f.; Senshō Murakami, *Bukkyō Ronri Gaku* (Buddhist Logic), 37, 88f.
32 K'uei-chi's *Commentary on Indian Buddhist Logic*, I. (*Taishō*, 101 c, and LXVIII, 212 a.)
33 Hakuju Ui, *Indo Tetsugaku Kenkyū*, V, 105; *Bukkyō Ronri Gaku*, 345.
34 Cf. Hakuju Ui, *Zenshū-shi Kenkyū* (A Study on the History of Zen Sects), 3ff.
35 *Tun-wu-yao-mên* (Essentials of Sudden Enlightenment), edited by Hakuju Ui (in Iwanami Bunko edition, 44–47).
36 *Ch'uan-hsin-fa-yao* (Essence of the Transmission of the *Dharma*), edited by Hakuju Ui (in Iwanami Bunko edition, 20).
37 Sayings of the Zen Master Lin-chi (Rinzai) (*Taishō*, XLVII, 497 a); Giving Men and Gods the Eyes For Seeing the Truth (*ibid.*, XLVII, 300f).
38 Records of the Transmission of the Lamp of Enlightenment, VI. (Taishō, LI, 246 a.)
39 Hakugen Ichikawa, *Zen no Kihonteki Seikaku* (The Fundamental Character of Zen), 49f.
40 *Cheng-tao Ko* (Praises on the Confirmed State of Enlightenment).
41 The attitude of avoiding any fixed dogmas and continuing to try practical experiments can be noticed in American pragmatism. The last word of William James was: "There is no conclusion. What has concluded, that we might conclude in regard to it? There are no fortunes to be told, and there is no advice to be given.—Farewell!" In the last words of so many Zen masters we find similar sayings. Van Meter Ames says, "This last word is a Zen word!" *Zen and American Thought* (Honolulu: University of Hawaii Press, 1962), 140.
42 Takeuchi, *op.cit.*, 299.
43 *T'sung-Yung Lu* (Record of Calmness of Mind and Enlightenment).

Chapter 17

1 Kōjirō Yoshikawa, *Shinajin no Koten to sono Scikatsu* (Chinese Classics and Way of Life), 70.
2 Arthur F. Wright, *Buddhism in Chinese History*, 47.
3 *Pi-yen-lu* (Zen Sayings), Chapter 12. English translation and edited with Commentary by R. D. M. Shaw, *The Blue Cliff Records: The Hekigan Roku*, containing 100 Stories of Zen Masters of Ancient China (London: Michael Joseph, 1961).
4 *Madhyamaka śāstra*, XXII, 15.
5 *Transmission of the Lamp*, X (*Taishō*, LI, 274 b).
6 Its equivalent is not found in either the dictionary of Buddhist technical terms, the *Mahāvyutpatti* (Unrai Ogiwara, *Bonkan Jiten*) or the *Index to the Laṅkāvatāra-sūtra* (compiled by Daisetz T. Suzuki, *Ryōgakyō Sakuin*), the companion volume to the translation of this sūtra.
6a *Wu-mên-kuan* (Gateless Gate), Chapter 3.
7 *Transmission of the Lamp*, VIII. (*Taishō*, LI, 255 a.)

8 *Pi-yen-lu*, Chapter 46.
9 Yoshikawa, *op.cit.*, 20. The characteristics of Chinese historiography are made clear in the light of individual studies, in *Confucian Personalities*, edited by Arthur F. Wright and Denis Twitchett (Stanford: Stanford University Press, 1962).
10 Tanaka; Watsuji; Jugaku [tr.]: *Girisha Seishin-no Yōsō* (Characteristics of Greek Thought and Culture), (Tokyo: Iwanami), 27.
11 Masson-Oursel, *La Philosophie Comparée*, 19.
12 Cf. Kikuya Nagasawa, *Shinagaku Nyūmon-sho Ryakukai* (Brief Explanation of Introduction to Sinology), 43f.
13 Biographies of Bodhisattvas Aśvaghoṣa, Nāgārjuna, Āryadeva, and Vasubandhu.
14 Only *Aśokāvadāna* (in the *Divyāvadāna*) remains at present.
15 Biographies of Aśoka by various Japanese writers.
16 Daijō Tokiwa, *Shina Bukkyō no Kenkyū* (A Study on Chinese Buddhism), III, 76 and 81f.
17 Tomojirō Hayashiya, *Kyōroku Kenkyū* (A Study on the Catalogues of Sūtras), I, 13f. Cf. Daijō Tokiwa, *Yakkyō Sōroku* (A Study of all the Catalogues of Sūtras in Chinese Translations).

Chapter 18

1 Sakae Takeda, "*Hiyu ni Tsuite*" ("On Metaphors"), *Kangakukai Zasshi* (Journal of the Chinese Classic Studies), X, No. 1.
2 Cf. Homer H. Dubs, translator, *The Works of Hsüntze* (London: 1928), and also Dubs' book on *Hsüntze, The Moulder of Confucianism* (London: 1927).
3 Kōjirō Yoshikawa, *Shinajin no Koten to sono Seikatsu* (Chinese Classics and Way of Life), 27.
4 *Ibid.*, 39–40.
5 *Ibid.*, 46.
6 Sōkichi Tsuda, *Shina Shisō to Nippon* (Chinese Intellectual History and Japan), (Tokyo: 1938), 29–30.
7 Sueo Gotō, *Shina Bunka to Shinagaku no Kigen* (Chinese Culture and the Origin of Chinese Studies), 376f.
8 The Lotus Sūtra, ch. III on Parables.
9 Hui-chao's Exposition of the Treatise on "Consciousness Only." (*Taishō*, XLIII, 671 b). Cf. *Madhyāntavibhāga-ṭīkā*, edited by S. Yamaguchi, 2f.
10 *San-lun-hsüan-i* (Profound Doctrines of the San-lun Sect), ed. by E. Kanakura, 157.
11 Official Collected Works of Pai-chang-ch'ing-kuei, VI. Cf. Dōgen, *Shuryō Shingi* (in *Eihei Shingi*). Rules Governing the Zen Order (in Rules of the Eihei Zen Temple).
12 *Sun-lun-hsüan-i*, 170.
13 *Ibid.*, 119, 125f.
14 *Mo-ho-chih-kuan* (On the Profound State of Quiescence), I, No. 1 (*Taishō*, XLVI, 1).

15 Platform Sūtra of the Sixth Patriarch, cf. Hakuju Ui, *Daini Zenshū-shi Kenkyū* (Studies on the History of Zen Buddhism), II, 164.

16 Tetsubun Miyasaka, *Zen ni okeru Ningen Keisei* (Formation of Human Character in Zen), 148f.

17 Cf. *Tarkajvālā, Commentary on the Madhyamaka-hṛdaya,* VIII, 47.

18 Cf. *Anthology on the Rise of Zen,* (edited by Hakuju Ui), 36.

19 Arthur Waley, *Three Ways of Thought in Ancient China* (Doubleday Anchor Books, 1962), 160f. Cf. David S. Nivison, "Protest against Conventions and Conventions of Protest," in *The Confucian Persuasion* (Stanford University Press, 1960), edited by Arthur F. Wright, 177–201.

20 Max Weber, *Konfuzianismus und Taoismus* (1924), 292.

21 *Ibid.*, 291–292.

22 *Ibid.*, 436.

23 Joseph R. Levenson, "Ill Wind in the Well-Field: The Erosion of the Confucian Ground of Controversy"; Tse-tsung Chow, "The Anti-Confucian Movement in Early Republican China," in Wright, *op.cit.*, 268–312.

24 Sōkichi Tsuda, *Rongo to Kōshi no Shiso* (*The Analects* and Thoughts of Confucius), 309–311.

25 Cf. *T'ien-t'ai Ssu-chiao-yi* (Four Doctrines of the T'ien-t'ai School), I.

Chapter 19

1 Li Ho (honorific name, Ch'ang chi). His poems are criticized as "uncanny and tricky" and therefore difficult to understand.

2 *Kanbun Taikei,* IV, 6. (Series of Texts of Chinese Literature, Selected Poems of the T'ang Period.)

3 *Shutsujō Kōgo* (Monologue after Meditation), ch. 8. *Jinzū* (On Divine or Miraculous Power).

4 *Ibid.*, ch. 24. *Sankyō* (Three Schools: Buddhism, Taoism, Confucianism).

5 Tao-an's Introduction to a Catalog of Annotated Texts, VIII; Introduction to the Abridged Chinese Version of the *Mahāprajñāpāramitā sūtra,* I.

6 *Anthology on the Rise of Zen,* edited by Hakuju Ui, I, 83.

7 Max Weber, *Konfuzianismus und Taoismus,* 432.

8 *Ibid.*, 239.

9 Max Weber (in his book *Hinduismus und Buddhismus,* 290) called Chinese Buddhism "Buchreligion" (Religion of Books).

10 The Zen sect also has such characteristics as it esteems highly the *Laṅkāvatāra Sūtra,* the *Prajñāpāramitā Hṛdaya Sūtra,* the *Vajracchedikā Sūtra,* and the *Yüan-chüeh* (Enlightenment) *Sūtra* among many sūtras.

11 *Taishō,* XXXVII, 1 c.

12 *Shōmangyō Kenshūshō* (Exposition of the *Śrīmālādevīsiṁhānanda-sūtra*) I, (*Nihon Daizō Kyō, Hōdōbu,* V, 8). Japanese Tripiṭaka, Vaipulya section.

13 Kōgaku Fuse, *Hokke Gensan Kaidai,* (*Kokuyaku Issaikyō, Kyōshobu,* IV, 3). (Explanation of the Profound Lotus Doctrine.)
14 Profound Doctrines of the *San Lun* (Three Treatises School), edited by Y. Kanakura, 174f.
15 Profound Treatise on the Mahāyāna, V. (*Taishō,* XLV, 73 c.)
16 Great Exposition of Indian Buddhist Logic (A Commentary on the *Nyāya-praveśaka*), I. (*Taishō,* XLIV, 92 a, 92 b.)
17 Profound Doctrines of the Avataṁsaka Sūtra. (*Taishō,* XXXV, 107 b.)
18 *Ibid.,* 121f.
19 Cf. Biographies of the Sung High Priests, III, Life of Man-Yüeh.
20 Cf. Max Weber, *Konfuzianismus und Taoismus,* 415.
21 *Maha Chih-kuan* (On the Profound State of Quiescence), III, Part 2. (*Taishō,* XLVI, 31 c.)
22 Daijō Tokiwa, *Shina Bukkyō no Kenkyū,* III, 115–116. (Studies on Chinese Buddhism.)

Chapter 20

1 Kōjirō Yoshikawa, *Shinajin no Koten to sono Seikatsu* (Chinese Classics and Way of Life), 89–94.
2 Although the term "five periods" was not used, Tsung-mi also systematized a similar scheme of classification (On the Rise of Zen), 116f. However, he did not criticize the method of classification but only its interpretation (Profound Doctrines of the San-lun [Three Treatises] School), edited by Y. Kanakura.
3 The third chapter of the *Avataṁsaka-sūtra* states that the Buddha preached it in the Hall of Truth of Universal Light. The Chinese version of the *Buddhāvataṁsaka-sūtra* in 60 vols., Chapter 3.
4 Explanations of the Teaching of the *Buddhāvataṁsaka-sūtra,* IV (*Taishō,* XLV, 584 a).
5 Chi-ts'ang divided all *abhidharma* into "general" and "detailed," another example of a classification (Profound Doctrines of the San-lun School, 133). He also showed the difference between the standpoints of the *Chung-lun* and the *Pai-lun* (*Ibid.,* 153).
6 Sōkichi Tsuda, *Shina Shisō to Nippon* (Chinese Thought and Japan), 25.
7 *Ibid.,* 10.
8 Shōichi Kuno in *Tōyō Gakuhō* (Oriental Studies), XXV, 582.
9 *Kan-hun-min-chi* (Supplementary Collection of Epistles), III. Cf. A. F. Wright, *The Confucian Persuasion,* 6–7.
10 *Yüan-jên-lun* (A Treatise on the Origin of Man), Chapter 2.
11 *Maha Chih-kuan,* VI, pt. 1 (*Taishō,* XLVI, 77 a-b).
12 *Fa-hua-i-chi* (Explanations on the Teachings of the Lotus Sūtra), V (*Taishō,* XXXIII, 635 a).
13 *Fa-hua-wên-chü* (Literal Word for Word Explanations of the Sentences in the Lotus Sūtra), VI, pt. 1 (*Taishō,* XXXIV, 81 b).
14 *Fa-hua-i-su* (Commentary on the Lotus Sūtra) VII (*Taishō,* XXXIV,

546 c). On Chi-tsang (549–623), cf. Fung Yu-lan, *A History of Chinese Philosophy* (Princeton; 1953), II, 293f.

15 *Fa-hua-i-chi,* V (*Taishō,* XXXIII, 635 c).

16 *Fa-hua-wen-chu,* VI, pt. 1 (*Taishō,* XXXIV, 82 b).

17 *Fa-hua-i-su,* VII (*Taishō,* XXXIV, 547 c).

Chapter 21

1 This problem is discussed by Tsu-lin Mei, "Chinese Grammar and the Linguistic Movement in Philosophy," *The Review of Metaphysics,* XIV, 3, (March 1961), 483f.

2 *Suttanipāta* (An Indian Buddhist scripture in Pali), 770.

3 The Chinese version of the *Arthavargīya-sūtra.*

4 Wan-li, *Introduction to Chinese Grammar,* in the Japanese translation *Chūgoku Bunpōgaku Shotan,* Chapter 6. Cf. Shō Saitō, *Tetsugaku Dokuhon* (Introduction to Philosophy), 76–77.

5 Kōjirō Yoshikawa, *Shinajin no Koten to sono Seikatsu,* 21.

6 Masson-Oursel, *La Philosophie Comparée,* 118.

7 *Ching-te-ch'uan-têng-lu* (Transmission of the Lamp of Enlightenment), III. (*Taishō,* LI, 255 a).

8 *Madhyāntavibhāgaṭīkā,* 29; "There is nothing to be taken away; there is nothing to be added. When one sees reality as it is, one can surely attain deliverance." *Buddhagotra-śāstra,* IV, ch. 10. (*Taishō,* XXXI, 312). Similar expressions can be found also in *Madhyamaka-śāstra,* 25–3; *Catuḥśatika,* XV, 350 (p. 513); *Māṇḍūkya-Kārikā,* III, 38.

9 Wing-tsit Chan, "Transformation of Buddhism in China," in *Philosophy East and West,* VII, 3 and 4 (October 1957–January 1958), 107–116.

10 *Analects,* XI, 12. " 'I do not say that the society as we know it *is* the whole,' wrote John Dewey, 'but I do emphatically suggest that it is the widest and richest manifestation of the whole accessible to our observation.' The statement would have suited Confucius perfectly." Huston Smith, *The Religions of Man* (The New American Library, 1961), 176.

11 Many such positivistic thoughts can be found in the teachings of Confucius.

12 Sōkichi Tsuda, *Shina Shisō to Nippon,* 11–12.

13 *Taishō,* L, 323 a-b; LV, 95 a.

14 *Ibid.,* L, 324 c.

15 *Ibid.,* 325 a.

16 His miraculous powers are mentioned in Biographies of High Priests of Liang Period (502–556), IX, (*Taishō,* L, 383 b), and also in *Tsin Shu* (Chin Dynasty Records), XCV, which is one of the authoritative historical records of China. It is unusual that a record of a person who is not a Chinese is mentioned in the authoritative history of China.

17 Tomojirō Hayashiya, *Kyōroku Kenkyū* (Studies of Catalogues of Buddhist Sūtras), Part 1, 338.

18 In the early periods of Chinese Buddhism, missionaries from An-hsi (Persia) mainly introduced Hīnayāna Buddhism and missionaries from Yüeh-chih mainly Mahāyāna Buddhism. However, in later periods, only Mahāyāna Buddhism spread and was followed in China. The following opinion is widely recognized as the reason why Mahāyāna Buddhism spread especially in the northern direction of India.

Aśvaghoṣa was invited by King Kaniṣka and introduced Mahāyāna Buddhism into Yüeh-chih country. It was this Mahāyāna Buddhism that was introduced into China. However, Hīnayāna Buddhism, especially Sarvāstivāda, was influential in Yüeh-chih at that time according to modern researches on inscriptions. There is no mention of Mahāyāna Buddhism among inscriptions of the Yüeh-chih period discovered in the modern age. (Cf. Sten Konow, *Kharoshṭhī Inscriptions,* passim.) It is also recognized by modern studies that Mahāyānistic thought cannot be found in the writings of Aśvaghoṣa. The author of *Discourses on Awakening of the Faith,* translated from the Chinese by D. T. Suzuki (Chicago: Open Court, 1900) must be distinguished from Aśvaghoṣa, the teacher of King Kaṇishka. According to an original Sanskrit manuscript which was discovered by Rāhula Sāṅkṛtyāyana in Tibet, Aśvaghoṣa was regarded as a Sarvāstivādin (*Journal of the Bihar and Orissa Research Society,* XXI [1935], 8 n). Therefore, it must not be understood that Mahāyāna Buddhism was introduced into China because it was influential in Yüeh-chih, but I have interpreted it to mean that the specific tendency of the ways of thinking of the Chinese was the reason for the choice of Mahāyāna Buddhism as their religion.

19 Biographies of priests who possessed such mystical and miraculous powers are found in *The Biographies of High Priests.*

20 *Taishō,* XLVI, 109 b.

21 Cf. Taiken Kimura, *Shina Bukkyō Jijō* (Some Information on Chinese Buddhism); *Shūkyo Kenkyū* (Journal of Religious Studies) (1924), 119; Shinyū Kichijō, *Shina Mikkyō no Genjo ni tsuite,* (On the Present State of Esoteric Buddhism in China); Chūgoku Bukkyō no Genjō (The Present State of Affairs in Chinese Buddhism), *Nikkwa Bukkyō Kenkyūkai Nenpō,* (Annual Publications of the Chinese and Japanese Buddhist Research Society, first year).

22 In the Chinese versions of the sūtras, there are many technical phrases and words of Taoism which cannot be found either in the original Sanskrit texts or in the Tibetan translations. Cf. Sōkichi Tsuda, *Shina Bukkyō no Kenkyū* (Study on Chinese Buddhism), 37–40, 85f.

23 De Groot, *Religious Systems in China,* translated into Japanese by K. Shimiżu H. Oginome, *Chūgoku Shūkyō Seido,* I, 69.

24 *Ibid.,* 116.

25 T'an-luan preferred the Chinese term for Tathāgata to the one for Amita, and used it frequently.

26 Zenryū Tsukamoto, "Shina ni okeru Muryōju-butsu to Amida-butsu," *Shūkyō Kenkyū* (1940), 1047. ("Amida Buddha and Amitāyus Buddha").
27 *Taishō*, XL, 835 c.
28 *Ibid.*, XLVI, 134 b.
29 Translated by Hakuji Ui, 110.
30 A praise of P'ang to the 42nd rule of *Pi-yen-chi;* cf. *The Blue Cliff Records.*
31 Cf. Hakuju Ui, *Zenshū-shi Kenkyū*, preface, 3.
32 De Groot, *op.cit.*, *Chūgoku Shūkyō Seido*, I, 218f.
33 *Essentials of Sudden Enlightenment*, 86.
34 Quoted from Forke, *Geschichte der neueren chinesischen Philosophie*, 190. Cf. J. P. Bruce, translator, *The Philosophy of Human Nature*, by Chu Hsi (same as Chu Tzŭ), (London: 1922).
35 This phrase is mentioned as the words of Ch'en P'ien in the *Spring and Autumn Annals Transmitted in the Family of Mr. Lü.* Yoshio Takeuchi, *Shina Shisō-shi*, 83.
36 Arthur Waley, *Three Ways of Thought in Ancient China* (New York: Doubleday Anchor Book, 1962), 30. Cf. Fung Yu-lan, *Chuang Tzŭ, A New Selected Translation with an Exposition of the Philosophy of Kuo Hsiang* (Shanghai: Commercial Press, 1933).
37 Takeuchi, *op.cit.*, 175. The following phrase has been conveyed as the words of Yang Wang Sun in the Records of the Former Han Dynasty, LXVII.
38 *Taishō*, L, 514 c-515 a. Although he was a descendant of a naturalized man, this fact did not influence the form of his thought.
39 A similar attitude can be noticed in Walt Whitman also. Cf. Van Meter Ames, *Zen and American Thought* (Honolulu: University of Hawaii Press, 1962), 97–105.
40 Keidō Itō, *Dōgen Zenji Kenkyū* (A Study of Zen Master Dōgen), I, 117.
41 De Groot, *op.cit.*, 4.
42 *Ibid.*, 5.
43 Kiyoko Takeda, *Ajia no Kirisuto-kyō to Kyōsan-shugi* (Christianity and Communism in Asia), *Shisō no Kagaku* (Science of Thought, July 1949).
44 Cf. Arthur F. Wright, *Buddhism in Chinese History, op.cit.*, 119.
44a Fung Yu-lan amply demonstrates in his *History of Chinese Philosophy*, 2 Volumes, translated by D. Bodde, (Princeton: 1953), that China did possess metaphysics. Whether or how far the Chinese developed metaphysics or not depends upon what one calls metaphysics. Cf. Yoshikawa, *op.cit.*, 70.
45 Sōkichi Tsuda, *Shina Shisō to Nippon* (Chinese Thought and Japan), 8.
46 Yoshikawa, *op.cit.*, 24–25.
47 *San-lun-hsüan-i:* "The confrontation of subject and object will be

brought to naught." Profound Doctrines of the Three Treatises School, *op.cit.*, 24.

48 *Yüan-jên-lun* (A Treatise on the Origin of Man), Chapter 1.

49 *San-lun-hsüan-i, op.cit.*, 24. *Shōbō Genzō* (Essence of Buddhist Teaching), *Shizen Biku* (Four Meditative Practices of a Zen Monk).

50 *Wan-shan-t'ung-kuei-chi* (Book of Myriad Good Things Leading to the Same Goal), Part 1. (*Taishō*, XLVIII, 987 c.)

51 Alfred Forke, *Geschichte der neueren chinesischen Philosophie*, 201.

52 Masson-Oursel, *Revue de Métaphysique et de Morale* (1912), 820.

53 *Ta-ch'êng-hsüan-lun* (Essentials of Mahāyāna). (*Taishō*, XLV, 15 a.) There are many similar statements mentioned in the writings of Chitsang.

54 Daitō Shimaji, *Nippon Bukkyō Kyōgaku-shi* (Historical Study of Teachings in Japanese Buddhism), 233. According to a work written by Ryōhen, (a scholar of the Hossō sect in the Kamakura period), there was only one temple which belonged to the Hossō sect (the school of the Vijñaptimātratā) in China at that time. In modern China, it is remarkable that the philosophy of the Vijñaptimātratā has been revived. This tendency originates from the fact that the necessity for a philosophical study of Buddhism has been recognized.

55 *Ch'an-yüan-chu-chüan-chi-tu-hsü* (Diagram of Hereditary Transmission of Zen from Master to Disciple), edited by Hakuju Ui, 205.

Chapter 22

1 Wing-tsit Chan, "Chinese Theory and Practice," *Philosophy and Culture East and West*, edited by Charles A. Moore, (Honolulu: University of Hawaii Press, 1962), 92.

2 *Analects*, IX, 25.

3 Frederick W. Mote, "Confucian Eremitism in the Yüan period." *The Confucian Persuasion*, edited by Arthur F. Wright (Stanford: Stanford University Press, 1960), 202ff. Also, cf. Wing-tsit Chan, *op.cit.*, 93.

4 *Wan-shan-t'ung-kuei-chi* (Book of Myriad Good Things Leading to the Same Goal), pt. 2 (*Taishō*, XLVIII, 987 c).

5 A saying of Yang-tzŭ in the *Huai-nan-tzŭ* (A compilation of various schools of thought by guests of Prince Huai-nan [d. 122 B.C.]).

6 Cf. Chuang-tzŭ; Y. Takeuchi, *Shina Shisō Shi* (History of Chinese Thought), 97.

7 Cf. Sōkichi Tsuda, *Shina Shisō to Nippon*, 13–15.

8 *Shōbō Genzō* (Subtleties of the True Buddhist Doctrine, by Dōgen). *Shizen Biku* (Four Meditative Practices of a Zen Monk).

9 Cf. Ryōshū Michibata, *Gaisetsu Shina Bukkyō-shi* (Introduction to the History of Chinese Buddhism), 51f, 98f; *Idem, Shina Bukkyō Jiin no Kinyū Jigyō* (Monetary Activities of Buddhist Temples in China), *Ōtani Gakuhō* (Journal of Otani University), 14–1; *Idem, Tōdai Jiin No Shakai Jigyō* (Social Activities of Temples in the T'ang Dynasty),

Eizan Gakuhō (Journal of Eizan College), 15; Hiroshi Yamazaki, *Shina Chūsei Bukkyō no Tenkai* (Development of Buddhism in the Medieval Ages of China), 677f.

10 Yoshio Takeuchi, *Shina Shisōshi* (History of Chinese Thought), 82.

11 *Hsi-ming* (Western Epigram).

12 This theory is the seventh theory of *Shih-pu-êrh-mên* (Ten Gates of Non-Duality) in the T'ien-t'ai school. Cf. *Taishō*, XXXIII, 918 b; XLVI, 704; 718 a.

13 For example, this thought can be found in the *Hsin-hsin-ming* (Epigrams of Faith). Again it is mentioned in the *Chêng-tao-ko* (Songs of Enlightenment): "One nature covers completely all natures, and one doctrine includes all doctrines. One moon is reflected on the water of any place and all reflections of the moon are namely one moon. True bodies of various Buddhas enter into the body of man and the body of man is identical with that of the Tathāgata."

14 *Santānāntarasiddhi*, edited by T. Stcherbatsky. Only the Tibetan translation of this text exists at present. Cf. Stcherbatsky, *Buddhist Logic*, I, 521f.

15 *Eihei Kōroku* (Discourses at the Eihei Temple), VIII. Cf. Daijō Tokiwa, *Shina Bukkyō no Kenkyū* (Study of Chinese Buddhism), III, 99–100.

16 Hui-yüan (334–416), the South Chinese founder of the Pure Land practice of the White Lotus Society, never left the Lu-shan Mountain during his life time. The eighth patriarch of the same society, Lien-ch'ih, also confined himself to the mountain.

17 *Op.cit.*, 20. Cf. *ibid.*, 240.

18 This thought is derived from the words in the 19th chapter of the Lao-tzŭ "*chüeh-hsüeh wu-yu*" ("banish cleverness and all desire for gain").

19 *Kenseiki* (Biography of Dōgen written by Priest Kensei), I. *Dai Nippon Bukkyō Zenshū* (Works of Japanese Buddhism), CXV, 544. Similar teachings can be found also in the Hōkyōki (a Treatise written in the Hōkyō Era in the Kamakura period).

20 Hui-yüan was especially respected and praised by the Chinese intelligentsia at the time. It is also very probable that the author of the *T'ang-shih-hsüan* selected and compiled only this sort of poems. Nevertheless, it can safely be said that such a way of thinking was influential during the T'ang and Ming dynasties.

21 The Lao-tzŭ, XVI.

22 The Chuang-tzŭ.

23 The Lieh-tzŭ.

24 Takeuchi, *op.cit.*, 82.

25 *Ibid.*, 85f.

26 In the *Biographies of High Priests* there are many mentions of priests who mastered the practice of meditation.

27 Chi-tsang attached great significance to the fact that in China the character *Kuan* was added to the title of *Chun-lun* written by Nāgārjuna. Namely, the Chinese used to designate *Chun-lun* as *Chun-kuan-lun*.

Kuan connotes observation or insight in meditation. (Cf. *op.cit.*, 172f.)

28 *Chan-yüan-chu-chüan-chi-tu-hsü* (Introduction to the Collection of Sayings on the Origin of Zen), 156.

29 *Ching-tê ch'uan-têng lu* (Transmission of Religious Lamps), VIII; *ibid.*, VI; *Pi-yen lu* (The Blue Cliff Records), Chapter 44.

30 *Tun-wu ju-tao-yao-mên lun* (Essentials of Sudden Enlightenment), 8.

31 *Chan-yüan-chu-chüan-chi-tu-hsü*, 14f.

32 *Tun-wu ju-tao-yao-mên lun*, 131.

33 *Ch'uan-hsin-fa-yao* (Transmission of the Enlightenment), 20.

34 *Ibid.*, 8.

35 Cf. *Tun-wu ju-tao-yao-mên lun*, part 1, p. 8.

36 Cf. *Ching-tê ch'uan-têng lu*, VII.

37 Wing-tsit Chan in *Philosophy East and West*, VII, 3–4, (October 1957—January 1958), 113.

38 Cf. Edwin O. Reischauer and John K. Fairbank, *East Asia: The Great Tradition* (Boston: 1958), 171ff.

39 Cf. *Mo-ho-chih-kuan*, II, Part 1. (*Taishō*, XLVI, 12 b.)

40 *The Platform Sūtra* by Hui-neng, the Sixth Patriarch, edited by Hakuju Ui: *Daini Zenshū-shi Kenkyū* (Studies on the History of Zen Buddhism), II, 147–148.

41 *Ibid.*, 125.

42 E.g., Book of Myriad Good Things Leading to the Same Final Goal, Part 1. (*Taishō*, XLVIII, 967 a.) This thought is also prominently mentioned in Collection of Pure Land Letters. (*Taishō*, XLVIII, 966 b.)

43 *Ibid.*

44 *Tun-wu ju-tao-yao-men lun*, 60.

45 Cf. R. F. Johnston, *Buddhist China* (London: 1913).

46 Cf. Daijō Tokiwa, *Shina Bukkyō no Kenkyū* (Studies in Chinese Buddhism) III, 108.

47 Of course, there are some exceptions concerning this tendency of the Chinese Buddhist sects. Cf. *ibid.*, III, 91.

48 *Ibid.*, 76.

49 For particulars, refer to Enjō Inaba, *Shina Bukkyō no Gensei to sono Yurai* (The Present State of Affairs in Chinese Buddhism and its Origin), *Mujintō*, XXIII, No. 1.

50 Cf. Chikusō Nihitsu, ("Two Letters at the Bamboo Window" by Yün-lu), and the thesis of Enjō Inaba, *loc.cit.*

51 According to the travel records of Daijō Tokiwa (*op.cit.*, III, 109): "When I visited famous temples in southern China, many of the head priests were absent. It seems that they went to the South Sea Islands to collect contributions from Chinese merchants overseas."

52 The Chinese word "*Tao*" has been used by most or all Chinese philosophic or religious schools. Each school has its own "way" of belief; e.g., there is the "Confucian Way," (Ju-tao) etc. Huston Smith mentions three senses of the word *tao*: (1) the way of ultimate reality; (2) the way of the universe; (3) the way man should order his life. This helps

us comprehend the connotations of the term, although it is not clear whether this interpretation will be approved by all sinologists. Cf. Huston Smith, *The Religions of Man* (Mentor Book, the New American Library, 1961), 184f.

53 Arthur Waley, *Three Ways of Thought in Ancient China* (New York: Doubleday Anchor Book, 1962), 48ff.

54 According to Chan-jan, the way to govern the family and save people is also mentioned in the Veda scriptures. [*Mo-ho-chih-kuan*, X, Part 1, (*Taishō*, XLVI, 134 b); Commentary on this work, X, Part 2 (*Taishō*, 440 b).] Cf. *Shōbōgenzō, Shizenbiku* (Four Meditative Practices of the Zen Monk).

55 Cf. Waley, *op.cit.*, 62f.

56 Wu-wai's preface to reprint of *Chan-yüan-chu-chüan-chi-tu-hsü* (Origins of the Rise of Zen). Wu-wai lived in the early part of 14th century, Yüan dynasty: *Kasante Zengensen wo Kokusuru Jo*, 161.

57 *En-ryō-roku*, pt. 2. *Ch'uan-hsin-fa-yao* (Transmission of the Essentials of the Heart of Enlightenment); *Den-shin-hō-yō*, edited by Hakuju Ui, 65.

58 Present-day Chinese Pure Land teachings regard the idea of concentration in the *Smaller Sukhāvatīvyūha-sūtra* as concentration as the One Practice, and they also regard this idea as the same as the idea of Tathatā-samādhi (concentration on thusness) in the *Mahāyāna-śraddhōtpāda-śāstra*). [Genmyō Hayashi, *Shina Genkon no Jōdo Kyōgi* (Pure Land Teaching in Present-day China), *Nikka Bukkyō Kenkyū-kai Nempō* (Annual Publication of the Association for Chinese and Japanese Buddhist Studies), 1st year, 9).]

59 *Tao-hsüan* asserted this. (*Taishō*, XLV, 833 b).

60 *Ch'an-yüan-chu-chüan-chi-tu-hsü*. 11.

61 *Ibid.*, 35.

62 This idea of the Chinese is mentioned by Enjō Inaba in detail in the *Mujintō* ("Infinite Light") (1918), 7f. On this point, a striking difference can be seen between the Chinese and the Japanese ways of thinking.

63 Needless to say, this thought can be found in the doctrine of the Lü (precepts) sect. Also Fa-tsang of the Hua-yen sect said that the "excellent behavior of all Bodhisattvas is based on the pure precepts." (*Taishō*, XXII, 602 c.)

64 One reason why Chinese Buddhism does not degenerate even at present is based on the fact that most of the temples are situated in mountains or valleys far away from villages or towns. However, it can also be thought that the ways of thinking of the Chinese would not cause the degeneration of Buddhism.

65 This fact is mentioned in detail in Taiken Kimura, *Shina Bukkyō Jijō* (The State of Affairs in Chinese Buddhism), *Shūkyō Kenkyū* (Religious Studies) (1924), 117, and Yūshō Tokushi, *Koji Bukkyō ni Tsuite* (On the Layman's Buddhism), *Nikka Bukkyō Kenkyū-kai Nempō*, 1st year, 20.

66 *Taishō*, XXII, 602 c.
67 *Ch'uan-hsin-fa-yao*, 44f. (Cf. 76f.)
68 Max Weber, *Hinduismus und Buddhismus*, 292.

Chapter 23

1 *Der Weg in die Philosophie*, by Georg Misch, states that Greek philosophy is physical (*physisch*), Indian philosophy is metaphysical (*metaphysisch*), and Chinese philosophy is ethical (*ethisch*).
2 *Taishō*, LIV, 220 a.
3 *Taishō*, LIV, 251 c.
4 It cannot be said that this idea cannot be found in Indian thought, e.g., *Chānd. Up.* V. 10. 7. However, the thought of the Indians in the later periods is generally metaphysical and both animals and men were included in the concept of "living beings."
5 *Taishō*, XXII, 602 c.
6 Chūsei Suzuki: *Bukkyō no Gonsetsu Kairitsu ga Sōdai no Minshū Seikatsu ni Oyoboshitaru Eikyō ni Tsuite* (*On the Influence of the Buddhist Precept "Abstaining from Killing" upon Public Life in the Sung Dynasty*), Shūkyō Kenkyū, III, No. 1.
7 Sāgara-nāgarāja-duhitā—tat strīndriyam antarhitaṃ puruṣendriyaṃ ca prādurbhūtaṃ bodhisattvabhūtaṃ c'ātmānaṃ saṁdarśayati. (*Saddh. P.* 277.)
8 Hajime Nakamura, *Shakuson no Kotoba* (Words of the Śākyamuni Buddha), 198f.
9 *Hua-yen-ching* (the Avataṁsaka Sūtra, translated in the Chin dynasty by Śikṣānanda), L. (*Taishō*, IX, 717 b.)
10 The *Gaṇḍavyūha-sūtra*, edited by Daisetz T. Suzuki & Hōkei Izumi, 204.
11 *Hua-yen-ching*, LXVIII. (*Taishō*, X, 366 a.)
12 The *Gaṇḍavyūha-sūtra*, 404–405.
13 *Hua-yen-ching*, LXXV. (*Taishō*, X, 408 b.)
14 *Hua-yen-ching*, LVI. (*Taishō*, IX, 756 c.)
15 Ye gṛhīta-paṁca-śiksā-padāḥ saṁto "bhāryāḥ pariṇayanti," vivāhayanti.
16 *Mo-ho-chih-kuan*, IV, Part 1. (*Taishō*, XLVI, 41 c.)
17 While it is true that Confucianism flourished in the time of Emperor Wu (140–87 B.C.), yet he personally was far from being a Confucian altogether. He accepted Taoists as well as Confucians in his bureaucracy. Not until the time of Emperor Ai (6–1 B.C.) or of the usurper Wang Mang (8–22 A.D.) was Confucianism required of all courtiers. Even then the common people were not Confucians, but followed their own beliefs. (Comment of Dr. Homer H. Dubs.)
18 *Taishō*, L, 361 b.
19 *Shutsujō Kōgo*, XIV, *Kai* (precepts).
20 Sōkichi Tsuda, *Rongo to Kōshi no Shisō* (The *Analects* and Thoughts of Confucius), 297f.
21 Senkurō Hiroike *Shina Bunten* (Chinese grammar), 125f.

22 Fully discussed in the *Li Chi*, II.
23 The different terms which express death were used in accordance with the social position of the dead.
24 Cf. *Li Chi* for details.
25 Yang Shu-ta, *Kōtō Kokubunpō* (Advanced Studies of Chinese Grammar), 412f.
26 *Mo-ho-chih-k'uan*, V, Part 1; *Taishō*, XLVI, 68 c.
27 *Ibid.*
28 *Ibid.*
29 This phrase was quoted in the Commentary on the *T'ien-t'ai's Four Divisions of Buddha's Teaching* by Ti-k'uan, I, Part 1, 19 a, as the words of Chan-j'an.
30 *Dīgha-Nikāya*, III, 191.
31 The Chinese Version of the *Dīrghagama-sūtra*, XI.
32 Yoshio Takeuchi, *Shina Shisō shi*, 268.
33 Cf. *Kuan-wu-liang-shou-ching-shu* (Commentary on the Larger Sukhāvatīvyūha Sūtra), Part 2. (*Taishō*, XXXVII, 186 b.) Hui-yüan called Buddhism itself the "Buddhist family" in his commentary.
34 *Ti-k'uan's* Commentary I, 35 b.
35 It seems that the Indian Buddhist did not call the Buddhist organization or school a family. In Jainism, the big school was called *Gotra* and the main school was called *Kula* or *Śākhā*. (Cf. The *Kalpasūtra* and many Jain inscriptions of the Kuṣāṇa dynasty.) However, Chia in Chinese Ch'an Buddhism had no relation to the Kula of Jainism.
36 Ti-k'uan's Commentary, I, 19 b.
37 *Ibid.*, II, 5 a.
38 In the original Pāli Buddhist text, filial piety is stated in the following texts: *Itivuttaka* 106 Gāthā—*AN*, I, 132 G; *SN*, I, 178 G. (It also states here that one has to respect one's elder brother. *Dhammapada*, 332; *SN*, I, 178 G; *Suttanipāta* vv. 98, 124, 262; *DN*, III, 191f.

In Pāli, one who is in allegiance with his parents is called "assavo putto." In Sanskrit, however, such a term cannot be found. "Metteyyatā" and "petteyyatā" in Pāli are rather similar to the idea of *Hsiao* (filial piety) in China. These terms do not correspond exactly to *Hsiao*, because filial piety to the father and the mother is explained in different terms in Pāli. Again these terms are seldom found in the Pāli texts. In the Mahāyāna sūtras translated into Chinese, gratitude to the parents is stated in the Chinese version of the *Saddharmasmṛtyupasthāna-sūtra*, LXI, and the *Ta-ch'êng-pên-shêng-hsin-ch'ih-k'uang-ching*, II.
39 Besides these, there are some sūtras which discuss filial piety, such as the *Hsiao-Tzŭ-ching* (*Taishō*, XVI, 708) and the *Fu-mu-ên nan-pao-ching* (*Taishō*, XVI, 778–779). These sūtras, however, are very short and not well-organized.
40 Max Weber, *Das antike Judentum*, 150.
41 *Ibid.*, 158.
42 *Hsing-li-ta-ch'üan* (A Treatise on Nature and Principle), XII, Part 6.

43 Tsung-mi, *Yü-lan-pên-ching-shu* (A Commentary on the Ullambana-sūtra), (*Taishō*, XXXIX, 512 b).
44 Cf. Arthur F. Wright, *Buddhism in Chinese History*, 105
45 Fully discussed by T'ang Chün-i in *Philosophy East and West*, XI, 4 (January 1962), 195–218.
46 Yoshikawa, *op.cit.*, 105–106.
47 Sōkichi Tsuda, *Shina Shisō to Nippon*, 18–19.
48 The *Chun-nan-tzŭ*.
49 Masson-Oursel, *La philosophie comparée*, 118.
50 Max Weber, *Konfuzianismus und Taoismus*, 285.
51 Zenryū Tsukamoto, *Shina Bukkyō-shi Kenkyū* (A Study on the History of Chinese Buddhism), 86.
52 Daijō Tokiwa, *Shina Bukkyō-no Kenkyū* (Studies on Chinese Buddhism), III, 97–98; Ryōshū Michibata, *Gaisetsu Shina Bukkyō-shi* (General Outline of the History of Chinese Buddhism), 74f; Hiroshi Yamazaki, *Shina Chūsei Bukkyō-no Tenkai* (The Development of Chinese Buddhism in the Medieval Age), 129f. Cf. Enichi Ōchō, *Shina Bukkyō-ni Okeru Kokka Ishiki* (National Sentiments in Chinese Buddhism). *Tōhō Gakuhō* (Series of Oriental Studies), XI, No. 3.
53 The Imperial version of the *Po-chang ch'ing-kuei* (Monastic Rules instituted by Master Po-ch'ing). (*Taishō*, XLVIII, 1112 c.)
54 The problem has been treated by Arthur F. Wright, *Buddhism in Chinese History*, 41ff., 60ff.
55 Tao-hsuan called Bodhiruci who came from India "Chinese Bodhiruci." (*Taishō* L, 470 b, 470 c.)
56 Eg., *Ch'an-yüan-chu-chüan-chi-tu-hsü* (Collection of Sayings on the Origin of Zen), I, 29, 83.
57 *Ibid.*, V.
58 Arthur F. Wright, "Fu-I and the Rejection of Buddhism," *Journal of the History of Ideas*, XII (January 1951), 42.
59 *Ibid.*, 44.
60 *Mo-ho-chih-k'uan*, VI, Part 2. (*Taishō*, XLVI, 80 a.)
61 Kōjirō Yoshikawa, *Shinajin no Koten to sono Seikatsu* (Chinese Classics and Way of Life Revealed in Them), 143–144.
62 Hajime Nakamura, *Shoki no Vedānta Tetsugaku* (Vedānta Philosophy in the Early Stages), 305f., 345f.
63 Arthur F. Wright, *Buddhism in Chinese History*, 93, 123.

Chapter 24

1 The ideogram *T'ien* is derived from the letter *Ta* by adding a line on the top. *Ta* is a hieroglyphic which originally meant man. Therefore, one may imagine that this ideogram *T'ien* indicates the sky which is above man.
2 Kōjirō Yoshikawa, *Chinese Classics and Way of Life*, 9.
3 *Ibid.*, 18. Cf. Masson-Oursel, "Etude de Logique Comparée," *Revue Philosophique* (1917), 67.

4 Fung Yu-lan, *History of Chinese Philosophy*, 61. Cf. A. Forke, *Yang Chu's Garden of Pleasures*, and J. Legge, *The Chinese Classics*, II, 92–99.
5 Fung Yu-lan, *op.cit.*, 169, 219, 238.
6 *Hsin-hsin-ming* (Epigrams of Faith).
7 The *Liu-Tsu Ta-shih fa-pao-t'an ching* (Jewelled Altar Sūtra, by the Sixth Patriarch) in Hakuju Ui, *Daini Zenshū-shi Kenkyū*, 149.
8 Rousselle asserted this opinion and A. Forke agreed with him. Alfred Forke, *Geschichte der mittelalterlichen chinesischen Philosophie* (Hamburg: 1934), 363.
9 The *San-lun hsüan-i*, 25.
10 This is stated in the chapter *San-hua-pin* of the *Mahā-prajñāpāramitā-sūtra;* also, the chapter *Shih-chi-pin* of the same sūtra mentions the identification of phenomena with reality. (*Taishō*, VIII, 277 b, 400–401.)
11 This thought is derived from the phrase in a version of the Prajñāpāramitāsūtra. (*Taishō*, VIII, 140 c.)
12 Concerning this poem, Dr. Hakuju Ui mentioned that this poem is quoted in the Collected Works of Ho-Tse Shen-hui, found at Tung-huang (30). However, its composer is unknown. In the old commentaries, this poem is attributed to a certain High Priest. It is quoted also in the *Ta-ch'êng yao-yü* (*Taishō*, LXXXV, 1206 a.)
13 The *Tun-wuju-tao-yao-menlun*, 86. Cf. *ibid.*, 96.
14 The *Hsin-hsin-ming*.
15 The *Wu-mên-kuan*, Chapter 19.
16 The *Ching-tê ch'uan-têng lu*, X. (*Taishō*, LI, 275 a.)
17 Another poem also expresses the same state of mind: Cf. Hakuju Ui: *Daini Zenshū-shi Kenkyū*, 450.
18 The *Chêng-tao-ko*.
19 The *Wu-men-kuan*, Chapter 19.
20 The *Pi-yen chi*, Chapter 6.
21 The *Ching-tê ch'uan-têng lu*, X. (*Taishō*, LI, 277 c.)
22 *Ibid.*, XI. (*Taishō*, LI, 284 b.)
23 *Ibid.*, XVII. (*Taishō*, LI, 337 a.)
24 Kōjirō Yoshikawa, *Chinese Classics and View of Life*, 28.
25 Masaaki Matsumoto, *Gi Shin ni okeru Mu no Shisō no Seikaku* (The Character of the Concept "Nothingness" in the Wêi and Chin dynasties) in *Shigaku Zasshi* (Journal of History) 1940.
26 Derk Bodde, "Dominant Ideas in the Formation of Chinese Culture," *Journal of American Oriental Society*, LXII (1942), 299.
27 Homer H. Dubs, "The Date of Confucius' Birth," *Asia Major* (1949), I, 139–146.
28 The *Suvarṇaprabhāṣa*, XXXVIII, Chapter 13.
29 Biographies of High Priests, III. (*Taishō*, L, 341 a.)

Chapter 25

1 Kōjirō Yoshikawa, *Chinese Classics and Way of Life*, 31–32.
2 *Ibid.*, 33.

3 The *Liu-tsu ta-shih fa-pao-t'an ching* (Jewelled Altar Sūtra) 35. Hakuju Ui, *Daini Zenshū-shi Kenkyū,* 168.
4 *Taishō,* XXXVII, 277 a.
5 *Taishō,* XLVII, 426 a. Cf. *Kyōgyōshinshō,* III, Part 2.
6 The *Analects of Confucius,* II.
7 Cf. Yoshikawa, *op.cit.,* 33–36.
8 Cf. The *San-lun hsüan-i* (edited by Yenshō Kanakura, 23).
9 The *Mo-ho-chih-kuan* VI, Part 1. (*Taishō,* XLVI, 77 a, b.)
10 *Ibid.,* 78 c. The thought of Yen Chih-T'ui is fully discussed by Albert E. Dien in *Confucian Personalities,* edited by Arthur F. Wright and Denis Twitchett (Stanford: Stanford University Press, 1962), 43–64.
11 The *Hung-min-chi,* VI, VII. (*Taishō,* LII, 41 b–49 a.)
12 This is based upon the *Yüan-jen-lun.* In the *Chan-yüan-chu-chüan-chi-tu-hsü* written by the same author (Tsung-mi), Taoism and Confucianism are completed ignored. (Edited by Hakuju Ui, in Iwanami Bunko, 51f.)
13 The *Tun-wu-ju-tao-yao-mên lun,* (edited by Hakuju Ui), 94.
14 Kyōdō Itō, *Dōgen Zenji Kenkyū,* (Studies on Dōgen Zenji), I, 65f. However, according to Dōgen, his master Ju-ching admonished him by saying "those who insist on the oneness of the three religions are those who destroy the holy teaching of the Buddha." (*Shōbō Genzō,* Shohōjissō.) Nevertheless, the analects of Ju-ching acknowledged the authority of Confucianism and Taoism, and furthermore, the phrases and words were quoted from the *Analects of Confucius* and *Lao-tzŭ-ching* in his writings. (Itō, *op.cit.,* I, 32f. 69f.)
15 *Wan Chih-hsin* (translated by Shizuhiko Tomita: *Shina Shūkyō Shisō-shi* (History of Religious Thoughts in China), 220.
16 The *Hung-min-chi,* VI. (*Taishō,* LII, 39 a.)
17 Daijo Tokiwa, *Shina ni okeru Bukkyō to Jukyō Dokyō* (Buddhism, Confucianism, and Taoism in China), 201.
18 The *Fu-chiao-p'ien,* Part 2. (*Taishō,* LII, 657 a.)
19 *Ibid.* (*Taishō,* LII, 660 a.)
20 Tokiwa, *op.cit.,* 401.
21 Wing-tsit Chan, "Chinese Theory and Practice," in *Philosophy and Culture/East and West,* edited by Charles A. Moore (Honolulu: University of Hawaii Press, 1962), 92.
22 P'ei-hsiu; preface to the *Ch'an-yüan-chu-chüan-chi-tu-hsü-hsü,* 4.
23 *Ibid.,* Part 1, 33.
24 "Concerning three sects of practical teaching and three sects of doctrinal teaching." Cf. *ibid.,* Part 1.
25 Cf. *ibid.,* 91, 51.
26 Cf. *ibid.,* 70f.
27 Gauḍapāda (*Māṇḍūkya Kārikā,* Chapter 4) and Bhartṛhari of India advance the same thought. Hegel and Dilthey interpreted it from the historical standpoint.
28 *Chu-fang-mên-jen-san-wêṇ-yü-lu,* Part 2. (*Tun-wu-yao-mên*), 94.
29 *Ch'an-yüan-chu-chüan-chi-tu-hsü,* 114.

30 *Ibid.*, 18.

31 *Chuan-hsin-fa-yao* (Essentials of Truth in the Transmission of Mind), 38f.

32 *Hsin-hsin-ming.*

33 It is said that the Chinese version of the *Saddharma-puṇḍarīka-sūtra* was frequently used in examinations for government officials in the Northern Sung dynasty.

34 Edwin G. Pulleyblank, "Neo-Confucianism in T'ang Intellectual Life," in *The Confucian Persuasion*, edited by Arthur F. Wright, 92.

35 *Fu-chiao-p'ien*, Part 1. (*Taishō*, LII, 649 a, 649 b.)

36 *Sun-ch'o, Yü-tao-lun, Hung-ming-chi*, III. (*Taishō*, LII, 17 a.)

37 *Hung-ming-chi*, VII. (*Taishō*, LII, 45 c–46 b.)

38 *Ibid.*, VI. (*Taishō*, LII, 38 c–39 a.)

39 *Tan-chin-wên-chi*, XIX. (*Taishō*, LII, 748 a.)

40 *San-chiao-p'ing-hsin-lun*, Part 1. (*Taishō*, LII, 781 c.)

41 *Shutsujō Kōgo* XXIV. *Sankyō.*

42 *P'o-hsich-lun*, Part 1 (*Taishō*, XXXII, 478 c); *Fo-tsu-t'ung-chi*, IV (*Taishō*, XLIX, 166 c); *ibid.*, XXXV (*Taishō*, XLIX, 333 b-c).

43 Cf. *Hung-ming-chi*, VI. (*Taishō*, LII, 42 c.)

44 Cf. *ibid.*, VII. (*Taishō*, LII, 46 a.)

45 Cf. *ibid.*, III. (*Taishō*, LII, 17 a.)

46 *Mo-ho-chih-kuan*, III, Part 2. (*Taishō*, XLVI, 31 b.)

47 *Shutsujō Kyōgo*, Chapter XXIV. *Sankyō.*

48 Sarvadarśanasaṃgraha; Sarvasiddhāntasaṃgraha, etc.

49 Yüeh Fei's biography and his mythologizing are discussed fully by Hellmut Wilhelm in Wright, *Confucian Personalities*, 146–161.

50 The features of Kuan Yü, a composite hero, discussed by Robert Ruhlmann in Wright, *The Confucian Persuasion*, 173ff.

51 Present day Chinese call both Taoist and Buddhist temples "*Miao*" (temple shrine). Daijō Tokiwa, *Shina Bukkyō no Kenkyū* (Study of Chinese Buddhism), III, 110f. Cf. "A Report by E. Inaba," *Mujintō* (1918), 10f.

PART III

Chapter 26

1 Max Weber, *Aufsätze zur Religionssoziologie*, II, 316.

2 Lamaism was introduced into Europe, too. As a result of the conquest of Russia proper by the "Golden Horde," i.e., the Buddhist kings of Tartary, Buddhism was propagated there and is thus still alive in European Russia. Among the Kalmuks in the basin of the Volga River, there are some people who call themselves Buddhists. Cf. L. A. Waddell, *The Buddhism of Tibet or Lamaism* (London: 1895), 9.

3 Due to the lack of opportunities to see the original texts of Tibetan works, and the fact that not many studies have been made along this line, it is rather difficult to carry out a complete study of Tibetan ways of thinking. Tibetology in Japan has been making some progress during the last two

decades. But most scholars consider it subsidiary to their main field of concern which is Indology or Buddhology. Such being the case, the following study consists of but a brief survey.

4 L. A. Waddell, "Lamaism," in *Encyclopaedia of Religion and Ethics*, Edited by James Hastings (Edinburgh: 1940), VII, 784 a.

5 *Ibid.*, 785b.

6 *tāsu puṣkariṇiṣu samantāc caturdisaṁ catvāri sopānāni.* The Smaller *Sukhāvatī-vyūha-sūtra*, 4, edited by F. Max Müller and Bunyiu Nanjio (Oxford: Clarendon Press, 1883). *rdsiṅ de dag gi phyogs bshi kun na them skas..............bshi bshi yod de.*

7 Translations from Chinese into Tibetan were made in ancient times. Cf. Shuki Yoshimura, *The Denkar-ma. An Oldest Catalogue of the Tibetan Buddhist Canons with Introductory Notes* (Kyoto: Ryukoku University, 1950), Introduction, 7. Cf. Charles Bell, *The Religion of Tibet* (Oxford: Clarendon Press, 1931), 26.

Chapter 27

1 Charles Bell, *The Religion of Tibet* (Oxford: Clarendon Press, 1931), 90–91.

2 *Ibid.*, 90.

3 Hisashi Satō, *Kodai Chibetto-shi Kenkyū* (Studies in the History of Ancient Tibet), II (Kyoto: 1959), 783.

4 Jirō Kawakita, *The Japanese Journal of Ethnology*, XIX, 1 (1955) and 3–4 (1956).

5 The Tibetan version of *Nāgānanda*. Cf. Vidhushekhara Bhattacharya, *bhoṭa-prākaśa. A Tibetan Chrestomathy* (University of Calcutta, 1939), 40. In Tibetan also there are some words meaning a prostitute, e.g. *ḥphyonma, smad-ḥtsoṅ-ma*, etc., but the translator did not use such a word.

6 Cf. the preceding "Ways of Thinking in China."

7 Shūki Yoshimura in *Ryūkoku Daigaku Ronshū*, 355 (1957), 91ff.

8 Satō, *op.cit.*, 791f.

9 J. F. Rock, *The Na-khi Nāga Cult and Related Ceremonies.* Série Orientale, IV. Roma Is. M.E.O. (Rome: 1952), 5.

10 Satō, *op. cit.*, I, 760.

11 *Ibid.*

12 Giuseppe Tucci, *The Tombs of the Tibetan Kings.* Série Orientale, I (Rome: 1950).

13 *Catuḥśataka*, XII, 25. (*Bhoṭaprakāśa*, 175.)

14 Satō, *op.cit.*, I, 160.

15 *rgyal po mihi lha shes pa / li tsa byi* (*Licchavi*) *rnams rigs su byuṅ.* (Deb-gter-sṅon-po. Satō, *op.cit.*, I, 218.)

16 *Taishō Tripiṭaka*, XXXII, 231 a-c.

Chapter 28

1 Shinkō Mochizuki, *Bukkyō Daijiten* (Dictionary of Buddhism), (Tokyo, 1935), 3612 c.

2 *Taishō Tripiṭaka*, LI, 977.
3 Hisashi Satō *Kodai Chibetto-shi Kenkyū* (Studies in the History of Ancient Tibet), II, 761.
4 *Ibid.*
5 Charles Bell, *The Religion of Tibet* (Oxford: Clarendon Press, 1931), 13–14. About this poem, cf. A. H. Francke, *Encyclopedia of Religion and Ethics*, VIII, 75–78.
6 Jane Caston Mahler, *The Westerners Among the Figurines of the T'ang Dynasty of China*. Série Orientale Roma. X (Roma: *Is. M.E.O.*, 1959), 149.
7 Edward Conze, *Vajracchedikā Prajñāpāramitā* (Roma: Is. M.E.O., 1957), 29. Cf. 42.
8 *Byaṅ chub sems dapḥ dṅos po la mi gnas par sbyin pa sbyin no.*
9 Vidhushekhara Bhattacharya, *Bhoṭa-prakāśa* (University of Calcutta, 1939), 132.
10 The Tibetan version of the *Samantamukha-parivarta* of the *Lotus Sūtra.*
11 *Udānavarga*, XIII, 7 (Bhattacharya, *op.cit.*, 76.)
12 Cf. my article on the Smaller Sukhāvatī-vyūha Sūtra in *Hirosato Iwai Commemoration Volume* (Tokyo: 1963), Section 40.
13 Satō, *op. cit.*, II, 760.
14 L. A. Waddell in *Encyclopedia of Religions and Ethics*, VII, 789.
15 *Pañcakrama* I, 57. Shinten Sakai, *Chibetto Mikkyō Kyōri no Kenkyū* (Studies in Tibetan Esoteric Teachings) (Koyasan: 1956), 132f, 186.
16 *Ibid.*, 63.
17 Hakuyū Hadano in *Tōhoku Daigaku Bungakubu Kenkyū Nenpō* (Proceedings of the Faculty of Letters, Tōhoku University, Sendai, No. 9, 1958), 33–36.
18 Sakai, *op.cit.*, 45.
19 *Ibid.*, 149–150.
20 Mochizuki, *op.cit.*, 3615.
21 Bell, *op.cit.*, 90.
22 A. Wayman, *Journal of the American Oriental Society*, LXXVIII, 1 (January–March 1958), 86.
23 Hadano, *op.cit.*, 37–38.
24 *Ibid.*, 38–39.
25 *Ibid.*, 59.
26 *Ibid.*, 49–50.
27 Bell, *op.cit.*, 41.
28 Hadano, *op.cit.*, 60–67., cf. Sakai, *op.cit.*, 27, 38.
29 *Ibid.*, 73.
30 Nāgānanda 11. (*Bhoṭaprakāśa*, 59.)
31 Hadano, *op.cit.*, 78–79.
32 *Nāpi Maithunadharma sarvaśaḥ* (*Saddharmapuṇḍarīka-sūtra*), edited by Wogihara (Tokyo: 1935), 373, line 7.
33 *Gyem-paḥi chos med do.*

34 Jitsugyō Kai, *Shūkyō Kenkyū* (*Journal of Studies in Religion*), New Series 4, No. 6, p. 141ff.
35 Waddell, *op.cit.*, 31. Cf. Koeppen, *Die Religion de Buddha* (1859) II, 71.

Chapter 29

1 Giuseppe Tucci, *The Tombs of the Tibetan Kings*. Série Orientale Roma, I (Roma: 1950), 16, 36, 91. Also *Minor Buddhist Texts*, pt. II, (Rome: 1958), 40.
2 *Ibid.*, 77 n. 37.
3 *Gnam gyi chos daṅ mtshuṅs par ni bakaḥ btsan te.* (*Ibid.*, 91.)
4 *Ibid.*, 97.
5 *Chos rgya cher thugs su chud nas.* (*Ibid.*, 101.)
6 Charles Bell, *The Religions of Tibet* (Oxford: Clarendon Press, 1931), 45.
7 *Pañca-krama*, I, 70. (Shinten Sakai, *Chiketto Mikkyō Kyōri no Kenkyū* [Studies in Tibetan Esoteric Teachings], 188.)
8 In some texts the appellation *bcom ladan ḥdas* (*bhagavat*) is added to *de bshin gśegs pa* (tathāgata).
9 Hakuyū Hadano in *Tōhoku Dargaku Bumgakubu Kenkyū Nenpō* (Proceedings of the Faculty of Letters, Fohoku University), 40.
10 Bell, *op.cit.*, 84.
11 Tōkwan Tada, *Chibetto* (Tibet), 2–3.
12 *Ibid.*, 5.
13 J. N. Ganhar and P. N. Ganhar, *Buddhism in Kashmir and Ladakh* (New Delhi: 1956), 192–193.
14 H. Hadano, *Zōgai Chibetto Seiten Mokoruku Hensan ni Tsuite* (On the Compilation of a Catalogue of Tibetan Works on Buddhism), *Bunka* (July 1944), 465.
15 Tada, *op.cit.*, 27–29.
16 Hadano, *op.cit.*, 13.
17 L. A. Waddell, in *Encyclopedia of Religion and Ethics*, VII, 787 b.
18 *Ibid.*, 788 a.
19 Helmut Hoffmann, *Mi-la Ras-pa. Sieben Legenden* (Munich: 1950,) 18.
20 H. Hadano, *Bunka*, XIX, 1 (1955), 46f.
21 Gadjin M. Nagao, *Chibetto Bukkyō Kenkyū* (Studies in Tibetan Buddhism) (Tokyo: Iwanami, 1954), 39.
22 Tada, *op.cit.*, 3–4.
23 Bunkyō Aoki, *Chibetto-yūki* (Record of a Journey in Tibet), 105. He calls himself an "avatāra" (Waddell, *op.cit.*, 242.)
24 Aoki, *op.cit.*, 247ff.
25 Bell, *op.cit.*, 181.
26 Tada, *op.cit.*, 24. In the case of the Dalai Lama, Tibetans treat his dead body with very great care. (Bunkyō Aoki, *op,cit.*, 343ff.)
27 G. Tucci, *Preliminary Report on Two Scientific Expeditions in Nepal.*

Materials for the Study of Nepalese History and Culture, 1. Série Orientale (Rome: 1956), 34.

28 The late Rev. Chiken Sumita, a high priest of the Higashi-Honganji Temple, Japan, said, as one of his dying wishes, that the recitation of scripture should be performed in front of the Buddha's image—an exceptional thing for Japan.

29 Tada, *op.cit.*, 26.

30 Yōkichi Takayama (translator), *Chibetto-Tanken-ki* (Record of the Expedition to Tibet), 73ff.

31 Tada, *op.cit.*, 89; Aoki, *op.cit.*, 192, 326.

32 R. O. Meisezahl, "Die Tibetischen Handschriften und Drucke des Linden-Museums in Stuttgart," *Tribus, Zetschrift für Ethnologie und ihre Nachbarwissenschaften.* N. F. VII (1957) 8f.

33 Sarat Chanda Das, *A Tibetan-English Dictionary* (Calcutta: 1902), 1002 a.

34 Aoki, *op.cit.*, 169.

35 Hadano, *Bunka* XXI, 6 (December 1957), 7.

The Buddha discouraged monks from having relationships with women. In a scripture of Early Buddhism the following passage illustrates the Buddha's attitude toward women:

Ānanda (a disciple) asked the Buddha, "How are we to conduct ourselves, O Lord, with regard to women?"

"Don't see them, Ānanda."

"But if we do see them, what are we to do?"

"Do not speak to them."

"But if they do speak to us, then what are we to do?"

"Keep wide awake, Ānanda."

From T. W. and C. A. F. Rhys Davids, *Dialogues of the Buddha* (London: Oxford University Press, 1910), pt. II, 154. (T. W. Rhys Davids, editor, *Sacred Books of the Buddhists,* III.)

36 Bell, *op.cit.*, 6–7.

37 Bu-ston's *History of Indian Buddhism,* edited by Dalai Lama the Thirteenth, 126 a.

Chapter 30

1 Bunkyō Aoki, *Chibetto-Yūki* (Record of a Journey in Tibet), 253, and according to his personal instruction.

2 Early Buddhism in India made a careful distinction between spiritual and worldly authority. Buddhist monasteries in India kept aloof from temporal involvements. But the Tibetan monasteries from the beginning were involved in a secular struggle for political paramountcy. To this end they allied themselves with various temporal authorities in their competition for power. In this struggle, the Yellow Sect, assisted by the Mongols, emerged victorious, with the result that the leader of that sect,

the Dalai Lama, came to assume both religious and civil authority. Kenneth Ch'en, "Transformations in Buddhism in Tibet," *Philosophy East and West,* VII, 3 and 4, (October 1957 and January 1958), 117–123.

3 H. A. Jäschke, *Tibetan Grammar* (New York: 1954), 35–36.

4 Vidhushekkara Bhattacharya, *Bhoṭaprakāśa,* 115.

5 Personal instruction to the author by Rev. Bsod-nams rgyamtsho, the Tibetan Lama.

6 Bhattacharya, *op.cit.,* 139, 464.

7 *Ibid.,* 204, 464.

8 T. Tada, *op.cit.,* 118.

9 *Ibid.,* 80, (cf. Tōhoku Catalogue, No. 360).

10 Tokwan Tada, *Chiketto* (Tibet), 80.

11 The above is according to the reports of Reverend Aoki and Tada. It seems quite opposite to the report of Ekai Kawaguchi referred to in the previous section. A common way of thinking in both reports, which superficially contradict each other, is the belief in religious charisma. Therefore it may be said that there is a consistent way of thinking in spite of the different forms of each idea due to historical and geographical conditions.

Chapter 31

1 Tōkwan Tada, *Chibetto* (Tibet), 168ff. Helmut Hoffman, *Quellen Zur Geschichte der tibetischen Bon-Religion.* (Akademie der Wissenschaften und der Literatur. Abhandlungen der Geistes und sozialwissenschaftlichen Klasse, 1950, no. 4.) The etymological meaning of "bon" is not clear (p. 137). The Bon religion exists in southwestern China and Nepal also. Cf. J. F. Rock, *The Na-khi Nāga Cult and Related Ceremonies, passim;* Giuseppe Tucci, *Preliminary Report on Two Scientific Expeditions in Nepal* (Materials for the History of Nepalese History and Culture, 1. Série Orientale, Roma, X. Is. M.E.O., 1956), 28–29.

2 According to Bunkyō Aoki's information, who guided this lama.

3 Susumu Yamaguchi, *Chibettogo no Keitō* (Tibetan Language), 33–35. (Contained in the Iwanami Kōza, "*Tōyō-shichō.*")

4 According to Reverend Tada's information, the *Bhadracaryā-praṇidhāna,* the *Mañjuśrī-paramārthanāmasaṁgīti,* the *Sitātapatrādhāraṇī* (*Tōhoku,* Nos. 1095, 4377; 360; 593) are most often used for ceremony, but the *Saddharmapuṇḍarīka* is scarcely recited.

5 Bunkyō Aoki, *Chibetto-yūki* (Record of a Journey in Tibet), 334.

6 Tada, *op.cit.,* 39; cf. Aoki, *op.cit.,* 270.

7 The following is according to Reverend Aoki's instruction.

8 Giuseppe Tucci, *Tombs of the Tibetan Kings,* 52f.

9 R. Nebesky de Wojkowitz, "State Oracle of Tibet," *The Modern Review,* (December 1950), 479–480.

Chapter 32

1 The *Mahāvyutpatti*, edited by Ryōzaburō Sakaki, No. 859. (Chinese equivalent to this Sanskrit is: "bringing about (?)—numberless—Buddha's land—adornment—vow.")

2 E.g., a Tibetan sentence: "*ṇaḥi gcen-po thams-cad bod-kyis bsad*" can be translated in two ways: (1) "Tibetans killed all my brothers." (2) "All my brothers were killed by Tibetans." The copula "*yin-pa*" is here to be supplied.

3 Cf. Tensen Yamagami, *Bukkyō-ronri no Kenkyū to Chibetto-zōkyō* (Studies on Buddhist Logic and the Tibetan Tripiṭaka), *The Wayūshi* (1908), XII.

4 Tibetan lama-students are required to study the five courses in the monastery, which require twenty years; the first three years are devoted to studies in logic. Tōkwan Tada, *Chibetto* (Tibet), 31ff.

5 According to Reverend Tada's information, Tibetan studies in logic are based upon the *Pramāṇavārttika* alone, while the *Nyāyabindu* and the *Pramāṇaviniścaya* are scarcely studied.

6 The following is according to Th. Stcherbatsky, *Buddhist Logic*, I (1932), 38, 57, 58.

7 *Ibid.*, 46. This is to be compared with the fact that Japanese and Chinese Buddhists had never maintained logic to be a secular science, but rather a study ancillary to theology.

8 According to Reverend Tada's instructions, students are required to learn by heart a short commentary of Haribhadra on the *Abhisamayālaṅkāra* (Tōhoku Catalogue No. 3793). It maintained an authority almost equivalent to the holy scriptures. Haribhadra belonged to the line of Bhavya (Bhāvaviveka), but his idea of *śūnyatā* is different from Bhavya's and rather nearer to that of Candrakīrti.

9 The texts which are often read in Tibet are more or less systematic. Cf. Shūki Yoshimura, *Tibetan Buddhistology: The Basic Original Texts of Historical Lamaism* (Kyoto: 1953), 5.

10 G. Tucci, *Minor Buddhist Texts*, II, 9, 21–2, 52–65.

11 Ekai Kawaguchi, *Nihon-Bukkyō to Chibetto-Bukkyō tono Busshin-kwan no Sōi ni tsuite* (On the difference of the Concept of Buddha in Japanese and Tibetan Buddhism), *Gendai-Bukkyō* (March 1928), 31.

Chapter 33

1 Owing to the spread of Buddhism, Sanskrit terms also found their way into Japanese. In the Man'yōshū collection of ancient poems (c. 8th century), for example, such terms as *tō* (*stūpa*, pagoda) and *Baramon* (Brahmin) are found, and the word *Śākya* appears in the *Bussokuseki* poems (*Buddha-Paduka* = footprints of Buddha). Other words gradually came to be used, but their number was never considerable.

2 Shinkichi Hashimoto, *Kokugogaku Gairon* (Survey of the Japanese language), (Tokyo: Iwanami Shōten, 1946), 91.
3 *Ibid.*, 98.
4 *Ibid.*, 101.
5 Daitō Shimaji, *Nihon Bukkyō Kyōgakushi* (History of Doctrines of Japanese Buddhism), (Tokyo: Meiji Shoin, 1935), 2.
6 Kanzan Matsumiya, *Sankyō Yōron* (1760), Essential Outlines of Three Religions [Shintoism, Confucianism, Buddhism] in *Nihon Jurin Sōsho,* (Series of Confucian Works in Japan), Kaisetsubu (Expository Section) II, 7.
7 "The Japanese gradually took over most of Chinese civilization but resolutely refused to accept rhymed tonal poetry, civil service examinations, footbinding, and a number of other particular Chinese features." A. L. Kroeber, *Anthropology* (New York: 1948), 416. On the influence of Chinese thought upon the Japanese, cf. *Sources of the Japanese Tradition,* compiled by Ryūsaku Tsunoda, Wm. Theodore de Bary, Donald Keene, edited by Wm. Theodore de Bary (New York: Columbia University Press, 1958), 54ff.
8 Cited in Taijō Tamamuro, *Nihon Bukkyōshi Gaisetsu* (An Outline of Japanese Buddhism) (Tokyo: Risōsha, 1942), 41. Cf. E. O. Reischauer and J. K. Fairbank, *East Asia, The Great Tradition* (Boston: 1960), 495: "With the Chinese writing system, the Japanese naturally adopted Chinese ways of thinking. Among these, Buddhism and the Chinese concept of centralized government. . . ."
9 Teikichi Kida in *Rekishi Chiri* (History and Geography), XL, no. 2, 96f.
10 Kōgatsuin Jinrei (1749–1817), *Kyōgyōshinshō Kōgi* (Lectures on Shinran's Teaching of Practice, Faith, Attainment) in the *Bukkyō Taikei* edition (Great Systems of Buddhism), 1334. Cf. the English translation of the original work of Shinran by Kōshō Yamamoto (Tokyo: Karinbunko, 1958).
11 For example, cf. Tetsurō Watsuji, *Nihon Seishinshi Kenkyū* (Studies in the Intellectual History of Japan), (Tokyo: 1953), 348–349.
12 Ten learned monks from the Tendai and Hossō sects took part in the religious debates held in a palace of the Imperial court of Japan. The Hossō school won and became the chief of the Six Sects of that time.

Chapter 34

1 Naoichi Miyaji, *Jingi-shi Taikei* (Great Outlines of the History of Shintoism), 6, 9.
2 Yōkyoku, *Taisha* (A Noh Song entitled "The Great Shrine").
3 *Fūkyō Hyakushu Kōsetsu* (Lecture on the "Wild Winds Eight-Hundred Fold"), in Genchi Katō, *Shintō no Shūkyō Hattatsushiteki Kenkyū* (A Study in the Religious Development of Shintoism), 935.
4 Cf. Doctrine of Tranquillity, I, Part 1. (*Taishō,* XLVI, 1 c.) Eun Mayeda, Proceedings of Philosophical Institute, *Tetsugakukan Kōgiroku* (*Shigaku Zasshi,* 1923, 373–374). (Journal of Philosophic Studies.)

5 *Kaimokushō,* part 2: "Awakening to the Truth," by Nichiren. (Tokyo: International Buddhist Society, 1941).

6 See Chapter 18, 7th *gāthā:* Saddharma-puṇḍarīka-sūtra (edited by Unrai Ogiwara), 251, line 25; Aṣṭasāhasrikā (cf. Unrai Ogiwara), 51, line 15; 572, lines 2–3; 666, line 7; etc.

7 *Shōbōgenzō,* Shohō-jissō (Dōgen's Essentials of the True Law), section on "The True Nature of the Law."

8 See "Profound Doctrine of the Lotus Sūtra," VIII, Part 2. (*Taishō,* XXXIII, 783 b.)

9 *Shōbōgenzō,* section on "Life and Death."

10 *Ibid.,* Busshō. Section on "The Buddha-Nature."

11 *Shasekishū,* X, Part 1.

12 This sentence was composed in China based upon such sentences as "In the milk there is the cream; in sentient beings there is the Buddha nature," and "If you have the desire to seek, you will find," in Mahā prajñā-pāramitrā-sūtra, XXVIII. (*Taishō,* XII, 532 a, 533 b.)

13 *Shōbōgenzō,* Busshō.

14 Kegon-sūtra, XXXVIII, chapter on the Ten Stages (Taishō, X, 194 a, 533 a).

15 *Bonbun Daihōkōbutsu-kegonkyō Jūjibon* (edited by Ryūko Kondō), 98.

16 *Shōbōgenzō,* Sangaiyuishin. (The Three Realms—Desire, Material Forms, Immaterial Forms—in Mind.)

17 *Ibid.,* Sokushin Zebutsu. (The Mind as the Buddha.)

18 *Ibid.,* Butsukōjōji. (Manifesting the Buddha-nature.)

19 *Ibid.,* Uji. (The Reality of Time.)

20 *Ibid.,* Setsushin Setsuchō. (Expounding the Mind is Expounding the Buddha-nature.)

21 *Ibid.,* Hosshō. (The Nature of the *Dharma.*)

22 *Ibid.,* Setsushin Setsushō.

23 *Ibid.,* Sanjūshichihon Bodaibunpō. (Chapter 37 on Steps to Enlightenment.)

24 Yasusada Hiyane, *Nihon Shūkyōshi,* 828–829. (History of Japanese Religions.)

25 *Gomō Jigi* (Explanations of Terms in the *Mencius*), I, 3.

26 *Dōjimon* (Children's Questions), II, 39.

27 Junsei Iwahashi, *Sorai Kenkyū,* 449. On Chu-tsu's *Li* and *Ch'i,* cf. Fung Yu-lan, *A Short History of Chinese Philosophy,* edited and translated from the Chinese by D. Bodde, (New York: 1961), 296–303.

28 Cf. Yaichi Haga, *Kokuminsei Jūron,* 91ff. (Ten Lectures on the National Character.)

29 R. H. Blyth, *Cultural East,* I (1947), 45.

30 *Man'yōshū,* III, 318.

31 *Ibid.,* VI, 919.

32 *Ibid.,* V, 822.

33 *Ibid.,* V, 824.

34 *Theragāthā,* 537, 538, 540, 544, 545.

35 Emperor Kazan (*Eiga Monogatari,* Mihatenu Yume). (*Tales of Splendor,* Futile Dreams.)
36 Emperor Kazan (*Zoku Kokinshū,* Shakukyōka). (*Supplementary Ancient and Modern Collection,* In Praise of Buddha.)
37 *Shōbōgenzō,* Hotsumujōshin. (Manifestation of the Supreme Mind.)
38 Nichiren also wrote a book named *Sōmoku Jōbutsu Kuketsu.* (Attaining of Buddhahood even by shrubs.)
39 This verse (*gāthā*) is not found in the Sūtra on Intermediate Existence (*Antarābhava-sūtra*). Perhaps someone composed this verse based upon this sūtra.
40 Daijō Tokiwa, *Nihon Bukkyō no Kenkyū,* 107ff. (Study of Japanese Buddhism.)
41 Hakujō Ui, *Bukkyō Hanron* (An Outline of Buddhism), II, 337.
42 See *supra,* Part I, Chapter 9.
43 Yaichi Haga, *Kokuminsei Jūron* (Ten Lectures on the National Character), 70.
44 *Ibid.,* 65–67.
45 Ryochū Shioiri, *Dengyō Daishi to Hokkekyō* (Master Dengyō and the Lotus Sūtra), (in *Nihon Bukkyō no Rekishi to Rinen* [History and Concepts of Japanese Buddhism], compiled by Seiichirō Ono and Shinshō Hanayama), 117ff.
46 See *Hokke Shūku* (Excellency of the Lotus Sūtra), by Saichō, II; *Dengyō Daishi Zenshū* (Complete Works of Master Dengyō), II, 265–266, 280.
47 *Sokushin Jōbutsugi Shiki* (Personal Remarks on the Doctrine of Becoming Buddha while One Is Living), [Tendaishū Sōsho (Collected Writings of the Tendai Sect), Annen Senshū (Works of Annen)], II, 210.
48 These words in *Bodai Shinron* (Treatise on the *Bodhi* mind) are said to have been written by Nāgārjuna.
49 *Myōichime Gohenji* (Reply to a woman Myōichi).
50 *Jushiki Kanjō Kudenshō* (Oral Teachings on the Consecration of a New Appointment).
51 *Shasekishū* ("Collection of Sands and Pebbles"—Anecdotes), II, Part 1.
52 "The Sacred Mountain" here is a Japanese equivalent for *Gṛdhrakūṭa.* See *Jimyō Hokke Mondōshō* (Questions and Answers on Keeping the Lotus Sūtra); *Toki dono Gohenji* (Reply to Esquire Toki), etc.
53 *Hōnen Shōnin Gyōjo Ezu* (Explanations and Pictures Illustrating the Acts of St. Hōnen), 26.
54 Cf. *Yuishinshō Mon-i* (Essentials of the Book of Faith).
55 *Shōbōgenzō Zuimonki* (Gleanings of the Sayings of Master Dōgen), II. Tsunoda, Keene, and De Bary, *Sources of Japanese Tradition,* 254–255. Dōgen refers here to Kūkai's assertion of the identity of mind and body, and the possibility of achieving liberation "in the body" in this life.
56 *Shōbōgenzō, op.cit.,* chapter on Busshō (Buddha-nature).
57 *Roankyō* (Lit. "Ass-Saddle Bridge"—Random Sayings, by Zen Priest Shōsan Suzuki), last part, 71.

58 *Sōan Zakki* (Miscellanies in a Hermitage, by Echū), Part II, 26.
59 *Shintō Gobusho* (Five Major Works of Shintoism), in *Kokushi Taikei* (Great Series of Japanese History), VII, 31.
60 *Hikosan Shugen Saihi Injin Kuketsushū* (Oral Teachings of Esoteric Shugen Practice in Mt. Hiko), Part 1, in Japanese Scriptures of Buddhism, Section on Shugen (*Nihondaizōkyō, Shugenshōshobu*, Part 2, 533, 549.)
61 Masatomo Manba, *Nihon Jukyōron* (Essays on Japanese Confucianism), 89.
62 *Taiheiki* (Chronicle of the Muromachi Period), XVI.
63 *Genkōshakusho* (Historiography of Japanese Buddhism), XIII.
64 *Shōbōgenzō, op.cit.*, chapter on Sanjūshichihon Bodaibumpō (37 chapters on Enlightenment Stages).
65 *Shutsujō Kōgo* (Monologue after Meditation), XXV, Zatsu.
66 *Āyāraṅga*, herausgegeben von W. Schubring, I, 27, 1, 28f.
67 *Ibid.*, I, 1, 6, 2 (p. 5, line 8).
68 *Shōbōgenzō, op.cit.*, chapter on Shōji (Life and death).
69 Yaichi Haga, *op.cit.*, 91–116.
70 *Man'yōshū* (Collection of Myriad Leaves), VIII (1959).
71 *Ibid.*, XX (4468).
72 Cf. Ichirō Hori, *Inton Shisō ni okeru Ningensei eno Shibo* ("Search for Humanity in a Life of Seclusion"), *Teiyū Rinri*, Nos. 7–8 (1947).
73 In *Tamakatsuma*, X, *Motoori Norinaga Zenshū* (Collected Works of Norinaga Motoori), IV, 236. See also Tsunetsugu Muraoka, *Motoori Norinaga* (1928), 430ff. Motoori's judgment on the *Shih Ching* is based, of course, on the moralizing interpretation of the songs in that book given by the Confucianists.
74 See Junsei Iwahashi, *Sorai Kenkyū* (Study on Sorai Ogyū), 433.
75 *Ibid.*, 331f.
76 See, e.g., Motoori Norinaga, *Genji Monogatari Tama-no-ogushi* (Jewels of the Comb [i.e. Commentary] on the Tale of Genji), in *Motoori Norinaga Zenshū*, V, 1135ff.
77 In *Bendō* (The Practice of the Way), *Nihon Jurin Sōsho, Ronben-bu*, 14.
78 In Dazai's *Keizai-roku* (Essays on Economy), I, fol. 10.
79 In *Seigaku Mondō* (Questions and Answers on Religious Scholarship), 3, quoted in Inoue Tetsujirō, *Nihon Kogakuha no Tetsugaku* (Philosophy in the Japanese Classical Study School), 693.
80 *Ibid.*, quoted in Inoue, *op.cit.*, 698.
81 *Gakusoku* (Rules for Study), 7, quoted in Iwahashi, *op.cit.*, 231.
82 *Okina Mondō* (Questions and Answers with an Elder), 1, a, *Tōju Sensei Zenshū* (Collected Works of Master Tōju), III, 76.
83 *Kodō-taii* (Outline of the Ancient Way), 3, *Hirata Atsutane Zenshū* (Collected Works of Atsutane Hirata), VIII, 69.
84 See the various versions of his works written in *Kana* characters, *Jiun Sonja Zenshū* (Collected Works of Master Jiun), III.
85 From the *Genji Monogatari* (Tale of Genji), quoted in Yasusada Hiyane, *Nihon Shūkyō-shi* (History of Japanese Religion), 410.

86 From the *Eiga Monogatari,* quoted in Hiyane, *op.cit.,* 410.
87 *Shaseki-shū,* III b, edited by Ebara Taizō, 106.
88 *Kōfukuji-sōjō* (Submitted Documents of the Kofuku Temple), in *Dai-Nippon Bukkyō Zensho* (The Great Collection of Japanese Buddhist Works) CXXIV, 107.
89 *Hōnen Shōnin Gyōjō-ezu,* XXI, in *Jōdo-shū Zensho,* XVI, 240.
90 *Shōgu Mondō-shō* (Questions and Answers on the Wise and Foolish), in *Shōwa Shinshū Nichiren Shōnin Imon-zenshū,* I, 474.
91 Fujiwara Arifusa, *Nomori no Kagami* (Mirror of a Field-Watcher), II, in *Gunsho-ruijū,* 2nd ed., XXI, 263.
92 See Master Butsujō Kokushi, *Daibai-zan Yawa* (Night Tales [i.e. Informal Sermons] in Mt. Daibai) in *Zenmon Hōgo-shū,* II, 603f.
93 *Hōnen Shōnin Gyōjo-ezu,* XXII, in *Jōdo-shū Zensho,* XVI, 20.
94 In his letter to Kingo Shijō, in *Shōwa Shinshū Nichiren Shōnin Imon-zenshū,* II, 1407.
95 In *Shugen Shimpi Gyōhō Fuju-shū* (Collection of Amulets in Esoteric Shugen Practices), VII, *Nihon Dai-zōkyō, Shugen Shōsho-bu,* II, 101. (Section of Commentary on Shugen's Works.)
96 *Nembutsu Myōgi-shū* (Collections of Nomenclatures of Invocation to Amitābha), II, in *Jōdō-shū Zensho* (Collected Works of Jōdo Sect), X, 376.
97 In his letter to Kingo Shijō, in *Shōwa Shinshū Nichiren Shōnin Imon-zenshū,* I, 866.
98 At the end of his play, *Sonezaki Shinjū,* in *Kindai Nihon Bungaku Taikei* (Great Series of Modern Japanese Literature), VI, 247f.
99 *Jakumetsu-iraku* in Japanese.
100 *Shibun-ritsu* (Books of Discipline in Four Sections), XXIII (*Taishō,* XXII, 153 a); see also *Shibun-ritsu Sampan Fuketsu Gyōji-shō Jo* (*ibid.,* XL, 2 a).
101 *Bassui Zenji Hōgo* (Buddhist Teachings of Zen Master Bassui) edited by D. T. Suzuki, 51.
102 A Bodhisattva is a future Buddha who wants to save all living beings.
103 *Shūgi-washo* (Books on Religious Doctrines), X.
104 *Kōshō Bosatsu Kyōkun Chōmon-shū* (Collection of Lectures by Kōshō Bodhisattva), in *Kokubun Tōhō Bukkyō Sōsho* (Collection of Japanese Buddhist Books), *Hōgo-bu* (Section on Sayings), 99–100.
105 Nissaggiya-pācittiya, 18–20; 23; 28; Pācittiya, 10–11. Cf. H. Nakamura, in *Nihon Rekishi* (Japanese History) (November–December 1949).
106 Hakujō Ui, *Zenshū-shi Kenkyū* (A Study on the History of the Zen Sect), 3ff. (Tokyo: Iwanami, 1939).
107 Eisai (1141–1215) was the founder of the Rinzai sect of Zen Buddhism in 1191.
108 *Taishō,* LXXX, 7 b.
109 *Ibid.,* 12 a.
110 *Sōtō Kyōkai Shushōgi,* 22. Cf. *Gleanings from Sōtō-Zen,* edited by Ernest Shikaku Hunt (Honolulu: Sōtō Mission, 1960), 27.
111 H. Nakamura, *Jihi* (Benevolence) (Kyoto: 1956), *passim.*

112 The Seventeen-Article Constitution attributed to Prince Shōtoku, X.

113 See Yaichi Haga, *Kokuminsei Jūron* (Ten Lectures on the National Character), 257.

114 The only parallel to this may be found in some ancient Indian countries to the west of the Ganges, as we are told in Fa-hsien's *Fa-kuo-chi* (Travel Records of the Buddhist Countries), and Hsüan-tsang's *Hsi-yü-chi* (Travel Records of the Western Lands), II.

115 See Masaharu Anesaki, *Kirishitan Hakugai-shi-chū no Jimbutsu-jiseki* (History of Christian Persecutions: Persons and Their Acts). 476f.

116 See Tōkan Tada, *Chibetto* (Tibet), 113ff.; Bunkyō Aoki, *Chibetto Yūki* (Travel in Tibet), 165ff.

117 In his *Ōjō-taiyō-sho* (An Outline of How to be Reborn into the Pure Land), *Shōwa Shinshū Hōnen Shōnin Zenshū* (Collected Works of Saint Hōnen), 61f.

118 *Hōnen Shōnin Gyōjō Ezu* (Illustrations of the Acts of Saint Hōnen), XXI, in *Shōwa Shinshū Hōnen Shōnin Zenshū,* XVI, 241.

119 See Ichirō Hori, *"Shinkō no Heizonsei ni tsuite"* (On the Co-existence of Different Faiths) in *Rinri,* No. 543 (October 1948).

120 See Shinshō Hanayama, *Hokke-gisho no Kenkyū* (Studies on the Commentary on the Lotus Sūtra) 664ff. This doctrine is called *The Teaching of Manzen Dōki.*

121 *Ibid.,* 117f.

122 *Ibid.,* 460.

123 In his *Jūshichi-jō no Kempō* (The Seventeen-Article Constitution).

124 In the *Kyōkijikoku-shō* (A Treatise on the Teaching, the Propensity, the Time, and the Country), *Shōwa Shinshū Nichiren Shōnin Imon-zenshū,* I, 450.

125 The *Ryōjin Hishō,* a poetical work ascribed to Emperor Go-Shirakawa (1127–1192). In *Nihon Koten-zensho* (Collection of Japanese Ancient Works), II, 71f.

126 See his *Keiranshūyō-shū,* quoted in Taijō Tamamuro, *Nihon Bukkyo-shi Gaisetsu* (Outline History of Japanese Buddhism), 221.

127 In his *Go-bunshō* 3, 10; see also *ibid.,* 2, 3; in *Kōchū Rennyo Shōnin O-fumi Zenshū,* 56ff.; cf. 24ff.

128 In the *Sekihei-kahō* (Disciplines of the Monastery at the Sekihei Mountain), quoted in Motosue Ishida, *Edo-jidai Bungaku Kōsetsu,* 14.

129 In the *Kōkiji-kitei* (The Regulations of the Kōkiji Temple), Article No. 13, quoted in Daijō Tokiwa, *Nihon Bukkyō no Kenkyū* (Studies of Japanese Buddhism), 526.

130 In the chapter on Emperor Yōmei in the *Nihonshoki* (Chronicles of Japan).

131 See Zennosuke Tsuji, *Nihon Bukkyō-shi no Kenkyū* (Studies on the History of Japanese Buddhism), 96.

132 *Ibid.,* 56.

133 In the *Ōmi Daifukuji-monjo* (Documents of the Daifuku Temple in Ōmi), quoted in Tsuji, *op.cit.,* 175.

134 See Yasusada Hiyane, *op.cit.*, 634.

135 See Kanshi Kagamishima, *Chūsei-bukkyōto no Jingikan to sono Bunka* (Concept of God among Medieval Buddhists and Their Culture), in *Shūkyō-kenkyū* (1940), 813.

136 *Shoku-nihonkōki* (Continued Chronicles of Japan), V, Asahi Shimbunsha, editor, 94.

137 In his preface to a poem in *Man'yōshū* (Collection of Myriad Leaves), V, in *Kokka Taikei* (Great Series of Japan), II, 156.

138 *Edo-bungaku-kenkyū* (Studies in the Literature of the Edo Period), 14.

139 *Fuju Fuse-ha* (Non-receiving, Non-giving School). This branch of the Nichiren sect, founded in 1595 by the bonze Nichiō, was forbidden together with the Christian religion in 1614.

140 Kitabatake Chikafusa (1293–1354), in his *Jinnōshōtōki* (A History of the Legitimate Line of the Divine Emperors), bk. 1, *Gunsho-ruijū*, XXIX, 1.

141 Quoted in Hiyane, *op.cit.*, 679f.

142 This material has been quoted from Genchi Katō, *Shintō no shūkyō-hattatushi-teki Kenkyū* (Studies on Shintoism from the Viewpoint of Historical Development), 950f., and Hiyane, *op.cit.*, 816ff.

143 From Prince Shōtoku's Seventeen-Article Constitution.

144 See his *Shōmangyō-gisho*, ch. *Ichijō;* cf. Shinshō Hanayama, *Nihon no Bukkyō* (Japanese Buddhism), 202ff.

145 *Eihei-shingi* (Rules of the Eihei Temple), *Bendō-hō, Dōgen Zenji Shingi*, edited by Dōshū Ōkubo, 43.

146 *Kyōgyōshinshō, op.cit.*, Chapter 2, *Taishō Shinshū Daizōkyō*, CXXXIII, 591 a.

147 *Honzon Mondō-shō* (Questions and Answers on the Main Buddha), *Shōwa Shinshū Nichiren Shōnin Imonzenshū, op.cit.*, II, 1721f.

148 In his *Letter to the Nun Kubo, ibid.*, II, 1768.

149 Daitō Shimaji, *Tendai Kyōgaku-shi* (History of Tendai Theology), 492.

150 *Sado-gosho* (Letters from Sado), *Shōwa Shinshū Nichiren Shōnin Imonzenshū, op.cit.*, I, 842.

151 In the *Kyōkijikoku-shō*, and the *Shōgu Mondō-shō, Shōwa Shinshū Nichiren Shōnin Imon-zenshū*, I, 447f. and 579f. In his two volume work, *Senji-shō* (Considerations on the Times), Nichiren elaborates on how other sects are not fit for his time; see *Shōwa Shinshū Nichiren Shōnin Imon-zenshū*, I, 1189–1241.

152 *Honchō-jinja-kō* (Discourses on Japanese Shrines), quoted in Masatomo Bamba, *Nihon Jukyō-shi* (History of Japanese Confucianism), 103ff.

153 In the preface to the *Honchō-jinja-kō, Razan Sensei Bunshū*, II, 118.

154 *Razan Bunshū* (Collected Essays of Razan), LVI.

155 *Okina Mondō* (Dialogues with an Elder), III, *Tōju Sensei Zenshū* (Collected Works of Master Tōju), III, 248.

156 *Ibid.*, 251.

157 In his *Miwa Monogatari* (Tales of the Miwa Shrine), VII, *Banzan Zenshū* (Collected Works of Banzan) V, 67. Elsewhere he says:

"If Chinese sages should come to Japan they would subscribe to Shintō which has been our traditional Way." (*Banzan Zenshū*, I, 12.)

158 Quoted in Hiyane, *op.cit.*, 943.

159 See Saburō Ienaga, *Chūsei Bukkyōshisō-shi Kenkyū* (Studies on the History of Medieval Buddhist Thought), 104, and Iwahashi, *op.cit.*, 301.

160 *Jindai-Kuketsu* (Oral Tradition on the Divine Age), quoted in Hiyane, *op.cit.*, 660.

161 *Kokuikō* (Discourses on the Genuine Thought of Japan), *Kamo Mabuchi Zenshū* (Collected Works of Kamo Mabuchi), X, 368.

162 *Okina no Fumi* (Letters of an Elderly Man), Chapter 6.

163 *Ibid.*, Chapter 1.

164 We do not contend that the Japanese thinkers mentioned above did not ever admit the universality of the Way. Banzan Kumazawa, for instance, said: "The Way is the Way of all gods, heaven and earth. It is universally valid throughout the whole world, China, and Japan." *Shūgi-washo* (Book of Righteousness and Harmony), Chapter 11, *Banzan Zenshū*, I, 286.

165 In colloquial Japanese, "*suru*" (to do).

166 See B. Spuler, *Die Goldene Horde* (Leipzig: 1943), and also *Die Mongolen in Iran* (Berlin: 1955).

167 At the rededication of a famous Buddhist temple in October 1958, the numerous *sake* barrels piled up as offerings in front of the temple and the booths advertising various brands of whisky certainly were in contrast to the original teaching of the Buddha.

168 Yaichi Haga, *op.cit.*, 121.

169 In the *Ryōjin Hishō* (a collection of popular songs), II, 1 c., 104.

170 *Hōjōki* (The Private Papers of Kamo no Chōmei of the *Ten-Foot-Square-Hut*), Iwanami Bunko edition, 61f.

171 In the introduction to the Iwanami Bunko edition of the *Hōjōki*, 4.

172 *Tsurezuregusa*, Chapter 10 (*Nihon Koten-Bungaku Taikei*, XXX, 97).

173 See Yaichi Haga, *op.cit.*, 126ff.

174 *Man'yōshū*, No. 3846.

175 See Otoo Fujii, *Edo Bungaku Kenkyū* (A Study of Literature in the Edo Era), 70ff.

176 *Ibid.*, 108ff.

177 *Kenshō-jōbutsu-gan-hōsho* (An Advertisement of the Pill for Becoming a Buddha), in *Zenmon-hōgo-shū* (Collection of Zen Buddhist Teachings), II, 239f.

178 *Hyakuhatchōki* (a pun on the three religions, each represented by a reason, in Japanese *ri*, which also stands for a distance of about 1/14 of a mile).

179 See Motosue Ishida, *Edojidai Bungaku Kōsetsu* (A Survey of Literature in the Edo Era), 9.

180 See Haga, *op.cit.*, *Kokuminsei Jūron* (Ten Essays on the National Character), 142ff.

181 See, for instance, H. Keyserling, *Reisetagebuch eines Philosophen* (Travel Diary of a Philosopher), 583.

Chapter 35

1 Izuru Shimmura, *Gengogaku Josetsu* (Introduction to Linguistics) (Tokyo: Kōbundō, 1923), 172.
2 *Nyojō Zenji Goroku* (Analects of Zen Master Ju-ching), I (*Taishō*, XLVIII, 121 c).
3 This can be seen in Sanskrit and German, for example.
4 In his novel, *Deutsche Liebe,* Max Müller relates the story of the pure love of a noble youth for a princess. The princess speaks to the youth as follows:

"We were close friends as children; and surely this relation between us has not changed. Then, I cannot say 'Sie' when I speak to you, as to a stranger. But it's not right for me to use the familiar word 'du,' so the only thing we can do is to talk in English. [In English] Do you understand me?"

Morimine Sagara, translator, *Ai wa Eien ni* (Love Is Everlasting), 33. This is the same problem we have in Japanese.
5 *Transactions of the Asiatic Society of Japan* (1925), 78–79.
6 A very similar phenomenon occurs in languages structurally close to Japanese, such as Mongolian and Manchurian.
7 Cf. *Makura-no-sōshi,* 21, in which the plural form *kodomo-domo* (children + plural) is used.
8 Is there not some relevance to this in the usage in Japanese dialect of *ware* ("I") in the sense of "you"? I wish specialists would instruct me on this point.
9 Dōshū Ōkubo, editor, *Dōgen Zenshi Shingi* (Rules Ordained by Master Dōgen), (*Iwanami Bunko* series), 95.
10 *Dhammapada* in Pali, No. 288.
11 *Ibid.*, No. 160
12 *Ibid.*, Nos. 236, 238, 380.
13 *Āyāraṅga,* 1. 3. 3. 4.
14 Prince Shōtoku's Seventeen-Article Constitution, 2.
15 Tetsurō Watsuji, *Sonnō Shisō To Sono Dentō* (The Idea of Reverence for the Emperor and Its Tradition), 94.
16 Fujiwara Teika, in his *Eika Taigai* (Principles of Poetic Composition), says: "There is no master of *waka* (Japanese poetry). We learn from older poems alone. Who, having steeped himself in the old style and learned words from our predecessors, will not be able to write poetry?"
17 The "pillow-word" (*makura-kotoba*) *chihayaburu* (greatly powerful) was prefixed both to *kami* (god) and *uji* (clan). This may be because the *uji-no-kami* (clan head) was originally a god. There are a good many questions concerning the *ujigami* (clan deity) which should be discussed further, but I cannot go into them here. Cf. E. O. Reischauer and J. K. Fairbank, *East Asia: The Great Tradition* (Boston: 1958), 469–471.

18 Cf. Naoichi Miyachi, *Jingishi Taikei* (Outline of the History of the Deities), 24. "There are cases where the *ujigami* is not an ancestral god, as for example, the Isonokami Shrine of the Mononobe clan. Then, too, there are *ujigami* who were ancestral gods, two important examples of which are the worship of Amenokoyane-no-mikoto by the Nakatomi clan at the Hiraoka Shrine in Kawachi province, and the worship of Futotama-no-mikoto by the Imibe clan at the Futotama Shrine in Yamato province" (*ibid.*, 25). Many points in connection with the clan system must unfortunately be omitted. Cf. Reischauer and Fairbank, *op.cit.*, 474.

19 Tetsurō Watsuji, *op.cit.*, *Sonnō Shisō To Sono Dentō* (Reverence to the Emperor and Its Tradition), 46–47.

20 *Kokuminsei Jūron, op.cit.*, 51ff. [Reischauer and Fairbank (*op.cit.*, 540, 628) insist on the subordination of the family in Japan to the clan and to the State.—Editor's note.]

21 *Man'yōshū*, XVIII.

22 *Gempei Seisuiki*, XXI (Record of the Rise and Fall of the Minamoto and Taira clans, 857–1185).

23 *Ushiuma* (Cows and Horses), *Suhajikami* (Vinegar Leaves).

24 *Sandai Jitsuroku* (Annals of the Reigns of the Three Emperors), under the 16th day of the 10th month of the second year of Jōkan (860 A.D.).

25 Kaoru Nakada, "*Waga Taiko ni Tochi no Sonraku Kyōyūsei ya Kazoku Kyōsansei ga atta ka*" ("Did Ancient Japan Have an Equal Division of Land Use and a Communal Family System?"), in the law-journal *Hōritsu Shimpō*, No. 737 (July 1947).

26 Based on a lecture delivered by Professor Takeyoshi Kawashima at the first conference of the Oriental Culture Institute (*Tōyō Bunka Kenkyū-kai*), November 8, 1947.

27 I am indebted to Professor Noboru Niida for facts on the adoption of children in recent China.

28 Masatomo Bamba, *Nihon Jukyō-ron* (A Study on Confucianism in Japan), 134, 188.

29 For example, the custom of *kaneoya* practiced in the vicinity of the city of Mishima in Shizuoka prefecture and in part of the Izu peninsula. *Kaneoya* (also known as *kanaoya*) means "the tooth-blackening parent." The name takes its origin from the fact that, at a wedding, someone was named *kaneoya* and presented the new bride with a tooth-blackening implement. (*Takeyoshi Kawashima*, Toshitaka Shiomi, "Kaneoya ni tsuite," in *Minzokugaku Kenkyū*, XII, No. 1, 33ff.)

30 One also finds such sentiments as "although the Perfect One desires to enter Nirvāṇa, a father cannot bear to cast his son into the flames and turn his back on him." Shinshō Hanayama, *Hokke Gisho no Kenkyū* (Studies on the Commentary on the Lotus Sūtra), 480.

31 *Kyōdaishō* (Treatise on Proper Brotherly Attitudes).

32 *Hyōeshi-dono Gohenji* (Reply to Mr. Hyōeshi).

33 "One forgets his own body and soul, placing himself in the home of Buddha; one relies on Buddha and follows him. Then, one uses no bodily

strength, nor exercises power of mind, but separates from birth and death, and becomes a Buddha."—*Shōbō Genzō* (Essence of Buddhism) by Dōgen.

34 "With the Christian persecution of the Tokugawa period, the household Buddhist shrine spread throughout the country. Ikkō (Jōdo Shin sect) believers call it the *naibutsu* (interior Buddha), which they worship in a thoroughgoing manner. At the morning and the evening services, the religious sentiments of the children are nurtured, and their character trained. In the Ikkō sect in particular the image of Buddha or the Holy Name is central and the ceremonies honoring ancestral spirits are *an accretion due to the racial characteristics of the faith of Japan.*" Quoted from Daijō Tokiwa, *Shina Bukkyō no Kenkyū* (A Study of Chinese Buddhism) (Tokyo: 1943), III, 80.

35 "Home Buddhist chapels (*butsudan*) are peculiar to Japan, and are generally not found in China or Korea. They are an expression of the ancestor-worship of the Japanese race. . . . I have not investigated every part of China, but, from my own casual observation, I never saw a home chapel centered about the Buddha. From late reports we learn that there are Buddhist altars in the gardens of middle- and upper-class homes in Shansi and Meng-chiang. Whether these have the same significance as the Japanese *butsudan* is yet to be investigated. I believe that the home Buddhist chapel centering about the Buddha may be a peculiarly Japanese phenomenon." Daijō Tokiwa, *Nihon Bukkyō no Kenkyū* (A Study of Japanese Buddhism), 61–62. "Since there is nothing corresponding to them in Korea, it is probably safe to assert that they are absent from the Korean tradition. [In China] in the homes of the gentry there are, of course, rooms in which the ancestors are worshiped, the question being whether such places are centered about the statue of the Buddha. Wherever you go, for instance, in niches at entrances, there are Taoist images, and there are also statues of Kuan-yin at appropriate spots in the house; but are they not quite apart from the worship of ancestral spirits?" (*Ibid.*, 80–81). The Chinese "*butsudan*" is a home altar, above which hangs a large colored triptych of the Buddha, the Law, and the Priesthood; on a table in front are offered cakes, fruit, and vegetables, but meat and fish are strictly prohibited. Here altars are adorned with a *dōban* (a part of banner used in Buddhist ceremonies). Cf. de Groot, *Religious Systems of China* (Leyden: 1892), 6 vols. (*Chūgoku Shūkyo Seido*, translated by Kinzaburō Shimizu and Hakudō Oginome), I, 123. "In Tibet, even the poorest households have *butsudan,* which are the center of the religious ceremonies of the family. *Butsudan* are placed in guest rooms." (Tōkan Tada, *Chibetto* [Tibet] in Iwanami Shinsho, 59). However, in Tibet, too, they appear to have no special connection with ancestor-worship.

36 *Tannishō*. English versions: *The Tannisho (Tract on Deploring the Heterodoxies)*: An Important Textbook of Shin Buddhism founded by Shinran (1173–1262), translated by Tosui Imadate (Kyoto: Eastern

Buddhist Society, 1928); *Tannisho: A Tract Deploring Heresies of Faith* (Kyoto: Higashi Honganji, 1961), in commemoration of the 700th anniversary of Shinran's death (1262).

37 Cf. Taijō Tamamuro, *Nihon Bukkyō-shi Gaisetsu* (Outline of the History of Japanese Buddhism), 194.

38 Yoshiharu Scott Matsumoto, "*Contemporary Japan: The Individual and the Group*," *Transactions of the American Philosophical Society*. New Series, L, Part 1 (January 1960).

39 *Ibid.*, 38.

40 *Ibid.*, 60.

41 E. O. Reischauer, *The United States and Japan* (Cambridge: Harvard University Press, 1950), 86.

41a Cf. H. Nakamura, "Basic Features of the Legal, Political, and Economic Thought of Japan" in Charles A. Moore, editor, *Philosophy and Culture* (Honolulu: University of Hawaii Press, 1962), 631–646.

42 The first article of the Injunctions reads as follows: "Harmony is precious; obedience is to be most honored. Men all have their particular interests, and there are few enlightened ones among them. Consequently they may disobey their lords and parents, and quarrel with the neighboring villages. But when those above are harmonious and those below are well disposed, and there is accord in their discussions, then matters progress spontaneously. If this is the case, what is there which will not succeed?"

43 Masatomo Bamba, *op.cit.*, 83.

44 *Ibid.*, 226–227.

45 Under the first day, *hinoe tora* of the 2nd month, spring, 2nd year of the reign of the Empress Suiko (594 A.D.).

46 "In the *Kaimokushō* it is said: 'Those of all sentient beings who must be respected are three, namely, master, teacher, and parent.' I say, these three occur in Confucianism, both orthodox and heterodox. The purpose of this book *Kaimokushō* is to reveal the master-parent-teacher doctrine in Buddhism. Although the teaching of master-parent-teacher indeed does appear among Confucians and pagans, yet, when the Buddhist doctrine of master-parent-teacher is revealed, all these become as retainers, pupils, and children. Therefore it is proper that the highest expression of the master-parent-teacher doctrine be found among Buddhists. It may be asked, what is the nature of this Buddhist doctrine of master-parent-teacher that you talk about: I answer, that is a further question, which I propose to deal with in due course." Nitchō, *Kaimokushō Shikemmon* (Private Comments on the Awakening to the Truth) No. 1, in *Nichirenshū Shūgaku Zensho* (Complete Works on the Religious Studies of the Nichiren Sect), *Chōshi Gosho Kemmonshū* (Comments on Nichiren's Works by Rev. Chō) No. 1, p. 191. There is also a work by Nichiren called *Shushishin Gosho* (Writings on Master-Teacher-Parent). On the question of the master-teacher-parent doctrine in the Nichiren sect, see, for example, Chiō Yamakawa, *Hokke Shisōshijō no Nichiren Shōnin* (Saint Nichiren in the History of *Hokke* Thought), 643ff.

47 He further says: "In my opinion, there are three authorities for the Japanese from the Emperor down to the masses of the people. These are first, parents; second, teachers; third, service of the lord." *Shimoyama Goshōsoku* (A Reply to the Constable of Shimoyama).

48 In the *jūdaijushō* (Chapter of the Ten Vows) of the Shōman Sūtra, there is this text: "From this day until enlightenment, in the various situations where veneration and respects are due, do not be arrogant." The *Shōman-gyō Hōkutsu* comments, "Parents and teachers are to be venerated, elder brothers and sisters are to be respected." (*Taishō,* XXXVII, 22 a.) However, Prince Shōtoku in his commentary *Shōman-gyō Gisho* (I, 14 b) says, "three categories are to be venerated, those of the rank of elder brother are to be respected." In other words, whereas the *Shōman-gyō Hōkutsu* lists only "parents and teachers" among those to be venerated, Prince Shōtoku mentions three, adding "sovereign" to the traditional two. (Shinshō Hanayama, *Shōman-gyō Gisho no Kenkyū,* 431.)

Myōkū comments " 'Three categories are to be venerated' means sovereign, parent and teacher. . . ." (*Nihon Bukkyō Zensho* edition, Complete Works on Japanese Buddhism, 11 b.)

Gyōnen, citing the text of Myōku, says, "The sovereign and the other two categories are all to be venerated; all those of the rank of elder brother are to be respected" (*Shōgenki* VI, in *Nihon Bukkyō Zensho* edition, 6 b). (Shinshō Hanayama, *op.cit.,* 468, note 217.)

49 *Hōonjō* (A Treatise on Reciprocation).

50 *Hagakurekikigaki* (Comments on the Way of the *Samurai*) No. 2 (*Iwanami Bunko* edition, 114).

51 Tetsubun Miyazaka, *Zen ni okeru Ningen Keisei* (Formation of Man in Zen), 210, 221.

52 Hakuon Saigusa, *Miura Baien no Tetsugaku* (Miura Baien's Philosophy), 530. See also 301, 517.

53 Masaharu Anesaki, *Kirishitan Hakugaishichū no Jimbutsu Jiseki* (Acts of Persons in the History of the Persecution of Christianity), 479. Also *Kirishitan Dendō no Kōhai* (Rise and Fall of Christian Missions), 789ff.

54 Anesaki, *Kirishitan Dendō no Kōhai,* 778.

55 *Ibid.,* 782ff. However, not all apostates from Christianity took their stand on the basis of the morality of rank. For example, the *Hakirishitan* of Suzuki Shōsan does not bring up morality of rank but criticizes Christianity in a rational manner. However, such an attitude is quite exceptional in the Tokugawa period. See also *Seiyō Kibun* (Records of the West), III.

56 Kemmyō Nakazawa, *Shijō no Shinran* (Shinran as a Historical Person). This work of pure scholarship has been refuted by Bunshō Yamada in his *Shinshūshikō* (Historical Studies on the Shin Sect), but the fact remains that there are no materials which constitute positive proof that Shiran was the son of Arinori Hino.

57 *Sado Gokanki Shō* (Sojourn in Sado).

58 *Honzon Mondō Shō* (Questions and Answers on the Principal Buddha).

59 Similar assertions are found elsewhere in the works of Nichiren. "Nichiren, in this incarnation, was born a poor and lowly man; he came forth from a family of Caṇḍāla" (*Sado Gosho*). "He who is 'born of a poor and lowly family' (prophesied in the Hatsunaion Sūtra) is I." *Kaimokushō* (Awakening to the Truth), II.

60 *Kokubun Tōhō Bukkyō Sōsho* (Series of Buddhist Works in Japanese); *Denkibu* (Section on Biography), Part 1, 432.

61 Zennosuke Tsuji, *Nihon Bunka to Bukkyō* (Japanese Culture and Buddhism), 56; Shōson Miyamoto, *Chūdo Shisō oyobi sono Hattatsu* (The Thought of the Middle Path and Its Development). Cf. Tsunoda, Keene, De Bary, editors. *Sources of Japanese Tradition,* 273f.

62 "Now, Great Nippon is the land of the gods. The gods come out from Paradise and assume the form of local manifestations of the Buddha. Naturally this should be the land where the Law of Buddha is most widespread." (Sakahoko.)

63 *Gessui Gosho* (Epistle of Nichiren).

64 *Hōjō Tokimune ni Atōru Sho* (Message Addressed to the Regent Tokimune).

65 *Kanke Bunsō,* III (*Kitano Bunsō,* II, 24 in *Kita-no-shi*) (Collected Writings of Michizane Sugawara [845–903], in Records of Kitano Shrine).

66 Sazan Kan (Reminiscences in Late Years) (1748–1827), *Fuyu no Hikage,* I, in *Nihon Jurin Sōsho, Kaisetsu-bu* (Japanese Series of Confucian Writings), II, 9–10.

67 *Kōmō Tōki,* Synopses of Lectures on Mencius, I, in *Yoshida Shōin Zenshū* (Collected Works of Yoshida Shoin), II, 263.

68 This account is based principally on the *Jōagon-kyō* (Sūtra of Long Discourses), XXII. (*Seki-kyō, Honnen-bon,* XII.) But similar notices are scattered through various scriptural texts. *Jōagon-kyō,* VI. *Shōen-kyō* (*Taishō,* I, 37–38); Pāli *Digha-Nikāya,* III, 91–94; *Dairutan-kyō,* VI (*Taishō,* I, 308); *Kise-kyō,* X (*Taishō,* I, 362–363); *Kise Inpon-kyō,* X (*Taishō,* I, 417); *Butsuhongyōju-kyō* (Biography of the Buddha), IV (*Taishō,* III, 672 c); *Shibunritsu,* XXXI (*Taishō,* XXII, 779); *Shōsho-chiron* (Explanations of Things to be Known) (*Taishō,* XXXII, 231 a); *Shukomakadai-kyō* (Sūtra of the Elected King) (*Taishō,* III, 933). Cf. *Sources of Indian Tradition,* edited by Wm. Theodore de Bary (New York: Columbia University Press, 1959), 131f.

69 *Kusha-ron,* XII, 14 a (Chinese Buddhist Exegesis of *Dharma*). Cf. Sir Charles Eliot, *Hinduism and Buddhism* in 3 volumes, and *Japanese Buddhism* (London: 1935).

70 Cf. the *Mahā-parinibbāna suttanta* (*Mahā-parinirvāṇa-sūtra*) and the various Chinese scriptures corresponding to it.

71 *Jinno Shōtō-ki* (On the Legitimate Succession of the Emperor), I; cf. Tsunoda, Keene, De Bary, *Sources of Japanese Tradition,* 279.

72 *Shutsujō-shōgo* (Critical Aspersions on Buddhism), by Atsutane Hirata.

73 Cf. *Konkōmyō Saishō-ō-kyō,* I (*Taishō,* XVI, 406 a); VI (*Taishō,* XVI, 432 b). Cf. also *Konkōmyō-kyō,* II (*Taishō,* XVI, 344 b, c). The corre-

spondence between the *Nihon shoki* and these sūtras was pointed out by Kenko Fujii, "*Kimmei-ki no Bukkyō Denrai no Kiji ni tsuite*" (On a Passage on the Advent of Buddhism in the Reign of Emperor Kimmei) in *Shigaku Zasshi* (Journal of Historical Science), XXXVI, 653–656. In passing, it should be noted that the passage of the *Kimmei-ki* (6th year, 9th month) which relates that Paikche built a 16-foot statue of the Buddha and presented it to the Emperor is a reproduction of the text of the *Kudara Hongi* (Hiroshi Ikeuchi, *Nihon Jōdaishi no Ichi Kenkyū* [A Study on the History Ancient Japan], 325).

74 Sten Konow, *Kharoṣṭhī Inscriptions* (Calcutta: 1929).

75 Tamamuro, *op.cit.*, 4.

76 *Shoku Nihongi* (Chronicles of Japan, Continued), 17.

77 Tamamuro, *op.cit.*, 17.

78 *Nihon Daizō-kyō, Hōdōbushōsho*, III, 2–4. (Japanese Tripiṭaka Collection of Buddhist *Vaipulya* Writings.)

79 *Kairitsu Denraiki* (A.D. 830), in *Dai Nihon Bukkyō Zensho*, 105. (Introduction of Vinaya, 830 A.D., in "Collected Works of Japanese Buddhism.")

80 The Eight Rules among the *Sange Gakushō Shiki* (Rules for Students *of Mt. Hiei*). Further, in the *Kenkairon Engi* we find the phrase "exalt Buddhism and protect the state," and in the *Rokusho Hōtō Gammon*, "establish and hold firmly to Buddhism and safeguard the state."

81 *Shoku Nihon-kōki*, IV, 2nd year of *Shōwa* (A.D. 835), 1st month, letter of Kūkai to the Emperor.

82 *Sandai Jitsuroku* (Records of Reigns of the Three Emperors), XLI, Reign of Emperor Yozei, 6th year of *Genkei* (A.D. 882), 5th month, 14th day.

83 *Shoku Nihon-kōki*, XII, 9th year of Shōwa (A.D. 842), 12th month, 17th day.

84 *Sandai Jitsuroku*, VII, Reign of Emperor Seiwa, 5th year of *Jōkan* (A.D. 863), 9th month, 6th day.

85 *Sandai Jitsuroku*, VII, Reign of Emperor Seiwa, 8th year of *Jōkan* (A.D. 866), 6th month, 21st day.

86 *Sandai Jitsuroku*, XI, Reign of Emperor Seiwa, 7th year of *Jōkan* (A.D. 865), 7th month, 19th day.

87 *Sandai Jitsuroku*, XII, Reign of Emperor Seiwa, 8th year of *Jōkan* (A.D. 866), 5th month, 29th day. Further, the following passage occurs in a letter addressed to the Emperor by Bishop Henjō; "When the sun of Buddhism is again at its height, the Imperial dignity will be safeguarded, the virtue of the Imperial House long endure, and the State will be peaceful and safe." *Sandai Jitsuroku*, XLVII, 1st year of Ninna (A.D. 885), 3rd month.

88 The pagoda of Eisai in the Kennin Temple, Higashiyama, Kyoto, is called *Kōzen gokoku-in* ("Exalt Zen, protect the nation").

89 Kyodō Itō, *Dōgen Zenji Kenkyū* (Study on the Zen Master Dōgen), I, 303.

90 *Kangyō Hachiman Shō* (Nichiren's Remonstrances Against the State's Attitude to Religion).

91 *Risshō Ankoku Ron.* However, the first of these quotes appears as the words of a guest addressed to the host. For an English translation of parts of this first great work of Nichiren, cf. Arthur Lloyd, *The Creed of Half Japan.*

92 *Ongikuden* (Rendition of the Esoteric Oral Doctrine), at the end.

93 *Ofumi* (Epistles), 2:10; cf. also 2:6, 3:10, 3:13, 4:1 and *Jōgai Ofumi* (Yūshō Tokushi, *Rennyo Shōnin Ofumi Zenshū* 48, 72). Rennyo's Complete Epistles.

94 *Rennyo Shōnin Goichidaiki Kikigaki* (Notes on Rennyo's Life), at the end.

95 This has been pointed out by Yukifusa Hattori. (*Kokudo,* I, 91.) *Shinran nōto* (Notes on Shinran), XXXII, 211.

96 *Hokke-kyō* (Lotus Sūtra), Anrakugyō section. A similar view is expressed in the *Shōbōnenjo-kyō,* L (*Taishō,* 294 c–295 a).

97 Based on Kazuo Higo, *Nihon Kokka Shisō* (The Concept of the Japanese Nation), 78–79.

98 Taiheiki (historical novel based on the "Great Peace"—really on the Civil Wars), XXI.

99 The Eighty Volume Kegon, XXVIII. (*Taishō,* X, 152 a-c; LIX, 312 a.)

100 Based on Yasusada Hiyane, *Nihon Shūkyō-shi* (The History of Japanese Religions), 648. Moreover, Takeshige, son of Kikuchi Taketoki, is said to have had the same concept (*ibid.,* 648–649).

101 But Jiun did not necessarily attempt to have Buddhists accept intact all the social ranks of Japanese society. Thus, in the same *Kōkiji kitei* (Kōki Temple Rules), he warns that "the adopted sons of the nobility should not seek public office." Cf. Daijō Tokiwa, *Nihon Bukkyō no Kenkyū* (History of Japanese Buddhism), 526ff.

102 When Chinese political thought was brought to ancient Japan, the Japanese ruling class, in order to govern the land, established the Taihō code in imitation of the T'ang system. This code, however, differed from the T'ang Model, in that it embodied considerations of social policy. In China, land was distributed to each family in proportion to the labor capacity of each. In accordance with the Taihō code, however, equal shares of land were allotted to boys of no labor capacity and even to girls. The huge income of the national treasury was spent for the welfare of the people and their cultural institutions. Cf. Tetsurō Watsuji, "Asuka Nara Jidai no Seijiteki Risō" (Political Ideals of the Asuka and Nara Periods), in his *Nihon Seishinshi Kenkyū* (Intellectual History of Japan).

103 *Dengyō Daishi Zenshū* (Collected Works of Dengyō), IV, 719.

104 *Tōshūyō,* in *Hōnen Shōnin Zenshū* (Collected Works of Saint Hōnen), edited by S. Mochizuki, 528.

105 *Tannishō* (Tracts Deploring Heterodoxies).

106 *Ibid.*

107 *Shōshinge* ("Hymn of True Faith"). Cf. *The Shoshin Ge: The Gāthā*

of *True Faith in the Nembutsu,* translated under the direction of Daien Fugen (Kyoto: 1961).

108 By the term *shinshū* Shinran meant the tradition of Pure Land Buddhism from Indian masters up to Hōnen, recorded in the *Kōsōwasan* (Hymns Extolling the High Priests) and the *Jōdo-monruiju-shō* (Anthology of Scriptural Passages Relevant to Pure Land).

109 The "Easy Way" stands in contrast to the "Difficult Way" and means the teaching of Pure Land Buddhism (or especially the *Shin-shu* teaching, in this context), which was thought by its followers to be the easiest and shortest road to salvation. Another's strength (or External Power) refers to the Original Vow of Amida (*Amitābha*) Buddha, relying on which we are sure of our final salvation and enlightenment.

110 In the beginning of the *Tannishō.*

111 Chiō Yamakawa, *Hokke-shisō-shi-jō no Nichiren Shōnin* (Saint Nichiren in the History of the Lotus Philosophy), 551.

112 Viśiṣṭacārita Bodhisattva, to whom Śākyamuni entrusted the propagation of the Lotus Sūtra in the future world.

113 In a letter of the year 1278.

114 According to T'ien-t'ai, all living beings, including holy persons, are divided into ten groups, each of them having its own sphere.

115 *Fa-hua-hsüan-i* (the Profound Teachings of the Lotus Sūtra), VII (*Taishō,* XXXIII, 771).

116 *Fa-hua-i-shu* (Commentary on the Lotus Sūtra), X (*Taishō,* XXXIV, 599).

117 *Jushiki-kanjō-kuden-shō* (Oral Teachings on a Consecration).

118 Nichiren's Letter to Ōta Kingo, *San-dai-hihō-rinshō no Koto* (On Inheriting the Three Great Esoteric Practices).

119 *Shōbō Genzō Zuimonki* (Gleanings of Master Dōgen's Sayings), II, edited by T. Watsuji (Tokyo: Iwanami), 34.

120 *Ibid.,* I, 20.

121 *Ibid.,* I, 12.

122 *Shōbō Genzō* (Subtleties of the Doctrine), chapter on Bendōwa, the sixth disputation.

123 *Shōbō Genzō Zuimonki,* VI, 104.

124 *Ju-ching-ho-shang-yü-lu* (Collected Works of Master Ju-ching), (*Taishō,* XLVIII, 130–131).

125 *Ju-ching-ch'an-shih-hsü-yü-lu* (Collected Works of Master Ju-ching, Continued) (*Taishō,* XLVIII, 135 a.).

126 Daijō Tokiwa, *Shina-bukkyō no Kenkyū* (A Study of Chinese Buddhism), III, 82.

127 At the end of the *Gaijashō* (Correction of Heresy).

128 *Jōdō-hōmon-genryū-shō* (Transmission of Pure Land Teaching), in *Jōdo-shū Zensho* (Complete Works of the Jōdo Sect), 15, 594.

129 Shinran, *Shūjishō* (On Desires).

130 E.g., *Mo-ho-chih-kuan* (A Tendai Work on Great Meditation), (Taishō, XLVI, 33.)

131 Daitō Shimaji, *Tendai-kyōgaku-shi* (A History of Tendai Philosophy), 468.

132 According to D. Shimaji, Shinran wrote the *Kyō-gyō-shin-shō* in the province of Hitachi under the influence of Buddhism in the Kantō District which had established the special tradition of the doctrine, practice, and illumination. Shinran added faith to the above-mentioned three.

133 *Nikka-Bukkyō-Kenkyūkai-Nempō* (Annual Publication of the Japanese-Chinese Association of Buddhist Studies), the first year, 9.

134 This sentence is also cited in the *Kyōgyōshinshō,* III, 1.

135 *Shōbō Genzō,* chapter on Sanjūshichi-hon Bodaibunpō (The 37 Constituents of Wisdom).

136 *Ibid.*, chapter on Bendōwa (Practice of the Way).

137 *Ibid.*, chapter on Shōji (Life and Death).

138 *Tun-yü-yao-mēn* (Essentials of Immediate Enlightenment), edited by H. Ui, (Tokyo: Iwanami), 61.

139 *Shōbō Genzō,* chapter on Keisei-sanshoku (Natural Scenery). This passage is often recited as the *Vow of Jōyō Daishi* (*Dōgen*).

140 *Ching-tê-chuan-têng-lu* (Transmission of the Lamps of Religion), XIV.

141 *Shōbō Genzō Zuimonki,* III.

142 *Roankyō* (literally, Ass-saddle Bridge), II, § 70.

143 *Fumoto no Kusawake* (Climbing at the Foot of a Mountain), in *Zen-mon-hōgo-shū* (Collected Works of Zen Masters), II, 545.

144 *Shishin-gohon-shō* (A Treatise on Four Faiths and Five Stages of Practitioners).

145 *Niike-gosho* (Reply to Esquire Niike).

146 *Himegoze Gohenji* (Reply to Lady Hime).

147 Daito Shimaji, *Nihon-bukkyō Kyōgaku-shi* (History of Japanese Buddhist Theology), 6.

148 *Soshitsujikyō-sho* (Commentary on the Susiddhikara Sūtra), in *Dainihon Bukkyō Zensho* (Complete Works of Japanese Buddhism), XLIII, 268.

149 *Kyakuhaibōki* (Notes in Oblivion) in Taizō Ebara (1894–1948), *Myōe Shōnin* (Saint Myōe), 25.

150 *Mujintō* (Infinite Light), (1918), 7f.

151 *Rokujō Gakuhō* (Bulletin of the Rokujō), (1917), 166.

152 The Chinese version of the *Mahāparinirvāṇa-sūtra,* XXXVI. (*Taishō,* XII, 575 c.)

153 Shōson Miyamoto, *Chūdo Shisō oyobi sono Hattatsu* (The Concept of the Middle Path and its Development), 68.

154 "When a man is satisfied only believing the words of the Buddha and neglecting his own efforts to seek after truth, his faith is superficial and of no avail for him." *Zengenshosenshūtojo* (ch'an-yüan-chu-chüan-chi-tu-hsü), edited by Hakuju Ui, 35.

155 Chiō Yamakawa, *op.cit.,* 355.

156 *Ibid.,* 652.

157 *Kōzen Gokoku Ron,* Preface.

158 *Shōbō Genzō,* chapter on Kenbutsu (Seeing the Buddha).

159 *Ibid.*, chapter on Bukkyō (Buddhism).
160 *Ibid.*, chapter on Bukkyō (Buddhist Sūtras).
161 *Shōbō Genzō Zuimonki,* IV.
162 See *supra,* Chapter 16.
163 In the *Hōkyōki* (Hōkyo Memoirs) the words of Dōgen's master Ju-ching are said to be as follows: "Besides Kāśyapa Mātaṅga, our master Bodhidharma came from the west to China to initiate us in the doctrines and the practices of Buddhism. This is the reason for the words '*kyō-ge-betsu-den.*' There cannot be two different teachings of the Buddha. Before our master came to this country of the East, there had been only the practice and no proper teacher to control it. The advent of our master to this country is comparable to the coronation of a king in a certain country. All the land, all the treasures and all the people are under the command of the king." This may not be, however, a faithful rendition of the words of Ju-ching. In the record of his sayings, there is no sentence expressing such an idea. On the contrary, we can find in it words like "to practice true Zen, one does not think about the masters." And we should be reminded of the fact that he criticized severely the proposition of the founding master Bodhidharma: "Nothing can be called holy" saying "He [Bodhidharma] created it only to violate it himself." It is very probable, therefore, that the above quotation, the authority of which Dōgen attributed to his master, are the words of Dōgen himself. Even if it is a faithful quotation of the words of his master Ju-ching, it is very significant (exhibiting the Japanese inclination to worship authority) that Dōgen selected this paragraph among many other sayings of his master and attached particular importance to it.
164 *Shōbō Genzō,* chapter on Shizenbiku (A Monk Practicing the Four Meditations).
165 *Hō-on Jo* (On Gratitude).
166 *Myōichime Gohenji* (Reply to a Woman Myōichi).
167 Sokichi Tsuda, *Shina Shisō to Nihon* (Chinese Philosophies and Japan), 43–66.
168 *Benmei* (Discussions on Names), I, the section on *Zenryō sansoku* (Three articles in goodness).
169 Tetsurō Watsuji, *Sonnō Shisō to sono Dentō* (Reverence for the Emperor and its Tradition), 230.
170 *Uiyamabumi* (First Climbing of a Mountain), in *Motoori Norinaga Zenshū* (Collected Works of Norinaga Motoori), edited by Hōei Motoori, IV, 607.
171 It is wrong to assume that none of the Japanese in the past took a critical attitude to established authority. I treated this subject in my recent work *Kinsei Nihon ni okeru Hihanteki Seishin no Ichikōsatsu* (A Study of the Critical Spirit in Modern Japan—Various Problems of Japanese Thought, 1949). Here, at least, we can say that the Japanese in the past were wanting in the spirit of criticism.
172 In the article of the *Goseibai Shikimoku* (Penal Law), customary law

which had been established prior to Yoritomo is frequently referred to as "established at the time of the great Shōgun (i.e. Yoritomo)"; this would seem to be an example of the same situation. Seijirō Takigawa, "*Nihon Hōritsu Shisō no Tokushitsu*" (Special Characteristics of Japanese Legal Thought), (*Iwanami Kōza, Tōyō Shichō*), 48–49. Cf. also Tsunoda, Keene, and De Bary, *Sources of Japanese Tradition*, 340–343.

173 *Kokuminsei Jūron* ("Ten Essays on the National Character"), 31–32.

174 *Ibid.*, 34.

175 "*Rājā rājyam*" (Kauṭilya, *Arthaśāstra*, edited by R. Shama Sastry, 2nd edition, 325).

176 *Ibid.*, 33–34.

177 *Kojiki*, Chapter 1.

178 *Ibid.*, 21.

179 Tetsurō Watsuji, *Sonnō Shisō to sono Dentō* (Emperor Worship and Its Tradition), 59ff. For comparable ideas in India, cf. my book, *Shūkyō to Shakai Rinri* (Religious and Social Ethics), (Tokyo: 1959), 286–326.

180 *Ibid.*, 49–51.

181 *Ibid.*, 67.

182 Cf. *Nakatomi-barai* (a kind of spell).

183 Emperor Shōmu, Edict on the construction of the Great Buddha, 10th month, 743.

184 However, in the very understanding of the content of the term "revolution" (*kakumei, ko-ming,*) there appears to have been a change in the course of time. For example, in the *Kakumei Kammon* (Considerations on Revolution) of Kiyoyuki Miyoshi (*Gunsho ruijū, zatsu*, Collection of Various Works and Miscellanies), the sense of *Kakumei* appears to be understood merely as "great change."

185 See various *Zuihitsu* (Essays) by Japanese writers (refer to the *Nihon Zuihitsu Sakuin* (Index to Japanese Essays) and the *Un tsa tsu* by a Ming author, etc.). Moku Kondō, *Shina Gakugei-daijiten* (Dictionary of Chinese Sciences and Arts).

186 *Kanke Ikai* (Family Administrations of Michizane Sugawara). But, as this passage does not occur in old manuscripts of this work, it would seem to be later interpolation. (Cf. *Kitano Bunsō*, VIII, 138, in *Kitano shi*, edited by the curator of the Kitano shrine.)

187 *Kōdōkan ki Jutsugi* (Commentary on the Chronicle of the Kōdōkan [school of Mito]). Contrary to general supposition, there were Confucianists who recognized and advocated the doctrines of "change of surname" (viz. dynasty) and "overturning of the mandate"; one, for example, was Totsuan Ōhashi; Shigeki Tōyama, *Ōsei Fukko no Imi* (Significance of the Restoration of Imperial Government), *Shisō*, V (1947), 33. However, he was exceptional.

188 Yukinari Iwahashi, *Sorai Kenkyū*, (Studies on Sorai), 444ff.

189 *Miwa Monogatari* (Tales at the Miwa Shrine), Part 1 (*Banzan Zenshū* [Collected Works of Banzan], V, 218 and 222).

190 Tetsurō Watsuji, *op.cit.*, 235–236.

191 Tō Yamada suggested that the oldest example is from the *Lü-shih-ch'un-chiu* (A Compendium of Various Schools of Philosophy, written under the direction of Lu in the 3rd century B.C.).

192 *Kōmōsakki* (Notes on Confucius and Mencius), IV; *Yoshida Shōin* Zenshū (Collected Works of Shōin Yoshida), II, 462.

193 *Kojiki,* Preface.

194 In Volume LXI of *Shōbō Neṅjo Kyō* (Sūtra of Meditation on the True Teaching), there is a discussion of the four benevolences of one's mother, one's father, the *Tathagāta* (Buddha), and teachers of the *dharma,* but the benevolence of the ruler is not mentioned.

195 *Sandai Jitsuroku* (Records of the Reigns of the Three Emperors), VI. Moreover, in the text under the date 865, 7th month, 19th day, there is the phrase, "the world of the four benevolences is the whole of mankind." (*Ibid.*, XI.)

196 *Gempei Seisuiki* (Records of the Rise and Fall of the Minamoto and Taira Clans), VI. Cf. also Volume II of *Heike Monogatari.*

196a *Takuan Zenshū* (Collected Works of Takuan), Vol. 5: *Tōkaiyawa* (Records of Takuan's Buddhist Teachings), last part.

197 Shinran said (*Kyōgyōshinshō,* Part 2) that "the doctrine of devotion is the imperial order of the call in the original vow;" again (*ibid.*, Part 3), he says the expression "a desire for birth" (in the *Daimuryōju kyō*), i.e., the desire for rebirth in the Pure Land, means "the Imperial Order of the *Tathāgata* calling all sentient beings." Probably his use of the expression "Imperial edict" enabled the Japanese to understand better.

198 Cf. *Kaimokushō* (The Awakening to the Truth), (Tokyo: 1941), Part II.

199 However, Nichiren did not regard the Emperor as absolutely divine because of his secular rank. In his view, religious authority stood above the authority of the Emperor. Even the Emperor, if he transgressed the law, would go to Hell. "Because of the bad *karma* of having despised the Buddha Śākyamuni and having neglected the Lotus Sūtra . . . the retired Emperor of Oki in the 82nd generation and also the retired Emperor of Sado . . . ended their lives in these islands, being dethroned by force. Because their spirits were wicked, they went down to Hell." (Reply to Sister Myōhō.)

200 *Hōonshō* (Treatise on Reciprocation of Benevolence).

201 *Sōryū Daiwajō Suiji* (Instructions by Great Master Sōryū), Part 2. *Jiunsonja Zenshū* (Collected Works of Master Jiun), XIII, 655.

202 *Shobō Shūyō-kyo* (Sūtra of Essentials of Doctrines). (*Taishō,* XVII, 516 a.)

203 *Shōbō Nenjo-kyō,* LV. (*Taishō,* XVII, 324 a.)

204 *Daijō Honshō Shinji kan-gyō,* II. (*Taisho,* III, 298 a.)

205 *Zatsuhōzōkyō* (Sūtra of Miscellaneous Treasure Stores), VIII. (*Taishō,* IV, 485 b-c.)

206 T'ang translation of the *Kegon* (*Avataṁsaka*) sūtra, LXVI (*Taishō,* X, 355 b); Volume XI of the 40-Volume *Kegon* has the following passage: "He commanded that all should desist from the Ten Evil Ways, and per-

fect themselves—the practice of the Ten Goods, just as did King Cakravarti." (*Taishō*, X, 712 c.)

207 Also, "His birth falling on a sacred day, he was molded by the influence of the Ten Virtues"—*Sandai Jitsuroku,* VI, paragraph under the date 862, 10th month of the reign of Emperor Seiwa.

208 Many former Japanese classical scholars explained such conceptions as "the Emperor of the Ten Virtues" as being applied to the Emperor on the basis of the Buddhist conception that a man who has kept the commandments of the Ten Virtues in a past life is reborn in present life as ruler of the land. Probably, Japanese classical scholars have interpreted the matter in the following way. Tokunō Oda, *Bukkyō Daijiten* (Great Dictionary of Buddhism), 922 a; *Kokubungaku Jūnishu Butsugo Kaishaku* [Explanation of Buddhist Terms in 12 books of Japanese Literature], 85). But literal expressions of this thesis are not to be found in Buddhist texts. Indeed, it is very often maintained in Buddhist texts that if a man does good he will be reborn in Heaven; and also there appears, although rarely, the thesis that one is born as ruler in this life because of merit accumulated in a past life. The Reverend Oda cites only the following examples, one quoted from the *Judaikakyō* (Sūtra of the Bodhi Tree) in Volume LII of *Hōen Shūrin* (Woods of Jewels in the Religious Garden): "How can one be reborn in Heaven? By practicing the Ten Virtues one is reborn in Heaven. How can one assume the human state? By observing the Five Injunctions one assumes the human state"; and another, quoted from *Make-bikuni-kyō* (Sūtra of a Demon Edifying a Nun) in Part 1 of *Benshōron* (Inquiry on Righteousness): "The Five Injunctions are the root of the human; the Ten Virtues are the root of the Heaven." In these it is not stated that through a cultivation of the Ten Virtues one is born an emperor. The foregoing interpretation resulted in the Japanese concept of the Emperor which identifies the notion of *tennō* (Ruler of Heaven) with that of *tenshi* (Son of Heaven) and was influenced by the Chinese idea of T'ien-Tzŭ (Son of Heaven).

209 Cf. Shinran's *Kōtaishi Shōtoku Hōsan* (A Eulogy of the Imperial Prince Shōtoku).

210 Y. Haga, *op.cit.,* 42.

211 *Jikkunshō* (Ten Instructions), Chapter 6. Cf. *Eiga Monogatari* (Tales of Prosperity), Chapter on *Hana yama* ("Flowers and Mountains").

212 Cited in *Genpei Seisuiki* (Rise and Fall of the Minamoto and Taira Clans), VIII, as a poem by the Lord of the Engi period, whereas in *Jikkunshō, op.cit.,* Chapter 5, as one by Prince Takaoka, Cf. *Yōkyoku, Hachi-no-ki* (Miniature Plant in a Pot).

213 Various similar poems by Emperors are collected in Mizumaro Ishida, *Rekidai Tennō Gyosei ni Haisuru Goshinkō* (Faith of Emperors Revealed in their Poems), ("Nihon Kyōgaku Kenkyūjo Kenkyū Hōkoku," No. 8).

214 *Sandai Jitsuroku,* II.

215 *Zoku Nihon Kōki* (Records of Japan, Continued), IX, S; *v.* the 9th year of the Shōwa period, in the reign of Emperor Ninmei.

216 *Monnō Kōtei Gaiki* (Anecdotes of Emperor Monnō), in *Zoku Gunsho Ruijū* (Collection of Various Works, Continued), Part VIII, Chapter 1, CXC, 44; cf. *Nanzen-ji-shi* (History of the Nanzen Temple), 41.

217 *Kudenshō* (Treatises Transmitted Orally), by Kakunyo (1270–1351), Kyoto, *Shinshū Shōgyō Zensho* (Complete Collection of the True Pure Land Sect), III. Kōkyō Shoin. 4th ed. *Shōwa,* 16 (1941), 9. The "Perfect One" is the English translation of "*Tathāgata*" which means the Buddha "thus come."

218 *Tannishō* (Tracts Deploring Heterodoxies), traditionally ascribed to Yuien, a disciple of Shinran. *Ibid.,* II, 776.

219 *Kudenshō,* 9.

220 Cf. *Tannishō, Kudenshō,* and *Gaijashō* (Treatise on Converting False Views), by Kakunyo.

221 *Gaijashō,* III, 84.

222 *Senkōji monjo* (Documents of the Senkō Temple) (T. Tamamuro, *op.cit.,* 321); n.b.—the book is *Nihon Bukkyōshi Gaisetsu* (Outline of Japanese Buddhist History)—79, note 22.

223 Cf. *Kyōgyōshinshō* (St. Shinran's major work, Teaching, Practice, Faith, and Confirmation).

224 "In Akao, situated on the upper reaches of the Shō-gawa in Etchū (Toyama prefecture), there remains an organization of a group of faithful which suggests the times of Rennyo." "In this village, a matter which has greatly impressed me is the fact that in each community there is a *dōjō* (sacred hall). Whereover there are as many as 20 households, there is a stately *dōjō.* A *dōjō* is not a temple. Although the eaves are higher than those of ordinary houses, and the interior is entirely in the style of a temple, there is no professional priest. Middle- and upper-class families of this village take charge in turn, and when necessary hold memorial services without a priest, and also perform funerals. Sometimes priests are invited to preach, but ordinarily there is none there; it is merely a place of worship for the community. In winter, since it is impossible to communicate with other settlements, the people of the community like to assemble here and talk together about their religion. This is the 'meeting of the dōjō' frequently mentioned in the *Ofumi* ("Letters") of Rennyo."—Daijō Tokiwa, *Nihon Bukkyō no Kenkyū* (Studies in Japanese Buddhism), 229.

225 Cf. *Shaseki-shū* (Collection of Sundry Reports), 1, b: "The followers of Jōdo think lightly of the Shintō gods." But as a contrary example there is the fact that Saint Ippen and others also showed respect for various gods and Buddhas.

226 Cf. Rennyo, *Ofumi* (*Shinshū Shōgyō Zensho* III, 402–518).

227 Dōgen maintained that such an attitude was derived from his teacher, Ju-ching (Nyojō); "The sentence, 'The Three Religions have one end,' is inferior to the talk of a little boy. (People who talk this way) are a group who would destroy Buddhism. There are many such people. They either appear as religious leaders of men and demi-gods, or become teachers of emperors. The present time (the Sung Dynasty) is a time

of decline of Buddhism as religious teachers and Buddhas of old forewarned." Dōgen (1200–1253), *Shōbō-genzō* (Essence of Buddhism), "Shohōjissō (True Nature of all dharmas)" Iwanami Bunko edition, II, 240.

228 When we look at the collected sayings of Ju-ching, we find that he recognizes the authority of Confucianism and Taoism also and quotes from the *Lun Yü*, the *Lao Tzŭ*, etc. Keidō Itō, *Dōgen Zenji Kenkyū* (A Study on Zen Master Dōgen) Chapter 1, 32ff., 69ff.

229 It is commonly considered that Dōgen's religion is a faithful continuation of its Chinese counterpart. But the fact that the thought of the *Shōbōgenzō* coincides with the teachings of Ju-ching, as recorded in the *Hōkyōki* (Record of Treasury Salutations), does not justify this opinion. [No. 1796 of Iwanami Bunko.] The *Hōkyōki* is a work by Dōgen, not by Ju-ching. Hence, it is to be feared that in the sayings of Ju-ching quoted there, Dōgen's wishful interpretations have probably been added. If we are to understand the thought of Ju-ching, we must in any case study his own collected sayings; but it is to be regretted that there is yet no study of the content of his thought beyond the bibliographical study of the collected sayings by Keidō Itō.

230 The emphasis on doctrinal lineage appears also in the T'ang Dynasty, China, and becomes strong with the Sung. But it is a much stronger tendency in Japan than in China.

231 Daitō Shimaji, *Tendai Kyōgakushi* (A History of Tendai theology), 466.

232 "In ancient India also, *sūtras* and *śāstras* were studied together; and in early times in China, the three schools were not separated, hence they must have had deep understanding." Accordingly, the priest Eisai (1141–1215) of the Kennin Temple "studied religious law and observed ceremonial rules, studied, and practiced Tendai, Shingon, and Zen alike, and also recommended to others the practice of Nembutsu." (*Shaseki-shū*, X, Part 2, *Kenninji Hongan Sōjō no Koto* [Anecdotes of the Abbot of Kennin Temple].) "Many examples can be found in the *Kao-seng-chuan* (Biographies of High Priests) of monks of different sects living together in one and the same temple in China."

233 The Jōdo sect usually called Zen the "School of the Sacred Way (Shōdōmon)," on the other hand, Hakuin vigorously attacked the Jōdo sect. Hakuin was a Zen master, whose full name was Hakuin Ekaku (1685–1768).

234 Daijō Tokiwa, *Shina-bukkyō no Kenkyū* (A Study of Chinese Buddhism), III, 76.

235 Kanzan Matsumiya (1686–1780), *Sankyō Yōron* (Introduction to the Essentials of the Three Teachings) (in *Nihon Jurin Sōshō* [Series of Japanese Confucian Works]), 3.

236 *Okina no Fumi* (Letters of an Elderly Man) by Nakamoto Tominaga (1715–1746), written in 1738, section 16.

237 Yoshio Mikami, *The Development of Mathematics in China and Japan* (New York: Chelsea Publishing Company, 1913), 324.

238 *Ibid.*, 161.
239 *Sankyō Yōron* (Outline of the Three Teachings), in *Nihon Jurin Sōsho* (Series of Japanese Confucian Works), 2.
240 *Kodō Taii* (Essence of the Ancient Way) *Hirata Atsutane Zenshū* (Collected Works of Atsutane Hirata), VII, 62 a.
241 A poem by Sakimori included in Volume XX of the *Man'yōshū* (Myriad Leaves) (Sakimori—a soldier defending the frontier).
242 This idea appears particularly in the epic poem *Mahābhārata* and in inscriptions on stone.
243 Cf. for example the *Bhagavadgītā*.
244 *Hagakure* (Iwanami Bunko edition, 114), sometimes called *Hagakure Kikigaki*, a book on the way of the *samurai*, is a book dictated by Yamamoto Tsunemoto (1649–1716) and written down by his disciple Tashiro Tsuramoto (1710–1776) and edited and annotated by Tetsuro Watsuji and Tesshi Furukawa.
245 Max Weber, *Hinduismus und Buddhismus*, 300.
246 *Nihon Saikyōshi* (History of Japanese Catholicism), (Taiyōdō edition), 37.
247 *Jōgai Ofumi* (by Rennyo—a supplementary group of his collection of letters, etc.); p. 30 of *Rennyo Shōnin Ofumi Zenshū* (Collected Works of Saint Rennyo) edited by Yūshō Tokushi. However, there is some doubt as to whether Rennyo himself wrote this letter.
248 The Fudō Myōō—the god of fire—is mentioned in the Sanskrit Buddhist scriptures only in the *Śikṣāsamuccaya* and the *Guhyasamājatantra*, by the name *acala*. Cf. *acala* in *Kanyaku Taishō Bonwa Daijiten* (Sanskrit-Japanese Dictionary with reference to Chinese Terms), edited by Unrai Ogiwara.
249 Daijō Tokiwa, *Shina Bukkyō no Kenkyū* (Studies in Chinese Buddhism), III, 83: "I want to add, that in spite of the fact that the Bodhisattva Kuan-yin is worshipped everywhere even in Taoist *Kuan* and *Miao*, one can nowhere find images of the god of fire (Fudō Myōō). . . . Since I do not recall seeing one example, in spite of the fact that I investigated relatively widely on foot, I assume that the worship of this god did not occur."
250 Chikamatsu Monzaemon (1653–1724), *Kaheiji Osaga Ikutama Shinju* (Double Suicide by Kaheiji and Osaga): "When we hear the phrase, 'The name of Amida is actually a sharp sword,' we understand that even the dagger of death (suicide) is Amida's means (of helping us enter the Pure Land)."
251 Cf. *Tsūgen Zenji Zenshū* (Collected Works of Zen Master Tsūgen), III, 55ff.; Keido Ito, *Dōgen Zenji Kenkyū* (Study of Zen Master Dōgen), I, 363ff.
252 *Roankyō* (Asses Bridge), Part 1, in *Zemmon Hōgo Shū* (Collection of Holy Sayings of the Zen Sect), I, 289.
253 *Bammin Tokuyū* (Significance of All Vocations), (*Zemmon Hōgo Shū*, III, 526).

254 In regard to this problem the *Hung Ming Chi* (Collected Essays on Buddhism) provides excellent material. See 181–182. Tetsurō Watsuji, *Nihon Rinri Shisō-shi* (A History of Ethical Thoughts in Japan), Iwanami Shoten, 1952, 2 volumes.

255 The term *shōjō* (lesser vehicle) is a translation of the Sanskrit *Hīnayāna*. Sometimes the word is translated *geretsujō* (ignoble vehicle), *gejō* (lower vehicle), *gejōhō* (the doctrine of the lower vehicle). Cf. *Bodhisattvabhūmi*, 223, Line 2 (*Taishō*, XXX, 531 b); *Madhyānta-vibhāgaṭīkā*, 216, line 8; 255, line 18 (*Kanzō-taishō-bon*, Chinese-Tibetan parallel edition, 104, 128); *Mahāvyutpatti* (Sasaki edition, 186, 1253). The term *Hīnayāna* is very seldom used in Sanskrit original texts now in existence; nevertheless, Chinese and Japanese Buddhists are fond of using the invidious term *shōjō* to refer to traditionalistic, conservative Buddhism.

256 "Japan is a pure Mahāyānist country, and is the country which has realized the Mahāyāna most perfectly" (Nichiren, *Jisshō-shō* [Commentary of Ten Chapters]). Also, according to tradition, Shinran in his 19th year went to the Mausoleum of Prince Shōtoku in Kawachi (Ōsaka area) to worship, and in a dream Prince Shōtoku appeared to him, pronouncing a *gāthā* (verse) containing the line, "Japan is the country most suited to Mahāyāna." Goten Ryōkū, *Takada Shinran Shōnin Shōtōden* (True Biography of Saint Shinranvat Takada), Chapter 1, *Shinaga Shōtoku-taishi-byō Mukoku Rokku Kimon* (The Six Phrases in the Dream at the Mausoleum of Prince Shōtoku at Shinaga), *Shinshū Zensho* (Complete Works of the Shin Sect), *Shidenbu* (Section on Historical Lineage), 337. Again in Hōkū, *Jōgū-taishi shūiki* (*Anecdotes of Prince Shōtoku*), the eulogy *"Hiketsu ni iwaku, Gobyō Sekimei no koto* (Account of the mausoleum inscription, according to the Secret Teaching [Hiketsu])" contains the line "the virtuous country most suited to the Mahāyāna." *Dainihon Bukkyō Zensho* (Complete Works of Japanese Buddhism), CXII, 142.

257 Shōson Miyamoto, *Chūdō Shisō oyobi sono Hattatsu* (The Idea of the "Middle Way" and its Development), 888–889.

258 Prince Shōtoku has at times used for the word *"bosatsu"* (bodhisattva) the modified translation *"Gishi."* (Shinshō Hanayama, *Shōmangy Gisho no Kenkyū* [Study on the Commentary on *Śrīmālādevīsiṁhanāda-sūtra*], 432–433.) In spite of the fact that the usual translation for the term *bosatsu* is *taishi* or *kaiji*, he used the translation *gishi* (literally, "man of righteousness"); this is probably to be understood as due to his interest in emphasizing especially the idea that the conduct of the Bodhisattva is to be realized throughout man's concrete moral life.

259 Shinshō Hanayama, *Hokke Gisho no Kenkyū* (Study on the Commentary on the *Saddharma-puṇḍarīka-sūtra*), 469.

260 *Yuimagyō Gisho* (Commentary on the *Vimalakīrti-nirdeśa-sūtra*), in *Dai Nihon Bukkyō Zensho*, ed., 141 a.

261 *Hokkye Gisho, Dainihon Bukkyō Zensho*, ed., 4 b.

262 *Ibid.*, 28 a. Further similar expressions may be found at random in many

places. "Every good action in the Six Spheres can lead man to become Buddha." (*Ibid.*, 5 a.) "Every [good] action is a cause leading to the effect of Buddhahood (becoming Buddha). (*Ibid.*, 34 a.) "Even those good actions which are of a purely secular mode occupy the religious status of the One Vehicle (viz. are on the highest religious plane)." (*Ibid.*, 28 b.) Cf. Shinshō Hanayama, *Hokke Gisho no Kenkyū*, 469, 489.

263 The clause which appears in the *Shōmangyō* (*Śrīmālā-devīsiṁhanāda-sūtra*) is commonly interpreted to read: "[The Buddhas and Bodhisattvas] enjoy especially distinguished reverence and support from all living beings." But Prince Shōtoku insisted that the word order should be changed to read: "[The Buddhas and Bodhisattvas] are caused to offer reverence and support for all especially distinguished living beings." Shinshō Hanayama, *Shōmangyo Gisho no Jogū-o-sen ni kansuru Kenkyū* (Study of Prince Shōtoku's Commentary of the Śrīmālā Sūtra), (Tokyo: 1944), 434–437). It goes without saying that this is a strained interpretation of the text, as he has read into the passage his own idea of altruism toward all living beings.

264 In regard to the clause in the *Sukhavihāraparivarta* (XIII of Sanskrit edition of the Lotus Sūtra), "always fond of *zazen* (sitting in meditation)," he makes the criticism, "If one is always fond of *zazen*, leaving this world to go and stay in the mountains, how will one have any time to propagate this sūtra throughout the world"; and he explains the meaning of the sūtra as being that "one should not associate with Hīnayāna Zen masters who are always fond of *zazen*." (Shinshō Hanayama, *op.cit.*, 437; also Shinshō Hanayama, *Shōtoku Taishi Gyosei Hokke Gisho no Kenkyū*, 386–387.) Also cf. Shinshō Hanayama, *Nippon Bukkyō no Engen* (Sources of Japanese Buddhism), 917–935 in *Bukkyōgaku no Shomondai* (Problems of Buddhist Studies), Iwanami, 1935.

265 Saburō Ienaga, *Chūsei Bukkyō Shinsoshi Kenkyū* (Studies in the History of Medieval Buddhist Thought, (Kyoto: Hōzkan, 1947), 23–27.

266 *Ibid.*, 78.

267 *Anrakushū* (Treatise on the Pure Land, by a Sui Buddhist of the Jōdo School, Tao-ch'o), Dōshaku, 562–645, Part 1.

268 *Mattōshō* (A Treatise on the Diminishing Lamp), by Shinran. Cf. beginning of *Shūjishō* (On Desires), by Kakunyo.

269 This sentence is also quoted in *Kyōgyōshinshō* (by Shinran), III, Part 2.

270 In the *Gutokushō* (A Treatise by an Idiot), by Shinran, Part 1 (Shinran, *Shinshū Shōgy Zenshū* II, 460, *Shūso-bu*, Section on the Founder), there is the passage, "*The moment of* the wholehearted belief in the original vow is the ending of (the ordinary) life (which is the terminal point) of the former invocation (of Amida, that which is proper to this earlier, ordinary life). (The principle that) one obtains right now a rebirth (in the Pure Land) is (what is meant by) the immediate rebirth (which is the beginning point) of the later invocation (of Amida—the *nembutsu* practiced in the new, recreated religious life)." This passage is

quoted in Book III B of the *Rokuyōshō* (A Treatise on Six Essentials, by Zonkaku, great-great-grandson of Shinran [1290–1373]), a commentary on Shinran's *Kyōgyōshinsō* (*Shinshū Shōgyō Zenshū*), III, 301, with the remark, "In regard to the principle of the realization of the true result (life) in the ordinary life, this passage makes evident the effect of (the principal that) the horizontal enlightenment is sudden." [Shinran argues that for the religious man who has attained salvation by achieving *nembutsu* with utterly sincere faith in the original vow—at which point his ordinary mind is cut away by the power of the vow and emptied, so that his calling upon Amida is identical with Amida's own continual calling of his own name, whereupon Amida's Pure Land Life enters into him—for such a man the ordinary life in this world and the life in the Pure Land are not two but one, and further that this pure life is not an other-worldly existence here and now but identical with this life. It is Shinran in principle that the *zennen* (former invocation) and the *gonen* (later invocation) (note the special senses of "former" and "later") constitute one and the same event in the individual's psychological and religious life. The metaphor describing enlightenment as Shinran conceives it is here geometrical (just as his notion of the identity of *zennen* and *gonen* is mathematical—a limiting point of two series).

The vertical direction from the "ordinary" to the "pure" life—called *Jiu-chō*—is gradual and difficult, dependent on one's own strength; it supposes the pure life to be separate from the "ordinary" one, whereas the horizontal direction called *Ōchō* ("horizontal enlightenment") shows the opposition between easy-going resting on faith and the sudden merging of the two "lives." Shinran calls these "two kinds of truth." Professor Abe here objects that if this were true, there would be no difference between Zen and Shin Buddhism—actually for Shinran, from the point of view of Amida the two lives are one; but from the point of view of man, they are utterly separate; he is hopelessly sinful—and just because he has an extreme consciousness of his sinfulness, Amida's love can help him, hence Shinran uses the expression "The two (lives) are one, and one (man) is two (lives)." Also the phrase *bonnō soku bodai:* "Defilements (kle'sa) are identical with bodhi" and *fudan bonnō toku nehan:* "Without stopping defilements one achieves Nirvāṇa"—this doctrine is called *Shōjōju no kurai.* This is the position from which *Sokutokuōjō* (immediate attainment of Rebirth in Pure Land) is possible—also called *Metsudo* (Nirvāṇa). Shinran says, Amida promises to help even good men, how much more so bad men! This is the point at which, due to Amida's promise and faith in it, one is guaranteed rebirth. In this sense one has it already and at the same time not yet.—D. Nivison.

271 Zonkaku, *Jōdo Shinyō Shō* (Essentials of Pure Land), Part I, (*Taisho* LXXXIII, 761 b).

272 *Ōjōronchū* (Commentary on the Rebirth Verses in the Commentary on the Endless Life), by Donran (476–542), *Shinshū Shōgyō Zensho,* 1, *Sangyō Shichi-so Bu,* section on the Three Sūtras and Seven Masters, 319.

273 Shōshinge (Poems of True Faith), *Kyōgyōshinshō* (*Shinshū Shōgyō Zensho* 2, *Shūso Bu*, 44).

274 *Shōshin-nembutsuge Kikigaki* (Notes on the Poems of True Faith), Part I, *Shinshū Zensho* (Complete Works of the Shin Sect), Supplement, VIII, 247; *Shōshin Nembutsuge Karohen* (Fireside Comments on the Poems of True Faith), Part II, in *ibid.*, 119; *Shōshin Nembutsuge Hoeiki* (Annotations on the Poems of True Faith), Part II, in *ibid.*, 25.

275 *Goichidaiki Kikigaki* (Notes on Biography), by Rennyo (1415–1499); *Shinshū Shōguyō Zensho* 3, *Ressobu* (Section on Chief Abbots), 582.

276 *Kyōgyōshinshō*, Part I (*Shinshū Shōgyō Zensho* 2, *Shūsobu*, 2). Cf. also *Jōdoron* (Treatise on the Pure Land) quoted in Part III of *Kyōgyōshinshō* (*ibid.*, 66). The two *ekō* (Parināmanā—"merit-transference") are also referred to in *Gutokushō*, Part II (*Shinshū Shōgyō Zensho*), *ibid.*, 475.

277 Cf. Kanji Naitō "*Shūkyo to Keizai Rinri, Jodō Shin-shū to Ōmi Shōnin*" (Religion and Business Ethics—Jōdo-shin sect and the Ōmi merchants). Cf. *Shakai Gaku* (the annual report of the Japan Sociological Association), 8 (1941), 243–286.

278 But perhaps we cannot say that National Master Daitō emphasized a life within the bonds of social morality. Razan Hayashi bitterly criticized Daitō's mode of monkhood as destructive of social morality. Tetsujirō Inoue, *Nihon Shushi-gakuha no Tetsugaku* (The Philosophy of the Chu Hsi School in Japan), 73ff. But it seems that his way of living together with beggars and other unattached elements was somewhat different from the way of life of Zen monks in China.

279 *Roankyō*, Part I, 107, in *Zenmon-hōgoshū*.

280 *Pāṭimokkha* (Rules of Discipline), 48–51, in the *Vinaya*.

281 *Roankyō*, Part I, 101.

282 A typical example of this way is the famous story of self-sacrifice of Prince Vessantara transmitted in Southern Buddhist countries (*Jātaka*, 547).

283 The phrase *shazai* ("giving up property") which occurs in the chapter "Shōju shōbo (Holding the Right Teaching)" of the *Shōmangyō* is interpreted by the Master Chia-hsiang (Chi-tsang) in the *Shōmangyō hōkutsu* ("Jewelled Cave of the Śrīmātā Sūtra) as meaning "to give to others everything except one's own body and life—country, castle, wife, and children" (*Taishō*, XXVII, 36 b-e); but Prince Shōtoku's commentary interprets it as "things other than one's own body" (Part 1, 36 b), deleting the phrase "to give country, castle, wife, and children to others." (Shinshō Hanayama, *Shōmangyō Gisho no Kenkyū*, 432.) Probably the interpretation of the Hōkutsu transmits the Indian idea faithfully.

284 "No teaching of *dharma*, when understood according to the proper sense, is at variance with the *jissō* (the real aspect). When popular books of secular thought, and political proverbs, and precepts about daily work are taught, all are in accord with the true *dharma*." This text is famous, and has been highly esteemed in Japan and China, but the original text is merely as follows:

"He should remain mindful and not forget the *dharma* which he will preach. Popular secular utterances—whether proverbs or mystic formulas—ought all to be explained in accordance with the true meaning of *dharma*."

In this phrase "precepts about daily work" does not occur. (Kern-Nanjō edition, 372; Ogiwara-Tsuchida edition, 315.)

285 *Ryōgon-kyō Chōsuisho* (Commentary on the Śūraṅgama-Sūtra, by Ch'ang-shui) I, last part. *Taishō,* XXXIX. According to tradition, Ch'ang-shui died in *Taihei* 9 (A.D. 1029), was a Kegon Buddhist of the Sung dynasty.

286 For example, in the *Muchū-mondō-shū* (Questions and Answers in Dreams) by National Master Musō Kokushi, a Kamakura Zen master, we read: "This (i.e. Ch'ang-shui's thought) has the same sense as the argument in the *Hokke-kyō* (Lotus Sūtra) that vocations also are all in accord with the *jisso*" (Real Aspect). Musō (1275–1351) was a brother of Ashikagu Takauji; Tadayoshi asked Musō questions, and this book contains 93 such questions, with Musō's answers. Cf. Iwanumi Bunko edition, p. 19.

287 *Shūi Waka Shū* (Collection of Gleanings of Poems), XX. The above poem is also quoted in Nichiren's *Minobusan Gosho* (*Nichiren-shōnin Zenshū*), II (Heirakuji Shoten: 1931), 840.

288 *Devadatta-parivarta* (Chapter of Devadatta), Chapter 13.

289 *Gyōki-bosatsu-den* (The Life of Gyōki Bosatsu, a monk in Nara, 668–749 A.D.) in *Zoku Gunsho ruijū* (Collection of Various Works, Continued), CCIV, Chapter 8, last part.

290 *Ritsuon Gyōji-monben* (Questions and Answers on Disciplines), *Nihon Daizōkyō, Kairitsu-shōsho,* III, 493.

291 *Shōbōgenzō* (by Dōgen), Jinzū (Miracles), Chapter 25.

292 *Ibid., Bendōwa* (Sermons on the Practice of the Way), Chapter 1.

293 *Loc.cit.*

294 *Eihei Shitsuchū Kikigaki* (Notes on Esoteric Practice in the Eihei Temple). Cf. Hanji Akiyama, *Dōgen no Kenkyū* (Studies on Dōgen), 281.

295 *Kanjin Honzon Shō* (Treatise on Meditation on the Principal Buddha, by Nichiren), *Nichiren Shōnin Zenshū* (Collected Works of Saint Nichiren), I, 342.

296 *Hokke-shū nai Buppō Ketsumyaku* (Transmission of Buddhism in the Lotus Sect), *ibid.*, VI, 2728.

297 *Ressei Zenshū* (Collected Writings of Japanese Emperors) *Shinkishū,* last part, 430.

298 *Ketsujō-shū* ("Connecting Ropes").

299 *Roankyō,* last part, 41 (by Shōsan Suzuki). Moreover in the *Banmin Tōkuyō* by Shōsan Suzuki, we read as follows: "In Buddhist scripture we are told that if we enter deeply into the secular world there will be nothing lacking in our withdrawal from the world. This passage means that through the secular law one may become a buddha. Thus, then, the secu-

lar law is the Buddhist law. In the Kegon doctrine we are told that 'The Buddhist law is not different from the secular law; the secular law is not different from the Buddhist law.' If one does not accept the truth that in the secular law itself one may attain buddhahood, then he is not one who fully understands the meaning of Buddhism. It is my prayer that the secular law and the Buddhist law be made one." [*Zenmon Hōgo-shū, op.cit.*, last part, 526.]

300 Shosan, Suzuki, *Roankyō* (*op.cit.*, p. 337); *Bammin Tokuyō* 5 (*Ibid.*, 536ff.).

301 *Yasen-kanwa* (Leisure Talks in a Night Boat); *Orategama.*

302 *Shōbōgenzō Keiteki* (NB. one of the best commentaries on *Shōbō Genzō* of Dōgen, by Fusan Soei, following lectures of Bokuzan Nishiari. Date of the lectures is Meiji 32 or A.D. 1900. *Bendōwa, op.cit.*, Ch. I, p. 153.

303 Yasusada Hiyane, *Nihon Shūkyōshi* (A History of Japanese Religions), 825.

304 H. Nakamura, *Kinsei Nihon ni okeru Hihan-teki Seishin no Ichi-kōsatsu* (Inquiry into the Critical Spirit in Modern Japan) Tokyo: Sanseido, 1949), 58f.

305 *Shōbōgenzō, "Jikuimbun"* (Letters to the Kitchen), p. 119 of Iwanami edition.

306 Zuihō Menzan (d. 1769), *Jujiki Gokan Kummō* (Instructions to Meditate in Five Ways before Dieting), 3. [Among the Hebrews, it is also sinful to waste food.—Editor's note].

307 *Rennyo Shōnin Goichidaiki Kikigaki* (Notes on the Biography of Saint Rennyo), Part 2. (*Shinshū Shōgyō Zensho*, III, Ressobu, 611.)

308 Tetsugen, *"Ke-en no Sho"* (A Book of Edification), *Tetsugen Zenji Keji Hōgo* (Buddhist Teachings of Zen Master Tetsugen), Iwanami Bunko edition, 50. Tetsugen Dōkō (1630–1682) belonged to the Ōbaku sect.

309 *"Kurushima Kō ni taisuru Tetsugen no Kyūmei Konseisho."* (A letter of Tetsugen to the *daimyō* Kurushima asking him to save men's lives), in *ibid.*, 77.

310 *Gomōjigi* (Gloss on the Mencius), by Jinsai Itō, I, 15.

311 *Ibid.*, I, 3.

312 *Rongo Kogi* (The Original Meaning of the Confucian Analects) by Jinsai Itō, V. Also cf. Kōjirō Yoshikawa, *Shinajin no Koten to sono Seikatsu*, 154.

313 Sorai Ogyu (1666–1728), *Bemmei* (Discussion on Names), last part, *"Sei Jō Sai Shichisoku,"* (The Seven Principles of Nature, Feeling, and Talent).

314 Sorai Ogyu, *Tōmonsho*, (Answers to Questions) Part 1, in *Nihon Rinri Ihen* (Compendium of Japanese Ethics), VI, 153.

315 Sorai Ogyu, *Rongo Chō* (Studies on the Confucian Analects), Junsei Iwahashi, *Sorai Kenkyū*, 300.

316 *Ibid.*, 446ff.

317 [Witness Japan's recent advances in industry, experimental sciences, and technology. However, by skipping over the centuries which Europe took to evolve a "scientific outlook," Japan has to face the educational problem

of preparing the minds of its people to adapt to the technological age. With the highest literacy in all Asia, Japan's prospects are very good.—Editor's note.]

318 Tetsurō Watsuji, *Sakoku* (Seclusion in the Country), 341.

319 *Kyōgyōshinshō,* Part III, end. (*Shinshū Shōgyō Zensho, Shūsobu,* II, 80.)

320 Cf. prophesies about monks in the final period of the *dharma* in various Buddhist sacred texts.

321 Cf. the works of Kumārajīva and various entries in the *Hung Ming Chi.*

322 *Daibutchōnyorai Mitsuin Shushō Ryōgi Shobosatsu Mangyō-shuryōgonkyō,* VII. (*Taishō,* XIX, 134ff.) *Sengen Sempi Kanzeonbosatsu Darani jin jugyō* (Magical Formula of Thousand-Headed and Thousand-Armed Avalokiteśvara)—*Beppon, Taishō Nilakanthā-tharani,* 1057, XX, 94 a. Also, there is an Essay on Magic in Volume 60 of *Hōon Jurin.* In this essay there is a spell for purging oneself of the sins of indulging the passions and of the "Five spicy things." The idea here of atonement being effected through magical rites is not essentially different from Brahmanism.

323 *Sanzengi* (A Treatise on Good Acts Achieved in Non-meditative State of Mind, Set Forth in the Amitāyur-Dhyāna-Sūtra), *more precisely, Kangyō Shōshū Bun Sanzengi,* IV, (*Taishō,* XXXVII, 270 c). In the *Hōnen-shōnin Gyōjo Ezu* (Portraits Illustrating the Career of St. Hōnen), Chapter 22, we read, "Do not maintain a saintly external appearance while keeping a deceitful mind within. Rather, regardless of what is external or internal, manifest or hidden, always maintain true sincerity." Shinkō Mochizuki, *Hōnen-shōnin Zenshū,* 897.

324 *Kyōgyoshinshō,* III, Part 2. (*Taishō,* V. 83, 601 c.) Shinran's *Gutokushō,* Part 2 (*Shinshū Shōgyō Zensho Shūsobu,* II, 464). The phrase "a saintly appearance" as discussed in detail is Shinran's *Yuishin-shōmon-i* (Purport of Mind-Only Treatise), 25ff. (*Shinshū Shōgyō Zensho,* II, *Shūsobu,* II, 635.) The phrase is interpreted by Hōnen, in the section entitled *San-shin Shaku* (Explanations on Three Minds) of his *Senjakuhongan-nembutsu-shū* (Treatise on the Invocation to Amitābha, Based upon Selected Original Vows), *Shinshū Shōgyo Zensho,* I, *Sangyō Shichisobu,* 957, as recommending that we maintain saintliness both within and without.

325 *Hitan Jukkai Wasan* (Japanese Poems of Lamentation, by Shinran). (*Taishō,* V. 83, 667 c.)

326 *"The Biography of Saint Hōnen"* in the Daigo Temple edition.

327 *Tannishō* (by *Yuien*), Chapter 3 (*Shinshū Shōgyō Zensho,* II, 775); also, *Kudenshō* (A Treatise on Oral Tradition, by Kakunyo), Chapter 19. *Shinshū Shōgyō Zensho,* III, *Ressobu,* 32.

328 Saburō Ienaga, *Chūsei-bukkyō Shisō-shi Kenkyū* (Studies on the History of Medieval Buddhist Thought), 67; 13–22.

329 *Wago Tōroku* (Works in Japanese, by Hōnen), IV (*Taishō,* V. 83, 218 c).

"Since we have heard that the original vow rejects not even a bad man, we should understand then how much more [Amida] rejoices in a good man." (*Ibid.*, 227 b.)

330 *Tōtaigishō* (A Treatise on the Essential Body, by Nichiren) (*Nichiren Shōnin Zenshū*, II, 1102). Further, in regard to the fact that Nichiren called himself "*mukai no sō*" (the monk who recognizes no law), cf. Saburō Ienaga, *op.cit.*, 75.

331 *Shō-hokke-daimoku Shō* (A Treatise on the Invocation of the Title of the Lotus Sūtra, by Nichiren), *Nichiren Shōnin Zenshū*, I, 489.

332 *Gessui no Gosho* (A Treatise on Menses, by Nichiren), *ibid.*, II, 871.

333 *Shōbō Genzō*, (Dōgen), Chapter 9, "*Keisei Sanshoku*" (the sound of brooks and the hue of mountains), Iwanami Bunko edition, I, 145. The same phrase is used also in the *Jōyō Daishi* [i.e., Dōgen] *Hotsugan-mon.* (Prayer by Master Dōgen). Cf. also Chapter 2 of *Sōtō-kyōkai Shushōgi* (Practice and Enlightenment in the Sōtō Sect). Cf. *Gleanings from Sōtō-Zen*, edited by Ernest Shinkaku Hunt, (Honolulu: Soto Mission, 1960), 20.

334 *Shōbō Genzō*, Chapter 92, "Shōji" (Life and Death), Iwanami edition, III, 240.

335 Cf. *Sōtō-kyōkai Shushōgi*, Chapter 3.

336 *Ju-ching Ho-shang* [Chinese Zen monk, teacher of Dōgen] *yü-lu*, (Collected Works of Ju-ching), last part. (*Taishō*, 48, 131 c.)

337 *Kinkaiwaka-shū, zatsu* (Miscellaneous Collection of Golden Poems). *Waka-shū* is ordinarily divided into sections for the seasons—*zatsu* section contains those not thus classifiable.

338 Junsei Iwahashi, *op.cit.*, *Sorai Kenkyū* (Studies on Sorai Ogyū), 280.

339 Tetsurō Watsuji, *op.cit.*, *Sakoku*, 341, 353, 474, 477.

340 Here I quote Master Jiun's own explanations as they appear—the *Jūzen Kaisō* (Aspects of the Ten Admonitions), also called *Jūzen Kana Hōgo.* (Sermons in Japanese on the Ten Admonitions). This book was dedicated by Jiun Sonja to Emperor Go-momozono in the 28th day of the 1st month of 1774. In other books of Jiun Sonja, also, there appear almost the same explanations. Jiun Sonja (1718–1804 A.D.), buddhist scholar, wrote a Sanskrit grammar—using *shittan* or Sanskrit letters—included in his *Bongaku Shinryō* (Compendium of Sanskrit Studies).

341 The following writings exist by Master Jiun himself, which deal solely with the Ten Admonitions: *Jūzen Kaisō* (Aspects of the Ten Admonitions), otherwise called *Jūzen-kai Kana Hōgo* (Religious Teachings in *kana* on the Ten Admonitions); *Jūzen-ryaku hōgo* (Informal [i.e. kana] teachings on the Ten Admonitions); *Jūzenkai Gohōgo* (Religious Teachings on the Ten Admonitions); *Hitotonaru Michi* (The Way of Character: The Way to Become a Fine Man). Also, there exists the *Hitotonaru Michi Zuikōki* (Records of Followers of Those Previously Mentioned), a record by Jiun's disciples of his religious teachings. (All of these are collected in Volume XIII of the *Jiun Sonja Zenshū.*) In his other writings, also, Jiun Sonja always emphasizes the 10 Admonitions.

342 Genchi Katō, *Shintō no Shūkyo-hattatsushi-teki Kenkyū* (Study of *Shintō* from the Point of View of the History of Religious Development), 874.

343 Tetsurō Watsuji, *Sonnō-shisō to sono Dentō* (The Idea of Reverence for the Emperor [*sonnō jōi,* one of the slogans of the Meiji Restoration—"expel foreigners"] and its Tradition), 103.

344 Genchi Katō, *op.cit.,* 1295.

345 *Jōdoronchū* (Commentary on the Treatise on Pure Land, by T'an-luan). *Jōdoron* (Treatise on Pure Land) was written by Vasubandhu—the *"Chū"* (commentary) is more important for Japanese Buddhism: "Honesty is called uprightness; through honesty is engendered a mind capable of compassion for all living creatures." Also in the chapter on "expedients" in the *Hokekyō,* "Among the many Bodhisattvas (the Buddha) is honest and discards expedients, teaching only the highest truth," i.e. among *bosatsu* (bodhisattva), as opposed to *shōmon* (Śravakas, those who emphasize orthodox teaching) and *engaku* (pratyekabuddhas, those who emphasize practical teaching)—the *bodhisattva* emphasizes both.

346 "The mind that has resolved to maintain honesty and discard expediency, is essentially good and upright, and since this is so, things are as they are." (*Yōkyoku*) (Kentarō Sanari, *Makiginu, Yōkyoku Taikan,* IV, 2808, Meiji Shoin, 1931.)

347 *Kyōgyōshinshō,* III, Part I.

348 Dōgen: "The word *ko* (ancient) in the term *kobutsu* (ancient or eternal Buddha) is identical with *ko* in *shin ko* (new and old); and yet also it transcends time. [The Kobutsu] is pure and upright eternally," *Shōbō Genzō,* Chapter 44, *"kobutsu shin* (Mind of Ancient Buddhas)," Iwanami Bunko edition, II, 177. *Shōjiki* ("honesty") here differs from "the virtue of *shōjiki"* in meaning, yet there is some connection between the usages.

349 *Nichimyō Shōnin Gosho* (A Letter to Saint Nichimyō, by Nichiren), *Nichiren Shōnin Zenshū,* 952ff.

350 *Kangyō-hachiman-shō* (A Treatise to Admonish the God Hachiman), *ibid.,* III, 1328.

351 *Hōmon Mōsarubekiyōno Koto* (How to Deliver Sermons, by Nichiren).

352 "In the notion *shōjiki* (honesty) there is what is superficial and what is profound. If we do not pervert true principles, maintain our duty, stand correctly in the way of the Five Social Virtues, accord with the natural order of things and have no selfish heart, this is the secular notion of *shōjiki.* This is the way to advance from the superficial into the profound. But, also, from the standpoint of Buddhism the notion of *shōjiki* is this, if all ordinary phenomenal law is recognized as illusory and artificial, and the essential truth (*dharmakāya*) is accepted as given by the natural true self, that is genuine honesty (*shōjiki*)." *Bammin tokuyō,* by Shōsan Suzuki.

353 The expression "In an honest head a god resides" (i.e. God defends the

right) appears to be a rather ancient proverb. It has been accepted also by Buddhists—"In the vow of the God Hachiman there are the words 'I will make the head of an honest man my home and I will not reside in the heart of a sycophant,' etc." (Nichiren, *Kangyō-hachiman-shō, Nichiren Shōnin Zenshū,* III, 1328.) "Among all people, high and low, it is said that 'The great Bodhisattva Hachiman resides in an honest head. But he does not make his home elsewhere,' etc." (*Hōmon mōsarubekiyō no Koto.*)

354 But there is the saying, "A lie is sometimes expedient" (e.g. a white lie).

355 Yoshio Takeuchi, *Eki to Chūyō no Kenkyū* (Studies on the Book of Changes and the Doctrine of the Mean), 325ff.

356 *Kojiki den* (Commentary on the Kojiki, Record of Ancient Matters), Chapter 2, edited by Motoori, I, 150ff., in *Motoori Norinaga Zenshū* (Collected Works of Motoori, 1730–1801). Cf. De Bary, Keene, Tsunoda, editors, *Source of The Japanese Tradition* (New York: 1958), 23f.

357 "Let us inquire what is the meaning of the word 'kami' as used of old in the language of our country: First of all, the various gods of heaven and earth which appear in the *Kojiki* (Record of Ancient Matters) and the *Nihonshoki* (History of Japan) were called *kami* and also the spirits residing in the shrines dedicated to these deities. Further, it was the ancient usage to apply the word to men, needless to say, and to birds, beasts, plants, trees, seas, mountains and anything else whatever, if that thing were out of the ordinary and had some distinctive virtue, or was to be revered or feared. The criterion of distinction was not that the thing or person should be honorable or good or meritorious; anything particularly august and dreadful, even something bad or strange, was called *kami*. Among those *kami* which are human, it goes without saying that the most august emperors of each generation, are all *kami;* thus in the anthology *Manyōshū* (Collection of Myriad Leaves) and other ancient poetry, they are called 'most high gods,' for they are far removed from, more honored by and against the ordinary people. So, in every successive age from antiquity to the present there have been human beings who are *kami*. Also, although they are not widely popular, each state, each province, each village and each family has its respective human *kami;* now many, even of the *kami* of 'the Age of Gods,' were men of that time; that age is called the 'Age of the Gods,' because the men of that age were all godlike." *Kodō Daii* (Outline of the Ancient Way), *Hirata Atsutane Zenshū,* VII, 37.

358 For example, such a phrase in the *Bommō-kyō* (*Brahmajāla-sūtra*) is quoted by Shinran in VI, Part 2, of the *Kyōgyōshinshō,* but, of course, it was never practiced.

359 The political power of the religious organization in Japan did not by any means extend as far as that of the Roman Pope in the Middle Ages.

360 According to Volume 9 of the *Ta T'ang Hsiyü-chi* (*Daitō Saiiki-ki,* Travel Records of Hsüan-tsang), King Bālāditya in the state of Magadha, when he became a monk, was obliged to occupy the last seat among the monks, and for this reason was highly dissatisfied. But the

Buddhist church did not go out of its way to break the traditional rules by giving him special honor. His seat was situated just above that of the novices who had not received their vows.

361 *Shōbōgenzō Zuimonki* (Notes on Dōgen's teachings on various occasions, by his disciple *Ejō*), V, 81, in Iwanami Bunko edition.

362 In the year 1250 A.D., the retired Emperor Gosaga (1220–1272), hearing of Dōgen's honorable character, presented him with a purple robe. Dōgen declined the gift two or three times, but when the Imperial messenger had come a third time to the Eiheiji Temple in Echizen, there was nothing he could do but accept it. Nevertheless, to the end of his life he never used it. The following poem is said to have been written by him on this occasion:

> Though the valley below the Eiheiji is not deep.
> I am profoundly honored to receive the Emperor's command.
> But I would be laughed out by monkeys and cranes.
> If I, a mere old man, were to wear this purple robe.

Dōgenzenji Gyōjō Zensho, (Collected Works on the Acts of Master Dōgen), 115, 555.

From this also we can see that he had no interest in riches and honor.

363 *Shin Sarugaku-ki* (New Critical Essays on *Sarugaku,* a vulgar form of dialogue), by Fujiwara-no-Akihira (989–1066)—(Latter Heian-reigns of Goichijō, Gosujaku, Goreizei, 1016–1068 A.D.)—in *Gunsho ruijū* (An Assortment of Writings).

364 T. Tamamuro, *Nippon Bukkyō Shi Gaisetsu* (Outline History of Japanese Buddhism), 87–88.

365 Hideyoshi Toyotomi (1536–1598), in collusion with the widow (*Nyoshunni*) of Kōsa (i.e. Kennyo), abbot of the Honganji, deposed his eldest son (Kyōnyo or Kōju) and installed the widow's own son (Junnyo or Kōsho) as an abbot. Ieyasu Tokugawa subsequently re-established Kyōnyo as an abbot of a temple—the Higashi Honganji—splitting the sect.

366 Max Weber, *Aufsätze zur Religionssozioligie,* II, 288.

367 *Tsurezuregusa* (Gleanings from My Leisure Hours), Part 1 by Kenkō Yoshida (1283–1350 A.D.)—of a family which hereditarily served in the Yoshida Shrine.

368 "There are countless comical varieties of *daruma* (the figure of Budhidharma, the founder of Zen Buddhism): figures moulded or carved in almost every kind of material, and ranging in size from the tiny metal *daruma,* half-an-inch long, designed for a pouch-clasp, to the big wooden *daruma,* two or three feet high, which the Japanese tobacconist has adopted for a shop-sign. Thus profanely does popular art deride the holy legend of the nine years meditation." Lafcadio Hearn, *A Japanese Miscellany* (Little Brown, 1901): *Studies Here and There, Otokichi's Daruma.* People of Southern Asia criticize severely the attitude of some Japanese who use the figure of the Great Buddha for a profanely commercial purpose.

369 Yoshiharu Scott Matsumoto, "*Contemporary Japan. The Individual and the Group,*" *loc.cit.*, 31.

370 Y. Haga, *Kokumin-sei Jūron* (Ten Lectures on the Japanese National Character), 140ff.

371 Cf. Tetsurō Watsuji, *Zoku Nihon Seishin-shi Kenkyū* (A Study of the Intellectual History of Japan), Part 2, 47, 49–50.

372 Christianity under the Goths in the 4th Century had already penetrated among the Germans. But Christianity as transplanted into the German world did not subsequently, in the 5th and 8th centuries, flourish very vigorously. In Japan, on the contrary, in the two and a half centuries after the introduction of Buddhism, such great scholars appeared as Saichō and Kūkai. (*Ibid.*, 76–78.)

Chapter 36

1 *Genkō-Shakusho* (History of Buddhism in Japan). XXX.

2 Izuru Shinmura, *Gengo-gaku Josetsu* (Introduction to Linguistics), 182.

3 Tetsuro Watsuji (1889–1960), *Zoku Nihon Seishin-shi Kenkyū* (Supplement to Research in Japanese Intellectual History), 397.

4 Takashi Ide (1892–), *Shijin Tetsugakusha* (Poet-Philosophers), 317.

5 The number of Chinese characters current in daily use was reduced in 1962 by the Ministry of Education of the Japanese Government to 1,850. These are called *Tōyō Kanji.*

6 Yoshio Yamada (1873–1960), *Inmyō yori idetaru Tsūyūgo* (Popular Words originally from Hindu Buddhist logic) in the journal *Geirin,* III, 22f.

7 Nevertheless Dr. Kanae Sakuma (1888–) maintains that the Japanese language contains combinations of words which perform the function of the relative pronoun; cf. "*Kyūchakugo no Mondai*" (The Problem of Agglutinative Languages), *Kokugo-Kokubun* (October 1938).

8 Tōkaidōchū Hizakurige (A Humorous Travel Diary on the Tōkaidō Road, by Jippensha Ikkyū), *Nippon Meicho Zenshū,* XXII, 101.

9 *Nyāyabinduṭīka,* 3, line 11. Tscherbatsky translated this line as: "[The act of cognition] has made him (= man) reach the object (i.e. reach it by his cognition)."

10 J. S. Speyer, *Vedische und Sanskrit-Syntax,* § 287.

11 Cf. Rev. Kusaka, *Bando Shinpon kyō-gyō-shin-shō* (Collected annotations to Shinran's works called *Kyō-gyō-shin-shō* based on the Bandō texts), 103.

12 Chikurō Hiroike, *Shina Bunten* (Chinese Grammar), 67. Cf. Y. Endō, *Kunten Shiryō to Kunten-go no kenkyū* (A Study on Kunten Material and Words), (Japanese Literature Association, 1952).

13 *Shōbōgenzō* (Subtleties of The True Doctrine, by Dōgen), chapter entitled *Gyōbutsu Igi* (High Demeanor of the Practice of Buddhas).

14 "cittamātram idam yad idaṃ traidhātukam", *Daśabhūmika-sūtra,* edited by J. Rahder, 49.

15 *Shōbōgenzō, Sangai Yuishin* (The Three Worlds of "Mind Only").
16 Two entrances and four practices; the two entrances (*ni nyū*) are the two courses of entry into enlightenment (i.e., the priesthood), namely, through contemplation (*ri*) and practice (*gyō*); the four practices of *gyō* are (1) righting of wrongs, (2) acceptance of the given, or resignation, (3) seeking nothing, (4) following *dharma*.
17 *Bendō* (Pursuit of the Way), by Sorai Ogyū.
18 *Tōmonsho* (Answers to Questions), Book 1, in *Nihon Rinri Ihen* (Collected Ethical Works of Japan), VI, 153.
19 *Ibid.*, 156.
20 *Nyūgaku Mondō* (Questions and Answers on Introduction to Study).
21 Seiichi Funabashi (1904–), "Language and Future of the Japanese People," *Orient/West*, VI, 9 (September 1961), 35.
22 *Naobi no Mitama* (The Holy Spirit).
23 *Ibid.*
24 Sōkichi Tsuda (1873–1961), *Shina Shisō to Nihon* (Chinese Thought and Japan), 37.
25 *In the Tetsugen Zenji Kajihōgo* (Discourse of doctrine in phonetic writing by the Zen master Tetsugen), his disciple has written a postscript in which he says, "Since the Zen sect was introduced into this country, there have been few other men who have in this fashion presented the essence of it in the Japanese language. The *Shaseki-shū* by the Zen master Mujū and the *Muchū Mondō-shū* (Dialogue in a dream) by the master Musō are about the only good books there are; although there are many others, few of them are worth mentioning."
26 *Shōbōgenzō* (Subtleties of the True Doctrine), chapter on *Busshō* (Buddha Nature).
27 *Ibid.*, chapter on *Shōji* (Life and Death).
28 *Muchū Mondō-shū* (Collection of Questions and Answers). In Tsunoda, De Bary, Keene, eds., *Sources of the Japanese Tradition* (New York: 1958), 261, a briefer translation is cited.
29 *Daigi-roku* (Record of Great Doubts), Part 2. *Ekiken Zenshū*, II, 156f.
30 Bemmei (Critical Study of Terms: 17 paragraphs on Heaven, destiny, God and spirits).
31 He was mentioned as *iruman*—not actually the man's name—from the Portuguese *irmão*, a lay preacher.
32 *Razan Sensei Bunshū* (Collected Writings of Hayashi Razan), Chapter 56.
33 *Uiyamabumi* (*Motoori Norinaga Zenshū*, Collected Works of Norinaga Motoori), IV, 601.
34 Eiichi, Matsushima, *Kinsei Nihon no Gakumonron no Ichi-seikaku* (A Characteristic of Discussions about Learning in Early Modern Japan), *Shisō*, No. 276 (Advice to Beginners).
35 The first four of the five volumes of Kakuken's *Inmyō-shō* (Commentary on Formal Logic) were made in preparation for the Jion meeting. Ennen wrote at the postscript of his work *Ichi-in-ishi* (One Line of Reasoning

and Four Types of Contradiction): "I have copied this work so that the Jion meeting of this year will be finished without trouble by the merit of copying."

36 Jakuhyō Koya (*Utaawase to Inmyō,* Lyrical Arrangement and Logic), *Misshū Gakuhō* (Journal of Esoteric Buddhism), June 1920, No. 84.

37 *Yat kṛtaṃ tad anityam dṛṣṭaṃ yathā ghaṭādir iti.*
Yan nityaṃ tad akṛtakaṁ dṛṣṭaṃ yathākaśādir iti. (Śaṅkarasvāmin's *Nyāyapraveśaka.*)

38 K. Kishigami, *Gōtō Inmyō Nisshōriron Kachū* (Commentary on the Inquiry into Correct Reasoning, with Annotations), 1888. K. Kira, *Kanchū Inmyō Nisshōriron-shō* (Commentary on the Inquiry into Correct Reasoning, with Annotations), II, 9; III, 4.

39 A Buddhist commented as follows: "As for Buddhist logic, one who is proficient in using ornate expressions skillfully can win in a debate even if his assertion is wrong. On the other hand, one who is awkward in expression is defeated even if his assertion is reasonable. So in Buddhist logic clever people win, whereas dull ones lose, and truths are difficult to defend." (*Inmyō Inu-sanshi,* 3 b.)

40 Daitō Shimaji, *Nihon Bukkyō Kyōgaku-shi* (History of Buddhist Doctrine in Japan), 231, 282.

41 Having pointed out the fact that in ancient Japan the scholarship of Buddhist logic flourished greatly, Echō (1780–1862) at the end of the Tokugawa period said: "Nowadays people who make it their business to debate with others have not come to know even the names of the three members of the syllogism (—the two propositions and conclusion). It argues the decline of Buddhist scholarship." (*Inmyō Inu-sanshi*), 4 b.

42 *Eshin Sōzu Zenshū* (Complete Works of Abbot Eshin), V, 284.

43 These materials have been drawn from Tokujō Ōya's article in *Mujintō,* XXI (1916), 937.

44 This work is a commentary by Jion (Tz'u-ēn) on Śaṅkarasvāmin's *Introduction to Logic* (*Nyāyapraveśaka*).

45 Hakuju Ui, *Indo Tetsugaku Kenkyū* (Studies in Indian Philosophy), I, 255, 265.

46 H. Saegusa, *Miura Baien no Tetsugaku* (Philosophy of Baien Miura), 204–209. Tsunoda, DeBary, Keene, editors, *Sources of the Japanese Tradition,* 489.

47 Hakuju Ui, *Bukkyō Ronrigaku* (Essays on Buddhist Logical Works), 168.

48 *Heike Monogatari* (Tale of the House of Taira). Yoshio Yamada has mentioned an abundance of other materials, in *Geirin,* III, Nos. 1, 2. Cf. also *Inmyō Inu-sanshi* (A Treatise on Indian Buddhist Logic), 19. But this term seems not to have been so important in original Indian Buddhist logic.

49 Tetsurō Watsuji, *Zoku Nihon Seishin-shi Kenkyū* (Research in Japanese Intellectual History, continued), 393.

50 E.g., *Shikishimano Yamatogokoroo Hitotowaba Asahini-niou Yamazakura-*

bana. (When one asks about the mind of Japan, / O! it is cherry blossoms, / Fragrant in the sunshine!)

51 Yaichi Haga, *Kokuminsei Jūron* (Ten Essays on the National Character), 211.

52 *Toganoo Myōeshōnin Ikun* (Last Word of Saint Myōe at Toganoo), in *Kokubun Tōhō Bukkyō Sōsho* (Collected Japanese Buddhist Works, in Japanese), *Hōgo-bu,* 57.

53 *Shōbōgenzō Zuimonki,* II, Iwanami Bunko edition, 37–38.

54 *Kichijōzan Eiheiji Shūryō Shingi* (Rules of the Buildings of the Eihei Monastery).

55 *Roankyō,* Part 2, No. 62.

56 E.g., Heijōshinze-dō, *Makotoshiku Hotokeno Michio Tazunureba Tada Yonotsuneno Kokoro Narikeri* (When we seek for the Way of Buddha earnestly, we find that it is simply the ordinary mind in the world), *Zoku Kokinshū,* Chapter 8.

57 *Chūron* (The *Madhyamaka-śāstra,* Treatise of the Middle Path), 24, 18.

58 Cf. Haga, *op.cit.,* 182–204. Ginō Tanaka, *Shintō Gairon* (Outline of Shintoism), 80.

59 *Daihōshakukyō* (The Chinese Version of the Mahā-ratnakūṭa-sūtra), CXIV. (*Taishō,* XI, 646 c.)

60 *Shōbōgenzō,* chapter on *Senmen* (Face Washing).

61 Hideki Yukawa, "Intuition and Abstraction in Scientific Thinking," *Annals of the Japan Association for Philosophy of Science,* II, 2 (March 1962), 94–97. Reprinted in *Basic Problems of Philosophy,* edited by Philip P. Wiener *et al.* (New York: Prentice-Hall, third edition, 1963).

62 *Jindai shi no Kenkyū* (Study on the History of Ancient Japan), 593.

63 *Ibid.,* 595.

64 *Kanmuryōju-kyō* (Sūtra of Meditation on the Amitāyus Buddha).

65 Taijo Tamamuro, *Nihon Bukkyō-shi Gaisetsu* (Outline History of Japanese Buddhism), 107.

66 Shinkō Mochizuki (editor), *Hōnen Shōnin Zenshū* (Collected Works of Saint Hōnen), 531.

67 *Taishō,* XLVII, 439 a. This is also quoted in the *Kyōgyōshinshō* (Shinran's Teaching, Practice, Faith, and Attainment), Part 2.

68 *Shōshinge* (Poems of the True Faith).

69 *Ippen Shōnin Goroku* (Collected Sayings of Saint Ippen).

70 Cf. *Daimuryōju-kyō* (Great Sūtra of the Pure Land), Part 1.

71 Tetsurō Watsuji, *Zoku Nihon Seishin-shi Kenkyū* (Supplementary Studies of Japanese History of Ideas), 88–89; 103–104.

72 Kojirō Yoshikawa, *Gakumon no Katachi* (Forms of Scholarship), in *Sekai,* May 1946.

73 *Shōbōgenzō, Bendōwa* (Practices of the Way).

74 *Shōbōgenzō Zuimonki* (Gleanings of the Master Dōgen's True Words) (Iwanami Bunko edition), VI, 108.

75 *Nyosetsu Shugyōshō* (Treatise on Ordained Practices). Cf. *Myōichini Gozen Gohenji* (Reply to Buddhist Sister Myōichi).
76 *Shutsujyōkōgo* (Monologue after Meditation), Chapter 8, *Jinzū* (Section on Miraculous Powers).
77 *Sankyo Yōron* (Essential Outlines of the Three Religions), 2.
78 Cf. Yasusada Hiyane, *Nihon Shūkyō Shi* (History of Japanese Religions), 248, 400.
79 Saburō Iyenaga, *Chūsei Bukkyō Shisō-shi Kenkyū* (A Study on Buddhist Thoughts in the Medieval Age), 42.
80 Cf. *Risshō Ankokuron* (Nichiren's Treatise on the Establishment of the True Faith for the Safety and Welfare of the Nation).
81 *Kangotōroku* (Collected Sayings of Saint Hōnen, in Chinese), X, *Hokuetsu ni Tsukawasu Sho* (A Letter sent to People in the Northern Province). (*Taishō*, LXXXIII, 169 b.)
82 Shōkaku, *Yuishinshō* (A Treatise on Pure Faith). (*Taishō*, LXXXIII, 915 b.)
83 *Mattōshō* (A Treatise on the Diminishing Lamp of Religion), last part.
84 *Kyōgyōshinshō*, Part 2.
85 Iyenaga, *op.cit.*, 34.
86 *Ippen Shōnin Goroku* (Collected Sayings of Saint Ippen).
87 *Rennyo Shōnin Goichidaiki Kikigaki*, No. 69.
88 Daijō Tokiwa, *Nihon no Bukkyō* (Buddhism in Japan), 43.
89 *Shuzenji Sōden Kubetsu* (Oral Tradition of the Transmission at Shuzen Temple), I. (*Dengyō Daishi Zenshū* [Collected Works of Master Dengyō], III, 666.) But this book was actually not written by Saichō.
90 *Ibid.*, II. (*Dengyō Daishi Zenshū*, III, 679.)
91 Iyenaga, *op.cit.*, 95.
92 *Gassui Gosho* (A Letter on Menses).
93 *Shōgu Mondō Shō*, Part 2.
94 *Shishin Gohon Shō*.
95 Cf. *Shōbōgenzō*, *Gyōji* (Demeanor), b.
96 *Ibid.*, *Bendōwa*.
97 *Ibid.*, *Bukkyō* (Buddhism).
98 *Shōbōgenzō Zuimonki*, I, 14.
99 *Ibid.*, I, 20, 21.
100 *Ibid.*, II, 41.
101 Daitō Shimaji, *Nihonbukkyō Kyōgakushi* (History of Buddhist Doctrine in Japan), 224.
102 *Ibid.*, 366.
103 *Miroku Kōshiki* (Rules on the Rites for Maitreya Buddha). (*Taishō*, LXXXIV, 889 a.)
104 *Shaseki Shū*, Chapter 2, Part 2.
105 Iyenaga, *op.cit.*, 42.
106 *Shin Sarugaku-ki* (*Gunshoruijū*, IX, 348).
107 Cf. *supra*, Chapter 34.
108 Watsuji, *op.cit.*; *Zoku Nihon Seishinshi Kenkyū*, 405, 411–412.

109 Frois, *Japanese History*, 449. Iyenaga, *op.cit.; Chūsei Bukkyō Shisōshi Kenkyū*, 142.

110 Masao Maruyama, *Fukuzawa ni okeru Jitsugaku no Tenkai* (The Development of Realistic Philosophy in Yukichi Fukuzawa), *Tōyō Bunka Kenkyū* (Studies on Eastern Culture), No. 3, 7.

Chapter 37

1 E.g., *Suttanipāta*, 927.

2 Ryōnin Sekiguchi, *Waga Kuni ni Okeru Bukkyō-Juyō ni tsuiteno ichi Kōsatsu* ("An Observation on the Introduction of Buddhism into Japan"), in the quarterly *Shūkyō Kenkyū*, IV, 210ff.

3 "The practice of Shingon and Tendai are fittest for Japan." *Keiranshūyōshū* (Collection of Fallen Leaves due to the Storm in a Valley), IX (*Taishō*, LXXVI, 539.

4 Cf. *Shugenshiyōben* (*Nihon Daizōkyō, Shugendō Shōsho*), III, 7.

5 Master Dengyō himself introduced Esoteric Buddhism. *Daitō Shimaji, Tendai Kyōgakushi* (History of Tendai Doctrine), 260f.

6 *Ibid.*, 345.

7 Some of them have been preserved in the Hōryū Temple.

8 Taijo Tamamuro, *Nihon Bukkyōshi Gaisetsu* (Historical Outline of Japanese Buddhism), 278, 279.

9 *Yōkyoku* (Noh-recitation), Enoshima.

10 *Kokonchomonshū* (Collection of Famous Stories, Ancient and Contemporary).

11 Cf. *Kitōshō* (A Treatise on Prayer).

12 *Nyosetsu-shugyōshō* (A Treatise on the Practice as Enjoined by Scriptures).

13 Tamamuro, *op.cit.*, 192.

14 *Eulogy to Kūya*, in *Zoku Gunshoruijū*, VIII.

15 *Tokujō Ōya*, "Some doubts on Kanezane Fujiwara's Faith," and *Jūnengokuraku-iōshū* (An Anthology on Rebirth in the Pure Land Through Invocation Ten Times), *Shirin*, IX, 26.

16 This aim is expressed in the chapter *Hōben-keshin-do* (the land magically produced as an expediency), of Shinran's *Kyōgyōshinshō*. Shundai Dazai said words to the same effect. *Seigaku Mondō* (Questions and Answers on Holy Scholarship), in *Nihon Rinri Ihen*, compiled by Tetsujirō Inouye and Yoshimaru Kaniye, VI, 292.

17 *Saṃyutta-nikāya*, edited by the Pali Text Society (London), IV, 118.

18 Naoichi Miyaji, *Jingishi Taikei* (System of the History of the Shinto Gods), 37.

19 *Benmei* (Discussion on Names), Part 2, in *Nihon Rinri Ihen*, VI, 84.

20 Kōjirō Yoshikawa, *Shinajin no Koten to sono Seikatsu*, 156.

21 Rei Saitō, *Ōchō-jidai no Onmyōdō* (The Way of Positive and Negative in the Court Period), 39.

INDEX